# The Voltaire Anthology
Voltaire
Translation by William F. Fleming

Start Publishing PD LLC
Copyright © 2024 by Start Publishing PD LLC

All rights reserved, including the right to reproduce this book or portions thereof in any form whatsoever.

Start Publishing PD is a registered trademark of Start Publishing PD LLC
Manufactured in the United States of America

Cover art: Shutterstock/Taisiya Kozorez

Cover design: Jennifer Do

10 9 8 7 6 5 4 3 2 1

ISBN 979-8-8809-2229-1

# Contents

Brutus. . . . . . . . . . . . . . . . . . . . . . . . . . . . . . . . . . . . . . . . . . . . . 4

Socrates. . . . . . . . . . . . . . . . . . . . . . . . . . . . . . . . . . . . . . . . . . 36

Alzire. . . . . . . . . . . . . . . . . . . . . . . . . . . . . . . . . . . . . . . . . . . . 59

Orestes. . . . . . . . . . . . . . . . . . . . . . . . . . . . . . . . . . . . . . . . . . . 86

Catiline. . . . . . . . . . . . . . . . . . . . . . . . . . . . . . . . . . . . . . . . . 122

Sémiramis. . . . . . . . . . . . . . . . . . . . . . . . . . . . . . . . . . . . . . . 151

Pandora. . . . . . . . . . . . . . . . . . . . . . . . . . . . . . . . . . . . . . . . . 187

The Scotch Woman. . . . . . . . . . . . . . . . . . . . . . . . . . . . . . . 198

Nanine. . . . . . . . . . . . . . . . . . . . . . . . . . . . . . . . . . . . . . . . . 237

The Prude. . . . . . . . . . . . . . . . . . . . . . . . . . . . . . . . . . . . . . 269

Mérope. . . . . . . . . . . . . . . . . . . . . . . . . . . . . . . . . . . . . . . . 316

Olympia. . . . . . . . . . . . . . . . . . . . . . . . . . . . . . . . . . . . . . . 361

The Orphan of China. . . . . . . . . . . . . . . . . . . . . . . . . . . . . 393

Mahomet. . . . . . . . . . . . . . . . . . . . . . . . . . . . . . . . . . . . . . 421

Amelia. . . . . . . . . . . . . . . . . . . . . . . . . . . . . . . . . . . . . . . . 456

Œdipus. . . . . . . . . . . . . . . . . . . . . . . . . . . . . . . . . . . . . . . 482

Mariamne. . . . . . . . . . . . . . . . . . . . . . . . . . . . . . . . . . . . . 509

Candide. . . . . . . . . . . . . . . . . . . . . . . . . . . . . . . . . . . . . . . 536

Zadig. . . . . . . . . . . . . . . . . . . . . . . . . . . . . . . . . . . . . . . . . 624

# Brutus

## Contents

Dramatis Personæ . . . . . . . . . . . . . . . . . . . . . . . . . . . . . . . . . . . . . . . . . . 4
Act I . . . . . . . . . . . . . . . . . . . . . . . . . . . . . . . . . . . . . . . . . . . . . . . . . . . . . 4
Act II . . . . . . . . . . . . . . . . . . . . . . . . . . . . . . . . . . . . . . . . . . . . . . . . . . . 11
Act III . . . . . . . . . . . . . . . . . . . . . . . . . . . . . . . . . . . . . . . . . . . . . . . . . . 17
Act IV . . . . . . . . . . . . . . . . . . . . . . . . . . . . . . . . . . . . . . . . . . . . . . . . . . 24
Act V . . . . . . . . . . . . . . . . . . . . . . . . . . . . . . . . . . . . . . . . . . . . . . . . . . . 29

## Dramatis Personæ

Junius Brutus, Consuls.
Valerius Publicola. Consuls.
Titus, Son of Brutus.
Tullia, Daughter of Tarquin.
Algina, Confidante of Tullia.
Aruns, Ambassador from Porsenna.
Messala, Friend of Titus.
Proculus, A military Tribune.
Albinus, Confidant of Aruns.
Senators. Lictors.

This tragedy was produced in 1730. It marks Voltaire's spirit of daring in treating a subject from which Shakespeare shrank as, perhaps, too painful for representation. When revived during the Revolution it was enthusiastically applauded.

## ACT I.

SCENE I.
Rome, Brutus in the Senate.
The scene represents part of the house appointed for the consuls on the Tarpeian mount: at a distance is seen the temple of the capitol. The senators are

assembled between the temple and the house, before the altar of Mars: the two consuls, Brutus and Valerius Publicola preside; the senators ranged in a semicircle, behind them the lictors with their fasces.

**Brutus**: At length, my noble friends, Rome's honored senate, The scourge of tyrants, you who own no kings But Numa's gods, your virtues, and your laws, Our foe begins to know us: this proud Tuscan, The fierce Porsenna, Tarquin's boasted friend, Pleased to protect a tyrant like himself; He who o'er Tiber's banks hath spread his hosts, And borne his head so loftily, now speaks In lowlier terms, respects the senate's power, And dreads the sons of freedom and of Rome: This day he comes, by his ambassador, To treat of peace, and Aruns, sent by him, Demands an audience: he attends even now Your orders in the temple: you'll determine Or to refuse or to admit him to us.

**Valerius Publicola**: Whate'er his errand be, let him be sent Back to his king; imperial Rome should never Treat with her foes till she has conquered them: Thy valiant son, the avenger of his country, Has twice repulsed Etruria's haughty monarch, And much we owe to his victorious arm: But this is not enough; Rome, still besieged, Sees with a jealous eye the tyrant's friends: Let Tarquin yield to our decrees; the laws Doomed him to exile; let him leave the realm, And purge the state of royal villainy; Perhaps we then may listen to his prayers. But this new embassy, it seems, has caught Your easy faith: can you not see that Tarquin, Who could not conquer, thinks he may deceive you. I never loved these king's ambassadors, The worst of foes beneath the mask of friendship; Who only bear an honorable title, And come to cheat us with impunity; Armed with state-cunning, or elate with pride, Commissioned to insult us, or betray. Listen not, Rome, to their deluding tongues; Stranger to art, thy business is, to fight; Conquer the foes that murmur at thy glory, Punish the pride of kings, or fall thyself; Such be thy treaties.

**Brutus**: Rome already knows How much I prize her safety and her freedom; The same my spirit, and the same my purpose, I differ in opinion from Valerius; And must confess, this first great homage paid The citizens of Rome, to me is grateful. I would accustom the despotic power Of princes on an easy level first To treat with our renowned commonweal, Till heaven shall crown our arms with victory, And make them subjects; then, Publicola, As such we'll use them: meantime, Aruns comes, Doubtless to mark the state of Rome, to count Her treasures, and observe her growing power, And therefore would I have him be admitted; Would have him know us fully: a king's slave Shall look on men; the novelty may please him: Let him at leisure cast his eyes o'er Rome, Let him behold her in your patriot breasts, You are her best defence; let him revere The God who calls us hither; let him see The senate, hear and tremble.

**Valerius Publicola:** I submit; [The senators rise and come forward to give their votes.] The general voice is yours: Rome and her Brutus Must be obeyed: for me, I disapprove it: Lictors, attend, and introduce him to us: Never may Rome repent of this! [To Brutus.] On thee Our eyes are fixed; on Brutus, who first broke Our chains; let freedom use a father's voice, And speak by thee.

SCENE II.

The Senate, Aruns, Albinus, Attendants.

[Aruns enters, preceded by two lictors, with Albinus, his friend; he passes by the consuls and senate, salutes them, and sits down on a seat prepared for him towards the front of the stage.]

**Aruns:** With pleasure I behold This great assembly, Rome's illustrious senate, And her sage consuls, famed for truth and justice, Which ne'er till now suffered reproach or blame: I know your deeds, and I admire your virtues; Unlike the wild licentious multitude, The vulgar crowd, whom party rage or joins Or disunites, who love and hate by turns, They know not why, taught in one changeful hour To boast or beg, to rail or to obey; Whose rashness—

**Brutus:** Stop, and learn with more respect To treat the citizens of Rome; for know, It is the senate's glory and her praise To represent that brave and virtuous people Whom thou hast thus reviled: for ourselves, Let us not hear the voice of flattery; It is the poison of Etrurian courts, But ne'er has tainted yet a Roman senate. On with thy message.

**Aruns:** Little doth the pride Of Rome affect me; but I own I feel For her misfortunes, and would plead her cause With filial love: you see the gathering storm Hangs o'er your heads, and threatens sure destruction: In vain hath Titus striven to save his country; With pity I behold that noble youth, Whose ardent courage labors to support Expiring Rome, and make her fall more glorious: His victories cost you dear; they thin your ramparts, And weaken your small force: no longer then Refuse a peace so needful to your safety. The senate bears a father's love to Rome, So does Porsenna to the hapless kings Whom you oppress: but tell me, you who judge Depending monarchs, you who thus determine The rights of all mankind, was it not here, Even at these altars, at this capitol, You called the gods to witness your allegiance, And bound your faith to your acknowledged king, To Tarquin? Say, what power has broken the tie? Who snatched the diadem from Tarquin's head? Who can acquit you of your oaths?

**Brutus**: Himself: Talk not of ties dissolved by guilt, of gods Whom he renounced, or rights which he has lost; We paid him homage, bound ourselves by oath, Oaths of obedience, not of slavery: But since thou bidst us call to our remembrance, The senate making vows for Tarquin's health, And kneeling at his feet, remember thou, That on this sacred spot, this altar here, Before the same attesting gods, that Tarquin Swore to be just; such was the mutual bond Of prince and people, and he gave us back The oath we made, when he forgot his own: Since to Rome's laws no more he pays obedience, Rome is no longer subject to his power, And Tarquin is the rebel, not his people.

**Aruns**: But, grant it true, that power unlimited, And absolute dominion, had misled The unhappy monarch from the paths of duty, Is there a man from human error free? Is there a king without some human weakness? Or if there were, have you a right to punish, You, who were born his subjects; you, whose duty Is to obey? The son doth never arm Against the sire, but with averted eyes Laments his errors, and reveres him still: And not less sacred are the rights of kings; They are our fathers, and the gods alone Their judges: if in anger heaven sometimes Doth send them down, why would you therefore call For heavier chains, and judgments more severe? Why violate the laws you would defend, And only change your empire to destroy it? Taught by misfortune, best of monitors, Tarquin henceforth, more worthy of his throne, Will be more wise and just; the legal bonds Of king and people now may be confirmed By happiest union; public liberty Shall flourish then beneath the awful shade Of regal power.

**Brutus**: Aruns, 'tis now too late: Each nation has its laws, by nature given, Or changed by choice: Etruria, born to serve, Hath ever been the slave of kings or priests; Loves to obey, and, happy in her chains, Would bind them on the necks of all mankind. Greece boasts her freedom; soft Ionia bends Beneath a shameful bondage; Rome had once Her kings, but they were never absolute: Her first great citizen was Romulus, With him his people shared the weight of empire; Numa was governed by the laws he made; Rome fell at last indeed beneath herself, When from Etruria she received her kings, Or from Porsenna; tyranny and vice From your corrupted courts flowed in upon us. Forgive us, gods, the crime of sparing Tarquin So many years! at length his murderous hands, Dyed with our blood, have broke the shameful chain Of our long slavery, and the Roman people Have through misfortune found the road to virtue: Tarquin restores the rights by Tarquin lost, And by his crimes has fixed the public safety: We've taught the Etruscans how to shake off tyrants, And hope they'll profit by the fair example. [The consuls descend towards the altar, and the senate rises.] O Mars, thou god of battles, and of Rome! Thou who dost guard these sacred walls, and fight For thy own people, on thy altar here Deign to accept our solemn oaths, for me And for the senate, for thy worthy sons: If in Rome's bosom there be found a traitor, Who weeps for banished kings, and seeks once more To be a slave, in torments shall he die; His guilty ashes, scattered to the winds, Shall leave behind a more detested name, Even than those tyrant kings which Rome abhors.

**Aruns**: [Stepping towards the altar.] And on this altar, which you thus profane, I call that god to witness, in the name Of him whom you oppress, the injured Tarquin, And great Porsenna, his avenger, here I swear eternal war with you, O Romans! And your posterity— [The senators are going off towards the capitol.] A moment stop Ere you depart, O senators! and hear What I have more to offer: Tarquin's daughter, Must she too fall a sacrifice to Rome? With ignommious fetters will ye bind Her royal hands, to triumph o'er her father, Whose treasures you detain? Ungenerous victors! As if the right of conquest gave them to you: Where are his riches? was it for the spoil You robbed him of his throne? let Brutus speak, And own the plunder.

**Brutus**: Little dost thou know Of Rome, her manners, and her noble nature; But learn, mistaken man, her great protectors, The friends of truth and justice, are grown old In honest poverty; above the pride Of wealth, which they disdain; it is their boast To conquer kings, who love such tinsel greatness. Take back your gold, it is beneath our notice; And for the hateful tyrant's hapless daughter, Though I abhor the wretched race, yet know The senate has consigned her to my care: She hath not tasted here the baneful cup Of flattery, that sweet poison of a court, Or viewed the pomp and dangerous luxury Of Tarquin's palace: little did her youth Profit by them; but all that to her age And sex was due, all her misfortunes claimed, She hath received: let her return this day To Tarquin; Brutus yields her back with joy: Naught should the tyrant have within these walls But Rome's fixed hatred, and the wrath of heaven: You have a day to carry off your treasures, That must suffice: meantime, the sacred rights Of hospitality await thee here; Beneath my roof thou mayest remain in safety: The senate thus by me decrees: bear thou Our answer to Porsenna, and then tell Proud Tarquin, you have seen a Roman senate. [Turning to the senators.] Let us, my friends, adorn the capitol With laurel wreaths, that round the brows of Titus Have spread their noble shade; the arrows too, And bloody ensigns, his victorious hand Hath wrested from the Etruscans: ever thus, From age to age, may the successful race Of Brutus still defend their much loved country: Thus, O ye gods, may you protect us ever; Guide the son's arm, and bless the father's councils!

### SCENE III.
Aruns, Albinus.

[Supposed to have retired from the hall of audience into an apartment of Brutus' house.]

**Aruns**: Didst thou observe the fierce unbending spirit Of this proud senate, which believes itself Invincible? and so perhaps it might be, Were Rome at leisure to confirm her sons In valor and in wisdom: liberty, That liberty, my friend, which all adore, And I admire, though I would wrest it from them, Inspires the heart of man with nobler courage Than nature gives, and warmth almost divine. Beneath the Tarquin's yoke, a slavish court Enfeebled their corrupted hearts, and spoiled Their active valor; whilst their tyrant kings, Busied in conquering their own subjects, left Our happier Etruscans in the arms of peace; But if the senate should awake their virtues, If Rome is free, Italia soon must fall: These lions, whom their keepers made so gentle, Will find their strength again, and rush upon us; Let us then stop this rapid stream of woes, Even at its source, and free a sinking world From slavery; let us bind these haughty Romans Even with the chains which they would throw on us, And all mankind.—But will Messala come, May I expect him here? and will he dare—

**Albinus**: My Lord, he will attend you; every minute We look for him; and Titus is our friend.

**Aruns**: Have you conferred; may I depend on him?

**Albinus**: Messala, if I err not, means to change His own estate, rather than that of Rome; As firm and fearless as if honor guided, And patriot love inspired him; ever secret, And master of himself; no passions move No rage disturbs him; in his height of zeal Calm and unruffled.

**Aruns**: Such he seemed to me When first I saw him at the court of Tarquin; His letters since—but, see, he comes.

### SCENE IV.
Aruns, Messala, Albinus.

**Aruns**: Messala, Thou generous friend of an unhappy master, Will neither Tarquin's nor Porsenna's gold Shake the firm faith of these rough senators? Will neither fear, nor hope, nor pleasure bend Their stubborn hearts? These fierce patrician chiefs. That judge mankind, are they without or vice Or passion? is there aught that's mortal in them?

**Messala:** Their boasts are mighty, but their false pretence To justice, and the fierce austerity Of their proud hearts, are nothing but the thirst Of empire; their pride treads on diadems; Yet whilst they break one chain, they forge another. These great avengers of our liberty, Armed to defend it, are its worst oppressors: Beneath the name of patrons they assume The part of monarchs; Rome but changed her fetters, And for one king hath found a hundred tyrants.

**Aruns:** Is there amongst your citizens a man Honest enough to hate such shameful bondage?

**Messala:** Few, very few, yet feel their miseries: Their spirits, still elate with this new change, Are mad with joy: the meanest wretch among them, Because he helped to pull down monarchy, Assumes its pride, and thinks himself a king: But I've already told you I have friends, Who with reluctance bend to this new yoke; Who look with scorn on a deluded people, And stem the torrent with unshaken firmness; Good men and true, whose hands and hearts were made To change the state of kingdoms, or destroy them.

**Aruns:** What may I hope from these brave Romans? say, Will they serve Tarquin?

**Messala:** They'll do anything; Their lives are thine; but think not, like blind vassals, They will obey a base ungrateful master: They boast no wild enthusiastic zeal, To fall the victims of despotic power, Or madly rush on death to save a tyrant, Who will not know them. Tarquin promises Most nobly, but when he shall be their master, Perhaps he then may fear, perhaps forget them. I know the great too well: in their misfortunes No friends so warm; but in prosperity, Ungrateful oft, they change to bitterest foes: We are the servile tools of their ambition; When useless, thrown aside with proud disdain, Or broke without remorse when we grow dangerous. Our friends expect conditions shall be made; On certain terms you may depend upon them: They only ask a brave and worthy leader To please their fickle taste; a man well known, And well respected; one who may have power To force the king to keep his plighted faith If we succeed; and if we fail, endued With manly courage to avenge our cause.

**Aruns:** You wrote me word the haughty Titus—

**Messala:** Titus Is Rome's support, the son of Brutus; yet—

**Aruns:** How does he brook the senate's base reward For all his services? he saved the city, And merited the consulship, which they, I find, refuse him.

**Messala:** And he murmurs at it. I know his proud and fiery soul is full Of the base injury: for his noble deeds, Naught has he gained but a vain empty triumph; A fleeting shadow of unreal bliss: I am no stranger to his throbbing heart, And strength of passion; in the paths of glory So lately entered, 'twere an easy task To turn his steps aside; for fiery youth Is easily betrayed: and yet what bars To our design! a consul, and a father; His hate of kings; Rome pleading for her safety; The dread of shame, and all his triumphs past. But I have stole into his heart, and know The secret poison that inflames his soul: He sighs for Tullia.

**Aruns:** Ha! for Tullia?

**Messala:** Yes: Scarce could I draw the secret from his breast; He blushed himself at the discovery, Ashamed to own his love; for midst the tumult Of jarring passions, still his zeal prevails For liberty.

**Aruns:** Thus on a single heart, And its unequal movements, must depend, Spite of myself, the fate of Rome: but hence, Albinus, and prepare for Tarquin's tent. [Turning to Messala.] We'll to the princess: I have gained some knowledge, By long experience, of the human heart: I'll try to read her soul; perhaps her hands May weave a net to catch this Roman senate.

# ACT II.

SCENE I.
The scene represents an apartment in the palace of the consuls.
Titus, Messala.

**Messala:** No: 'tis unkind; it hurts my tender friendship: He who but half unveils his secrets, tells Too little or too much: dost thou suspect me?

**Titus:** Do not reproach me; my whole heart is thine.

**Messala:** Thou who so lately didst with me detest The rigorous senate, and pour forth thy plaints In anguish; thou who on this faithful bosom Didst shed so many tears, couldst thou conceal Griefs far more bitter, the keen pangs of love? How could ambition quench the rising flame, And blot out every tender sentiment? Dost thou detest the hateful senate more Than thou lovest Tullia?

**Titus:** O! I love with transport, And hate with fury; ever in extreme; It is the native weakness of my soul, Which much I strive to conquer, but in vain.

**Messala:** But why thus rashly tear thy bleeding wounds? Why weep thy injuries, yet disguise thy love?

**Titus:** Spite of those injuries, spite of all my wrongs, Have I not shed my blood for this proud senate? Thou knowest I have, and didst partake my glory; With joy I told thee of my fair success; It showed, methought, a nobleness of soul To fight for the ungrateful, and I felt The pride of conscious virtue: the misfortunes We have o'ercome with pleasure we impart, But few are anxious to reveal their shame.

**Messala:** Where is the shame, the folly, or disgrace: And what should Titus blush at?

**Titus:** At myself: At my fond foolish passion, that o'erpowers My duty.

**Messala:** Are ambition then, and love, Passions unworthy of a noble mind?

**Titus:** Ambition, love, resentment, all possess The soul of Titus, and by turns inflame it: These consul kings despise my youth; deny me My valor's due reward, the price of blood Shed in their cause: then, midst my sorrows, seize All I hold dear, and snatch my Tullia from me. Alas! I had no hope, and yet my heart Grows jealous now: the fire, long pent within, Bursts forth with inextinguishable rage. I thought it had been o'er; she parted from me, And I had almost gained the victory O'er my rebellious passion: but my race Of glory now is run, and heaven has fixed Its period here: Gods! that the son of Brutus, The foe of kings, should ever be the slave Of Tarquin's race! nay, the ungrateful fair Scorns to accept my conquered heart: I'm slighted; Disdained on every side, and shame o'erwhelms me.

**Messala:** May I with freedom speak to thee?

**Titus:** Thou mayest; Thou knowest I ever have revered thy prudence; Speak therefore, tell me all my faults, Messala.

**Messala:** No: I approve thy love, and thy resentment: Shall Titus authorize this tyrant senate, These sons of arrogance? if thou must blush, Blush for thy patience, Titus, not thy love. Are these the poor rewards of all thy valor, Thy constancy, and truth? a hopeless lover. A weak and powerless citizen of Rome, A poor state-victim, by the senate braved, And scorned by Tullia: sure a heart like thine Might find the means to be revenged on both.

**Titus:** Why wilt thou flatter my despairing soul? Thinkest thou I ever could subdue her hate, Or shake her virtue? 'tis impossible: Thou seest the fatal barriers to our love, Which duty and our fathers place between us: But must she go?

**Messala:** This day, my lord.

**Titus:** Indeed! But I will not complain: for heaven is just To her deservings; she was born to reign.

**Messala:** Heaven had perhaps reserved a fairer empire For beauteous Tullia, but for this proud senate, But for this cruel war, nay but for Titus: Forgive me, sir, you know the inheritance She might have claimed; her brother dead, the throne Of Rome had been her portion—but I've gone Too far—and yet, if with my life, O Titus, I could have served thee, if my blood—

**Titus:** No more: My duty calls, and that shall be obeyed: Man may be free, if he resolves to be so: I own, the dangerous passion for a time O'erpowered my reason; but a soldier's heart Braves every danger: love owes all his power To our own weakness.

**Messala**: The ambassador From Etruria is here: this honor, Sir—

**Titus**: O fatal honor! what would he with me? He comes to snatch my Tullia from my sight; Comes to complete the measure of my woes.

## SCENE II.
Titus. Aruns.

**Aruns**: After my long and fruitless toils to serve The state of Rome, and her ungrateful senate, Permit me here to pay the homage due To generous courage, and transcendent virtue; Permit me to admire the gallant hero Who saved his country on the brink of ruin: Alas! thou hast deserved a fairer meed, A cause more noble, and another foe; Thy valor merited a better fate: Kings would rejoice, and such I know there are, To trust their empire with an arm like thine, Who would not dread the virtues they admire, Like jealous Rome and her proud senate: O! I cannot bear to see the noble Titus Serving these haughty tyrants; who, the more You have obliged them, hate you more: to them Your merit's a reproach; mean vulgar souls, Born to obey, they lift the oppressive hand Against their great deliverer, and usurp Their sovereign's rights; from thee they should receive Those orders which they give.

**Titus**: I thank you, Sir, For all your cares, your kind regard for Titus, And guess the cause: your subtle policy Would wind me to your secret purposes, And arm my rage against the commonweal; But think not to impose thus on my frankness; My heart is open, and abhors design: The senate have misused me, and I hate them, I ought to hate them; but I'll serve them still: When Rome engages in the common cause, No private quarrels taint the patriot breast; Superior then to party strife, we rush United on against the general foe: Such are my thoughts, and such they ever will be; Thou knowest me now: or call it virtue in me, Or call it partial fondness, what you please, But, born a Roman, I will die for Rome, And love this hard unjust suspicious senate, More than the pomp and splendor of a court Beneath a master, for I am the son Of Brutus, and have graved upon my heart The love of freedom, and the hate of kings.

**Aruns**: But does not Titus soothe his flattered heart With fancied bliss, and visionary charms? I too, my lord, though born within the sway Of regal power, am fond of liberty; You languish for her, yet enjoy her not. Is there on earth, with all your boasted freedom, Aught more despotic than a commonweal? Your laws are tyrants; and their barbarous rigor Deaf to the voice of merit, to applause, To family, and fame, throws down distinction; The senate grind you, and the people scorn; You must affright them, or they will enslave you: A citizen of Rome is ever jealous Or insolent; he is your equal still, Or still your foe, because inferior to you: He cannot bear the lustre of high fortune; Looks with an eye severe on every action; In all the service you have done him, sees Naught but the injury you have power to do; And for the blood which you have shed for him, You'll be repaid at last with—banishment. A court, I own's a dangerous element, And has its storms, but not so frequent; smooth Its current glides, its surface more serene: That boasted native of another soil, Fair liberty, here sheds her sweetest flowers: A king can love, can recompense your service, And mingles happiness with glory; there Cherished beneath the shade of royal favor, Long mayest thou flourish, only serve a master, And be thyself the lord of all beside: The vulgar, ever to their sovereign's will Obedient, still respect and honor those Whom he protects, nay love his very faults: We never tremble at a haughty senate, Or her harsh laws: O! would that, born as thou art, To shine with equal lustre in a court Or in a camp, thou wouldst but taste the charms Of Tarquin's goodness! for he loved thee, Titus, And would have shared his fortunes with thee; then Had the proud senate, prostrate at thy feet—

**Titus**: I've seen the court of Tarquin, and despise it: I know I might have cringed for his protection, Been his first slave, and tyrannized beneath him; But, thanks to heaven, I am not fallen so low: I would be great, but not by meanness rise To grandeur: no, it never was my fate To serve: I'll conquer kings, do thou obey them.

**Aruns**: I must approve thy constancy; but think, My lord, how Tarquin, in thy infant years, Guided thy tender youth: he oft remembers The pleasing office, and but yesterday, Lamenting his lost son, and sad misfortunes, "Titus," said he, "was once my best support, He loved us all, and he alone deserved My kingdom and my daughter."

**Titus**: Ha! his daughter! Ye gods! my Tullia! O unhappy vows!

**Aruns**: Even now I carry her to Tarquin; him Whom thou hast thus deserted, far from thee, And from her country, soon must Tullia go; Liguria's king accepts of her in marriage: Meantime thou, Titus, must obey the senate, Oppress her father, and destroy his kingdom: And may these vaulted roofs, these towers in flame, And this proud capitol in ashes laid, Like funeral torches, shine before your people, To light the Roman senate to its grave. Or serve to grace our happy Tullia's nuptials!

**SCENE III.**
Titus, Messala.

**Titus**: Messala, in what anguish hath he left me! Would Tarquin then have given her to my arms! O cruel fate! and might I thus—O no, Deceitful minister! thou camest to search My foolish heart; alas! he saw too well, Read in my eyes the dear destructive passion, He knows my weakness, and returns to Tarquin To smile at Titus, and insult his love: And might I then have wedded her, possessed That lovely maid, and spent a life of bliss Within her arms, had heaven allotted me So fair a fate! O I am doubly wretched.

**Messala**: Thou mightest be happy; Aruns would assist thee, Trust me, he would, and second thy warm wishes.

**Titus**: No: I must bid adieu to my fond hopes; Rome calls me to the capitol; the people Who raised triumphal arches to my glory, And love me for my labors past, expect me, To take with them the inviolable oath, The solemn pledge of sacred liberty.

**Messala**: Go then, and serve your tyrants.

**Titus**: I will serve them; It is my duty, and I must fulfil it.

**Messala**: And yet you sigh.

**Titus**: 'Tis a hard victory.

**Messala**: And bought too dearly.

**Titus**: Therefore 'tis more glorious. Messala, do not leave me in affliction. [Exit Titus.]

**Messala**: I'll follow him, to sharpen his resentment, And strike the envenomed dagger to his heart.

SCENE IV.
Brutus, Messala.

**Brutus**: Messala, stop; I'd speak with you.

**Messala**: With me?

**Brutus**: With you. A deadly poison late hath spread Its secret venom o'er my house: my son, Tiberius, is with jealous rage inflamed Against his brother; it appears too plain; Whilst Titus burns with most unjust resentment Against the senate: the ambassador, That shrewd Etruscan, has observed their weakness, And doubtless profits by it: he has talked To both: I dread the tongues of subtle statesmen, Grown old in the chicanery of a court: To-morrow he returns: a day's too much To give a traitor, and ofttimes is fatal: Go thou, Messala, tell him he must hence This day: I'll have it so.

**Messala**: 'Tis prudent, Sir, And I obey you.

**Brutus**: But this is not all: My son, the noble Titus, loves thee well; I know the power that sacred friendship hath O'er minds like his; a stranger to distrust Or diffidence, he yields his artless soul To thy experience; and the more his heart Relies on thee, the more may I expect, That, able as thou art to guide his steps, Thou wilt not turn them from the paths of virtue, Or take advantage of his easy youth To taint his guiltless heart with fond ambition.

**Messala**: That was even now the subject of our converse; He strives to imitate his godlike sire; Rome's safety is the object of his care: Blindly he loves his country, and his father.

**Brutus**: And so he ought; but above all, the laws; To them he should be still a faithful slave; Who breaks the laws, can never love his country.

**Messala**: We know his patriot zeal, and both have seen it.

**Brutus**: He did his duty.

**Messala**: Rome had done hers too, If she had honored more so good a son.

**Brutus**: Messala, no: it suited not his age To take the consulship; he had not even The voice of Brutus: trust me, the success Of his ambition would have soon corrupted His noble mind, and the rewards of virtue Had then become hereditary: soon Should we have seen the base unworthy son Of a brave father claim superior rank, Unmerited, in sloth and luxury, As our last Tarquin but too plainly proved. How very seldom they deserve a crown Who're born to wear it! O! preserve us, heaven, From such destructive vile abuse of power, The nurse of folly, and the grave of virtue! If thou indeed dost love my son, (and much I hope thou dost) show him a fairer path To glory; root out from his heart the pride Of false ambition: he who serves the state Is amply recompensed: the son of Brutus Should shine a bright example to the world Of every virtue: he is Rome's support, As such I look upon him; and the more He has already done to serve his country, The more I shall require of him hereafter. Know then by what I wish the love I bear him, Temper the heat of youth; to flatter Titus Were death to him, and injury to Rome.

**Messala**: My lord, I am content to follow Titus, To imitate his valor, not instruct him: I have but little influence o'er your son; But, if he deigns to listen to my counsels, Rome soon will see how much he loves her glory.

**Brutus**: Go then, be careful not to soothe his errors; For I hate tyrants much, but flatterers more. [Exit Brutus

### SCENE V.

**Messala**: [Alone.] There's not a tyrant more detestable, More cruel than thy own relentless soul; But I shall tread perhaps beneath my feet The pride of all thy false insulting virtue: Yes, thou Colossus, raised thus high above us By a vile crowd, the thunder is prepared, Soon shall it fall, and crush thee into ruin.

# ACT III.

**SCENE I.**
Aruns, Albinus, Messala.

**Aruns**: [A letter in his hand.] At length, my friend, a dawn of fair success Breaks in upon us; thou hast served me nobly, And all is well: this letter, my Albinus, Decides the fate of Tarquin, and of Rome. But, tell me, have you fixed the important hour? Have you watched closely the Quirinal gate? If our conspirators to-night should fail To yield the ramparts up, will your assault Be ready? Is the king well satisfied, Thinkest thou, Albinus, we shall bring him back To Rome subjected, or to Rome in blood?

**Albinus**: My lord, by midnight all will be prepared; Tarquin already reaps the promised harvest; From you, once more, receives the diadem, And owns himself indebted more to Aruns Than to Porsenna.

**Aruns**: Or the envious gods, Foes to our hapless sovereign, must destroy Our fair design, well worthy of their aid; Or by to-morrow's dawn rebellious Rome Shall own a master; Rome perhaps in ashes, Or bathing in her blood. But better is it A king should rule o'er an unhappy people, Who are obedient, than in plenty's lap, O'er a proud nation, who are still perverse And obstinate, because they are too happy. Albinus, I attend the Princess here In secret—Stay, Messala.

**SCENE II.**
Aruns, Messala.

**Aruns**: Touching Titus, What has thou done? couldst thou prevail on him To serve the cause of Tarquin? couldst thou bind His haughty soul?

**Messala**: No: I presumed too far; He is inflexible: he loves his country, And has too much of Brutus in him; murmurs Against the senate, but still dotes on Tullia: Pride and ambition, love and jealousy, Opened, I thought, a passage to his soul, And gave my arts some promise of success; But, strange infatuation! liberty Prevailed o'er all: his love is desperate, Yet Rome is stronger even than love: in vain I strove, by slow degrees, to efface the horror Which Rome had taught his foolish heart to feel Even at the name of king; in vain opposed His rooted prejudice; the very mention Of Tarquin fired his soul; he would not hear me, But broke off the discourse: I must have gone Too far, had I persisted.

**Aruns**: Then, Messala, There are no hopes of him.

**Messala**: Much less reluctant I found his brother; one of Brutus' sons, At least is ours.

**Aruns**: Already hast thou gained Tiberius? by what lucky art, Messala—

**Messala:** His own ambition did it all: long time, With jealous eye, hath he beheld the honors Heaped on his brother, that eclipse his own; The wreath of laurel, and the pomp of triumph, The waving ensigns, with the people's love, And Brutus' fondness, lavished all on Titus, Like deepest injuries, sunk into his soul, And helped to fill the poisoned cup of envy; Whilst Titus, void of malice or revenge, Too much superior to be jealous of him, Stretched forth his hand from his triumphal car, As if he wished to give his brother part Of all his glories: I embraced, with joy, The lucky minute; pointed out the paths Of glory; promised, in the name of Tarquin, All the fair honors Rome could give, the throne Alone excepted: I perceived him stagger, And saw him bend, by slow degrees, before me: He's yours, my lord, and longs to speak with you

**Aruns:** Will he deliver the Quirinal gate, Messala?

**Messala:** Titus is commander there, And he alone can give it us: already His virtues have been fatal to our purpose; He is the guardian deity of Rome: The attack is dangerous: without his support Success were doubtful, with it all is certain.

**Aruns:** If he solicited the consulship, Thinkest thou he would refuse the sovereign power The sure reversion of a throne with Tullia?

**Messala:** 'Twere an affront to his exalted virtue To offer him a throne.

**Aruns:** And Tullia with it?

**Messala:** O he adores her; and even loves her more, Because he strives to hate; detests the father, And rages for the daughter; dreads to speak, Yet mourns in silence; seeks her everywhere, Yet shuns her presence, and drinks up his tears In secret anguish: all the rage of love Possesses him; sometimes in storms like these A lucky moment turns the wavering mind. Titus, I know, is turbulent and bold; And, if we gain him, may, perhaps, go further Even than we wish: who knows but fierce ambition May yet rekindle by the torch of love! His heart would glow with pleasure, to behold The trembling senate prostrate at his feet. Yet, let me not deceive you with the hopes, That Titus ever will be ours; once more, However, I shall try his stubborn virtue.

**Aruns:** If still he loves, I shall depend on him: One look of Tullia's, one sweet word from her, Will soften his reluctant heart much more, Than all the arts of Aruns or Messala: For, O, believe me, we must hope for naught From men, but through their weakness and their follies: Titus and Tullia must promote our cause; The one's ambition, and the other's love: These, these, my friend, are the conspirators That best will serve the king: from them I hope Much more than from myself. [Exit Messala.]

## SCENE III.
Tullia, Aruns, Algina.

**Aruns**: This letter, Madam, With orders to deliver it to your hands, I have received from Tarquin.

**Tullia**: Gracious heaven! Preserve my father, and reverse his fate! [She reads.] "The throne of Rome may from its ashes rise, And he who was the conqueror of his king Be his restorer: Titus is a hero, He must defend that sceptre which I wish To share with him. Remember, O my Tullia, That Tarquin gave thee life; remember too, My fate depends on thee; thou mayest refuse Liguria's king: if Titus be thy choice, He's mine; receive him for thy husband." Ha! Read I aright! Titus! impossible! Could Tarquin, could my father, still unmoved In all his sorrows, thus at last relent? How could he know, or whence— [Turning to Messala.] Alas, my lord, 'Tis but to search the secrets of my heart You try me thus: pity a wretched princess, Nor spread your snares for helpless youth like mine.

**Aruns**: Madam, I only mean to obey your father, And serve his honored daughter; for your secrets, In me it were presumption to remove The sacred veil which you have drawn before them; My duty only bids me say, that heaven By you determines to restore our empire.

**Tullia**: And is it possible, that Tullia thus Should be the friend of Tarquin, and the wife Of Titus?

**Aruns**: Doubt it not: that noble hero Already burns to serve the royal race: His generous heart abhors the savage fierceness Of this new commonweal; his pride was hurt By their refusal of his just demand: The work's half done, and thou must finish it. I have not looked into his heart; but sure, If he knows Tullia well, he must adore her: Who could behold, unmoved, a diadem By thee presented, and with thee adorned? Speak to him then, for thou alone hast power To triumph o'er this enemy of kings: No longer let the senate boast of Titus, Their best support, the guardian god of Rome; But be it Tullia's glory to possess The great defender of her father's cause, And crush his foes to ruin.

## SCENE IV.
Tullia, Algina.

**Tullia**: Gracious heaven! How much I owe to thy propitious goodness! My tears have moved thee: all is changed; and now Thy justice, smiling on my passion, gives New strength and freedom to the glorious flame. Fly, my Algina, bring him hither: gods! Does he avoid me still, or knows he not His happiness?

But stay, perhaps my hopes Are but delusions all: does Titus hate The senate thus? alas! and must I owe That to resentment which is due to love?

**Algina**: I know the senate have offended him; That he's ambitious; that he burns for Tullia.

**Tullia**: Then he'll do all to serve me: fly, Algina, Away, begone. [Exit Algina.] And yet this sudden change Alarms me: O! what anguish racks my heart! Now, love, do thou assist and guide my virtue! My fame, my duty, reason, all command it And shall my father owe his crown to me, Shall Tullia be the chain to bind their friendship; And all Rome's happiness depend on mine? O, when shall I impart to thee, my Titus, The wondrous change we little thought to see, When shall I hear thy vows, and give thee mine, Without a pain, a sorrow, or a fear? My woes are past; now, Rome, I can forgive thee; If Titus leaves thee, Rome, thou art a slave: If he is mine, proud senate, thou art no more: He loves me; tremble therefore, and obey.

SCENE V.
Titus, Tullia.

**Titus**: May I believe it? wilt thou deign once more To look on this abhorred Roman, long The object of thy hatred, and thy foe?

**Tullia**: The face of things, my lord, is strangely altered; Fate now permits me—but first tell me, Titus, Has Tullia still an interest in thy heart?

**Titus**: Alas! thou canst not doubt thy fatal power; Thou knowest my love, my guilt, and my despair; And holdest a cruel empire o'er a life Which I detest; exhaust your rage upon me; My fate is in your hands.

**Tullia**: Know, mine depends On thee.

**Titus**: On Titus? never can this trembling heart Believe it: am I then no longer hated? Speak on, my Tullia: O, what flattering hope Thus in a moment lifts me to the height Of mortal bliss?

**Tullia**: [Giving him the letter.] Read this, and make thyself, Thy Tullia, and her father happy—Now May I not hope—but wherefore that stern brow And frowning aspect? gods!

**Titus**: Of all mankind Titus is sure the most accursed: blind fate, Bent on my ruin, showed me happiness, Then snatched it from me: to complete my woes, It doomed me to adore, and to destroy thee: I love thee, and have lost thee now forever.

**Tullia**: How, Titus!

**Titus**: Yes; this fatal hour condemns me To shame and horror: to betray or Rome Or Tullia: all that's left to my sad choice Is guilt, or misery.

**Tullia:** What sayest thou, Titus? When with this hand I offer thee a throne; Now when thou knowest my heart, for no longer Will I conceal my virtuous passion for thee; When duty yields a sanction to our love; Alas! I thought this happy day would prove The fairest of my life, and yet the moment When first my fearful heart, without a blush, Might own its passion, is the first that calls For my repentance. Darest thou talk to me Of guilt and misery? Know, thus to serve Ungrateful men against their lawful prince, To scorn my proffered bounties, and oppress me, These are my miseries, Titus, these thy crimes. Mistaken youth, weigh in the even balance What Rome refused, and what she offers thee: Or deal forth laws, or meanly stoop to obey them: Be governed by a rabble, or a king; By Rome, or me: direct him right, ye gods!

**Titus:** [Giving her back the letter.] My choice is made.

**Tullia:** And fearest thou to avow it? Be bold, and speak at once; deserve my pardon, Or merit my revenge: what's thy resolve?

**Titus:** 'Tis to be worthy of thee, of myself, And of my country; to be just, and faithful; 'Tis to adore and imitate thy virtues; It is to lose, O Tullia, yet deserve thee.

**Tullia:** Forever then—

**Titus:** Forgive me, dearest Tullia; Pity my weakness, and forget my love: Pity a heart foe to itself, a heart A thousand times more wretched now than even When thou didst hate me: O! I cannot leave, I cannot follow thee; I cannot live Or with thee or without thee; but will die Rather than see thee given to another.

**Tullia:** My heart's still thine, and I forgive thee, Titus.

**Titus:** If thou dost love me, Tullia, be a Roman; Be more than queen, and love the commonweal: Bring with thee patriot zeal, the love of Rome, And of her sacred laws, be that thy dowry: Henceforth let Brutus be thy father, Rome Thy mother, and her loved avenger, Titus, Thy husband: thus shall Romans yield the palm Of glory to an Etruscan maid, and owe Their freedom to the daughter of a king.

**Tullia:** And wouldst thou wish me to betray—

**Titus:** My soul, Urged to despair, hath lost itself: O no! Treason is horrible in every shape, And most unworthy of thee: well I know A father's rights; his power is absolute, And must not be disputed: well I know That Titus loves thee, that he is distracted.

**Tullia:** Thou knowest what duty is, hear then the voice Of Tullia's father.

**Titus:** And forget my own! Forget my country!

**Tullia:** Canst thou call it thine Without thy Tullia?

**Titus:** We are foes by nature; The laws have laid a cruel duty on us.

**Tullia:** Titus and Tullia foes! how could that word E'er pass thy lips!

**Titus:** Thou knowest my heart belies them.

**Tullia:** Dare then to serve, and if thou lovest, revenge me.

SCENE VI.

Brutus, Aruns, Titus, Tullia, Messala, Albinus, Proculus, Lictors.

**Brutus:** [Addressing himself to Tullia.] Madam, the time is come for your departure; Whilst public tumults shook the commonweal, And the wild tempest howled around us, Rome Could not restore you to your household gods: Tarquin himself, in that disastrous hour, Too busy in the ruin of his people To think on Tullia, ne'er demanded thee. Forgive me if I call thus to remembrance Thy sorrows past: I robbed thee of a father, And meet it is I prove a father to thee: Go, princess, and may justice ever guard The throne which heaven hath called thee to possess! If thou dost hope obedience from thy subjects, Obey the laws, and tremble for thyself, When thou considerest all a sovereign's duty: And if the fatal powers of flattery e'er Should from thy heart unloose the sacred bonds Of justice, think on Rome; remember Tarquin: Let his example be the instructive lesson To future kings, and make the world more happy. Aruns, the senate gives her to thy care; A father and a husband at your hands Expect her. Proculus attends you hence, Far as the sacred gate.

**Titus:** [Apart.] Despair, and horror! I will not suffer it—permit me, sir, [Advancing towards Aruns.] [Brutus and Tullia with their Attendants go out, leaving Aruns and Messala.] Gods! I shall die of grief and shame: but soft, Aruns, I'd speak with you.

**Aruns:** My lord, the time Is short; I follow Brutus, and the princess; Remember, I can put off her departure But for an hour, and after that, my lord, 'Twill be too late to talk with me; within We may confer on Tullia's fate, perhaps On yours. [Exit.]

SCENE VII.

Titus, Messala.

**Messala:** O cruel destiny! to join And then divide us! Were we made, alas! But to be foes! My friend, I beg thee stop The tide of grief and rage.

**Messala:** I weep to see So many virtues and so many charms Rewarded thus: a heart like hers deserved To have been thine, and thine alone.

**Titus:** O no! Titus and Tullia ne'er shall be united.

**Messala:** Wherefore, my lord? what idle scruples rise To thwart your wishes?

**Titus**: The ungenerous laws She has imposed upon me: cruel maid! Must I then serve the tyrants I have conquered, Must I betray the people I had saved? Shall love, whose power I had so long defied, At last subdue me thus? Shall I expose My father to these proud despotic lords! And such a father, such a fair example To all mankind, the guardian of his country, Whom long I followed in the paths of honor, And might perhaps even one day have excelled; Shall Titus fall from such exalted virtue To infamy and vice? detested thought!

**Messala**: Thou art a Roman, rise to nobler views, And be a king; heaven offers thee a throne: Empire and love, and glory, and revenge Await thee: this proud consul, this support Of falling Rome, this idol of the people, If fortune had not crowned him with success, If Titus had not conquered for his father, Had been a rebel: thou hast gained the name Of conqueror, now assume a nobler title; Now be thy country's friend, and give her peace. Restore the happy days, when, blessed with freedom, Not unrestrained by power, our ancestors Weighed in the even scale, and balanced well The prince's honors and the people's right: Rome's hate of kings is not immortal; soon Would it be changed to love if Titus reigned: For monarchy, so oft admired, so oft Detested by us, is the best or worst Of human governments: A tyrant king Will make it dreadful, and a good, divine.

**Titus**: Messala, dost thou know me? Dost thou know I hold thee for a traitor, and myself Almost as guilty for conversing with thee?

**Messala**: Know thou, the honor thou contemnest shall soon Be wrested from thee, and another hand Perform thy office.

**Titus**: Ha! another! who?

**Messala**: Thy brother.

**Titus**: Ay! my brother.

**Messala**: He has given His faith to Tarquin.

**Titus**: Could Tiberius e'er Betray his country?

**Messala**: He will serve his king, And be a friend to Rome: in spite of thee, Tarquin will give his daughter to the man Who shall with warmest zeal defend her father.

**Titus**: Perfidious wretch! thou hast misled my steps. And left me hanging o'er the precipice; Left me the dreadful choice or to accuse My brother, or partake his guilt; but know, Sooner thy blood—

**Messala**: My life is in thy power, Take it this moment; I deserve to die For striving to oblige you: shed the blood Of friend, of mistress, and of brother; lay The breathless victims all before the senate, And for thy virtues ask the consulship: Or let me hence, and tell them all I know, Accuse my fellow-traitors, and myself Begin the sacrifice.

**Titus:** Messala, stop, Or dread my desperate rage.

### SCENE VIII.

Titus, Messala, Albinus.

**Albinus:** The ambassador Would see you now, my lord; he's with the princess.

**Titus:** Yes, I will fly to Tullia: O ye gods Of Rome, ye guardians of my much-loved country! Pierce this corrupted, this ungrateful heart: Had Titus never loved, he had been virtuous: And must I fall a sacrifice to thee, Detested senate! let us hence. [Turning to Messala.] Thou seest, Messala, this proud capitol replete With monuments of Titus' faith.

**Messala:** 'Tis filled By a proud senate.

**Titus:** Ay: I know it well: But hark! I hear the voice of angry heaven, It speaks to me in thunder, and cries, stop, Ungrateful Titus, thou betrayest thy country: No, Rome, no, Brutus, I am still thy son: O'er Titus' head the sun of glory still Hath shed his brightest rays; he never yet Disgraced his noble blood: your victim, gods, Is spotless yet; and if this fatal day Shall doom me to involuntary crimes, If I must yield to fate, let Titus die Whilst he is innocent, and save his country.

# ACT IV.

### SCENE I.

titus, aruns, messala. **Titus:** Urge me no more: I've heard too much already: Shame and despair surround me, but begone, I am resolved: go, leave me to my sorrows, And to my virtue: reason pleads in vain, But Tullia's tears are eloquent indeed: One look from her will more unman my soul Than all your tyrant's threats: but never more Will I behold her; let her go: O heaven!

**Aruns:** I stayed but to oblige you, sir, beyond The time which you so earnestly requested, And which we scarce could gain.

**Titus:** Did I request it?

**Aruns:** You did, my lord, and I in secret hoped A fairer fate would crown your loves; but now 'Tis past; we must not think on't.

**Titus:** Cruel Aruns! Thou hast beheld my shame, and my disgrace, Thou hast seen Titus for a moment doubtful: Thou artful witness of my folly, hence! And tell thy royal masters all my weakness; Tell the proud tyrants, that their conqueror, The son of Brutus, wept before thy face; But tell them too, that, spite of all my tears, Spite of thy eloquence, and Tullia's charms, I yet am free, a conqueror o'er myself: That, still a Roman, I will never yield To Tarquin's blood, but swear eternal war Against the race of her whom I adore.

**Aruns**: Titus, I pity and excuse thy grief; And, far from wishing to oppress thy heart With added sorrows, mix my sighs with thine; Only remember, thou hast killed thy Tullia Farewell, my lord.

**Messala**: O heaven!

## SCENE II.

Titus, Messala.

**Titus**: She must not go: On peril of my life I'll keep her here.

**Messala**: You would not—

**Titus**: No: I'll not betray my country: Rome may divide her from me, but she never Can disunite our fate; I live, and breathe For Tullia only, and for her will die. Messala, haste, have pity on my woes, Gather our troops, assemble all our friends. Spite of the senate I will stop her; say She must remain a hostage here at Rome; I'll do it, Messala.

**Messala**: To what desperate means Doth passion urge you? What will it avail To make this fond avowal of your love?

**Titus**: Go to the senate, and appeal to them, Try if thou canst not soften the proud hearts Of these imperious kings. Messala, tell them The interest of Brutus, of the state— Alas! I rave, 'tis idle, and all in vain.

**Messala**: I see you're hurt, my lord, and I will serve you. I go—

**Titus**: I'll see her: speak to her, Messala, She passes by this way, and I will take My last farewell of her.

**Messala**: You shall.

**Titus**: 'Tis she Now I am lost indeed.

## SCENE III.

Titus, Messala, Tullia, Algina.

**Algina**: Madam, they wait.

**Tullia**: Pity my hard, my cruel fate, Algina; This base ungrateful man still wounds my heart; And Brutus, like a vengeful god, appears To torture us: love, fear and grief, at once Distract my soul: let us begone.

**Titus**: O no! Stay, Tullia, deign at least—

**Tullia**: Barbarian, hence! Thinkest thou with soothing words—

**Titus**: Alas! my Tullia, I only know in this disastrous hour What duty bids me do, not what I would: Reason no longer holds her empire here, For thou hast torn her from me, and usurpest The power supreme o'er this distracted mind: Reign, tyrant, stretch thy cruel power; command Thy vassal; bid thy Titus rush on guilt; Dictate his crimes, and make him wretched; No; Sooner than Titus shall betray his country, Give up his friends, his fellow citizens, Those whom his valor saved to fire and slaughter, Sooner than leave his father to the sword Of Tarquin, know, proud woman—

**Tullia**: Shield me, heaven! Thou pleadest the cause of nature, and her voice Is dear to me as to thyself: thou, Titus, Taughtest me long since to tremble for a father; Brutus is mine; our blood united flows: Canst thou require a fairer pledge than love And truth have given thee: if I stay with thee, I am his daughter, and his hostage here. Canst thou yet doubt? thinkest thou in secret Brutus Would not rejoice to see thee on a throne? He hath not placed indeed a diadem On his own brows, but is he not a king Beneath another name? and one year's reign Perhaps may bring—but these are fruitless reasons. If thou no longer lovest me—one word more, Farewell: I leave, and I adore thee, Titus: Thou weepest, thou tremblest; yet a little time Is left for thee. Speak, tell me, cruel man, What more canst thou desire?

**Titus**: Thy hatred; that Alone remains to make me truly wretched.

**Tullia**: It is too much to bear thy causeless plaints; To hear thee talk of fancied injuries, With idle dreams of visionary ties: Take back thy love, take back thy faithless vows, Worse than thy base refusal: I despise them. Think not I mean to search in Italy The fatal grandeur which I sacrificed To Titus' love, and in another's arms Lament the weakness which I felt for thee; My fate's determined: learn, proud Roman, thou Whose savage virtue rises but to oppress A helpless woman, coward, when I ask Thy aid, and only valiant to destroy me, Fickle and wavering in thy faith, of me Learn to fulfill thy vows; thou shalt behold A Woman, in thy eyes however contemned, However despised, unshaken in her purpose, And by her firmness see how much she loved thee. Titus, beneath these walls, the reverend seat Of my great ancestors, which thou defendest Against their rightful lord; this fatal spot Where thou hast dared to insult and to betray me; Where first thy faithless vows deceived me; there, Even there, by all the gods who store up vengeance For perjured men, I swear to thee, O Titus, This arm, more just than thine, and more resolved, Shall punish soon my fond credulity, And wash out all my injuries in my blood: I go—

**Titus**: No, Tullia, hear and then condemn me; You shall be satisfied; I fly to please you, Yet shudder at it: I am still more wretched, Because my guilty soul has no excuse, No poor delusion left. I have not even The joy of self-deceit to soothe my sorrows: No, thou hast conquered, not betrayed me, Tullia; I loathe

the fatal passion which I feel, And rush on vice, yet know and honor virtue. Hate me, avoid me, leave a guilty wretch Who dies for love, yet hates himself for loving; Nor fears to mix his future fate with thine, Midst crimes, and horrors, perjury, and death.

**Tullia**: You know too well your influence o'er my heart; Mock my fond passion, and insult my love; Yes, Titus, 'tis for thee alone I live, For thee would die: yet, spite of all my love, And all my weakness, death were far more welcome Than the reluctant hand of cruel Titus, Who is ashamed to serve his royal master, And blushes to accept a kingdom from me. The dreadful hour of separation comes, Think on it, Titus, and remember well That Tullia loves, and offers thee a throne. The ambassador expects me; fare thee well, Deliberate and determine: an hour hence Again thou shalt behold me with my father: When I return to these detested walls Know, Titus, I'll return a queen, or perish.

**Titus**: Thou shalt not die: I go—

**Tullia**: Stop, Titus, stop; If thou shouldst follow me, thy life's in danger, Thou'lt be suspected; therefore stay: farewell; Resolve to be my murderer, or my husband.

### SCENE IV.

**Titus**: [Alone.] O Tullia, thou hast conquered, Rome's enslaved: Return to rule o'er her, and o'er my life, Devoted to thee: haste, I fly to crown thee, Or perish in the attempt: the worst of crimes Were to abandon thee. Now, where's Messala? My headstrong passion hath at length worn out His patient friendship; mistress, Romans, friends, All in one fatal day, hath Titus lost.

### SCENE V.

Titus, Messala.

**Titus**: O my Messala, help me in my love, And my revenge: away; haste, follow me.

**Messala**: Command, and I obey: my troops are ready At the Quirinal mount to give us up The gates, and all my gallant friends have sworn To acknowledge Titus as the rightful heir Of Tarquin: lose no time; propitious night Already offers her kind shade to veil Our great design.

**Titus**: The hour approaches: Tullia Will count each minute: Tarquin, after all, Had my first oaths: away, the die is cast. [The lower part of the stage opens and discovers Brutus.] What do I see; my father!

## SCENE VI.

Brutus, Titus, Messala, Lictors.

**Brutus**: Titus, haste, Rome is in danger; thou art all our hope: Secret instructions have been given the senate That Rome will be attacked at dead of night, And I have gained for my beloved Titus The first command, in this extremity Of public danger. Arm thyself, my son, And fly, a second time, to save thy country; Hazard thy life once more in the great cause Of liberty; or victory or death Must crown thy days, and I shall envy thee.

**Titus**: O heaven!

**Brutus**: My son!

**Titus**: To other hands commit The senate's favors, and the fate of Rome.

**Messala**: What strange disorder has possessed his soul!

**Brutus**: Dost thou refuse the proffered glory?

**Titus**: I! Shall I, my lord—

**Brutus**: Ha! doth thy heart still burn With proud resentment of thy fancied wrongs? Is this a time, my son, for fond caprice? Can he who saved his country be unhappy? Immortal honor! will not that suffice Without the consulship? The laws, thou knowest, Refused it, Titus, to thy youth alone, Not to thy merit: think no more of that: Go; I have placed thee in the post of honor; Let tyrants only feel thy indignation; Give Rome thy life; ask nothing in return, But be a hero; be yet more, my son, A Roman: I am hastening to the end Of my short journey; thy victorious hands Must close my eyes; supported by thy virtues, My name shall never die; I shall revive And live once more in Titus: but perhaps It is decreed that I must follow thee; Old age is weak; but I will see thee conquer, Or perish with thee, Rome's avenger still, Free, and without a master.

**Titus**: O Messala!

## SCENE VII.

Brutus, Valerius, Titus, Messala.

**Valerius**: My lord, let all retire.

**Brutus**: [To Titus.] Run, fly, my son—

**Valerius**: Rome is betrayed.

**Brutus**: What do I hear?

**Valerius**: There's treason; We're sold, my lord, the author's yet unknown; But Tarquin's name is echoed through our streets, And worthless Romans talk of yielding to him.

**Brutus**: Ha! would the citizens of Rome be slaves!

**Valerius:** Yes: the perfidious traitors fled from me; I've sent in quest of them: much I suspect Menas and Lælius, the base partisans Of tyranny and kings, the secret foes Of Rome, and ever glad to disunite The senate and the people: if I err not, Protected by Messala, who himself, But for his friendship with the noble Titus, I almost think, has joined them.

**Brutus:** We'll observe Their steps with caution; more cannot be done: The liberty and laws which we defend Forbid that rigor which I fear is needful; But to detain a Roman on suspicions Were to resemble those usurping tyrants Whom we would punish: let us to the people, Awake the fearful, give the virtuous praise, Astonish the perfidious: let the fathers Of Rome and liberty revive the warmth Of Roman courage: who will not be bold When we appear? O rather give us death, Ye gods! than slavery: let the senate follow.

### SCENE VIII.

Brutus, Valerius, Proculus.

**Proculus:** A slave, my lord, desires a private audience.

**Brutus:** At this late hour of night!

**Proculus:** He brings you news, He says, of highest import.

**Brutus:** Ha! perhaps Rome's safety may depend on it: away. [To Proculus.] A moment's loss might hazard all—go thou And seek my son: let the Quirinal gate Be his first care: and may the world confess, When they behold his glorious deeds, the race Of Brutus was decreed to conquer kings.

## ACT V.

### SCENE I.

Brutus, Senators, Proculus, Lictors. Vindex (A Slave).

**Brutus:** A little more and Tarquin, armed with vengeance, This night had rushed upon us; Rome had fallen, And freedom sunk beneath the tyrant's power: This subtle statesman, this ambassador, Had opened wide the fatal precipice: Would you believe it, even the sons of Rome United to betray her: false Messala Urged on their furious zeal, and sold his country To this perfidious Aruns; but kind heaven, Still watchful o'er the fate of Rome, preserved us. [Pointing to Vindex.] This slave o'erheard it all; his faithful counsels Awaked my fears, and filled my aged breast With double vigor: I had scized Messala, And hoped by tortures to have wrested from him The names of his associates; but, behold, Surrounded by my lictors, on a sudden He from his bosom drew a poniard forth, Designed no doubt for other purposes, And cried, if you would know Messala's secrets, Look for them here, within this bleeding breast; He who has courage to conspire against you, Can keep the counsel which he gives, and die: Then, as tumultuously they gathered round him, Pierced his false heart, and like a Roman died, Though he had lived unworthy of the name. Already Aruns was beyond the walls Of Rome; our guards pursued him to the camp, Stopped him with Tullia, and ere long will bring The traitor here, when heaven, I trust, will soon Unravel all their dark and deadly purpose. Valerius will detect them: but remember Friends, Romans, countrymen, I charge you all, When ye shall know the names of these vile slaves, These parricides, nor pardon nor indulgence Be shown to friends, to brothers, nay to children; Think on their crimes alone, preserve your faith, For liberty and Rome demand their blood, And he who pardons guilt like theirs, partakes it. [To the slave.] Thou, whose blind destiny and lowly birth Made thee a slave, who shouldst have been a Roman; Thou, by whose generous aid the senate lives, And Rome is safe, receive that liberty Thou hast bestowed; henceforth let nobler thoughts Inspire thy soul; be equal to my sons, The dread of tyrants, the delight of Rome. But whence this tumult? Hark!

**Proculus**: The ambassador Is seized, my lord, and they have brought him hither.

**Brutus**: How will he dare—

SCENE II.

Brutus, Senators, Aruns, Lictors.

**Aruns**: How long, insulting Romans, Will you thus violate the sacred rights Of all mankind? How long by faction led Thus in their ministers dishonor kings? Your lictors have with insolence detained me: Is it my master you thus treat with scorn, Or Aruns? Know, my rank respectable In every nation—

**Brutus**: The more sacred that, More guilty thou: talk not of titles here.

**Aruns**: A king's ambassador—

**brutus**: Thou art not one: Thou are a traitor, with a noble name, Emboldened by impunity: for know That, true ambassadors interpret laws, But never break them; serve their king, but ne'er Dishonor him: with them reposed in safety Lie the firm ties of faith 'twixt man and man; And of their holy ministry the fruit Is grateful peace: they are the sacred bonds That knit the sovereigns of the earth together; And, as the friends of all, by all revered. Ask thy own heart if thou art such; thou darest not: But if thy master bade thee learn our laws, Our virtues, and our treasures, we will teach thee Now what Rome is, and what a Roman senate: Will teach thee that this people still respects The law of nations, which thou hast dishonored: The only punishment inflicted on thee, Shall be to see thy vile associates bleed, And tell thy king their folly and their fate. When thou returnest, be sure inform thy friends Of Rome's resentment, and thy own disgrace: Lictors, away with him.

SCENE III.
Brutus, Valerius, Proculus, Senators.
Well, my Valerius, They're seized, I hope, at least you know the traitors: Ha! wherefore is that melancholy gloom Spread o'er thy face, presaging greater ills? Thou tremblest too.

**Valerius**: Remember thou art Brutus.

**Brutus**: Explain thyself.

**Valerius**: I dare not speak it: take [Gives him the tablets.] These tablets, read, and know the guilty.

**Brutus**: Ha! My eyes deceive me; sure it cannot be! O heavy hour! and most unhappy father! My son! Tiberius! pardon me, my friends, Unlooked for misery! Have you seized the traitor?

**Valerius**: My lord, with two of the conspirators, He stood on his defence, and rather chose To die than yield himself a prisoner: close By them he fell all covered o'er with wounds: But O there still remains a tale more dreadful For thee, for Rome, and for us all.

**Brutus**: What is it?

**Valerius**: Once more, my lord, look on that fatal scroll Which Proculus had wrested from Messala.

**Brutus**: I tremble, but I will go on: ha! Titus! [He sinks into the arms of Proculus.]

**Valerius**: Disarmed I found him, wandering in despair And horror, as if conscious of a crime Which he abhorred.

**Brutus**: Return, ye conscript fathers, Straight to the senate; Brutus hath no place Amongst you now: go, pass your judgment on him, Exterminate the guilty race of Brutus; Punish the father in the blood of him Who was my child: I shall not follow you, Or to suspend or mitigate the wrath Of injured Rome.

SCENE IV.
**Brutus**: [Alone.] Great gods! to your decrees I yield submissive, to the great avengers Of Rome, and of her laws: by you inspired I reared the structure of fair liberty On justice and on truth; and will you now O'erthrow it? will you arm my children's hands Against your own work? Was it not woe enough That fierce

Tiberius, blind with furious zeal, Should serve the tyrant, and betray his country? But that my Titus too, the joy of Rome, Who, full of honor, but this very day Enjoyed a triumph for his victories, Crowned in the capitol by Brutus' hand, Titus, the hope of my declining years, The darling of mankind, that Titus—gods!

## SCENE V.

Brutus, Valerius, Lictors, Attendants.

**Valerius**: My lord, the senate has decreed, yourself Should pass the sentence on your guilty son.

**Brutus**: Myself!

**Valerius**: It must be so.

**Brutus**: Touching the rest, Say, what have they determined?

**Valerius**: All condemned To death; even now perhaps they are no more.

**Brutus**: And has the senate left to my disposal The life of Titus?

**Valerius**: They esteem this honor Due to thy virtues.

**Brutus**: O my country!

**Valerius**: What Must I return in answer to the senate?

**Brutus**: That Brutus knows the value of a favor He sought not, but shall study to deserve. But could my son without resistance yield? Could he—forgive my doubts, but Titus ever Was Rome's best guard, and still I feel I love him.

**Valerius**: Tullia, my lord—

**Brutus**: Well, what of her?

**Valerius**: Confirmed Our just suspicions.

**Brutus**: How!

**Valerius**: Soon as she saw, In her return, the dreadful preparation Of torture for the offenders, at our feet She fell, and soon in agonies expired; The last poor victim of the hated race Of tyrants: doubtless 'twas for her, my lord, Rome was betrayed: I feel a father's grief, And weep for Brutus; but in her last moments This way she turned her eyes, and called on Titus.

**Brutus**: Just gods!

**Valerius**: Thou art his judge, perform thy office, Or strike, or spare; acquit him, or condemn; Rome will approve what Brutus shall determine.

**Brutus**: Lictors, bring Titus hither.

**Valerius**: I retire, And trust thy virtue; my astonished soul Admires and pities thee: I go to tell The senate, naught can equal Brutus' grief But Brutus' firmness.

## SCENE VI.

Brutus, Proculus.

**Brutus:** No: the more I think, The less can I believe my son could e'er Conspire with traitors to betray his country: No: he loved Rome too well; too well he loved His father: sure we cannot thus forget Our duty and ourselves in one short day: I cannot think my son was guilty still.

**Proculus:** 'Twas all conducted by Messala; he Perhaps designed to shelter his own crimes Beneath the name of Titus; his accusers Envy his glory, and would fain obscure it.

**Brutus:** O! would to heaven it were so!

**Proculus:** He's thy son, Thy only hope; and innocent or guilty, The senate has to thee resigned his fate: His life is safe whilst in the hands of Brutus; Thou wilt preserve a great man for his country; Thou art a father.

**Brutus:** No: I am Rome's consul.

SCENE VII.
Brutus, Proculus.
**Titus:** [At the farther end of the stage, guarded by Lictors.]
**Proculus:** He comes.
**Titus:** [Advancing.] 'Tis Brutus: O distressful sight! Open, thou earth, beneath my trembling steps! My lord, permit a son—

**Brutus:** Rash boy, forbear: I was the father of two children once, And loved them both; but one is lost: what sayest thou? Speak, Titus, have I yet a son?

**Titus:** O no: Thou hast not.

**Brutus:** Answer then thy judge, thou shame To Brutus; say, didst thou betray thy country, Give up thy father to a tyrant's power, And break thy solemn vows? Didst thou resolve To do this, Titus?

**Titus:** I resolved on nothing. Filled with a deadly poison that possessed My frantic mind, I did not know myself, Nor do I yet; and my distempered soul, In its wild rage, was for a moment guilty; That moment clothed me with eternal shame, And made me false to what I loved, my country: 'Tis past; and anguish and remorse succeed To avenge their wrongs, and scourge me for the crime. Pronounce my sentence: Rome, that looks upon thee, Wants an example, and demands my life: By my deserved fate she may deter Those of her sons, if any such there be, Who might be tempted to a crime like mine. In death at least thus shall I serve my country; Thus shall my blood, which never till this hour Was stained with guilt, still flow for liberty.

**Brutus:** Unnatural mixture! perfidy and courage; Such horrid crimes with such exalted virtue! With all thy dear-bought laurels on thy brow, What power malignant could inspire thee thus With vile inconstancy?

**Titus**: The thirst of vengeance, Ambition, hatred, madness; all united—

**Brutus**: Go on, unhappy youth.

**Titus**: One error more, And worse than all the rest; one cruel flame; That fired my guilt, and still perhaps augments it, Completed my destruction: to confess it Is double shame, to Rome of little service, And most unworthy of us both: I own it: But I have reached the summit of my guilt, And of my sorrows too: end with my life My crimes, and my despair, my shame and thine. [Kneeling.] But if in battle I have ever traced Thy glorious steps; if I have followed thee, And served my country; if remorse and anguish Already have o'erpaid my crimes; O deign Within thy arms once more to hold a wretch Abandoned and forlorn: O say, at least, "My son, thy father hates thee not": that word Alone my fame and virtue shall restore, And save my memory from the brand of shame. The world will say, when Titus died, a look From you relieved him from his load of grief, And made him full amends for all his sorrows; Spite of his guilt, that still esteemed by thee, He bore thy blessing with him to the grave.

**Brutus**: O Rome! his pangs oppress me: O my country! Proculus, see they lead my son to death. Rise, wretched Titus, thou wert once the hope Of my old age, my best support; embrace Thy father who condemned thee; 'twas his duty. Were he not Brutus, he had pardoned thee; Believe my tears that trickle down thy cheeks Whilst I am speaking to thee: O my Titus, Let nobler courage than thy father shows Support thee in thy death; my son, farewell: Let no unmanly tears disgrace thy fall, But be a Roman still, and let thy country, That knows thy worth, admire while she destroys thee.

**Titus**: Farewell: I go to death; in that at least Titus once more shall emulate his father.

## SCENE VIII.

Brutus, Proculus.

**Proculus**: My lord, the senate, with sincerest grief, And shuddering at the dreadful stroke—

**Brutus**: No more: Ye know not Brutus who condole with him At such a time: Rome only is my care; I feel but for my country: we must guard Against more danger: they're in arms again: Away: let Rome in this disastrous hour Supply the place of him whom I have lost For her, and let me finish my sad days, As Titus should have done, in Rome's defence.

**SCENE the LAST.**
**Brutus**, Proculus, a Senator.
**Senator**: My lord—
**Brutus**: My son is dead?
**Senator**: 'Tis so: these eyes—
**Brutus**: Thank heaven! Rome's free; and I am satisfied.
**End**

# Socrates

## Contents

Dramatis Personæ . . . . . . . . . . . . . . . . . . . . . . . . . . . . . . . . . . . . . 36

Act I . . . . . . . . . . . . . . . . . . . . . . . . . . . . . . . . . . . . . . . . . . . . . . . . 36

Act II . . . . . . . . . . . . . . . . . . . . . . . . . . . . . . . . . . . . . . . . . . . . . . . 44

Act III . . . . . . . . . . . . . . . . . . . . . . . . . . . . . . . . . . . . . . . . . . . . . . 52

## Dramatis Personæ

Socrates.
Anitus, High Priest of Ceres.
Melitus, one of the Judges of Athens.
Xantippe, Wife of Socrates.
Aglae, a young Athenian Lady, brought up by Socrates.
Sophronimus, a young Athenian Gentleman, brought up by Socrates.
Drixa, Terpander, Acros, Friends of Anitus.

## ACT I.

*Judges, Disciples of Socrates, and three Pedants, Protected by Anitus.*

### SCENE I.
Anitus, Drixa, Terpander, Acros.

**Anitus**: My dear confidante, and you my trusty friends, you well know how much money I have put into your pockets this last feast of Ceres: I am now going to be married, and I hope you will all do your respective duties on this great occasion.

**Drixa**: That, my lord, we most certainly shall, provided you give us an opportunity of getting a little more by it.

**Anitus**: I shall want of you, Madam Drixa, two fine Persian carpets; from you, Terpander, I must have two large silver candlesticks; and from you, half a dozen robes.

**Terpander**: A considerable demand, my lord; but there is nothing which we would not do to merit your holy protection.

**Anitus**: O you will be rewarded for it a hundred fold: 'tis the best means to gain the favor of the gods: give much, and much you shall receive; but above all fail not, I beseech you, to stir up the people against all the rich and great, who are deficient in paying their vows, and presenting their offerings.

**Acros**: On that, my lord, you may depend; it is a duty too sacred ever to be neglected by us.

**Anitus**: 'Tis well, my friends; may heaven continue to inspire you with the same just and pious sentiments, and be assured you will prosper; you, your children, and your children's children, to all posterity.

**Terpander**: You have said it, my lord, and therefore it must be so.

SCENE II.
Anitus, Drixa.

**Anitus**: Well, my dear Drixa, I believe you will have no objection to my marrying Aglae; I shall not love you the less, and we may still live together as we used to do.

**Drixa**: O my lord, I am not jealous; as long as trade goes on well, I am contented. While I had the honor of being one of your mistresses, I was a woman of some consequence in Athens: but if you are in love with Aglae, I, in my turn, am as fond of young Sophronimus: and Xantippe, Socrates's wife, has promised that he shall marry me. I shall be always, notwithstanding, as much at your service as ever. I am only vexed that this young fellow has been brought up with that rascal Socrates, and that Aglae is still in his hands. We must take them both out as fast as we can. Xantippe will be glad to get rid of them. The beautiful Sophronimus and the fair Aglae have a sad time of it with the surly Socrates.

**Anitus**: I am in great hopes, my dear, that Melitus and I together shall soon be able to destroy this dangerous fellow, who preaches nothing but virtue and divinity, and has taken the liberty to laugh at some certain adventures that happened at the mysteries of Ceres: but he is Aglae's tutor: her father, Agathon, they tell me, has left her a great fortune: in short, Aglae is a charming girl; I love her, and I will marry her; and as to Socrates, I shall take care of him.

**Drixa**: Do what you please with Socrates, so I can but get my dear Sophronimus: but how could that fool Agathon leave his daughter in the hands of this old flat-nosed Socrates, that intolerable reasoner, who corrupts all our young men, and keeps them away from courtesans and the mysteries?

**Anitus**: Agathon himself was tainted with the same vile principles: he was one of your sober, serious fools, whose manners differed in every respect from ours; a man, in short, of another age, one of our sworn and inveterate enemies, who think they have fulfilled every duty when they worship God, assist man, cultivate friendships, and study philosophy; one of those ridiculous creatures who insolently deny that the gods prognosticate future events by the liver of an ox; those merciless reasoners, who find fault with priests for sacrificing young girls, or passing a night with them on occasion. These you see, Drixa, are a kind of people not fit to live. As to Socrates, I should have been glad to have him strangled long ago. However, I have agreed to meet him here in the portico, and talk with him about the marriage.

**Drixa**: Here he comes: you do him too much honor: but I must leave you, and talk to Xantippe about my young man.

**Anitus**: The gods conduct you, my dear Drixa; remember to serve them, and don't forget my two fine Persian carpets.

## SCENE III.

Anitus, Socrates.

**Anitus**: Good morning, my dear Socrates, thou favorite of the gods, and wisest of men; methinks every time I see you I am raised above myself; in you I look up with admiration to the dignity of human nature.

**Socrates**: O my lord, I am a plain simple man, as void of knowledge, and as full of weakness, as any of my fellow-creatures; it is enough for me if you can bear with me.

**Anitus**: Bear with? I admire you, and would it were possible I could resemble you! To convince you of it, and that I may oftener be a witness to your virtues, and improve by your instructions, I am willing to espouse your fair pupil Aglae, whom I find you have the entire disposal of.

**Socrates**: It is true indeed that her father Agathon, who was my friend, the dearest of all relations, bequeathed to my care, by his last will, this amiable and virtuous orphan.

**Anitus**: With a considerable fortune no doubt, for I hear she is one of the best matches in all Athens.

**Socrates**: With regard to that I can give you no information; her father, my dearest friend, whose will is ever sacred to me, forbade me to divulge the situation of her affairs in that point.

**Anitus:** This respect and discreet veneration for the last will of your friend are worthy of your noble soul; but it is well enough known that Agathon was rich.

**Socrates:** He deserved to be so, if riches are a mark of the divine favor.

**Anitus:** They tell me a young coxcomb, named Sophronimus, makes love to her on account of her fortune; but I am persuaded you will not give encouragement to such a fellow, and that Anitus will have no rival.

**Socrates:** I know in what light I ought to consider a person like you; but it is not for me to thwart the inclinations of Aglae. I would supply the place of a father to her, but I am not her master: she has a right to dispose of her own heart: I look upon restraint in this case as a crime: talk to her: if she hearkens to your proposal, with all my heart, I have no objection.

**Anitus:** I have your wife's consent already; without doubt she is acquainted with Aglae's sentiments, and therefore I look upon the affair as good as concluded.

**Socrates:** But I never look upon things as done till they are really so.

## SCENE IV.

Socrates, Anitus, Aglae.

**Socrates:** Come hither, Aglae, and determine for yourself. Here is a person of considerable rank, who offers himself to you for a husband: you are at liberty to explain yourself to him: my presence might perhaps be a restraint upon you: whatever choice you make I shall approve: Xantippe will prepare everything for your nuptials.

**Aglae:** Generous Socrates! I am sorry you leave me.

**Anitus:** You seem, charming Aglae, to place great confidence in the good Socrates.

**Aglae:** It is my duty, sir; he has been a father to me; he has educated and instructed me.

**Anitus:** And pray, my dear, as he has instructed you, tell me what is your opinion of Ceres, Cybele, and Venus?

**Aglae:** Of them, sir, I will think just as you please.

**Anitus:** 'Tis well said, and you will do as I please, too, then I hope.

**Aglae:** No, sir, that is quite another affair.

**Anitus:** You see, the wise Socrates consents to our marriage, and Xantippe above all things wishes for it. You know my passion for you, and are no stranger to my rank and fortune; my happiness, perhaps your own too, depends on one word, therefore determine.

**Aglae**: I will answer you, sir, with that truth and sincerity which the great man who just now left us taught me never to depart from: I respect your dignity, know but little of your person, and, in a word, can never be yours.

**Anitus**: Never? cruel Aglae, are you not free? you will not then?

**Aglae**: No, sir, I cannot.

**Anitus**: What an affront, what an indignity is this! but 'tis to Socrates I am obliged for it: he dictated your answer, I know he did; he prefers Sophronimus to me, that unworthy rival, that impious—

**Aglae**: Sophronimus is not impious, not unworthy; Socrates has loved him from his infancy; he has been a father to us both. Sophronimus is all beauty and all virtue; I love, and am beloved by him; it is in my power to marry him if I think proper; but I shall no more be his than yours.

**Anitus**: You astonish me: what! own you love Sophronimus?

**Aglae**: Yes, sir, I own it, because it is true.

**Anitus**: And yet when it is in your power to make yourself happy with him, refuse him you hand?

**Aglae**: That, sir, is no less true.

**Anitus**: Then I suppose your fear of displeasing me prevents your engaging with him?

**Aglae**: No such thing, I assure you: for having never wished to please, I have no fear of displeasing you.

**Anitus**: You dread then perhaps the displeasure of the gods, at seeing you prefer a profane wretch, like Sophronimus, to a high-priest?

**Aglae**: Not in the least. I am persuaded it is matter of very little concern to the supreme being, whether I marry you, or not.

**Anitus**: The supreme being! my dear child, you should not talk in this manner; you should say the gods and goddesses: take care, for I see you entertain some very dangerous opinions; but I know too well from whom they came. Learn then that Ceres, whose priest I am, may punish you for thus despising her worship, and her minister.

**Aglae**: I despise neither the one nor the other. I have been told that Ceres presides over the harvest, and I believe it; but she has nothing to do with my marriage.

**Anitus**: She has to do with everything; you know it; but I hope I shall be able to convert you. Are you indeed resolved not to marry Sophronimus?

**Aglae**: Yes; I am resolved, and am very sorry for it.

**Anitus**: I cannot understand a word of all these contradictions: but observe me; I love you, would have made you happy, and advanced you to rank and dignity: be advised, and reject not the offers which kind fortune thus courts you to accept: remember that everything should be sacrificed to our real interest; that youth will pass away, but riches remain: that wealth and honors should be your first concern, and that I speak to you on the part of the gods. I beg you will reflect seriously on what I have said: farewell; my dear girl, I shall pray to Ceres that she would inspire you, and still flatter myself she will touch your heart. Once more adieu, remember, you have promised me never to marry Sophronimus.

**Aglae**: I promised myself, but not you. [Exit Anitus]

**Aglae**: [Alone.] This man but makes me more unhappy. I know not why it is, but I never see him without shuddering: but here comes Sophronimus: alas! whilst his rival fills my heart with terror, he increases my tenderness and doubles my disquietude.

## SCENE V.

Aglae, Sophronimus.

**Sophronimus**: My dear Aglae, I met Anitus, the priest of Ceres, that worst of men, the sworn enemy of Socrates, just coming from you: your eyes seem bathed in tears.

**Aglae**: Is he the enemy of our benefactor too? then indeed I wonder not at my aversion to him, even before he spoke.

**Sophronimus**: And is he the cause of your tears, my Aglae?

**Aglae**: No, Sophronimus, he can inspire nothing but hatred and disgust: my tears can flow for you alone.

**Sophronimus**: For me? O gods, for me, who would repay them with my blood, for me who adore you, who hope to be beloved by Aglae, who only live for and would die for you? shall I reproach myself with having embittered one moment of your life? Aglae weeps, and Sophronimus is the cause. What have I done? what crime have I committed?

**Aglae**: None, my Sophronimus: you could not do it: 'tis not in your nature. I wept because you merit all my tenderness, because you have it, and because I must renounce you.

**Sophronimus**: What dreadful sentence have you pronounced against me? I cannot believe you: you love me, you said you did, and Aglae can never change. You have promised to be mine, you cannot wish my death.

**Aglae**: No; I would have thee live and be happy: but, alas! I cannot make you so: I hoped I could, but fortune has deceived me. I swear to you, Sophronimus, since I cannot be yours, I never will be another's. I have declared so to Anitus, who courts me, and whom I despise; and here I declare the same to you, with a heart full of grief, tenderness, and love.

**Sophronimus**: Since you love me, I must live; but if you refuse me your hand, it will be death to Sophronimus; therefore, my dearest Aglae, in the name of love, of all your charms, and all your virtues, explain to me this dreadful mystery.

### SCENE VI.

Socrates, Sophronimus, Aglae.

**Sophronimus**: O my honored master, my father, and my friend, behold in Sophronimus the most unfortunate of men, though in the presence of the only two beings upon earth who could make me happy: Socrates first taught me wisdom, and from Aglae I learned to love; you consented to our marriage, and this beauteous fair one, who seemed so desirous of it, now refuses me; and whilst she says she loves, plunges a dagger in my heart: she has broke off the match without assigning any cause of her cruel caprice: O Socrates, prevent my misery, or teach me, if possible, how to bear it.

**Socrates**: Aglae is mistress of herself; her father made me her tutor, but not her tyrant; to see you united would have made me happy: if she has changed her mind I am surprised and sorry for it: but let us hear her reasons; if they are good, we must submit to them.

**Sophronimus**: It is impossible they should.

**Aglae**: To me however they appear so, but you shall hear them. When you first opened my father's will, most noble Socrates, you told me he had left me a sufficient competency; from that moment I resolved to bestow my fortune on the good Sophronimus, who has no support but you, no riches but his virtue: you applauded my resolution. How great was my happiness, in promoting that of him whom you have so long regarded as your own son! full of this pleasing hope I laid open the situation of my heart to Xantippe, who at once undeceived me. She treated me as an idle visionary; showed me the will of my father, who died a beggar, and left me nothing but your friendship to depend on. Awakened from my dream of promised happiness, nothing remained for me but the melancholy reflection that it was no longer in my power to make the fortune of Sophronimus: I would not oppress him with the weight of my misfortunes.

**Sophronimus**: I told you, Socrates, her reasons were poor and insufficient. If she loves me, am I not rich enough? Hitherto, it is true, I have subsisted from your bounty; but there is no employment, however irksome, which I would not undertake, to provide for my dearest Aglae: I ought indeed to make her a sacrifice of my passion, to find out some richer, happier lover for her: but I own my weakness, I cannot do it, there I am indeed unworthy of her; but if she could content herself with my low estate, if she could stoop to my humble condition: but I dare not hope so much; I sink beneath a misfortune which her fortitude is able to bear.

**Socrates**: My dear children, it was very indiscreet in Xantippe to show you the will; but believe me, Aglae, she deceived you.

**Aglae**: Indeed she has not: I saw it with my own eyes: I know my father's hand too well to have the least doubt of it: but be assured, Socrates, I shall be able to bear poverty as I ought: these hands will support me; if I can but live, it is enough for me, but it is not for Sophronimus.

**Sophronimus**: It is too much, a thousand times too much for me: thou tender, noble soul, worthy of thy illustrious master: a virtuous and laborious poverty is the natural state of man. I wish I could have offered you a throne, but if you will condescend to live with Sophronimus, our respectable poverty will be superior to the throne of Crœsus.

**Socrates**: Your generous sentiments at once delight and distress me: I behold with transport those virtues budding forth in your heart, which I myself had sown: never were my hopes better fulfilled than in Aglae and Sophronimus: but once more believe me, Aglae, my wife has misinformed you: you are richer than you think you are: it was not to her, but to me your father entrusted you. May he not have left you a fortune which Xantippe knows nothing of?

**Aglae**: No, Socrates, he says expressly in his will, that he has left me poor.

**Socrates**: And I tell you that you are deceived, that he has left you a sufficient competency to enable you to live happily with the virtuous Sophronimus, and that I desire therefore you would come, and sign the contract immediately.

### SCENE VII.

Socrates, Xantippe, Aglae, Sophronimus.

**Xantippe**: Come, come, child, don't stand amusing yourself there with my husband's visions and nonsense: philosophy to be sure is a mighty pretty thing when folks have nothing else to do: but you are a beggar, child; and must study how to live first, and philosophize afterwards. I have concluded your marriage with Anitus, a worthy priest, and a man of fortune. Come, child, follow me, let me have no delays nor contradiction; I love to be obeyed: quick, quick, my dear, 'tis for your good, therefore let me have none of your reasonings, but follow me.

**Sophronimus**: O heaven! my dear Aglae!

**Socrates**: Let her talk, and trust to me for your happiness.

**Xantippe:** Let me talk indeed! I shall talk and do too, I assure you. You are a pretty one to be sure, with your wisdom, your familiar demon, your irony, and all your nonsense that signifies nothing, to trouble yourself about matrimony: you are a good sort of a man, but you really know nothing of the world; happy is it for you that I am able to govern you. Come, Aglae, I must settle you as soon as possible: And you, sir, there, that seem as if you were thunderstruck, I have taken care of you too: Drixa is the woman for you: you will both of you thank me by and by: I shall have done it all in a minute: I am very expeditious: let us lose no time therefore, by rights it should have been all over before this.

**Socrates:** My children, don't thwart or provoke her, but pay her all kind of deference: we must comply with since we can't mend her: it is the triumph of reason to live well with those who have none.

# ACT II.

### SCENE I.
Socrates, Sophronimus.

**Sophronimus:** Divine Socrates, I know not how to believe my own happiness: how can Aglae, whose father died in extreme poverty be possessed of so considerable a fortune?

**Socrates:** I told you before, she had more than she thought she had: I knew her father's affairs better than herself: let it suffice that you both enjoy a fortune which you deserve: the secrets of the dead should be preserved as religiously as those of the living.

**Sophronimus:** I am only afraid the priest of Ceres, to whom you have preferred Sophronimus, will endeavor to avenge Aglae's refusal upon you: he is a man whom we have reason to dread.

**Socrates:** What has he to fear who does his duty? I know the malice of my enemies, I know all their calumnies; but when we take care never to offend God, and endeavor to do all the good we can to mankind, then is it that we are afraid of nothing, or whilst we live, or when we die.

**Sophronimus:** I know it well; yet I should die with grief if the happiness you bestowed on me should induce your enemies to put your virtue to the trial.

### SCENE II.
Socrates, Sophronimus, Aglae.

**Aglae:** O my benefactor, my father, let me fall at your feet, thou more than man; join me, Sophronimus, in mutual acknowledgments; 'tis he, 'tis Socrates who marries us at his own expense, and gives us best part of his own fortune to support us: but we must not suffer him, we must not be rich on these conditions; no, if our hearts have any gratitude, let them imitate his generosity.

**Sophronimus:** O Socrates, with her I throw myself at thy feet; like her I am charmed, astonished and confounded at thy goodness; we will not, must not abuse it: look on us as your children, but do not let those children be a burden to their kind parent; thy friendship is fortune sufficient, 'tis all that we desire: you are not rich, and yet you do more than all the great ones of the earth; but were we to accept thy bounties, we should be unworthy of them.

**Socrates:** Rise, my children, you affect me too deeply: are we not bound to respect the will of the dead? did not your father, Aglae, whom I always considered as part of myself, did he not enjoin me to treat you as my daughter? Had I not done so, I had betrayed the confidence of friendship: I took upon me the performance of his will, and I have executed it: the little I bestow on you would have been useless to my old age, which has not many wants to supply. If it was my duty to obey my friend, it is yours to obey your father. I am that father now, and by that sacred name command you not to make me unhappy by your refusal: but retire, I see Xantippe coming this way; I have reasons for desiring you to avoid her at present.

**Aglae:** Your commands are cruel, but they must be obeyed.

### SCENE III.
Socrates, Xantippe.

**Xantippe:** A fine piece of work you have made here; upon my word, my dear husband, I must put a stop to your proceedings. Here had I promised Aglae to Anitus the high-priest, a man of interest amongst the great, and Sophronimus to the rich Drixa, who has extensive influence in the whole nation; and you marry your two fools together, and make me break my word to both: not content with this, you must needs give them best part of your fortune too. Twenty thousand drachms! good gods! twenty thousand drachms! are you not ashamed of yourself? at the age of threescore and ten too? Who's to pay your physicians when you are sick? or your lawyers when you have a law-suit? What am I to do, when that villainous wry-necked fellow, Anitus, whom you might have had on your side, if he should join his party to persecute you, as they have done so often already? confusion to all philosophy and philosophers I say, and to my own foolish regard for you! You pretend to direct others, and want leading-strings yourself; always reasoning without a grain of common sense. If you were not one of the best men in the world, you would be the most ridiculous and the most insupportable: but mind me, you have only one way left, break off this foolish match, and do what your wife bids you.

**Socrates:** You talk well, my dear Xantippe, and with great moderation; but hear what I have to say in return. I did not propose this marriage myself, but Aglae and Sophronimus love and are worthy of each other. I have already made over everything to you that the laws will allow me, and have given almost all that remained to the daughter of my friend: the little which I keep is enough for me. I have no physician to pay because I live sober; no lawyers because I have neither debts nor reversions: and with regard to that philosophy you reproach me with, it will teach me to bear the malice of Anitus, and your treatment of me; nay, even to love you, in spite of your ill-humor. [Exit.]

### SCENE IV.

**Xantippe:** [Alone.] The old fool! and yet, spite of myself, I can't help esteeming him; for after all, there is something great even in his follies: but his coolness and indifference make me mad. To scold him is but lost labor: for these thirty years past I have been perpetually pecking at him; and when I have tired myself with it, he bids me go on, and I am dumbfounded. Surely there must be something in that soul of his superior to mine.

### SCENE V.

Xantippe, Drixa.

**Drixa:** So, Madam Xantippe, I see you are mistress at home: fie! fie! how mean it is to be governed by a husband! this vile Socrates, to prevent my making a young fellow's fortune; but I'll be revenged.

**Xantippe:** My dear Madam Drixa, don't be so angry with my husband, I am angry enough with him myself: he's a poor, weak man, I confess; but I verily believe has one of the best hearts in the world; has not the least degree of malice, and does a thousand foolish things without designing, and with so much honesty, that one can't help forgiving him: then indeed he is as obstinate as a mule: I have done nothing but tease and torment him my whole life; nay, I have even beat him sometimes, and yet I have never been able to mend him, nay, not so much as to put him into a passion. What can I do with him?

**Drixa:** I tell you, I'll be revenged; under yonder portico I perceive his good friend Anitus, and some more of our party: let me alone with him.

**Xantippe**: My god! I am dreadfully afraid these folks, all together, will do my poor husband some mischief: I must go and tell him of it, for after all one can't help loving him.

## SCENE VI.
Anitus, Drixa, Terpander, Acros.

**Drixa**: Most noble Anitus, we have all been wronged: you are tricked as well as myself: this vile Socrates has given away three parts of his fortune on purpose to spite you: you must take ample revenge of him.

**Anitus**: I design it: heaven itself requires it of me: this man treats me with contempt, and of course must despise the gods. Already we have had several accusations against him, we must repeat them, you will all assist me: we will put him in danger of his life, then will I offer him my protection, on condition that he resigns Aglae to me, and to you the beautiful Sophronimus: thus we shall all gain our several points: he will be sufficiently punished by the fright we shall put him into: I shall get my mistress, and you your lover.

**Drixa**: Wisdom herself speaks in Anitus: sure some divinity inspires you: but tell us, how are we to proceed?

**Anitus**: This is about the time when the judges go to the tribunal, with Melitus at the head of them.

**Drixa**: That Melitus is a little pedant, a sad fellow, and your enemy.

**Anitus**: He is so; but he is still a greater enemy to Socrates; 'tis a rascally hypocrite who supports the rights of the Areopagus against me: but we always hold together when our mutual interest and business is to destroy these pretended wise men, who want to open the eyes of people on our conduct: hearken, my dear Drixa, you are a devotee.

**Drixa**: Certainly, my lord, I love money, and I love pleasure with all my soul, but in matters of devotion I yield to none.

**Anitus**: Go then immediately, and get together as many bawling enthusiasts as you can, and cry out, impiety! impiety.

**Terpander**: Is there anything to be got by it? if there is, we are all ready.

**Acros**: Ay, ay, that we are; but what sort of impiety?

**Anitus**: O every kind: however, we had best accuse him at once of not believing in the gods; that's the shortest way.

**Drixa**: O let me alone then.

**Anitus**: You shall be well supported; go, and stir up your friends under the portico: I'll inform meantime some of my news-loving friends of it, who come frequently to dine with me, a parcel of contemptible fellows they are, to be sure, but such as, if properly directed, can do a good deal of mischief on occasion: we must make use of every expedient to promote a good cause: away, my friends, recommend yourselves to Ceres, and be ready to cry out when I give you the signal: 'tis the only way for you to live happy here, and gain heaven hereafter.

SCENE VII.
Anitus, Graphius, Chomus, Bertillus.

**Anitus**: Most indefatigable Graphius, profound Chomus, and delicate Bertillus, have you finished those little works as I commanded you against the impious Socrates?

**Graphius**: My lord, I have labored: he'll never hold up his head again.

**Chomus**: I have proved the fact against him; struck him dumb.

**Bertillus**: I have only mentioned him in my journal, and it has done for him.

**Anitus**: Graphius, beware, you know I forbad your prolixity: you are naturally tedious, and that may wear out the patience of the court.

**Graphius**: My lord, 'tis all in one leaf: wherein I have proved that the soul is an infused quintessence; that tails were given to animals to drive away flies; that Ceres works miracles; and consequently, that Socrates is an enemy to the state, and ought to be exterminated.

**Anitus**: A most excellent conclusion! remember to carry your accusation to the second judge, who is a complete philosopher. I'll answer for it, you'll soon get rid of your enemy Socrates.

**Graphius**: My lord, I am not his enemy: I am only vexed that he has so great a reputation: all that I do is for the glory of Ceres, and the good of my country.

**Anitus**: Well, well, make haste and be gone: and you, learned Chomus, what have you done?

**Chomus**: My lord, finding nothing reprehensible in the writings of Socrates. I shall accuse him point-blank of thinking directly opposite to what he says, and shall show the poison he intends to spread in everything he is to say hereafter.

**Anitus**: Wonderful indeed! carry your piece to the fourth judge: he has not common sense, and therefore will understand you perfectly: now for you, Bertillus.

**Bertillus**: My lord, here is my last journal upon the Chaos. I have proved, by a regular series from the Chaos to the Olympics, that Socrates perverts the youth of Athens.

**Anitus**: Admirable! go you from me to the seventh judge, and tell him I desire he'd take care of Socrates; so; here comes Melitus already, the first of the eleven; there's no necessity of practising any art with him, we know each other too well.

## SCENE VIII.
Anitus, Melitus.

**Anitus**: Mr. Judge, one word with you: this Socrates must be destroyed.

**Melitus**: Indeed, Mr. High Priest, I have long thought so: let us agree in this point; we may quarrel, you know, notwithstanding, about everything else.

**Anitus**: I know we hate each other most cordially: but at the same time we may lay our heads together to govern the commonwealth.

**Melitus**: With all my heart, nobody can overhear us: therefore, to speak freely, I know you are a rogue, and you don't look upon me as a very honest man: I can't hurt you because you are high priest, nor you me because I am first judge; but Socrates may do us both a mischief, by exposing us to the world; our first business, therefore, is to destroy him, and then we may be at leisure to fall upon each other the first opportunity.

**Anitus**: [Aside.] 'Tis well observed: how I could rejoice now to see this rascally judge upon an altar, his arms hanging on one side and his legs on the other, whilst I with my golden knife was ripping up his guts and consulting his liver at leisure!

**Melitus**: [Aside.] Shall I never be able to send this villainous high priest to jail, and make him swallow a pint of hemlock by my command?

**Anitus**: O my friend, here come our noble assistants. I have taken care to prepare the populace.

**Melitus**: Very well, my dear friend, you may depend upon me in this affair, not forgetting old scores.

## SCENE IX.
Anitus, Melitus, some of the Judges of Athens passing along under the portico. [Anitus whispers Melitus.]

**Drixa, Terpander,** and **Acros** together: Justice, justice, scandal, impiety, justice, justice, irreligion, impiety, justice!

**Anitus**: What's the matter, my friends, what's your complaint?

**Drixa, Terpander,** and **Acros**: Justice! in the name of the people.

**Melitus**: Against whom?

**Drixa, Terpander,** and **Acros**: Against Socrates.

**Melitus**: Ha! ha! against Socrates? that fellow has been often accused: what has he done now?

**Acros**: I don't know what.

**Terpander**: They say he gives money to young girls in marriage.

**Acros**: Ay, he corrupts our youth.

**Drixa**: O he's a wicked wretch: he has offered up no cakes to Ceres; he says there is a great deal of useless gold and silver in the temple.

**Acros**: Ay, and he says the priests of Ceres get drunk sometimes; that's true; he's a wicked wretch indeed.

**Drixa**: He's a heretic; he denies the plurality of gods; he's a deist: he believes only in one God; he's an atheist.

**All Three Together**: Yes; he's a heretic, a deist, and an atheist.

**Melitus**: Dreadful accusations indeed, and all extremely probable: I have heard as much before.

**Anitus**: The state is in danger if we leave such crimes unpunished: Minerva will withdraw her protection from us.

**Drixa**: Ay, that she will, I have heard him laugh at Minerva's owl.

**Melitus**: At Minerva's owl! O heaven! gentlemen, is not it your opinion he ought to be sent to prison immediately?

**The Judges**: [All together.] To prison with him, to prison.

**Melitus**: Guards, carry Socrates to prison this instant.

**Drixa**: And afterwards let him be burned without a hearing.

**One of the Judges**: No, no; we must hear him; we must not go against the law.

**Anitus**: No, no; that's what the good woman meant: we must hear him, but not let what he says have too much effect on us; you know these philosophers are devilish subtle: 'tis they who have disturbed all those nations which we have endeavored to render peaceable and quiet.

**Melitus**: To prison with him, to prison.

### SCENE X.

Xantippe, Sophronimus, Aglae, Socrates, in chains. [Entering.]

**Xantippe**: O mercy, mercy, my poor husband is going to prison; aren't you ashamed, Mr. Judges, to treat a man of his years in this manner? What harm could he do? Alas! it is not in his power, he is more fool than knave, God knows; have pity on him, good gentlemen. O my dear, I told you you would draw yourself into some bad affair. This comes of portioning young girls. What an unhappy creature I am!

**Sophronimus**: O my lords, respect his age, respect his virtue; give me his chains! I am ready to yield up my liberty, my life for his.

**Aglae**: Yes; we will go to prison in his stead; we will die for him: do not destroy the noblest, best of men: take us rather for your victims.

**Melitus:** You see how he corrupts our youth.

**Socrates:** No more, my wife, no more, my children; do not oppose the will of heaven, which speaks by the laws: he who resists the law, is no longer a citizen. God wills that I should be put in bondage; I submit to his divine decree without murmur, or repining. In my own house, in Athens, or in a prison, I am equally free; and whilst I behold in you so much gratitude, and so much friendship, I am happy. What matters it whether Socrates sleeps in his own chamber, or in a prison? Everything is as the supreme will ordains, and my will should submit to it.

**Melitus:** Take away this reasoner.

**Anitus:** Gentlemen, what he says I must own has affected me; the man seems to have a good disposition; I flatter myself I should be able to convert him; let me have a little private conversation with him; please to order his wife and these young folks to retire.

**One of the Judges:** Most venerable Anitus, you have our consent to parley with him before he appears at the tribunal.

## SCENE XI.

Anitus, Socrates.

**Anitus:** Most virtuous Socrates, my heart bleeds to see you in this condition.

**Socrates:** And have you a heart?

**Anitus:** I have, and one that feels for you: I am ready to do everything for you.

**Socrates:** I think you have done enough already.

**Anitus:** Hark ye, Socrates, your situation is worse than you think it is; let me tell you, your life is in danger.

**Socrates:** That is of very little consequence.

**Anitus:** To your noble soul it may appear so, but it is otherwise in the eyes of all those who, like me, admire your virtue: believe me, however you may be armed by philosophy, it is dreadful to die a death of ignominy: but that is not all: your reputation, which should be dear to you, will be sullied in after ages: the religious of both sexes will laugh at your fall, and insult you: if you are burned, they'll light the pile; if you're strangled, they'll tie the cord; if you're poisoned, they'll pound the hemlock; and not only that, but they'll make your memory execrable to all posterity. Now it is in your own power to prevent all this: I will promise not only to save your life, but even to persuade your judges to say with the oracle, that you are the wisest of men: you have nothing to do but to give me up your young pupil, Aglae, with the portion; you understand me: as to her marriage with Sophronimus, we shall find means to set it aside:

thus you will enjoy a peaceful and honorable old age, and the gods and goddesses will bless you.

**Socrates**: Soldiers, conduct me to prison immediately. [He is carried off.]

**Anitus**: This fellow is incorrigible; but it's not my fault; I have done my duty, and have nothing to reproach myself with: he must be abandoned as a reprobate, and left to die in his sins.

# ACT III.

SCENE I.

The judges seated on the tribunal, Socrates below:

**Judge**: [To Anitus.] You should not sit here, you are priest of Ceres.

**Anitus**: I am only here for edification.

**Melitus**: Silence there: Socrates, you are accused of being a bad citizen, of corrupting youth, of denying a plurality of gods, of being a heretic, deist, and atheist: answer to the charge.

**Socrates**: Judges of Athens, I exhort you all to be as good citizens as I have always myself endeavored to be: to shed your blood for your country, as I have done in many a battle: with regard to youth, guide them by your counsels, and, above all, direct them by your example; teach them to love true virtue, and to avoid the miserable philosophy of the schools: the article concerning a plurality of gods is a little more difficult to discuss, but hear what I have to say upon it. Know then, ye judges of Athens, there is but one God.

**Melitus and Another Judge**: O the impious wretch!

**Socrates**: I say, there is but one God, in his nature infinite, nor can any being partake of his infinity. Turn your eyes towards the celestial globes, to the earth and seas; all correspond together, all are made one for the other: each being is intimately connected with other beings, all formed with one design, by one great architect, one sole master, and preserver: perhaps he hath deigned to create genii, and demons, more powerful and more wise than men; if such exist, they are creatures like you, his first subjects, not gods: but nothing in nature proves to us that they do exist, whilst all nature speaks one God and one father: this God hath no need of Mercury and Iris to deliver his commands to us: he hath only to will, and that is enough. If by Minerva you understand no more than the wisdom of God; if by Neptune you only mean his immutable laws, which raise or depress the sea, you may still reverence Neptune and Minerva, provided that under these emblems you adore none but the supreme being, and that the people are not deceived by you into false opinions. Be careful above all not to turn religion into metaphysics, its essence is morality: dispute not, but worship. If our ancestors believed that the supreme God came down into the arms of Alcmene, Danæ, and Semele, and had children by them, our ancestors imagined dangerous and idle fables. 'Tis an insult on the divinity to conceive that he could possibly, in any manner whatsoever, commit with woman the crime which we call adultery. It is a discouragement to the rest of mankind to say that, to be a great man, it is necessary to be produced from the mysterious union of Jupiter and one of our own wives and daughters. Miltiades, Cimon, Themistocles, and Aristides, whom you persecuted, were perhaps much greater than Perseus, Hercules, or Bacchus. The only way to become the children of God, is to endeavor to please him. Deserve therefore that title, by never passing an unjust sentence.

**Melitus**: What insolence! what blasphemy!

**Another Judge**: What absurdities! one can't tell what he means.

**Melitus**: Socrates, you are always too fond of argument: answer briefly, and with precision: did you, or did you not, laugh at Minerva's owl?

**Socrates**: Judges of Athens, take care of your owls; when you propose ridiculous things as objects of belief too many are apt to resolve that they will believe nothing: they have sense enough to find out that your doctrine is absurd, though they have not elevation of mind sufficient to discover the law of truth; they know how to laugh at your little deceits, but not to adore the first of beings, the one incomprehensible, incommunicable being, the eternal, all-just, and all-powerful God.

**Melitus**: O the blasphemer! the monster! he has said too much already: I condemn him to death.

**Many of the Judges**: And so do we.

**One of the Judges**: Several of us are of another opinion; Socrates has spoken wisely; we believe men would be more wise and just if they thought like him: for my part, far from condemning him, I think he ought to be rewarded.

**Many of the Judges**: We think so too.

**Melitus**: The opinions seem to be divided.

**Anitus**: Gentlemen of the Areopagus, permit me to interrogate him a little. Do you believe, Socrates, that the sun turns round, and that the Areopagus acts by divine right?

**Socrates**: You have no authority to ask any questions, but I have authority to teach you what you are ignorant of: it is of little importance to society, whether the sun or the earth turns round, but it is of the utmost consequence, whether the men who turn with them be just or unjust: virtue only acts from the right divine, and you and the Areopagus have no rights but those which your country has bestowed on you.

**Anitus**: Illustrious and most equitable judges, let Socrates retire. [Melitus makes a sign, Socrates is carried out.]

**Anitus**: [Proceeds.] Most august Areopagus, instituted by heaven, you hear what he says: this dangerous fellow denies that the sun turns round, and that you act by right divine: if these opinions prevail, adieu to magistracy, and adieu to the sun: you are no longer judges appointed by Minerva; you will become accountable for your proceedings; you must no longer determine but according to the laws; and if you once depend on the laws, you are undone: punish rebellion therefore, revenge earth and heaven: I am going: dread you the anger of the gods if Socrates is permitted to live. [Anitus goes out, and the Judges demur.]

**One of the Judges**: I don't care to quarrel with Anitus; he is a dangerous man to offend. If he troubled himself with the gods only it would not signify.

**Another Judge**: [To his brother sitting near him.] Between you and me, Socrates is in the right; but then he should not be in the right so publicly. I care no more for Ceres and Neptune than he does; but he should not speak out to the whole Areopagus what he ought to have whispered: yet after all, what is there in poisoning a philosopher, especially when he is old and ugly?

**Another Judge**: If there be any injustice in condemning Socrates, it is Anitus' business and not mine: I lay it all upon his conscience: besides, it grows late, we lose our time; let us talk no more about it: to death with him.

**Another Judge**: Ay, ay, they say he's a heretic, and an atheist; to death with him.

**Melitus**: Call Socrates. [He is brought in.] Blessed be the gods, the plurality of voices is for death; Socrates, the gods by us condemn you to drink hemlock.

**Socrates**: We are all mortal: nature condemns you also to death in a short time, probably you may meet with a more unhappy end than mine: the distempers which bring on death are much more painful than a cup of hemlock. I thank those amongst my judges who pleaded in favor of innocence; for the rest, they have my pity.

**One of the Judges**: [Going out.] Certainly this man deserved a pension from the state, rather than a cup of poison.

**Another Judge**: I think so too; but why would he quarrel with a priest of Ceres?

**Another**: After all, it is best to get rid of a philosopher: those fellows have always a certain fierceness of spirit which should be damped a little.

**Another**: One word with you, gentlemen: would not it be right, whilst our hand is in, to make an end of all the geometricians, who pretend that the three angles of a triangle are equal to two right ones? they are a mighty scandal to the foolish people that read their works.

**Another**: Ay, ay, we'll hang them all the next session; let's go to dinner.

## SCENE II.

**Socrates**: [Alone.] I have been long prepared for death; all I fear at present is, that my wife Xantippe will be troubling me in my last moments, and interrupt me in the sweet employment of recollecting my soul, and preparing myself for eternity: I ought to busy myself only in the contemplation of that supreme being, before whom I am soon to appear: but here she comes; I must be resigned to all things.

## SCENE III.

Socrates, Xantippe, with the Disciples of Socrates.

**Xantippe**: Well, my poor man, what have these gentlemen of the law concluded? have they fined you, are you banished, or acquitted? my God! how uneasy have I been about you! pray take care this don't happen a second time.

**Socrates**: No, my dear, this will not happen a second time, I'll answer for it; give yourself no uneasiness about anything. My dear disciples, my friends, welcome.

**Crito**: [At the head of his disciples.] You see us, beloved Socrates, no less concerned for you than Xantippe; we have gained permission of the judges to visit you; just heaven! must we behold Socrates in chains! permit us to kiss those bonds which reflect shame on Athens. How could Anitus and his friends reduce you to this condition?

**Socrates**: Let us think no more of these trifles, my friends, but continue the examination we were making yesterday into the soul's immortality. We observed, I remember, that nothing could be more probable, or at the same time more full of comfort and satisfaction, than this sweet idea; in fact, matter we know changes, but perishes not; why then should the soul perish? can it be that, raised as we are to the knowledge of a God through the veil of this mortal body, we should cease to know him when that veil is removed? no, as we think now, we must always think; thought is the very essence of man; and this being must appear before a just God, who will recompense virtue, punish vice, and pardon weakness and error.

**Xantippe**: Nobly said: but what does this fellow here with his cup? [Enter the Jailer, or Executioner of the Eleven, carrying a cup of Hemlock.]

**Jailer**: Here Socrates, the senate have sent you this.

**Xantippe**: Thou vile poisoner of the commonwealth, would you kill my husband before my face? monster, I'll tear you to pieces.

**Socrates**: My dear friend, I ask your pardon for my wife's rude behavior: she has scolded me all her life; she only treats you as she does her husband; excuse her impertinence: give me the cup. [He takes the cup.]

**One of the Disciples**: O divine Socrates! why may not we take that poison for you? horrible injustice! shall the guilty thus condemn the innocent, and fools destroy the wise? you go then to death!

**Socrates**: No, my friends, to life: this is the cup of immortality: it is not this perishable body that has loved and instructed you; it is my soul alone that has lived with you, and that shall love you forever. [He is going to drink.]

**Jailer**: I must take off your fetters first: 'tis always done.

**Socrates**: Do it then, I beg you. [He scratches his leg.]

**One of the Disciples**: You smile!

**Socrates**: I smile at the reflection, that pleasure should arise from pain: thus it is that eternal felicity shall spring from the miseries of this life. [Drinks the poison.]

**Crito**: Alas! what have you done?

**Xantippe**: Ay, for a thousand ridiculous discourses of this kind the poor man has lost his life: indeed, my dear, you will break my heart; I could strangle all the judges with my own hands. I did use to scold you indeed, but I always loved you notwithstanding; these polite well-bred gentlemen have put you to death: O my dear, dear husband!

**Socrates**: Be calm, my good Xantippe; weep not, my friends; it becomes not the disciples of Socrates to shed tears.

**Crito**: How can we avoid it on so dreadful an occasion? this legal murder!

**Socrates**: Thus it is that men will often behave to the worshippers of one true God, and the enemies of superstition.

**Crito**: And must Socrates be one of those unhappy victims?

**Socrates**: 'Tis noble to be the victim of the deity: I die contented. I wish indeed that, to the satisfaction of seeing you, my friends, I could have added the happiness of embracing Sophronimus and Aglae: I wonder they are not here: they would have made my last moments more welcome.

**Crito**: Alas! they know not that you have already undergone the judges' dreadful sentence: they have been talking to the people, and praising those magistrates who would have acquitted you. Aglae has laid open the guilt of Anitus, and published his shame and dishonor: they perhaps might have saved your life: O dear Socrates, why would you thus precipitate your fate?

**SCENE THE LAST**
Aglae, Sophronimus.

**Aglae:** [Entering.] Divine Socrates, be not afraid: be comforted, Xantippe: worthy disciples of Socrates, do not weep.

**Sophronimus:** Your enemies are confounded: the people rise in your defence.

**Aglae:** We have been talking to them; we have laid open the intrigues and jealousy of the wicked Anitus: it was my duty to demand justice for his crime, as I was the cause of it.

**Sophronimus:** Anitus hath saved himself by flight from the rage of the people: he and his accomplices are pursued: solemn thanks have been given to those judges who appeared in your favor: the people are now at the gates of the prison, and wait to conduct you home in triumph.

**Xantippe:** Alas! 'tis lost labor!

**One of the Disciples:** O Socrates, why would you so hastily obey?

**Aglae:** Live, dear Socrates, the benefactor of your country, the model of future ages; O live for the general happiness of mankind!

**Crito:** Ye noble pair, my virtuous friends, it is too late.

**Xantippe:** You stayed too long.

**Aglae:** Alas! too late? what mean you? just heaven!

**Sophronimus:** Has he then already drunk the fatal draught?

**Socrates:** Sweet Aglae and dear Sophronimus, the law ordained that I should take the poison: I obeyed the law, unjust as it is, because it oppressed myself alone: had the injustice been done to another, I would have resisted it. I go to death, but the example of friendship which you give the world, and your nobleness of soul shall never perish: your virtue is greater, much greater, than the guilt of those who accused me. I bless that fate which the world may call misfortune, because it hath set in the fairest light the goodness of your hearts. My dear Xantippe, be happy; and remember, that to be so, you must curb your impetuous temper. My beloved disciples, listen always to the voice of that philosophy which will teach you to despise your persecutors, and pity human weakness: and you, my daughter Aglae, and my son Sophronimus, be always what you now are.

**Aglae:** How wretched are we that we cannot die for you!

**Socrates:** Your lives are valuable, mine would have been useless: take my tender last farewell; the doors of eternity are opened to receive me.

**Xantippe:** He was a great man! O I will rouse up the whole nation.

**Sophronimus:** May we raise up temples to Socrates, if ever mortal man deserved it!

**Crito:** At least may his wisdom teach mankind that temples should be raised to God alone!

**End**

# Alzire

## Contents

Dramatis Personæ. . . . . . . . . . . . . . . . . . . . . . . . . . . . . . . . . . . . . . 59

Act I. . . . . . . . . . . . . . . . . . . . . . . . . . . . . . . . . . . . . . . . . . . . . . . 60

Act II. . . . . . . . . . . . . . . . . . . . . . . . . . . . . . . . . . . . . . . . . . . . . . 65

Act III. . . . . . . . . . . . . . . . . . . . . . . . . . . . . . . . . . . . . . . . . . . . . 71

Act IV. . . . . . . . . . . . . . . . . . . . . . . . . . . . . . . . . . . . . . . . . . . . . 76

Act V. . . . . . . . . . . . . . . . . . . . . . . . . . . . . . . . . . . . . . . . . . . . . . 81

## Dramatis Personæ

Don Guzman, Governor of Peru.
Don Alvarez, [Father of Guzman, and late Governor].
Zamor, Sovereign of a Part of Potosi.
Montezuma, Sovereign of another Part.
Alzire, Daughter of Montezuma.
Emira, Attendant on Alzire.
Cephale. Attendant on Alzire
Spanish Officers.
Americans.

In his preface to this play Voltaire says; "This tragedy, the fable of which is invented, and almost of a new species, was written with a view of showing how far superior the spirit of true religion is to the light of nature. The religion of a barbarian consists in offering up to his gods the blood of his enemies; a Christian badly instructed has seldom much more humanity: to be a strict observer of some unnecessary rites and ceremonies, and at the same time deficient in the most essential duties, to say certain prayers at particular times, and carefully to conceal his vices; this is his religion: that of a true Christian is to look upon all mankind as his brethren, to do them all the good in his power and pardon their offences: such is Guzman at the hour of death, and Alvarez during the whole course of his life; such a man was Henry IV., as I have described him, even with all his foibles: in every part of my writings I have endeavored to enforce that humanity which ought to be the distinguishing characteristic of a thinking being: the reader will always find in them (if I may venture to say so much of my own works) a desire to promote the happiness of all men, and an abhorrence of injustice and oppression: it is this, and this alone, which hath hitherto saved them from that obscurity to which their many inperfections would otherwise long since have condemned them."

# ACT I.

SCENE I.
Alvarez, Guzman.

**Alvarez**: At length, for so the council hath decreed, Guzman succeeds Alvarez; long, my son, Mayest thou preserve for heaven and for thy king This better half of our new conquered world, This fertile source of riches and of crimes! Joyful to thee I yield the post of honor, That suits but ill with feeble age like mine; In youth thy father trod the paths of glory; Alvarez first our winged castles bore To Mexico's astonished sons; he led Spain's gallant heroes to this golden shore: After a life spent in my country's service, Could I have formed these heroes into men, Could I have made them virtuous, mild, and good, I had been amply paid for all my toils: But who shall stop the haughty conqueror? Alas! my son, their cruelties obscure The lustre of their fame; I weep the fate Of these unhappy victors, raised by heaven To greatness but to be supremely wicked. O Guzman, I am verging to the grave, Let me but live to see thee govern here As justice shall direct thee, and I die With pleasure.

**Guzman**: By thy great example fired, With thee I fought and conquered for my country; From thee must learn to rule: it is not mine To give the wise and good Alvarez laws, But to receive them from him.

**Alvarez**: No; my son, The sovereign power can never be divided: Worn down with years and labor, I resign All worldly pomp; it is enough for me If yet my feeble voice be sometimes heard To counsel and direct thee; trust me, Guzman, Men are not creatures one would wish to rule: To that almighty being, whom too long I have neglected, would I consecrate My poor remains of life; one boon alone, As friend, I ask of thee, as father claim; To give me up those slaves who by your order Are here confined; this day, my son, should be A day of pardon, marked by clemency, And not by justice.

**Guzman**: A request from you Is a command; but think, my lord, I beg, What dangers may ensue: a savage people, But half subdued, and to the yoke of slavery

Bending reluctant, ready for revolt, Should never be familiar with their conquerors, Or dare to look on those they should be taught To tremble at: unarmed with power and vengeance They would despise us: these untutored Indians, Fiery and bold, ill brook the galling rein Of servitude, by chastisement alone Made tame, and humble, pardoned once, they think You fear them; power, in short, is lost by mildness; Severity alone insures obedience. The brave Castilian serves in honor's cause, With cheerful resignation, 'tis his pride, His glory; but inferior nations court Oppression; force and only force constrains them: Did not the gods of these barbarians drink The blood of men, they would not be adored.

**Alvarez:** And can a Christian, as thou art, approve These tyrant maxims, the detested offspring Of narrow policy? are these the means To win the wild barbarian to our faith? Thinkest thou to rule them with an iron hand, And serve a God of peace with war and slaughter? Braved I for this the burning tropic's rage, And all the terrors of a world unknown, To see our country cursed, our faith disgraced? God sent us here for other purposes, Sent us to make his holy name revered, His sacred laws beloved: whilst we, my son, Unmindful of that faith which we profess, The laws we teach, and all the tender ties Of soft humanity, insatiate still For blood and gold, instead of winning o'er These savages by gentle means, destroy them. All is confusion, death, and horror round us, And nought have we of heaven but its thunder; Our name indeed bears terror with it; Spain Is feared, but hated too: we are the scourge Of this new world, vain, covetous, unjust; In short, I blush to own it, we alone Are the barbarians here: the simple savage, Though fierce by nature, is in courage equal, In goodness our superior. O my Guzman, Had he, like us, been prodigal of blood, Had he not felt the throbs of tender pity, Alvarez had not lived to speak his virtues: Hast thou forgot that day, when by a crowd Of desperate natives I was circled in On every side, and all my faithful band Of followers cut off; alone I stood, And every moment looked for death, when, lo; At mention of my name, they dropped their arms; And straight a young American approached me, Embraced my knees, and bathed them with his tears; And "is it you," he cried, "is it my friend? Live, good Alvarez, virtue pure as thine May be most useful to us; be a father To the unhappy; let thy tyrant nation, That would enslave us, learn from hence—to pardon, And own a savage capable of virtue." I see you are moved; O hearken to the voice Of mild humanity, by me she speaks, By me addresses Guzman; O my son, Canst thou expect the object of thy wishes, The fair Alzire ever will crown thy hopes, If thou art cruel? thinkest thou to cement

The dearest bonds of nature in the blood Of her loved countrymen, or shall their groans Be heard, and Guzman soften into mercy?

**Guzman**: 'Tis your command, my lord, and I submit; They have their freedom, but on this condition, For so our laws require, they must be Christians: To quit their idols, and embrace our faith, Alone can save them; we must bend by force Their stubborn hearts, and drag them to the altar; One king must be obeyed, one God adored.

**Alvarez**: Hear me, my son, I wish, as much as Guzman, That truth may fix her sacred empire here, That neither heaven nor Spain henceforth may find A foe on earth; but know, the heart oppressed Is never conquered: I force none, yet I Have conquered many; the true God, my son, The God of Christians is a God of mercy.

**Guzman**: You've conquered, sir, the father over his son Is absolute; and you, my lord, would soften The hardest heart, whilst virtue by Alvarez In mildest accents pleads her powerful cause: O since kind heaven to thee hath lent the art Of soft persuasion, use it for thy son, On thee alone depends the happiness Of Guzman's life: the proud Alzire scorns My proffered hand: I love her but too well, Heaven knows how dearly! but I cannot stoop Meanly to sooth a haughty woman's pride, I cannot make myself a poor tame slave To her imperious will; but thou hast power O'er the fair tyrant's father; talk to him For the last time; let him command his daughter To take my hand, and make your Guzman happy; And yet it hurts my soul to think Alvarez Should stoop so low, and be a suppliant for me.

**Alvarez**: Already I have spoke, and Montezuma Hath seen his daughter; she will soon be thine. I've been a friend to his unhappy race, And soothed the sorrows of captivity: Already he hath quitted his false gods; Alzire too, a convert to our faith, To this new world shines forth a bright example. She only can unite the jarring nations, And make us happy; thy long wished-for nuptials Shall join two distant globes; these fierce barbarians, Who now detest our laws, when they shall see The daughter of their king in Guzman's arms, Cheerful beneath thy easy yoke shall bend Their willing hearts, and soon be all our own: But Montezuma comes; away, my son, Expect me with Alzire at the altar.

## SCENE II.

Alvarez, Montezuma.

**Alvarez**: At length, obedient to a father's will, Alzire yields, I hope, to thy persuasion.

**Montezuma:** If yet my daughter trembles at the thought Of wedding him who has destroyed her race, Alvarez will forgive a woman's weakness; For thou hast been a father to the wretched: Thy gentle manners teach us to revere That holy faith from whence they sprung; by thee The will of heaven to this new world revealed, Enlightened our dark minds; what mighty Spain Unconquered left, thy virtue has subdued: Thy cruel countrymen's remorseless rage Had rendered even thy God detestable, But that in thee His great perfections shine, His goodness, and His mercy; in thy heart We trace his image; Montezuma's thine, His daughter, and his house; the good Alvarez Shall have them all: Potosi and Peru, With my Alzire, shall descend to **Guzman:** Prepare the nuptial rites, adorn your temple, And let your son be ready to receive her: Methinks it is as if the immortal beings Had deigned to visit earth, and mix with men.

**Alvarez:** O Montezuma, let me live to see This blest event, and I shall die content. O God, whose gracious hand conducted us To this new world, enlighten and preserve it; Propitious smile on these first holy vows Made at thy altar here! adieu, my friend, To thee I owe my Guzman's happiness.

### SCENE III.

**Montezuma:** [Alone.] O thou true God, whose powerful arm destroyed Those idle deities I once adored, Watch o'er the poor remains of my sad life, And sooth my sorrows; I have lost my all, All but Alzire, O protect her youth, Watch o'er her steps, and guide her tender heart!

### SCENE IV.

Montezuma, Alzire.

**Montezuma:** Daughter, the hour is come to make thyself And the world happy, to command the conqueror, And make the vanquished smile, restore thy country To her lost honor, and to regal power Rise from the bosom of adversity. Alzire will obey, I know she will; Dry up thy tears, a father must not see them.

**Alzire:** I have no will but yours; yet, O my lord, See my despair, and look into my soul.

**Montezuma:** No more of that; thy word is passed, Alzire, And I depend on it.

**Alizire:** 'Twas extorted from me; The cruel sacrifice: is this a time To plight my faith, and think of nuptial joy, This hapless day, when all I held most dear Was ravished from me, when our wide-stretched empire And all her hosts, the children of the sun, Inglorious fell beneath the cruel Guzman? O 'twas a day marked by the hand of heaven As most unfortunate.

**Montezuma:** Our days, Alzire, Are happy or unhappy from ourselves, And not from circumstance or accident, As superstition taught our ancestors To credit; think no more on it.

**Alzire:** On this day My Zamor fell, our country's great avenger, My lover, chosen by thee, by thee, my father, To be Alzire's husband.

**Montezuma:** I have paid The debt of sorrow due to Zamor's ashes, And hold his memory dear; but death has cancelled Your mutual bonds; therefore no longer shed Those fruitless tears, but carry to the altar A free and cheerful heart; thy God commands, He calls thee to him; if thou art a Christian, Now hear his voice.

**Alzire:** Alas! my lord, I know A father's power, and know my duty to him, 'Tis to obey, to fall a sacrifice Before him; I have passed the utmost bounds Which nature ever prescribed; thy will alone Hath been my law, nor did I ever stain With disobedience my true faith, for thee I left my country's gods, and am a Christian: Alas! my father, why wouldst thou deceive me, Why tell me, the new deity I serve Would bring me peace, that his all-healing power Would ease my tortured heart? delusive promise! For O my lord, the deadly poison still Lurks in my veins, still Zamor's image dwells In his Alzire's heart, nor time nor death Can e'er efface it: well I know Alvarez Condemns that passion which he once approved: But I will make him ample recompense By my obedience:—wed me to the tyrant, Give me to Guzman, 'tis a sacrifice I owe my country; but remember, sir, How dreadful 'tis, and tremble at the thought Of such unnatural, such detested bonds, Thou who condemnest me to these fatal nuptials, Who bidst Alzire give her hand to Guzman, And at the altar promise him a heart Which is not hers to give.

**Montezuma:** What says my child? O in the name of every tender tie That binds thee to me, spare a wretched father! Pity my age, and do not, by the woes Which thou alone, Alzire, canst remove, Let me entreat thee, O embitter not The sad remainder of Alvarez's life! Have I not ever strove to make thee happy, And wilt thou not return it? O my daughter, Let virtue guide thy steps in duty's path, And lead thee on to bliss! thy country calls, Wilt thou betray her? learn henceforth, Alzire, To be the mistress of thyself.

**Alzire:** And must I Learn to dissemble then? ungrateful task!

### SCENE V.
Guzman, Alzire.

**Guzman:** These long delays, Alzire, are unkind, And, let me add, ungenerous, to the man Who lives but to oblige you: for thy sake I stopped the hand of justice; all those captives, Whose pardon you solicited, are free: But I should blush to think that Guzman owed Thy kind compliance to so poor a service; 'Tis on thyself, and thy consenting heart, He founds his hopes, nor thought I ever till now My happiness could make Alzire wretched.

**Alzire:** Wretched indeed! O grant, kind heaven, this day May not prove fatal to us both! you see I am abashed, confounded, left a prey To horror and despair: do not these eyes Alone betray the anguish of a mind Oppressed with grief? canst thou not read it there? I know thou canst: such is my nature, Guzman; Ne'er did Alzire's face belie her heart: Dissimulation and disguise, my lord, Are European arts, which I abhor.

**Guzman:** I love thy frankness, but lament the cause; Zamor is still beloved, his memory lives Within thy breast, my rival even in death: This is too much, Alzire; duty, honor, Virtue forbid it: weep no more, it wounds My heart, and I am jealous of thy tears.

**Alizire:** Jealous of him, my lord, who in the grave Is mouldering now, my loved, lamented Zamor? For I confess I loved him, we were bound By mutual vows, and still I weep his fate: If thou art a friend to constancy and truth, Thou wilt not blame my passion, but approve it. By this, and this alone, may Guzman gain Alzire's heart.

SCENE VI.
**Guzman:** [Alone.] Her pride astonishes, And yet I know not how her freedom charms me: There is a savage beauty in her heart That suits the wildness of her native clime; But softer manners may subdue her mind, And bind her stubborn fierceness to the yoke Of duty; Guzman now is lord of all, And nought remains unconquered but **Alzire:** Resolved by force or art to make her mine, Our hands, if not our hearts, shall be united.

# ACT II.

SCENE I.
Zamor, Americans.
**Zamor:** My noble friends, and fellow-sufferers, Whom dangers strengthen, and misfortunes make But more illustrious, shall we ne'er obtain Our sweet revenge, or honorable death? Still must we live unable or to serve Alzire, or our country; shall we never Find out the hated Guzman, and destroy That fell destroyer? O my country's gods, Powerless and vain, ye gave up this fair land Of liberty to hostile deities; And tamely suffered a few wandering Spaniards To spoil your

altars, lay your temples waste, And desolate our empire; I have lost A kingdom and Alzire; all is gone But shame, and sorrow, and resentment, those I carried with me to the burning sands And gloomy deserts; there I cherished long The secret hopes of vengeance: you, my friends Revived your drooping Zamor, and inspired His soul with flattering thoughts of better days: Deep in the forest's shade we left a band Of chosen spirits, resolute and bold, And hither came, impatient to observe The walls upraised by our tremendous foe. They watched, and seized us: in a dungeon long Confined, at length our tyrant masters grant us Leave to walk forth, and breathe the wholesome air, Yet will not deign to let us know our fate: Can none inform me where we are, who dwells Within this seat of sorrow? where's Alzire, Where's Montezuma, lives he, is he free, Or a vile slave like Zamor? say, my friends, And partners in affliction, know ye not?

**An American:** Like you, my lord, in chains, and hither led By secret paths, we're ignorant of all: Great Cacique, worthy of a better fate, If 'tis decreed that thou must fall, at least Thou shalt find friends prepared to perish with thee, And own them not unworthy of their master.

**Zamor:** After a glorious victory, my friends, A glorious death is most to be desired; But O, to die in vile obscurity, To perish thus in ignominious bondage, To leave our bleeding country thus enslaved By European robbers, those assassins Whose thirst for blood and gold, these proud usurpers, Who would extort by every cruel art Of punishment those riches which we hold More cheap, more worthless than themselves, to leave My loved Alzire, Zamor's dearer half, To their licentious fury, O my friends, 'Tis worse than death: I tremble at the thought.

### SCENE II.

Alvarez, Zamor, Americans.

**Alvarez:** Live, and be free.

**Zamor:** Good heavens, what do I hear? O unexpected sound! what God art thou In human shape? a Spaniard, and forgive! It cannot be: art thou the ruler here?

**Alvarez:** No, captive; I am only the protector Of innocence oppressed.

**Zamor:** Thou good old man, What is thy office here?

**Alvarez:** To aid the wretched.

**Zamor:** What could inspire thee with a thought so noble?

**Alvarez:** My gratitude, religion, and my God.

**Zamor:** God and religion! what! these cruel tyrants, These ruffians, that still bathed in human blood Depopulate earth, and change the smiling face Of nature to a dreary desert, they Who worship avarice alone! their God Cannot be thine!

**Alvarez:** It is the same, my son, But they offend him, they disgrace his name, And are indeed more guilty; they abuse Their new-got power: thou knowest their crime, but know My duty too: twice hath the travelling sun Enlightened in his course our world and yours Since a brave Indian, who he was I know not, Stepped from amidst his fellow-savages, And saved me from their fury; from that moment I felt your sorrows, pitied your misfortunes, And held you as my brethren and my friends; Could I but meet my kind deliverer, That gallant stranger, I should die in peace.

**Zamor:** His age, his features, his transcendent virtue, All, all conspire to say it is **Alvarez:** Behold, and mark us well, canst thou distinguish The hand that saved thee?

**Alvarez:** Gracious heaven! come near. O Providence! it is, it must be he, The wished-for object of my gratitude; He whom these eyes, grown dim with age, have sought So long in vain; my son, my benefactor, What shall I do to serve thee? thou shalt live With old Alvarez; he shall be thy father, Thy guardian and protector here: kind heaven In gracious pity hath prolonged my days, That I might pay the debt I owe to thee.

**Zamor:** O if thy barbarous nation had possessed But half the virtues that adorn Alvarez, Our willing world had bowed submissive down Before them; but their souls are not like thine, For they delight in blood, whilst nature's self Abhorring shudders at their cruelty; Death were more welcome far than life with them: Urge me not therefore, good Alvarez, all I wish to know is this, have they destroyed My noble friend, the wretched Montezuma? Where's my Alzire's father? O my lord, Forgive these tears, the memory of past griefs Sits heavy on me.

**Alvarez:** Let them flow my son, 'Tis the best mark of our humanity: The heart that feels not for another's woe Is fit for every crime: thy friend survives, And full of years and honors lives with us In happiness and peace.

**Zamor:** Might I behold him?

**Alvarez:** Yes; thou shalt see him soon: may his persuasion Induce thee to think better of us all, And follow his example!

**Zamor:** Can he live With Christians, Montezuma live with Christians?

**Alvarez:** Have patience, son, and he shall tell thee all, Touching our union, and the sacred bonds That soon shall bind in cords of amity Our world to thine—but I must to my son, And let him know my happiness; I leave thee But for a moment; fare thee well.

### SCENE III.

Zamor, Americans.

**Zamor:** At last Heaven seems to smile on Zamor; I have found Amongst these vile barbarians one just man, Honest and true: Alvarez is a god, Sent down from heaven to soften this rude world, And bless mankind: he said he had a son, That son shall be my brother and my friend, If he is worthy of his noble father: O glorious hope! shall I again behold Great Montezuma after three long years? Alzire too, my dear, my loved Alzire, Shall I embrace thee, hast thou kept thy faith, That first of virtues, to reward thy Zamor? The heart oppressed is ever diffident: Another old man comes this way: my soul It still perplexed.

### SCENE IV.

Montezuma, Zamor, Americans.

**Zamor:** O noble Montezuma, Do I once more embrace thee? see thy Zamor Snatched from the jaws of death; he lives to save And to defend his prince: behold thy friend, Thy soldier, and thy son: O where's Alzire? Be quick, and tell me, let me know her fate, My life depends on that.

**Montezuma:** Unhappy Cacique, With grief sincere we have lamented thee; Thy fellow-soldiers to thy memory raised The decent tomb, and every honor paid Due to thy virtues: but thank heaven! thou livest, Henceforth may happier days await thee, Zamor! But say, why camest thou hither?

**Zamor:** To avenge My gods, myself, my father and Alzire.

**Montezuma:** What sayst thou?

**Zamor:** Call to mind that dreadful day When the fierce Spaniard, terrible in arms, Rushed through our powerless hosts, o'erthrew our bulwarks, And laid our empire waste; his name was **Guzman**: That name, thou well rememberest, was the signal Given for destruction; at that name they snatched The sweet Alzire, thy loved daughter, from me, And bore her to captivity with thee And all thy race; destroyed the holy altar, Where I had hoped to make Alzire mine, Then dragged me to the tyrant: shall I tell thee What cruel torments that insatiate monster Inflicted on me, to extort confession Of hidden gold, the Christian's deity, Which we despise and trample on? half-dead They left me and retired: time, Montezuma, Can never bury injuries like mine; Thou seest me here, prepared for great revenge: Some chosen friends, attached to Zamor's cause, By equal wrongs provoked, with equal hate Inspired, await me in the neighboring forest, Resolved with me to conquer or to die.

**Montezuma:** O Zamor, whither would thy headlong passion Transport thee? wherefore wouldst thou thus pursue That death which seems so willing to avoid thee? What can thy friends do for thee? their weak arms, Their fish-bone spears, their sabres made of stone, Their soldiers naked, and ill-disciplined, Against these giants armed with mortal steel, And launching their dread thunder bolts against thee? Swift as the winds, their fiery coursers bear them To certain victory; the world is theirs, And we, my Zamor, must submit.

**Zamor**: Whilst life Shall animate these veins, I never will: No, **Montezuma**: their destructive thunder, Their coats of steel, their fiery coursers taught Like them to fight, and share their master's glory, This might affright, and terrify a while Our gaping savages, but I behold This pompous scene unruffled: to subdue Our haughty foe one thing alone's required, And that is, not to fear them; novelty, That conquers cowards, only has enslaved us: Gold, that pernicious native of our soil, Draws Europe hither, but defends us not Against her; niggard nature has denied us A nobler metal, her all-conquering steel, And given it to barbarians; but kind heaven, In lieu of this indulgence, hath bestowed Virtues on us which Europe never knew. I come to fight and conquer for Alzire.

**Montezuma**: Urge it no more, my Zamor, heaven declares Against us, calm thy rage; the times are changed.

**Zamor**: Changed, didst thou say, my lord? it cannot be, If Montezuma's heart is still the same, If my Alzire's faithful, if I live Still in her memory.—Thou turnest aside And weepest.

**Montezuma**: Unhappy Zamor!

**Zamor**: Am I not Thy son? our tyrants have not altered thee? They cannot, sure they cannot have corrupted An old man's heart, and made it false as theirs?

**Montezuma**: I am not guilty, Zamor, nor are all These conquerors tyrants; some were sent by heaven To guide our footsteps in the paths of truth, To teach us arts unknown, immortal secrets, The knowledge of mankind, the arts, my son, To speak, to think, to live, and to be happy.

**Zamor**: O horrid! canst thou praise these ruffians, whilst Thy daughter, thy Alzire, is their slave?

**Montezuma**: Zamor, Alzire's free.

**Zamor**: Ha! Montezuma, Alzire free? forgive me, but remember, She's mine, my lord, by every solemn tie; You promised me, before the gods you promised, To give her to me; they received our vows; She is not perjured?

**Montezuma**: Call not on those gods, For they are vain, and fancied idols all; I have abjured them, and henceforth must worship That power supreme which hath subdued them.

**Zamor**: Ha! The law of thy forefathers, thy religion, Is that deserted?

**Montezuma:** I have found its weakness, And left its vain chimeras: may the God Of Gods convert thee, and inspire with truth Thy unenlightened soul! unhappy Zamor, Soon mayest thou know that Europe thou condemnest, Her virtues, and her faith!

**Zamor:** What mighty virtues Has she to boast? thou art indeed a slave If thou hast lost thy gods, thy faith, thy honor, And broke thy sacred word: Alzire too, Has she betrayed me? O take heed!

**Montezuma:** My heart Reproaches me for nothing: fare thee well! I bless my own good fate, and weep for thine.

**Zamor:** If thou art false, thou hast cause to weep indeed: Pity the torments which I feel for thee, And for thy guilt; pity a heart distracted By love and vengeance; let me find out Guzman Let me behold Alzire, let me fall Beneath her feet; O do not hide her from me: Conduct me, urge me not thus to despair, Put on a human heart, let thy lost virtue—

SCENE V.

Montezuma, Zamor, Guards.

**Guard:** [To Montezuma.] The ceremony waits, my lord.

**Montezuma:** I come.

**Zamor:** Thou wilt not leave me? tell me, Montezuma, What ceremony's this.

**Montezuma:** No more: away, And leave this fatal place.

**Zamor:** Though heaven itself Forbade me, I would follow thee.

**Montezuma:** Forgive My rude denial, Zamor, but you must not, I say you must not—guards, prevent him—pagans Must not profane our Christian altars; I Command not here, but Guzman speaks by me: You must obey: farewell.

SCENE VI.

Zamor, Americans.

**Zamor:** What do I hear? Guzman? O shameful treason! Montezuma The slave of Guzman! where is virtue fled? Alzire too, is my Alzire guilty? Has she too drank corruption's poisonous bowl From these vile Christians?—that destroyer Guzman Rules here, it seems; what's to be done?

**First American:** Permit me To counsel you, my lord; the good old man Who saved thee with his son will soon return, He can deny you nothing; ask of him Safe conduct to the city gates; that done, We may return and join our noble friends Against the foe: I doubt not of success: We will not spare a man of them except Alvarez, and his son: I've marked, my lord, With most observant eye, their fosses, ramparts, And brazen thunders, European arts That fright not me:

alas! our countrymen Forge their own shameful chains, and tamely bend Beneath these sons of pride; but soon, my lord, When they shall see their great avenger here, Then will they rise indignant, and destroy This ignominious work of slavery: Yes; on the bleeding bodies of our foes We'll make a path to glory; on the heads Of these vile Christians turn the fiery tempest, And with their own destructive instruments Of murder shake this all-usurping power, Founded by pride on ignorance and fear.

**Zamor:** O how I joy, ye great unfortunate, To find your kindred breasts thus nobly beat With sympathetic fury! let us punish The haughty Guzman, let his blood atone For our lost country's: O thou deity Of injured mortals, sweet revenge, O come, Assist thy servants, let but Guzman perish And we are satisfied! but O my friends, We talk of vengeance, yet are captives still, Still groan beneath the yoke of shameful bondage: Deserted by Alvarez, and betrayed By Montezuma, all I love perhaps Is in the power of him whom most I hate, The only comfort left me is—to doubt. But hark! what noise is that? the torches flame On every side, and yield a double day: This barbarous people's brazen thunder speaks Some horrid rites, or pompous sacrifice Preparing: look around, and see if Zamor Shall save his much-loved friends, or perish with them.

# ACT III.

### SCENE I.
**Alizire:** [Alone.] Ye manes of my dear departed Zamor, Forgive me, O forgive the wife of Guzman! The holy altar hath received our vows, And they are sealed in heaven: pursue me not, Indignant shade! O if Alzire's tears, Her bitter anguish, her remorse, the pangs Of her reluctant soul, can reach the dead, If in a happier world thou still retainest Thy generous noble spirit, thou wilt pardon My weakness; 'twas a father's cruel will, A people's happiness required it of me; Could I refuse the dreadful sacrifice? Thou art at peace, my Zamor, do not thus Distract my soul, but leave me to my fate; Alas! already it has cost me dear.

### SCENE II.
Alzire, Emira.

**Alizire:** And shall I not behold my countrymen, The loved companions of my infant years, Those wretched captives, may I not enjoy The mournful privilege to mix with theirs My friendly tears, and mourn their cruel fate?

**Emira:** O madam, we have cause indeed to weep, To dread the wrath of Guzman, to lament And tremble for our country; for the hour Of slaughter and destruction is at hand: Again I saw the bloody flag displayed, The proud tribunal's met, and Montezuma Is summoned to appear: all dreadful omens! What will become of us?

**Alizire**: Unpitying heaven! I've been deceived, betrayed:—cruel O Guzman! Was it for this I gave him at the altar My long reluctant hand? that fatal bond I shall repent of to my latest hour: O under what malignant star, my father, Madest thou these cruel, these detested nuptials?

### SCENE III.

Alzire, Emira, Cephanes.

**Cephanes**: One of those slaves, whom this propitious day Restored to freedom, begs admittance to you In secret.

**Alizire**: Let him enter; 'twill rejoice My heart to see him; he and all his friends Are welcome to **Alzire**: but why comes he Alone?

**Cephanes**: Some secret labors in his breast, Which you and only you, he says, must know. 'Twas he, it seems, whose heaven-directed arm Saved the good father of thy valiant lord, The noble Guzman.

**Emira**: He has sought you long; But Montezuma's private orders were, He should not see you: melancholy sits On his dark brow, as if he were intent On some great purpose.

**Cephanes**: Grief and anguish seem To rack his soul: at mention of your name He sighed, and wept, as if yet ignorant Of your new honors and the rank you bear.

**Alizire**: Unworthy rank, and honors I despise! Perhaps the hero knows my wretched race. And is no stranger to Alzire's woes: Perhaps he knew my Zamor; who can tell But he might be a witness of his death, And comes to tell the melancholy tale? A dreadful duty! that would but renew A lover's pangs, and double my distress; But let him come: I know not why my heart Should flutter thus; this hateful palace ever Hath been a scene of sad disquietude And trouble to me: bid him enter.

### SCENE IV.

Alzire, Zamor, Emira.

**Zamor**: Yes; It is **Alzire**: is she then restored?

**Alizire**: Such were his features, voice, and motion: heaven! It cannot be: O Zamor!—O support me. [She faints.]

**Zamor**: 'Tis he.

**Alizire**: Ha! Zamor at Alzire's feet? 'Tis all delusion.

**Zamor**: No; I live for thee, And at thy feet reclaim thy plighted faith; O my Alzire, idol of my soul, Wilt thou not hear me? where are all thy vows, The sacred ties that bound us fast together? Thou hast not broke them?

**Alizire**: Thou dear fatal object Of grief and joy, of rapture and despair, In what a dreadful moment hast thou chose To meet Alzire? every word thou utterest But plunges a new dagger in my heart.

**Zamor**: Thou weepest, yet lookest on Zamor!

**Alizire**: 'Tis too late:

**Zamor**: I know you thought me dead: e'er since that hour Of terror, when those European tyrants Deprived me of my gods, my throne and thee, I've been a poor unhappy wanderer. Knowest thou, my love, that savage murderer, Guzman, With ignominious stripes, and cruel torture, Insulted me? the husband of thy choice, Thy once loved happy Zamor, fell a prey To ruffians:—how it wounds thy tender heart! Thou burnest with fierce resentment of my wrongs, And thou wilt join with Zamor to avenge them: Some guardian god, propitious to our loves, Saved me from death, that we might meet again In happiness: I hope Alzire's true: Thou hast not left thy gods, betrayed thy country, Thou art not grown a false perfidious Spaniard? They tell me I shall meet with Guzman here, I come to free thee from that proud barbarian: Thou lovest me, my Alzire, and wilt give The victim to my wrath.

**Alizire**: Thou hast been wronged; Revenge thyself and see thy victim—here.

**Zamor**: What sayest thou?—ha! thy faith, thy vows—

**Alizire**: No more, But strike—I merit not life or thee.

**Zamor**: O cruel Montezuma! what thou toldest me Was but too true.

**Alizire**: And could he tell thee all; Named he the wretch for whom I quitted Zamor?

**Zamor**: He did not, durst not name him; that remains For thee: O speak it: I shall be surprised At nothing.

**Alizire**: Hear then all my guilt.

**Zamor**: Alzire!

**Alizire**: That Guzman—

**Zamor**: Gracious heaven!

**Alizire**: Thy murderer, Within this hour received my guilty hand; He is—my husband.

**Zamor**: Guzman!

**Alizire**: Montezuma, Alvarez—they betrayed my easy youth, And urged me to the deed: the lost Alzire Did at the Christian altar give up all That she held dear on earth, her gods, her country, Her—**Zamor**: O by those dear injured names I beg thee, take this hated life.

**Zamor**: Alzire, Can it be true? is Guzman then thy husband?

**Alizire**: To plead a father's undisputed right, To say how long I struggled with my duty, To number o'er the fruitless tears I shed For three long years lamenting Zamor's death, That still I loved thee, that I left in wrath Those powerless gods that had deserted thee. And from despair alone became a Christian, Perhaps might mitigate Alzire's crime; But I disdain it, I acknowledge all, Confess my guilt, and sue for punishment. Who shall absolve the wretch whom love condemns? Take then a life that is not worth my care Without thee; dost thou not abhor me, Zamor?

**Zamor**: No: if thou lovest me still, thou are not guilty: May I yet hope that Zamor has a place In his Alzire's heart?

**Alizire**: When old Alvarez And Montezuma led me to the altar I thought on Zamor, thought him then no more, But reverenced, but adored his memory: Our tyrants, our usurpers know I loved thee; I told them all, told heaven and earth, nay told My husband—and O take this last farewell, I love thee still.

**Zamor**: Is this then our last hour Of happiness, and must we part so soon, So lately met? O if the voice of love—

**Alizire**: 'Tis Guzman and his father.

## SCENE V.

Alvarez, Guzman, Zamor, Alzire, Attendants.

**Alvarez**: [To Guzman.] Son, behold With thy Alzire stands my great preserver, My benefactor, my deliverer. [To Zamor.] O noble youth, to thee I owe my life, Let me embrace thee, be my second son, And share the pleasures of this happy day With Guzman and Alvarez.

**Zamor**: He thy son; Guzman then thy son, that proud barbarian?

**Alizire**: Avert the terrors of this dreadful moment, Indulgent heaven!

**Alvarez**: In what astonishment—

**Zamor**: How could a father, brave and good, like thee Be cursed with such a son?

**Guzman**: Insulting slave, Who gave thee license thus to spurn thy master? Thou knowest not who I am.

**Zamor**: I know thee well; And thou among the wretches thou hast made Perhaps mayest one day meet the injured Zamor.

**Guzman**: And art thou he?

**Alvarez**: Ha! Zamor!

**Zamor:** 'Tis the same, 'Tis Zamor, whom thy cruel hand oppressed With ignominious tortures, he whose eye Thou darest not meet; thou tyrant ravisher, Comest thou at last to rob me of my best And dearest treasure? with thy ruthless sword Make sure thy vengeance, and prevent the fate Which thou deservest, ere Zamor, who preserved The father, shall chastise the guilty son.

**Alvarez:** [To Guzman.] What sayest thou, Guzman, canst thou answer this?

**Guzman:** It were beneath me; punishment alone Should answer insolence, and, but for thee, Ere this he should have met with it. [Turning to Alzire.] You, madam, For your own honor might have more regard, If not for mine, than thus to parley with A traitor: come, no more of this, Alzire, Thy tears offend me: husbands may be jealous; Remember that and tremble.

**Alizire:** [To Guzman.] Cruel Guzman! My kind protector, [Turning to Alvarez.] Good Alvarez, hear me: And thou, [To Zamor.] In better days my dearest hope, O look with pity on the lost Alzire! [Pointing to Zamor.] Behold the husband whom my father chose; Long ere this hapless country bowed the neck To European tyrants, Zamor fell, So fame reported, and with him Peru, Then first subdued: my wretched father, old And full of sorrows, to the Christian's God, Forsaken by his own, indignant fled; The Christian altar saw Alzire's hand Given to her lover's murderer: thy new faith, Which yet I know not, may condemn Alzire, But virtue will forgive me when I add, That still I love thee, Zamor; but my oath, My marriage vow, rash fatal marriage! says I never must be thine—nor can I now Be Guzman's—false to both, ye both have cause To hate me: which of you will kindly end My wretched being? Guzman's hand, already Stained with the blood of my unhappy race, Were fittest to revenge the injured rights Of honor and of love; be just for once, And strike the guilty.

**Guzman:** Darest thou thus abuse The goodness thou deservest not? but remember 'Twas thy request; thy punishment is ready: My rival dies;—away with him.

**Alvarez:** Inhuman! O stop, my son, consider what is due To him who saved thy father—ye are both My children—let that tender name inspire Your breasts with pity for an aged father: At least—

SCENE VI.

Alvarez, Guzman, Alzire,

**Zamor:** don Alonzo, a Spanish officer.

**Alonzo:** My lord, the foe is at our gates; On every side their brazen bucklers ring With barbarous dissonance: aloud they cry, Revenge, and Zamor, whilst with measured steps, Solemn and slow, the close-wedged phalanx moves, As if these savages had learned from us The arts by which we conquered them.

**Guzman**: Away: Let us be gone; my presence soon shall teach These slaves their duty—heroes of Castile, Ye sons of victory, this new world was made To wear your chains, to fear, and to obey you.

**Zamor**: To fear and to obey? 'tis false, proud Guzman; Ye are but mortals like ourselves, no more.

**Guzman**: Guards, drag him hence.

**Zamor**: [To the Spaniards surrounding him.] Ye dare not: are ye gods, And must we worship deities thus bathed In our own blood?

**Guzman**: Obey me, slaves.

**Alizire**: My lord!

**Alvarez**: Remember, son, that Zamor saved thy father.

**Guzman**: My lord, I shall remember your instructions, You taught me how to conquer, and I fly Once more to victory: farewell!

### SCENE VII.

Alvarez, Alzire.

**Alizire**: [Kneeling.] My lord, Behold me at your feet, accept the homage Due to thy virtues! Guzman's injured honor Calls for revenge, Alzire was to blame; But I was bound to Zamor by the ties Of sacred love, long ere I knew thy son; We cannot give our hearts a second time: Zamor had mine, and ever must preserve it: O he is good and virtuous, for he saved Thy life, Alvarez—O forgive me!

**Alvarez**: Rise Alzire, I forgive and pity thee; Feel as a father and a friend thy sorrows, Lament thy Zamor's fate, and will protect him: But let the solemn vow thou madest to Guzman Be graved within thy heart; thou are no longer The mistress of thyself: remember well Thou art my daughter—Guzman was most cruel, I know he was, but still he is—thy husband: Perhaps he may relent; heaven grant he may!

**Alizire**: Alas! why art not thou my Zamor's father?

# ACT IV.

### SCENE I.

Alvarez, Guzman.

**Alvarez**: Fortune, my son, has crowned thee with success, Endeavor to deserve it; do not stain The laurel wreath with blood, but let fair mercy, That adds new lustre to the conqueror's glory, Inspire thy breast with pity; be a man, A Christian, and forgive: Alvarez asks thee To pardon Zamor—shall a father plead In vain? O Guzman, shall I never soften Thy savage manners, never teach my son To conquer hearts?

Guzman: Alvarez has pierced mine Most deeply; ask my life, and it is yours, But leave my honor, leave me my revenge; How can I pardon Zamor, when I know Alzire loves him?

Alvarez: Therefore he deserves Thy pity more.

Guzman: O to be pitied thus, And thus beloved, Guzman would die with pleasure.

Alvarez: With all that fierce resentment, feelest thou too The pangs of jealousy?

Guzman: And canst thou blame An injured husband? I have too much cause For jealousy, and yet thou pitiest not The unhappy Guzman.

Alvarez: Thou art wild, impetuous, And bitter in thy wrath; Alzire's virtues Deserve a milder treatment; when opposed, Her open heart, rough as her native soil, Resists with stubborn firmness, but would yield To soft persuasion; gentle means, my son, Are ever the most powerful.

Guzman: Must I soothe The pride of beauty, wear a brow serene, And cover my resentment, to expose My easy heart to new indignities? I should have thought that, jealous of my honor You would approve, and not condemn my rage: Is it not shame enough that I am wedded To a proud slave who hates me, braves my power, And owns her heart is given to another? Whom yet, to make me more accursed, I love.

Alvarez: Why blush at that? it is a lawful passion, Indulge, but keep it within proper bounds, For all excess is guilty—only promise You will determine nothing till I've seen her Once more.

Guzman: A father's will must be obeyed; I will suspend my wrath, but urge me, sir, No further.

Alvarez: All I want is time: farewell. [Exit.]

Guzman: [Alone.] And have I lived to envy Zamor's fate, To envy a vile slave, who scarce deserves The name of man!—What do I see? Alzire!

SCENE II.
Guzman, Alzire, Emira.

Alizire: 'Tis I, my lord, 'tis the afflicted wife Of Guzman; she who honors, who reveres And yet has injured thee: I come, my lord, To throw me at your feet, to own my crime, And beg forgiveness: nought have I disguised, My open heart confessed its fatal passion For the unhappy Zamor; if he dies, He dies because Alzire was sincere; But I shall more astonish thee, I come To plead for him: I know that Guzman's proud, Resentful, and severe, and yet I hope He may be generous, 'tis a conqueror's pride, His glory to forgive: an act like this Would gain thee more than conquest can bestow, Win every heart, perhaps even change Alzire's. A fawning Spaniard might have promised more, Have sighed, and wept, and softened thee with tears, Which I disdain; the hand of nature formed My plain untutored heart, if ought can move it, 'Tis generosity: let Guzman try If it is made of penetrable mould.

**Guzman**: If you're so fond of virtue, 'twould become you To know and practise it, to study, madam, Those manners you condemn, to learn your duty, To treat yourself, your honor, and your fame With more respect; nor dare to name a rival Whom I abhor, but wait in humble silence Till I determine what shall be his fate; It is enough if I forgive **Alzire**: This heart is not insensible; but know, Those who believe shall always find me cruel.

## SCENE III.
Alzire, Emira.

**Emira:** He loves you still, and yet may be persuaded.

**Alizire**: Ay, but he's jealous, that destroys my Zamor, I lost his life by asking it; but say, Emira, canst thou save him? shall he live, Though far from his Alzire? didst thou try That soldier?

**Emira**: Yes; the grand corrupter, gold, Has bought him to our interest; he is ready.

**Alizire**: Thank heaven, that metal doth not always prove The instrument of ill: but haste, Emira.

**Emira**: Is Zamor then devoted to destruction? Cannot Alvarez save him? have the council—

**Alizire**: I have a thousand fears for him: alas! These tyrants think the world was made for them, That they were born the sovereigns of mankind, That Zamor is a rebel and a slave: Barbarians as they are—this cruel council— But I'll prevent their murderous purposes: That soldier, my Emira, how he lingers!

**Emira**: Be not alarmed; night's friendly shade protects him, And he will soon be here with Zamor; sleep Hath closed the tyrant's eyes, and we are safe.

**Alizire**: O let him lead me to the prison gate That I may set him free.

**Emira**: Behold, he comes: But should ye be discovered, foul dishonor, Disgrace, and infamy—

**Alizire**: Attend on her Who would betray the man she loves; this shame Thou talkest of is a European phantom, Which fools mistake for virtue! 'tis the love Of glory not of justice, not the fear Of vice but of reproach; a shame unknown In these untutored climes, where honor shines In its own native light, and scorns the aid Of such false lustre; honor bids me save A lover and a hero thus deserted.

SCENE IV.
Alzire, Zamor, Emira, A Soldier.
**Alizire**: O Zamor, all is lost, thy punishment Already is prepared, and thou art doomed To instant death; lose not a moment's time, But haste away, this soldier will conduct thee: Alas! thou seest my grief and my despair, O save my husband from the guilt of murder, Save thy dear self, and leave me to my fate.

**Zamor**: Thou bidst me live, I must obey **Alzire**: But wilt thou follow the poor friendless Zamor? A desert and this heart are all I now Have left to offer; once I had a throne.

**Alizire**: What were a throne and empire without thee? Alas! my Zamor, to the gloomy desert My soul shall follow thee; but I am doomed To wander here alone, to drag a life Of bitterness and woe, to spend my hours In sad reflections on my wretched state, To be another's, and yet burn for thee: I bid farewell to Zamor and to joy; Away, and leave me to my duty; fain Would I preserve my honor, and my love, They both are sacred.

**Zamor**: What's this idle honor, This European phantom, that deludes thee; This Christian altar, those detested oaths Extorted from thee, this triumphant God; What have they done to rob me of Alzire?

**Alizire**: My sacred promise—

**Zamor**: 'Twas a guilty vow, And binds thee not; perdition on thy oaths, And thy false God, whom I abhor! farewell!

**Alizire**: O stop, my Zamor.

**Zamor**: Guzman is thy husband.

**Alizire**: Do not upbraid but pity me.

**Zamor**: O think On our past loves.

**Alizire**: I think but on thy danger.

**Zamor**: Thou hast betrayed me.

**Alizire**: No; I love thee still: If 'tis a crime, I own, nay glory in it; But hence, and leave me here to die alone; Some dreadful purpose labors in thy breast: How thy eyes roll! O Zamor—

**Zamor**: 'Tis resolved.

**Alizire:** Where art thou going?

**Zamor:** Glorious liberty, I'll use thee nobly.

**Alizire:** If thou diest remember I perish with thee.

**Zamor:** In this hour of terror Thou talkest to me of love: but time is precious, Conduct me, soldier; fare thee well.

### SCENE V.

**Alizire:** He's gone; But where I know not: dreadful moment! Guzman, For thee I quitted **Zamor**: haste, Emira, Follow him, fly, return, and tell me all. Thinkest thou that soldier will be faithful to us? [Exit Emira.] I know not why, but something tells me here, This day, for me, will be a day of horror. O God of Christians, thou all-conquering power, Whom yet I know not, O remove the cloud From my dark mind; if by my fatal passion I have offended thee, pour all thy vengeance On me, but spare my Zamor; O conduct His wandering footsteps through the dreary desert! Is Europe only worthy of thy care? Art thou the partial parent of one world, And tyrant o'er another? all deserve Thy equal love, the victor and the vanquished Are all the work of thy creating hand. But hark! what dreadful cry is that? methought They called on Zamor—hark! again that noise! It comes this way: my Zamor's lost.

### SCENE VI.

Alzire, Emira.

**Alizire:** Emira, I'm glad thou art come: what hast thou seen, what done? Where is he? speak, and ease my troubled soul.

**Emira:** O it is past all hope; he cannot live: Conducted safely by the faithful soldier He passed the guards, then darting from him rushed Towards the palace; trembling I pursued him, Amidst the horrors of the silent night, Almost to Guzman's chamber; there he escaped me, Though oft I called on him, oft looked in vain: I heard a dreadful shriek, some cried aloud, He's dead: the palace is in arms: fly, madam, And save yourself.

**Alizire:** Let us begone, and help My Zamor.

**Emira:** What can we do for him?

**Alizire:** Die.

### SCENE VII.

Alzire, Emira, Don Alonzo, Guards.

**Alonzo:** I've orders, madam, to secure you.

**Alizire:** Slave, What meanest thou? where's my Zamor?

**Alonzo:** That I know not: Permit me to conduct you.

**Alizire:** Cruel fate! I must not die then? Zamor is no more, And yet I live, a captive, and in chains: O ignominious!—dost thou weep, barbarian? I must indeed be wretched, if my woes Can touch a heart like thine; I'll follow thee; If death awaits me, I obey with pleasure.

End of the Fourth Act.

# ACT V.

### SCENE I.
Alzire, Guards.

**Alizire:** Prepare your tortures, you who call yourselves The judges of mankind; why am I left In dread suspense, uncertain of my fate? To live, or die? if I but mention Zamor The guards around me tremble, and look pale, His very name affrights them.

### SCENE II.
Montezuma, Alzire.

**Alizire:** Ha! my father!

**Montezuma:** O my Alzire, what a scene of woe Hath thy imprudent fatal passion brought Among us! we were pleading for thy Zamor, The good Alvarez had well nigh prevailed, When on a sudden an armed soldier rushed With violence in, and bore down all before him; 'Twas Zamor's self; with fury in his aspect, And wild distraction, on he sprang to Guzman, Attacked, and plunged the dagger in his breast: The blood that issued from your husband's wound Gushed on your father: Zamor then resigned, With calm submission at Alvarez's feet Fell humble; "take," he cried, "this guilty sword, Stained with thy Guzman's blood, I am revenged; Now nature calls on thee to do thy duty, As I have mine; strike here;" then bared his breast To the expected blow: the good Alvarez Sunk breathless in my arms; confusion followed And cries and horror; Guzman's friends upraised him, Bound up his wounds, and tried by every art Of medicine to preserve his life; the people Accuse thee as accomplice in the deed, And call for justice on thee.

**Alizire:** And couldst thou—

**Montezuma:** O no; my heart suspects thee not, Alzire, Thy soul I know is capable of error, But not of guilt: alas! thou didst not see The precipice before thee: Guzman dies By Zamor's hand, thy husband by thy lover; They will condemn thee to a shameful death, But I will try if possible to move The council in thy favor.

**Alizire**: Do not sue For me, my father, of these cruel tyrants, Let but Alvarez live, and love me still, I ask no more: Guzman's untimely fate I must lament, because 'twas horrible, Because, more dreadful still, he had deserved it: Zamor avenged his wrongs, I cannot blame Nor can I praise him for it; he must die; Alzire wishes but to follow him.

**Alvarez**: O heaven, assist me in this work of mercy!

## SCENE III.

**Alizire**: Now end all gracious power, this wretched being! Alas! Alzire, the new God thou servest Withholds thy hand, and says thou must not finish Thy hated life; the deities I left Denied me not the privilege to die. Is it a crime to hasten on, perhaps A few short years, the universal doom Appointed for us all? and must we drink The bitter cup of sorrow to the dregs? In this vile body is there aught so sacred That the free spirit should not leave at will Its homely mansion? this all-conquering nation, Shall they depopulate earth, destroy my race, Condemn Alzire, and I not be mistress Of my own life? Barbarians! Zamor then Must die in tortures.

## SCENE IV.
Zamor in Chains, Alzire, Guards.

**Zamor**: Yes, it is decreed: We both must die; beneath the specious name Of justice, the tribunal hath condemned us; Guzman yet lives, my erring hand had left Its work unfinished; the barbarian lives To glut his vengeance with Alzire's blood, To taste a tyrant's savage joy, and see us Perish together—to pronounce our doom Alvarez comes: I am the guilty cause; Thou diest for me, Alzire.

**Alizire**: Then no more, For death is welcome if it comes with **Zamor**: O bless the happy hour that shall dissolve My ties to Guzman; I may love thee now Without a crime, without remorse; receive The heart that's due to thee, and thee alone: Yon dreadful scaffold, for our death prepared, Shall be the altar of my love; there, Zamor, I'll offer up my faith, and expiate there My crime of infidelity—the worst Of all our sentence is, that it must come From good Alvarez.

**Zamor**: See, he's here; his cheeks Are bathed in tears.

**Alizire**: Alas! who most deserves Compassion? this will be a dreadful parting.

## SCENE V.
Alzire, Zamor, Alvarez, Guards.

**Zamor**: From you we both expect to hear our fate, Pronounce it, we are not afraid to die: Zamor deserves it, he has slain thy son, The son of good Alvarez, of my friend; But what, my lord, has this fair innocent, What has Alzire done? thou art not cruel, Proud, and revengeful, like thy countrymen, Distinguished by thy clemency, we loved Alvarez; wilt thou give up the fair title Of just and good, and bathe thee in the blood Of innocence?

**Alizire**: Avenge thyself, avenge Thy son; but do not thus condemn the guiltless: I am the wife of Guzman, that alone Should tell thee, I would save, and not betray him, Even though I hated, I respected him, And swerved not from my faith, thou knowest I did not: Careless of what the slandering multitude May think, I rest my character on thee; Acquitted by Alvarez, for the rest 'Tis equal all: if Zamor dies, Alzire Must go with him: I pity thee alone.

**Alvarez**: Amazing scene of tenderness and horror! That he should be the murderer of my son Who was my kind deliverer! O Zamor, To thee I owe a life which I abhor; It was a fatal gift, and bought too dear: I am a father, yet I am a man; Spite of a parent's grief that cries aloud For vengeance on thee, gratitude pleads strongly; She will be heard:—and thou who wert my daughter, Whom yet I call by that dear tender name; Think not I joy in the inhuman pleasure Of fell revenge; I lose a friend, I lose A daughter, and a son: the council dooms thee To death, and bids a wretched father pass The cruel sentence; I could not refuse The dreadful task, and now am come, my children, To save you both: it is in Zamor's power.

**Zamor**: To save Alzire? say, what's to be done?

**Alvarez**: Believe in Him who now inspires Alvarez; One word will change your fate: the law decrees, Whoe'er becomes a Christian meets forgiveness, The God of pardon will himself o'ershade Thy every crime, and take thee to his mercy; Spain will protect and love thee as a brother; Alzire shall be safe, ye both shall live; I'll answer for her life as for thy own; Zamor, to thee I speak; of thee I ask Another life, I owe thee one already; A father asks thee only to be happy, To be a Christian, and to save Alzire.

**Alizire**: What says my love? say, should we purchase life So dearly? Shall I quit my gods for Guzman's, And be a traitor? tell me, thou sage tyrant, When I was master of thy fate, wouldst thou, Had Zamor sued, have quitted thy own gods For mine?

**Alvarez**: I should have done as now I do, Implored the almighty being to enlighten A heart like thine, and make thee a true Christian.

**Zamor:** O cruel contest! what am I to choose, Or life or death, Alzire, or my gods, Which must I leave? Alzire, 'tis thy cause, Determine it; I think thou wouldst not bring Dishonor on thy Zamor.

**Alizire:** Hear me then: Thou knowest that, to obey a father's will, I gave another what to thee alone I had devoted; I embraced his faith, And worshipped Montezuma's God; perhaps It was the error of my easy youth, And thou wilt blame me for it; but methought The law of Christians was the law of truth, And therefore only did I make it mine But to renounce those gods our heart adores; That is no venial error, but a crime Of deepest die; it is to give up both, The God we worship, and the God we leave; 'Tis to be false to heaven, to the world, And to ourselves: no, Zamor, if thou diest, Die worthy of Alzire; hear the voice Of conscience; act as she alone directs thee.

**Zamor:** Thou hast determined as I thought thou wouldst, Zamor shall die with honor.

**Alvarez:** Then ye scorn Our proffered mercy: hark! those mournful cries—

### SCENE VII.

Alvarez, Guzman, Zamor, Americans, Soldiers.

**Zamor:** O save Alzire; let me perish.

**Alizire:** No: I will be joined to Guzman, and to thee.

**Alvarez:** My son is in the agonies of death; O Guzman, hear me.

**Zamor:** Look on Zamor, learn Of him to die.

**Guzman:** [To Zamor.] Perhaps I may teach thee Another lesson: I have owed the world A good example long, and now I mean To pay the debt. [Turning to Alvarez.] My soul is on the wing, And ere she takes her flight but waits to see And imitate Alvarez; O my father, The mask is off, death has at last unveiled The hideous scene, and showed me to myself; New light breaks in on my astonished soul: O I have been a proud, ungrateful being, And trampled on my fellow-creatures: heaven Avenges earth: my life can never atone For half the blood I've shed: prosperity Had blinded Guzman, death's benignant hand Restores my sight; I thank the instrument Employed by heaven to make me what I am. A penitent: I yet am master here; And yet can pardon: Zamor, I forgive thee, Live and be free; but O remember how A Christian acted, how a Christian died. [To Montezuma, who kneels to him.] Thou, Montezuma, and ye hapless victims Of my ambition, say my clemency Surpassed my guilt, and let your sovereigns know, That we were born your conquerors. [To Zamor.] Observe The difference, Zamor, 'twixt thy God and mine: Thine teach thee to revenge an injury, Mine to forgive and pity thee.

**Alvarez**: My son, Thy virtue's equal to thy courage.

**Alizire**: Heaven! How wonderful a change! amazing goodness!

**Zamor**: Thou wilt oblige me to repent.

**Guzman**: Yes, Zamor, I will do more, thou shalt admire and love me: Guzman too long hath made Alzire wretched, I'll make her happy; with my dying hand I give her to thee, live and hate me not, Restore your country's ruined walls, and bless My memory. [To Alvarez.] Alvarez, be once more A father to them, let the light of heaven Shine forth upon them; Zamor is thy son, Let him repair my loss.

**Zamor**: Amazed, confounded, And motionless I stand; can Christians boast Of such exalted virtue? 'twas inspired By heaven; the Christian's law must be divine: Friendship, and faith, and constancy I knew Already; but this soars above them all: I must indeed admire and love thee, Guzman [Falls at his feet.]

**Alizire**: My lord, permit me to embrace thy knees: O I could die for Guzman; will you then Forgive my weakness?

**Guzman**: Yes: I pardon all, I cannot see thee weep and not forgive thee. Come near, my father, take my last farewell! [Dies.]

**Alvarez**: [To Montezuma.] I see the hand of God in all our woes, And humbly bend myself before that power Who wounds to heal, and strikes but to forgive.

**End**

# Orestes

## Contents

Dramatis Personæ. . . . . . . . . . . . . . . . . . . . . . . . . . . . . . . . . . . . . . . 86
Act I. . . . . . . . . . . . . . . . . . . . . . . . . . . . . . . . . . . . . . . . . . . . . . . . . . 88
Act II. . . . . . . . . . . . . . . . . . . . . . . . . . . . . . . . . . . . . . . . . . . . . . . . . 95
Act III. . . . . . . . . . . . . . . . . . . . . . . . . . . . . . . . . . . . . . . . . . . . . . . 101
Act IV. . . . . . . . . . . . . . . . . . . . . . . . . . . . . . . . . . . . . . . . . . . . . . . 109
Act V. . . . . . . . . . . . . . . . . . . . . . . . . . . . . . . . . . . . . . . . . . . . . . . . 115

## Dramatis Personæ.

Ægisthus.
Orestes, Son of Agamemnon and Clytemnæstra.
Electra, Sisters of Orestes.
IPHISA, Sisters of Orestes.
ClytemnÆstra, Wife of Ægisthus.
Pylades, Friend of Orestes.
Pammenes, an old Man, attached to the Family of Agamemnon.
Dimas, an Officer of the Guards.
Attendants.

*Orestes* was produced in 1750, an experiment which intensely interested the literary world and the public. In his Dedicatory Letters to the Duchess of Maine, Voltaire has the following passage on the Greek drama:

"We should not, I acknowledge, endeavor to imitate what is weak and defective in the ancients: it is most probable that their faults were well known to their contemporaries. I am satisfied, Madam, that the wits of Athens condemned, as well as you, some of those repetitions, and some declamations with which Sophocles has loaded his *Electra*: they must have observed that he had not dived deep enough into the human heart. I will moreover fairly confess, that there are beauties peculiar not only to the Greek language, but to the climate, to manners and times, which it would be ridiculous to transplant hither. Therefore I have not copied exactly the *Electra* of Sophocles—much more

I knew would be necessary; but I have taken, as well as I could, all the spirit and substance of it. The feast celebrated by Ægisthus and Clytemnæstra, which they called the feast of Agamemnon; the arrival of Orestes and Pylades; the urn which was supposed to contain the ashes of Orestes; the ring of Agamemnon; the character of Electra, and that of Iphisa, which is exactly the Chrysothemis of Sophocles; and above all, the remorse of Clytemnæstra; these I have copied from the Greek tragedy. When the messenger, who relates the fictitious story of the death of Orestes, says to Clytemnæstra: 'I see, Madam, you are deeply affected by his death;' she replies, 'I am a mother, and must therefore be unhappy; a mother, though injured, cannot hate her own offspring:' she even endeavors to justify herself to Electra, with regard to the murder of Agamemnon, and laments her daughter. Euripides has carried Clytemnæstra's repentance still further. This, Madam, was what gained the applause of the most judicious and sensible people upon earth, and was approved by all good judges in our own nation. No character, in reality, can be more natural than that of a woman, criminal with regard to her husband, yet softened by her children; a woman, whose proud and fiery disposition is still open to pity and compassion, who resumes the fierceness of her character on receiving too severe reproaches, and at last sinks into submission and tears. The seeds of this character were in Sophocles and Euripides, and I have only unfolded them. Nothing but ignorance, and its natural attendant, presumption, can assert that the ancients have nothing worthy of our imitation: there is scarcely one real and essential beauty and perfection, for the foundation of which, at least, we are not indebted to them.

"I have taken particular care not to depart from that simplicity so strongly recommended by the Greeks, and so difficult to attain; the true mark of genius and invention, and the very essence of all theatrical merit. A foreign character, brought into Œdipus or Electra, who should play a principal part and draw aside the attention of the audience, would be a monster in the eyes of all those who have any knowledge of the ancients, or of that nature which they have so finely painted. Art and genius consist in finding everything within the subject, and never going out of it in search of additional ornaments: but how are we to imitate that truly tragic pomp and magnificence which we find in the verses of Sophocles, that natural elegance and purity of diction, without which the piece, howsoever well conducted in other respects, must after all be but a poor performance!

"I have at least given my countrymen some idea of a tragedy without love, without confidants, and without episodes: the few partisans of good taste acknowledge themselves obliged to me for it, though the rest of the world withhold their approbation for a time, but will come in at last, when the rage of party is over, the injustice of persecution at an end, and the clouds of ignorance dissipated. You, Madam, must preserve among us those glittering sparks of light which the ancients have transmitted to us; we owe everything to them: not an art was born among us: everything was transplanted: but the earth that bears these foreign fruits is worn out, and our ancient barbarism, by the help of false taste, would break out again in spite of all our culture and improvement: and the disciples of Athens and Rome become Goths and Vandals, corrupted with the manners of the Sybarites, without the kind favor and protection of persons of your rank. When nature has given them either genius, or the love of genius, they encourage this nation, which is better able to imitate than to invent; and which always looks up towards the great for those instructions and examples which it perpetually stands in need of. All that I wish for, Madam, is, that some genius may be found to finish what I have but just sketched out; to free the stage from that effeminacy and affectation which it is now sunk into; to render it respectable to the gravest characters; worthy of the few great masterpieces which we already have among us; worthy, in short, the approbation of a mind like yours, and all those who may hereafter endeavor to resemble you."

# ACT I.

**SCENE I.**
Scene, the seashore, a wood, a temple, a palace and a tomb, on one side: on the other, Argos at a distance.
Iphisa, Pammenes.

**Iphisa:** Sayest thou, Pammenes? shall these hated walls, Where I so long have dragged a life of woe, Afford at least the melancholy comfort Of mingling sorrow with my dear Electra? And will Ægisthus bring her to the tomb Of Agamemnon, bring his daughter here, To be a witness of the horrid pomp, The sad solemnity, which on this day Annual returns, to celebrate their crimes, And make their guilt immortal?

**Pammenes:** O Iphisa, Thou honored daughter of my royal master, Like thee, confined within these lonely walls, The secrets of a vile abandoned court Do seldom reach Pammenes; but, 'tis rumored, The jealous tyrant brings Electra here, Fearful lest Argos, by her cries alarmed, Should rise to vengeance; every heart, he knows, Feels for the injured princess, therefore much He dreads her clamors; with a watchful eye Observes her conduct, treats her as a slave, And leads the captive to adorn his triumph.

**Iphisa**: Good heaven! and must Electra be a slave! Shall Agamemnon's blood be thus disgraced By a barbarian? Will her cruel mother, Will Clytemnæstra bear the vile reproach That on herself recoils, and all her race? Perhaps my sister is too fierce of soul, She mingles too much pride and bitterness Of keen resentment with her griefs; alas! Weak are her arms against a tyrant's power: What will her anger, what her pride avail her? They only irritate a haughty foe, And cannot serve our cause: my fate at least Is milder, and this solitary state Shields me from wrongs which must oppress Electra. Far from my father's foes, these pious hands Can pay due offerings to his honored shade: Far from his murderer, in this sad retreat Freely I weep in peace, and curse Ægisthus: I'm not condemned to see the tyrant here, Save when the Sun unwillingly brings round The fatal day that knit the dreadful tie, When that inhuman monster shed the blood Of Agamemnon, when base Clytemnæstra—

SCENE II.
Electra, Iphisa, Pammenes.
**Iphisa**: O my Electra! art thou here? my sister—
**Electra**: The day of horror is returned, Iphisa: The dreadful rites, the guilty feast prepared, Have brought me hither; thy Electra comes, Thy captive sister, comes a wretched slave, To bear the tidings of their guilty joy.

**Iphisa**: To see Electra is a blessing still, It pours some joy into the bitter cup Of sorrow, thus to mix my tears with thine.

**Electra**: Tears, my Iphisa! I have shed enough Of them already: O thou bleeding ghost Of my dead father, ever-honored shade, Is that the tribute which I owe to thee? I owe thee blood, and blood thou hast required; Amidst the pomp of this dire festival, Dragged by Ægisthus here, I will collect My scattered spirits, shake off these vile chains, And be my own avenger: yes, Iphisa, This feeble arm shall reach the tyrant's heart: Did not the cruel Clytemnæstra shed A husband's blood? did I not see her lift Her barbarous hand against him, and shall we Suspend the blow, and let a murderer live? O vengeance, and thou, animating virtue, That dost inspire me, art thou not as bold As daring guilt? we must revenge ourselves, We must, Iphisa: fearest thou then to strike, Fearest thou to die? shall Clytemnæstra's daughter, The blood of Atreus fear? O rather lend Thy aid, and join the desperate Electra!

**Iphisa**: My dearest sister, moderate thy rage, And calm thy troubled mind: against our foes What can we bring but unavailing tears? Who will assist us? who will lend us arms? Or how shall we surprise a watchful king, For guilt is ever fearful, by his guards Surrounded? why, Electra, wilt thou court Perpetual danger? should the tyrant hear Thy loud complaints, I tremble for thy life.

**Electra:** Why let him hear them? I would have my grief Sink to his heart, and poison all his joys: Yes; I would have my cries ascend to heaven, And bring the thunder down; would have them raise A hundred kings, who never yet have dared, Unworthy cowards as they are, to avenge Great Agamemnon: but I pardon thee, And the vain terrors of thy fearful soul, That shrinks at danger; for he favors you, I know he does, and only crushes me Beneath his iron yoke: thou hast not been, Like me, a wretched persecuted slave; Thou didst not see the impious parricide, The horrid[1] feast, the dire solemnity, When Clytemnæstra—O the dreadful image Is still before me, in this place, Iphisa, Where now thou tremblest to declare thy wrongs, There did these eyes behold our hapless father Caught in the deadly snare: Pammenes heard His dying groans, and ran with me to save him: But when I came, what did I see! my mother Plunging her ruthless dagger in his breast, To rob him of the poor remains of life. [Turning to Pammenes.] Thou sawest me take Orestes in my arms, My dear Orestes; little knew he then Of danger, but as near his murdered father He stood, called out for aid to Clytemnæstra: She, midst the horrors of the guilty scene, Stopped for a moment short, and gave us time Safe to convey the victim from Ægisthus. Whether the tyrant has completed yet The imperfect vengeance in Orestes' blood, I know not: O my brother, dost thou live, Or hast thou followed thy unhappy father? Alas! I weep for him, and fear for thee. These hands are loaded with inglorious chains, And these sad eyes, forever bathed in tears, See naught but guilt, oppression, and despair.

**Pammenes:** Ye dear remains of Atreus' honored race, Whose splendor I have seen, whose woes I feel, Permit a friend to fill your weeping souls With cheerful hope, that ever waits propitious To soothe affliction: call to mind what heaven Long since hath promised, that its vengeful hand Should one day lead Orestes to the place Where we preserved him; that Ægisthus there, Even at yon tomb, and on the fatal day Marked for his impious triumph o'er the dead, Should pay the forfeit of his crime: the Gods Can ne'er deceive; in darkness still they veil Their secret purpose from the eyes of men, And punishment with slow but certain steps, Still follows guilt.

**Iphisa:** But wherefore stays so long Their tardy vengeance? I have languished here In grief and anguish many a tedious hour; Electra, still more wretched, is in chains: Meantime the proud oppressor lives in peace, And glories in his crimes.

**Electra:** Thou seest, Pammenes, Ægisthus still renews his cruel triumph, And celebrates the fatal nuptials; still A wretched exile lives my dear Orestes, Forgetful of his father, and Electra.

**Pammenes:** But mark the course of time: he touches now The age when manly strength, with courage joined, May aid your purpose; hope for his return, And trust in heaven.

**Electra:** We will: thou son of wisdom, Thou good old man, O thou hast darted forth A ray of hope on my despairing soul! If with unpitying eye the gods beheld Our miseries here, and proud oppression, still Unpunished, trampled on the tender feet Of innocence, what hand would crown their altars With incense and oblation! but kind heaven Will give Orestes to a sister's arms, And blast the tyrant: hear my voice, Orestes, O hear thy country's, hear the cries of blood, That call thee forth; come from thy dreary caves, And pathless deserts, where misfortune long Hath tried thy courage; leave thy savage prey, And all the roaming monsters of the forest, To chase the beasts of Argos, to destroy The tyrants of the earth, the murderers Of kings; O haste, and let me guide thy hand Even to the traitor's breast.

**Iphisa:** No more: repress Thy griefs, Electra; see, thy mother comes.

**Electra:** And have I yet a mother?

### SCENE III.

Clytemnæstra, Electra, Iphisa.

**Clytemnæstra:** Hence, and leave me; You may retire, Pammenes; stay, my daughters.

**Iphisa:** Alas! that sacred name dispels my fears.

**Electra:** And doubles mine.

**Clytemnæstra:** Touching your fate, my children, I came to lay a mother's heart before you. Barren, thank heaven, hath been my second bed, Nor brought a race of jealous foes to sow Division here. Alas! my little race Is almost run; the secret grief that long Hath preyed on my sad heart will finish soon A life of woe: spite of Ægisthus, still I love my children; spite of all his rage, Electra, thou who in thy infant years So oft hast given me comfort, when the loss Of Iphigenia, and her cruel father Oppressed my soul; though now thy pride disdains me, And braves my power, thou art my daughter still; Unworthy as thou art, there's still a place In Clytemnæstra's heart for her Electra.

**Electra:** For me! O heaven, and am I yet beloved; And dost thou feel for thy unhappy daughter? O, if thou dost, behold her chains, behold Yon tomb—

**Clytemnæstra:** Unkind Electra, thus to wake The sad remembrance! thou hast plunged a dagger Into thy mother's breast; but I deserve it.

**Electra:** Thou hast disarmed Electra, nature pleads A mother's cause; I own myself to blame For all the bitterness of sorrow poured In dreadful execrations on thy head. By thee delivered to the tyrant's power, I would have torn thee from him; I lament, But cannot hate thee. O, if gracious heaven Hath touched thy soul with wholesome penitence, Obey its sacred will, and hear the voice Of conscience, that commands thee to unloose The horrid ties that bind thee to a wretch Despised and hated; follow the great God Who leads thy footsteps to the paths of virtue; Call back your son, let him return to fill The throne of his great ancestors, to scourge A tyrant, to avenge his murdered father, His sisters, and his mother: haste and send For my Orestes.

**Clytemnæstra:** Talk no more of that, Electra, nor speak thus of my Ægisthus: I grieve to see thee in these shameful bonds; But know, a sovereign cannot tamely brook Repeated insults, or embrace a foe: You had provoked him to, be cruel; I, Who am but his first subject, oft have tried To soothe his anger, but in vain: my words, Instead of healing, but inflamed the wound: Electra is indebted to herself For all her deep-felt injuries; henceforth bend To thy condition; let thy sister teach thee That we must yield submissive to our fate, If e'er we hope to change it. I could wish To end my days in peace amongst my children; But if thy rapid and imprudent zeal Should bring Orestes here before the time, His life might answer for it, and thy own, If the king see him: though I pity thee, Electra, yet I owe a husband more Than a lost son, whom I have cause to fear.

**Electra:** O heaven, that monster! he thy husband, he! And is it thus thou pitiest me? alas, What will this poor, this light remorse avail thee, This fleeting sorrow? was thy tenderness But for a moment, dost thou threaten me, [To Iphisa.] Is this, Iphisa, this a mother's love? [To Clytemnæstra.] It seems thou threatenest my Orestes too; Thou hast no cause to fear, nor I to hope For him: alas! perhaps he is no more; Perhaps Ægisthus, the detested tyrant, He whom but now thou didst not blush to call Thy husband, hath in secret ta'en his life.

**Iphisa:** Believe me, Madam, when I call the gods To witness, poor Electra and myself Are strangers to the fate of dear Orestes; Have pity then on your afflicted daughter, Pity your helpless son and spare Electra: She has been wronged; her tears and her reproaches Suit well her fate, and ought to be forgiven.

**Electra:** I must not hope it, must not even complain; And if Orestes lives but in my thoughts 'Tis deemed a crime. I know Ægisthus well, Know his fierce nature; if he fears my brother, He'll soon destroy him.

Clytemnæstra: Know, thy brother lives; If he's in danger, 'tis from thy imprudence; Therefore be humble, moderate thy transports, Respect thy mother: thinkest thou I come here, Elate with joy, to lead the splendid triumph? O no, to me it is a day of sorrow; Thou weepest in chains, and I upon a throne. I know the cruel vows thy hatred made Against me: O, Electra! cease thy prayers, The gods have heard thee but too well already: Retire, and leave me.

## SCENE IV.

Clytemnæstra: [Alone.] How it shocks my soul To see my children! O the guilty bed! My fatal marriage, and long prosperous crimes, Adultery and murder, horrid bonds! How ye torment me now! my little dream Of happiness is o'er, and conscience darts Its sudden rays on my affrighted soul. How can Ægisthus live so long in peace! Fearless he leads me on to share with him These cruel triumphs; but my spirits fail, My strength forsakes me, and I tremble now At every omen; fear my subjects, fear All Argos, Greece, Electra, and Orestes. How dreadful 'tis to hate the blood that flowed Congenial with our own, to dread the names Which mortals hold so sacred and so dear! But injured nature, banished from my heart, Indignant frowns, and to avenge herself Now bids me tremble at the name of son.

## SCENE V.

Ægisthus, Clytemnæstra.

Clytemnæstra: Cruel Ægisthus, wherefore wouldst thou lead me To this sad place, the seat of death and horror?

Ægisthus: Is then the solemn pomp, the feast of joy, The sweet remembrance of our prosperous days, Grown hateful to thee? is our marriage day A day of horror?

Clytemnæstra: No: but here, Ægisthus, There may be danger: my unhappy children Have filled this heart with anguish: poor Iphisa Weeps her hard lot; Electra is in chains; This fatal place reminds me of the blood We shed, reminds me of my dear Orestes, Of Agamemnon.

Ægisthus: Let Iphisa weep, And proud Electra rave; I bore too long Her bitter taunts, 'tis fit her haughtiness Should now be humbled; I'll not suffer her To stir up foul rebellion in my kingdom, To tell the factions that Orestes comes, And call down vengeance on me; every hour That hated name is echoed in my ear, I must not bear it.

Clytemnæstra: Ha! what name was that? Orestes! O, I shudder at the thought Of his approach: an oracle long since Declared, that here, even at the fatal tomb

Whither thou leadest, his parricidal hand Should one day rise vindictive, and destroy us. Why therefore wouldst thou tempt the gods, why thus Expose a life so dear to Clytemnæstra?

Ægisthus: Be not alarmed; Orestes ne'er shall hurt thee: His be the danger; for I have sent forth Some friends in search of him, and soon I hope Shall see him in the toils; a wretched exile From clime to clime he roams, and now it seems In Epidaurus' gloomy forest hides His ignominious head; but there perhaps We have more friends than Clytemnæstra thinks of; The king may serve us.

Clytemnæstra: But, my son—

Ægisthus: I know He's fierce, implacable, revengeful; stung By his misfortunes, all the blood of Atreus Boils in his breast, and animates his rage.

Clytemnæstra: Alas! my lord, his rage is but too just.

Ægisthus: Be it our business then to make it vain; Thou knowest I've sent my Plisthenes in secret To Epidaurus.

Clytemnæstra: But for what?

Ægisthus: To fix My throne in safety, and remove thy fears: Yes, Plisthenes, my son, by thee adopted Heir to my kingdom, knows too well how much His interest must depend on the event E'er to neglect his charge: he is thy son, Think of no other: had Electra's heart Submissive yielded to another's counsels, She had been happy in my Plisthenes: But she shall feel the power which she contemns, She and her haughty brother, her Orestes, He may be found perhaps.—You seem disturbed.

Clytemnæstra: Alas! Ægisthus, must we sacrifice More victims? must I purchase length of days With added guilt? Thou knowest whose blood we shed— And must my son too perish, must I pay So dear a price for life?

Ægisthus: Remember—

Clytemnæstra: No: First let me ask the sacred oracle—

Ægisthus: What canst thou hope from gods or oracles, Were they consulted on the blissful day That gave Ægisthus to his Clytemnæstra?

Clytemnæstra: Thou hast recalled a time when heaven, I fear, Was much offended: love defies the gods, But fear adores them; guilt weighs down my soul, Do not oppress my feeble spirits; time, That changes all, hath altered this proud heart; The hand of heaven is on me, and subdues The haughty rage that once inspired my breast; Not that my tender friendship for Ægisthus Can e'er decay, our interests are the same; But to behold my daughter made a slave, To think on my poor lost abandoned son, To think that now, even now, perhaps he dies

By vile assassins, or, if living, lives My foe, and hates the guilty Clytemnæstra, Is it not dreadful? pity me, Ægisthus, I am a mother still.

**Ægisthus:** Thou art my wife; Thou art my queen; resume thy wonted courage, And be thyself again; indulge no more This foolish fondness for ungrateful children, Who merit not thy love; consult alone Ægisthus' safety, and thy own repose.

**Clytemnæstra:** Repose! the guilty mind can ne'er enjoy it.

# ACT II.

### SCENE I.
Orestes, Pylades.

**Orestes:** Whither, my Pylades, hath cruel fate Conducted us? alas! Orestes lives But to increase the sorrows of his friend: Our arms, our treasures, and our soldiers lost In the rude storm; here on this desert coast, No succor near, deserted and forlorn We wander on, and naught but hope remains. Where are we?

**Pylades:** That I know not; but since fate Hath led us hither, let us not despair; It is enough for me, Orestes lives: Be confident; the barbarous Ægisthus In vain pursued thy life, which heaven preserved In Epidaurus, when thy arm subdued The gallant Plisthenes: let naught alarm Or terrify thy soul, but boldly urge Thy way, protected by that guardian God Who watches o'er the just, the great avenger, Who hath already to thy valor given The son, and promised that ere long the father Shall follow him.

**Orestes:** Alas, my friend, that God In anger now withdraws his powerful aid, And frowns upon us, as thy cruel fate Too plainly shows; a terrible example! But say, within the rock didst thou conceal The urn, which to Mycenæ, horrid seat Of murder, by the gods command, we bear; That urn which holds the ashes of my foe, Of Plisthenes; with that we must deceive The tyrant.

**Pylades:** I have done it.

**Orestes:** Gracious heaven! When shall we reap the fruits of our obedience? When will the wished-for day of vengeance come? Shall I again behold my native soil, The dear, the dreadful place where first I saw The light of day? Where, shall I find my sister, The pride, the glory, of admiring Greece; That generous maid, whom all unite to praise, But none will dare to succor? She preserved My life; and, worthy of her noble father, Hath never bent beneath the oppressive hand Of power, but braved the fury of the storm. How many kings, how many heroes, fought For Menelaus! Agamemnon dies, And Greece forgets him, whilst his hapless son, Deserted, wanders o'er a faithless world, To seek some blest asylum for repose. Alas, without thy friendship I had been The most distressed, most abject of mankind: But heaven, in pity to my woes, hath sent My Pylades; it would not let me perish, But gave me to subdue my hated foe, And half avenge my father: say, my friend, What path will lead us to the tyrant's court?

**Pylades**: Behold that palace, and the towering height Of yon proud temple, the dark grove overgrown With cypress, and the tomb, rich images Of mournful splendor all: and see! this way Advancing, comes a venerable sage, Of mildest aspect, and whose years, no doubt, Have long experience of calamity; His soul will melt at thy disastrous fate.

**Orestes**: Is every mortal born to suffer? hark! He groans, my Pylades.

SCENE II.
Orestes, Pylades, Pammenes.

**Pylades**: Whoe'er thou art, Stop, and inform us: we are strangers here. Two poor unhappy friends, long time the sport Of winds and waves, now on this unknown shore Cast helpless, canst thou tell us if this place Will be or fatal to us, or propitious?

**Pammenes**: I am a simple, plain old man, and here Worship the gods, adore their justice, live In humble fear of them, and exercise The sacred rights of hospitality; Ye both are welcome to my little cottage, There to despise with me the pride of kings, Their pomp and riches; come, my friends, for such I ever hold the wretched.

**Orestes**: Generous stranger, May gracious heaven inspire us with the means To recompense thy goodness! but inform us What place is this; who is your king?

**Pammenes**: Ægisthus: I am his subject.

**Orestes**: Terrors, crimes, and vengeance! O heaven, Ægisthus!

**Pylades**: Soft: do not betray us; Be careful.

**Orestes**: Gods, Ægisthus! he who murdered—

**Pammenes**: The same.

**Orestes**: And Clytemnæstra, lives she still After that fatal blow.

**Pammenes**: She reigns with him; The rest is known too well.

**Orestes**: That tomb before us, And yonder palace—

**Pammenes**: Is inhabited Now by Ægisthus; built, I well remember, By worthier hands, and for a better use. The tomb thou seest, forgive me if I weep At the remembrance, is the tomb of him I loved, my lord, my king—of Agamemnon.

**Orestes:** O 'tis too much! I sink beneath it.

**Pylades:** Hide Thy tears, my friend. [To Orestes, who turns away from him.]

**Pammenes:** You seem much moved, and fain Would stop the tide of grief: O give it way, Indulge thy sorrows, and lament the son Of gods, the noble conqueror of Troy; Whilst they insult his sacred memory here, Strangers shall weep the fate of Agamemnon.

**Orestes:** A stranger as I am, I cannot look With cold indifference on the noble race Of Atreus, 'tis a Grecian's duty ever To weep the fate of heroes, and I ought— But doth Electra live in Argos still?

**Pammenes:** She doth, she's here.

**Orestes:** I run, I fly to meet her.

**Pylades:** Ha! whither wouldst thou go! What! brave the gods Hazard thy precious life! forbear, my lord. [To Pammenes.] O, sir, conduct us to the neighboring temple, There will we lay our gifts before the altar In humble duty, and adore that God Who ruled the waves, and saved us from destruction.

**Orestes:** Wilt thou conduct us to the sacred tomb Where lie the ashes of a murdered hero? There must I offer to his honored shade A secret sacrifice.

**Pammenes:** O heavenly justice, Thou sacrifice to him! amidst his foes! O noble youth! my master had a son, Who, in Electra's arms—but I forbear, Ægisthus comes: away; I'll follow you.

**Orestes:** Ægisthus! ha!

**Pylades:** We must avoid his presence.

SCENE III.

Ægisthus, Clytemnæstra, Pammenes.

**Ægisthus:** [To Pammenes] Who are those strangers? one of them methought Seemed, by his stately port and fair demeanor, Of noble birth, a gloom of melancholy Hangs on his brow: he struck me as he passed: Is he our subject? knowest thou whence he came?

**Pammenes:** I only know they are unfortunate; Driven by the tempest on those rocks, they came For shelter here; as strangers I relieved them; It was my duty: if they tell me truth, Greece is their country.

**Ægisthus:** Thou shalt answer for them On peril of thy life.

**Clytemnæstra:** Alas! my lord, Can these poor objects raise suspicion?

**Ægisthus:** Yes: The people murmur; everything alarms me.

**Clytemnæstra:** Such for these fifteen years hath been our fate, To fear, and to be feared; the bitter poison To all my happiness.

**Ægisthus:** Away, Pammenes; Let me know who and whence they are; why thus They come so near the palace; from what port Their vessel sailed, and wherefore on the seas Where I command: away, and bring me word.

SCENE IV.
Ægisthus, Clytemnæstra.

**Ægisthus:** Well, madam, to remove thy idle fears, The interpreters of heaven it seems at length Have been consulted; but in vain: their silence Doubles thy grief, and heightens thy despair; For to thyself, thy restless spirit ne'er Will know repose; thou tremblest at the thought Of thy son's death, yet fearest his dangerous life: Consult no more thy doubtful oracles, And hesitating priests, that brood in secret O'er the dark bosom of futurity; But hear Ægisthus, he shall give thee peace, And satisfy thy soul: this hand determines, This tongue pronounces Clytemnæstra's fate: If thou wouldst live and reign, confide in me, And me alone, and let me hear no more Of your unworthy son; but for Electra, She's to be feared, and we must think of her: Perhaps her marriage with my Plisthenes Might stop the mouth of faction, and appease The discontented people: thou wouldst wish To see the deadly hatred, that so long Hath raged between us, softened into peace; To see our interests and our hearts united: Let it be so. Go thou, and talk with her; But take good heed her pride refuses not The proffered boon, that were an insult soon She might repent of; but I hope with you, That slavery hath bowed down her haughty spirit, That this unhoped for, unexpected change From poverty and chains to rank and splendor, Joined to a mother's kind authority, And above all, to Ambition, will persuade her To seize the golden minutes, and be wise: But if she spurns the happiness that courts her, Her insolence shall meet its due reward. Your foolish fondness, and her father's name, Have fed her pride too long; but let her dread, If she submits not, a severer fate, Chains heavier far, and endless banishment.

SCENE V.
Clytemnæstra, **Electra: Clytemnæstra:** Come near, my daughter, and with milder looks Behold thy mother: I have mourned in secret, And wept with thee thy hard and cruel bondage, Though not unmerited; for sure thy hatred Was most unjust, Electra: as a queen, I was offended; as a mother, grieved; But I have gained your pardon, and your rights Are all restored.

**Electra:** O madam, at your feet—
**Clytemnæstra:** But I would still do more.
**Electra:** What more?

**Clytemnæstra**: Support Your race, restore the honored name of Pelops, And re-unite his long-divided children.

**Electra**: Ha! talkest thou of Orestes? speak, go on.

**Clytemnæstra**: I speak of thee, and hope at last Electra Will be Electra's friend: I know thy soul Aspires to empire, be thyself again, And let thy hopes transport thee to the throne Of Argos and Mycenæ; rise from chains And ignominious slavery to the throne Of thy great ancestors: Ægisthus yields To my entreaties, as a daughter yet He would embrace thee, to his Plisthenes Would join Electra; every hour the youth From Epidaurus is expected here; When he returns he weds you: look, my daughter, Towards the bright prospect of thy future glory, And bury all the past in deep oblivion.

**Electra**: Can I forget the past, or look with joy On that which is to come? O cruel fate, This is the worst indignity that e'er Electra bore: remember whence I sprang, Remember, I am Agamemnon's daughter, And wouldst thou bind me to his murderer's son? Give me my chains again, oppress my soul With all the horrors of base servitude; All that the tyrant e'er inflicted on me, Shame and reproach suit with my sad condition; I have supported them, and looked on death Without a fear: a thousand times Ægisthus Hath threatened me with death, but this is worse; Thou art more cruel far to ask my vows, My love, my honor; but I see your aim, I know your purpose; poor Orestes slain, His murderer trembles at a sister's claim, And dreads my title to a father's throne: The tyrant wants my hand to second him, To seal his poor precarious rights with mine, And make me an accomplice in his guilt: O, if I have a right Ægisthus fears, Let him erase my title in my blood, And tear it from me: if another arm Be needful to his purpose, lend him thine; Strike here, and join Electra to her brother; Strike here, and I shall know 'tis Clytemnæstra.

**Clytemnæstra**: It is too much: ungrateful as thou art, I pitied thee; but all my hopes are past: What have I done, what would I do, to bend Thy stubborn heart? tears, menaces, reproaches, And love and tenderness, the throne itself, Which but for me thou never couldst have hoped, Prayers, punishment, and pardon, naught availed, And now I yield thee to thy fate: farewell! Thou sayest that thou shalt know me for thy mother, For Clytemnæstra, by my cruelty: I am thy mother, and I am thy queen, Remember that; to Agamemnon's race Naught do I owe but hatred and revenge; I will not warm a serpent in my breast To sting me: henceforth storm, complain, and weep, I shall not heed the clamors of a slave: I loved thee once, with grief I own I loved thee; But from this hour remember Clytemnæstra Is not thy mother, but Ægisthus' wife; The bonds are broken that united us, Electra broke them; nature hath disclaimed, And I abjure them.

### SCENE VI.

**Electra**: [Alone.] Gracious heaven! is this A mother's voice? O day the bitterest sure That ever rose since my dear father's death! I fear I said too much, but my full heart, Spite of myself, would pour its venom forth: She told me my Orestes was no more; Could I bear that? O if a cruel mother Has robbed me of my best, my dearest treasure, Why should I court my worst of foes, why fawn And cringe to her, to live a vile dependant On her precarious bounties; to lift up These withered hands to unrelenting heaven, To see my father's bed and throne usurped By this base spoiler, this inhuman tyrant, Who robbed me of a mother's heart, and now Hath taken Orestes from me?

### SCENE VII.

Electra, Iphisa.
**Iphisa**: O Electra, Complain no more.
**Electra**: Why not?
**Iphisa**: Partake my joy.
**Electra**: Joy is a stranger to this heart, Iphisa, And ever shall be.
**Iphisa**: Still there is hope.
**Electra**: O no, Still must we weep: for if I may believe A mother, our dear brother, our Orestes, Is dead.
**Iphisa**: And if I may believe these eyes, He lives, he's here, Electra.
**Electra**: Can it be? Good heaven! O do not trifle with a heart Like mine: Iphisa, didst thou say Orestes?
**Iphisa**: I did.
**Electra**: Thou wouldst not with a flattering dream Deceive me, my Iphisa—but, go on, For hope and fear distract me.
**Iphisa**: O my sister, Two strangers, cast by some benignant God On these unhappy coasts, are just arrived, And hither, by the care of good Pammenes, Conducted; one of them—
**Electra**: I faint: die— Well, one of them—
**Iphisa**: I saw the noble youth: O what a lustre sparkled in his eye! His air, his mien, his every gesture bore The perfect semblage of a demi-god; Even as they paint the illustrious Grecian chief, The conqueror of Troy; such majesty And sweet deportment ne'er did I behold; But with Pammenes he retired, and hid His beauteous form from my desiring eyes: Struck with the charming image, and

amazed, I ran to seek thee here, beneath the shade Of this dark grove, to tell the pleasing tale: But mark what followed—on the sacred tomb, Where we so oft have mingled our sad tears, I saw fresh garlands, saw the votive wreath, The water sprinkled over it, and the hair Doubtless of those whom I so late had seen, The illustrious strangers: near to these was laid, What most confirmed my hopes, a glittering sword, That spoke methought the day of vengeance near: Who but a son, a brother, and a hero, Raised by the gods to save his falling country, Would dare to brave the tyrant thus? 'Tis he, Electra, heaven hath sent him to our aid, The lightning glares upon us, and the thunder Will soon be heard.

**Electra**: I must believe Iphisa, And hope the best; but is it not a snare Laid by the tyrant? Come: we'll know the truth, Let us away—I must be satisfied.

**Iphisa**: We must not search him in the dark retreat Where he is hid. Pammenes says, his life Would answer for it.

**Electra**: Ha! what dost thou say? Alas! we are deceived, betrayed, Iphisa, By cruel heaven: thus, after fifteen years, Restored, Orestes would have run with joy To the dear arms that saved him, would have cheered Electra's mournful heart, he ne'er had fled From thee, Iphisa: O that sword thou sawest, Which raised thy sanguine hope, alarms my fears; A cruel mother would be well informed, And in her eyes I read the barbarous joy She felt within: O dart one ray of hope, Ye vengeful gods, on my despairing soul! Will not Pammenes yield to my entreaties? He will; he must: away, I'll speak to him.

**Iphisa**: Do not, Electra; think what cruel eyes Watch o'er our steps, and mark our every action. If he is come, we shall discover him By our fond zeal, and hazard his sweet life: If we're deceived, our search but irritates The tyrant, and endangers good Pammenes; But let us pay our duty at the tomb, There we at least may weep without offence. Who knows, Electra, but the noble stranger May meet us in that blest asylum; there That heaven, whose goodness thy impatient rage Hath called in question, may yet hear my vows, And give him to our wishes and our tears: Let us be gone.

**Electra**: Thou hast revived my hopes: But O, I die with grief, if thou deceivest me!

# ACT III.

### SCENE I.

Orestes, Pylades, Pammenes [A slave at the farther end of the stage carrying an urn and a sword.]

**Pammenes**: Blest be the day that to our wishes thus Restores the long-expected hope of Greece, My royal master's son, the minister Of heaven's high will, to execute swift vengeance On Agamemnon's foes! The tyrant long Hath dreaded, long foreseen the impending blow; Conscious of guilt, in every face unknown Still he beholds his master and his judge, And still Orestes haunts his troubled soul: Much he inquires concerning you, and longs To see you both. I have a thousand fears, A thousand hopes; heaven grant we may succeed! Meantime I have obeyed your orders, sounded The people's hearts, and strove to animate Their zeal; inspired them with the distant hope Of an avenger; soon or late the race Of rightful kings must prosper: every heart Glowed with warm transport at Orestes' name; Awakened from her slumber, vengeance rises With double vigor; my few faithful friends, Who dwell in this lone desert with Pammenes, Lift up their hands to heaven, and call on thee; And yet I tremble to behold thee here Unarmed and unassisted, lest some chance Discover thee, and blast our hopes: the foe Is barbarous, active, vigilant, and bold; One fatal stroke may ruin all; whilst thou, Against a tyrant seated on his throne, Bringest nothing but Orestes, and his friend.

**Pylades**: And are not they sufficient? 'Tis the work Of heaven that oft fulfils its own designs By means most wonderful, that in the deep O'erwhelmed our little all, and here alone Hath left us to perform the sacrifice. Sometimes it arms the sovereigns of the earth With tenfold vengeance; sometimes, in contempt Of human valor, strikes in awful silence; Nature and friendship then assert the rights Of heaven, and vindicate its power divine.

**Orestes**: Orestes asks no other aid, no arm But thine, my Pylades.

**Pylades**: Take heed, my friend, Quit not the paths of safety pointed out By the just gods; remember thou art bound By solemn oath to hide thee from Electra; Thy peace, thy happiness, thy kingdom, all Depend upon it: O refrain thy transports, Dissemble, and obey; 'tis fit Electra Should be deceived, even more than Clytemnæstra.

**Pammenes**: Thank heaven, that thus ordained it for thy safety. Already hath Electra, bathed in tears, And calling for her great avenger, filled These solitary mansions with her cries; Importunate and bold, she sought me out, And with imprudent warmth, demanded loud, Where was her brother, where her dear Orestes: Nature had whispered to her anxious heart He was not far from his Electra: scarce Could I withhold her eager steps.

**Orestes**: Ye gods! Must I refrain? O insupportable!

**Pylades**: You hesitate; O think, my dear Orestes, Think on the menaces of angry heaven, Think on its goodness that preserved thy life From every danger;

if thou shouldst oppose Its sacred will, eternal wrath awaits To blast thy purpose; tremble, son of Atreus And Tantalus, remember what thy hapless race Hath suffered, nor expect a milder doom.

**Orestes:** What power invincible presides unseen O'er human actions, and directs our fate? Is it a crime to listen to the voice Of fond affection? O eternal justice, Thou deep abyss, unsearchable to man! Shall not our weakness and our guilt by thee Be still distinguished? shall the man who wanders From virtue's paths unknowing, and who braves Thy power, shall he who yields to nature's laws, And he who breaks them, share an equal fate? But shall the slave condemn his master? heaven Gave us our being, and can owe us nothing: Therefore no more: in silence I obey. Give me the urn, the ring, and bloody sword, Which thou hast hither brought, they shall be offered Far from Electra's sight: let us be gone; I'll see my sister when I have avenged her. [Turning to Pammenes.] Go thou, Pammenes, and prepare the hearts Of thy brave followers for the great event Which Greece awaits, and I must execute: Deceive Ægisthus, and my guilty mother; Let them enjoy the transitory bliss, The short-lived pleasure of Orestes' death, If an unnatural mother can behold With joy the ashes of a murdered son: Here will I wait, and stop them as they pass.

### SCENE II.

Electra and Iphisa on one side of the stage Orestes and Pylades on the other, with a slave carrying an urn and a sword.

**Electra:** [To Iphisa.] Hope disappointed is the worst of sorrows. O my Iphisa, all thy flattering dreams Are vanished, and Pammenes, with a word, Hath undeceived us; the fair day that shone So bright is clouded o'er, and darkness spreads On every side: alas! our wretched life Is but a round of never-ending woes.

**Orestes:** [To Pylades.] Two women, and in tears!

**Pylades:** Alas, my lord, Beneath a tyrant all things wear the face Of grief and misery.

**Orestes:** In Ægisthus' court Nothing should reign but sorrow.

**Iphisa:** [To Electra.] Look, Electra, The strangers come this way.

**Electra:** Unhappy omen! They did pronounce Ægisthus' hated name.

**Iphisa:** One is that hero whom I told thee of, The noble youth—

**Electra:** [Looking at Orestes.] Alas! I too, like thee, Have been deceived. [Turning to Orestes.] Who are ye, wretched strangers; And what hath led you to this fatal shore?

**Orestes**: We come to see the king who reigns in Argos, And take our orders from him.

**Electra**: Are ye Grecians, And call ye him a king, the murderer Of Agamemnon?

**Orestes**: He is sovereign here, And heaven commands us to respect his throne, Not to dispute his title.

**Electra**: Horrid maxim! And what have you to ask of this proud king, This bloody monster here?

**Orestes**: We come to bring him Some happy tidings.

**Electra**: Dreadful then to us They must be.

**Iphisa**: [Seeing the Urn.] Ha! an urn! O grief, O horror!

**Pylades**: Orestes—

**Electra**: O ye gods! Orestes dead! I faint, I die.

**Orestes**: What have we done, my friend! They could not be mistaken, for their grief Betrays them: O! my blood runs cold.—Fair princess, Be comforted, and live.

**Electra**: Orestes dead? And can I live? O no, barbarians, here Complete your cruelty.

**Iphisa**: Alas! you see The poor remains of Agamemnon; we Are his unhappy daughters, the sad sisters Of lost Orestes.

**Orestes**: O Electra! O Iphisa! O where am I? cruel gods! [To the slave carrying the urn.] Take from their sight those monuments of woe, That fatal urn, which—

**Electra**: [Running towards the urn.] Wouldst thou take it from me? Wouldst thou deprive me of the little all That's left Electra by offended heaven? O give it me. [She takes the urn, and embraces it.]

**Orestes**: Forbear; what wouldst thou do?

**Pylades**: Away: Ægisthus only must receive These precious relics.

**Electra**: Must I then behold My brother's ashes in a tyrant's hand, And are Orestes' murderers before me?

**Orestes**: Horrid reproach! it shocks my very soul: I can no longer—

**Electra**: Yet you weep with me: O, in the name of the avenging gods, If ye are guiltless, if your generous hands Collected his dear ashes—

**Orestes**: Gracious heaven!

**Electra**: If ye lament his death, O answer me: Who told you of his fate: art thou his friend? Speak, noble youth: both dumb! yet both afflicted: Even whilst your words plant daggers in my heart, Ye seem to pity me.

**Orestes**: It is too much; The gods have been obeyed enough already.

**Electra**: What sayest thou?

Orestes: Leave those poor remains.

Electra: O no: I never will: alas! is every heart Inflexible? I tell thee, cruel stranger, I must not, cannot give thee back again The fatal gift thy pity hath bestowed: 'Tis my Orestes; and I will embrace him: Behold his dying sister.

Orestes: Cruel gods! Where are your thunders now? O strike: Electra, I can no longer—

Electra: Ha!

Orestes: I ought—

Pylades: O heaven!

Electra: Go on—

Orestes: Know then—

SCENE III.

Ægisthus, Clytemnæstra, Orestes, Pylades, Electra, Iphisa, Pammenes, Guards.

Ægisthus: O glorious spectacle! Fortune, I thank thee: Can it be, Pammenes? My rival dead! it is, it must be true, Electra's grief confirms it.

Electra: Dreadful hour?

Orestes: To what am I reserved?

Ægisthus: Seize on the urn, And wrest it from her. [They take the urn from her.]

Electra: O thou hast robbed me of the only good This life could e'er afford me, barbarous monster! O take Electra too, tear forth this heart And join me to Orestes; father, son, Sister, and brother, all thy wretched victims Unite to satiate thy revenge: now, tyrant, Enjoy thy happiness, enjoy thy crimes: And thou, inhuman mother, look with him On the delightful spectacle, it suits Thy nature, and is worthy of you both. [Iphisa leads her off.]

SCENE IV.

ægisthus, clytemnæstra, orestes, pylades, Guards. **Clytemnæstra**: Must I bear this?

Ægisthus: She shall be punished for it: Let her complain to heaven, for heaven itself Will justify Ægisthus; it approves Where it forbids not; therefore I am guiltless, And happy too: my throne stands firmly now, My life's in safety; but I must reward The zeal and valor of these noble Grecians.

Orestes: It was our duty, royal sir, to lay These proofs before you: take this sword, this ring, You must remember it: 'twas Agamemnon's.

Clytemnæstra: And was it then by thee Orestes fell?

Ægisthus: If thou hast served me, thine be the reward: But, say, who art thou, of what race?

Orestes: My name Must not as yet be known; perhaps hereafter It may be: in the fields of Troy my father Distinguished shone amongst the great avengers Of Menelaus; in those days of glory He fought, and fell: deserted and forlorn, Left by a cruel mother, and pursued By most inhuman foes, this friend alone Supported me; was fortune, father, all; With him I still have trod the paths of honor, With him defied the malice of my fate: Such is my story.

Ægisthus: But say where thy arm Avenged me of this hated prince: inform me.

Orestes: 'Twas a word that to the temple leads Of Epidaurus, near Achemor's tomb.

Ægisthus: The king had set a price upon his head: How came you not to ask for your reward?

Orestes: Because I hated infamy, and fought For vengeance, not for hire; I did not mean To sell his blood; a private motive raised This arm against him, as my friend well knows, And I revenged myself without the aid Of kings, nor shall I boast the victory: Forgive me, sir: I tremble; for the widow Of Agamemnon's here; perhaps I've served, Perhaps offended her; I'll take my leave.

Ægisthus: Thou shalt not; stay, I charge thee.

Clytemnæstra: Let him go: That urn, and the sad story he has told, Have filled my soul with horror: heaven, my lord, Protects your throne and life, be thankful for it, And leave a mother to indulge her sorrows.

Orestes: Madam, I thought that Agamemnon's son Was hateful to you.

Clytemnæstra: I must own I feared him.

Orestes: Feared him?

Clytemnæstra: I did indeed; for he was born To be most guilty.

Orestes: Guilty? and to whom?

Clytemnæstra: The wretched wanderer, thou knowest, was doomed To hate a mother, doomed to shed the blood From whence he sprang; such was his horrid fate: Perhaps he had fulfilled—and yet, his death, I know not why, affrights me, and I tremble To look on you who saved me from his vengeance.

Orestes: Alas! a son against a mother armed! O who could loose that sacred tie? perhaps He wished—

Clytemnæstra: O heaven!

Ægisthus: What sayest thou? didst thou know him?

Pylades: [Aside.] He will discover all. [To Ægisthus.] He did, my lord, The wretched soon unite, and soon divide: At Delphi first we saw him.

Orestes: Yes: I know His purpose well.

Ægisthus: What was it?

Orestes: To murder thee.

Ægisthus: I've seen his malice long, but I despised it. Meantime Electra used Orestes' name To spread division o'er my kingdom; she Was my worst foe: thou hast avenged me of her, Take thy reward, I yield her to thy power; She shall be thine: the haughty maid, who spurned The great alliance with Ægisthus' son; Henceforth she is thy slave: the wretched race Of Priam long beneath the conqueror's yoke Submissive bowed, and dragged the servile chain; And wherefore should not Agememnon's blood Bend in its turn, and share an equal fate?

Clytemnæstra: Would Clytemnæstra suffer that!

Ægisthus: Thou wouldst not Defend thy worst of foes; proscribe Orestes, Yet spare Electra. [To Orestes.] Leave the urn with me.

Orestes: We will, my lord, and shall accept your offer.

Clytemnæstra: That were to carry our resentment further Than justice warrants: let him hence, and bear Some other recompense: we too must go: Let us, my lord, I beg thee, let us quit These horrid mansions of the dead, where naught But dreadful images on every side Surrounds me: O we never can prepare The bloody feast between the father's tomb And the son's ashes! How shall we invoke The household gods, whom we have injured; how, Amidst our cruel sports, give up the blood Of Clytemnæstra to the murderer Of her Orestes? O it must not be! I tremble at the thought: my fears, Ægisthus, Should waken thine: this stranger rives my heart; His very sight is deadliest poison to me. Away, my lord, and let me be concealed From every eye; would it were possible To hide me from myself! [Exit Clytemnæstra]

Ægisthus: [To Orestes.] Stay thou, and wait Till time befriend thee; nature for a moment Is clamorous and loud, but soon as reason Shall reassume its empire, interest then Must plead thy cause, and she alone be heard. Meantime remain with us, and celebrate Our nuptial day: [To one of his attendants.] Haste you to Epidaurus, And hither bring my son; let him confirm The welcome tidings.

SCENE V.

Orestes, Pylades.

Orestes: Yes, Orestes comes To join the cruel pomp, and make thy feast A feast of blood.

Pylades: O how I trembled for thee! I feared thy love; I feared thy tenderness; And, more than all, thy honest rage, that burst In transports forth when thou beheldest the tyrant: I saw thee ready to insult him; saw Thy soul take fire at Agamemnon's name, And dreaded the sad consequence.

**Orestes:** My mother, O, Pylades, my mother pierced my heart. Didst thou not mark the workings of her soul Whilst I was speaking? O I felt them all! Scarce could my voice in faltering accents tell The melancholy tale, whilst Clytemnæstra Still gazed, and trembled still: a father's murder; A sister unrevenged; a tyrant yet Unpunished; and a mother to be taught Her interest and her duty; what a weight Of secret cares! great heaven complete thy work! Urge on the lingering moments that retard My vengeance; O, let me perform the task Of love, and hatred; let me mix the blood Of base Ægisthus with the vile remains Of Plisthenes; let sweet Electra see The cruel tyrant gasping at my feet, And know her dear deliverer in Orestes!

## SCENE VI.

Orestes, Pylades, Pammenes.

**Orestes:** What hast thou done, Pammenes, may we hope—

**Pammenes:** O my dear lord, never, since the fatal day When Agamemnon fell, did greater perils Threaten thy precious life.

**Orestes:** Ha! what hath happened?

**Pylades:** Still Must I have cause to tremble for Orestes?

**Pammenes:** This instant is arrived a messenger From Epidaurus, and ere this related The death of Plisthenes.

**Pylades:** Immortal gods!

**Orestes:** And knows he that Orestes slew his son?

**Pammenes:** They speak of nothing but his death; ere long Fresh tidings are expected; and the news Meantime concealed from Greece that she has lost One of her tyrants; the king, still in doubt, Shuts himself up with Clytemnæstra: this I learned from one, who, to the royal blood Still faithful, pines in loathsome servitude Beneath the proud usurper.

**Orestes:** I have gathered At least the first fair fruits of promised vengeance; Grant me, ye gods, to reap a plenteous harvest! Thinkest thou, my friend, they would uplift this arm In vain, and only prosper to deceive me; To my successful valor give the son, And after yield me to the father's power? Let us away: danger should make us bold; Who fears not death is master of his foe; I'll seize the moment of uncertainty, Ere the full day of truth glares in upon him, And points his rage.

**Pammenes:** Away: you must be known To those few noble spirits who will die To serve their prince; this secret place conceals Some faithful friends, who may be still more useful, Because unknown.

**Pylades:** Haste then; and if the tomb Of thy dear father, if thy honored name Joined to Electra's, if the wrath of heaven Against usurpers, if the gracious gods Who hither led thee, if they all should fail, If this detested spot is doomed by fate To be thy grave, O take a wretched life To thee devoted, we will die together, That comfort's left; for Pylades shall fall Close by thy side, and worthy of Orestes.

**Orestes:** Strike me, kind heaven! but O for pity save His matchless valor, and protect my friend!

# ACT IV.

### SCENE I.
Orestes, Pylades.

**Orestes:** Perhaps the vigilance of good Pammenes May for awhile remove the king's suspicions; And gracious heaven, in pity to our woes, Deceive Ægisthus to a fond belief, That the devoted race of Tantalus Is now no more; but, O my Pylades, The sword I offered at my father's tomb Is stolen by sacrilegious hands, that reach Even to the sacred mansions of the dead: If it be carried to the tyrant, all Will be discovered; let us haste, my friend, And seize him, ere it be too late.

**Pylades:** Pammenes Is watchful o'er our interest: we must wait For him: when we have gathered the few friends That mean to serve us, be this tomb the place Of meeting for us all, Pammenes then Will join us here.

**Orestes:** O Pylades, O heaven! This barbarous law that forces me to wound A tender heart that lives but for Orestes! And must I leave Electra to her sorrows?

**Pylades:** Yes: thou hast sworn it, therefore persevere; Thou hast more cause to dread Electra now Than all thy foes; she may destroy, but never Can serve us, and the tyrant's eyes may soon Be opened: O subdue, if possible, The pangs of nature, and conceal thy love: We came not here to comfort thy Electra, But to avenge her.

**Orestes:** See, my Pylades, She comes this way, perhaps in search of me.

**Pylades:** Her every step is watched: you must not see her: Begone; and doubt not, I'll observe her well; The eyes of friendship seldom are deceived.

## SCENE II.

Electra, Iphisa, Pylades.

**Electra**: The villain hath escaped me; he avoids My hated sight, and leaves me to my fate, To fruitless rage, and unavailing tears, Without the hope of vengeance: say, barbarian, Thou vile accomplice in his crimes, where went The murderer, my tyrant, my new lord, (For so it seems Ægisthus has decreed) Where is he gone?

**Pylades**: To do the will of heaven, In dutiful obedience to the gods, And well would it become the royal maid To follow his example: fate ofttimes Deceives the hearts of men, directs in secret, And guides their wandering steps through paths unknown; Ofttimes it sinks us in the deep abyss Of misery, and then raises us to joy; Binds us in chains, or lifts us to a throne, And gives us life midst horrors, tombs, and death. Complain no more, but yield to thy new sorrows; Be patient, and be happy: fare thee well.

## SCENE III.

Electra, Iphisa.

**Electra**: He swells my rage to fury and despair: Thinks he I'll tamely bear these cruel insults? Could not a father's and a brother's death Fill up the measure of Electra's woes; But she must bend beneath the vile assassin Of her Orestes; be a common slave To all the murderers of her hapless race? Thou dreadful sword, wet with Orestes' blood, Exposed in triumph at the sacred tomb, Thou execrable trophy, for a moment Thou didst deceive me, but thou hast insulted The ashes of the dead; I'll make thee serve A nobler purpose: though Ægisthus hides His guilty head, and with the queen in secret Plans future crimes, and meditates destruction, Still we may find the murderer of Orestes: I cannot bathe me in the blood of both My tyrants, but on one at least my soul Shall be revenged.

**Iphisa**: I cannot blame the grief Which I partake; but hear me, hear the voice Of reason; every tongue speaks of Orestes; They say, he lives, and the king's fears confirm it. You saw Pammenes talking with this stranger In secret, saw his ardent zeal to serve And to attend him: thinkest thou, our best friend, Our comforter, the good old man, would e'er Associate with a murderer? never, never, He could not be so base.

**Electra**: He may be false, Or weak; old age is easily deceived: We are betrayed by all; I know we are: Did not the cruel stranger boast his deed? Did not Ægisthus yield me up a victim? Was not Electra made the price of guilt, The murderer's reward? Orestes calls me To join him in the tomb: now then, my sister, If e'er thou lovest Electra, pity her In her last moments; bloody they must be, And terrible. Away; inform thyself Touching Pammenes; see if the assassin Be with the queen: she flatters all my foes; She heard unmoved the murder of her son, And seemed, O gods! a mother seemed, to share The guilty transport with her savage lord. O that this sword could reach him in her arms, And pierce the traitor's heart! I'll do it.

**Iphisa:** No more: Indeed you wrong her; for the sight of him Offends her: be not thus precipitate And rash, Electra; I will to Pammenes, And talk with him: or I am much deceived, Or by their silence they but mean to hide Some mystery from us: your imprudent warmth (Yet who would not forgive it in the wretched?) Perhaps alarms them, and they would conceal From you their purpose; what it is, I know not: Pammenes seems to shun you, let me go And speak to him; but do not, my Electra, Hazard a deed thou wilt too late repent of.

## SCENE IV.

**Electra:** The subtle tyrants have gained o'er Pammenes; Old age is weak and fearful: what can faith Or friendship do against the hand of power? Henceforth Electra to herself alone Shall trust her vengeance: 'tis enough: these hands, Armed with despair, shall act with double vigor. Arise ye furies, leave your dark abode For seats more guilty, and another hell, Open your dreary caverns, and receive Your victims: bring your flaming torches here, Daughters of vengeance, arm yourselves and me; Approach, with death and terror in your train; Orestes, Agamemnon, and Electra Invoke your aid: and lo! they come, I see Their glittering swords, and unappalled behold them; They are not half so dreadful as Ægisthus: The murderer comes; and see, they throng around him; Hell points him out, and yields him to my vengeance.

## SCENE V.

**Electra:** [At the bottom of the stage.]

**Orestes:** [On the other side at a distance from her.] Where am I? hither they directed me: O my dear country! and thou, fatal spot That gave me birth, thou great but guilty race Of Tantalus, for ever shall thy blood Be wretched? horror here on every side Surrounds me: wherefore am I punished thus? What have I done? why must Orestes suffer For his forefathers' crimes?

**Electra:** [Advancing a little from the bottom of the stage.] What power withholds me? I cannot lift my arm against him; but I will go on.

**Orestes:** Methought I heard a voice: O my dear father, ever-honored shade, Much injured Agamemnon, didst thou groan?

*Electra:* Just heaven! durst he pronounce that sacred name? And see he weeps: can sighs and penitence Find entrance here? but what is his remorse To the dire horrors that Electra feels! [She comes forward.] He is alone; now strike—die, traitor—O I cannot—

*Orestes:* Gods! Electra, art thou here, Furious and trembling?

*Electra:* Sure thou art some god Who thus unnervest me—thou has slain my brother: I would have taken thy life for it, but the sword Dropped from my hand; thy genius hath prevailed; I yield to thee, and must betray my brother.

*Orestes:* Betray him, no! O, why am I restrained?—

*Electra:* At sight of thee my resolution dies, And all is changed: could it be thou who filled My soul with terror?

*Orestes:* O, I would repay Thy precious tears with hazard of my life!

*Electra:* Methought I heard thee speak of Agamemnon. O gentle youth, deceive me not, but speak: For I had well nigh done a desperate deed; O show me all the guilt of it! explain The mystery; tell me who thou art.

*Orestes:* O sister Of dear Orestes, fly from me, avoid me.

*Electra:* But wherefore? speak.

*Orestes:* No more—I am—take heed They see us not together.

*Electra:* Gracious heaven! Thou fillest my heart with terror and with joy.

*Orestes:* O if thou lovest thy brother—

*Electra:* Love him! yes: And O in thee I hear a father's voice, And see his features; nature hath unveiled The mystery: O be kind and speak for her, Do not deny it; say thou art my brother: Thou art, I know thou art—my dear Orestes; How could a sister seek thy precious life?

*Orestes:* [Embracing her.] Heaven threatens in vain, and nature will prevail: Electra is more powerful than the gods.

*Electra:* The gods have given a sister to thy vows, And dost thou fear their wrath?

*Orestes:* Their cruel orders Would have deprived me of my dear Electra, And may perhaps chastise a brother's weakness.

*Electra:* Thy weakness there was virtue; O rejoice With me, Orestes; wherefore wouldst thou force me To that rash act? it might have cost thee dear.

*Orestes:* I've broken my sacred promise.

*Electra:* 'Twas thy duty.

*Orestes:* A secret trusted to me by the gods.

*Electra:* I drew it from thee; I extorted it; Mine be the guilt; an oath more sacred far Binds me to vengeance: what hast thou to fear?

*Orestes:* My destiny, the oracles, the blood From whence I sprung.

**Electra:** That blood henceforth shall flow In purer streams; haste then, and join with me To scourge the guilty; oracles and gods Are all propitious to our great design, And the same power that saved will guide Orestes.

## SCENE VI.

electra, orestes, pylades, pammenes. **Electra:** Rejoice with me, my friends, for I have found My dear Orestes.

**Pylades:** [To Orestes.] Hast thou then revealed The dangerous secret? Couldst thou think—

**Orestes:** If heaven Expects obedience, it must give us laws We can obey.

**Electra:** Canst thou reproach him thus Only for making poor Electra happy? Wouldst thou adopt the cruel sentiments Of persecuting foes, and hide Orestes From my embraces? what unjust decree What harsh commands—

**Pylades:** I meant to save him for thee, That he might live, and be thy great avenger.

**Pammenes:** Princess, thou knowest, in this detested place They watch thee nearly; every sigh is heard, And every motion carefully observed: Those private friends, whose humble state eludes The tyrants search, adore this noble youth, And would have served him; everything's prepared; But thy imprudence now will hazard all.

**Electra:** Did not Ægisthus give me to a hand, Stained, as he thought, with my Orestes' blood? [To Orestes.] Thou art my master; I am bound to serve thee; I will obey the tyrant; his commands, For once, are welcome, and the prospect brightens On every side.

**Pammenes:** It may be clouded soon, Ægisthus is alarmed, and we have cause To tremble; if he but suspects us, death Must be our portion, therefore let us part.

**Pylades:** [To Pammenes.] Hence, good Pammenes, bring our friends together, The hours are precious; haste and finish soon Thy noble work; 'tis time we should appear, And—like ourselves.

## SCENE VII.

ægisthus, clytemnæstra, electra, orestes, pylades, Guards. **Ægisthus:** Slaves, execute your office, And bear these traitors to the dungeon.

**Orestes:** Once There ruled o'er Argos those who better knew The rights of hospitality.

**Pylades:** Ægisthus, What is our crime? Inform us, and at least Respect this noble youth.

**Ægisthus:** Away with them; Ye stand aghast, as if ye feared to touch His sacred person: hence, I say, take heed Ye disobey me not: guards, drag them off.

**Electra:** O stay, barbarian, stay; for heaven itself Pleads for their sacred lives—they tear them from me, O gods!

**Ægisthus:** Electra, tremble for thyself, Perfidious as thou art, and dread my wrath.

## SCENE VIII.

Electra, Clytemnæstra.

**Electra:** O hear me, if thou art a mother, hear; Let me recall thy former tenderness, Forgive my guilty rage, the sad effect Of unexampled sorrows; to complain, Is still, the mournful privilege of grief: Pity these wretched strangers; heaven perhaps, Whose dreadful vengeance thou so long hast feared, May for their sakes forgive thy past offences; The pardon thou bestowest on them may plead For thee: O save them, save them.

**Clytemnæstra:** Why shouldst thou Be thus solicitous? What interest prompts Thy ardent zeal?

**Electra:** Thou seest, the gods protect them, Who saved them from the Ocean's boisterous rage, And brought them here: heaven gives them to thy care, And will require them at thy hands—to one, O if thou knewest him—but they both are wretched. Are we in Argos, or at Tauris, where The cruel priestess bids her altars smoke With stranger's blood? What must I do to save him? Command, and I obey: to Plisthenes You'd have me wedded; I submit, though death Were far more welcome; lead me to his bed.

**Clytemnæstra:** You mean to mock us: knowest thou not, he's dead?

**Electra:** Just heaven! and hath Ægisthus lost a son?

**Clytemnæstra:** I see the joy that sparkles in thy eyes; Thou art pleased to hear it.

**Electra:** No: I am too wretched To be delighted with another's woe: I pity the unhappy, nor would shed The blood of innocence: O save the strangers! I ask no more.

**Clytemnæstra:** Away: I understand thee, And know thee but too well; thou hast confirmed The king's suspicions, and revealed the secret: One of these strangers is—Orestes.

**Electra:** Well, Suppose it were; suppose that gracious heaven, In tender pity, had restored thy son—

**Clytemnæstra:** O dreadful moment! how am I to act?

**Electra:** Is it a doubt, and canst thou hesitate? Thy son! O heaven! think on his past misfortunes, Think on his merits; but if still thy mind Is doubtful, all is lost: farewell Orestes.

**Clytemnæstra:** I'm not in doubt; I am resolved; even thou, With all thy fury, canst not change the love, The tenderness I bear him: I will guard, Save, and protect him—he may punish me, Perhaps he will; I tremble at his name; No matter—I'm a mother still, and love My children; thou mayst yet preserve thy hate.

**Electra:** No: I will fall submissive at thy feet, And thank thy bounty: now, indulgent heaven, Thy mercy shines superior to thy wrath; For thou hast given a mother to my vows, Changed her resentful heart, and saved Orestes.

# ACT V.

### SCENE I.

**Electra:** I am forbid to enter here; oppressed With fears, in vain I lift these hands to heaven: Iphisa comes not; but behold the gates Are opened: ha! she's here, I tremble.

### SCENE II.

Electra, Iphisa.

**Electra:** Say, My dear Iphisa, what have I to hope, Will Clytemnæstra dare to be a mother? Has she the power, has she the will to make us Some poor amends for all the cruel evils She has inflicted on us? Could she e'er— But she's a slave to guilt, and to Ægisthus: I am prepared to hear the worst; O speak, Say, all is past, and we must die.

**Iphisa:** I hope, And yet I fear: Ægisthus hath received Some dark suggestions, but is doubtful still, Whether Orestes is his prisoner here, And Clytemnæstra never named her son: She seems to feel a mother's fondness for him, And, pierced with anguish, trembles for his life: She struggles with herself, and fears alike To speak or to be silent; strives to soothe The tyrant's rage, and save them from his vengeance: But should Orestes once be known, he dies.

**Electra:** O cruel thought! perhaps when I implored My barbarous mother I destroyed Orestes; Her grief will but enrage the fierce Ægisthus; Nature is ever fatal here: I dread Her silence, and yet would not have her speak; Danger is on every side: but say, Iphisa, What hath Pammenes done?

**Iphisa:** His feeble age Seems strengthened by misfortune, and our dangers But breathe new spirit o'er his ardent zeal To serve our cause; he animates our friends With double vigor; even the servile throng, That cringe around the tyrant's throne, begin To murmur at the name of great Orestes: Veterans, who served beneath the father, burn With honest ardor to support the son: Such power have justice and the sacred laws O'er mortal minds, howe'er by vice corrupted.

**Electra:** O that Electra could inflame their souls With glowing virtue, breathe her own fierce spirit Into their timid hearts, and animate Their cold resentment! would I had but known, Ere he arrived on this detested shore, That my Orestes lived! or that Pammenes Had further urged—

### SCENE III.
Ægisthus, Clytemnæstra, Electra, Iphisa, Guards.

**Ægisthus:** Guards, seize that hoary traitor, And let him be confronted with those strangers Whom I have doomed to death; he is their friend, And confidant, the accomplice in their crimes: How dreadful was the snare which they had laid! O, Claytemnæstra, 'tis the cursed Orestes, It must be he; do not deceive thyself, Do not defend him: O, I see it all, It is too plain: alas! this urn contains The ashes of my son: the murderers brought This fatal present to his weeping father.

**Clytemnæstra:** Canst thou believe—

**Ægisthus:** I can; I must rely On the sworn hatred 'twixt the unhappy children Of Atreus and Thyestes; must believe The time, the place, the rage of fierce Electra, Iphisa's tears, your undeserved compassion, Your ill-timed pity for these base assassins; Orestes lives, and I have lost my son; But I have caught him in the toils; whiche'er It be, for yet I know not, I'll be just, I'll sacrifice the murderer to my son, And to his mother.

**Clytemnæstra:** Horrid sacrifice! I must not see it.

**Ægisthus:** Horrible to thee?

**Clytemnæstra:** O yes; already blood enough hath flowed In this sad scene of slaughter: O 'tis time To end the woes of Pelops' hapless race: If after all it should not be Orestes, Wouldst thou, on dark suspicion's vague report, Murder the innocent? and if it be Indeed my son, my lord, I must defend him, Must gain his pardon at thy hands, or perish.

**Ægisthus:** I cannot, dare not yield to thy request; For thy own sake I dare not; thy fond pity May be thy ruin; all that melts thy heart To soft compassion, sharpens mine to rage And fierce resentment: one of them I know Must be

Orestes, therefore both shall die; I ought not even to hesitate a moment: Guards, do your office.

**Iphisa:** O, my lord, behold me Low at your feet; must all our hapless race Thus humbly bend, thus supplicate in vain? Electra, kneel with me, embrace his knees, Thy pride destroys us.

**Electra:** Can I stoop so low? Shall I bring foul disgrace on thee, my brother, And ignominy, and shame? it shocks my soul; But I will suffer all to save Orestes. [Turning to Ægisthus.] It thou wilt save him, here I promise thee, (Not to forget my father's murder, that I never can, but) in respectful silence To pay thee homage, still to live with thee A willing slave, let but my brother live.

**Ægisthus:** Thy brother dies, and thou shalt live a slave; My vengeance is complete: thy pride is humbled, And sues in vain.

**Clytemnæstra:** Ægisthus, 'tis too much, To trample thus on the unhappy race Of him who was thy master once; away, Spite of thy rage, I will defend my son; Deaf as thou art to a fond sister's prayers, A mother's may prevail: O think, my lord, Think on thy happy state, above the reach Of adverse fortune no, Orestes ne'er Can hurt thee, and Electra bends submissive Beneath thy power, Iphisa at thy feet; Can nothing move thee? I have gone too far Already with thee in the paths of guilt, And offered up a dreadful sacrifice. Thinkest thou I'll yield thee up my purest blood To glut thy rage? Am I forever doomed To take a murderous husband to my arms? At Aulis one a lovely daughter slew, The other threatens to destroy my son Before my eyes, close to his father's tomb: O rather let this fatal diadem, Hateful to Greece, and to myself a load Of misery, fall with me, and be no more Remembered! O Ægisthus, well thou knowest, I loved thee, 'tis amongst my blackest crimes, And stands the foremost; but I love my children, And will defend them; against thy arm upraised To shed their blood will lift my vengeful hand, And blast thy purpose: tremble, for thou knowest me: The bands are sacred that united us, Thy interest is most dear to Clytemnæstra: Remember still, Orestes is my son, And fear his mother.

**Electra:** You surpass my hopes. Surely a heart like thine could ne'er be guilty; Go on, my honored mother, and avenge Your children, and your husband.

**Ægisthus:** Slave, thou fillest The measure of thy crimes: gods! shall Ægisthus Withhold his vengeance for a woman's cries, For Agamemnon's widow, and her children? Unhappy queen! say, whom dost thou accuse? Whom dost thou plead for? hear me and obey. Away with them to instant death.

### SCENE IV.
Ægisthus, Clytemnæstra, Electra, Iphisa, Dymas.

**Dymas:** My lord?

**Ægisthus:** Thou seemest disordered: what has happened? Speak.

**Dymas:** Orestes is discovered.

**Iphisa:** Ha! where is he?

**Clytemnæstra:** My son!

**Electra:** My brother?

**Ægisthus:** Have you punished him As he deserves?

**Dymas:** My lord, as yet he lives.

**Ægisthus:** And wherefore were my orders disobeyed?

**Dymas:** His friend and fellow-captive, Pylades, Pointed him out, and to the soldiers showed Great Agamemnon's son; they seemed much moved; I dread the consequence.

**Ægisthus:** I must prevent it, For they shall die: who dares not to revenge me Shall feel my justice: Dymas, follow me: Stay thou and guard his sisters; I defy The blood of Agamemnon: from the father Of Plisthenes, and great Thyestes' son, What mortal, or what god, shall save Orestes?

## SCENE V.

clytemnæstra, electra, iphisa. **Iphisa:** Fear not, but follow him; Electra, speak, Exhort our friends, and animate their zeal.

**Electra:** [To Clytemnæstra.] O, in the name of powerful nature, now Complete thy noble work; conduct us, fly—

**Clytemnæstra:** You must not hence, the guards will not permit it: Stay here, my children, and rely on me, On a fond mother, and a tender wife: I will perform the double task, and take Orestes and Ægisthus to my care.

## SCENE VI.

Electra, Iphisa.

**Iphisa:** Alas! the avenging god pursues us still; Though she defends Orestes, still Ægisthus Is at her heart; perhaps the tender cries Of pity and remorse shall naught avail Against the tyrant; he is proud, revengeful, Implacable, and furious; who shall save If he condemns? we must submit, and die.

**Electra:** O that before my death I had not fallen So low as to entreat him, to belie My honest heart, and supplicate the tyrant! Despair and horror sink me to the tomb With infamy and shame; my vain endeavors To save Orestes but urge on his fate. Where are these boasted friends Pammenes talked of, Who, with fell rancor, and determined hate, Pursued Ægisthus? Where those vengeful gods Who hid Orestes from my sight, upraised His righteous arm, and promised to support him? Where are ye now, infernal goddesses, Daughters of night, ye who so lately shook Your dreadful torches here? all nature once United seemed to guard and to protect us, But all desert us now, all court Ægisthus, And men and gods, and heaven and hell betray me.

### SCENE VII.
Electra, Pylades, Iphisa.

**Electra**: What sayest thou, Pylades? the deed is done?
**Pylades**: It is: Electra's free, and heaven obeyed.
**Electra**: How?
**Pylades**: Yes, Orestes reigns: he sent me hither.
**Iphisa**: Just gods!
**Electra**: Orestes! is it possible! I faint, I die with joy.
**Pylades**: Orestes lives, And has avenged the blood of innocence.
**Electra**: What wondrous power hath wrought this strange event.
**Pylades**: His father's name, Electra's, and his own; His valor, and his virtue; our misfortunes, Justice, and pity; and the power that pleads In human hearts for wretchedness like thine. Pammenes, by the tyrant's order bound, Was led with us to death; in weeping crowds The people followed, and deplored our fate: I saw their rage was equal to their fears, But the guards watched them closely: then Orestes Cried, "Strike, ye slaves, and sacrifice the last Of Argos' kings; ye dare not." When he spoke, On his fair front such native majesty And royal lustre shone, we almost thought Great Agamemnon's spirit from the tomb Had risen, and came once more to bless mankind. I spoke, and friendship's happy voice prevailed; The people rose, the soldiers stood aghast, And dropped the uplifted falchions from their hands; The crowd encircled us, and desperate love, With friendship joined, fought nobly for Orestes; The joyful people bore him off in triumph: Ægisthus flew to seize his destined prey, And in the slave he meant to punish, found A conqueror: pleased I saw his humbled pride; His friends deserted, and his guards betrayed him: The insulting people triumphed in his fall. O glorious day! O all discerning justice! Ægisthus wears the chains that bound Orestes; The queen alone attends, protects, and saves him From the mad crowd, that press tumultuous on, Big with revenge, and thirsting for his blood; While Clytemnæstra holds him in her arms, And shields him from their rage, implores Orestes To save her husband: he respects her still, Fulfils the duties of a son and brother: Safe from the foe you will behold him soon Triumphant here, a conqueror and a king.

**Iphisa:** Let us away, to greet the loved Orestes, And comfort our afflicted mother.

**Electra:** Gods! What unexpected bliss! O Pylades, Thou best of friends, thou kind protector, haste, Let us begone.

**Pylades:** [To his attendants.] Take off those shameful bonds; [They take off her chains.] Fall from her hands, ye chains, for they were made To wield a sceptre.

### SCENE VIII.

Electra, Iphisa, Pylades, Pammenes.

**Electra:** O Pammenes, where, Where is my Orestes, my deliverer? Why comes he not?

**Pammenes:** This is a dreadful moment, And full of terror, for his father's spirit Demands a sacrifice, and justice waits To pay it, so hath heaven decreed: this tomb Must be the altar where the victim's blood Shall soon be shed; that sacred duty done, He will attend thee; but thou must not see A sight so terrible: thou knowest the laws Of Argos suffer not thy spotless hands To join with her ere the appointed time.

**Iphisa:** But say, Pammenes, what of Clytemnæstra, How acts she in this dreadful crisis?

**Pammenes:** Vainly She deprecates the wrath of fierce Orestes, And strives to save Ægisthus; kneels for pardon, And craves that boon she never will obtain: Meantime the furies, deaf to her entreaties, And thirsting for the cruel murderer's blood, Throng round Orestes, and demand his life.

**Iphisa:** O may this day of terror be a day Of pardon and forgiveness; may it finish The cruel woes of our unhappy race! Hark, Pylades, Electra, heard ye not A dreadful groan?

**Electra:** My mother's sure.

**Pammenes:** 'Tis she.

**Clytemnæstra:** [Behind the scenes.] O spare me!

**Iphisa:** Heaven!

**Clytemnæstra:** [Behind the scenes.] My son!

**Electra:** He kills Ægisthus. O hear her not, Orestes, but go on, Revenge, revenge, dissolve the horrid tie, And sacrifice the murderer in her arms: Strike deep.

**Clytemnæstra:** My son! O, thou hast slain thy mother.

**Pylades:** O cruel fate!

**Iphisa:** O guilt!

**Electra:** O wretched brother! Crimes punish crimes; forever be this day Lamented by us!

## SCENE IX.

**Orestes:** [Enters.] Open wide, thou earth, And swallow me: O Clytemnæstra, Atreus, And Tantalus, I come, I follow you To Erebus, a partner in your crimes, To share your tortures.

**Electra:** O what hast thou done?

**Orestes:** She strove to save him, and I smote them both— I can no more—

**Electra:** She fell then by thy hand! O dreadful stroke! and couldst thou—

**Orestes:** 'Twas not I; 'Twas not Orestes; some malignant power Guided my hand, the hateful instrument Of heaven's eternal wrath: Orestes lives But to be wretched; banished from my country, When my dear father fell, my mother slain, And by my hand; an exile from the world, Bereft of parents, country, fortune, friends, Now must I wander: all is lost to me: O thou bright orb, thou ever glorious sun, Shocked at our crimes, and Atreus's horried feast, Thou didst withdraw thy beams, and yet thou shinest On me! O wherefore in eternal night Dost thou not bury all? O tyrant gods, Merciless powers, who punished me for guilt Yourselves commanded, O for what new crime Am I reserved? speak—ye pronounce the name Of Tauris, there I'll seek the murderous priestess, Who offers blood alone to the angry gods, To gods less cruel, less unjust than you.

**Electra:** Stay, and conjure their justice and their hate.

**Pylades:** Where'er the gods may lead, thy Pylades Shall follow still, and friendship triumph o'er The woes of mortals, and the wrath of heaven.

### End

[1] Nothing could add more to the horror of the crime than such a circumstance. Clytemnæstra, not content with murdering her husband, instituted a solemn feast in commemoration of the happy event, and called it, with cruel raillery, "the supper of Agamemnon" Dinias, in his *History of Argos*, informs us, it was on the thirteenth of the month Gamelion, which answers to the beginning of our January.

# Catiline

## Contents

Dramatis Personæ. . . . . . . . . . . . . . . . . . . . . . . . . . . . . . . . . . . . . . . . . . . . 122
Act I. . . . . . . . . . . . . . . . . . . . . . . . . . . . . . . . . . . . . . . . . . . . . . . . . . . . . . 123
Act II. . . . . . . . . . . . . . . . . . . . . . . . . . . . . . . . . . . . . . . . . . . . . . . . . . . . . 129
Act III. . . . . . . . . . . . . . . . . . . . . . . . . . . . . . . . . . . . . . . . . . . . . . . . . . . . 135
Act IV. . . . . . . . . . . . . . . . . . . . . . . . . . . . . . . . . . . . . . . . . . . . . . . . . . . . 140
Act V. . . . . . . . . . . . . . . . . . . . . . . . . . . . . . . . . . . . . . . . . . . . . . . . . . . . . 147

## Dramatis Personæ

Cicero
Septimus
Cæsar
Crassus
Catiline
Clodius
Aurelia
Cethegus
Cato
Lentulus-Sura
Lucullus
Conspirators
Martian
Lictors

In his preface to this play Voltaire says:
"The learned will not here meet with a faithful narrative of Catiline's conspiracy: a tragedy, they very well know, is not a history, but they will see a true picture of the manners of those times: all that Cicero, Catiline, Cato and Cæsar do in this piece is not true, but their genius and character are faithfully represented: if we do not there discover the eloquence of Cicero, we shall at

least find displayed all that courage and virtue which he showed in the hour of danger. In Catiline is described that contrast of fierceness and dissimulation which formed his real character; Cæsar is represented as growing into power, factious, and brave; that Cæsar who was born at once to be the glory and the scourge of Rome."

# ACT I.

### SCENE I.

The Scene represents, on one side, the palace of Aurelia; on the other the temple of Tellus, where the senate assembled: At a distance, a gallery communicating to some private passages that lead from the palace of Aurelia to the vestibule of the temple.

[Soldiers at the bottom of the stage.] Yes, thou proud talker, thou vile instrument Of a deluded people, soon thy power Shall be no more; and thou whose savage virtue, Inflexibly severe, destroys the nation It means to save, imperious Cato, know Thy doom is passed, thou and the tyrant senate Must fall together; they who keep the world In bondage shall themselves be slaves; their chains Are forged already, and usurping Pompey Shall pay for dear bought honors with his blood. Cæsar, his haughty rival, shall oppose him, His equal Cæsar: he who, like myself, Was ever factious, shall assist my cause; The snare is laid, and Cæsar shall prepare The throne for Catiline; I'll make them all Subservient to my purpose: Cicero's self, The man whom most I hate, shall be my friend: My wife too may be useful, and may prove A step to greatness: fathers, husbands, all Those empty names mistaken mortals call Most sacred, hence, I give you to the winds: Ambition, I am thine.

### SCENE II.

Catiline, Cethegus.

**Catiline**: Well, my Cethegus, Whilst Rome and our designs are hid in night, Say, hast thou called together our brave chiefs?

**Cethegus**: Even here, my lord, beneath this portico, Safe from the consul's prying eyes, and near That impious scene where our proud tyrants sit, Thy friends shall meet—already they have signed The solemn compact, and are sworn to serve thee. But how stands Cæsar, will he second us?

**Catiline**: He is a turbulent unruly spirit, And acts but for himself.

**Cethegus**: And yet without him We never shall succeed.

**Catiline:** I've laid a snare He cannot escape: my soldiers, in his name, Shall seize Præneste—he's been long suspected. This will confirm his guilt—the furious consul Shall soon accuse him to the senate—Cæsar Will hazard all to satiate his revenge. I'll rouse this sleeping lion from his den, And make him roar for me.

**Cethegus:** But Nonnius still Rules in Præneste; he's a friend to Rome. In vain already thou hast tried to tempt His stubborn virtue—what must be his fate?

**Catiline:** Thou knowest I love his daughter, though I hate Her surly father: long he strove in vain To thwart our mutual passion, and prevent Our private marriage, which at last the churl Unwillingly consented to: he feared To incur his angry party's high displeasure And the proud consul's—but I've made his pride Subservient to our purpose—he is bound By solemn oaths to keep our marriage still A secret: Sura only and Cethegus Are privy to it: this perhaps may serve More purposes than one: Aurelia's palace Conducts us to the temple; there I've placed My instruments of ruin, arms, and firebrands, To execute our great design: thy zeal To friendship much I owe, but more to love. Beneath the senate's sacred vault, beneath The roof of Nonnius will we sacrifice These tyrants—you, my friends, must to Præneste; You to the capitol; remember whom You serve, the oath that binds you, and the cause You are engaged in—thou, my loved Cethegus, Must watch o'er all, and guide the great machine.

### SCENE III.
Aurelia, Catiline.

**Aurelia:** O Catiline, my lord, my husband, ease My troubled heart, remove my doubts, my fears, My horror, my despair—alas! what means This dreadful preparation?—every step I tread alarms me; why these soldiers, why With arms and torches is my palace filled? The days of Marius and of Sulla sure Are now returned, and discord reigns amongst us: Explain, my lord, this dreadful mystery: Do not turn from me—by the sacred tie That joins our hearts, by the dear babe thou lovest, I talk not to thee of its mother's danger, For thee alone I tremble: pity me, Pity a wretched wife, and tell me all.

**Catiline:** Know then, my life, my fortune, and my fame, Thy safety, and my own, the common cause, Demand a conduct which thy fears condemn: But if thou lovest me, let whate'er thou seest Be buried in thy breast: I mean to save Rome's better part; the senate and the people Are disunited—danger threats the state On every side; I've taken the best means To make all well again.

**Aurelia:** I hope thou hast; But can we hide our hearts from those we love? Canst thou deceive me? yet what thou hast said Doubles my fears. Alas! thy looks are wild, And full of horror. What will Nonnius say When he shall see these dreadful preparations? The voice of nature, and the tender names Of father and brother oft have passed Unheard and unregarded when the cause Of Rome required it—well thou knowest our marriage Gave much offence, and when my angry father Returning, shall behold these sad effects Of our unhappy union, what, my lord, Must I expect? O why wilt thou abuse The power which love has given thee o'er a heart Devoted to thy service?—thou hast gained A party, but consider well my father, Cato, and Cicero, and Rome, and heaven, Are all thy foes: Nonnius perhaps may come This very day on purpose to destroy thee.

**Catiline**: Be not afraid, I know he cannot.

**Aurelia**: How?

**Catiline**: Whene'er he comes he must approve our purpose: I am not left at liberty to tell thee What we design, suffice it that his interest And mine are one: I know when he shall find The fair result, he then will join with me To pull down the proud tyrants he obeys: Trust me, Aurelia, what I do shall prove The fertile spring of everlasting glory And honor to you both—

**Aurelia**: Alas! the honor I fear is doubtful, and the danger certain: What seekest thou? wherefore wouldst thou urge thy fate? Is it not enough to rank among the first Of human kind, and rule the subject world? Why wouldst thou mount the giddy heights of power, And court destruction? my foreboding heart Already sees, and trembles at thy danger. Are these the promised joys of flattering love? The peace I hoped for? I have lost it now For ever: O, my lord, when last these eyes Were in a short and broken slumber closed, Methought I saw in flames imperial Rome; Saw murders, deaths, and rivers stained with blood, My father massacred in open senate, And thee, my Catiline, amidst a band Of vile assassins, breathing forth thy soul In dreadful agonies: I rose, and fled From these sad images to find my lord, My guardian, my protector—thou art here, And I, alas! am but the more unhappy.

**Catiline**: Away—thy omens fright not Catiline; Complain not, but be resolute: I want Thy courage, not thy tears, when I am serving Thee and my country.

**Aurelia**: Is it thus thou meanst To serve her? O, my lord, I know not what Thy purpose is, but were it fair and just Perhaps I might long since have been consulted; Our mutual interest claimed it from a husband: If thou dissemblest with me, I have cause To doubt, and to be wretched—Cicero Has long suspected thee, and Rome thou knowest Adores him.

**Catiline**: Whom? my hated rival?

## SCENE IV.

Catiline, Aurelia, Martian.
One of the Conspirators.

**Martian**: Sir, The consul comes this way—by his command The senate meet; he wishes first to see And speak with you.

**Aurelia**: I tremble at his name.

**Catiline**: Why tremble at the name of Cicero? Let Nonnius fear and reverence him, disgrace His rank and character by mean submission; I pity the weak senator, but hoped To find in thee a noble soul: not thus, Remember, acted thy brave ancestors: Gods! that a woman, and a Roman, sprung From Nero's blood, should thus be void of pride Or of ambition! noble minds are ne'er Without them.

**Aurelia**: Mine perhaps thou thinkest is mean And timid; cruelty alone with thee Is courage; thy reproach is most unkind; But know me better; know that this fond wife, Whom thou contemnest, who has not power to change Or soften thee, has more of Roman in her Than thou canst boast; and, coward as she is, Can teach thee how to die.

**Catiline**: How many cares At once surround me!—Cicero comes—but him I fear not: this Aurelia.—

## SCENE V.

Cicero, Catiline, Chief of the Lictors.

**Cicero**: [To the Chief Lictor.] Do as I Command you—I'll try if I can sound This faithless heart; leave me alone with him: Sometimes a villain may be wrought by fear To better counsel, and renounce his purpose. Who's there? the proud plebeian, chosen by Rome To be her master? [Turns to Cataline.] Ere the senate meet, Catiline, I come for the last time to hold The friendly torch, and save thy wandering steps From the dread precipice of guilt and ruin.

**Catiline**: Who, thou?

**Cicero**: Yes, I.

**Catiline**: And is it thus thy hate Pursues me?

**Cicero**: Call it pity—but observe me. The capitol is weary of thy plaints, Thy factious cries, and bold impertinence; Rome, and the senate have, it seems, debased The consul's dignity by choosing me: Thy pride we know expected it, but how Hadst thou deserved it? was it by the name, Or family, thy valor, or the pride Of a loose prodigal in shows and feasts And idle pomp; could these entitle thee To such exalted honors? couldst thou hope To be the great dispenser of the laws, To guide the mistress of the world who rules O'er prostrate kings? had

Catiline been what He ought to be, I might perhaps to him Have yielded the contested palm.—Hereafter Thou mayest support the state, but to be consul 'Tis fit thou first shouldst be—a citizen. Thinkest thou by vile reflections on my birth, My fortune, and my fame, to taint my honor, Or weaken the firm basis of my power? In our corrupted days it is not name, Or family, that Rome has need of: no: 'Tis virtue; and the pride of Cicero Hath ever been, that he should nothing owe To his forefathers—my nobility Springs from myself, and thine may end in thee.

**Catiline**: It ill becomes a temporary power, Like thine, to boast of its authority.

**Cicero**: Had Cicero used that power as thou deservest, Thou wouldst not have been here to question it: Thou who hast stained our altars with pollution And sacrilegious rage, thy days are numbered But by thy crimes: thy merit is to dare, To strike at all, dissemble, and betray: Thou hast abused the precious gifts that heaven Bestowed on thee for other purposes: Sense, beauty, courage, and heroic warmth, All the fair ornaments of human nature, In thee are but the instruments of ill. My voice, which still is raised to scourge the wicked, And plead for the oppressed, hath spared thee yet; Nor with the odious Verres ranked the name Of Catiline: but long impunity Hath made thee shameless, and insensible Of all reproof—thou hast betrayed the state: At Rome, and in Etruria all is discord, And foul confusion; Umbria is revolted; Præneste staggers in her faith; the soldiers Of barbarous Sulla, drenched in blood, come forth From their dark caves prepared for slaughter, armed By cruel Mallius; all are leagued with thee; Thy partisans declared, or secret friends, All are united in one guilty bond, And sworn to the destruction of their country: I know thee for their chief, for I have eyes On every side, and hands too, thou shalt find, That, spite of thee, shall vindicate the cause Of injured Rome; thy guilty friends shall feel My justice too: thou hast beheld me long But as thy rival, now behold thy judge, And thy accuser, who will force thee soon To answer for thy actions by those laws Which thou so oft hast trampled on unpunished, Those laws which thou contemnest, and I revenge.

**Catiline**: I've told you, sir, already, that your office But ill excuses this indecent freedom: But for that country's sake, whom both are bound To serve, I pardon your unjust suspicions; Nay, I do more, I honor your warm zeal; Blind though it be, in such a cause 'tis just: But do not thus reproach me for past errors, For the wild follies of impetuous youth, That soon are o'er; your senate is to blame, I followed their example; pomp and pride, Excess and luxury, the fruits of conquest, Are the time's vices, not the native bent Of Catiline's heart:

I served the commonweal In Asia as a soldier, as a judge In Africa: spite of our domestic feuds, Did I not make the name of Rome revered Among the nations? I who have defended Shall ne'er betray her.

**Cicero**: Sulla too and Marius Both served their country well, and then destroyed her. Tyrants have all some specious show of virtue, And ere they break their country's laws support them.

**Catiline**: If you suspect each brave and gallant soldier, Let Cæsar, Pompey, Crassus be accused: Why fix on me amongst so many? why Am I the only object of your fears? Have I deserved it?

**Cicero**: That you best can tell. But wherefore deign I thus to answer you?

**Catiline**: The more I plead in my defence, the more Will Cicero condemn me: if as friend Thou talkest to me, thou but deceivest thyself, I am thy foe; if as a citizen, So too is Catiline; if as a consul, A consul's not a master, he presides But in the senate, I defy him there.

**Cicero**: Thou durst not; for I there can punish guilt: If thou art innocent, I will protect thee; If not, I charge thee, be not seen in Rome.

**Catiline**: This is too much: I will no longer bear Thy insults, though I scorn thy vague suspicions: Yet know I think the worst affront that thou Couldst put on Catiline, would be to protect him.

**Cicero**: [Alone.] Insolent traitor! means he thus to prove His innocence by false affected pride? Perfidious wretch, I'm not to be deceived, Nor shalt thou thus escape the watchful eye Of vengeance.

### SCENE VI.

Cicero, Cato.

**Cicero**: Well, my friend, hast thou prepared For Rome's defence?

**Cato**: Your orders are obeyed; I have disposed the chiefs, and all are ready To march as you direct them; but I fear The people, nay the senate.

**Cicero**: Ha! the senate?

**Cato**: Ay—they are swollen with pride—and foul division Will soon enslave them.

**Cicero**: Much indeed I fear Our vices will avenge the conquered world; Our liberty and virtue are no more; But Rome may still have hope whilst Cato lives.

**Cato**: Alas! who serves his country often serves A most ungrateful mistress—even thy merit Offends the senate; with a jealous eye It views thy greatness.

**Cicero**: Cato's approbation Is recompense enough; thy honest praise Will more than balance their ingratitude; On that and on posterity alone I shall rely; let us perform our duty, And leave the rest to heaven.

**Cato**: How shall we stem The torrent of corruption? when I see, Even in this sacred temple, raised to virtue, Infamous treason rise with shameless front: Can we suppose that Manlius, that proud rebel, Would dare advance his standard, and blow up The flames of civil war, if greater powers Did not support him, if some secret foe Abetted not their vile conspiracy? The leaders of the senate may betray us; From Sulla's ashes may new tyrants rise: My just suspicions light on Cæsar.

**Cicero**: Mine On Catiline; perfidious, sordid, rash, And bold; he loves rebellion, and delights In novelty; more dangerous than Cæsar; I know him well; even now I parted from him: What passed between us but confirms me more In my suspicions; on his face I read Rage and resentment, the determined pride Of his fierce spirit, that no longer deigned To hide its purpose, but stood forth, and owned Its enmity to Rome.—I must discover His bold compeers, perhaps I may prevent His future crimes, and save my falling country.

**Cato**: Catiline has friends, and much I fear the power Of these united tyrants may prove fatal: Our forces are in Asia, and at Rome We are corrupted; but one upright man May save the state.

**Cicero**: If we unite, our country Has naught to fear—in factions discord soon Dissolves the tie: Cæsar perhaps may join them; But, if I know him right, his noble soul Will never stoop to serve a worthless tyrant; He loves his country still, and hates a master; Though soon the time will come when he shall strive To be one; both are eager for applause, And both ambitious: both are raised too high To meet in friendship long; by their division Rome may be saved; let us not tamely wait To see our country's ruin, or behold In shameful chains the masters of mankind.

# ACT II.

SCENE I.

Catiline, Cethegus.

**Cethegus**: At length the torch is lit to set on fire Rome and the subject world; our army's nigh, And all is ready for the great event. Knowest thou meantime, my friend, what passes here?

**Catiline**: I know the consul's prudence, so he calls His cowardice, which deeply ruminates On future ills: like an unskilful pilot He sets up every sail for every wind, But knows not or which way the tempest comes, Or whither it may drive him—for the senate, I fear it not; that many-headed monster, So proud of conquest and nobility, Looks with an evil eye on Cicero; I know it hates him, so does Cæsar; Crassus Would gladly yield him up a sacrifice To our resentment; on their jealousy Depend my hopes—he's like a dying man, With feeble arm he struggles for a while, But soon shall sink beneath us and expire.

**Cethegus:** Envy I know attacks him, but his tongue Can soften all; he leads the captive senate.

**Catiline:** I brave him everywhere; despise his clamors, And smile at his resentment: let him rail To his last hour, and triumph in the shouts Of his admirers, I have other cares That sit more heavy on me.

**Cethegus:** What should stop Thy rapid progress in the paths of glory And happiness? Canst thou have aught to fear?

**Catiline:** My numerous foes I heed not, 'tis my friends I have most cause to dread; the jealousy Of Lentulus, the aspiring soul of Cæsar, And, above all, my wife.

**Cethegus:** Shall Catiline Be frightened at a woman's tears?—for shame, Leave her to indulge her visionary fears: I thought thou lovest her as a master should, And madest her but the servile instrument Of thy ambition.

**Catiline:** 'Tis a dangerous one: Rome and her child divide with me her love. Curse on the name of Rome, that even beneath The roof of Catiline those should dwell who love Their country! But before the important hour That must decide our fate, she shall be moved, She and her son—be that thy care, Cethegus: Our wives and children must not trouble us In those distressful moments—but for Cæsar—

**Cethegus:** What's to be done? if he refuse to join Our cause, shall we proscribe him; shall the names Of Cicero and of Cæsar be united?

**Catiline:** Let me consider—to cut Cæsar off— That were a dreadful sacrifice; methinks I cannot but admire him, and revere In him the honor of the Roman name: But where is Lentulus?

**Cethegus:** O fear not him; His pride we know will prompt him to believe That thou with him wilt share the sovereign power.

**Catiline:** Let him believe it still! the credulous fool! Thou seest, Cethegus, with what sublety I'm forced to manage these imperious spirits; Their rage, resentment, pride and jealousy: Knowest thou he dares even to be Cæsar's rival? To keep my friends within the pale of prudence Will cost me much more trouble than the ruin Of Cicero and Rome—to guide a party Is of all tasks the hardest.—

**Cethegus**: Lentulus Is here, my lord.

## SCENE II.
Catiline, Cethegus, Lentulus-Sura.

**Sura**: In spite of my remonstrance You will rely on Cæsar, and confide In him alone; Præneste's in his power. And I must yield to him; but know I scorn it, The blood of Scipio was not made to yield.

**Catiline**: I've joined with Cæsar, but depend not on him; He may support our cause, or he may hurt it; I use his name, but 'tis for your advantage.

**Sura**: And what is there in Cæsar's name superior To yours or mine? why must we meanly court His favor? but because he's Pompey's rival Rome makes a God of him.—I am thy friend; Sura and Catiline may defy them all, And without Cæsar make the world their own.

**Catiline**: We may—thy conduct and approved valor Have ever been my best and surest hope; But Cæsar is beloved, respected, feared; The senate and the people all admire And court him; statesman, general, magistrate; In peace revered, and terrible in war; A thousand ways he charms the multitude; In short he will be necessary.—

**Sura**: Say Destructive rather—if to-day he shines Our equal, by to-morrow he will prove Our rival, and ere long perhaps our master; Trust me, I know him well, and therefore think Our party has not a more dangerous foe: Perhaps his haughty soul may yield to thee, But play the tyrant o'er the rest; for me, I cannot, will not, brook it—I've devoted My honor and my fortunes to thy service; But I renounce my plighted faith, renounce Thee and thy cause, if Cæsar is preferred.

**Catiline**: And so thou shalt—I'd sacrifice my life Rather than e'er permit a haughty rival To soar above us—Cæsar is our tool, Our instrument; to-day I flatter him, To-morrow can bring down his pride, perhaps Do more—thou knowest our mutual happiness And interest are my first and dearest care. [To Cethegus.] Away, and let Aurelia be prepared: Go; or her fond intruding love may ruin Our deep laid schemes, and mar the great design: Return some private way and meet me here, I wait for Cæsar.

**Sura**: Nothing's to be done. I find, without him—but I'll wait the event.

**Catiline**: Farewell: remember I rely on thee More than on Cæsar.—

**Cethegus**: I shall execute Your high command, and gather all our friends Before the standard of great Catiline.

## SCENE III.
Catiline, Cæsar.

**Catiline**: Hail, godlike Cæsar, thou whom from the days Of Sulla I have ranked amongst my best And dearest friends, whose fortunes I foretold: Born as thou art to be the first of Romans, How suits it with thy pride to be the slave Of a plebeian, who forever thwarts And braves thee to thy face? I know thou hatest him; Thy piercing eye observes impatient Rome Contending for her freedom, will not Cæsar Assist his country to shake off her chains? The cause is noble, and the fate of millions Depends on this important crisis; thou Wilt join us—lookest thou not with jealous eye On Pompey still? dost thou not still abhor The surly Cato? canst thou serve the gods With half thy wonted zeal when the proud consul Presides at the altar? will thy noble spirit Bear these imperious rulers; soft Lucullus, Sunk in the arms of luxury and sloth; The greedy Crassus, grasping his large heaps Of ill-got wealth, enough to purchase Rome And all her venal sons? on every side Or faction or corruption reigns; the world Calls out on Cæsar; wilt thou hear her voice? Wilt thou redress and save thy falling country? Will Cæsar listen to his friend?

**Cæsar**: He will; And if the senate do thee wrong, step forth To plead thy cause; I never will betray thee; But ask no more.

**Catiline**: Are these the utmost bounds Of Cæsar's friendship, but to talk for him?

**Cæsar**: I've weighed the projects, and shall not oppose them; I may approve, but would not execute.

**Catiline**: I understand you, you are on that side Which fortune favors, and would stand aloof To mark the progress of our civil wars, And raise your fortunes on the common ruin.

**Cæsar**: No—I have nobler views; my hate of Cato, My jealousy of Pompey, the renown Of Cicero, conspire to make me wish I might surpass them all; fair glory calls, The banks of Seine, the Tagus, and the Rhine; I pant for honor, and for victory.

**Catiline**: If conquest is thy aim, begin with Rome; To-morrow we may reign the masters of her.

**Cæsar**: The enterprise is great, perhaps too bold; But, to be open with thee, though 'tis worthy Of Catiline, it suits not Cæsar.

**Catiline**: How!

**Cæsar**: I do not choose to serve.

**Catiline**: To share with Cæsar Were no dishonor to the most ambitious.

**Cæsar:** But power supreme is not to be divided: I'll not be dragged at Catiline's chariot wheels To grace his triumph: as a friend I love thee; But know that friend shall never be—my master: Even Pompey shall not—Sulla, whom thy valor Hath nobly followed in the race of glory, Whose courage I admire, whose lawless rage I ever shall abhor, enslaved proud Rome: But he deserved the glorious prize, subdued The Hellespont, and made Euphrates tremble: Asia was conquered: Mithridates owned His martial genius—but what noble deeds Hast thou to boast? what kings hast thou subdued? What seas has Catiline passed, what lands explored? Thou hast the seeds of greatness in thy nature; But to enslave thy country is above Thy present powers, above the powers of Cæsar: We have not strength, authority or name For such an enterprise. Rome soon must fall: But ere I will attempt to be her master, I will extend her empire and her glory; And if I forge my country's chains, at least Will cover them with laurels.

**Catiline:** Mine, perhaps, Is, after all, the shortest path to glory: How did your boasted Sulla rise to empire? He had an army, so has Catiline; Raised by myself alone, and not, like his, The gift of fortune; he observed with care The favorable hour, and well improved it: I have done more; have made the times and seasons Subservient to me. Sulla was a king. Wouldst thou be one? wilt thou be Cicero's slave, Or rule with Catiline?

**Cæsar:** Neither. To be free, For I no longer will dissemble with you, I esteem Cicero; but love him not, Nor fear him: though I love, I dread not thee. Divide the senate if thou canst, pull down The proud oppressors; thou hast my consent; But hope no more, nor dare to think that Cæsar Will ever be thy slave: I'll keep thy secret, And be thy friend or foe, as thou deservest it.

## SCENE IV.

**Catiline:** If he supports us not, even let him fall The victim of his folly: Sulla knew And would have cut him off, but Sulla dared not: I know he is my secret enemy, As such I shall beware of him.

## SCENE V.

Catiline, Cethegus, Lentulus-Sura.

**Sura:** What says The mighty Cæsar? is he friend or foe?

**Catiline:** His barren friendship only offers me A feeble aid; but we can do without him: Perhaps he may repent it; and meantime We've better pillars to support the fabric. Behold, the heroes come.

SCENE VI.
Catiline, the Conspirators.

**Catiline**: Hail, bold Statilius, Valiant Autronius, noble Piso, hail, Vargontes, and the rest of my brave friends, The first of men, the conquerors of kings, The great avengers of a world oppressed, This seat of empire soon shall be your own: The vanquished nations, which your valor gained, Were ravished from you by usurping tyrants; For the proud senate still your blood hath flowed; For them Tigranes, Mithridates fell; For them alone; and all your poor reward Was but to stand at distance, and adore Your haughty masters; but at length the hour Of vengeance is approaching: be prepared For no inglorious enterprise: I know Your souls would scorn a victory cheaply bought; But I will bring you noble conquests, full Of danger and of glory: seize, my friends, The golden opportunity: already I see your foes expiring at your feet. Rush on your prey, burn, plunder, and destroy; But, above all, let union guide your counsels: Even now Præneste falls: the brave remains Of Sulla's scattered forces march towards us: I shall command them, and Rome must be yours Petreius vanquished, I shall clear my way Even to the capitol: then you, my friends, Shall rise to empire, to a throne disgraced By worthless Romans, and by you restored To its true lustre: Curius and his band Will open me the gates; but tell me, friend, The gladiatorian cohorts, where are they? Will those brave veterans join our cause?

**Lentulus-Sura**: They will: Myself shall lead them in the dead of night, And arm them in this secret place.

**Catiline**: Mount Cælius— Is that secured?

**Statilius**: I've bribed the sentinels, And all is safe.

**Catiline**: You to mount Aventine Repair, and soon as Mallius shall display His colors, light your torches, spread destruction On every side; let the proscribed perish. Let Cicero—ye have sworn it—be my first My darling victim: Cæsar too must die, And Cato; these removed, the senate soon Will tremble and obey: already fortune Declares for us, and blinds them to their ruin: Within their walls, and almost in their sight We lay the snares of death, and mark them out For sacrifice: remember not to take up arms Before the appointed time: we must surprise Ere we destroy: let Cicero and Rome Perish together, and the lightning blast Before the thunder's threatening voice alarms them. Call not this deed a foul conspiracy; 'Tis a just war declared against the foes Of Rome and all mankind; reclaim your rights, The empire of the world, which base usurpers Had ravished from you. [To Cethegus and Lentulus-Sura.] Haste, ye gallant leaders, Haste to the senate; see your victims there: Hear your proud consul roar; 'tis the last time That he shall triumph there—now, worthy Romans, Swear by this sword, that with the blood of tyrants Shall soon be stained, to perish, or to conquer, With Catiline.

**Martian**: By thee and by this sword We swear with thee to perish or to conquer.

**Another Conspirator**: Perish the senate! perish all who serve, All who defend them! if there be amongst us A traitor, let him die.

**Catiline**: Away, this night Will finish all, and Rome shall be our own.

# ACT III.

### SCENE I.

catiline, cethegus, martian, septimus. **Catiline**: Are all things ready? do our troops advance?

**Martian**: Even so, my lord; the faithful Mallius comes Prepared to circle these devoted walls; Our friends impatient brook not dull delay, But urge each other to the bloody scene; We wait but thy command; appoint the hour When Rome must fall.

**Catiline**: Soon as I quit the senate Begin the sacrifice: let this great day Be sacred to destruction: but meantime Take special care the consul's busy friends Do not observe our motions.

**Cethegus**: Were it not Most prudent to destroy him in the senate? He has alarmed the people, and foresees Our every action.

**Catiline**: Knows he the revolt Of Mallius? knows he Catiline's deep designs? Knows he an army is approaching for me? Fear not, my friends, ours is no common cause, 'Tis fit the means should be proportioned to it: When vulgar mortals, grovelling and obscure, Form ill-digested schemes, and idle plans Of future greatness, if one slender wheel Is broke, it overthrows the whole machine: But souls like ours, a firm and chosen band, Plans deeply laid, the conquerors of kings, The sons of Mars, united to support And raise each other, these must be superior To Cicero's art, or Cicero's vigilance: We've naught to fear.

**Cethegus**: But is Præneste ours In Cæsar's name?

**Catiline**: Ay; that was my first stroke Of policy: the unsuspecting senate Will be deceived: I've whispered it abroad, That Nonnius hath conspired against the state, And half our credulous fools believe the tale. Ere he can clear his innocence, my army Will be in Rome, and all secured: away, Remove Aurelia: let no little cares Intrude to stop or hurt the great design.

## SCENE II.

Aurelia, Catiline, Cethegus, etc.

**Aurelia:** [A letter in her hand.] There, Catiline, read Aurelia's fate and thine, Thy crime and thy just sentence.

**Catiline:** What rash hand— Ha! 'tis thy father's.

**Aurelia:** Read it.

**Catiline:** [Reads the letter.] "Death too long Hath spared me, and the child I loved too well Must finish my sad days: at length I suffer For my own follies, and that hapless marriage Which I consented to; I know the plots Of thy vile husband: Cæsar has betrayed us, And would have seized Præneste: thou partakest The treason: but repent, or perish with them." But how could Nonnius e'er discover that Which even the consul knows not?

**Cethegus:** This may prove Our ruin.

**Catiline:** [To Cethegus.] It may turn to our advantage. Aurelia, I must tell thee all: this day The world is armed in Catiline's defence: Say, in the hour of danger wilt thou serve A father or a husband?

**Aurelia:** To be silent, And trouble thee no more, were the commands Which Catiline laid on his neglected wife, Spite of her fond entreaties, prayers, and tears: What hast thou further to desire?

**Catiline:** Away: This moment, send that letter to the consul; I have my reasons; I would have him know, That Cæsar is as much to be suspected As I am: he's accused, and Catiline not So much as named: it is as I could wish. Take with thee our loved infant, and return not To bleeding Rome, till I am master there: Then thou shalt reign with me: our marriage yet Is kept a secret: I'll not have it known, 'Till at the head of our victorious army I shall proclaim it loud to Italy, And to the world: then shall thy haughty father, As our first subject, humbly bend before thee, And sue to be forgiven: begone, Aurelia, And leave me to my fate. I would not wish Thou shouldst partake my dangers or my cares: This night prepare to meet a conqueror.

**Aurelia:** O Catiline, meanest thou to destroy thy country? Is this the day appointed for destruction?

**Catiline:** To-day I purpose to chastise my foes; All is prepared.

**Aurelia:** Begin then with Aurelia; For I had rather perish by thy hand, Than live to share thy guilt.

**Catiline:** O let the tie That binds us—

**Cethegus:** Drive not thus to desperation A husband and a friend, who trusts his all To thee; thou art entered in the paths of glory, And to retreat were fatal.

**Aurelia:** Misery And sure destruction were Aurelia's fate: From that unhappy moment, when by thee And thy vile counsels led, I gave my hand To Catiline; despised, neglected, long Have I beheld, with eyes of detestation, Your horrid plots: spite of myself you made me A vile accomplice; but you know I loved, And basely have imposed upon my weakness: I blush to think how grossly you abused A woman's fond credulity; but know I'll no longer be guilty of a crime Which I abhor: no longer serve a tyrant: No, I renounce my vows, my faith to thee; These hands shall rise against thee, thou vile traitor: Henceforth I am thy foe. Strike, Catiline, strike; Destroy me; carry into burning Rome, For thy first victim, an expiring wife Slain by thy hand; destroy the hapless infant, Sad pledge of our detested nuptials: then, Barbarian as thou art, complete thy guilt, And in the blood of millions glut thy vengeance.

**Catiline:** And is the gentle, kind Aurelia then Amongst my foes? thus in the noblest war, That e'er was waged for freedom and for empire, When Pompey, Cæsar, Cato, are subdued, My worst of enemies at last are found In my own house; I am deserted there For an unworthy father: threatened too.

**Aurelia:** I threaten guilt, and tremble for—a husband: Even in my rage thou seest my tenderness; Abuse it not, it is my only weakness: But I would have thee fear—

**Catiline:** That word, Aurelia, Was never made for Catiline—but hear me: I love thee; yet presume not on thy power, Nor think I e'er will sacrifice my friends, My noble cause, my interest, and my fame, Glory and empire: no, it is enough If I forgive and pity thee, but know—

**Aurelia:** The crown thy pride looks up to I despise: I should behold it as the shameful mark Of infamy: thou showest thy love for me By pity and forgiveness; and I mine, By holding back, if possible, thy hand From guilt and error—therefore will I go—

## SCENE III.
Catiline, Cethegus, Lentulus-Sura, Aurelia, etc.

**Lentulus-Sura:** We are discovered, lost, undone; our friends Betrayed, our plots unravelled all; Præneste Not yielded to us; Nonnius is in Rome; One of our spies is seized, and has confessed; Nonnius in open senate will accuse His son-in-law; he's gone to Cicero, Who knows too much already.

**Aurelia:** Now behold The fruits of guilt, and all thy great designs, Thy boasted fortunes, empire, and the throne, Which I despised: are thy eyes opened yet?

**Catiline:** [After a long pause.] This is a blow I thought not of; but say, Wilt thou betray me?

**Aurelia**: 'Tis what thou deservest: My country claims, and heaven demands it of me; But I'll do more, I'll save both Rome and thee; And though I have not all thy rage, may boast Some of thy courage; love will make me brave: Long since I saw thy danger, Catiline: 'Tis come, and now I will partake it with thee; I'll see my father, and obtain thy life, Or lose my own; I know he is forgiving, Gentle, and mild: I know he loves Aurelia, And will not urge too far a foe like thee, Desperate and brave; I'll talk to Cicero Who fears, and to the senate who adores thee; They will be glad to think thee innocent; Those whom we fear we readily forgive: But let sincerest penitence atone For thy past crimes: convicted guilt by that, And that alone, can hope for pardon; though I know it hurts thy pride, it must be done: At least I hope I shall procure thee time, Or to quit Rome, or to defend thyself: I'll not reproach thee; even when most guilty I loved, and in misfortune will not leave thee; But rather die to save thy life and glory. Farewell; let Catiline learn henceforth to trust me; I have deserved it.

**Catiline**: Sad alternative; It is most dreadful—but I yield to thee: Remember that a husband's plea is stronger, Much stronger than a father's: if I err, The crime is thine.

**Aurelia**: I'll take it all upon me; Nay, even thy hatred, if it must be so; I act for thee, and I'm satisfied. Daughter, and wife, and Roman, every duty Shall be performed; remember thine, and keep Thy heart as pure and spotless as Aurelia's.

SCENE IV.

Catiline, Cethegus, Lentulus-Sura, Freedmen.

lentulus-**Sura**: Is this the bold and fearless Catiline, Or Nonnius' timid son; a woman's slave; Appalled by phantoms? how thy great soul shrunk Soon as Aurelia spoke!

**Cethegus**: It cannot be; Catiline will never change; his noble soul By opposition grows but more resolved: Præneste lost, the senate our accusers, We may be conquerors still, and make them tremble Whilst they condemn us; we have noble friends, And will deserve them.

**Lentulus-Sura**: Ere the signal's given We may be seized; thou knowest at dead of night, Just as the senate part, we had agreed To execute our purpose: what, my friends, Must be resolved on?

**Cethegus**: [To Catiline.] Catiline, thou art silent, And tremblest too.

**Catiline**: I tremble at the blow Which I shall strike; my fate demands it of me.

**Lentulus-Sura**: I've no dependence on Aurelia: all That we can hope for is to sell our lives As dearly as we can.

*Catiline:* I count the moments, And weigh each circumstance; Aurelia's tears And flattery will a while suspend our fate; Cicero on other business is detained, And all is safe; let me have arms and men, No matter who they are, or slaves or free, Assassins, robbers, if they will but fight, We'll have them: thou brave Septimus, and thou My dearest Martian, whose approved zeal I shall depend on, must observe Aurelia; And Nonnius; when they're parted, talk to him About his daughter; tell him of her danger, Draw him by artful means to the dark path That leads to the Tiber, seize the lucky moment, And hurl him—ha! who's this?

## SCENE V.
Cicero, Catiline, Cethegus, etc.

*Cicero:* Audacious traitor, Where art thou going? speak, Cethegus, who Assembled you?

*Catiline:* We'll tell thee in the senate.

*Cethegus:* There we shall see if thou art authorized Thus to pursue us.

*Lentulus-Sura:* Or what right The son of Tullius has to question us.

*Cicero:* At least I have a right to ask of these, Who brought them here: these are not like yourselves, Of senatorial rank; away with them. To prison.

*Catiline:* Darest thou thus on mere suspicion Confine a Roman; where's our liberty?

*Cicero:* They are of thy council, that's sufficient cause; Tremble, thyself; lictors, obey. [The lictors carry off Septimus and Martian.]

*Catiline:* 'Tis well: Go on, proud consul, and abuse thy power, The time will come when thou shalt answer for it.

*Cicero:* Instant I will examine them, hereafter Thus may I treat their masters; Nonnius knows All thy designs, Præneste's mine, and Rome Prepared for her defence; we soon shall see Which most prevails, or Catiline's artifice Or Cicero's vigilance: I do not preach Repentance and forgiveness to thee; no, I talk of punishment, thou mayest expect it: Come to the senate; follow if thou darest.

## SCENE VI.
Catiline, Cethegus, Lentulus-Sura.

*Cethegus:* Must we at last then bend to Cicero, And own his hated power?

*Catiline:* To the last hour I will defy him: still his curious soul Pries into all, but can discover nothing: Our friends will only lead him more astray, By holding out false lights that will misguide His wandering footsteps: in that fatal scroll Cæsar's accused; the senate is divided, And Manlius with his army's at the gate:

You think that all is lost, but follow me. And mark the event; we shall be conquerors still.

**Lentulus-Sura**: Nonnius, I fear, will make it all too plain.

**Catiline**: But he and Cicero shall never meet; Depend on that; away, address the senate With confidence, and leave the rest to me: But whither am I going?

**Cethegus**: Ha!

**Catiline**: Aurelia! O gods! what shall I do with that proud heart? Remove her from me: if I see my wife, Bold as I am, I shall relapse: away.

# ACT IV.

### SCENE I.

The Scene represents the place prepared for the reception of the Senate, with part of the gallery leading from Aurelia's palace to the temple of Tellus; a double row of benches in a circular form, with a raised seat for Cicero in the middle of it.

Cethegus, Lentulus-Sura.

**Lentulus-Sura**: These reverend fathers are exceeding slow, I thought ere this they would have met; perhaps Uncertain yet, and trembling for their fate, They know not how to act.

**Cethegus**: The oracle Of Rome, (for so he deems himself,) engaged In a continued round of toil, is busied In questioning his prisoner Septimus, Who will perplex him more; 'tis that retards Their meeting.

**Lentulus-Sura**: Would to heaven that we already Had taken up arms! I own I dread the senate. That reverence and attachment to the state, That sacred name of country, which awakes The sense of honor in each patriot breast; I like it not.

**Cethegus**: 'Tis nothing but a name, A word without a meaning; in the days Of our forefathers men respected it. Save a few stubborn stoics, none retain The memory of it; Cicero has raised Suspicions only; Cato's credit's lost; Cæsar is for us, what have we to fear? Defend yourselves, and Rome will be your own.

**Lentulus-Sura**: But what if Catiline, by an artful wife Seduced, at last should leave us; we have all Our weaknesses, and well thou knowest Aurelia Can lead him as she lists; he loves, esteems, And may be ruled by her.

**Cethegus**: His love will yield To his ambition.

**Lentulus-Sura**: Thou beheldest him tremble. In short, my friend, when tender ties like these—

**Cethegus:** [Taking him aside.] Cato approaches, let us listen to him. [Lentulus-Sura and Cethegus sit down at one corner of the Senate-house.]

## SCENE II.

Cato enters the Senate With Lucullus, Crassus, Favonius, Clodius, Murena, Cæsar, Catullus, Marcellus, etc. **Cato:** [Observing the two conspirators.] Lucullus, mark those dangerous men; behold them In secret conference; see, the blush of guilt Glows on their cheeks at sight of me; already Treason with bold and shameless front stalks forth Amongst us, and the senate still dissemble Their knowledge of it; Sulla's demon sure Hath breathed its baneful influence o'er the souls Of our blind rulers.

**Cethegus:** Cato, thy rash censure May cost thee dear.

**Cato:** [Sits down, the other senators take their places.] The gods of Rome sometimes Permit a traitor's crimes to pass unpunished; They crushed our ancestors beneath the yoke Of cruel tyrants; shall imperial Rome, The mistress of the world, again submit To slavery? no: the guilt she spared in Sulla, In Catiline and Cethegus she may punish.

**Cæsar:** Cato, what meanest thou? thy outrageous virtue Can serve no purpose but to make thee foes.

**Cato:** [To Cæsar.] Cæsar is still the factious leader's friend, The patron of corruption, and preserves A soul unmoved whate'er his country suffers.

**Cæsar:** When danger calls, my country will not say I am too calm, therefore complain not, Cato.

**Cato:** I must complain, must weep the fate of Rome, Deserted and betrayed: now where is Pompey? Would he were here to save us!

**Cæsar:** Why not call On Cæsar?

**Cato:** Pompey loves his country.

**Cæsar:** That Would I dispute with him.

## SCENE III.

**Cicero:** [Entering with precipitation, the senators rise.] Why waste ye thus in idle altercation, The precious time when Rome is on the brink Of ruin, whilst on you she calls for succor, When the dread signal is already given? Already is this land of freedom stained With senatorial blood.

**Lucullus:** O heavens!

**Cato:** What sayest thou?

**Cicero:** The equestrian cohort, formed by my command, Were posted where they best might quell the foe; Nonnius, my friend, that generous old man, Who, amidst the crimes of this degenerate age, Still uncorrupted, from Præneste came, To guide us through this labyrinth of treason, And lead our wandering steps to peace and safety, When lo! two bloody ruffians rushed upon him, And plunged their daggers in his faithful heart: He fell: confusion followed, and wild uproar Amongst the people: we pursued the traitors, Spite of the multitude that thronged around them, And night's dark shade to favor their escape: One I have seized, and bound in chains; already He has confessed that Catiline set him on.

### SCENE IV.

**Catiline**: [Standing up between Cato and Cæsar, Cethegus next to Cæsar, the Senate seated.] Yes, reverend fathers, know, the deed was mine; I slew your foes; 'twas Catiline who revenged His injured country, and destroyed a traitor.

**Cicero**: Barbarian, thou?

**Cato**: And darest thou boast of it?

**Cæsar**: Remember, fathers, we've no right to punish Before we hear him.

**Cethegus**: Speak, defend thyself, And triumph o'er the malice of thy foes.

**Cicero**: Romans, where are we?

**Catiline**: Amidst evil days And evil men, the horrors of foul discord And civil war; amidst determined foes, Whom I alone must conquer; Sulla's spirit Inspires once more the haughty sons of Rome: With grief I see expiring liberty, With grief behold this reverend senate torn By discord, horrors spread on every side, And Cicero pouring in the senate's ear Unjust suspicions: Cicero talks for Rome, But I avenge her: I have shown her cause Is dearer far to me than e'er it was To your proud consul. Nonnius was the soul, The leader of this foul conspiracy: It was a dangerous crisis; I stepped forth And saved you all: thus by a soldier fell The daring Spurius; thus was Gracchus slain By the brave Scipio: who shall punish me For acting like a Roman? which of you Will dare accuse me?

**Cicero**: I, who know thy crime; I, who can prove it—bring those freedmen here, Let them be heard. Fathers, behold the man Who has destroyed a senator of Rome: Will ye permit him thus to speak, to boast Of his foul deed, and call his crime a virtue?

**Catiline**: And will ye, Romans, let this vile accuser Thus persecute your fellow-citizens, Your best, your noblest friends? but know from me What Cicero could not tell you, and improve The important secret to your best advantage: In his own palace, know, this impious man, This vile betrayer, Nonnius, had concealed Arms, torches, all the instruments of death Designed for our destruction: if Rome lives, She lives by me, and to this arm you owe Your safety:

send and seize them, and then say What's due to Catiline from his thankless country.

**Cicero:** [To the lictors.] Go you to the palace, bring with you the daughter Of Nonnius—ha! thou tremblest.

**Catiline:** I? 'tis false: Know, I despise this mean, this last resource Of disappointed malice—fathers, say, Have I not cleared myself? are you convinced!

**Cicero:** I am, that thou art guilty: can ye think That good old man was ever capable Of such detested fraud? it was thy art, Thy cunning, miscreant, to conceal from me Thy treachery; therefore didst thou choose the palace Of Nonnius to secrete thy instruments Of vengeance; there thou wouldst have hid thy guilt: Perhaps thou hast seduced his wretched daughter: Alas! his family is not the first Where thou hast carried sorrows, crimes, and death; And now thou wouldst destroy thy country too; Yet boldly darest, instead of punishment, To call for approbation and reward. O thou abandoned traitor, murderer, Reviler, hypocrite; such titles suit Thy boasted services. O you, who once Stood forth the happy patrons of mankind, The sovereign judges of the world, at length Will you submit, to let a tyrant hold Dominion o'er you, will you shut your eyes And rush into the precipice? awake, Revenge yourselves, or you partake his guilt: This day or Rome or Catiline must perish: Lose not a moment therefore, but determine:

**Caesar:** Judgments too quickly made are oft unjust: This is the cause of Rome, and therefore merits Our strict attention: when our equals lag Beneath the stroke of censure, we should act With caution, and in them respect ourselves: Too much severity suits none but tyrants.

**Cato:** Too much indulgence here suits none but traitors. What! balance 'twixt a murderer and Rome! Is it not Cicero speaks, and shall we doubt?

**Caesar:** These are suspicions only; give us proof: The arms once found, and Nonnius' guilt confirmed, Catiline deserves our praise. [Turning to Catiline.] Thou knowest I'll keep My word with thee in all things.

**Cicero:** O my country! O Rome! O gods! thus shall a hero plead A traitor's cause; art thou the senate's friend, And canst be Catiline's? henceforth Rome has naught To fear but from her own ungrateful sons.

**Clodius:** Rome is in safety; Caesar loves his country, And we should think with him.

**Cicero:** It well becomes A man like Clodius to unite with those Who plan destruction, and delight in ruin: But wheresoe'er I turn my eyes, they meet With bold conspirators, or citizens Cold and inactive in the cause of Rome: Catiline, without or fear or danger, drives The storm upon us; he proscribes the senate;

Already reaps in thought the bloody harvest; Marks out his victims, threatens, and commands; And when I point out the dread consequence, Then Cæsar talks of senatorial rights, And Clodius joins him: Cicero must be dumb: Catiline has murdered Nonnius; he who takes Another's life should lose his own; no rights, No laws should plead for him: the first great care Is to defend our country; but, alas! That country is no more.

### SCENE V.
The Senate, Aurelia.

**Aurelia:** Ye great avengers Of innocence oppressed, my only hope, And thou, O consul, virtue's kind protector, To thee my murdered father calls for vengeance: O let me wash thy feet with tears—assist, [She falls at Cicero's feet; he raises her up.] Avenge me: tell me, if thou canst, who slew My father.

**Cicero:** There he stands. [Pointing to Catiline.]

**Aurelia:** O gods!

**Cicero:** 'Twas he Who did the deed, and boasts of it.

**Aurelia:** Good heaven! Can it be Catiline? did I hear aright? O bloody monster, didst thou murder him? [The Lictors support her.]

**Catiline:** [Turning to Cethegus, and fainting in his arms.] This is a dreadful sight—support me—this Is punishment enough.

**Cethegus:** Why droops my friend? Aurelia calls for vengeance: but if Catiline Has served his country, what has he to fear?

**Catiline:** [Turning to Aurelia.] Aurelia, 'tis too true—my cruel duty— My country—think me not so base; Aurelia Thou knowest my love, my tenderness—but ties Of a more sacred nature, ties—

### SCENE VI.
The Senate, Aurelia, Chief of the Lictors.

**Chief Lictor:** My lord, We've seized these arms.

**Cicero:** At Nonnius's?

**Chief Lictor:** His house Was the receptacle of all: our prisoners Accuse him as the chief conspirator.

**Aurelia:** Malice and calumny! the lying slaves First take his life, and then destroy his fame: The wretch whose murderous hand—

**Cicero:** Go on—

**Aurelia:** Just gods. For what have ye reserved me?

**Cicero**: Speak: let truth In open day appear: but at the sight Of him you tremble; your dejected eyes, And sudden silence, show how much you dread The tyrant.

**Aurelia**: I have been to blame; Aurelia Alone is guilty.

**Catiline**: No; thou art not.

**Aurelia**: Hence, Detested monster, I abhor thy pity, Disclaim all converse, all relation with thee: Alas! too late, I see my guilt; too late Confess my crimes; yes, reverend fathers; yes, Aurelia knew the traitor, and concealed him: I asked for aid, but merit punishment; My weakness may be fatal; Rome's in danger; The world this day may be subverted: thou, Thou traitor, ledst me to the dark abyss Of infamy; thou madest my tenderness Subservient to thy wicked purposes; Curse on the guilty hour that gave my heart To Catiline; to thee I have been faithful, But false to heaven, and to my country; false To my unhappy father: I betrayed, And I destroyed him. [Whilst Aurelia is speaking, Cicero seems deeply affected.] Ye avenging gods, Ye sacred walls, and thou much injured spirit Of my dear father, Romans, senators, Behold my husband, your inveterate foe. [Turning to Catiline.] Now, miscreant, mark, and imitate Aurelia. [Stabs herself.]

**Catiline**: O wretched Catiline!

**Cato**: O dreadful day!

**Cicero**: [Rising.] 'Tis worthy of this guilty age.

**Aurelia**: O consul! There was a letter sent you—murder threatens On every side—take heed—alas!—I die. [Aurelia is carried off.]

**Cicero**: Let her have needful succor: Aufidus, Search for that paper—still are ye in doubt; Still will ye suffer this vile murderer To lord it o'er the senate, shall the deaths Of Nonnius and Aurelia pass unpunished?

**Catiline**: The guilt was thine: thy rancor and fell hatred Of Catiline urged him to the deed; ambition Inspired us both; thy happier fortune soared Above me, thou hast been the cause of all: I hate thee, Cicero, hate Rome itself For loving thee: long have I sought thy ruin, And I will seek it still: the wrongs I suffer Shall be revenged on thee; thy blood shall pay For mine; inconstant Rome, that now adores thee, Shall one day see with joy the mangled limbs Of her proud consul scattered o'er the senate: Remember Catiline has foretold thy fate; I hasten to accomplish it: farewell.

**Cicero**: Guards, seize the traitor.

**Cethegus**: Let them if they dare.

**lentulus-Sura**: The senate is divided: we defy thee.

**Catiline:** The war then is declared: friends, follow me, We must to battle: the uncertain senate Will think on't, and determine at their leisure. [He goes out with some senators of his party.]

**Cicero:** Now, ye illustrious conquerors of the world, Which will ye choose, or slavery or empire: Where is the freedom, where the majesty Of ancient Rome? where is her lustre now? 'Tis faded all: awake, my slumbering country; Lucullus, Cæsar, and Murena, listen; O listen to the voice of Rome; she calls Aloud for help, demands some gallant leader To fight for her; equality of rank Must be reserved for happier times, the Gauls Are here, Camillus must be found, we want A chief, a warrior, a dictator; now Name the most worthy, and I'll follow him.

### SCENE VII.

The Senate, Chief Lictor.

**Chief Lictor:** My lord, I found this letter to Aurelia From Nonnius: all our cares for her were vain.

**Cicero:** [Reading the letter.] More dangers threatening! "Cæsar, who betrays us, Would seize Præneste," ha! [Turning to Cæsar.] Art thou too, Cæsar, A vile accomplice? this completes our woes; And wilt thou bend beneath a tyrant?—read it.

**Cæsar:** I have: I am a Roman, ruin comes Upon us, danger is on every side; 'Tis well: I must be gone: you have my answer.

**Cato:** It was a doubtful one: most certainly He is their friend.

**Cicero:** Away: let us defend The state against them all: O Senators! If Nonnius' death, if poor Aurelia's pangs, If bleeding Rome, if a subverted world Have power to stir up your resentment, rise, Fly to the capitol, defend your gods, Defend your country, punish Catiline. I'll not reproach you; though 'twas most unkind, To spurn at Cicero, and embrace a villain. But to avoid a tyrant, name your chief: You, who are friends to virtue, separate From traitors. [The Senators separate themselves from Cethegus and Lentulus-Sura.] Now let us unite, my friends, Never let quarrels, jealousies, and strife, Divide us; 'twas by them that Sulla triumphed. For me, wherever danger calls, I go Intrepid and inflexible: O gods! Strengthen this arm, and animate this voice: O grant me still to save ungrateful Rome!

# ACT V.

### SCENE I.
Cato, with Part of the Senate in Arms.

**Clodius:** [To Cato.] What! whilst the senate armed for its own safety From busy faction's power can scarce preserve These sacred walls; thus shall a proud plebeian Insult us? shall a people, born to freedom, Be treated like dependent slaves? by him, Shall Rome's best friends, the conquerors of the world, Be put in chains? because he is a consul, Shall he condemn his masters? Catiline's self Were less despotic, and less dangerous: With you I feel my country's wretchedness, And weep her fate; but cannot, will not, see The senate thus disgraced.

**Cato:** Disgrace attends On those alone who merit it—but know, The blood of nobles, your patrician friends, Debased by guilt, should rank below the meanest; Those who betrayed us are condemned to death: Cicero condemned them; he who saved your country, The glorious consul, whom ye dare accuse, Because he loved you but too well: yet fear And tremble all, ungrateful as ye are To join with traitors, for an equal fate Shall soon o'erwhelm you; Catiline's at our gates. What Cæsar hath determined yet we know not; Whether he means to save, or to destroy His country: Cicero bravely acts alone, And hazards all for Rome, whilst you despise Your best of friends, and treat him as a foe.

**Clodius:** Cato has more severity than courage, And ever rigorous, hates not guilt so much As he loves punishment: reproach us not, Nor act the censor when we want a friend. Whilst the destructive flames of war surround, 'Tis not a consul's edict can defend us. What can your lictor and his fasces do, Against a band of fierce conspirators? You talk of dangers, and of Cæsar's power: Who does not know that Cæsar is the friend Of Catiline? you have pointed out the ills That threaten Rome; it were a nobler task To show us how we may remove them.

**Cato:** Yes; And so I will: I would advise the senate To be aware of Cæsar, and of—thee; Nay, more—but see our father comes.

### SCENE II.
Cicero, Cato, Part of the Senate.

**Cato:** [To Cicero.] Behold Great Cicero, the sons of thankless Rome: Approach and save us; envy's self shall soon Fall at thy feet, in humble admiration Of such transcendent virtue.

**Cicero:** Friends and Romans, The love of glory is my ruling passion, Fame is the fair reward of human toil, And I would wish to merit it from you: I have done little yet, perhaps hereafter I may do more to serve my country: Rome Was full of open and of secret foes; Patricians, and plebeians, citizens And soldiers, all in wild confusion, seemed To thirst for blood: I saw the gathering storm That threatened universal ruin; saw The bold conspirators tumultuous rise, And bear down all before them: at their head Were Sura and Cethegus; them I seized, And gave to justice; but the Hydra faction Hath many heads which still successive rise, And mock my labors: Catiline boldly pushed To the Quirinal gate; by gallant deeds, Almost incredible, he kept the field, And forced a passage to his army; Rome Beheld him with amazement; Antony In vain opposing Sulla's hardy veterans, Was baffled and subdued; Petreius strove To succor him, but with unequal force And fruitless valor: thus on every side, Surrounded by calamities, great Rome, The mistress of the world, is on the brink Of ruin; Cicero trembles for her fate.

**Crassus:** What part hath Cæsar taken?

**Cicero:** He hath behaved As Cæsar must, with most undaunted courage, Yet not as Rome could wish a zealous friend Would act in her defence. I saw him quell The rebel foe; yet after that, stir up Seditious spirits, and by every art Of smooth insinuation, work himself Into the people's hearts. Amidst this scene Of blood, methought a secret joy o'erspread His glowing cheek, whilst his all-soothing voice Courted applause, inviting Rome to be His slave hereafter.

**Cato:** I was ever fearful Of Cæsar's power; he is not to be trusted.

### SCENE III.

The Senate, Cæsar.

**Cæsar:** Well: am I still suspected in the senate? Is Cato's stubborn virtue still my foe? Of what does he accuse me?

**Cato:** As a friend To Catiline, the sworn enemy of Rome; You have protected him, and leagued with those It had become you better to chastise.

**Cæsar:** I would not stain my laurels with the blood Of such vile miscreants: Cæsar fights with none But warriors.

**Cato:** What are these conspirators?

**Cæsar:** A dastard crowd, contemptible and vile: They fled like slaves before me; but the soldiers Of Sulla are a formidable band, And boast an able chief; from them indeed Rome hath some cause to fear; Petreius sinks Beneath his wounds, and Catiline marches onward; Our soldiers are alarmed: what says our consul? And what has he resolved?

**Cicero**: I'll tell thee, Cæsar: Grant, heaven, we may succeed!—thou hast deserved Suspicion, but I'll give thee the fair means To clear thy honor, and avenge thy country. I know thee well, thy virtues and thy frailty; Know what thou canst, and what thou darest not do; Know Cæsar would command, but not betray, A noble friend, and a most dangerous foe: Whilst I condemn I cannot but esteem thee. Away: remember that the eyes of Rome, And of the world, are on thee: go, support Petreius, save the empire, and deserve The love of Cato: we have men, but want A general to conduct them; Cæsar best Can lead them, and to him alone we trust The safety and the glory of mankind.

**Cæsar**: Cicero on Cæsar safely may depend; Farewell: I go to conquer or to die. [Exit.]

**Cato**: You've touched him in the tenderest part; ambition Will urge him on.

**Cicero**: Great souls must ever thus Be treated: I have bound him to the state By this firm confidence; I know his valor Will now support us: the ambitious still Should be distinguished from the traitor; I Shall make him virtuous if he is not so Already. Courage, as directed, forms The mighty hero, or the mighty villain; And he who is renowned for guilt alone, Had glory fired his breast, to him had been The incense poured, to him the temple raised For his exalted merit: Catiline's self, By me conducted, had like Scipio shone: Though many a Sulla is in Cæsar hid, Yet doubt I not but Rome shall find in him Her best support. [Turning to the chief of the Lictors, who enters armed.] Well: these conspirators, What have they done?

**Chief Lictor**: My lord, they met the fate They merited, but other foes rise up, Sprung from their blood; like Ætna's flames, that burst From the parched entrails of the burning mount: Another Hannibal, but far more dreadful, Because amongst the guilty sons of Rome He finds his traitorous friends, is at our gates. A hundred voices roar for Catiline, Condemn your laws, and curse your tardy senate; Demand their ancient rights, and cry aloud For vengeance on the consul.

**Clodius**: Well indeed They may, while Cicero tramples on the laws, And spurns his equals thus; perhaps the senate—

**Cicero**: Clodius, no more; restrain thy envious tongue, Nor rashly blame the guiltless; my short power Will soon be wrested from me; whilst it lasts It shall not be controlled; you will have time Enough to vex and persecute hereafter; But whilst the state's in danger, Cicero claims The tribute of respect: I know too well This fickle world to hope for constancy And candor from it; foul ingratitude Is all that I expect; on false surmises Great Scipio was accused; he thanked the gods, And quitted Rome: I too will pay my vows To gracious heaven, but will not leave you; no; My days are all devoted to my country, And all shall be expended in her service.

**Cato:** Suppose I were to show myself in Rome, Perhaps my presence might disperse the crowd, And be a check on Cæsar, whom I own I much suspect: if fortune frowns upon us—

**Cicero:** We cannot do without you in the senate; I've given my orders; Cæsar's in the field; Thy great example may be useful here, And Rome's expiring glory be restored By Cato's virtue—but behold he comes, And crowned with victory. [Cæsar enters; Cicero embraces him.] Most noble Cæsar, Hast thou preserved the state?—

**Cæsar:** I hope so: now The consul will believe me—brave Petreius Has gained immortal glory: here we fought, Beneath this sacred rampart, in the sight Of our domestic gods that fired each soul With nobler rage: Metellus, and Murena, With the brave Scipios showed in Rome's defence The same exalted courage that subdued Asia and Carthage; they have merited Most nobly of their country: touching Cæsar Let others speak: the desperate remains Of Sulla's army seemed to brave their fate, And in the agonies of death breathed forth Their curses on us: midst the general slaughter, The fiery Catiline long undaunted stood, Fought through a host of circling foes, till spent With ceaseless toil, and covered o'er with wounds, Bravely he fell: I must admire the soldier, Though I detest the rebel: once I loved him, I own it; but let Cicero judge, if ever To friendship Cæsar sacrificed his honor.

**Cicero:** Cæsar is all that Cicero could desire, All that he wished, and all he hoped to find him: Go on, brave youth, preserve thy noble spirit, And be thy country's friend; may heaven protect And guard thee: never may thy generous soul Be stained with vice, nor false ambition urge Thy spotless youth to quit the paths of virtue!

**End**

# Sémiramis

## Contents

Dramatis Personæ . . . . . . . . . . . . . . . . . . . . . . . . . . . . . . . . . . 151

Act I. . . . . . . . . . . . . . . . . . . . . . . . . . . . . . . . . . . . . . . . . . . . . 151

Act II. . . . . . . . . . . . . . . . . . . . . . . . . . . . . . . . . . . . . . . . . . . . 159

Act III. . . . . . . . . . . . . . . . . . . . . . . . . . . . . . . . . . . . . . . . . . . 166

Act IV. . . . . . . . . . . . . . . . . . . . . . . . . . . . . . . . . . . . . . . . . . 173

Act V. . . . . . . . . . . . . . . . . . . . . . . . . . . . . . . . . . . . . . . . . . . 180

## Dramatis Personæ

Sémiramis.
Arsaces, or Ninias.
Azema, a Princess of the Family of Belus.
Assur, a Prince of the Family of Belus.
Oroes, High Priest.
Otanes, a Favorite of Semiramis.
Mitranes, Friend of Arsaces.
Cedar, Friend of Assur. Guards, Magi, Slaves, Attendants.
This was produced in 1748 and a burlesque upon it was played at Fontainebleau.

## ACT I.

The scene represents a large peristyle, at the bottom of which is the palace of Sémiramis. Gardens with fine hanging terraces, raised above the palace: on the right hand the temple of the magi, and on the left a mausoleum adorned with obelisks.

SCENE I.
Arsaces, Mitranes.
[Two slaves at a distance carrying a coffer.]

**Arsaces**: Once more, Mitranes, thou beholdest thy friend, Who, in obedience to the royal mandate In secret sent, revisits Babylon, The seat of empire; how Sémiramis Imprints the image of her own great soul On every object! these stupendous piles, These deep enclosures, where Euphrates pours His tributary waves; the temple's pride, The hanging gardens, and the splendid tomb Of Ninus, wondrous monuments of art! And only less to be admired than she Who raised them! here, in all her splendid pomp, More honored than the monarchs of the East, Arsaces shall behold this glorious queen.

**Mitranes**: O my Arsaces, credit not the voice Of Fame, she is deceitful oft, and vain; Perhaps hereafter thou mayest weep with me, And admiration on a nearer view May turn to pity.

**Arsaces**: Wherefore?

**Mitranes**: Sunk in grief, Sémiramis hath spread o'er every heart The sorrows which she feels; sometimes she raves, Filling the air with her distressful cries, As if some vengeful God pursued her; sits Silent and sad within these lonely vaults, Sacred to night, to sorrow, and to death, Which mortals dare not enter; where the ashes Of Ninus, our late honored sovereign, lie: There will she oft fall on her knees and weep: With slow and fearful steps she glides along, And beats her breast besprinkled with her tears: Oft as she treads her solitary round, Will she repeat the names of son and husband, And call on heaven, which in its anger seems To thwart her in the zenith of her glory.

**Arsaces**: Whence can her sorrow flow?

**Mitranes**: The effect is dreadful: The cause unknown.

**Arsaces**: How long hath she been thus Oppressed, Mitranes?

**Mitranes**: From the very time When first her orders came to bring **Arsaces**: Arsaces: Me, saidst thou?

**Mitranes**: You, my lord: when Babylon Rejoicing met to celebrate thy conquests, And saw the banners thy victorious arm Had wrested from our vanquished foes; when first Euphrates brought to our delighted shore The lovely Azema, from Belus sprung, Whom thou hadst saved from Scythian ravishers, Even in that hour of triumph and success, Even in the bosom of prosperity, The heart of majesty was pierced with grief, And the throne lost its lustre.

**Arsaces**: Azema Was not to blame; she could not be the cause Of sorrow or distress; one look from her Would soothe the wrath of gods: but say, my friend, Sémiramis is still a sovereign here, Her heart is not forever sunk in grief?

**Mitranes**: No: when her noble mind shakes off the burden, Resumes its strength, and shines in native lustre, Then we behold in her exalted soul Powers that excel whatever flattery's self Hath e'er bestowed on kings; but when she sinks Beneath this dreadful malady, loose flow The reins of empire, dropping from her hand; Then the proud satrap, fiery Assur, guides The helm and makes the nations groan beneath him: The fatal secret never yet hath reached The walls of Babylon: abroad we still Are envied, but, alas! we mourn at home.

**Arsaces**: What lessons of instruction to weak mortals, When happiness is mingled thus with woe! I, too, am wretched, thus deprived of him Whose piercing wisdom best could give me council, And lead me through the mazes of a court. O I have cause to weep: without a father, Left as I am to all the dangerous passions Of heedless youth, without a friendly guide, What rocks encompass and what shoals affright me!

**Mitranes**: I weep with thee the loss of him we loved, The good old man; Phradates was my friend; Ninus esteemed and gave to him the care Of Ninias, his dear son, our country's hope: But O! one fatal day destroyed them both, Father and son: to voluntary exile Devoted, long he lived: his banishment Was fortunate to thee, and made thee great: Close by his side, in honor's glorious field, Arsaces fought, and conquered for his country: Now, ranked with princes, thy exalted virtue Claims its reward by merit all thy own.

**Arsaces**: I know not what may be my portion here: Perhaps, distinguished on Arbazan's plains With fair success, my name is not unknown: On Oxus' banks to great Sémiramis, When vanquished nations paid the homage due, From her triumphant cars she dropped a ray Of her own glory on Arsaces' head: But oft the soldier, honored in the field, In courts neglected lies, and is forgotten. My father told me in his dying hour The fortune of Arsaces here depended Upon the common cause; then gave to me These precious relics, which from every eye He had preserved: I must deliver them To the high priest, for he alone can judge, And know their value: I must talk with him In secret, touching my own fate, for he Can best conduct me to Sémiramis.

**Mitranes**: He seldom sees the queen: in solitude Obscure he lives: his holy ministry Engrosses all his care; without ambition, Fearless, and void of art: is always seen Within the temple, never at the court: Never affects the pride of rank and title, Nor his tiara near the diadem Immodest wears: the less he seeks for greatness, The more is he admired, the more revered: I have access to every avenue Of his retirement in this sacred place, And can this moment talk to him in secret; Ere day's too far advanced I'll bring him hither.

## SCENE II.

**Arsaces**: [Alone.] Immortal gods! for what am I reserved? Make known your will: why did my dying father Thus send me to the sanctuary, me A soldier, bred amidst the din of arms? A lover, too? How can Arsaces serve The gods of the Chaldæans?—Ha! what voice From yonder tomb in plaintive accents strikes My frighted ear, and makes my hair to stand On end with horror! Near this place I've heard The spirit of Ninus dwells—again it shrieks— It shocks my soul—Ye dark and dreary caves, And thou, the shade of my illustrious master, Thou voice of heaven, what wouldst thou with Arsaces?

### SCENE III.

Arsaces, Oroes, the High Priest, the Magi Attending Him, Mitranes.

**Mitranes**: [Speaking to Oroes.] He's here, my lord, and waits to give you up Those precious relics.

**Arsaces**: Most revered father, Permit a soldier to approach your presence, Pleased to fulfil a father's last command, One whom you deigned to love; thus at your feet, Obedient to his will, I here resign them.

**Oroes**: Welcome! thou brave and noble youth! that God Who governs all, and not a father's will, Guided thee here: Phradates was my friend; Dear is his memory to me; thou shalt know Perhaps hereafter how I love his son: Where are the gifts he sent me?

**Arsaces**: [The slaves deliver the coffer to two of the magi, who place it on an altar.]

Here, my lord.

**Oroes**: [Opening the coffer, bowing reverentially to it, and seeming greatly affected.]

Ye sacred relics! do these eyes at length Behold you! O, I weep for joy to press These monuments of woe, whilst tears recall My solemn oath: Mitranes, let no ear Profane disturb our holy mystery: We would be private. [The magi retire.] Mark this seal, Arsaces: 'Tis that which to the laws of Ninus gave Their public force, and kept the world in awe: The letter, too, which with his dying hand He wrote: Arsaces, view the wreath that crowned His royal brows, and his victorious sword: The vanquished Medes and Persians felt its power: It comes at last to vindicate its master, And to revenge him; useless instrument Against base treachery, and destructive poison, Whose mortal—

**Arsaces**: Heaven! what sayest thou?

**Oroes**: The dread secret Hath long been hid in darkness from the eyes Of men within the sepulchre; the shade Of Ninus, and offended heaven, long time Have raised their voice in vain, and called for vengeance.

**Arsaces**: It must be as thou sayest: for know, but now, Even on this spot, I heard most dreadful groans.

**Oroes**: It was the voice of Ninus.

**Arsaces**: Twice the noise Affrighted me.

**Oroes**: 'Twas he: he calls for vengeance.

**Arsaces**: He has a right to ask it: but on whom?

**Oroes**: On the vile murderers, whose detested hands Had of the best of sovereigns robbed mankind; No tracks are left behind of the base treason, But all with him lies buried in the tomb: With ease might they deceive the sons of men, But not the all-seeing eye of watchful heaven, Which pierces the deep night of human falsehood.

**Arsaces**: O would to heaven this feeble hand had power To punish crimes like these! I know not wherefore, But when I cast my eyes towards you tomb, New horrors rise: O might I not consult That venerable shade, the inhabitant Of those dark mansions?

**Oroes**: No; it is forbidden: An oracle severe long since denounced The wrath of heaven against whoe'er should press Into this vale of tears, inhabited By death and the avenging gods: await With me, Arsaces, for the day of justice: Soon will it come, and all shall be accomplished: I can no more: sequestered from the world, I pray in secret to offended heaven, Which, as it wills, commissions me to speak, Or close my lips in silence: I have said All that I dare, and all I ought: be careful Lest in these walls a word, or look, or gesture, Betray the secret which the god by me Hath trusted with thee; for on that depends His glory, Asia's welfare, and thy life. Approach, ye magi, hide these sacred relics Beneath the altar. [The great gate of the palace opens, Assur appears at a distance, surrounded by attendants and guards on every side.] Ha! the palace opens: The courtiers crowding to the queen: behold The haughty Assur with his servile throng Of flatterers round him! O almighty power! On whom dost thou bestow thy bounties here? O monster!

**Arsaces**: Ha! what meanest thou?

**Oroes**: Fare thee well: When night shall cast her sable mantle o'er These guilty walls, I'll have more converse with thee, Before the gods: revere them, my Arsaces, For know, brave youth, their eyes are fixed on thee.

SCENE IV.

Arsaces, Mitranes, in the front of the stage, Assur, Cedar, with attendants, on one side.

**Arsaces**: His words are dreadful; they affright my soul: What horrid crimes! and what a court is here! How little known! my royal master poisoned, And Assur, but too well I see, suspected!

**Mitranes:** Assur is sprung of royal race, and claims The deference due to his authority: He is the favorite of Sémiramis, And thou, without a blush, mayest pay him homage.

**Arsaces:** Homage to him!

**Assur:** [To Cedar.] Ha! do my eyes deceive me, Or is Arsaces here without my order? Amazing insolence!

**Arsaces:** What haughtiness!

**Assur:** [Advancing.] Come hither, youth: what new engagements here Have brought you from the camp?

**Arsaces:** My duty, sir, And the queen's orders.

**Assur:** Did the queen send for you?

**Arsaces:** She did.

**Assur:** But, know you not, with her commands You should have asked for mine?

**Arsaces:** I know not that, And should have thought the honor of her crown Debased by such a mean submission to thee: My lord, you must forgive a soldier's roughness, We are bad courtiers: bred up in the plains Of Arbazan and Scythia, I have served Your court, but am not much acquainted with it.

**Assur:** Age, time, and place, perhaps, may teach you, sir. What would you with the queen? for know, young man, Assur alone can lead you to her presence.

**Arsaces:** I come to ask my valor's best reward, The honor still to serve her.

**Assur:** Thou wantest more, Presumptuous boy! I know thy bold pretences To Azema, but that thou wouldst conceal.

**Arsaces:** Yes: I adore that lovely maid: her heart Would I prefer to empire: my respect, My tenderest love—

**Assur:** No more: thou knowest not whom Thou art insulting thus: what! join the race Of a Sarmatian to the demigods Of Tigris and Euphrates! mark me well: In pity to thy youth I would advise thee Ne'er, on thy peril, to Sémiramis Impart thy insolent request; for know, Rash boy, if thou shouldst dare to violate The rights of Assur, 'twill not pass unpunished.

**Arsaces:** I'll go this instant: thou hast given me courage: Thus threatenings always terrify Arsaces: Thou hast no right, whate'er thy power may be, To affront a soldier who has served his queen, The state, and thee: perhaps my warmth offends; But thou art rasher than myself, to think That I would bend beneath thy servile yoke, Or tremble at thy power.

**Assur:** Perhaps thou mayest; I'll teach thee what a subject may expect For insolence like this.

**Arsaces:** We both may learn it.

## SCENE V.

Sémiramis, at the farther end of the stage, leaning on her women.
Otanes, Assur, Arsaces, Mitranes, in the Front.

**Otanes:** [Advancing.] My lord, the queen at present would be private: You must retire, and give her sorrows way: Withdraw, ye gods, the hand of vengeance from her!

**Arsaces:** How I lament her fate!

**Assur:** [To one of his attendants.] Let us begone, And study how we best may turn her griefs To our advantage. [Sémiramis comes forward, and is joined by **Otanes:** Otanes: My royal mistress, be yourself again, And wake once more to joy and happiness.]

**Sémiramis:** O death! when wilt thou come with friendly shade To close these eyes that hate the light of day? Be shut, ye caves; horrible phantom, hence! Strike if thou wilt, but threaten me no more. Otanes, is Arsaces come?

**Otanes:** Ere morn Rose on the temple, madam, he was there.

**Sémiramis:** That dreadful voice, from heaven or hell I know not, Which in the dead of night so shakes my soul, Told me, my sorrows, when Arsaces came, Would soon be o'er.

**Otanes:** Rely then on the gods, And let the cheerful ray of hope dispel This melancholy.

**Sémiramis:** Is Arsaces here? Methinks, when I but hear his name, my soul Is less disturbed, and guilt sits lighter on me!

**Otanes:** O! quit, forever quit the sad remembrance: Let the bright days of great Sémiramis, Replete with glory, blot one moment out That broke the chain of thy ill-fated nuptials: Had Ninus driven thee from his throne and bed, All Babylon with thee had been destroyed; But happily for us, and for mankind, That wanted such distinguished virtues, you Prevented him; and fifteen years of toil, Spent in the service of thy country, lands Desert and waste made fertile by thy care, The savage tamed, and yielding to the laws, The useful arts, obedient to thy voice, Uprising still, the glorious monuments Of wealth and power, the wonder of mankind, And the loud plaudit of a grateful people, All plead thy cause before the throne of heaven; But if impartial justice hold the scale, If vengeance is required for Ninus' death, Why thus should Assur brave the angry gods, And live in peace? He was more guilty far Than thou wert, yet the ruthless hand that poured The fatal draught never shakes with fear: he feels No stings of conscience, no remorse affrights him.

**Sémiramis**: Our duties different, different is our fate: Where ties are sacred, crimes are heavier far: I was his wife, Otanes, and I stand Without excuse; my conscience is my judge And my accuser: but I hoped the gods, Offended at my crimes, had punished me Enough, when they deprived me of my child; Hoped my successful toils, that made the earth Respect my name, had soothed the wrath of heaven: But months on months have passed in agony Since this dire spectre hath appalled my soul: My eyes forever see him, and my ears Still hear his cries: I get me to the tomb, But dare not enter: trembling I revere His ashes, and invoke his honored shade, Which only answers me in dismal groans. Some dread event is nigh: perhaps the time Is come to expiate the offence.

**Otanes**: But thinkest thou The spirit of thy lord hath left indeed The mansions of the dead, and stalks abroad? Ofttimes the soul, by powerful fancy led, Starts at a phantom of its own creation; Still it beholds the objects it has made, And everything we fear is present to us.

**Sémiramis**: O no! it was not the wild dream of fancy By slumber wrought, I saw him but too well: The stranger, Sleep, had long withheld from me His sweet delusions; watchful as I stood, And mused on my unhappy fate, a voice Close to my bed, methought, cried out, "Arsaces!" The name revived me: well thou knowest, long time Assur has pierced this heart with deadly grief: I shudder at his presence, and the blushes That show my guilt increase my punishment, Hate the reproachful witness of my shame, And wish I could—but wherefore should I add To crimes like mine fresh guilt? I sought Arsaces To punish Assur, and the thought of him Awhile relieved me! but in the sweet moment Of consolation, sudden stood before me That minister of death, all bathed in blood, And in his hand a falchion: still I see, Still hear him: comes he to defend, or punish? 'Twas at that very hour Arsaces came. This day was fixed by heaven to end my sorrows, But peace is yet a stranger to my soul, And hope is lost in horror and despair: The load of life is grown too heavy for me, My throne is hateful, and my glories past But add fresh weight to my calamities. Long time I've hid my sorrows from the world And blushed in secret, fearful to consult That reverend sage whom Babylon adores: I would not thus degrade the majesty Of sovereign power, or let Sémiramis Betray her fears before a mortal's eye, But I have sent to Libya's sands in secret There to consult the oracle of Jove: As if removed from man, the God of truth Had hid in desert plains his will divine. Alas! Otanes, that dread power which dwells Within these lonely walls, hath long received My fears and adorations; at his altars My gifts were offered, and my incense rose; But gifts and incense never can atone For crimes like mine: to-day I shall receive Answers from Memphis.

### SCENE VI.
Sémiramis, Otanes, Mitranes.

**Mitranes:** An Egyptian priest Is at the palace gate, and begs admittance.

**Sémiramis:** Then will my woes be ended, or complete. Let us begone, and hide from Babylon Her queen's disgraceful sorrows: let Arsaces Be sent to me: soon may his presence calm This storm of grief, and soothe my troubled soul!

# ACT II.

### SCENE I.
Arsaces, Azema

**Azema:** To thee, Arsaces, this great empire owes Its lustre, I my liberty and life. When vanquished Scythia, thirsting for revenge, From its wild desert rushed indignant forth, And bore down all before it; when my father, Oppressed by numbers, fell, and left me there A hapless slave; then, armed with thunder, thou, Piercing their dark retreats, didst break my chains, And give me ample vengeance on my foes. Thou wert my great deliverer, Arsaces, And in return I give thee all my heart; I will be thine, and only thine; but O! Our fatal passion will destroy us both: Thy generous heart, too open and sincere, Believed that gallant deeds, and fair renown In arms, would gain thee honors in a court; And, fearless of success, thou bringest with thee A hero's fierceness and a lover's heart. Assur is incensed: alas! thou dost not know him: He is too powerful for us; he rules all At Babylon; and much, I fear, abuses His fatal influence o'er Sémiramis: He is thy great inexorable–rival.

**Arsaces:** Ha! does he love thee?

**Azema:** No; that savage mind, Subtle and dark, a foe to every virtue, Insensible to love and every charm But those ambition boasts, could never feel A real passion for me: but he knows That Azema is descended from the race Of our Assyrian kings, and soon may claim My right of empire here, as next the throne; And therefore means to blend his interest here With mine, and gain the sceptre for himself: But if the youth whom Ninus had decreed, Even from my infant years, to be my husband, The son of great Sémiramis, and heir Of Babylon, were living now, and here Would offer me his heart and half his empire, By love I swear, and by thy precious self, Ninias should sue in vain, and see me quit A throne with him for banishment with thee. Even Scythia's bleak inhospitable plains Would yield a sweet asylum to our love; For they would echo my Arsaces' name, And sound his praise; those barren wilds, where first Our passion grew, would be to me a court, Nor should I cast a thought on Babylon. But much I fear this subtle statesman means To carry his resentment further still: I've searched his soul, and know the blackness of it: Or I mistake, or guilt sits lightly on him; Already he is jealous of thy glory, He fears, and hates thee.

**Arsaces**: And I hate him more, But fear him not, since Azema is mine: Keep thou thy faith, and I despise his anger. At least I share with him the royal favor: I saw the queen, and her humanity Equalled the pride of Assur: when I fell Prostrate before her, gently she upraised me, And called me the support of Babylon: With pride I heard the flattering voice of her Whose name contending kings unite to honor: The distance 'twixt her royal state and mine Was lessened soon by mildest condescension; It touched, it melted me; and, after thee, To me she seemed, of all the human race, Most nearly to resemble the divine.

**Azema**: If she protects us, Assur's threats are vain: I heed them not.

**Arsaces**: Inspired by thee, I went, Fearless and brave, to lay before the feet Of my great mistress, that aspiring passion Which Assur dreads, and Azema approves; When lo, that very moment came a priest From Egypt with Ammonian Jove's decree: Trembling she opened quick the awful scroll, First fixed her eyes on me, then sudden turned Her face aside, and wept: stood fixed in grief Like one distraught, then sighed, and vanished from me. They tell me, she is fallen into despair, And hath of late been dreadfully pursued By some avenging god: I pity her: 'Tis wonderful that after fifteen years, Heaven, that so long defended, should at last Oppress her thus: by what hath she offended The angry gods, and wherefore are they changed?

**Azema**: We hear of naught but dreadful spectres, omens, And vengeance from above: the queen of late Lets loose the reins of empire: we had cause To fear for Babylon, least subtle Assur, Who knows her weakness, in this dangerous time, Should seize the helm, and bury all in ruin; But the queen came, and all was calm again; All owned the power of her despotic sway. If I have any knowledge of the court, The queen hates Assur, but keeps fair with him, And watches close; they're fearful of each other, Would quarrel soon, but that some secret cause, Some mutual interest, still prevents a rupture: I saw her fire indignant at his name; The blushes on her cheeks betrayed her thoughts, And her heart seemed to glow with deep resentment: But sudden changes happen in a court; Return, and speak to her.

**Arsaces**: I will; but know not Whether again I e'er shall gain admittance.

**Azema**: Thou hast my vows, my wishes, and my prayers For thy success: I glory in my love, And in my duty: let Sémiramis Rule o'er the vanquished East, I envy her Nor fame nor conquest; let the world be hers, Arsaces mine: but Assur comes this way.

**Arsaces:** The traitor! how I shudder at his presence! My soul abhors him.

## SCENE II.
Assur, Arsaces, Azema.

**Assur:** Your reception, sir, I find, was noble, such as kings have oft Solicited in vain: you saw the queen In secret, did she not reprove a conduct Injurious to my honor and her own? Did she not tell thee Azema's designed For Assur, not for thee? Long since her hand To Ninias given was for the blood of kings Alone reserved; and therefore is my right, As next to the throne: did she acquaint you, sir, Into what fatal snares your pride would lead you, That neither fame nor honors will excuse Your bold pretensions?

**Arsaces:** I well know what's due To your high birth, and to the rank you bear, And should have paid it, though you had not thus Instructed me; but as a master here I own you not: your royal ancestors, From Belus sprung, perhaps may give you claim To Azema; the welfare of the state, Present and future, all, I own, conspire To raise your hopes of bliss, and make her yours: These are your claims, and I acknowledge them: But I have one that's worth them all: I love her: I might have added this, that I avenged And saved her, gave new lustre to the throne Which she was born to fill, if I had chosen, Like thee, to boast of my exploits before her. But I must leave thee, to perform her orders. Sémiramis and her I shall obey, And them alone: a day perhaps may come When thou shalt be our master: heaven sometimes In anger sends us kings: but thou art deceived, At least in one of thy ambitious views, If amongst thy subjects thou hast ranked **Arsaces: Assur:** The measure's full: thou courtest thy own destruction.

## SCENE III.
Assur, Azema.

**Assur:** I've borne his insolence too long already, 'Tis time we enter on a nobler subject, And worthier thy attention.

**Azema:** Can there be one? But speak.

**Assur:** Ere long all Asia shall attend On our resolves, and low concerns like these Must pass unheeded by: a world demands Our mutual care: Sémiramis is now The shadow of herself, her glory's past, That star which shone with such transcendent lustre, Declining now, sends forth a feeble ray; The people see and wonder at her fall, Whilst every tongue demands a—successor: That word sufficeth: you well know my right: 'Tis not for love to deal forth sovereign power, And point out who shall rule in Babylon; Not that my soul, to beauty blind, would make A virtue of insensibility; But I should blush for thee and for myself, To see the welfare of a nation thus Dependent on a sigh: thoughts worthier both Must guide my fortune, and determine thine: Our ancestors the same, we should offend Their venerable shades, and lose the world By not uniting: I astonish you: These are harsh words for tender age like thine; But I address me to the kings and heroes From whom you sprung, to all those demigods Whom here you represent: too long trod down Beneath a woman's feet their ashes lay, Their glories she eclipsed, usurped their power, And fettered vanquished nations with her laws; But she is gone, and thou must now support The building she had raised: she had thy beauty, And thou must have her courage: let not love Or folly wrest the sceptre from thy hand, But grasp it close: you will not sacrifice To a Sarmatian's idle passion for you The name you ought to honor, and the throne You should ascend, of universal empire.

**Azema**: Let not Arsaces be the theme, my lord, Of your reproaches, but depend on me To vindicate the honor of my race, And to defend, whene'er occasion calls, The rights of my loved ancestors; I know Their worth and virtues, but I know not one Amongst the heroes which Assyria boasts More great, more virtuous, more beloved, than he, Than this Sarmatian, whom you thus disdain. Do justice to his merit: for myself, When I shall bend to Hymen's laws, the queen Must guide my choice, and at her hands alone Will I receive a master: for the crowd, The babbling echo of one secret voice, I heed it not; nor know I if the people Are tired of their obedience to a woman, But still I see them bow the knee before her; And if they murmur, murmur in the dust: The hand of heaven, they say, is raised against her: I am a stranger to her guilt, but think That heaven would never have made choice of thee To tell its high commands, or minister Its justice to mankind: Sémiramis Is still a queen, and you who lord it here Receive from her the laws which you dispense: For me, I own her power, and hers alone: My glory is to obey, be thine the same.

SCENE IV.
Assur, Cedar.

**Assur**: Obey! I blush to think how long already I have obeyed: O insupportable! But say, hast thou succeeded, are the seeds Of hatred sown in secret through the realm? Will they spring up into a fruitful harvest Of discord, and rebellion?

**Cedar**: All is well: The people, long deluded by the arts And dazzling glory of Sémiramis, At length have lost their idle veneration: No longer chained to silence, they demand A successor: each lover of his country Calls for a master, and looks up to thee.

**Assur:** Heart-burning care! and ever-during shame! Still must my hopes, my fate depend on her? Was it for this that Ninus and his son Fell by my hand, that Assur might be still Only her first of slaves? So near the throne, To languish in illustrious servitude, And only be the second of mankind! The queen was satisfied with Ninus' death, But I went further, and pursued my blow: Ninias, in secret murdered by my order, Opened my passage to the throne; but she Denied me entrance.—A long time in vain I soothed her pride with flattery on her charms; Still hoped one day to gain upon her youth That happy influence which assiduous care And humble adoration seldom fail To win o'er artless minds that bend with ease: I little knew the firmness of her soul, Inflexible, and bold; the world alone Could satisfy her pride: she seemed indeed Most worthy of it: spite of my resentment, I own she was, and yield the praise she merits. The reins of empire, that flowed loose before, Strongly she held; appeased the murmuring crowd, Silenced their plaints, and quashed conspiring rebels; Fought like a hero, like a monarch ruled: She led her army and her people captive, And spite of fame, with more than magic art, Chained down the minds of men: the universe Astonished stood, and trembled at her feet. In short, her beauty, woman's best support, Strengthened the laws which power and valor made; And when I strove to raise conspiracies My friends stood mute, and only could admire her. At length the charm is broke: her power decays; Her genius droops; remorse, and idle fears, And fond credulity have bound her faith To lying oracles, which knavish priests Had taught to speak in Egypt's barren plain: She pours her daily incense at their altars, And wearies heaven with vows: Sémiramis Creeps on a level now with common mortals, And condescends to fear: I know her weakness: Know, till she falls, Assur can never rise: But I have raised the people's voice against her, And she must yield: this blow decides her fate: If she consents to give me Azema, She is no longer queen; if she refuses, The kingdom will revolt: on every side The snare is laid, and nothing now can save her. Yet, after all, perhaps I am deceived, And fortune, so long called for, comes at last But to betray me.

**Cedar:** If the queen is forced To name a successor, and yields the princess To Assur's bed, what can he have to fear, When the divided branch of Asia's kings Shall be united? all conspires to pave Your way to empire.

**Assur:** Azema is safe; She must be mine; but wherefore send so far For this Arsaces? she supports him too; And when I would chastise his insolence, Her interposing hand prevents me still: A minister without the power, a prince

Without a subject, girt around with honors, And yet a poor dependent, what is Assur? All, all unite to persecute me now: A peevish mistress, and a haughty rival, Consulted priests that teach their gods to speak Against me; with Sémiramis, who strives To free herself, yet trembles at my presence: But we shall see how far this proud ingrate Will urge an angry rebel who defies her.

SCENE V.
Assur, Otanes, Cedar.
**Otanes**: My lord, the queen commands you to attend her In secret, and alone.
**Assur**: I shall obey Her sacred orders, and with care perform My sovereign's will.

SCENE VI.
Assur, Cedar.
**Assur**: Whence springs this sudden change? These three months past she has avoided me, Even as the object of her hatred: oft When she beheld me she would cast her eyes Down on the earth, as if she loathed the sight: Whene'er we met, 'twas in a gaping crowd Of hearers; when she spoke, her sighs and tears Would interrupt our converse, or perchance Silence was all the answer she would give me. What can she want? What can she say to me? But here she comes: 'tis she—wait you within. [To Cedar.]

SCENE VII.
Sémiramis, Assur.
**Sémiramis**: My lord, I come to ease a troubled heart Of its long hidden woes, and pour it all Before you: I have ruled o'er Asia long, And not ingloriously: Babylon perhaps May pay this tribute to my memory, And say Sémiramis deserved to rank Among the greatest of her kings: thy hands Have helped me to support the weight of empire; With absolute dominion have I ruled, Adored by all, and crowned with victory On every side: intoxicated long With flattery's pleasing incense, I forgot The crimes that raised me to this envied state; Forgot the justice of high heaven: it comes; It speaks to me: Sémiramis must yield: This noble structure, which I fondly thought Superior to the injuries of time, Is tottering now, and shakes from its foundation; Means must be found to strengthen and support it.
**Assur**: The work is yours, and you must finish it: Foresee the attacks of time, and stop his rapine: Who shall obscure the lustre of thy days, Or wherefore fearest thou heaven whilst earth obeys thee?

**Sémiramis:** Yonder the ashes of my husband lie; Canst thou look there, and wonder at my fears?

**Assur:** I cannot bear to hear the noisy crowd Still talk of Ninus: wherefore should remembrance Call back the thoughts of that inglorious reign? Can they believe, that, after fifteen years, His angry spirit still calls out for justice? Ere now he would have taken due vengeance on us, Had he the power: why from the peaceful realms Of dark oblivion wouldst thou call the dead, Or search for truth in lying oracles? I am astonished too, but 'tis at thee, And thy vain fears: to make the gods propitious, We must be resolute: this idle phantom, At once the child and parent of your fears, Why should it thus alarm you? Prodigies Never appear to those who dread them not: Baits to allure the unthinking multitude, By knaves invented, and by fools believed; The great despise them: but if nobler views Inspire thy soul to immortalize the blood Of Belus, if the beauteous Azema Claims her high rank.—

**Sémiramis:** Assur, on that I came To speak with thee: our Babylon demands, For such is Ammon's will, a successor: Heaven and my people will be satisfied When I shall take a partner to my throne: Thou knowest, my pride could never condescend To a divided sway; 'twas my resolve To rule alone, while the impatient world Urged me in vain; and when the people's voice, Which now is echoed by the voice of heaven, Still presses me, in the bloom of youth, to give A sovereign to mankind, I still refused: If I had yielded then to any claim, It had been thine; you had a right to hope, And to expect it; but you knew too well, How much Sémiramis abhorred a master. Without submitting to a tie so fatal, I made thee then the second of mankind, And only not my equal; 'twas enough, I thought, to satisfy even thy ambition. At length the gods make known their will divine, And I obey them: hear the oracle: "All shall again be well at Babylon, When Hymen's torch a second time shall blaze Propitious; then shalt thou, O cruel wife, And wretched mother, then shall thou appease The shade of Ninus." Thus the voice of heaven Declares its sacred will: I know thy arts; Know, thou hast formed a party in the state, And mean to oppose me with the royal blood From whence you sprung: from thee and Azema My successor, it seems, must rise; I know You look that way, and she perhaps aspires To equal honors; but, observe me well: I shall not suffer your united claims To rob me of my right: remember, sir, You know my will; 'tis constant, and as fate Irrevocable: thinkest thou now the God Whose arm is lifted o'er me hath deprived My soul of all its wonted strength and spirit, Or dost thou still behold Sémiramis, Who can support the honor of her throne? Know, Babylon ere long shall at my hands Receive a master: whether the high choice Shall fall on thee, or be another's lot,

I'll take a sovereign as a sovereign ought: Bring me the magi and the princess here To join their voices with Sémiramis. To give away my freedom and my empire Is the first, greatest act of royal power, And therefore let it be performed with awe And silence due to my authority. Heaven hath appointed this great day to show Its mercy to me, and the gods at length Remit their anger; nothing can disarm it But my repentance; 'tis the only virtue: Trust me, it is, howe'er you may despise it, Remaining for the guilty: weak, I know, And fearful thou esteemest me; but henceforth Remember, Assur, guilt alone is weakness: Think not that fear can e'er disgrace a throne, It has done good to kings, and might to thee; I tell thee, statesman, to obey the gods, And tremble at their power, is no abasement.

### SCENE VIII.

**Assur**: [Alone.] Astonishment! such language, such designs! Or is it artifice, or weakness in her, Or cowardice or courage? Does she mean, By yielding thus, to prop her tottering power, And by our union to defeat my purpose? I must not think, it seems, of Azema, Because, perhaps, I'm destined for herself. It must be so. What all my cares in vain Solicited, my flattery of her charms, My deep intrigues, and our united crimes, With all her fears, could never gain, at length An idle dream, and a dark oracle From Egypt have performed. What power unknown Decrees the fate of mortals? Great events Hang on the slenderest thread: still I am doubtful: I'll see Sémiramis again; she seemed Too much in haste; such sudden resolutions Betray an overanxious mind, and those Who change with ease are either weak, or wicked.

# ACT III.

### SCENE I.

Sémiramis, **Otanes**: [The scene represents an apartment in the palace.]

**Sémiramis**: Who would have thought, Otanes, that the gods, Offended as they were, at length should smile Propitious thus, and threaten but to save! Should drop the uplifted thunder from their hand, And pardon me; should send Arsaces hither To change my fate! for know it is their will That I should wed, and by a second tie Expiate the crimes of my first fatal nuptials. They are the great disposers of our hearts, And mine with pleasure yields to their decrees: It even outruns their purposes: Arsaces, I'm thine; for thou wert born to rule o'er me, And o'er the world.

**Otanes**: Arsaces! he!

**Sémiramis:** Thou knowest, In Scythia's plains, when I avenged the Persian, And conquered Asia, this young hero fought Beneath his father's banners, and, surrounded With captives, brought to me the bloody spoils, And, blushing, laid his victims at my feet. When first I saw him, I could feel his heart, As by some secret power, attracting mine Insensibly towards him; all mankind, Besides Arsaces, seemed not worth my notice. Assur grew jealous of him, and ever since Has fired with indignation at his name; Whilst his dear image still employed my thoughts, Before that voice which guides my every word And every action named him for my husband, Before the gods had pointed out Arsaces Otanes. It was indeed a noble conquest, thus To bend that haughty spirit which disdained The proffered homage of our Eastern monarchs, Who as her subjects, not as lovers, still Accepted kings! You who contemned those charms, That sovereign beauty, which extended wide Your universal empire; whilst your eyes Pierced every heart, you scarce would condescend To mark their power; and dost thou yield at last To love's imperious sway; to fears and horror Succeed the tender passions? Can it be?

**Sémiramis:** O, no; it is not love: I am not fallen So much beneath myself, as to bestow On beauty the reward that's due to virtue; I feel a nobler passion in my breast: Alas! such weakness would but ill become Sémiramis: unhappy as I am, For me to think of love, Otanes, how Couldst thou suppose it? Once I was a mother, But scarce had studied to deserve the name By my fond cares, when heaven in anger snatched My child away, and left me here alone A prey to anguish. I had nothing near me That I could love; and, midst my grandeur, felt An aching void within my soul. I fled The court, endeavored to avoid myself, And sought relief in these proud monuments, Amusing flatterers of a restless heart That shunned reflection: rest was still a stranger, And long remained so; but he comes once more, I feel him now, and wonder at the power That charmed him hither: 'twas Arsaces; he Shall hold the place of husband and of son, A conquered world, and all my glories past. How much I owe to thee, celestial power, Who thus propitious leadest me to the altar So long abhorred; and hast thyself inspired That passion which alone can make me happy!

**Otanes:** But what will be the rage and grief of Assur? Hast thou reflected on it, when he hears Thy new resolves? He is not without hopes: The people have already fixed thy choice On him, and his resentment will not end In mere complaints.

**Sémiramis:** I never have deceived, And therefore fear him not: these fifteen years, Whate'er his views have been, I've taught him still To rank but with my subjects, though the first Amongst them; and set bounds to his ambition,

Which he hath never o'erleaped: I reigned alone; And if this feeble hand so long could guide The helm of power, and curb his haughtiness, What can his courage or his cunning do Against Arsaces and Sémiramis? Yes: Ninus hath accepted my repentance, And leaves the mansions of the dead to urge Our happy union: his illustrious shade Again would rage to see his murderer seize His throne and bed: this calls him from the tomb, And Ammon's oracles unite with him To crown my bliss: no more the awful virtue Of Oroes affrights me; I've sent for him To be a witness of the great event, And soon expect him here.

**Otanes**: His honored name And sacred character may give indeed A sanction to your choice.

**Sémiramis**: I know it will, And establish my resolves.

**Otanes**: Behold, he comes.

### SCENE II.

Sémiramis, Oroes,

**Sémiramis**: Great successor of Zoroaster, welcome: To-day must Babylon receive a king; Thy office is to crown him; is all ready For the solemnity?

**Oroes**: The magi wait Thy pleasure, and the nobles all attend: To pay obedience to the sovereign power Is all my duty, and I shall fulfil it: I am not to judge kings, for that belongs To heaven alone.

**Sémiramis**: By this mysterious language, It seems you disapprove my purpose.

**Oroes**: Madam, I know it not, but wish it fair success.

**Sémiramis**: Thou canst interpret heaven's high will: these signs Which I have seen, can they be fatal to me? A spectre hath of late, perhaps some god, Appeared, and in the bosom of the earth Re-entered soon: what power hath thus broke down The eternal barrier that divides the light From darkness? wherefore should a mortal thus Rise from the tomb to visit me?

**Oroes**: Know, heaven Doth oft suspend its own eternal laws When justice bids, reversing death's decree; Thus to chastise the sovereigns of the earth, And terrify mankind.

**Sémiramis**: The oracles Demand a sacrifice.

**Oroes**: It shall be offered.

**Sémiramis**: Eternal justice, thou whose piercing eye Beholdest my naked heart, O fill it not Again with horror, bury in oblivion My first unhappy nuptials! Oroes, stay. [To Oroes, who is retiring.]

**Oroes**: [Returning.] I thought my presence might disturb you, madam.

**Sémiramis**: Return, and answer me: this morning, say, Did not Arsaces offer at your altars Gifts to the gods?

**Oroes**: He did; and precious were they: Arsaces is the favorite of heaven.

**Sémiramis**: I know he is, and I rejoice to hear it. Can I be wretched if I trust to him?

**Oroes**: He is the empire's best support; the gods Conducted him; his glory is their care.

**Sémiramis**: With transport I accept the fair presage, Whilst hope and peace return to calm my breast. Away: again let purest incense rise Before your altars; let your magi come And sanctify the choice; bring down the smiles Of the assenting gods, and make us happy. Henceforth may Babylon with me revive, And shine amongst the nations of the earth With double splendor! Go thou, and prepare The solemn pomp.

## SCENE III.

Sémiramis, Otanes.

**Sémiramis**: Heaven seconds my design, And I am only the interpreter Of its high will, to give the world a master: Thus to receive a kingdom at my hand Will strike him with astonishment: even now How little thinks he of the approaching greatness! How will proud Assur and his fawning crowd Be humbled! But a word, and the whole earth Falls at his feet; and, grateful as he is, I know he will repay me: I shall wed him, And for my portion carry him a world; My glory's pure, and now I shall enjoy it.

## SCENE IV.

Sémiramis, Otanes, Mitranes. An Officer of the Palace.

**Otanes**: Arsaces begs admittance to your presence, To lay his sorrows at your feet.

**Sémiramis**: Arsaces! What sorrows can Arsaces feel when I Am near him, he who thus hath banished mine? Quick, let him come: he knows not yet his power O'er the fond heart of his Sémiramis. O thou dread shade whose voice alarmed my soul, Whose blood no more calls out for vengeance on me, And you, the guardian gods of this great empire. Of the Assyrians, Ninus, and my son, Unite to bless Arsaces! Ha! the sight Alarms me; whence can these strange terrors rise?

## SCENE V.

Sémiramis, Arsaces.

**Arsaces**: O queen, I am devoted to thy service; My life is thine; and when I shed this blood, I am rewarded if it flows for thee. My father had some small renown in arms; I saw him perish bravely in the field, And at the head of thy victorious bands; He left his hapless son a fair example, Perhaps but ill pursued: I'll not recall The memory of my father's services. 'Twould ill become me; at your royal knees, Though here I sue for favor and protection: Pity the rashness of a guilty youth, Who listened to the dictates of imprudence. And even in serving feared he might offend you.

**Sémiramis**: Offend me! thou, Arsaces! fear it not.

**Arsaces**: To-day you give your kingdom and your hand: My heart, I know, should on the great event Keep secret all its fears, and humbly still In silence, with depending monarchs, wait To know our master; but this Assur steps So haughtily, and triumphs in his conquest, We cannot brook his pride: the people call him Already their new sovereign; his high blood And rank support him: may he prove himself Worthy of both! but I have still a soul Too proud to bend beneath him, or adore The power I had defied: his jealous heart I know detests Arsaces: let me then Retire in safety, far from him, and thee: Permit me to revisit the dear climes Where first I served my royal mistress, there His tyranny can never reach: perhaps I may hereafter—

**Sémiramis**: Wilt thou leave me then, And fearest thou Assur?

**Arsaces**: No: Arsaces fears Naught but the anger of Sémiramis. Perhaps thou knowest my fond ambition, then I've cause indeed to tremble.

**Sémiramis**: Hope the best, And know that Assur ne'er shall be thy master.

**Arsaces**: I own it shocked my soul to look on him As Ninus' successor: but is he then Designed for Azema? forgive this bold Presumptuous questioner: long since I know She was to Ninias given, proud Assur sprung From the same race, and claims her as his own: I am but a poor subject, yet I dare—

**Sémiramis**: Such subjects are my kingdom's best support; I know thee well; thy noble soul, superior To vulgar minds, hath sought Sémiramis, Not for her fortunes, but herself; thy eyes Are fixed on her true interest, and on thee I shall depend: Assur and Azema Shall never meet; their union would be dangerous: But their designs are known, and by my care Will be prevented.

**Arsaces**: Since my heart at length Is open to thee, and thou hast discovered—

**Azema**: [Enters suddenly, and throws herself at the feet of Sémiramis.] O queen, permit me thus—

**Sémiramis**: Rise, Azema: Where'er my choice may light, thou mayest depend On my protection, and shalt find respect Due to thy birth; for, destined as thou wert To be the wife of my lamented son, I look upon thee with a mother's eye: [To them both.] Go, place yourselves with those whom I have called To witness my resolves, and mark my choice. [To Arsaces.] Be thou, my best protector, near the throne.

## SCENE VI.

The apartment of Sémiramis opens into a magnificent saloon richly ornamented; a number of officers in their proper habits on the steps of the throne, which is raised in the middle; the satraps on each side: the high priest enters with the magi, and places himself between Assur and Arsaces: the queen in the midst with Azema, and her attendants: guards at the lower end of the saloon.

**Oroes:** Ye princes, magi, warriors, the support Of Babylon, assembled by command From great Sémiramis, the will of heaven Soon shall ye know: the gods that guard our empire Have fixed on this important hour to work A great and mighty change; whoe'er the queen Shall here appoint her sovereign and our own It is our duty to obey; and here I bring my tribute to the throne, my prayers And wishes for the glory and the welfare Of them, and of their kingdom: may these days Of joy and gladness ne'er be changed to hours Of grief and sorrow, nor these songs of mirth To mournful plaints!

**Azema:** A king, my lords, will soon Be named; whoe'er he be, the choice will injure Myself alone; but Azema was born And must remain a subject; I submit To the queen's pleasure, and on her protection Shall still depend; nor with the dark presage Of future ills shall interrupt your joy: But leave you my example of obedience.

**Assur:** Howe'er the queen may choose, and heaven determine, We must consult the public good alone; Let us then swear by this imperial throne, And great Sémiramis, to yield submissive, And without murmuring to obey her will.

**Arsaces:** I swear it; and this arm that fought for her, This heart obedient ever to her voice, Which next the voice of heaven I still revered, This blood which flowed with pleasure for her sake, Shall be devoted to that royal master Whom she appoints.

**High Priest:** I wait the great award Of heaven and **Sémiramis: Sémiramis:** Enough: Each to his place, and now attend, my people. [She seats herself on the throne. Azema, Assur, Oroes (the high priest) and Arsaces take their places, and she proceeds.] If in that hand which custom and the laws Of an imperious husband had confined To homely cares, and to a distaff chained, I bore aloft the sceptre and the sword, Beyond my subjects' hope, nor sunk beneath The weight of empire, let me now extend To latest times its glory: 'tis my purpose This day to take a partner in the throne: The gods must be obeyed, whose dread command At length subdued my long unconquered heart: They who deprived me of my son, perhaps May one day raise an heir to Babylon Worthy of empire, who shall follow me Through all the thorny paths that I have trod, Finish my work, and make my reign immortal. I might have chosen a sovereign from the kings That dwell around me, but they are all my foes, Or tributary slaves: a foreign hand Shall never wield this sceptre: my own subjects Are better than the kings which they have conquered: Belus was born a subject; if he gained The diadem, he owed it to the people, And to himself: by rights like his I hold The power supreme; and, mistress of a kingdom Larger than his, have bent beneath my yoke The nations of the East, which Belus ne'er Had seen or heard of: what he but attempted Sémiramis performed; for they who found A kingdom, and they only, can preserve it. You want a king who may be worthy of you, Worthy of such an empire, shall I add Worthy the hand that crowns him, and the heart Which I shall give: I have consulted heaven, My country's weal, the interest of mankind, And choose a king to make the world more happy. Adore the hero, see in him revived The princes of my honored race; observe him, And know, this king, this hero, is—Arsaces. [She descends from the throne, and they all rise.]

**Azema:** Arsaces! the perfidious—

**Assur:** Rage and vengeance!

**Arsaces:** Believe me, Azema—

**Oroes:** Just heaven! avert These omens.

**Sémiramis:** Thou who sanctifiest my choice, Confirm it at the altar: see in him Ninus and Ninias both restored. [It thunders, and the tomb shakes.] O heaven! What do I hear?

**Oroes:** Great gods, protect us now!

**Sémiramis:** The thunder comes, in anger or in love I know not: pardon, gracious gods! Arsaces Must win them to forgiveness. Ha! what voice Distracts me thus? and see, the tomb is open. O heaven! I die. [The ghost of Ninus comes out of the tomb.]

**Assur:** The shade of Ninus' self. Gods! is it possible?

**Arsaces:** What sayest thou? speak, Thou god of terrors.

**Assur:** O unfold thy tale.

**Sémiramis:** Comest thou to pardon, or to punish me? It is thy sceptre and thy bed which here I have bestowed: speak, is he worthy of it? Determine: I obey thee.

**The Ghost of Ninus:** [To Arsaces.] Thou shalt reign, Arsaces, but there are some dreadful crimes Which thou must expiate: hie thee to the tomb, And to my ashes offer sacrifice: Serve me and Ninias: remember well Thy father: listen to the pontiff.

**Arsaces**: O! Thou venerable shade, thou demigod, Who dwellest within these walls, the sight of thee Inspires but does not amaze Arsaces: Yes, I will go, on peril of my life, And meet thee in the tomb: but tell me, what Must be the sacrifice? O speak! he's gone. [The ghost retires towards the entrance of the mausoleum.]

**Sémiramis**: Thou honored spirit of my lord, permit me Thus on my knees to pour my sorrows forth, Permit me in the tomb to—

**Ghost:** [At the entrance of the tomb.] Stop: no farther: Respect my ashes: when the time is come I'll send for thee. [The ghost goes into the tomb, and the mausoleum closes.]

**Assur**: Amazing!

**Sémiramis**: Follow me, My people, to the temple: be not thus Dismayed: for know, the gentle shade of Ninus Is not implacable; it loves your king, And therefore will it spare Sémiramis: Heaven that inspired my choice will now support it: Haste then, and pray for me, and for Arsaces.

# ACT IV.

**SCENE I.**
Representing the porch of the temple.
Arsaces, Azema.

**Arsaces**: Do not oppress me in this hour of grief, And aggravate my sorrows; I have borne Enough already: this dread oracle Affrights me; prodigies on every side Disturb the course of nature: heaven deprives me Of all, if Azema is lost.

**Azema**: No more, False man, nor to the horrors of this day Add the remembrance of thy perfidy; No more the terrors of Sémiramis, The walking spectre, and the opening grave, Appal me now; of all the prodigies Which I have seen, thy base inconstancy Hath shocked me most: go on, appease the shade Of Ninus, and begin the sacrifice With Azema; behold, and strike the victim.

**Arsaces**: It is too much; my heart was not prepared Against this cruel stroke: thou knowest, my soul Prefers thee to the empire of the world: What was the object of that fame in arms I held so dear, of all my victories? All my ambition hoped for was at last To merit thee: Sémiramis, thou knowest, Was dear to both; thy tongue unites with mine To praise her; she was still the guardian god That cherished and protected us; as such We both revered her with that pious zeal And chaste regard which mortals bear to heaven: Judge of my spotless faith by my surprise At the queen's choice, and mark the precipice It leads us to, thence learn our future fate.

**Azema**: I know it.

**Arsaces**: Learn, that neither thou nor empire Were destined for Arsaces; know, that son Whom I must serve, the child of Ninus, he Who must inherit here—

**Azema**: Well; what of him?

**Arsaces**: That Ninias, he who from his cradle lit The torch of Hymen with thee, who was born My rival and my master—

**Azema**: Ninias!

**Arsaces**: Lives; And will be with us soon.

**Azema**: Ha! then the queen—

**Arsaces**: Even to this day deceived, laments his death.

**Azema**: Ninias alive!

**Arsaces**: It is a secret yet Within the temple, and she knows it not.

**Azema**: But Ninus crowns thee, and his widow's thine.

**Arsaces**: Ay, but his son was born for Azema; He is my king, so says the oracle, And I must serve him.

**Azema**: But love claims his own, And will be heard in spite of all, Arsaces: His orders are not doubtful, or obscure. Love is my oracle, and that alone Shall be obeyed. Ninias, thou sayest, yet lives, Let him appear, and let Sémiramis Recall her plighted faith to him; let Ninus Rise from the tomb, to join the fatal knot Made in our infant years; let Ninias come, My king, thy master, and thy rival, fired With all the love which once Arsaces had For Azema, then see how I will slight His proffered vows; then shalt thou see me scorn The sceptre at my feet, and spurn a crown Which is my due: where is he now? What secret, What mystery veils him from us? Let him come; But know, nor Ninias, nor Sémiramis, No, nor the sacred spirit of his father Risen from the tomb, nor all the powers of nature Thrown in confusion, from my heart would wrest The image of my perjured dear Arsaces: Go, ask thy own, if it will dare to act As mine hath done. What are those dreadful crimes Which thou must expiate? if thou e'er shouldst break The sacred tie that binds us, if thou art false, I know no crime, no treachery like thy own. I see the sage interpreter of fate This way advancing, love will never plead Thy cause with heaven, if thou betrayest me: go, From Ninus' hand receive thy doom; remember, Thy fate depends on heaven, and mine on thee. [Exit **Azema**: **Arsaces**: Arsaces still is thine: stay, cruel maid:] How mingled is our happiness and woe! What strange events that contradict each other—

## SCENE II.

Arsaces, Oroes, the Magi Attending.

**Oroes:** [To Arsaces.] Let us retire to yonder lonely walk; I see you are much moved: prepare yourself For strokes more dreadful. [To the magi.] Bring the royal wreath. [The magi bring the coffer.] This letter, and this sacred sword, to thee, Arsaces, I deliver.

**Arsaces:** Reverend father, Wilt thou not save me from the precipice That gapes before me? wilt thou not at length Uplift the veil, that from my eyes conceals My future fate?

**Oroes:** 'Twill be removed, my son; The hour is come, when in his dreary mansions, Ninus from thee expects a sacrifice That shall appease his angry spirit.

**Arsaces:** What Can Ninus ask, what sacrifice from me? Must I be his avenger, when his son Still lives? Let Ninias come; he is my king, And I will serve him.

**Oroes:** 'Tis his father's will, Thou must obey him: an hour hence, Arsaces, Be at his tomb, armed with this sacred sword, And with this wreath adorned, which Ninus wore, And which thyself did bring to me.

**Arsaces:** The wreath Of Ninus!

**Oroes:** 'Tis his royal will that thus Thou shouldst appear, to offer up the blood That must be shed; the victim will be there: Strike thou, and leave the rest to him, and heaven.

**Arsaces:** If he requires my life, I'll give it him: But where is Ninias? thou speakest naught of him: Thou hast not told me how his father gives To me his kingdom and his queen.

**Oroes:** To thee His queen! O heaven, to thee Sémiramis Be given! Arsaces, the important hour Which I had promised thee is come, when thou Shalt know thy fate, and this abandoned woman.

**Arsaces:** Great gods!

**Oroes:** 'Twas she who murdered Ninus.

**Arsaces:** She, Saidst thou, the queen?

**Oroes:** Assur, that foul disgrace Of human nature, Assur gave the poison.

**Arsaces:** I'm not surprised at Assur's cruelty, But that a wife, a queen, and such a queen, The pride of sovereigns, the delight of nations, That she should e'er be guilty of a crime So horrible! it passes all belief. How can such virtues and such guilt as hers Subsist together!

**Oroes:** How indeed! the question Is worthy of thy noble heart: but now 'Twere needless to dissemble, every moment Is big with some new secret, horrible To nature, who already whispers to thee Her soft complaints; thy generous heart, I see, Spite of thyself, is shocked, and mourns within thee: But wonder not that Ninus from the tomb Indignant rises on this seat of guilt; He comes to break the horrid nuptial tie, Woven by the furies, and expose to light Unpunished crimes; to save his son from incest: He speaks to, he expects thee: know thy father, For thou art Ninias, and the queen's thy mother.

**Arsaces:** Thou hast o'erpowered me in one dreadful moment With such repeated wonders, that I stand Astonished, and the night of death surrounds me. Am I his son, and can it be?

**Oroes:** Thou art: Ninus, the morn before he died, foresaw His end approaching; knew the deadly draught Which he had drunk was ministered to thee By the same hand, and, dying as thou wert, Withdrew thee from this wicked court: for Assur Had poisoned thee that he might wed thy mother, Thought to exterminate the royal race, And open thus his passage to the throne: But whilst the kingdom mourned thy loss, Phradates, Our faithful friend, secreted and preserved thee; With skilful hand the precious herbs prepared, O'er Persia spread by her benignant God, Whose wondrous power drew forth the latent venom From thy parched limbs: his own son dying, you Supplied his place, and still wert called Arsaces. He waited patient for some lucky change, But the great judge of kings had otherwise Determined; truth at length descends from heaven, And vengeance rises from the tomb.

**Arsaces:** O God! Enough already hast thou tried thy servant, Or must I yield that life which you restored? Yes: I was born midst grandeur, shame, and horror: My mother—Ninus! O what deadly purpose— But if the traitor Assur was alone To blame, if he—

**Oroes:** [Giving him the letter.] Behold this paper here, Too faithful witness of her guilt, then say If yet a doubt remains.

**Arsaces:** Haste, give it me, And clear them all. [He reads.] Ha! "Ninus to Phradates: I die by poison, guard my Ninias well, Defend him from his foes: my guilty wife—"

**Oroes:** Needest thou more proof? this witness came from thee. He had not finished; death, thou seest, broke off The imperfect scroll, and stopped his feeble hand; Phradates hath unfolded all the rest, Read this, and learn the whole. [Gives him another paper.] It is enough That Ninus hath commanded thee, he guides Thy steps, and leads thee to the throne, but says He must have blood.

**Arsaces:** [After reading the paper.] O day of miracles, And you, ye dreadful oracles from hell, Dark as the tomb which I must visit, how Shall I unveil your secret purposes, When he who is to make the sacrifice Knows not his victim! Who shall guide my choice? I tremble at it.

**Oroes:** Tremble for the guilty. Amidst the horrors that oppress thy soul, The gods will guide thee; deem not thou thyself A common mortal, from the race of men Thou art distinguished, set apart by heaven, And noted by its signature divine, Walk thou secure, though night conceals thy fate, The gods of thy great ancestors employ thee But as their instrument. What right hast thou To litigate their power, and to oppose Thy masters? Saved from death, as thou hast been, Be thankful still; complain not, but adore.

### SCENE III.
Arsaces, Mitranes.

**Arsaces:** I cannot reconcile this strange event: Sémiramis my mother! can it be?

**Mitranes:** [Entering in haste.] My lord, the people in this hour of terror Demand their king: permit me first to hail thee The husband of Sémiramis, and lord Of Babylon: the queen is hasting hither In search of thee; I bless the happy hour That gave her to thee: ha! not answer me! Despair is in thy looks, thy lips are closed In dreadful silence, thou art pale with terror, And thy whole frame's disordered: what has passed? What have they said?

**Arsaces:** I'll fly to Azema: **Mitranes:** Amazing! can it be Arsaces? fly A queen's embraces; scorn her proffered love; Insult her choice; the royal hand that spurned Kings for thy sake! thus are her hopes betrayed?

**Arsaces:** Gods! 'tis Sémiramis herself; O Ninus, Now let thy tomb in its dark bosom hide Her crimes, and me!

### SCENE IV.
Sémiramis, Arsaces.

**Sémiramis:** Arsaces, all is ready, We want but thee, great master of the world, Whose fate, like mine, depends on thee; O haste, And make our bliss complete! with joy I see Thy brows encircled with that sacred wreath: The priest, I know, was by the gods commanded To crown thee with it; heaven and hell at once Approve my choice, and by these signs confirm it: Assur's seditious party, struck with awe And holy reverence, tremble at my presence; Ninus, at length propitious, hath required A sacrifice, O haste, and give it him, That we may soon be blest: the people's hearts Are all with us, and Assur's threats are vain.

**Arsaces:** [Walking about with great emotion.] Assur! away! in his perfidious blood The parricide—we will revenge thee, Ninus.

**Sémiramis:** What do I hear? just heaven! speakest thou of him, Of Ninus?

**Arsaces**: [Wildly.] Saidst thou not, his guilty hand [Coming to himself.] Had shed—to arm against his queen! the slave, That was enough to make me hate him.

**Sémiramis**: Haste then, Receive my hand, and thus begin thy vengeance.

**Arsaces**: My father!

**Sémiramis**: Ha! what looks are those, Arsaces? Is this the soft submissive tender heart Which I expected from thee, when I gave My willing hand? That fearful prodigies, And spectres rising from their dark domain, Should leave the marks of horror on thy soul, Alarms me not, I feel them too, but less When I behold Arsaces: do not thus O'erspread this fairest dawn of happiness With sorrow's gloomy shade, but still appear Such as thou wert when trembling at my feet, Lest Assur e'er should be thy master; fear Nor him, nor Ninus and his angry shade; My dear Arsaces, thou art my support, My lord, my husband.

**Arsaces**: [Turning aside from her.] 'Tis too much, O stop: Her guilt o'erwhelms me.

**Sémiramis**: How his soul's disturbed! Alas! he wants that peace which he bestowed On me.

**Arsaces**: Sémiramis—

**Sémiramis**: What wouldst thou? speak.

**Arsaces**: I cannot: leave me, leave me: hence! begone.

**Sémiramis**: Amazing! leave thee! can I e'er forsake Arsaces? O explain this mystery to me, And ease my tortured soul: it makes us both Unhappy:—ha! despair is in thy aspect; Thou chillest my veins with horror, and thy eyes Are dreadful; they affright me more than heaven And hell united to oppose my vows: Scarce can my trembling lips pronounce, I love thee: Some power invisible now leads me on Towards thee, now withholds me from thy arms, And mingles, how I know not, tenderest love With sentiments of horror and despair.

**Arsaces**: Hate me, abhor me.

**Sémiramis**: Canst thou bid me hate thee? Cruel Arsaces, no: I still must trace Thy footsteps, still my heart must follow thine: What is that paper which thou lookest on thus With horror, whilst thy eyes are bathed in tears, Does that contain a reason for thy coldness?

**Arsaces**: It does.

**Sémiramis**: Then give it me.

**Arsaces**: I must not: darest thou—

**Sémiramis**: I'll have it.

**Arsaces**: Leave to me that dreadful scroll, To thee 'twere fatal, I have use for it.

Sémiramis: Whence came it?

Arsaces: From the gods.

Sémiramis: And wrote by whom?

Arsaces: Wrote by my father.

Sémiramis: Ha! what sayest thou?

Arsaces: Tremble.

Sémiramis: Give it me, let me know at once my fate.

Arsaces: Urge it no more; there is death in every line.

Sémiramis: No matter: clear my doubts, or I shall think That thou art guilty.

Arsaces: Ye immortal powers That guide our steps, it is to your decrees That I submit.

Sémiramis: For the last time, Arsaces, I here command thee, listen, and obey.

Arsaces: [Giving her the letter.] O may thy justice, heaven, be satisfied! And this the only punishment that e'er Shall be inflicted on her! now 'tis past, And thou wilt know too much. [She reads.]

Sémiramis: [To Otanes.] What do I read? Support me, or I die. [She faints.]

Arsaces: She sees it all.

Sémiramis: [Coming to herself, after a long silence.] Delay not, but fulfil thy destiny: Punish this guilty, this unhappy wretch, And in my blood wash out the deadly stain. Nature deceived is horrible to both, Avenge thy father, strike, and punish me.

Arsaces: No: let the sacred character I bear, The name of son, preserve me from that crime! Much rather would I pierce the heart of him Who still reveres thee, the poor lost Arsaces: Sémiramis: [Kneeling.] Be cruel as Sémiramis; she felt No pity, therefore be the son of Ninus, And take my life: thou wilt not; nay, thy tears Even mix with mine: O Ninias, 'tis a day Of horrors, yet there's pleasure in this pain. Before thou givest me what I have deserved, The stroke of death, let nature's voice be heard: O let a guilty mother's tears bedew That dear, that fatal hand.

Arsaces: I am thy son, 'Tis not for thee, whate'er thy guilt, to fall Thus at my feet: O rise, thy Ninias begs, He loves thee still, still vows obedience to thee, Respect and purest love: consider me As a new subject, only more submissive, More humble, than the rest; I hope, more dear. Heaven that restores thy son is sure appeased: The gods who pardon thee reserve their vengeance For Assur; leave him to his fate.

Sémiramis: Receive My crown and sceptre, I have much disgraced them.

Arsaces: Still, I beseech you, hold me ignorant Of all, and let me with the world adore you.

**Sémiramis**: O no: my guilt's too flagrant.

**Arsaces**: But repentance May blot it out.

**Sémiramis**: Ninus hath given to thee The reins of empire, thou must not offend His vengeful spirit.

**Arsaces**: O it will relent At thy remorse, and soften at my tears. Otanes, in the name of heaven, preserve My mother, and conceal the horrid secret.

# ACT V.

SCENE I.

Sémiramis, Otanes.

**Otanes**: O 'twas some god that smiled propitious on thee, Who thus prevented these abhorred nuptials; Whilst nature shuddered at the approaching danger, Gave thee a son, and saved thee thus from incest. The oracles of Ammon, and the voice From hell, the shades of Ninus, all declared The day appointed for thy second marriage Should end thy sorrows, but they never said That marriage e'er should be accomplished: No: The nuptials were prepared: thou hast fulfilled Thy destiny: thy son reveres thee still: Mild is the justice of offended heaven, Which only asks a private sacrifice: This day Sémiramis shall still be happy.

**Sémiramis**: Alas! there is no happiness for me, Otanes: Ninias smiles indeed upon me: A mother's sorrows for a time will plead More strongly with him than the blood of Ninus, And my past crimes; but soon his tenderness And filial love may change perhaps to wrath And fierce resentment for a murdered father.

**Otanes**: What fearest thou from a son? what dire presage—

**Sémiramis**: Fear is the natural punishment of guilt, And still attends it: this detested Assur, Has he attempted aught, say, does he know What passed of late, and who Arsaces is?

**Otanes**: The dreadful secret still remains unknown; The shade of Ninus is by all revered; But how to comprehend the oracle They know not; how they must avenge his ashes; How serve his son—the minds of men are struck With wild astonishment, in silence now They wait the hour when the self-opened tomb Shall banish all their fears, and make them happy. Meantime the soldiers are in arms, the people Crowd to the altars; wretched Azema, Trembling and pale, with terror in her looks, Walks round the tomb, and lifts her hands to heaven; Whilst Ninias stands astonished in the temple, Prepared to strike his victim yet unknown: The gloomy Assur meditates revenge, Unites the remnants of his scattered party, And forms some dark design.

**Sémiramis:** I have kept fair Too long already with him: seize the traitor, Otanes, bear him to my son in chains; Ninias shall soon appease eternal justice, At least with Assur's blood, my vile accomplice. Ninus, thou seest I am a mother still; Thou seest my heart, O take it, take it all, And may it rise a grateful sacrifice! Ha! who approaches with such hasty steps? How everything appals my fluttering soul!

## SCENE II.
Sémiramis, Azema, Otanes.

**Azema:** O Queen, forgive me if I come uncalled; But terrors worse than death have forced me thus To clasp thy knees, and beg thy royal mercy—

**Sémiramis:** What wouldst thou, princéss? speak.

**Azema:** To snatch a hero From instant danger, stop a traitor's hand, And save Arsaces: **Sémiramis:** Ha! what hand? Arsaces!

**Azema:** He is thy husband, Azema's betrayed, He lives for you alone; no matter—

**Sémiramis:** He My husband! gods!

**Azema:** The sacred tie that binds you—

**Sémiramis:** The tie is dreadful, impious, and abhorred: Arsaces is—but speak, go on; I tremble: What dangers? haste, and tell me.

**Azema:** Well thou knowest, Perhaps this very moment, whilst I ask Thy aid, perhaps—

**Sémiramis:** Well, what?

**Azema:** That demigod Whom we adore, demands the sacrifice Within the dreary labyrinths of the tomb: What are the crimes Arsaces must atone for I know not.

**Sémiramis:** Crimes! just heaven!

**Azema:** But impious Assur Hath sworn to violate that sacred place Which mortals dare not enter.

**Sémiramis:** Ay! indeed! Hath Assur sworn it?

**Azema:** In the dead of night The wily traitor had long since secured A safe retreat, if e'er occasion called, Within the secret windings of the tomb, Where now he means to do the bloody deed, To brave the powers of hell, and wrath of heaven; With sacrilegious hand he would destroy The generous **Arsaces:** **Sémiramis:** Heaven! what sayest thou? By what detested means?

**Azema:** Believe a heart By love enlightened, and by love inspired: I know the traitor's rank envenomed hatred, Marked how the trembling faction by his zeal Revived; I pried into their secret councils, Pretended to unite his cause with mine, And join our interests; I have looked into him, Have wrested from his heart the fatal secret. Boldly he marches on, and hopes to pass Unpunished: well he knows that none dare enter That holy place, not Oroes himself: Thither he's gone: meantime his slaves report Arsaces is the victim that must die For Babylon, and Ninus in his blood Shall satiate his revenge: the nobles meet, The people murmur; Ninus, Assur, heaven, Are all incensed: I tremble for **Arsaces**:

**Sémiramis**: My dearest Azema, heaven speaks by thee: It is enough: I see what must be done. Repose thyself with safety on a mother; Daughter, our danger is the same; go thou, Defend thy husband, I will save my son.

**Azema**: O heaven!

**Sémiramis**: I meant to wed him, but the gods In mercy have forbade it: they inspire A hapless mother now—but time is precious; Go: leave me here, and in my name command The nobles, priests, and people, to attend me. [Azema goes into the porch of the temple, and Sémiramis advances toward the tomb.] Thou shade of Ninus, lo! I fly to avenge thee; The hour is come when thou didst promise me Admittance to thy tomb; I have obeyed thee, Called by thy voice, behold me here to save My son. Ye guards that wait around my throne Approach: henceforth Arsaces is your king; No more obedient to Sémiramis, Observe his laws, to him the sovereign power I here resign: be you his subject now, And his defenders. [Guards appear, and range themselves on each side at the further part of the stage.] Gracious heaven! protect me. [She goes into the tomb.]

### SCENE III.

**Azema**: [Returning from the porch of the temple to the front of the stage.] What can she purpose? O it is too late To save him now; I know not what to think: 'Tis wondrous all; O 'tis a dreadful moment, Arsaces! Ninias! ye immortal powers Who guide our fate, O say, did you restore My loved Arsaces but to snatch him from me?

### SCENE IV.

Azema, Ninias.

**Azema**: Ha! Ninias! can it be? Art thou indeed Great Ninus' son, my sovereign, and my husband?

**Ninias**: O! thou beholdest me, Azema, ashamed To know myself, sprung from the blood of gods, And shuddering at the thought: O! Azema, Remove my terrors, calm my troubled soul, Strengthen my arm upraised to avenge a father.

**Azema**: Take heed how thou performest that dreadful office.

**Ninias:** He hath commanded, and I must obey.

**Azema:** Ninus would never sacrifice his son: Impossible!

**Ninias:** What says my Azema?

**Azema:** Ne'er shalt thou enter that abhorred place, For know, a traitor lies in wait for thee.

**Ninias:** Who shall withhold or terrify Arsaces?

**Azema:** Thou art the victim to be offered there: With sacrilegious steps the impious Assur Profanes the sacred tomb, and rashly dares To violate its privilege divine: He waits thee there.

**Ninias:** Good heaven! then all is plain; I'm satisfied: the victim is prepared; My father, poisoned by the wicked Assur, Demands the traitor's blood: instructed thus By Oroes, and conducted by the gods, Armed by the hand of Ninus' self, I go To punish the assassin: thither led By heaven's eternal justice, my weak hand Is but the instrument of power divine: The gods do all, and my astonished soul Yields to that voice which must decree my fate: Spite of ourselves, our ways are noted down, Marked, and determined: prodigies are spread Around the throne, and spirits called from hell To wander here: but fearless I obey. Believe, and trust in heaven.

**Azema:** Whate'er the gods Have done but fills my soul with sad dismay: Ninus was loved by them; yet Ninus perished.

**Ninias:** But now they will avenge him: cease thy plaints.

**Azema:** Oft have they chose the purest victim, oft Have shed the blood of innocence.

**Ninias:** No more; They will defend whom thus they have united: They by a father's voice exhorted us, Gave me a throne, a mother, and a wife. Soon shalt thou see me sprinkled with the blood Of the vile murderer; from the tomb those gods Shall lead me to the altar; I obey; It is enough: the rest be left to heaven.

SCENE V.

**Azema:** [Alone.] O guard his footsteps in this fatal tomb! Ye powers inscrutable, whose blood must flow This day? I tremble for the event, and dread The hand of Assur, long inured to slaughter; Even on his father's ashes may he shed The blood of Ninias: O may the dark womb Of hell receive and swallow up his rage! Ye lightnings blast him! O illustrious shade Of Ninus, wherefore wouldst thou not permit A wretched wife to go with her dear lord? O guide, support him in this place of darkness! Did I not hear the voice of Ninias mixed With deadly groans? O would this sacred tomb, Which I profane, but open to my wishes The gate of death!—I will descend:—I go— Hark! the earth shakes, and dreadful lightnings flash Athwart the skies: fear, hope, despair—he comes.

## SCENE VI.

Ninias, a Bloody Sword in His Hand, Azema.

**Ninias:** O heaven! Where am I?

**Azema:** O! my lord, you're pale, And bloody, frozen with horror.

**Ninias:** 'Tis the blood Of the vile parricide: I wandered down Even to the bottom of the tomb; my father Still led me onward through its winding paths, He walked before, and pointed out the place Of my revenge: there, by the imperfect light That glimmered through the dreary vault, I saw, Or thought I saw, upraised the murderer's sword: Methought he trembled; guilt is ever fearful: Twice did I plunge my sword into his heart, And with my bloody arm, which rage had strengthened, Had dragged him in the dust towards the place Whence the dim rays of light appeared: and yet I own to thee, his deep heart-rending sighs, The mournful sounds, imperfect as they were, That reached my ears, his humble vows to heaven, With that repentance which in his last hour Seemed to possess his soul, the hallowed place, The voice of pity, which, revenge once o'er, Calls loudly on us, with I know not what Of dark mysterious terror, shook my soul, And made me leave the bleeding victim there. What can this trouble, this strange horror mean That dwells upon me, Azema? My heart Is pure, ye gods, my hands are innocent, Stained only with the blood you bid me shed; I've served the cause of heaven, and yet am wretched.

**Azema:** The dead are satisfied, and nature too: Come let us quit this horrid place, and seek Thy mother, she shall calm thy troubled mind: Since Assur is no more—

## SCENE VII.

Ninias, Azema,

**Assur:** [Assur appears at a distance with Otanes, surrounded by guards.]

**Azema:** O heaven! he's there.

**Ninias:** Assur!

**Azema:** O haste, ye ministers of heaven, Ye servants of the king, defend your master.

## SCENE VIII.

Oroes, the High Priest, with the Magi and People Assembled, Otanes, Ninias, Azema, Mitranes, Assur. [Disarmed.]

**Otanes**: They need not: by the queen's command I've seized The traitor, who attempted to profane Yon sacred monument, and enter there: I shall deliver him to thee.

**Ninias**: Alas! What victim then hath Ninias sacrificed?

**Oroes**: Heaven is appeased, and vengeance now complete. Behold, ye people, your king's murderer. [Pointing to Assur.] Behold, ye people, your king's successor. [Pointing to Ninias.] 'Tis Ninias, Babylon's lost prince, restored: He is your sovereign, know him, and obey.

**Assur**: Thou Ninias!

**Oroes**: Ay; 'tis he: the guardian god, Who saved him from thy rage, hath brought him hither; That god whose vengeance hath o'erthrown thee.

**Assur**: Ha! did Sémiramis then give thee life?

**Ninias**: She did, and power withal to punish thee: Guards take him hence, and rid me of a monster. He was not worthy of my sword; to fall By Ninias' hand had been a death too glorious. The victim hath escaped me; let him die, Even as he lived, with infamy: away.

**Assur**: It is my heaviest punishment to see Ninias my sovereign: but 'tis pleasure still To leave thee more unhappy than myself; [Sémiramis appears at the foot of the tomb, wounded, and almost dead, one of the magi supporting her.] Look yonder, and behold what thou hast done. [Pointing to Sémiramis: Ninias.] Whom have I slain?

**Azema**: Fly, my dear Ninias, fly This fatal place.

**Mitranes**: What hast thou done?

**Oroes**: [Placing himself between Ninias and the tomb.] Away; And cleanse those bloody hands: give me the sword, That fatal instrument of wrath divine.

**Ninias**: No: let me plunge it to my heart. [He attempts to destroy himself, the guards interpose.]

**Oroes**: Disarm him.

**Sémiramis**: [Brought forward and seated on a sofa.] Revenge me, O my son; some base assassin Has slain thy mother.

**Ninias**: O unhappy hour; Unheard of guilt! for know, that base assassin, That monster was—thy son: this hand hath pierced The breast that nourished and supported me: But soon thou shalt have vengeance, Ninias soon Shall follow thee.

**Sémiramis**: I went into the tomb To save thee, Ninias; thy unhappy mother— But from thy hands, I have received the fate I merited.

**Ninias**: This last, this fatal stroke, Sinks deep into my soul: but here I call Those gods to witness who conducted me, Those who misled my steps—

**Sémiramis:** No more, my son: Freely I pardon thee, and only make This last request, that those dear hands may close My dying eyes. [He kneels.] A mother begs it of thee: Thy heart I know was stranger to the deed: O would that I had been as innocent When Ninus died! but I have suffered for it. Henceforth let mortals know, that there are crimes Offended heaven never can forgive. O Ninias, Azema, let your blessed union Blot out my crimes; come near your dying mother; Give me your hands; long may ye live and reign In happiness! that hope still gives me comfort, And mingles joy even with the pangs of death. It comes, I feel it. O! my children, think On your Sémiramis, O do not hate My memory,—O my son, my son—'tis past.

**Oroes:** Her eyes are sunk in darkness: help the king And guard his life. Learn from her sad example, That heaven is witness to our secret crimes: The higher is the criminal, remember, The gods inflict the greater punishment; Kings, tremble on your thrones, and fear their justice.

**End**

# Pandora

## Contents

Dramatis Personæ............................................. 187
Act I. ......................................................... 187
Act II. ........................................................ 189
Act III. ....................................................... 191
Act IV. ....................................................... 193
Act V. ........................................................ 194

## Dramatis Personæ

Prometheus, a Son of Heaven and Earth, A Demi-God.
Pandora.
Jupiter.
Mercury.
Nemesis.
Nymphs.
Titans.
Celestial Deities.
Infernal Deities.

## ACT I.

The scene represents a fine country, with mountains at a distance.

**SCENE I.**
Prometheus, Chorus of Nymphs, Pandora.
[At the farther end of the stage, lying down in an alcove.]
**Prometheus:** In vain, Pandora, do I call on thee, My lovely work; alas! thou hearest me not, All stranger as thou art to thy own charms, And to Prometheus' love: the heart I formed Is still insensible; thy eyes are void Of motion; still the ruthless power of Jove Denies thee life, and drives me to despair: Whilst nature

breathes around thee, and the birds In tender notes express their passion, thou Art still inanimate; death holds thee still Beneath his cruel empire.

SCENE II.

Prometheus, the Titans, Enceladus, Typhon, etc.

**Enceladus and Typhon**: Child of Earth And Heaven, thy cries have raised the forest; speak; Who amongst the gods hath wronged Prometheus?

**Prometheus**: [Pointing to Pandora.] Jove Is jealous of my work divine; he fears That altars will be raised to my Pandora; He cannot bear to see the earth adorned With such a peerless object; he denies To grant her life, and makes my woes eternal.

**Typhon**: That proud usurper Jove did ne'er create Our nobler souls; life, and its sacred flame, Come not from him.

**Enceladus**: [Pointing to his brother Typhon.] We are the sons of Night And Tartarus: To thee, eternal night, we pray, Thou wert long before the day; Let then to Janarus Olympus yield.

**Typhon**: Let the unrelenting Jove Join the jealous gods above; Life and all its blessings flow From hell, and from the gods below.

**Prometheus and the Two Titans**: Come from the centre, gods of night profound, And animate her beauty; let your power Assist our bold emprize!

**Prometheus**: Your voice is heard, The day looks pale, and the astonished earth Shakes from its deep foundations: Erebus Appears before us. [The scene changing represents chaos; all the gods of hell come upon the stage.]

**Chorus of Infernal Deities**: Light is hateful to our eyes, Jove and heaven we despise; The guilty race, as yet unborn, must go With us to hell's profoundest depths below.

**Nemesis**: The waves of Lethe, and the flames of hell, Shall ravage all: speak, whom must Janarus In its dark womb embrace?

**Prometheus**: I love the earth, And would not hurt it: to that beauteous object [Pointing to Pandora] Have I given birth; but Jove denies it power To breathe, to think, to love, and to be happy.

**The Three Parcæ**: All our glory, and our joy, Is to hurt, and to destroy; Heaven alone can give it breath, We can nought bestow but death.

**Prometheus**: Away then, ye destroyers, ye are not The deities Prometheus shall adore; Hence to your gloomy seats, ye hateful powers, And leave the world in peace.

**Nemesis**: Tremble thou, for thou shalt prove Soon the fatal power of love: We will unchain the fiends of war, And death's destructive gates unbar. [The infernal deities disappear, and the country resumes its verdure: the nymphs of the woods range themselves on each side of the stage.]

**Prometheus:** [To the Titans.] Why would ye call forth from their dark abyss The foes of nature, to obscure the light Of these fair regions? From hell Pandora never shall receive That flame divine which only heaven should give.

**Enceladus:** Since, good Prometheus, 'tis thy dear delight To scatter blessings o'er this new abode, Thou best deservest to be its master: haste To yon blest regions, and snatch thence the flame Celestial, form a soul, and be thyself The great Creator.

**Prometheus:** Love's in heaven; he reigns O'er all the gods: I'll throw his darts around, And light up his fierce fires: he is my god, And will assist Prometheus.

**Chorus of Nymphs:** Fly to the immortal realms above, And penetrate the throne of Jove; The world to thee shall altars raise, And millions celebrate thy praise.

# ACT II.

The scene represents the same country; Pandora inanimate reclining in the alcove; a flaming chariot descends from heaven.

Prometheus, Pandora, Nymphs, Titans, etc.

**A Dryad:** Ye woodland nymphs, rise from your fair abode, And sing the praises of the demi-god; Who returns from above In the chariot of love?

**Chorus of Nymphs:** Ye verdant lawns, and opening flowers, Ye springs which lavish nature's powers; Ye hills that bear the impending sky, Put on your fairest forms to meet his eye.

**Prometheus:** [Descending from the chariot, with a torch in his hand.] Ravished from heaven I bring to happier earth Love's sacred flame, more brilliant than the light Of glittering day, and to Jove's boasted thunder Superior.

**Chorus of Nymphs:** Go, thou enlivening, animating soul, Through nature's every work, pervade the whole; To earth, to water, and to air impart, Thy vivid power, and breathe o'er every heart.

**Prometheus:** [Coming near to Pandora.] And may this precious flame inspire thy frame With life and motion! earth, assist my purpose! Rise, beauteous object, love commands thee; haste, Obey his voice; arise, and bless Prometheus! [Pandora rises, and comes forward.]

**Chorus:** She breathes, she lives; O love, how great thy power!

**Pandora:** Whence, and what am I? to what gracious powers Owe I my life and being? [A symphony is heard at a distance.] Hark! my ears Are ravished with enchanting sounds; my eyes With beauteous objects filled on every side: What wonders hath my kind creator spread Around me! O where is he? I have thought And reason to enlighten me: O earth, Thou art not my mother; some benignant god Produced me: yes, I feel him in my heart. [She sits down by the side of a fountain.] What do I see! myself, in this fair fountain, That doth reflect the face of heaven? the more I see this image, sure the more I ought To thank the gods who made me.

**Nymphs and Titans**: [Dancing round her.] Fair Pandora, Daughter of heaven, let thy charms inspire An equal flame, and fan the mutual fire.

**Pandora**: What lovely object that way draws my eyes? [To Prometheus.] Of all I see in these delightful mansions, Nought pleases like thyself; 'twas thou alone Who gavest me life, and I will live for thee.

**Prometheus**: Before those lovely eyes could see Their author, they enchanted me; Before that tongue could speak, Prometheus loved thee.

**Pandora**: Thou lovest me then, dear author of my life, And my heart owns its master; for to thee It flies with transport: have I said too much, Or not enough?

**Prometheus**: O thou canst never say Too much; thou speakest the language of pure love And nature: thus may lovers always speak!

**Duet**: God of my heart, eternal power, Great love, enliven every hour; Thy reign begins, and may thy transports prove The reign of pleasure is the reign of love!

**Prometheus**: But hark! the thunder rolls; thick clouds of darkness, As envious of the earth's new happiness, Disturb our joys: what horrors throng around me! Hark! the earth shakes, and angry lightnings pierce The vault of heaven: what power thus moves the world From its foundations? [A car descends, on which are seated Mercury, Discord, Nemesis, etc.]

**Mercury**: Some rash hand hath stolen The sacred fire from heaven: to expiate The dire offence, Pandora, thou must go Before the high tribunal of the gods.

**Prometheus**: O cruel tyrant!

**Pandora**: Dread commands!

**Mercury**: Obey: Thou must to heaven.

**Pandora**: I was in heaven already, When I beheld the object of my love.

**Prometheus**: Have pity, cruel gods!

Prometheus and Pandora, Barbarians, stay.

**Mercury**: Haste, offenders, haste away, Jove commands, you must obey: Bear her, ye winds, to heaven's eternal mansions. [The car mounts and disappears.]

**Prometheus**: The cruel tyrants, jealous of my bliss, Have torn her from me; she was the lovely work Of my own hands: I have done more than Jove Could ever do: Pandora's charming eyes, Soon as they opened, told me that she loved: Thou jealous god! but thou shalt feel my wrath, And I will brave thy power: for know, usurper, Less dreadful far will all thy thunders prove, Than bold Prometheus fired by hopeless love.

# ACT III.

The scene represents the palace of Jupiter.

Jupiter, Mercury.

**Jupiter**: O Mercury, I've seen this lovely object, Earth's fair production; heaven is in her eye, The graces dwell around her, and my heart Is sacrificed a victim to her charms.

**Mercury**: And she shall answer to thy love.

**Jupiter**: O no: Terror is mine, and power; I reign supreme O'er earth, and hell, and heaven; but love alone Can govern hearts: malicious, cruel fate, When it divided this fair universe, Bestowed the better part on mighty love.

**Mercury**: What fearest thou? fair Pandora scarce hath seen The light of day; and thinkest thou that she loves?

**Jupiter**: Love is a passion learned with ease; and what Cannot Pandora do? she is a woman, And handsome: but I will retire a moment, Enchant her eyes, and captivate her heart: Ye heavens! in vain, alas! ye shine, for nought Have you so fair, so beauteous as Pandora. [He retires.]

**Pandora**: Scarce have these eyes beheld the light of day, Scarce have they looked on him I loved, when lo! 'Tis all snatched from me; death, they say, will come And take me soon: O I have felt him sure Already: is not death the sudden loss Of those we love? O give me back, ye gods, To earth, to that delightful grove where first I saw my kind creator, when at once I breathed and loved: O envied happiness! [The gods, with their several attributes, come upon the stage.]

**Chorus of Gods**: Let heaven rejoice At the glad voice Of heaven's eternal king.

**Neptune**: Let the sea's bosom—

**Pluto**: And the depths of hell—

**Chorus of Gods**: To distant worlds his endless praises tell. Let heaven rejoice, etc.

**Pandora**: How all conspires to threaten and alarm me! O how I hate and fear this dazzling splendor! Another's merit how can I approve, Or bear the praise of aught but him I love?

**The Three Graces**: Love's fair daughter, here remain, Thou in right of him shalt reign; Heaven thy chosen seat shall be, Earth in vain shall wish for thee.

**Pandora**: All affrights me, Nought delights me, Alas! a desert had more charms for me. Hence, ye idle visions; cease, Discordant sounds, [A Symphony is heard.] And give me peace. [Jupiter comes forth out of a cloud.]

**Jupiter**: Thou art the best and fairest charm of nature, Well worthy of eternity: from earth Sprang thy weak body; but thy purer soul Partakes of heaven's unalterable fire, And thou wert born for gods alone: with Jove Taste then the sweets of immortality.

**Pandora**: I scorn thy gift, and rather would be nothing, From whence I sprang; thy immortality, Without the lovely object I adore, Is but eternal punishment.

**Jupiter**: Fair creature, Thou knowest not I am master of the thunder: Canst thou in heaven look back to earth?

**Pandora**: That earth Is my abode; there first I learned to love.

**Jupiter**: 'Twas but the shadow of it, in a world Unworthy of that noble flame, which here Alone can burn unquenchable.

**Pandora**: Great Jove, Content with glory and with splendor, leave To earthly lovers happiness and joy: Thou art a god; O hear my humble prayer! A gracious god should make his creatures happy.

**Jupiter**: Thou shalt be happy, and in thee I hope For bliss supreme: ye powerful pleasures, you Who dwell around me, now exert your charms, Deceive her lovely eyes, and win her heart. [The Pleasures dance around her and sing.]

**Chorus of Pleasures**: Thou with us shalt reign and love, Thou alone art worthy Jove.

**A Single Voice**: Nought has earth but shadows vain, Of pleasures followed close by pain; Soon her winged transports fly, Soon her roses fade and die.

**Chorus**: Thou with us shalt reign and love, Thou alone art worthy Jove.

**Single Voice**: Here the brisk and sportive hours Shall cull thee ever-blooming flowers; Time has no wings, he cannot fly, And love is joined to immortality.

**Chorus**: Thou with us shalt reign and love, Thou alone art worthy Jove.

**Pandora**: Ye tender pleasures, ye increase my flame, And ye increase my pain: if happiness Is yours to give, O bear it to my love.

**Jupiter**: Is this the sad effect of all my care, To make a rival happy? [Enter Mercury.]

**Mercury**: Assume thy lightnings, Jove, and blast thy foe; Prometheus is in arms, the Titans rage, And threaten heaven; mountain on mountain piled, They scale the skies; already they approach.

**Jupiter**: Jove has the power to punish; let them come.

**Pandora**: And wilt thou punish? thou, who art the cause Of all his miseries; thou art a jealous tyrant: Go on, and love me; I shall hate thee more; Be that thy punishment.

**Jupiter**: I must away: Rive them, ye thunder-bolts.

**Pandora**: Have mercy, Jove!

**Jupiter**: [To Mercury.] Conduct Pandora to a place of safety: The happy world was wrapped in peace profound, A beauty comes, and nought is seen but ruin. [He goes out.]

**Pandora**: [Alone] O fatal charms! would I had ne'er been born! Beauty and love, and every gift divine, But make me wretched: if, all-powerful Love, Thou didst create me, now relieve my sorrows; Dry up my tears, bid war and slaughter cease, And give to heaven and earth eternal peace.

# ACT IV.

The scene represents the Titans armed, mountains at a distance, with giants throwing them on each other.

**Enceladus**: Fear not, Prometheus, nature feels thy wrongs, And joins with us in just revenge: behold These pointed rocks, and shaggy mountains; soon The jealous tyrants all shall sink beneath them.

**Prometheus**: Now, earth, defend thyself, and combat heaven: Trumpets and drums, now shall ye first be heard: March, Titans, follow me: the seat of gods Is your reward; be fair Pandora mine. [They march to the sound of trumpets.]

**Chorus of Titans**: Arm, ye valiant Titans, arm, Spread around the dread alarm: Let proud immortals tremble on their thrones.

**Prometheus**: Their thunder answers to our trumpets' voice. [Thunder is heard; a car descends, bearing the gods towards the mountains: Pandora is seated near Jupiter; Prometheus speaks.] Jove gives the dreadful signal; haste, begin The battle. [The giants rise towards heaven.]

**Chorus of Nymphs**: Earth, and hell, and heaven confounded, All with terrors are surrounded: Cease, ye gods, and Titans, cease Your cruel wars, and give us peace.

**Titans**: Yield, cruel tyrants.

**Gods**: Rebels, fly.

**Titans**: Yield, heaven, to earth.

**Gods**: Die, rebels, die.

**Pandora**: O heaven! O earth! ye Titans, and ye gods, O cease your rage, all perish for Pandora: I have made the world unhappy.

**Titans**: Draw Your arrows now.

**Gods**: Strike, thunders.

**Titans**: Hurl down heaven.

**Gods**: Destroy the earth.

**Both**: Yield, cruel tyrants—rebels fly— Yield, earth, to heaven—die, rebels, die. [A dead silence for a time; a bright cloud descends; Destiny appears, seated in the middle of it.]

**Destiny**: Cease, hostile powers, attend to me, And hear the will of Destiny. [Silence ensues.]

**Prometheus**: Unalterable being, power supreme, Speak thy irrevocable doom; attend, Ye tyrants, and obey.

**Chorus**: Speak, the gods must yield to thee; Speak, immortal Destiny.

**Destiny**: [In the middle of the gods, who throng round him.] Hear me, ye gods; another world this day Brings forth: meantime let every gift adorn Pandora; and you, Titans, who 'gainst heaven Have raised rebellious war, receive your doom, Beneath these mountains sunk forever groan. [The rocks fall upon them; the chariot of the gods descends to earth; Pandora is restored to Prometheus.]

**Jupiter**: O fate, my empire yields to thee, Jove submits to destiny: Thou art obeyed; but from this hour let earth And heaven be disunited: Nemesis, Come forth. [Nemesis advances from the bottom of the stage, and Jupiter proceeds.] Nemesis, thy aid impart, Pierce the cruel beauty's heart; My vengeance let Pandora know, In the gifts that I bestow: Let heaven and earth henceforth be disunited.

## ACT V.

The scene represents a grove, with the ruins of rocks scattered about it. Prometheus, Pandora.

**Pandora**: [Holding a box in her hand.] And wilt thou leave me then? art thou subdued, Or art thou conqueror?

**Prometheus**: Victory is mine: If yet thou lovest me, love and destiny Speak for Prometheus.

**Pandora**: Wilt thou leave me then?

**Prometheus**: The Titans are subdued: lament their fate: I must assist them; let us teach mankind To succor the unhappy.

**Pandora:** Stay a moment: Behold thy victory: let us open this, It was the gift of Jove.

**Prometheus:** What wouldst thou do? A rival's gift is dangerous; 'tis some snare The gods have laid.

**Pandora:** Thou canst not think it.

**Prometheus:** Hear What I request of thee, and stay at least Till I return.

**Pandora:** Thou biddest, and I obey: I swear by love still to believe Prometheus.

**Prometheus:** Wilt thou then promise?

**Pandora:** By thyself I swear: All are obedient where they love.

**Prometheus:** Enough: I'm satisfied: and now, ye woodland nymphs, Begin your songs; sing earth restored to bliss; Let all be gay, for all was made for her.

**First Nymph:** Come, fair Pandora, come and prove An age of gold, of innocence, and love; And, like thy parent Nature, be immortal.

**Second Nymph:** No longer now shall earth affrighted mourn, By cruel war her tender bosom torn: Pleasures now on pleasures flow, Happiness succeeds to woe: The flowers their fragrant odors yield; Who would wither the fair field? The blest creation teems with mirth and joy, And nature's work what tyrant would destroy?

**The Chorus:** [Repeats.] Come, fair Pandora, come and prove An age of gold, etc.

**First Nymph:** See! to Pandora Mercury appears, And ratifies great Nature's kind decree. [The nymphs retire: Pandora advances with Nemesis, under the figure of Mercury.]

**Nemesis:** Already I have told thee, base Prometheus Is jealous of thee, and exerts his power Like a harsh tyrant.

**Pandora:** O he is my lord, My king, my god, my lover, and my husband.

**Nemesis:** Why then forbid thee to behold the gift Of generous heaven?

**Pandora:** His fearful love's alarmed, And I would wish to have no will but his.

**Nemesis:** He asks too much, Pandora, nor hath done What thou deservest: he might have given thee beauties Which now thou hast not.

**Pandora:** He hath formed my heart Tender and kind; he charms and he adores me; What could he more?

**Nemesis:** Thy charms will perish.

**Pandora:** Ha! Thou makest me tremble.

**Nemesis:** This mysterious box Will make thy charms immortal; thou wilt be Forever beauteous, and forever happy: Thy husband shall be subject to thy power, And thou shalt reign unrivalled in his love.

**Pandora:** He is my only lord, and I would wish To be immortal, but for my Prometheus.

**Nemesis:** Fain would I open thy fair eyes, and bless thee With every good; would make thee please forever.

**Pandora:** But dost thou not abuse my innocence? And canst thou be so cruel?

**Nemesis:** Who would hurt Such beauty?

**Pandora:** I should die with grief, if e'er I disobliged the sovereign of my heart.

**Nemesis:** O in the name of Nature, in the name Of thy dear husband, listen to my voice!

**Pandora:** That name has conquered, and I will believe thee. [She opens the box; darkness is spread over the stage, and a voice heard from below.] Ha! what thick cloud thus o'er my senses spreads Its fatal darkness? thou deceitful god! O I am guilty, and I suffer for it.

**Nemesis:** I must away: Jove is revenged, and now I will return to hell. [Nemesis vanishes: Pandora faints away on the grass.]

**Prometheus:** [Advancing from the farther end of the stage.] O fatal absence! dreadful change! what star Of evil influence thus deforms the face Of Nature? where's my dear Pandora? why Answers she not to my complaining voice? O my Pandora! but behold, from hell Let loose, the monsters rise, and rush upon us. [Furies and demons running on the stage.]

**Furies:** The time is come when we shall reign: Fear and grief, remorse and pain, From this great decisive hour, O'er the world shall spread their power; Death shall come, a bitter draught, By the Furies hither brought.

**Prometheus:** That cruel guest shall powers infernal bring? And must the earth lose her eternal spring? To time, and dire disease, and horrid vice, Shall mortals fall a helpless sacrifice? The nymphs lament our fate: Pandora, hear And answer to my griefs! she comes, but seems Insensible.

**Pandora:** I am not worthy of thee: I have destroyed mankind, deceived my husband, And am alone the guilty cause of all: Strike: I deserve it.

**Prometheus:** Can I punish thee?

**Pandora:** Strike, and deprive me of that wretched life Thou didst bestow.

**Chorus of Nymphs:** Tenderest lover, dry her tears, She is full of lover's fears; She is woman, therefore frail, Let her beauty then prevail.

**Prometheus:** Hast thou then, spite of all thy solemn vows, Opened the fatal box?

**Pandora:** Some cruel god Betrayed me: fatal curiosity! The work was thine: O every evil sprung From that accursed gift: undone Pandora!

**Love:** [Descending from heaven.] Love still remains, and every good is thine: [Scene changes, and represents the palace of love.] [Love proceeds.] For thee will I resist the power of fate; I gave to mortals being, and they ne'er Shall be unhappy whilst they worship me.

**Pandora:** Soul of my soul, thou comforter divine, O punish Jove; inspire his vengeful heart With double passion for the blessed Pandora.

**Prometheus and Pandora:** Heaven shall pierce our hearts in vain With every grief, and every pain; With thee no pains torment, no pleasures cloy; With thee to suffer is but to enjoy.

**love:** Lovely hope, on mortals wait; Come, and gild their wretched state; All thy flattering joys impart. Haste, and live in every heart; Howe'er deceitful thou mayest be, Thou canst grant felicity, And make them happy in futurity.

**Pandora:** Fate would make us wretched here, But hope shall dry up every tear; In sorrow he shall give us rest, And make us even in anguish blest: Love shall preserve us from the paths of vice, And strew his flowers around the precipice.

**End**

# The Scotch Woman

## Contents

Dramatis Personæ. . . . . . . . . . . . . . . . . . . . . . . . . . . . . . . . . . . . . . . . . . . 198
Act I. . . . . . . . . . . . . . . . . . . . . . . . . . . . . . . . . . . . . . . . . . . . . . . . . . . . . . 198
Act II. . . . . . . . . . . . . . . . . . . . . . . . . . . . . . . . . . . . . . . . . . . . . . . . . . . . . 207
Act III. . . . . . . . . . . . . . . . . . . . . . . . . . . . . . . . . . . . . . . . . . . . . . . . . . . . 217
Act IV. . . . . . . . . . . . . . . . . . . . . . . . . . . . . . . . . . . . . . . . . . . . . . . . . . . . 224
Act V. . . . . . . . . . . . . . . . . . . . . . . . . . . . . . . . . . . . . . . . . . . . . . . . . . . . . 231

Represented at Paris in 1760.

## Dramatis Personæ

Mr. Fabrice, master of a Coffee-house.
Miss Lindon, a Scotchwoman.
Lord Montross, a Scotchman.
Lord Murray.
Polly, maid to Miss Lindon.
Freeport, a Merchant of London.
Wasp, a Writer.
Lady Alton.
Several English Gentlemen frequenting the Coffee-house, Servants, Messengers, &c.

Voltaire dashed off this comedy in eight days, to ridicule Fréron, who had unfavorably criticised Candide. It was first published as by Hume, or Home, author of the tragedy "Douglas."

## ACT I.

SCENE I.
Scene London.

# Voltaire

The scene represents a coffee-house, with apartments on the same floor on each side communicating with it.

**Wasp:** [At one corner of the room reading the papers. Coffee, pen and ink, etc., on the table before him.] A plague on this vile news! here are places and pensions given to above twenty people, and nothing for me! a present of a hundred guineas to a subaltern for doing his duty! a great merit indeed! so much to the inventor of a machine to lessen the number of hands; so much to a pilot; so much settled on men of letters, but nothing for me! here's another pension, and another—but the deuce a farthing for Wasp [he throws down the paper and walks about] and yet I have done the state some service; I have written more than any one man in England; I have raised the price of paper; and yet nothing is done for me: but I will be revenged on all those whom the world calls men of merit: I have got something already by speaking ill of others; and if I can but contrive to do them a real mischief, my fortune is made. I have praised fools, and calumniated every good quality and perfection of human nature, and yet can scarce live by it: in short, to be a great man, you must not be content with slander and destruction, but endeavor to be really hurtful. [To the master of the coffee-house.] Good morrow to you, Mr. Fabrice. Well, Mr. Fabrice, everybody's affairs, I find, go well but mine; it is intolerable.

**Fabrice:** Indeed, indeed, Mr. Wasp, you make yourself a great many enemies.

**Wasp:** I believe I excite a little envy.

**Fabrice:** On my soul I believe not; but rather a passion of a very different kind: to be free, for I have really a friendship for you, I am extremely concerned to hear people talk of you as they do: how do you contrive to be so universally hated?

**Wasp:** It is because I have merit, Mr. Fabrice.

**Fabrice:** That may possibly be; but you are the only person who ever told me so: they say you are a very ignorant fellow: but that is nothing; they say, moreover, that you are ill-natured and malicious; that gives me concern, as it must every honest man.

**Wasp:** I assure you I have a good and tender heart. I do indeed now and then speak a little freely of the men; but for the women, Mr. Fabrice, I love them all, provided they are handsome. As a proof of it, I must absolutely insist on your introducing me to your amiable lodger, whom I have never yet been able to converse with.

**Fabrice:** Upon honor, Mr. Wasp, that young lady will never do for you; for she never praises herself, or speaks ill of anybody else.

**Wasp**: She speaks ill of nobody, because, I suppose, she knows nobody: are you not in love with her, Fabrice?

**Fabrice**: Not I indeed, sir; she has something in her air so noble, that I dare not think of it—besides, her virtue—

**Wasp**: [Laughing.] Ha! ha! ha! her virtue indeed!

**Fabrice**: Why so merry, sir? think you there is no such thing as virtue?—but I hear a coach at the door, and yonder is a livery servant with a portmanteau in his hand; some lord coming to lodge with me, perhaps.

**Wasp**: Be sure, my dear friend, you recommend me to him as soon as possible.

## SCENE II.

Lord Montross, Fabrice, Wasp.

**Montross**: You, sir, I suppose, are Mr. Fabrice.

**Fabrice**: At your service, sir.

**Montross**: I shall stay here only a few days. (Protect me, heaven, unhappy as I am!) I am recommended to you, sir, as a worthy honest man.

**Fabrice**: So, sir, we ought all to be. You will here, sir, I believe, meet with all the conveniences of life; a tolerably good apartment, and my own table, if you choose to do me the honor to dine at it, and the amusement of coffee-house conversation.

**Montross**: Have you many boarders with you at present?

**Fabrice**: Only one young lady, sir, very handsome and extremely virtuous.

**Wasp**: O mighty virtuous, ha! ha!

**Fabrice**: Who lives quite retired.

**Montross**: Beauty and youth are not for me. Let me have an apartment, sir, if possible, entirely to myself. (What do I feel!) Have you any remarkable news in London?

**Fabrice**: This gentleman, sir, can inform you: he talks and writes more than any one man in England, and is extremely useful to foreigners.

**Montross**: [Walking about.] I have other business.

**Fabrice**: I'll step out, sir, and get things ready for you. [Exit.]

**Wasp**: [Aside.] This gentleman, I suppose, is just arrived in England: he must be some great man, for he seems to care for nobody. [Turning to Montross.] Permit me, my lord, to present to your lordship my respects; my pen and self, my lord, are at your lordship's service.

**Montross:** I am no lord, sir: to boast of a title, if we have one, is the part of a fool; and to assume one when we have no right, that of a knave. I am what I am; but pray, sir, what may be your employment in this house?

**Wasp:** I don't belong to the house, sir; but I spend most of my time in the coffee-room; write news, politics, and so forth, and am always ready to do an honest gentleman service. If you have any friend you want to have praised, or any enemy to be abused; any author you want to protect or to decry; 'tis but one guinea per paragraph: if you are desirous of cultivating any acquaintance for profit or pleasure, sir, I am your man.

**Montross:** And have you no other business, friend?

**Wasp:** O sir, it is a very good one, I assure you.

**Montross:** And have you never been shown in public with a pretty iron collar about your neck?

**Wasp:** This fellow has no notion of literature.

### SCENE III.

**Wasp:** [Sitting down to the table] several people walking about the coffee-house; Montross comes forward.

**Montross:** Will my misfortunes never have an end? proscribed, banished, condemned to lose my head in Scotland; in my dear native country: I have lost my honors, my wife, my son, my whole family; except one unhappy daughter, like myself a miserable wanderer, perhaps dishonored; and must I die without taking revenge on Murray's barbarous family? I am razed out of the book of life; I am no more; even my name is wrested from me by that cruel decree: I am but a poor departed ghost, that hovers round its tomb. [One of the gentlemen in the coffee-house slapping Wasp on the shoulder.] Well! you saw the new piece yesterday, it met with great applause; the author is a young fellow of merit, but has no fortune, the public ought to encourage him.

**Another:** Rot the new piece; public affairs are strangely carried on; stocks rise; the nation's rich, and I'm ruined, absolutely undone.

**Wasp:** [Writing.] The piece is good for nothing; the author's a fool, and so are all those that support him: public affairs are in a wretched condition: the nation's ruined: I shall prove it in my pamphlet.

another gentleman. Your pamphlet's nonsense: philosophy is the most dangerous thing in the world; it was that which lost us the island of Minorca.

**Montross:** [At a distance from them.] Lord Murray's son shall pay dearly for it. O that before I die I could avenge the father's injuries in the son's blood!

**A Gentleman:** I thought the comedy last night was an excellent one.

**Wasp:** Detestable: our taste grows worse and worse.

**Another Gentleman:** Not so bad as your criticisms.

**Another:** Philosophers sink the public funds: we must send another ambassador to Porte.

**Wasp:** We should always hiss a successful piece, for fear anything good should appear. [Four of them talk at once.]

**First Gentleman:** If there was nothing good, you would lose all the pleasure of satirizing it: now I think the fifth act has great beauties.

**Second Gentleman:** I can't sell any of my goods.

**Third Gentleman:** I am in pain for Jamaica this year: depend on't, these philosophers will make us lose it.

**Wasp:** The fourth and fifth acts are both contemptible.

**Montross:** What a riot is here.

**First Gentleman:** It is impossible the government can exist as it is.

**Second Gentleman:** If the price of Barbadoes water is not lowered, the nation's undone.

**Montross:** How happens it, that in every country when men meet they all talk together, though they are certain of not being heard or attended to!

**Fabrice:** [Enters with a napkin in his hand.] Dinner's on the table, gentlemen; but pray, let us have no disputes there, if you mean to dine with me any more. Sir, [Turning to Montross.] shall we have the honor of your company?

**Montross:** What, with this tribe? no, friend, let me have something in my own room. Hark'ee, sir, [Whispering to him.] Is my Lord Falbridge in London?

**Fabrice:** No, sir, but I believe he will be here soon.

**Montross:** Does he come to your house sometimes? I think I have heard so.

**Fabrice:** He has done me that honor.—

**Montross:** Very well. Good morrow to you.—How hateful is life to me! [Exit.]

**Fabrice:** This man seems lost in grief and thought; I should not be surprised to hear he had made away with himself; 'twould concern me, for he has the appearance of a worthy gentleman. [The gentlemen leave the coffee-house, and go to dinner; Wasp continues at the table writing: Fabrice knocks at Mrs. Lindon's door.]

SCENE IV.
Fabrice, Polly, Wasp.

**Fabrice:** Mrs. Polly, Mrs. Polly.

**Polly:** Who's there, my landlord?

**Fabrice:** Will you be so obliging as to favor us with your company to dinner?

**Polly:** I dare not, my mistress eats nothing. How indeed should we eat! we have too much grief.

**Fabrice:** O it will give you spirits, and make you cheerful.

**Polly:** I can't be cheerful: when my mistress suffers, I must suffer with her.

**Fabrice:** Then I'll send you up something privately. [Exit.]

**Wasp:** [Rising from the table.] I'll follow you, Mr. Fabrice—well, and so, my dear Polly, you will not introduce me to your mistress—still inflexible?

**Polly:** 'Tis a fine thing for you to pretend to make love to a woman of her condition.

**Wasp:** Pray what is her condition?

**Polly:** A respectable one, I assure you, sir. I should think a servant was good enough for you.

**Wasp:** That is to say, if I were to court you, you would be thankful.

**Polly:** Not I, indeed.

**Wasp:** And what, pray, is the reason why your mistress positively refuses to see me, and her waiting-maid treats me so contemptuously?

**Polly:** We have three reasons for it. First, you are a wit; secondly, you are very tiresome; and thirdly, you are a wicked fellow.

**Wasp:** And what right has your mistress, pray, who is kept here on charity, to despise me?

**Polly:** Upon charity? who told you so, sir? my mistress, sir, is very rich: if she is not expensive, it is because she hates pomp: she is plainly clad, out of modesty, and eats little, because temperance is prescribed to her: in short, sir, you are very impertinent.

**Wasp:** Don't let her give herself so many airs; we know her conduct, her birth, and her adventures.

**Polly:** You, sir, who told them you? what do you know?

**Wasp:** O, I have correspondents in every part of the world.

**Polly:** [Aside.] O heaven! this man will ruin us. [Turning to him.] Mr. Wasp, my dear Mr. Wasp, if you know anything, don't betray us.

**Wasp:** O ho! there is something then, and now I am dear Mr. Wasp: well, well, I shall say nothing, but you must—

**Polly:** What?

**Wasp:** You must love me.

**Polly:** Fie, fie, sir, that's impossible.

**Wasp:** Either love or fear me. You know there is something—

**Polly:** There is nothing, sir, but that my mistress is as respectable as you are hateful. We are truly easy. We fear nothing, and only laugh at you.

**Wasp:** They are very easy: from that I conclude they are almost starved: they fear nothing, that is to say, they are afraid of being discovered—I shall get to the bottom of it by and by, or—I shall not. I'll be revenged on them for their insolence. Despise me!

SCENE V.

**Miss Lindon:** [Coming out of her chamber dressed very plainly.]

Miss Lindon, Polly.

**Miss Lindon:** O my dear Polly, you have been with that vile fellow, Wasp; he always makes me uneasy; a destestable character, whose pen, words, and actions are all equally abominable: they tell me he works himself into families to bring in misery where there is none, and to increase it where it is: I had left this house because he frequents it, long since, but for the honesty and good heart of our landlord.

**Polly:** He absolutely insisted on seeing you, and I would not let him.

**Miss Lindon:** To see me! where is my Lord Murray, he has not been here these two days!

**Polly:** True, madam, but because he does not come, are we never to dine?

**Miss Lindon:** Remember, Polly, to conceal my misery from him, and from all the world: I am content to live on bread and water: poverty is not intolerable, but contempt is: I am satisfied to be in want, but I would not have it known I am so.

**Polly:** Alas! my dear mistress, whoever looks at me will easily perceive it: with you it is a different thing; your nobleness of soul supports you, you seem to rejoice in calamities, and only look the handsomer for it: but I grow thinner and thinner, you may see me fall away every minute; I am so altered within this last year that I scarcely know myself.

**Miss Lindon:** We must not part with our courage nor our hopes: I can support my own poverty, but yours indeed affects me. My dear girl, let the labor of my hands relieve you, we will have no obligations to anybody. Go and sell this embroidery which I have done lately. I think I succeed pretty well in this kind of work. You have assisted me, and in return my hands shall feed and clothe you: It is noble to owe our subsistence to nothing but our virtue.

**Polly:** Let me kiss, let me bathe with my tears the dear hands that have labored in my service O! I had rather die with my dear mistress in poverty, than be servant to a queen. Would I could administer some comfort to you!

**Miss Lindon:** Alas! Lord Murray is not come: he whom I ought to hate, the son of him who was the author of all my misfortunes: alas! the name of Murray will be forever fatal to me: if he comes, as he certainly will, let him not know my country, my condition, or my misfortunes.

**Polly**: Do you know, that villain, Wasp, pretends to be well acquainted with him?

**Miss Lindon**: How is it possible he should know anything of him, when even you are scarcely acquainted with him? Nobody writes to me, I am locked up in my chamber as closely as if I were in my grave: he only pretends to know something in order to make himself necessary: take care he does not so much as find out the place of my birth. You know, my dear Polly, I am an unfortunate woman whose father was banished in the late troubles, and whose family is ruined: my father is wandering from desert to desert in Scotland. I should have left London to join him in his misfortunes, but that I have still some hopes in Lord Falbridge; he was my father's friend: our true friends never desert us. He has returned from Spain, and is now at Windsor: I wait but to see him: but alas! Murray comes not. I have opened my heart to thee, remember the most fatal blow thou canst give to it would be the disclosure of my condition.

**Polly**: To whom should I disclose it; I never go from you; besides that, the world is very indifferent about the poor and unfortunate.

**Miss Lindon**: The world is indifferent, Polly, in this respect; but still it is always inquisitive, and loves to tear open the wounds of the wretched: besides that, the men assume a right over our sex when they are unhappy, and abuse their power. I would make even my miseries respectable: but alas! Lord Murray will not come.

## SCENE VI.

Miss Lindon, Polly, Fabrice.

**Fabrice**: Forgive me, madam, I am not acquainted with your name or quality; but I have, I know not why, the greatest respect for you. I have left the company below to wait on you, and know your commands.

**Miss Lindon**: The regard which you express for me, my dear sir, deserves my most grateful acknowledgments: but what are your commands with me?

**Fabrice**: I came, madam, only to know yours: you had no dinner yesterday.

**Miss Lindon**: I was sick, sir, and could not eat.

**Fabrice**: You are worse than sick, madam, you are melancholy: you will pardon me, but I cannot help thinking your fortune is not equal to your person and appearance.

**Miss Lindon**: Why should you think so? I never complained of my fortune.

**Fabrice**: Notwithstanding that, madam, I am sure it is not what you could wish it were.

**Miss Lindon**: What say you?

**Fabrice**: I say, madam, that the world you seem to shun, admires and pities you. I am but a plain man, madam, but I can see all your merit as well as the finest courtier. Let me entreat you, my dear lady, to take a little refreshment: there is above stairs an elderly gentleman who would be glad to eat with you.

**Miss Lindon**: What, sit down to table with a stranger!

**Fabrice**: The gentleman, I am sure, would be agreeable to you: you seem afflicted, and so does he. The communication of your grief might, perhaps, give mutual consolation.

**Miss Lindon**: I cannot, will not, see anybody.

**Fabrice**: At least, madam, permit my wife to pay her respects to you, and keep you company: permit her—

**Miss Lindon**: I return you thanks, sir, but I want nothing.

**Fabrice**: You will pardon me, madam, but I cannot think you want nothing, when you stand in need even of common necessaries.

**Miss Lindon**: Who could make you believe so? indeed, sir, you are imposed upon.

**Fabrice**: You will forgive me, madam.

**Miss Lindon**: O Polly, 'tis two o'clock, and Lord Murray not come yet!

**Fabrice**: That lord you speak of, madam, is one of the best of men; you never received him here but before company. Why would not you permit me to furnish out a little repast for you both? he is, perhaps, a relative of yours.

**Miss Lindon**: My dear sir, you are mistaken.

**Fabrice**: [Pulling Polly by the sleeve.] Go, child, there is a good dinner for you in the next room. This woman is incomprehensible: but who is yonder lady in the coffee-room with a masculine air? I should have taken her for a man: how wildly she looks!

**Polly**: O my dear mistress! 'tis Lady Alton, who wanted to marry my lord—I remember I saw her once before this way: 'tis certainly she.

**Miss Lindon**: And my lord not come! then I am undone. Why am I still condemned to live? [She goes in.]

SCENE VII.

**Lady Alton**: [Walking across the stage in a violent passion, and taking Fabrice by the arm.] Follow me, sir, I must talk with you.

**Fabrice**: With me, madam?

**Lady Alton**: With you, wretch.
**Fabrice**: What a devil of a woman!

# ACT II.

### SCENE I.
Lady Alton, Fabrice.

**Lady Alton**: I don't believe a word you say, Mr. Coffeeman; you will absolutely drive me out of my senses.

**Fabrice**: Then pray, madam, get into them again.

**Lady Alton**: You have the impudence to affirm to me, that this fortune-hunter here is a woman of honor, though she has received visits from a nobleman. You ought to be ashamed of yourself.

**Fabrice**: Why so, madam? when my lord came, he never came in privately; she received him publicly, the doors of her apartment were open, and my wife present. You may despise my condition, madam, but you should respect my honesty; and as to the lady you are pleased to call a fortune-hunter, if you knew her, you would esteem her.

**Lady Alton**: Leave me, sir, you grow impertinent.

**Fabrice**: What a woman!

**Lady Alton**: [Goes to Miss Lindon's door, and knocks rudely.] Open the door.

### SCENE II.
Miss Lindon, Lady Alton.

**Miss Lindon**: Who knocks so? what do you want, madam?

**Lady Alton**: Answer me, madam. Does not Lord Murray come here sometimes?

**Miss Lindon**: What's that to you? what right have you to ask me? am I a criminal, and you my judge?

**Lady Alton**: I am your accuser. If my lord still visits you, if you encourage that wretch's passion, tremble: renounce him, or you are undone.

**Miss Lindon**: If I had a passion for him, your menaces, madam, would but increase it.

**Lady Alton**: I see you love him; that the perfidious villain has seduced you; he has deceived you, and you brave me: but know, there is no vengeance which I am not capable of executing.

**Miss Lindon:** Then, madam, know, I do love him.

**Lady Alton:** Before I revenge myself I will astonish you. There, know the traitor, look at these letters he wrote to me: there is his picture too which he gave me; but let me have it back, or—

**Miss Lindon:** [Giving her back the picture.] What have I seen? unhappy woman! madam—

**Lady Alton:** Well.

**Miss Lindon:** I no longer love him.

**Lady Alton:** Keep your resolution and your promise; know, he is inconstant, cruel, proud, the worst of characters.

**Miss Lindon:** Stop, madam; if you continue to speak ill of him, I may relapse, and love him again. You are come here on purpose to take away my wretched life: that, madam, will easily be done.—Polly, 'tis all over; come and assist me to conceal this last and worst of all my miseries.

**Polly:** What is the matter, my dear mistress, where is your courage?

**Miss Lindon:** Against misfortune, injustice, and poverty, there are arms that will defend a noble heart; but there is an arrow that always must be fatal. [They go out.]

## SCENE III.
Lady Alton, Wasp.

**Lady Alton:** To be betrayed, abandoned for this worthless little wretch. [To Wasp.] You, news-writer, have you done what I ordered you? have you employed your engines of intelligence, and found out who this insolent creature is that makes me so completely miserable?

**Wasp:** I have fulfilled your ladyship's commands, and have discovered that she is a Scotchwoman, and hides herself from the world.

**Lady Alton:** Prodigious news indeed!

**Wasp:** I can find out nothing else at present.

**Lady Alton:** What service then have you been of?

**Wasp:** When we discover a little, we add a little; and one little joined to another, makes a great deal. There's a hypothesis for you.

**Lady Alton:** How, pedant, a hypothesis!

**Wasp:** Yes, I suppose she is an enemy to the government.

**Lady Alton:** Certainly, nothing can be worse inclined; for she has robbed me of my lover.

**Wasp:** You plainly see, therefore, that in troublesome times, a Scotchwoman, who conceals herself, must be an enemy to the state.

**Lady Alton**: I can't say I see it altogether so clearly, but I heartily wish it were so.

**Wasp**: I would not lay a wager about it, but I'd swear to it.

**Lady Alton**: And would you venture to affirm this before people of consequence?

**Wasp**: I have the honor of being related to many persons of the first fashion. I am intimate with the mistress of a valet de chambre to the first secretary of the prime minister: I could even talk with the lackeys of your lover, Lord Murray, and tell them that the father of this young girl has sent her up to London, as a woman ill disposed. Now observe, this might have its consequences, and your rival, for her bad intentions, might be sent to the same prison where I have so often been for my writings.

**Lady Alton**: Good, very good: violent passions must be served by people who have no scruples about them. Let the vessel go with a full sail, or let it go to the bottom. You are certainly right; a Scotchwoman who conceals herself at a time when all the people of her country are suspected, must certainly be an enemy to the state. You are no fool, as you have been represented to me. I thought you had been only a smatterer on paper, but I see you have genius. I have already done something for you; I will do a great deal more. You must let me know everything that passes here.

**Wasp**: Let me advise you, madam, to make use of everything you know, and of everything you do not know. Truth stands in need of some ornament: downright lies indeed may be vile things, but fiction is beautiful. What after all is truth? a conformity with our own ideas; what one says is always conformable to the idea one has whilst one is talking; therefore, properly speaking, there is no such thing as a lie.

**Lady Alton**: You seem to be an excellent logician, I fancy you studied at St. Omer's. But go, only tell me whatever you discover, I ask no more of you.

SCENE IV.

Lady Alton, Fabrice.

**Lady Alton**: This is certainly one of the vilest and most impudent scoundrels; dogs bite from an instinct of courage, and this fellow from an instinct of meanness. Methinks, now I am a little cool, his behavior makes me out of love with revenge. I could almost take my rival's part against him. She has in her low condition a pride that pleases me; she is decent, and I am told, sensible: but she has robbed me of my lover, and that I can never pardon. [To Fabrice, whom she sees in the coffee-room.] Honest man, your servant, you are a good kind of fellow, but you have got a sad rascal in your house.

**Fabrice**: I have heard, madam, from many, that he is as wicked as Miss Lindon is virtuous and amiable.

**Lady Alton**: Amiable! that wounds my heart.

SCENE V.

Fabrice, Mr. Freeport.

**Fabrice**: [Dressed plainly, with a large hat.] Heaven be praised, Mr. Freeport, I see you safe returned: how are you since your voyage to Jamaica?

**Freeport**: Pretty well, I thank you, Mr. Fabrice, I have been very successful, but am much fatigued. [To the waiter.] Boy, some chocolate and the papers—one finds it more difficult to amuse oneself than to get rich.

**Fabrice**: Will you have Wasp's papers?

**Freeport**: No: what should I do with such stuff? It is no concern of mine if a spider in the corner of a wall walks over his web to suck the blood of flies. Give me the Gazette! What public news have you?

**Fabrice**: None at present.

**Freeport**: So much the better; the less news the less folly. But how go your affairs, my friend? have you a good deal of business? who lodges with you now?

**Fabrice**: This morning an old gentleman came who won't see anybody.

**Freeport**: He's in the right of it: three parts of the world are good for nothing, either knaves or fools, and as for the fourth, they keep to themselves.

**Fabrice**: This gentleman has not so much as the curiosity to see a charming young lady who is in the same house with him.

**Freeport**: There he's wrong. Who is she, pray?

**Fabrice**: She is something more singular even than himself: she has now been with me these four months, and has never stirred out of her apartment: she calls herself Lindon, but I believe that is not her real name.

**Freeport**: I make no doubt but she's a woman of virtue, or she would not lodge with you.

**Fabrice**: O she is more than you can conceive; beautiful to the last degree, greatly distressed, and the best of women. Between you and me she is excessively poor, but of a high spirit and very proud.

**Freeport**: If that be the case she is more to blame even than your old gentleman.

**Fabrice**: By no means: her pride is an additional virtue. She denies herself common necessaries, and at the same time would let nobody know she does:

works with her own hands to get money to pay me; never complains, but hides her tears: it is with the utmost difficulty I can persuade her to expend a little of her money, due for rent, on things she really wants; and am forced to make use of a thousand arts before she will suffer me to assist her. I always reckon what she has at half the price it cost me, and when she finds it out, there is always a quarrel between us, which indeed is the only quarrel we have ever had: in short, sir, she is a miracle of virtue, misfortune, and intrepidity: she frequently draws from me tears of tenderness and admiration.

**Freeport:** You are naturally tender; I am not. I admire none, though I esteem many: but I will see this woman; I am a little melancholy, and she may divert me.

**Fabrice:** O sir, she scarcely ever receives any visitors. There is a lord indeed who comes now and then to see her, but she will never speak to him unless before my wife. He has not been here for some time, and now she lives more retired than ever.

**Freeport:** I love retirement too, and hate a crowd as much as she can: I must see her, where is her apartment?

**Fabrice:** Yonder: even with the coffee-room.

**Freeport:** I'll go in.

**Fabrice:** You must not.

**Freeport:** I say I must: why not go into her chamber? bring in my chocolate and the papers. [Pulls out his watch.] I have not much time to lose, for I am engaged at two.

SCENE VI.

Freeport, Fabrice.

**Miss Lindon:** [frightened, Polly following her.] My God! who is this? sir, you are extremely rude; I think you might have shown more respect to my sex than thus to intrude on my retirement.

**Freeport:** You will pardon me, madam, [To Fabrice] bring me the chocolate.

**Fabrice:** Yes, sir, with the lady's consent.

**Freeport:** [Seats himself near a table, reads the newspaper, and looks up to Miss Lindon and Polly, takes off his hat, and puts it on again.

**Polly:** This gentleman seems pretty familiar.

**Freeport:** Why won't you sit down, madam? you see I do.

**Miss Lindon:** Which I think, sir, you ought not to do. I am astonished, sir: I never receive visits from strangers.

**Freeport**: A stranger, madam! I am very well known; my name's Freeport, a merchant, and rich: inquire of me on 'Change.

**Miss Lindon**: Sir, I know nobody in this country, I should be obliged to you if you would not intrude on a person to whom you are an utter stranger, and to whom as a woman you should have shown more respect.

**Freeport**: I don't mean to incommode you, madam: be at your ease, as I am at mine; you see I am reading the news, take up your tapestry, or drink chocolate with me, or without me, just as you please.

**Polly**: This is an original!

**Miss Lindon**: Good heaven! what a visit! and my lord not come. This whimsical fellow distracts me, and I don't know how to get rid of him. How could Fabrice let him in! I must sit down. [She sits down, and works, chocolate is brought in; Freeport takes a dish without offering her any; he sips, and talks by turns.

**Freeport**: Hark'ee, madam, I hate compliments, I have heard one of the best of characters of you: you are poor and virtuous, but they tell me you are proud; that's a fault.

**Polly**: And pray, sir, who told you all this?

**Freeport**: The master of this house, who is a very honest man, and therefore I believe him.

**Miss Lindon**: O sir, 'tis all a fable; he has deceived you; not indeed with regard to pride, which always accompanies true modesty: nor as to virtue, which is my first duty; but with regard to that poverty of which he suspects me. Those who want nothing can never be poor.

**Freeport**: You don't stick to truth, which is even a worse fault than being proud: I know better, I know you are in want of everything, and sometimes deny yourself so much as a dinner.

**Polly**: That's by order of the doctor.

**Freeport**: Hold your tongue, hussy, do you pretend to give yourself airs too?

**Polly**: What an original!

**Freeport**: In a word, whether you are proud or not, is nothing to me. I have made a voyage to Jamaica that has brought me in five thousand pounds: now, you must know, it is a law with me, and ought to be a law with every good Christian, always to give away a tenth part of what I get: it is a debt which I owe to the unfortunate. You are unhappy, though you won't acknowledge it. There's five hundred pounds for you: now, remember, you're paid: let me have no curtseys, no thanks, keep the money and the secret. [Throws down a large purse on the table.]

**Polly:** In faith this is more original still.

**Miss Lindon:** [Rising.] I never was so astonished in my life—alas! how everything conspires to humble me! what generosity! and yet what an affront!

**Freeport:** [Reading the news and drinking his chocolate.] This impertinent writer! a ridiculous fellow to talk such nonsense with an air of consequence—"The king is arrived: he makes a most noble figure, being extremely tall." The blockhead! what signifies it whether he is tall or short? could not he have told us the plain fact?

**Miss Lindon:** [Coming up to Freeport.] Sir—

**Freeport:** Well, madam—

**Miss Lindon:** What you have done, sir, surprises me still more than what you said: but I cannot possibly accept the money, as it may not, perhaps, ever be in my power to repay it.

**Freeport:** Who talks of repaying it?

**Miss Lindon:** I thank you, sir, for your goodness, from the bottom of my heart: you have my sincere acknowledgments, my admiration; I can no more.

**Polly:** You are more extraordinary than the gentleman himself. Surely, madam, in the condition you are in, deserted by all the world, you must have lost your senses to refuse an unexpected succor, thus offered you by one of the most generous, though whimsical and absurd men I ever met with.

**Freeport:** What do you mean by that, madam! whimsical and absurd!

**Polly:** If you won't accept of it for your own sake, take it for mine. I have served you in your ill-fortune, and have some right to partake of the good: in short, sir, this is no time to dissemble, we are in the utmost distress; and if it had not been for our kind landlord, must have perished with cold and hunger. My mistress concealed her condition from all those who might have been of service to us: you became acquainted with it in spite of her: in spite of herself, therefore, oblige her to accept of that which heaven hath sent her by your generous hand.

**Miss Lindon:** Dear Polly, you will ruin my honor.

**Polly:** You, my dear mistress, would ruin yourself by your folly.

**Miss Lindon:** If you love me, consider my reputation. I shall die with shame.

**Freeport:** [Reading.] What are these women prating about?

**Polly:** And if you love me, madam, don't oblige me to perish with hunger.

**Miss Lindon:** O Polly, what think you my lord would say, if still he loves me? could he believe me capable of such meanness? I always pretended to him that I wanted nothing; and shall I receive a present from another, from a stranger?

**Polly**: Your pretence was wrong, and your refusal still more so: as to my lord, he'll say nothing about it, for he has deserted you.

**Miss Lindon**: My dear Polly, by our sorrows I entreat you, do not let us disgrace ourselves: contrive in some way to excuse me to this strange man, who means well, though he is so rude and unpolished: tell him, when an unmarried woman accepts such presents, the world will always suspect she does it at the expense of her virtue.

**Freeport**: [Reading.] What does she say?

**Polly**: [Coming close to him.] O sir, something mighty ridiculous; she talks of the suspicions of the world, and that an unmarried woman—

**Freeport**: Is she unmarried then?

**Polly**: Yes, sir, and I too

**Freeport**: So much the better. So she says that an unmarried woman—

**Polly**: Cannot take a present from a man—

**Freeport**: She does not know what she says. Why am I to be suspected of a dishonest purpose, because I do an honest action?

**Polly**: Do you hear him, madam?

**Miss Lindon**: I hear, and I admire him, but am still resolved not to accept it: they would say I loved him; that villain. Wasp, would certainly report it, and I should be undone.

**Polly**: [To Freeport.] She is afraid, sir, you are in love with her.

**Freeport**: In love with her! how can that be, when I know nothing of her? indeed, madam, you may make yourself easy on that head; and if perchance some years hence I should fall in love with you, and you with me, well and good; as you determine, I shall determine also; and if you think no more of it, I shall think no more of it; if you tell me I am disagreeable to you, you will soon be so to me; if you desire not to see me, you shall never see me again; and if you desire me to return, I will. [Pulls out his watch.] So fare you well. I have a little business at present. Madam, your, servant.

**Miss Lindon**: Your servant, sir, you have my esteem and my gratitude; but take your money with you, and once more spare my blushes.

**Freeport**: The woman's a fool.

**Miss Lindon**: Mr. Fabrice, Mr. Fabrice, for heaven's sake come and assist me.

**Fabrice**: [Coming in a violent hurry.] What's the matter, madam?

**Miss Lindon**: [Giving him the purse.] Here, take this purse: the gentleman left it by mistake, give it him again, I charge you; assure him of my esteem, and remember I want no assistance from any one.

**Fabrice:** [Taking the purse.] O Mr. Freeport, I know you by this generous action; but be assured this lady means to deceive you: she is really in want of this.

**Miss Lindon:** 'Tis false: and is it you, Mr. Fabrice, who would betray me?

**Fabrice:** I will obey you, madam. [Aside to Freeport.] I will keep this money; it may be of service to her without her knowing it. My heart bleeds to see such virtue joined to such misfortunes.

**Freeport:** I feel for her too, but she is too haughty: tell her it is not right to be proud. Adieu.

SCENE VII.

**Polly: Polly:** Well, madam, you have made a fine piece of work of it; heaven graciously offered you assistance, and you resolve to perish in indigence; I too must fall a sacrifice to your virtue, a virtue which is not without its alloy of vanity: that vanity, madam, will destroy us both.

**Miss Lindon:** Death is all I have to wish for: Lord Murray no longer loves me; he has left me these three days; he has loved my proud and cruel rival; perhaps, he loves her still. I was to blame to think of him, but 'tis a crime I shall not long be guilty of. [She sits down to write.]

**Polly:** She seems in despair, alas! she has but too much reason to be so; her condition is far worse than mine: a servant has always some resource, but a woman like her can have none.

**Miss Lindon:** [Folding up her letter.] 'Tis no great sacrifice. There, Polly, when I am no more, carry that letter to him—

**Polly:** What says my dear mistress?

**Miss Lindon:** To him who is the cause of my death. I have recommended you to him, perhaps he may comply with my last request: go, Polly, [embracing her] and be assured, that amongst all my misfortunes, that of not being able to recompense you as you deserve, is not the least which this wretched heart has experienced.

**Polly:** O my dear mistress, I cannot refrain from tears, you harrow up my soul: what is your dreadful purpose? what means this letter? God forbid I should ever deliver it! [she tears the letter.] Alas! madam, why would not you open your heart to Lord Murray? perhaps your cold reserve has disgusted him.

**Miss Lindon:** Perhaps so, indeed: my eyes are open now, I must have offended him: but how could I disclose my condition to the son of him who ruined my father and family?

**Polly:** How, madam! was it my lord's father who—

**Miss Lindon**: Yes, it was he who persecuted my father, had him condemned to death, deprived us of our nobility, and took away everything from us: left as I am without father, mother, or fortune, I have nothing but my reputation and my fatal love. I ought to detest the son of Murray: misfortune, that still pursues me, brought me acquainted with him. I have loved him, and I ought to suffer for it.

**Polly**: O madam, you grow pale, your eyes are dim.

**Miss Lindon**: May grief perform that office for me, which sword or poison—

**Polly**: Help here, Mr. Fabrice, help: my mistress faints.

**Fabrice**: Help, help here! where are ye all, my wife, my servants, come down: tell the gentlemen above—help here— [Fabrice's wife, her maids, and Polly, carry off Miss Lindon into her chamber.]

**Miss Lindon**: [As she is going out.] Why will ye bring me back to life again? let me die in peace.

## SCENE VIII.

Montross, Fabrice.

**Montross**: What's the matter, landlord?

**Fabrice**: That beautiful young lady, sir, I told you of, fainted away just now: but it will be over soon.

**Montross**: O the mere effect of vapors in young girls; they are not dangerous: what service could I be of? why call me down for this? I thought the house must have been on fire.

**Fabrice**: I had rather it were, than this sweet creature should be hurt. If Scotland has many such beauties as her, it must be a charming country.

**Montross**: Is she Scotch then?

**Fabrice**: So it seems; though I knew it but to-day: our news-writer tells me so, and he knows everything.

**Montross**: And what's her name?

**Fabrice**: She calls herself Lindon.

**Montross**: That's a name I'm not acquainted with. [He walks about.] The bare mention of my country rives my heart. Was ever man treated with such cruelty and injustice as I have been? Barbarous Murray, thou art dead; but thy son survives: I will have justice or revenge. O my dearest wife, my children, my daughter! I have lost all. This sword had long since ended all my cares, did not the hopes of sweet revenge force me still to bear the detestable load of life.

**Fabrice**: [Returning.] Thank God! all is well again.

**Montross**: What sudden change has happened then?

**Fabrice**: O, sir, she has recovered her senses, and is pretty well; looks still pale, but always beautiful.

**Montross**: O it's nothing. I must go out—I must run the hazard—I will. [Exit.]

**Fabrice**: This man does not trouble himself much about young ladies that faint; but if he had seen Miss Lindon, he would not be so indifferent.

# ACT III.

### SCENE I.

Lady Alton, Andrew.

**Lady Alton**: Yes: since I can't see the villain at home, I'll see him here: he'll certainly come. This news-writer told me truth, and was in the right of it: a Scotchwoman concealed in these dangerous times! she must be in a conspiracy against the state; she shall be seized; the order is given; at least I am too sure she conspires against me: but here comes Andrew, my lord's servant; I will know the whole of my misfortune. Andrew, you have got a letter from my lord, have not you?

**Andrew**: Yes, madam.

**Lady Alton**: For me.

**Andrew**: No, madam.

**Lady Alton**: How? have not you brought me several from him?

**Andrew**: Yes, madam: but this is not for you; 'tis for a certain person whom he is most desperately in love with.

**Lady Alton**: Well, and was not he most desperately in love with me when he used to write to me?

**Andrew**: O no, madam, he loved you calmly and coldly; 'tis quite another thing here; he neither sleeps nor eats, runs about day and night, and does nothing but talk of his dear Lindon. O there's a great deal of difference, I assure you.

**Lady Alton**: Perfidious wretch! but no matter: I tell you that letter is for me: 'tis without a superscription, is not it?

**Andrew**: Yes, madam.

**Lady Alton**: Were not all the letters you brought me without a superscription too?

**Andrew**: Yes, madam; but this I know is for Miss Lindon.

**Lady Alton**: I tell you 'tis for me, and to prove it to you, here are ten guineas for you.

**Andrew:** Indeed, madam, I begin to think the letter was for you; I was certainly mistaken: but if after all it is not, I hope you will not betray me; you may say you found it at Miss Lindon's.

**Lady Alton:** O leave that to me.

**Andrew:** After all, where is the harm in giving a love letter designed for one woman to another? they are all alike; and if Miss Lindon does not receive this letter, she may have twenty others. I have executed my commission, and made a pretty good hand of it too.

**Lady Alton:** [Opens the letter, and reads.] Now for it—"My dear, amiable, and truly virtuous Miss Lindon"—that's more than ever he said to me—" 'tis now two days, an age to me, since I had the happiness of seeing you: but I have denied myself that pleasure with the hopes of serving you. I know what you are, and what I owe you. I will change the face of your affairs, or perish in the attempt. My friends are zealous for you. Depend on me as on the most faithful of lovers, and one who will endeavor to prove himself worthy of your affection."

This is an absolute conspiracy; there can be no doubt of it: she is a Scotchwoman, and her family ill disposed to the government. Murray's father commanded in Scotland: his friends, he says, are zealous; he runs about day and night: 'tis certainly a conspiracy. Thank God, I am as zealous as he, and if she does not accept my offers, she shall be seized in an hour's time, before her vile lover comes to her assistance.

## SCENE II.

Lady Alton, Miss Lindon, Polly.

**Lady Alton:** [To Polly, who is passing from her mistress's apartment towards the coffee-room.] You, madam, go immediately and tell your mistress I must speak with her; she need not be afraid; I shall say nothing to her but what will be agreeable, and concerns her happiness: let her come immediately, immediately, do you hear? she need not be afraid, I say.

**Polly:** O madam, we are afraid of nothing; but your looks make me tremble.

**Lady Alton:** I'll see if I can't persuade this virtuous lady to do as I would have her: I'll make my proposals, however.

**Miss Lindon:** [Comes in trembling, supported by Polly.] What are your commands with me, madam? are you come again only to insult me in my distress?

**Lady Alton:** No: I come to make you happy. I know you are worth nothing; I am rich; I now make you an offer of one of my seats on the borders of Scotland, with all the lands belonging to it; go and live there, you and your family, if you have any; but you must immediately quit my lord forever, nor must he know of your retreat as long as you live.

**Miss Lindon:** Alas! madam, he has abandoned me: be not jealous of a poor unfortunate: in vain you offer me a retreat; I shall soon find one without you, an eternal one, in a place where I need not blush at my obligations to you.

**Lady Alton:** Rash woman, is this an answer for me?

**Miss Lindon:** Rashness, madam, would ill suit with my condition; firmness and intrepidity will much better become it: my birth, madam, is as good as yours; my heart, perhaps, much better; and as to my fortune, it shall not depend on any one, much less on my rival. [Goes out.]

**Lady Alton:** [Alone.] It shall depend on me. I am sorry she reduces me to this extremity, and am ashamed to make use of this rascal, Wasp; but she obliges me to it. Faithless lover! unhappy passion! O! I am choked with rage.

**SCENE III.**
Fabrice, Lady Alton, Freeport, Montross [in the coffee-room, with Fabrice's wife, and servants putting things in order.]

**Lady Alton:** [To Fabrice.] Mr. Fabrice, you see me here often; but 'tis your own fault.

**Fabrice:** On the contrary, madam, we could wish—

**Lady Alton:** I am more concerned than you can be; but you shall see me again, I assure you. [She goes out.]

**Fabrice:** So much the worse. What would she be at now? What a difference there is betwixt her and the beautiful patient Miss Lindon!

**Freeport:** True; she is, as you say, beautiful and virtuous.

**Fabrice:** I am sorry this gentleman never saw her; I am sure he would be greatly affected with her behavior.

**Montross:** [Aside.] Wretch that I am! I have other things to think of.

**Freeport:** I am always either on 'Change or at Jamaica; but one can't help liking now and then to see a fine woman: she is really a fine creature, a sweet behavior, a charming countenance, and has something noble in her air and demeanor.—I must see her again one day or other. 'Tis pity she's so proud.

**Montross:** My landlord here informs me you behaved to her in a most generous manner.

**Freeport:** Who I? no. Would not you, or any man in my place, have done the same?

**Montross:** If I had been rich, and she had merit, I believe I might.

**Freeport**: What is there in it then to be wondered at? [He takes up the papers.] Well, what news have we to-day? How's this? Lord Falbridge dead!

**Montross**: Falbridge dead! the only friend I had on earth, or from whom I could expect relief? O fortune, fortune, wilt thou ever persecute me?

**Freeport**: Was he your friend? I am sorry for you.—"Edinburgh, April 14. Great search is being made after Lord Montross, condemned to lose his head about eleven years ago."

**Montross**: Just heaven! what do I hear? What's that, sir, Lord Montross condemned—

**Freeport**: Yes, sir, Lord Montross; there, sir, read it yourself.

**Montross**: [Looking on the paper.] 'Tis so indeed. [Aside.] I must get away as fast as I can; this place is too public: sure, earth and hell conspired together never heaped so many misfortunes on one man. [To his servant.] John, let my horses be saddled, perhaps I may be going towards evening—how bad news flies!

**Freeport**: Bad news, why so? what signifies it whether Lord Montross is beheaded or not? everything passes away—to-day a head is cut off, to-morrow we have it in the newspapers, and next day we talk no more of it. If this Miss Lindon was not so proud, I would go and ask her how she did; she is very handsome, and a very worthy creature.

## SCENE IV.

To them a King's Messenger.

**Messenger**: Is your name Fabrice, sir?

**Fabrice**: Yes, sir, your commands with me?

**Messenger**: You keep a coffee-house, and let lodgings?

**Fabrice**: I do, sir.

**Messenger**: You have a young Scotch lady in your house, named Lindon?

**Fabrice**: I have, sir, and esteem it a great happiness.

**Freeport**: A most beautiful and virtuous lady; everybody tells me so.

**Messenger**: I come to seize her by order of the government; there's my warrant.

**Fabrice**: Amazing! I shudder at the thought.

**Montross**: A young Scotchwoman seized on the very day of my arrival! O my unhappy family, my country, what will become of my unfortunate daughter! she is, perhaps, the victim of my misfortunes, languishing in poverty and a prison: why was she ever born?

**Freeport**: I never heard of young girls being seized by order of the government: I am afraid, Mr. Messenger, you are a rascal.

**Fabrice:** If she is a fortune-hunter, as Wasp said, it will ruin my house; I am undone: this court lady had some reasons I see plainly—and yet she must be good and virtuous.

**Messenger:** Let's have none of your reasons, sir, to prison, or give bail, that's the rule.

**Fabrice:** I'll give you bail, myself, my house, my goods, my person.

**Messenger:** Your person's nothing; the house, perhaps, not your own—your goods, where are they? I must have money.

**Fabrice:** Good Mr. Freeport, shall I give him the five hundred pounds which she so nobly refused, and which are still in my possession?

**Freeport:** Ay, ay, I'll give five hundred, a thousand, two thousand; I'll be answerable for it, my name's Freeport. I believe the girl's strictly virtuous; but she should not be so proud.

**Messenger:** Come, sir, give us your bond.

**Freeport:** With all my heart.

**Fabrice:** 'Tis not every one employs their money thus.

**Freeport:** To spend it in doing good is putting it out to the best interest. [Freeport and the Messenger retire to the corner of the coffee-room to count out the money.]

### SCENE V.

Montross, Fabrice.

**Fabrice:** You are astonished, sir, at Mr. Freeport; but 'tis his constant practice: happy are those whom he takes a fancy to! he is no complimenter, but does a man a service in less time than others spend in making protestations about it.

**Montross:** [Aside.] There are still in the world some noble souls—what will become of me?

**Fabrice:** We must take care not to let the poor young lady know anything of the danger she has been in.

**Montross:** I must be gone this night.

**Fabrice:** One should never tell people of their danger till it is past.

**Montross:** The only friend I had in London is dead: what should I do here?

**Fabrice:** We should make her faint away a second time.

### SCENE VI.

**Montross:** A young Scotchwoman is seized, a person who lives retired, and is suspected by the government. I don't know why, but this adventure throws me into deep reflections. Everything conspires to awaken the memory of my sorrows, my afflictions, my misfortunes, and my resentment.

SCENE VII.

**Montross**: [Seeing Polly crossing the stage.] One word with you, madam, are you that pretty amiable young lady, born in Scotland, who—

**Polly**: Yes, sir—I, I am tolerably young, and a Scotchwoman; and as to pretty they say I am not amiss.

**Montross**: Have you any news from your own country?

**Polly**: No, sir, I have left it a long time.

**Montross**: And what are your relations, pray?

**Polly**: My father was an excellent baker, as I have heard, and my mother waiting-maid to a woman of quality.

**Montross**: O, now I understand you. You, I suppose, are servant to that young lady I have heard so much of. I was mistaken.

**Polly**: O sir, you do me too much honor.

**Montross**: You know who your mistress is, I suppose?

**Polly**: Yes, sir, the sweetest and most amiable of her sex, and one too who has the most fortitude in affliction.

**Montross**: She is in distress then?

**Polly**: Yes, sir, and so am I: but I had rather serve her in affliction than be ever so happy.

**Montross**: But don't you know her family?

**Polly**: My mistress, sir, desires to remain unknown: she has no family: sir, why do you ask me these questions?

**Montross**: To remain unknown! say you? O heaven, if I could at last—but 'tis a vain imagination. Tell me, pray, how old is your mistress?

**Polly**: One may safely tell her age. She is just eighteen.

**Montross**: Eighteen! the very age of my dear Montross, my lovely infant, the only remaining hope of my unhappy family—eighteen sayest thou?

**Polly**: Yes, sir, and I am but two and twenty, there's no great difference between us. I see no reason why you should make so many reflections on her age.

**Montross**: Eighteen, and born in my country, desires to remain unknown! I cannot contain myself—by your permission I must see and talk to her immediately.

**Polly**: Telling him of a girl of eighteen has turned this old gentleman's brain.—You can't possibly see her at present, sir, she's in the greatest distress.

**Montross**: For that very reason I must see her.

**Polly**: O, sir, fresh griefs and calamities have torn her heart, and deprived her of her senses. She is not one of those I assure you, sire, who faint away for nothing; she is but just now come to herself, and the little rest she now enjoys is mixed with grief and bitterness. Have pity, sir, on her condition.

**Montross**: All you say but increases my desire. I am her countryman, and partake of her afflictions, perhaps I may be able to lessen them; permit me, I beg you, before I leave this place, to have an interview with her.

**Polly**: You affect me deeply, sir; stay here a few minutes. It is impossible a young lady, who has just fainted away, should be able to receive visits immediately. I'll go to her, and come back to you soon.

## SCENE VIII.

Montross, Fabrice.

**Fabrice**: [Pulling him by the sleeve.] Sir, is there nobody near us?

**Montross**: With what impatience shall I wait for her return!

**Fabrice**: Can nobody hear us?

**Montross**: I can never support this anxiety.

**Fabrice**: They are in search of you, sir,—

**Montross**: Who, where, what?

**Fabrice**: I say, sir, they are in search of you; I cannot help interesting myself in the safety of those who lodge in my house. I don't know who you are, sir, but I have been asked a thousand questions about you. They have surrounded the house, passing, and repassing, getting all the information they can. In short I shall not be surprised if in a little time they should pay you the same compliment as they did the young lady, who, it seems, is of the same country.

**Montross**: I must speak with her before I go.

**Fabrice**: Take my advice, sir, and get away as fast as you can; our friend, Freeport, perhaps might not be in the humor to do as much for you as for a girl of eighteen.

**Montross**: Pardon me, but I know not where I am; I scarce heard you—what must I do, or where can I go? my dear sir, I cannot go without seeing her: let me talk to you a little in private: I must beg you some how or other to let me have an opportunity of seeing this young lady.

**Fabrice**: I told you before, you would want to see her. I assure you nothing can be more beautiful, more virtuous, or more agreeable.

# ACT IV.

**SCENE I.**

**Fabrice, Wasp:** [At a table in the coffee-room.]

**Freeport:** [Smoking a pipe.]

**Fabrice:** I must be so free as to tell you, Mr. Wasp, if I may believe all that is said of you, you would do me a favor by never coming to my house again.

**Freeport:** All that is said is generally false: what fly has stung you, Mr. Fabrice?

**Fabrice:** You come, and write your papers here, Mr. Wasp; and my coffee-house will be looked on as a poison shop.

**Freeport:** [To Fabrice.] This fellow seems to deserve what you say.

**Fabrice:** [To Wasp.] They say you speak ill of all mankind.

**Freeport:** Of all mankind! that's too much indeed.

**Fabrice:** They begin even to say you are an informer, and a scoundrel, but I am loth to believe them.

**Freeport:** [To Wasp.] Do you hear, sir? this is past raillery.

**Wasp:** I am an illustrious writer, sir, a man of taste.

**Fabrice:** Taste or no taste, sir, I say you have done me an injury.

**Wasp:** So far from it, sir, that I have helped off your coffee, made it fashionable to come to your house, 'tis my reputation that has brought you custom.

**Fabrice:** A fine reputation indeed! that of a spy, a bad author, and a worse man!

**Wasp:** Stop, Mr. Fabrice, if you please. You may attack my morals, but my works—I will never suffer that.

**Fabrice:** Your writings, sir, are not worth my consideration; but you are suspected of a design against the amiable Miss Lindon.

**Freeport:** If I thought so, I would drown the dog with my own hands.

**Fabrice:** 'Tis said, you accused her of being Scotch, and the honest gentleman too who lives above stairs.

**Wasp:** Well, and suppose I had, what harm is there in being of any particular country?

**Fabrice:** 'Tis moreover reported that you have had several conferences with the agents of a certain choleric lady who comes here, and with the servants of a noble lord, who used to frequent this house: that you tell tales, and blow up quarrels.

**Freeport:** [To Wasp.] Are you really such a rogue? then shall I detest you.

**Fabrice**: O thank God! here comes my lord, if I am not mistaken.

**Freeport**: A lord, is it? then your humble servant, I hate a lord, as much as I do a bad writer.

**Fabrice**: He's not like other lords, I assure you.

**Freeport**: Like other lords or not, 'tis no matter. I never love to be disturbed, so fare you well. I don't know how it is, my friend, but I am always thinking of this young Scotchwoman—I'll come back presently—immediately. I want to talk seriously to her—your servant. This Scotchwoman is handsome, and a good creature.—Adieu—[returning] tell her, I intend to serve her greatly.

## SCENE II.

**Lord Murray**: [Pensive and in great agitation.]

**Wasp**: [Bowing to him, of which he takes no notice.]

**Fabrice**: [At a distance from him.]

**Lord Murray**: [To Fabrice.]

I'm glad to see you, friend: how is that charming girl you have the pleasure to boast of as your lodger here?

**Fabrice**: She has been very ill, sir, since she saw you: but I'm sure she will be better now.

**Lord Murray**: Great God, thou protector of innocence, I implore thee for her; O deign to make me an instrument in doing justice to virtue, and sheltering the unfortunate from oppression! Thanks to thy goodness, and my own endeavors, I have hopes of success. Hark'ee, friend, I would talk a little with that man. [Pointing to Wasp.]

**Wasp**: [To Fabrice.] You see, sir, you were mistaken, and I have some credit still at court.

**Fabrice**: [Going out.] That's not quite so clear.

**Lord Murray**: [To Wasp.] Well, my friend—

**Wasp**: [Bowing.] Permit me, my lord, to dedicate a volume to your lordship—

**Lord Murray**: No, sir, we are not talking about dedications: you are the person that informed my servants of the arrival of the old gentleman just come from Scotland; you described him, and made the same report to the minister of state.

**Wasp**: My lord, I only did my duty.

**Lord Murray**: [Giving him a purse.] You have done me a service without knowing it: but I don't consider the intention. Some folks say you meant to hurt, and have done good: there's something for your service. But if ever from this time forward you so much as pronounce the name of that gentleman, or of Miss Lindon, I'll throw you out at window,—away, be gone, sir.

**Wasp**: My lord, I return you thanks; everybody abuses me, and gives me money; I am certainly a cleverer fellow than I thought I was.

### SCENE III.

**Lord Murray**: [Alone.] An old gentleman just arrived from Scotland; Miss Lindon born in the same country! alas! if it were possible to repair the cruel injuries my father did—if heaven would graciously permit—but I'll go in. [To Polly, who comes out of Miss Lindon's apartment.] Polly, were not you surprised at not seeing me for so long a time? two whole days! I should not have forgiven myself had I not been engaged in my dear Miss Lindon's service: the ministers of state were at Windsor, and I was obliged to follow them there. Heaven surely inspired thee, when thou toldst me, Polly, the secret of her birth.

**Polly**: I'm frightened yet, my mistress so often forbade me: were I to give her the least uneasiness I should die with grief. Alas! sir, your absence this very day threw her into a fainting fit, and I believe I should have fainted too, if I had not exerted all my strength to assist her.

**Lord Murray**: There, Polly, there's something for the fainting fit you had like to have fallen into. [Gives her money.]

**Polly**: My lord, I thank you; I am not so high spirited as my mistress, who refuses to accept of anything; and pretends to be quite at her ease, when she is absolutely starving.

**Lord Murray**: Good heaven! the daughter of Montross reduced to poverty! how guilty am I! but I will repair everything, her condition shall soon be changed: why would she so long conceal it from me?

**Polly**: 'Tis the only thing in which she deceived you, or I believe ever will.

**Lord Murray**: But let us go in, I long to throw myself at her feet.

**Polly**: O my lord, not yet; she is now with an old gentleman, a very old gentleman, who is her countryman, and they are saying such tender things.

**Lord Murray**: Who is this old gentleman? methinks I am already interested in his favor.

**Polly**: I know nothing of him.

**Lord Murray**: Would to God he were the person I wish him to be! and what did they say to each other?

**Polly**: They began to grow very serious, the gentleman seemed to wish me out of the room, and so I came away.

## SCENE IV.

Lady Alton, Lord Murray, Polly:

**Lady Alton**: So, sir, at last I've caught you: thou base perfidious man, now sir, I am convinced of your inconstancy, and my own disgrace.

**Lord Murray**: True, madam, you are so. [Aside.] what an unseasonable intrusion!

**Lady Alton**: Perfidious monster!

**Lord Murray**: A monster I may appear in your eyes, and I am glad of it; but perfidious I never was; 'tis not my character: before I loved another, I frankly told you I had no longer any regard for you.

**Lady Alton**: After a promise of marriage, wretch, after so many protestations of love!

**Lord Murray**: When I made those protestations I loved you, and when I promised to marry you, I meant to do so.

**Lady Alton**: And why then did not you keep your word? what prevented you?

**Lord Murray**: Your character, your fiery temper and disposition: marriage was intended to make us happy, and I saw too plainly we were not made for each other.

**Lady Alton**: And so you have quitted me for a wandering lady errant, a poor fortune-hunter.

**Lord Murray**: No, madam, I leave you for softness and good-nature, for every grace, and every virtue.

**Lady Alton**: But you are not yet possessed of her: know, traitor, I will be revenged, and speedily too.

**Lord Murray**: I know your vindictive temper, know you have more envy than jealousy, more rage than tenderness, but you will be forced to honor and respect the woman I love.

**Lady Alton**: I know the object of your affection, sir, better than you do; know I who she is; I know too who that stranger is, who came hither yesterday: yes sir, I am acquainted with it all, and so are they who have more power and authority than Lord Murray: that unworthy rival, for whom I am despised, shall soon be seized and taken from you.

**Lord Murray**: What says she, Polly? I'm terrified at the thought.

**Polly**: And so am I. We are undone, sir.

**Lord Murray**: Stay, madam, explain yourself—hear me.

**Lady Alton**: I'll hear nothing, answer nothing, explain nothing: you are an inconstant, false-hearted, perfidious villain. [Exit.]

## SCENE V.
Lord Murray, Polly.

**Lord Murray:** What does this fury mean? her jealousy is terrible: heaven grant I never may be jealous! she talks of having my dear girl seized, and pretends to know this stranger. What would she be at?

**Polly:** To tell you the truth, my mistress has been taken up by order of the government, and I too, I believe; and if it had not been for an honest fat man, who is goodness itself, and who gave in bail for us, we had both been in prison at this very time. They had made me swear not to tell you anything of it: but how can I conceal it from you?

**Lord Murray:** What do I hear? misfortune on misfortune! your mistress's very name I find is suspected. Alas! my family was born to be the destruction of hers: heaven, fortune, justice, and love would repair all, but guilt opposes me. It shall not, must not triumph; do not alarm my dear girl. I'll go myself to the ministry! Try everything, do everything to save her. I'll deny myself the happiness of seeing her till I can assure her of success. I fly, Polly, to serve her, and will return immediately. Tell her I have left only because I adore her. [Going out.]

**Polly:** This is a strange adventure. I see this world is nothing but a perpetual contest between the virtuous and the wicked, and we poor girls are always the sufferers.

## SCENE VI.

**Miss Lindon:** [Nods to Polly, who goes out.]

**Montross:** Every word you utter pierces my soul: born in Lochaber! persecuted, oppressed, and deserted! a woman with such noble sentiments!

**Miss Lindon:** Those sentiments, sir, perhaps are owing to my misfortunes: had I been brought up in ease and luxury, my soul, which is fortified by adversity, had been weak and vain.

**Montross:** O thou art worthy of a nobler fate. You acknowledge to me you are sprung from one of the proscribed families, whose blood was shed on a scaffold in our civil wars. But still you conceal from me your name and birth.

**Miss Lindon:** Duty binds me to silence. My father himself was proscribed: they are even now in search of him, and were I to name perhaps I might destroy him. You inspire me, I own, with uncommon tenderness and respect, but I know you not, and I have everything to fear. You see I am myself suspected, and am a prisoner here. One word might ruin me.

**Montross:** One word perhaps might give me the greatest comfort: but tell me only what age you were of when you parted from your father, who was afterwards so unhappy?

**Miss Lindon:** I was then but five years old.

**Montross:** Great God, have mercy on me! everything she says contributes to throw new light on my dark paths! O providence, do not withdraw thy goodness from me!

**Miss Lindon:** You weep, sir, alas! nor can I help joining my tears with yours.

**Montross:** [Wiping his eyes.] Go on, I conjure you: after your father had quitted his family to see it no more, how long did you remain with your mother?

**Miss Lindon:** I was ten years old when she died in my arms, oppressed with grief and misery, and after she had heard that my brother was killed in battle.

**Montross:** O, I faint; what a dreadful moment! O thou dear, unhappy wife, and thou more fortunate son, to die without seeing so much misery! do you remember this picture? [Takes a picture out of his pocket.]

**Miss Lindon:** What do I see? is this a dream? surely 'tis my mother's picture.

**Montross:** It is, it is your mother; and I am that unhappy father who is condemned to death, whose trembling arms now embrace thee.

**Miss Lindon:** Do I live? where am I? O, sir, behold me at your knees: this is the first happy moment of my life: O, my father! alas! how darest you venture hither? I tremble for you, even whilst I am thus happy in your sight.

**Montross:** My dearest child, you know the misfortunes of our family; you know that the house of Murray, still jealous of ours, plunged us into these calamities. I have lost all: one friend alone remained, who by his interest and power might have restored me, and had promised it; but on my arrival here, I find that friend is dead, that I am searched after in Scotland, and a price put on my head. 'Tis, no doubt, the son of my old enemy who still persecutes me: I will die by his hand, or be revenged on him.

**Miss Lindon:** And come you then with a resolution to kill Lord Murray?

**Montross:** Yes: I will avenge you and my family, or die. I only hazard a life already devoted to the scaffold.

**Miss Lindon:** O fortune, in what new horrors dost thou involve me! what must I do? O my father!

**Montross:** My dearest daughter! how cruel is thy fate to be born of such a wretched father!

**Miss Lindon:** O sir, I am much more unhappy than you think me: are you resolved on this fatal enterprise?

**Montross:** Ay, to death.

**Miss Lindon:** O, my dear father, let me conjure you by that life which you gave me, by your misfortunes, by my own, which are, perhaps, still greater, do not expose me to the dread of losing you; have pity on me, spare your own life, and preserve mine.

**Montross:** Your voice reaches to my inmost soul: methinks I hear in thee, thy much-loved mother; speak, what would you?

**Miss Lindon:** Do not expose your precious life, but quit this dangerous place, dangerous for us both: yes, I am resolved I will renounce all for my dear father's sake. I am ready to follow you, I will accompany you, sir, to some far distant island, and there these hands shall labor to support you. It is my duty, and I will perform it: 'tis done, away.

**Montross:** I must not then avenge you?

**Miss Lindon:** No, sir, that vengeance would destroy me: come, let us be gone.

**Montross:** Well, I submit. The father's love prevails over all: since you have the courage to accompany me, I will go: I will prepare everything for our departure from London within this hour: be ready: one more embrace, and farewell.

SCENE VII.
Miss Lindon, Polly:

**Miss Lindon:** 'Tis all over, Polly: I shall never see Lord Murray again.

**Polly:** Indeed, madam, but you will; he'll be here in a few minutes: he is but just gone from hence.

**Miss Lindon:** Gone from hence! and not see me; this is worse than all. O my unhappy father! why did we not go before?

**Polly:** If he had not been interrupted by that detestable Lady Alton.

**Miss Lindon:** What! did he meet her here after all to insult me! after leaving me for three days without so much as writing! to affront me so grossly. O if my life were not necessary to my dear father, this moment would I part from it.

**Polly:** But hear me, madam, I swear to you my lord.—

**Miss Lindon:** Perfidious wretch! but all men are so. O my poor father! hereafter I will think on none but thee.

**Polly:** On my soul, madam, you are wrong; my lord is not false or perfidious, but one of the best of men: he loves you from his soul, and has given me convincing proofs of it.

**Miss Lindon:** Nature should be superior to love. I know not whither I am going, or what will become of me; but certainly I can never be more miserable than I am at present.

**Polly**: My dear mistress, you will hear nothing; recover your spirits a little: I tell you, you are beloved.

**Miss Lindon**: O Polly, will you follow me?

**Polly**: To the end of the world, madam: but hear me; you are beloved, indeed you are.

**Miss Lindon**: Let me alone; talk no more to me of my lord: alas! if he did love me, I must leave him—that gentleman you saw with me—

**Polly**: Well—

**Miss Lindon**: Come in, and I'll tell you all: tears and sighs will not let me speak: follow me, and get everything ready for our departure.

# ACT V.

### SCENE I.

Miss Lindon, Freeport, Fabrice.

**Fabrice**: Polly, I find, is packing up your things; you are going to leave us: you can't imagine, madam, the concern it gives me.

**Miss Lindon**: My dear landlord, and you, sir, to whom I am so much indebted for your unmerited generosity, I am sorry it is not in my power to return it; but be assured I shall never, whilst I have life, forget you.

**Freeport**: What is all this, what is all this? if you like us, why do you leave us? you aren't afraid of anything are you? a girl, like you, can have nothing to fear.

**Fabrice**: Mr. Freeport, the old gentleman, who it seems is her countryman, is going too. The lady wept, and he wept, at parting; and I am ready to weep too.

**Freeport**: Ridiculous! I never wept in my life: our eyes were never given us for that purpose: I own I'm sorry. Though she is a little proud, as I told you, yet she is such a good creature, one can't help being concerned at losing her. If you go, madam, you must write to me; I shall always be glad to do you any service: perhaps we may meet again one day or other, who knows! but be sure you don't forget to write to me.

**Miss Lindon**: I assure you, sir, I will; and if ever fortune—

**Freeport**: Fabrice, I'm sure this woman is well-born. I shall expect a letter from you, but don't put too much wit into it.

**Fabrice**: You will forgive me, madam, but I really don't think you are at liberty to go hence, as Mr. Freeport is bail for you, and must lose five hundred pounds if you leave us.

**Miss Lindon:** O heaven! another distress! another humiliation! must I then remain here? and my lord—my father too.—

**Freeport:** [To Fabrice.] O don't let that stop her—there is something in her that charms me—but let her go as soon as she pleases: you don't suppose I value five hundred pounds. Hark'ee, Fabrice, put five hundred more into her portmanteau. I beg, madam, [to Miss Lindon] you will go whenever it is agreeable to you; write to me, and let me see you when you return; for I have really conceived a great esteem and affection for you.

## SCENE II.

Lord Murray and Servants at One Part of the Stage, Miss Lindon and the Rest at the Other.

**Lord Murray:** [To his servants.] Stay you here: and do you run to the court of chancery, and bring me those parchments as soon as they are finished: go you and get things ready at my new house. [Pulls a paper out of his pocket, and reads.] What happiness it will be to make her happy!

**Miss Lindon:** [To Polly.] O Polly, I am distracted at the sight of him.

**Freeport:** This lord always comes in unseasonably: he is handsome and well-made, and yet I don't like him: but what's that to me? I have certainly some regard for her; but I am not in love with her.—Madam, your servant.

**Miss Lindon:** I shall not go, sir, without paying my respects to you.

**Freeport:** O pray, madam, no ceremony; perhaps it may affect me too much. Don't think I'm in love with you, madam; but I should be glad to see you once more before you go: I shall be in the house, and must see you set out. Go, Fabrice, and help the good gentleman above. I find I have a prodigious regard for this young lady.

## SCENE III.

Lord Murray, Miss Lindon

**Lord Murray:** At length once more I am happy in the sight of all I hold dear on earth. What a house is this for Miss Lindon! but one more worthy of her is prepared: you look down and weep: for heaven's sake what has happened to you? who was that surly looking fellow talking with you? if he is the cause of your uneasiness, he shall soon repent it.

**Miss Lindon:** Alas! my lord, he is one of the best of men; one who has taken pity on my misfortunes; who has never abandoned, never insulted me; one who never talked to my rival without deigning to look on me; one who, if he had loved me, would not have let three days pass without writing.

**Lord Murray**: Believe me, when I tell you, I had rather die than merit the least of those cruel reproaches. I absented myself but for your sake, thought of nothing but you, and have served you in spite of yourself: if, on my return here, I found that clamorous revengeful woman, could I help it? I went back again immediately to counteract her fatal designs. My God, not write to you!

**Miss Lindon**: No.

**Lord Murray**: I see she has intercepted my letters; her baseness increases, if possible, my passion; may it recall yours! how unkind was it in you to conceal from me your name and condition! a condition so unworthy of you.

**Miss Lindon**: Who disclosed them to you?

**Lord Murray**: [Pointing to Polly.] She, your confederate.

**Miss Lindon**: Did you betray me?

**Polly**: You betrayed yourself, madam; I served you.

**Miss Lindon**: You know me then; you know what hatred hath always divided our families: your father was the cause of mine being condemned to death; he reduced me to that wretched state which I endeavored to conceal from you; and you, his son, now dare avow a passion for me!

**Lord Murray**: I do; I adore you; 'tis what I owe you: my love shall repair the injuries my father did: 'tis the justice of providence: my heart, my fortune, and my life, are at your disposal: let us unite these hostile names. Here is a contract of marriage; shall I hope to see it executed?

**Miss Lindon**: Alas! my lord, it is impossible; I am going this moment to leave you forever.

**Lord Murray**: Going? to leave me forever? sooner shall you behold me perish at your feet: am I at last rejected then?

**Polly**: I say, madam, you must not go; you are always making some desperate resolution: but I shall bring you to yourself again. My lord, you must second me.

**Lord Murray**: Who could inspire you with this cruel design to fly from me, to render all my cares abortive?

**Miss Lindon**: My father.

**Lord Murray**: Your father? where is he? what does he mean to do with you? inform me quickly.

**Miss Lindon**: He's here, and means to carry me away with him; it is resolved.

**Lord Murray**: No: by thy dear self I swear, it must not, shall not be: where is he? conduct me to him.

**Miss Lindon**: My dearest lord, take care; let him not see you: he is come hither to finish his misfortunes by taking away your life, and I have consented to fly with him to divert him from this dreadful resolution.

**Lord Murray:** Yours is more cruel still; but be assured I fear him not, nay hope one day to make him my friend.—This fellow not returned yet! O heaven! how swift is every evil thing, how slow is every good!

**Miss Lindon:** My father comes: if you love me, do not let him see you; spare him the horror of such an interview: for heaven's sake retire, at least for a while.

**Lord Murray:** 'Tis with the utmost regret that I submit; but you command, and I must obey. I will go in, and return with arms that shall make his drop out of his hand.

SCENE IV.
Montross, Miss Lindon.

**Montross:** Come, my dear daughter, my only comfort and support, let us be gone.

**Miss Lindon:** O thou unhappy father of a more unhappy daughter, never, never will I leave you; but permit me to stay here a little longer.

**Montross:** What! after your urgent entreaties that I would go immediately; after having promised to follow me to some desert solitude, where I may forget my disgrace! have you changed your design? have you so soon forgot the tender sentiments you so lately expressed?

**Miss Lindon:** Indeed, sir, I am not changed: I am incapable of such baseness; I will follow you: but once more let me entreat you, stay a little while: grant but this favor to her who owes to you a life of sorrows; do not refuse me a few precious moments.

**Montross:** They are indeed precious, and yet you would lavish them away: consider we are every moment in danger of being discovered, that you have yourself been seized, that they are even now in search of me, and that to-morrow you may see your father given up to an ignominious death.

**Miss Lindon:** Those words are as a clap of thunder to me. I submit, sir: I am ashamed to have stayed so long; but I had a distant hope—no matter; you are my father, and I'll follow you. O me!

SCENE V.
Freeport and Fabrice on One Side of the Stage, Montross and His Daughter on the Other.

**Freeport:** [To Fabrice.] Her servant has carried the portmanteau back to her chamber: they'll not go yet; I'm glad of that, however. I began to have a sort of liking for her; not that I'm in love with her; but she is so well-bred, there is no parting from her without some uneasiness; a kind of anxiety that I never felt before: there's something very extraordinary in it.

Montross: [To Freeport.] Sir, your servant; we are just going to set out, with hearts full of gratitude to you for past favors: I assure you I never met with a worthier man than yourself: you almost reconcile me to mankind.

Freeport: You are going then, sir, and this lady I suppose: I'm sorry for it: you should have staid a little longer; indeed you should. I have just now thought of something, that, perhaps, might not be disagreeable to you: pray, stay.

## SCENE VI.

Lord Murray: [To them, taking a roll of parchment from his servant.] 'Tis well: thank heaven! I have at last got the pledge of my future happiness.

Freeport: [Aside.] A plague on this lord, here he is again: I hate him for being so agreeable.

Montross: [To his daughter, while Lord Murray is talking to his servant.] Who is that man, my dear?

Miss Lindon: It is, sir—it is—O heaven! have mercy on me!

Fabrice: 'Tis my Lord Murray, sir, one of the finest gentlemen in this kingdom, and the most generous.

Montross: Murray! O heaven! my fatal enemy, who comes to insult me, to triumph over my misfortunes [draws his sword] but he shall have my life, or I his.

Miss Lindon: O stop, my father, what would you do?

Montross: Cruel daughter! and is it thus you have betrayed me?

Fabrice: [Stepping between them.] No violence, I beg, sir, in my house; you will ruin me.

Freeport: Why should you hinder people from fighting, if they have a mind to it?

Lord Murray: [At a distance from Montross.] You are the father of that charming woman?

Miss Lindon: O, I die.

Montross: I am, sir; I'll not deny it. Come then, thou cruel son of a still more cruel father, I know thy purpose; come, and take my life.

Fabrice: Again, sir—

Lord Murray: Stop him not: I have that which will disarm him. [Draws his sword.]

Miss Lindon: [Sinking into the arms of Polly.] Cruel man! and dare you—

**Lord Murray**: Yes, I dare—I am the son of your inveterate foe; and thus [throwing away his sword] I attack you.

**Freeport**: Here's another for you, sir.

**Lord Murray**: Now, sir, with one hand strike this guilty breast, and with the other receive this paper—read, and know me.

**Montross**: What do I see? my pardon signed, my honors restored, my family re-established! O heaven! and is it to you, to Lord Murray, I owe it all. O! my friend, my benefactor, now you triumph more, much more, than if I had fallen by your sword.

**Miss Lindon**: O unexpected happiness! my lover then is worthy of me.

**Lord Murray**: O my father, permit me to embrace you.

**Montross**: How shall I repay such generosity?

**Lord Murray**: [Pointing to Miss Lindon.] There, sir, is my reward.

**Montross**: The father and the daughter are both yours forever.

**Freeport**: [To Fabrice.] My friend, I was afraid this lady was not made for me: however, she is fallen into good hands, and I am satisfied.

**End**

# Nanine

## Contents

Dramatis Personæ . . . . . . . . . . . . . . . . . . . . . . . . . . . . . . . . . . . . . 237

Act I . . . . . . . . . . . . . . . . . . . . . . . . . . . . . . . . . . . . . . . . . . . . . . . 237

Act II . . . . . . . . . . . . . . . . . . . . . . . . . . . . . . . . . . . . . . . . . . . . . . 248

Act III . . . . . . . . . . . . . . . . . . . . . . . . . . . . . . . . . . . . . . . . . . . . . 259

## Dramatis Personæ

The Count d'Olban, a nobleman retired into the country.
The Baroness de l'Orme, a relation of the Count's, a haughty, imperious woman, of a bad temper, and disagreeable to live with.
The Marchioness d'Olban, mother of the Count.
Nanine, a young girl, brought up in the Count's house.
Philip Hombert, a peasant in the neighborhood.
Blaise, the gardener.
Germon, servant.
Marin, servant.
Scene, the Count d'Olban's country seat.
This Comedy is called in the French Nanine, ou le Préjugé Vaincu (Nanine, or Prejudice Overcome). It is written, as we are told in the title-page, in verses of ten syllables. The absurdity of comedies in rhyme I have already remarked. The original begins thus:

Il faut parler, il faut, Monsieur le Comte,

Vous expliquer nettement sur mon Compte.

The reader cannot but observe, what villainous rhymes Comte and Compte are, and perhaps will more readily forgive my reducing this comedy into plain prose. It was produced in 1749.

## ACT I.

**SCENE I.**
The Count D'Olban, the Baroness De L'Orme.

**Baroness**: In short, my lord, it is time to come to an explanation with regard to this affair; we are no children; therefore, let us talk freely: you have been a widower for these two years past, and I, a widow about as long: the lawsuit in which we were unfortunately engaged, and which gave us both so much uneasiness, is at an end; and all our animosities, I hope, now buried with those who were the causes of them.

**Count**: I am glad of it; for lawsuits were always my aversion.

**Baroness**: And am not I as hateful as a lawsuit?

**Count**: You, madam?

**Baroness**: Yes, I, sir: for these two years past we have lived together, with freedom, as relations and friends; the ties of blood, taste, and interest, seem to unite us, and to point out a more intimate connection.

**Count**: Interest, madam? make use of some better term, I beseech you.

**Baroness**: That, sir, I cannot; but with grief I find, your inconstant heart no longer considers me in any other light than as your relative.

**Count**: I do not wear the appearance, madam, of a trifler.

**Baroness**: You wear the appearance, sir, of a perjured villain.

**Count**: [Aside.] Ha! what's this?

**Baroness**: Yes, sir: you know the suit my husband began against you, to recover my estate, was, by agreement, to have been terminated by a marriage; a marriage you told me, of choice; you are engaged to me, you know you are; and he who defers the execution of his promise seldom means to perform it.

**Count**: You know, I wait for my mother's consent.

**Baroness**: A doting old woman: well, sir, and what then?

**Count**: I love and respect her yet.

**Baroness**: But I do not, sir. Come, come, these are idle, frivolous excuses for your unpardonable falsehood: you wait not for her, or for anybody; perfidious, ungrateful man!

**Count**: Who told you so, madam, and whence all this violence of passion? who told you so? whence comes your information, madam?

**Baroness**: Who told me? yourself, yourself. Your words, your manner, your air, your whole behavior, put on on purpose to affront me: it shocks me to see it: act in another manner, or find some better excuses for your conduct: can you think me blind to the shameful, unworthy passion that directs you, a passion for the lowest, meanest object? you have deceived me, sir, basely deceived me.

**Count**: 'Tis false, I cannot deceive; dissimulation is no part of my character. I own to you, there was a time when you were agreeable to me; I admired you, and flattered myself that I should have found in you a treasure to make amends for that which heaven had deprived me of; I hoped in this sweet asylum to have tasted the fruits of a peaceful and happy union: but you have found out the means to destroy your own power. Love, as I told you long since, has two quivers: one filled with darts, tipped with the purest flame, which inspires the soul with tender feelings, refines our taste and sentiments, enlivens our affection, and enhances our pleasures; the other is full of cruel arrows, that wound our hearts with quarrels, jealousy, and suspicion, bring on coldness and indifference, and remove the warmth of passion to make room for disgust and satiety: these, madam, are the darts which you have drawn forth, against us both, and yet you expect that I should love.

Baroness: There, indeed, I own myself in the wrong: I ought not to expect it: it is not in your power: but you are false, and now would reproach me for it, and I must suffer your insults, your fine similes and illustrations: but pray, sir, what is it I have done to lose this mighty treasure? what have you to find fault with?

Count: Your temper, your humors, madam: beauty pleases the eye alone, softness and complacency charm the soul.

Baroness: And have not you your humors, too, sir?

Count: Doubtless, madam; and, for that very reason, would have an indulgent wife; one whose sweet complying goodness would bend a little to my frailties, and condescend to reconcile me to myself, to heal my wounds without burning them, to correct without assuming, to govern without being a tyrant, to insinuate herself by degrees into my heart, as the light of a fine day opens gradually on the weak and delicate eye: he who feels the yoke that is put on him will always murmur at it; and tyrannic love is a deity that I abjure: I would be a lover, but not a slave: your pride, madam, would make me contemptible: I have faults, I own I have; but heaven made woman to correct the leaven of our souls, to soften our afflictions, sweeten our bad humors, soothe our passions, and make us better and happier beings: this was what they were designed for; and, for my part, I would prefer ugliness and affability to beauty with pride and arrogance.

Baroness: Excellently well moralized, indeed; and so when you insult, abuse, and betray me, I in return, with mean complacency, must forgive the shameful extravagance of your passion; and your assumed air of grandeur and magnanimity must be a sufficient excuse to me for all the baseness of your heart.

Count: How, madam?

Baroness: Yes, sir: I know you: it is the young Nanine who has done me this injury; a child, a servant, a field beggar, whom my foolish tenderness nourished and supported; whom your fond, easy mother, touched with false pity, took up out of the bosom of penury and sorrow. O you blush, sir, do you?

**Count**: I, madam? I wish her well.

**Baroness**: You love her, sir: I know you do.

**Count**: Well, madam, and if I did love her, know, I would openly avow it.

**Baroness**: Nay, I believe you are capable of it.

**Count**: I am so.

**Baroness**: And would you break thus through all the bounds of decency, degrade your rank, demean your birth, and, plunged as you are in shame and infamy, laugh at and defy all honor?

**Count**: Call it prejudice: whatever you, or the world may think, madam, I never mistake vanity for honor and glory: you love pomp and splendor, and place grandeur and nobility in a coat of arms: I look for it in the heart. The man of worth, who has modesty with courage, and the woman who has sense and spirit, though without fortune, rank, or title, are, in my eyes, the first of human kind.

**Baroness**: But surely they ought to have some rank and condition in life. Would you treat a low-born scholar, or an honest man of the meanest birth, because he had a little virtue, in the same manner and with the same respect as you would a lord?

**Count**: The virtuous should always have the preference.

**Baroness**: This extravagant humility is insupportable: do we owe nothing then to our rank?

**Count**: Yes: to be honest.

**Baroness**: My noble blood would aspire to a higher character.

**Count**: That is a high one which defies the vulgar.

**Baroness**: Thus you degrade all quality.

**Count**: No: thus I do honor to humanity.

**Baroness**: Ridiculous! what then becomes of the world? what is fashion?

**Count**: Fashion, madam, is despised by wisdom: I will obey its ridiculous commands in my dress perhaps, but not in my sentiments: no: it becomes a man to act like a man, to preserve to himself his own taste and his own thoughts: am I ridiculously to ask of others what I am to seek, or to avoid, to praise, or condemn? must the world decide my fate? surely I have my reason, and that should be my guide: apes were made for imitation only, but man should act from his own heart.

**Baroness**: Why, this, to be sure, is freedom of sentiment, and talking like a philosopher. Go, then, thou noble and sublime soul, go, and fall in love with village damsels, be the happy rival of plowmen and hedgers: go, and support the honor of your race.

Count: Good heaven! what must I do? How am I to act?

## SCENE II.

The Count, the Baroness, Blaise.

Count: Well, sir, what do you want?

Blaise: Your poor gardener, sir, humbly beseeches your honor—

Count: My honor! well, Blaise, and what wouldst thou have of my honor?

Blaise: And please, your honor, I would fain—be married and—

Count: With all my heart, Blaise, you have my consent; I like your design, and will assist you. It is well folks should marry. Well, and thy spouse elect, Blaise, what is she? handsome?

Blaise: O yes, sir, a delicate little morsel.

Baroness: And does she like you, Blaise?

Blaise: O yes.

Count: Well, and her name is?

Blaise: Yes, 'tis—

Count: What?

Blaise: The pretty Nanine.

Count: Nanine?

Baroness: Well, very well indeed! I approve of the match extremely.

Count: [Aside.] O heaven! how am I sunk! it cannot, must not be.

Blaise: I'm sure, master will like it.

Count: What! did you say she loved you, rascal?

Blaise: I beg pardon, sir, I—

Count: Did she tell you that she loved you, sir?

Blaise: Why, no, sir, not absolutely, sir; not directly; but she seemed to have a little sort of a sneaking kindness for me, too: a hundred times has she said to me in the prettiest, softest, most familiar tone, "Help me, my dear friend Blaise, to make a fine nosegay for my lord, that best of masters;" then would she make the nosegay with such a pretty air, and look so thoughtful, and so absent, and so confused, and so—O it was plain enough.

Count: [Aside.] Away, Blaise, get thee gone—Oh! and am I agreeable to her then?

Blaise: Nay, master, now don't put off this little affair of mine.

Count: Ha!

Blaise: You shall see how this little spot of land will thrive under our hands soon: why won't you answer me, sir? You say nothing.

Count: [Aside.] Oh! my heart is too full: I must retire—madam, your servant.

## SCENE III.

The Baroness, Blaise.

**Baroness:** [To herself.] He loves her to distraction, of that I'm positive: by what charms, by what happy address, could she thus steal his heart from me? Nanine! good heaven! what a choice! what madness! Nanine! no! I shall burst with disappointment.

**Blaise:** What did you say, madam, about Nanine?

**Baroness:** [To herself.] Insolent creature!

**Blaise:** Is not Nanine a charming girl?

**Baroness:** No.

**Blaise:** Well, I say no more; but do speak for me, speak for poor Blaise.

**Baroness:** What a dreadful stroke is this!

**Blaise:** I have a little money, madam, a few crowns: my father left me three good acres of land, and they shall be hers; money, and land, everything I have, body and soul, Blaise and all.

**Baroness:** Believe me, Blaise, I wish you as well as you can wish yourself, and should be glad to serve you: I should be glad to see you married this very night: nay, what's more, I'll give her a portion.

**Blaise:** O good, dear baroness! how I do love you! is it possible you can make me so happy?

**Baroness:** Alas! Blaise, I am afraid I cannot; we shall never succeed.

**Blaise:** O but you must, madam.

**Baroness:** I wish to God she was your wife: wait for my orders.

**Blaise:** And must I wait? not long I hope.

**Baroness:** Be gone.

**Blaise:** Servant, madam: I shall have hear, I shall have her.

## SCENE IV.

**Baroness:** [Alone.] What a strange adventure! could I have received a more cruel injury? a more shameful affront? the Count d'Olban rivalled by a gardener—here, boy, [she calls out to her servant] fetch Nanine to me: since I am so unhappy, I must examine her: where could she have learned this art of flattery? who taught her to gain hearts, and to preserve them, to light up a strong and a lasting flame? where? doubtless, in her eyes, in plain and simple nature: but this shameful and unworthy passion of his is still a secret; it has not dared as yet to appear openly. D'Olban, I see, has his scruples about it: so much the worse; if he had none, I might still have hopes; but he has all the symptoms of true love: O here she comes, the sight of her hurts me; nature is most unjust, to bestow so much beauty on such a creature; 'tis an affront to nobility: come this way, madam.

SCENE V.
The Baroness, Nanine.
**Nanine**: Madam.
**Baroness**: And yet, after all, she is not so very handsome; those great black eyes of hers express nothing; but if they have said, I love; ay, there's the danger: but I must—come this way, child.
**Nanine**: I come, madam, as is my duty.
**Baroness**: Yes: but you make me wait a little for you; prithee, child, step on: how awkwardly she is made! what a mien there is! he was never made for such a creature as you.
**Nanine**: 'Tis very true, madam: I assure you; I have often blushed in secret when I looked on these fine clothes: but they were your first present to me, the effect of that goodness which I shall ever acknowledge, and of that generous care with which you were pleased to honor me: you took a pride in dressing me: O madam, remember how often you have protected me: believe me, madam, I am still the same: why should you wish to humble a submissive heart, which can never forget itself?
**Baroness**: Bring that couch nearer to me—O I am distracted: whence come you? what have you been about?
**Nanine**: Reading, madam.
**Baroness**: Reading what?
**Nanine**: An English book that was given me.
**Baroness**: What's the subject of it?
**Nanine**: 'Tis extremely interesting: the author would have us believe that we are all brethren, all born equal, and on a level with each other; but 'tis an idle chimera, I can't reconcile myself to his doctrine.
**Baroness**: [Aside.] She will soon, I suppose—what vanity! [To Nanine] bring me my standish, and pen and ink.
**Nanine**: Yes, madam.
**Baroness**: No; stay: give me something to drink.
**Nanine**: What, madam?
**Baroness**: Nothing: it's no matter: take my fan. Go and get my gloves—or—stay—it does not signify, you need not: come hither: I desire you to take care never to think yourself handsome.

**Nanine**: That, madam, is a lesson you have so often taught me that if I had so much vanity, and self-love had such influence over my foolish heart, you would soon have cured me of it.

**Baroness**: [Aside.] Where can she have learned all this? how I hate her! beauty and wit together! 'tis intolerable—hark'ee, child, you know the tenderness I had for you in your infancy.

**Nanine**: Yes, madam, and I hope my youth will be honored with equal goodness from you.

**Baroness**: Be careful then to deserve it: it is my intention now, this very day, nay, this very hour, to fix and establish your happiness; judge then whether I love you.

**Nanine**: To fix my happiness?

**Baroness**: Yes: I will give you a portion: the husband I design for you is well-made, and in every way worthy of you; a proper match for you in every particular, and the only one that at present could suit you: you ought to thank me for the choice: in a word, 'tis Blaise, the gardener.

**Nanine**: Blaise, madam?

**Baroness**: Yes: why that simpering? do you hesitate a moment to consent? my offers, madam, I would have you know, are commands; obey, or expect my resentment.

**Nanine**: But, madam—

**Baroness**: Let me have no buts; they offend me: a pretty thing indeed, for your impertinence to refuse a husband at my hands! that simple heart of yours is swelled to a fine degree of vanity: but your boldness is a little premature, and your triumph will be of short duration: you take advantage of the capricious fortune of one lucky day, but shall soon see what will be the event. You ungrateful little wretch, have you the insolence to please? you understand me, madam, but I'll bring you back to that nothingness whence you came, and you shall lament your folly and your pride: I'll shut you up for the rest of your life in a convent.

**Nanine**: On my knees I thank you, madam; do shut me up, my fate will be too mild: yes, madam, of all the benefits you have ever bestowed on me, this, which you call a punishment, I shall esteem the greatest favor: shut me up forever in a cloister; there, I will thank you for your goodness, and bless my dear master: there I shall learn to calm those cruel fears, those dreadful alarms, those worst of evils, those passions that are far more dangerous to me even than your resentment, which fill me with terror and astonishment: O madam, by that anger, I entreat you, deliver me, save me, save me, if possible, from myself; this moment I am ready to go.

*Baroness:* What do I hear? can it be? are you in earnest, Nanine, or mean you to deceive me?

*Nanine:* No: indeed I do not. O do me this charming, this divine favor; my heart stands too much in need of it.

*Baroness:* [With transport.] Rise then, and let me embrace you. O happy hour! my dear Nanine, my friend, I'll go this instant and prepare your sweet retreat; O 'tis a charming thing to live in a convent!

*Nanine:* 'Tis at least a shelter from the world, and all its cares.

*Baroness:* O my dear, 'tis a delightful situation.

*Nanine:* Do you think so, madam?

*Baroness:* This world is a hateful place—jealous—

*Nanine:* [Sighing.] 'Tis so indeed.

*Baroness:* Foolish, wicked, vain, deceitful, inconstant, and ungrateful: O 'tis a horrid place.

*Nanine:* Yes, I see it would be fatal to me, I ought to flee from it.

*Baroness:* You ought indeed: a good convent is the best haven of security. Now, my good lord, I think I shall be beforehand with you.

*Nanine:* Did you say anything about my master, madam?

*Baroness:* O Nanine, I love you even to madness: this moment I would, if possible, lock you up never to come out again: but to-night it is too late, we must wait till morning. Hark'ee, child, come to me at midnight to my apartment, and we will set off secretly for the convent: be ready by five at the latest.

### SCENE VI.

*Nanine:* [Alone.] How distressful is my condition! what trouble and uneasiness do I feel! and what various passions rise in my soul! to leave so good, so amiable a master, perhaps to offend him by it: and yet, if I had stayed, this excess of his goodness might have brought on worse calamities, and put his whole family in confusion. The baroness seems apprehensive that he has a particular regard for me: but his heart could never stoop so low; I must not, dare not think of it: and my lady seems desperately angry about it: am I hated then, and should I be afraid of being beloved? O but myself, myself I have most reason to fear, and my foolish heart, that beats so at the thought of him. What will become of me? taken out of my humble state, my notions now are too refined and too exalted: it is a misfortune, nay, and it is a fault, too, to have a mind above one's condition. I must go: I know it will kill me: but no matter.

### SCENE VII.

The Count, Nanine, a Servant.

**Count**: Stay at that door there somebody, d'ye hear? bring chairs here, quick, make haste. [He bows to Nanine, who makes him a low courtesy.] Come, sit down.

**Nanine**: Who, I, sir?

**Count**: Yes: I will have it so: I mean to pay you, Nanine, that respect which your conduct, your beauty, and merit deserve: shines the diamond with less lustre, or is it less valuable, because found in a desert? What's the matter? your eyes seem bathed in tears: O I see it but too plainly; our angry baroness, jealous of your charms, has been venting her ill-humors on you, and left my poor girl weeping.

**Nanine**: No, sir, no: her goodness, I assure you, to me was never greater than at present; but everything here softens and affects me.

**Count**: I'm glad to hear it; I was afraid it was some of her malice.

**Nanine**: Why so, sir?

**Count**: O my dear girl, jealousy reigns in every breast: every man is jealous when he is in love, and every woman even before she is so. A young and beautiful girl, who at the same time is good-natured and sincere, is sure to displease her whole sex: men are more just, and we endeavor as well as we can to revenge ourselves on you for your jealousy: but, with regard to Nanine, I only do her justice, I love that heart which is void of artifice; I admire the display of those extraordinary talents which you have so finely cultivated; and I am both surprised and charmed at the ingenuous simplicity of your manners.

**Nanine**: O sir, my merit is small indeed; but I have seen you, have heard and been instructed by you: you have raised me too high above my humble birth: I owe you but too much: from you only I have learned to think.

**Count**: O Nanine, wit and good sense are not to be taught.

**Nanine**: I think too much, I fear, for one in my station: my fortune designed me for the lowest rank in life.

**Count**: Your virtues have placed you in the highest: but tell me ingenuously, what effect had that English book I lent you?

**Nanine**: Not convinced me at all, sir: I am more than ever of opinion, that there are hearts so noble and so generous, that all others must appear mean and vile when put in comparison with them.

**Count**: True, Nanine, and you are yourself a proof of it: but permit me to raise you for the future to a rank and station here less unworthy of you.

**Nanine:** My condition, sir, is already too high, and too desirable for me.

**Count:** No, Nanine, that cannot be: henceforward I shall consider you as one of the family; my mother is coming, she will look on you as her daughter, my esteem, and her tender friendship, will put you on a different footing, and place you in a better rank than you have hitherto held under a proud and imperious woman.

**Nanine:** [Aside.] She only taught me my duty, sir—and a hard one it is to fulfil.

**Count:** What duty? yours, Nanine, is only to please, and that you always perform; would I could do so, too! but you should be more at your ease, and appear with more splendor; you are not yet in your proper sphere.

**Nanine:** I am indeed quite out of it, and it is that which makes me unhappy; 'tis my misfortune, perhaps an irreparable one. [Rising.] O my lord, my master, remove, I beseech you, from me all these vanities: I am confused, overwhelmed with your excess of goodness; let me live unknown and unenvied; heaven formed me for obscurity, and humility has nothing in it that to me is grating or disagreeable: leave me to my retreat; what should I do in the world, what should I wish to see there, after the admiration of your virtues?

**Count:** [To himself.] It is too much, I can resist no longer. [To Nanine.] You remain in obscurity? you?

**Nanine:** Whatever I may do, permit me to ask one favor of you.

**Count:** What is it? speak.

**Nanine:** For some time past you have loaded me with presents.

**Count:** Pardon me, Nanine, I acted but as a tender father who loved his child: I have not the art to set off my presents by flattery, I aim not at gallantry, and only desire to be just: fortune had done you wrong, and I meant to avenge the injury: but nature, in recompense for it, lavished all her bounties on you, and her I strove to imitate.

**Nanine:** You have done a great deal too much; but I flatter myself I may be permitted, without being thought ungrateful, to dispose of those noble presents, which I shall ever hold dear because they came from you.

**Count:** You mean to affront me, sure.

## SCENE VIII.

The Count, Nanine, Germon.

**Germon:** My lady wants you; she waits.

**Count:** Let her wait then: what! can't I speak a moment to you without being interrupted?

**Nanine:** It gives me pain to leave you; but you know, sir, she was my mistress.

**Count**: No: I know it not, nor ever will.

**Nanine**: She has still a power over me.

**Count**: No such thing: she shall have none—you sigh, Nanine, there's something at the bottom of that heart; what's the matter?

**Nanine**: I am sorry to leave you, sir—but I must—O heaven, now all is over. [She goes out.]

SCENE IX.
The Count, Germon.

**Count**: [To himself.] She wept as she left me; for a long time she has groaned beneath the tyrannical caprice of this peevish baroness, who insults her: and by what right, or what authority? but 'tis an abuse which I will never suffer: this world is nothing but a lottery of wealth, titles, dignities, rights, and privileges, bartered for without legal claim, and scattered without distinction—here, you—

**Germon**: My lord.

**Count**: To-morrow morning lay this purse of a hundred louis d'ors on her toilette; be sure you don't fail; you must then go and see after her servants below, they'll wait there.

**Germon**: The baroness shall certainly have them on her toilette according to your orders.

**Count**: Blockhead, they're not for her: for Nanine, I tell you.

**Germon**: O very well, sir, I beg pardon.

**Count**: Begone, leave me. [Germon goes out.] This tenderness of mine can never be a weakness in me: true, I idolize her; but my heart was not touched by her beauty only, her character is to the last degree amiable: I admire her soul; but then her low condition—it is too high; were she lower, I should love her yet more: but can I marry her? doubtless I may; can one pay too dear for being happy? shall I fear the censure of an idle world, and let pride deprive me of all I wish for? but then custom—a cruel tyrant: nature has a prior right, and should be obeyed: and so I am Blaise's rival, too; and why not? Blaise is a man; he loves her, and he is in the right of it: she can be but in the possession of one, though the desire of all: gardeners may sigh for her, and so may kings: my happiness will justify my choice.

# ACT II.

SCENE I.
The Count, Marin.

**Count:** [To himself.] Well; this night is a whole year to me: not once have I closed my eyelids: everybody is asleep but me; Nanine sleeps in peace, a sweet repose refreshes her charms, while I wander from place to place, and can find no rest: I sit down to write, but can't: then strive to read, but all in vain; I don't know the words before me while I am looking on them, nor can my mind retain a single idea: methinks, in every page, I see the name of Nanine imprinted by some hand divine—hullo! who's there? all asleep? German, Marin.

**Marin:** [Behind the scenes.] Coming, sir.

**Count:** You idle rascals, make haste, it's broad daylight; come, come.

**Marin:** Lord, sir, what spirit has raised you up so early this morning?

**Count:** Love.

**Marin:** O ho! my lady will let none of us sleep long in this house; what did you want, sir?

**Count:** Why, Marin, I must have, let me see, by to-morrow at the latest, six new horses, a new equipage, a clever chambermaid, notable and careful, a valet de chambre, and two footmen, young and well-made, and no libertines; some diamonds, some very fine buckles, some gold trinkets, and some new stuffs; therefore, be gone, ride post to Paris this instant, never mind killing a few horses.

**Marin:** O ho, I see how it is; you are caught; my lady baroness is to be our mistress to-day, I suppose; you are going to be married to her at last?

**Count:** Whatever my intention is, go you about your business; fly, and make haste back.

**Marin:** I'm gone, sir.

SCENE II.

The Count, Germon.

**Count:** [To himself.] And shall I then enjoy the sweet pleasure of honoring, of making happy the dear object of my love? The baroness, I know, will be in a rage: with all my heart, let her rave as long as she will; I despise her, and the world, and its opinion; and am afraid of nobody: I will never be the slave of prejudice; it is an enemy whom we ought to subdue, those who make a rational mind more virtuous, and those only are respectable: but hark! what noise is that in the court? a chariot sure: it must be so; yet who could come at this time in the morning? my mother perhaps. Germon—

**Germon:** Sir.

**Count:** What is that?

**Germon:** A chariot, sir.

**Count:** Whose is it? anybody coming here?

**Germon:** No, sir, they're going.

**Count:** Going? who? where?

**Germon:** The baroness, sir, going out immediately.

**Count:** O with all my heart, let her go forever if she pleases!

**Germon:** Nanine and she are this minute setting out.

**Count:** O heaven! what sayest thou? Nanine?

**Germon:** So the maid says, sir.

**Count:** How is this?

**Germon:** My lady, sir, is going with her this morning, to put her into a neighboring convent.

**Count:** Away: fly: let us begone: but what am I about? I am too warm to talk to them: no matter, I'll go; I ought—but stop, that must not be, I should at once discover all my passion: no—go, Germon, stop them, let everything be fast; bring Nanine to me, or answer it with your life. [Germon goes out.] So they would have carried her off! what a dreadful stroke! ungrateful, cruel, unjust woman! how have I deserved this! what have I done! I only loved and adored her; but never declared my passion; never endeavored to force her inclinations, or to alarm her timid innocence: why should she fly from me? the more I think of it, the more I am astonished.

### SCENE III.

The Count, Nanine.

**Count:** My sweet girl, is it you? what, run away from me? answer me, explain this mystery to me: terrified, I suppose, with the baroness's threats, you were willing to escape; and that tender regard which I have long had for your virtues, I know, has quickened her resentment; surely you could not yourself have thought of leaving me, of depriving this place of its fairest ornament: last night, when I saw you in tears, tell me, Nanine, had you any intention of this? answer me, tell me, why would you have wished to leave me?

**Nanine:** Behold me on my knees, and trembling before you.

**Count:** [Raising her up.] Rise, Nanine, and tell me—I tremble more myself.

**Nanine:** My lady, sir—

**Count:** Well—what of her?

**Nanine:** That lady, sir, whom I honor and esteem, did not, I assure you, force me to the convent.

**Count:** And could it then be your own choice? O misery!

**Nanine**: It was, I own it was: I entreated her to restrain my wandering thoughts—she wanted to marry me.

**Count**: Indeed? to whom?

**Nanine**: To your gardener.

**Count**: O the worthy choice!

**Nanine**: I, sir, was ashamed, and to the last degree unhappy: I who in vain endeavor to stifle sentiments far above my condition, I whom your bounty had raised too high, must now be punished by the loss of that goodness which I never deserved.

**Count**: You punish yourself, Nanine, and for what?

**Nanine**: For having dared to raise the resentment of your relation, sir, who was once my mistress; I know, sir, I am disagreeable to her; the very sight of me disgusts her: she has reason indeed, for when I was near her, I was guilty of a weakness which I shall ever feel; it grows on me every hour: but I would have torn it from my breast; I would have humbled, by the austerities of a convent, this proud heart, exalted by your goodness, and revenged on it the involuntary crime: but the bitterest grief I felt, was my fear of offending you.

**Count**: [Turning from her, and walking about.] What sentiments! what a noble and ingenuous mind! Can she be prejudiced in my favor? was she afraid of loving me? O exalted virtue!

**Nanine**: If I have offended you, I beg a thousand pardons; but permit me, sir, in some deep retreat to hide my sorrows, and to reflect in secret on my own duty, and your goodness to me.

**Count**: No more of that: now, observe me, the baroness is your friend, and out of her generosity has provided you with a servant, a rustic, a boor, for your husband. I know of one who will at least be less unworthy of you: in birth and fortune far superior to Blaise; young, honest, and well provided for: a man, I assure you, of sense and reflection: his character very different from those of the present age: if I am not much mistaken, he'll make you an excellent husband: is not this better than a convent?

**Nanine**: No: sir, I own to you, this new favor which you would bestow on me has nothing in it that can give me any real satisfaction: you know my grateful heart, read there my real sentiments, and see why I wish to retreat from the world: a gardener, or the monarch of the whole world, who should offer marriage to me, would be equally displeasing.

**Count**: You have determined me: and now, Nanine, know the man for whom I have designed you: you already esteem him: he is yours; he adores you: that husband is—myself. I see, you are troubled and surprised: but speak to me; my life depends on you: O recollect yourself, you are strangely agitated.

**Nanine**: What do I hear? can it be?

**Count**: It is no more than you deserve.

**Nanine**: In love with me? O do not think, do not imagine I will ever dare to claim my conquest: no, sir, never will I suffer you to descend thus low for me: such marriages, believe me, sir, are always unhappy: fancy vanishes, and repentance alone remains. No, I will call your ancestors to witness—alas! sir, think not on me: you took pity on my youth: this heart, which you have formed, which is your own work, would be unworthy of your care, if it could accept from you this noblest present. No, sir, I owe you at least this refusal: my heart shall sacrifice itself for your sake.

**Count**: No more: for I am resolved, and you shall be my wife. Did you not this moment assure me you would refuse every other man, though he were a prince?

**Nanine**: I did, and repent not of the resolution.

**Count**: Do you hate me then?

**Nanine**: Should I have fled, should I have avoided, should I have feared, if I had hated you?

**Count**: It is enough, and I am fixed.

**Nanine**: What then have you determined on?

**Count**: Our marriage.

**Nanine**: Think, sir.

**Count**: I have thought of everything.

**Nanine**: And foreseen too?

**Count**: I have.

**Nanine**: If you love me, believe me, sir—

**Count**: I do believe—that I have resolved on the only means to make myself happy.

**Nanine**: But you forget—

**Count**: I have forgotten nothing: everything is ordered, and everything shall be ready.

**Nanine**: What! in spite of all I say, will your obstinate passion—

**Count**: Yes, in spite of you, my impatient love must urge the happy moment. I will quit you for a minute, that henceforth we may never part: adieu, my dear Nanine.

## SCENE IV.

**Nanine:** [Alone.] Good heaven! do I dream? or am I indeed arrived at the summit of earthly happiness? 'tis not the honor, great as it is; 'tis not the splendor that dazzles me: no: I despise it all: but to wed the most generous of men, the dear object of all my timid wishes, him whom I was so much afraid of loving, him whom I adore, yet I love him too much to wish he should demean himself for my sake: but it is impossible to avoid it; I cannot now escape him: what can I do? heaven, I trust, will direct me, and support my weakness, perhaps even—but I'll write to him—and yet how to begin, and what to say—what a surprise! I will write immediately before I enter into this solemn engagement.

## SCENE V.

Nanine, Blaise.

**Blaise:** O there she is: well, my little maid, my lady has spoken to you in my favor, has she not? ha! she writes on, and takes no notice of me.

**Nanine:** [Writing on.] O Blaise, good morrow to you.

**Blaise:** Good morrow is but a cold compliment.

**Nanine:** [Writing.] Every word I write doubles my distress, and my whole letter is full of doubts and uneasiness.

**Blaise:** How she writes offhand! O she's a great genius; and a monstrous wit: I wish I was a wit too, then I'd tell her—

**Nanine:** Well, sir.

**Blaise:** Lackaday, she's so clever, I'm afraid to speak: I shall never be able to break my mind to her—yet I was hot upon't, and came here o' purpose; that I did.

**Nanine:** Dear Blaise, you must do me a piece of service.

**Blaise:** Marry, two an' you will.

**Nanine:** I shall trust to your discretion, to your good heart, Blaise; nay, I do you but justice.

**Blaise:** O no ceremony; for look you, ma'am, Blaise is ready to serve you, and there's an end of it. Come, come, make no secret.

**Nanine:** You often go to the neighboring village, to Remival, the right hand side of the road.

**Blaise:** Yes, yes.

**Nanine:** Could you find one Philip Hombert for me there?

**Blaise:** Philip Hombert? I know nothing of him: what sort of a man is he?

**Nanine:** He came there, I believe, but yesterday evening; do you look him up, and give him immediately this money, and this letter.

**Blaise**: Oh, money is it?

**Nanine**: And at the same time deliver him this packet: go on horse-back that you may return the sooner: away, make haste, and be assured I'll remember you for it.

**Blaise**: I would go for you to the world's end—this Philip Hombert is a happy rogue: the purse is full: all ready rhino. What, is it a debt?

**Nanine**: Yes: and well proved; nothing can be more sacred, therefore take care of it: hark'ee, Blaise, Hombert may not be known in the village, perhaps he is not yet returned: if you can't give the letter into his own hands, bring it me back again: my dear friend, remember that.

**Blaise**: My dear friend!

**Nanine**: I shall depend on you.

**Blaise**: Her dear friend! O lud!

**Nanine**: I rely entirely upon you, and expect everything from your fidelity.

## SCENE VI.

The Baroness, Blaise.

**Blaise**: What a message! and where the deuce could this money come from? it would have been of service to me in housekeeping: but she has a friendship for me, and that's better than money, so away we go. [As he is putting the money and letter into his pocket, he meets the baroness, and runs full against her.]

**Baroness**: How now, booby? a little more and you'd have broken my head.

**Blaise**: I beg your pardon, madam.

**Baroness**: Where are you going? have you heard anything of Nanine? what is she about? is the count in a violent passion? what have you got there, a letter?

**Blaise**: O that's a secret: poise on her!

**Baroness**: Let me look at it.

**Blaise**: Nanine will be angry.

**Baroness**: Nanine! could she write, and send it by you? give it me this minute, or I'll break off your match immediately; give it me, I say.

**Blaise**: [Laughing.] He! he!

**Baroness**: What do you laugh at?

**Blaise**: [Still laughing.] Ah! ah!

**Baroness**: I must know the contents of this;—[Breaks open the letter] if I am not mistaken, they concern me nearly.

**Blaise**: [Laughing.] Ah! ah! ah! how she is nicked now! she has got nothing there but a scrap of paper: but I shall keep the money, and carry it to Philip Hombert: yes, yes, must obey my mistress. Servant, ma'am.

## SCENE VII.

**The Baroness:** [Alone.] Now let's see what we have got. [Reads.] "Both my joy and tenderness are unspeakable, as is my happiness also: what a moment was this for you to come in! when I cannot see or hear you, cannot throw myself into your arms: but, I conjure you, take these packets, and accept the contents of them. Know, I have been offered a most noble and truly enviable condition in life, such as I might well be dazzled with the prospect of: but there is nothing which I would not sacrifice to the only one on earth whom my heart ought to love." Very fine indeed! upon my word, Nanine, an excellent style: how prettily she writes! the innocent orphan: her passion speaks most eloquently: a rare billet this! O thou sly jade: thus you deceived poor Blaise, and thus deprived me of my lover: this going into a convent, I find, was all a feint, a pretence; and the count's money, it seems, is for Philip Hombert: thou little coquette! but I am glad of it: the count's perfidiousness to me deserved this return: I thought indeed Nanine's heart was as mean as her birth, and now I am satisfied of it.

## SCENE VIII.

The Count, Baroness.

**Baroness:** But here comes the philosopher, the sentimental Count d'Olban, the wise lover, the man above prejudice: your servant, noble count, approach and laugh, my dear lover, at the most ridiculous circumstance: do you know Philip Hombert, of Remival? but, to be sure, you can't be a stranger to your—rival.

**Count:** What is all this, pray?

**Baroness:** This billet perhaps will inform you: this Hombert must be a handsome lad.

**Count:** You are too late, madam, now with your schemes; my resolution once made, I am not to be shaken: be satisfied, madam, with the shameful trick you wanted to play me this morning.

**Baroness:** You'll find this new one worse, I believe: there, read: [Gives him the letter] you'll like it vastly: you know the hand, and you know the virtue of the dear nymph that has subdued you: [While he is reading it he seems confounded, grows pale and angry] well, sir, what think you of the style?—he sees nothing, says nothing, hears nothing: poor man! but he deserves it.

**Count:** Did I read aright? it cannot be. I am astonished, thunder-struck; ungrateful sex! perfidious creature!

**Baroness:** [Aside.] I know his temper well; naturally violent, quick and resolute: he'll do something immediately.

SCENE IX.

The Count, Baroness, Germon.

**Germon:** Yonder comes Madam d'Olban: she's in the avenue already.

**Baroness:** Is the old woman returned?

**Germon:** Sir, sir, my lady, your mother, is coming.

**Baroness:** His anger has taken away his hearing: the letter operates finely.

**Germon:** [Bawling out to him.] Sir.

**Count:** Does she think—

**Germon:** [Aloud.] My lady, sir, your mother.

**Count:** What is Nanine doing at this instant?

**Germon:** Writing in her own apartment—but, sir—

**Count:** [With an air of coolness.] Go, seize her papers; bring me what she writes, and then let her be sent away.

**Germon:** Who, sir?

**Count:** Nanine.

**Germon:** I can never have the heart to do it, sir: O sir, if you knew how she charms us all, so noble, so good!

**Count:** Do it, sir, or see my face no more.

**Germon:** I obey, sir. [He goes out.]

SCENE X.

The Count, Baroness.

**Baroness:** Now, the day is ours: I give you joy, sir, of your return to reason: now, sir, is it not true as I told you, the low-bred always retain something of their former condition, and persons of family alone have hearts truly noble? Blood, sir, let me tell you, does everything, and meanness of birth will inspire Nanine with sentiments you never suspected her of.

**Count:** That I don't believe: but come, we'll talk no more about it, but endeavor to make amends for past errors: every man has his follies, at some part of his life; we all go wrong; and he is least to blame who repents the soonest.

**Baroness:** 'Tis well observed.

**Count:** Never mention her to me again: be silent on that head, I entreat you.

**Baroness:** Most willingly.

**Count:** I beg this subject of our dispute may be entirely forgotten.

**Baroness:** But will you remember then your former vows?

**Count:** Well, well, I understand you, I will.

**Baroness:** And quickly, too, or you will not repair the injury: our marriage so shamefully deferred is an affront—

Count: That shall be made amends for; but, madam, we must have—
Baroness: Have what? we must have a lawyer.
Count: You know, madam, that—I waited for my mother.
Baroness: And here she comes.

SCENE XI.
The Marchioness D'olban, the Count, Baroness.
Count: [To his mother.] Madam, I should have—[Aside] O Philip Hombert! [To his mother] but you have prevented me: my respect and tenderness—[Aside] with that air of innocence too! perfidious wretch!
Marchioness: Why, you rave, child; I heard indeed, as I passed through Paris, that your head was a little touched, and I find there was some truth in it; how long has this misfortune—
Count: Good heaven! how confused I am!
Marchioness: Does it seize you often?
Count: It never will again, madam.
Marchioness: I should be glad to speak with you alone. [Turns to the baroness and makes her a formal courtesy.] Good morrow, madam.
Baroness: [Aside.] The old fool! [Turning to the Marchioness] Madam, I leave you the pleasure of entertaining the count at your leisure, and retire. [She goes out.]

SCENE XII.
The Marchioness, the Count.
Marchioness: [Talking very fast, and in the manner of a little prattling old woman.] Well, sir, and so you intend to make the baroness my daughter-in-law: 'twas this, to tell you the truth, that brought me here so soon: she's a peevish, impertinent, proud, opinionated creature, and one who never had the least regard for me: last year, when I supped with the Marchioness Agard, she said before all the company, I was a babbler. Lord forbid I should ever sup there again: a babbler! besides, I know, between you and me, she is not so rich; and that, let me tell you, son, is a great point, and we ought to be well-informed about it: they tell me that the Château d'Orme did but half of it belong to her husband, and that the other half was disputed by a long lawsuit, that is not finished to this day: that I had from your grandpapa, and he always told the truth: ay, he was a man; there are few such nowadays: there is nothing now at Paris but a set of half-men, vain, foolish, impertinent coxcombs, talking on every subject, and laughing at times past. Oh, their eternal clack distracts me, prating

about new kitchens, and new fashions: we hear of nothing now but bankrupts, and distress, and ruin: the wives, in short, are licentious, and the husbands simpletons: everything grows worse and worse.

**Count:** [Reading the letter over again.] Who could have thought it? this is a desperate stroke indeed. Well, Germon?

SCENE XIII.

The Marchioness, the Count, Germon.

**Germon:** Here's your lawyer, sir.

**Count:** O let him wait.

**Germon:** And here's the paper, sir, she sent you.

**Count:** [Reading.] Give it me—well, let me see: she loves me, she says here, and refuses me out of—respect. Faithless woman! thou hast not told me the true reason of that refusal.

**Marchioness:** My son's head is certainly turned: 'tis the baroness's doing: love has taken away his senses.

**Count:** [To Germon.] Is Nanine gone! shall I be rid of her?

**Germon:** Alas! sir, she has already put on her old rustic garb with the greatest modesty, and never murmured or complained.

**Count:** Very likely so.

**Germon:** She bore her misfortune with the utmost tranquillity, while everybody about her was in tears.

**Count:** With tranquillity, sayest thou?

**Marchioness:** Whom are you talking about?

**Germon:** O madam, poor Nanine, she is going to be driven away, and everybody laments the loss of her.

**Marchioness:** To be driven away? how is this? I don't understand it: what! my little Nanine go! call her back again: my charming orphan! what has she done, pray? why, Nanine was my present to you. O I remember, at ten years of age she delighted everybody that saw her: our baroness took her, and I said then she would be ill-used; I knew it would be so: but you never mind what I say; you will do everything of your own head: but let me tell you, turning Nanine out of doors thus is a very bad action.

**Count:** Alone, on foot, without money, without assistance!

**Germon:** O sir, I forgot to tell you: an old man asked after you below, and says he wants to speak to you on an affair of importance, which he can communicate to none but yourself: he wants to throw himself at your feet.

Count: In my present unhappy situation of mind, am I fit to converse with anybody?

Marchioness: You are uneasy enough, I believe, child, and so am I, too, to drive away poor Nanine, and make up a marriage which you knew would be disagreeable to me: come, it was not a wise thing: in three months' time you will be weary of one another: I'll tell you what happened exactly like this to my cousin the Marquis of Marmure: his wife was as sour as verjuice, though, by the by, yours is worse; when they married, they thought they loved one another, and in two months after they were parted. My lady went to live with her gallant, a foolish, sharking, extravagant fop; and my lord took a vile, tricking, ridiculous coquette! fine suppers, country houses, horses, clothes, a rascally steward, new trinkets bought on trust, lawyers, contracts, interest-money, all together soon ruined them, and in two years both went together to the hospital. O, and now I think of it, I remember another story, more tragical, and more extraordinary than the other, it was of a—

Count: My dear mother, we must go in to dinner: come—could I ever have suspected such infidelity!

Marchioness: 'Tis really dreadful: but I'll tell it you all at table: in proper time and place, son, it may be of great use to you. Away.

# ACT III.

SCENE I.
Nanine, Clothed as a Country Girl, Germon.

Germon: We are all in tears at the thought of losing you.

Nanine: It is time to go: I've staid too long already.

Germon: But you won't leave us forever, I hope, and in this dress, too?

Nanine: Obscurity was my first condition.

Germon: What a change! and only from this morning: to suffer is nothing, but to be degraded is terrible.

Nanine: No, no, there are a thousand times worse misfortunes.

Germon: I admire your patience and humility; surely my master must have been ill-advised: our baroness has certainly abused her power: she must have done you this injury, the count could never have the heart.

Nanine: I am indebted to him for everything; and, if he thinks fit to banish me, I must submit; his favors are his own, and he has a right to recall them.

Germon: Who would ever have expected such a change? what do you intend to do with yourself?

**Nanine**: To retire, and repent.

**Germon**: How we shall all detest the baroness!

**Nanine**: They have made me miserable, but I forgive them.

**Germon**: But what shall I tell my master from you when you are gone?

**Nanine**: Tell him, I thank him for restoring me to my former condition: tell him that, forever sensible of his goodness, I shall forget nothing but his—cruelty.

**Germon**: You melt my very soul; I could leave this house immediately to go along with you wherever you went: but Blaise is beforehand with us all: he will go and live with you, and we are all ready to follow him.

**Nanine**: No, Germon, that I'm sure you are not. O Germon, to be driven out in this manner—and by whom?

**Germon**: The devil is certainly at the bottom of this business: you are leaving us, and my master is going to be married.

**Nanine**: Married, sayest thou? indeed? nay, then let us be gone: O he was too dangerous for me—farewell.

**Germon**: Well! after all, my master must have a cruel heart, to banish so sweet a creature: she seems a most amiable girl, but in this world one should swear to nothing.

### SCENE II.

The Count, Germon.

**Count**: Well, is she gone at last?

**Germon**: Yes, sir, 'tis done.

**Count**: I'm glad of it.

**Germon**: Then, sir, you have a heart of iron.

**Count**: Did Philip Hombert meet and give her his hand?

**Germon**: What Philip Hombert, sir? alas! sir, poor Nanine went off without a creature to give her his hand; she would not even accept of mine.

**Count**: And where is she gone?

**Germon**: That I know not; most probably to her friends.

**Count**: Ay, at Remival, I suppose.

**Germon**: Yes, I believe she went that road.

**Count**: Go, Germon, immediately, and conduct her to that convent where the baroness was going this morning, I'll lodge her in that safe retreat: these hundred louis d'ors will secure her reception; carry them to her, but take care she does not know they come from me: tell her 'tis a present from my mother: on no account mention my name to her.

**Germon**: Very well, sir, I shall obey your orders. [He goes towards the door.]

**Count:** Germon, you saw her as she went off?

**Germon:** I did, sir.

**Count:** Did she seem dejected? did she weep?

**Germon:** She behaved still better, sir; a few tears dropped from her, but she strove as much as she could to repress them.

**Count:** Did she let fall anything that betrayed her sentiments? did you remark—

**Germon:** What, sir?

**Count:** Did she say anything of me?

**Germon:** Yes, sir; a great deal.

**Count:** Tell me, then, rascal, what did she say?

**Germon:** That you were her master, her best and kindest benefactor; that she shall forget everything—but your cruelty.

**Count:** Away—be sure you take care she never returns; [Germon going out] and hark'ee, Germon.

**Germon:** Sir.

**Count:** One word more: remember, if, by chance, as you are conducting her, one Philip Hombert should follow you, that you treat him in a proper manner.

**Germon:** O, sir, I'll use him most politely, and treat him with a good drubbing, that you may depend on: I'll do the business honestly, I warrant you: young Hombert, you say?

**Count:** The same.

**Germon:** Very well: I have not the honor to know him, but the first man I see will I trim most heartily, and afterwards make him tell me his name. [He goes towards the door and comes back.] This young Hombert, I'll lay my life, is some lover of hers, a beau, a prig, I suppose, the cock of the village. Let me alone to deal with him.

**Count:** Do as I bid you, and immediately.

**Germon:** I thought there was some lover in the case—and Blaise, too, puts in his claim, I suppose. Ay: they always love their equals better than their masters.

**Count:** Begone, I tell you.

### SCENE III.

The Count: [Alone.] He's in the right, and has hit on the true cause of my unhappiness, but I shall myself be the punisher of my own folly. I must now marry the baroness; it is determined, and I can't avoid it: 'tis dreadful; but I have deserved it; 'twill at least be a convenient match: she's not very tractable indeed, but every man may rule, if he has a mind to it; and he who has resolution may, at any time, be master in his own house.

SCENE IV.
The Count, Baroness, Marchioness.
**Marchioness**: Well, son, you are going to marry this lady here?
**Count**: Yes, madam.
**Marchioness**: This night she is to be your wife and my daughter-in-law?
**Baroness**: If you approve of it, madam; I suppose I shall have your consent.
**Marchioness**: Why, I must give it, I think: but to-morrow I shall take my leave of you.
**Count**: Your leave, madam, why so?
**Marchioness**: I shall take my Nanine with me: since you have thought fit to turn her out of doors, I shall take her under my protection: I have a match in my eye for ner: I propose marrying her to the young chief justice, nephew to the attorney-general, Jean Roc Souci; he whose father met with that comical adventure at Corbeil; you must have heard of him: yes, I will take care of this poor child, I'm determined: she is a jewel, and deserves to be well set. I'll marry her off immediately. Your servant.
**Count**: My dear mother, don't be in a passion: leave me to manage my own affairs, and let Nanine go into a convent.
**Baroness**: Indeed, madam, you may believe us, such a girl as Nanine is not fit to go into a family.
**Marchioness**: Ha! why, what's the matter?
**Baroness**: O a little affair only.
**Marchioness**: But pray—
**Baroness**: O nothing at all.
**Marchioness**: Nothing! a great deal, I'm afraid: I understand you mighty well: some little indiscretion I suppose: nothing more likely, for to be sure, she's very handsome. Ay, ay, we are all frail; we tempt, and are tempted; the heart has its weakness: young girls are always a little coquettish: but come, it is not so bad as you make it; tell me fairly, what my poor child has done?
**Count**: I tell you, madam?
**Marchioness**: You seem, after all, at the bottom to have some regard for the girl, and perhaps you may—

SCENE V.
The Count, Marchioness, Baroness, Marin. [Booted.]

**Marin:** I've done it, sir; it's all agreed for.

**Marchioness:** What's agreed for?

**Baroness:** Ay, what, sir, what?

**Marin:** Why, sir, I've done as you ordered me, spoke to the tradesmen, and you'll have your equipage tomorrow.

**Baroness:** What equipage?

**Marin:** Everything, madam, that your future spouse had ordered; six fine horses, and a charming berlin; I'm sure your ladyship will like it; it's very fine; the panels all varnished by Martin: the diamonds, too, are brilliant, and well-chosen; and the new stuffs quite in taste.—O nothing comes up to them.

**Baroness:** [To the count.] And had you ordered all this?

**Count:** I had–[Aside] but for whom!

**Marin:** Everything will come to-morrow morning in the coach, and will be ready for your wedding in the evening: O there's nothing like Paris for getting everything at a minute's warning, if you have but money. As I came back, I called on the lawyer; he's just by, finishing your affair.

**Baroness:** It has hung a long time in suspense.

**Marchioness:** [Aside.] I wish it would hang these forty years.

**Marin:** In the hall I met a poor old man, sighing and in tears; he has waited a long time, he says, and begs to speak to you.

**Baroness:** An impertinent fellow! let him go about his business: he has chosen the wrong time to trouble us now.

**Marchioness:** Why, so, madam? have a little consideration: son, let me tell you, it's very wrong to repulse poor people in this manner; I have told you over and over, when you were a child, you ought to treat them with indulgence; hear what they have to say; be courteous, and affable to them: are not they men as well as yourself? we don't know perhaps whom we affront, and may repent our hardness of heart: the proud never prosper. [To Marin.] Go, see to that old man.

**Marin:** I will, ma'am. [He goes out.]

**Count:** Forgive me, madam, my respects are always due to you, and I am ready to see this man, in spite of my present embarrassment.

## SCENE VI.

The Count, Marchioness, Baroness, A Peasant.

**Marchioness:** [To the Peasant.] Come, come, speak, don't be afraid.

**Peasant:** O my lord, for heaven's sake, hear me; permit me to fall at your feet, and to give you back–

**Count**: Rise, friend; I'll not be knelt to; do not imagine me capable of such pride: you seem to be an honest man, do you want employment in my family? who are you?

**Marchioness**: Cheer up, man.

**Peasant**: Alas! sir, I am the father of—Nanine.

**Count**: You?

**Baroness**: Your daughter's a slut.

**Peasant**: This, sir, is what I feared: this is the cruel stroke that has wounded my poor heart: I thought indeed so much money could not fairly belong to one in her condition: we little folks soon lose our integrity when we come among the great.

**Baroness**: There he's right enough: but still he's a deceiver, for Nanine is not his daughter, she was an orphan.

**Peasant**: It is too true, she was so: I left her with her poor relatives in her infant years, having lost her mother, with all my fortune; obliged by necessity, I went to serve abroad; and as I would not have her pass for the daughter of a soldier, forbade her ever to mention my name.

**Marchioness**: Why so? for my part, I respect a soldier: we stand in need of them sometimes.

**Count**: What is there shameful in the profession?

**Peasant**: It meets indeed with less honor than it deserves.

**Count**: The prejudice against them is inexcusable. I own, I esteem an honest soldier, who hazards his life in the defence of his king and country, much more than an important, self-sufficient scoundrel, whose knavish industry sucks up the blood of his fellow subjects.

**Marchioness**: You must have been in a great many battles: let me have an account of them all; I long to hear it.

**Peasant**: In my present unhappy condition you must excuse me: let it suffice to inform you, that I received a thousand promises of advancement; but, without friends, how was it possible to rise? thrown amongst the common crowd, all I could do was to distinguish myself, and honor my only reward.

**Marchioness**: You were then well-born?

**Baroness**: Fie: how can you think so! well-born indeed!

**Peasant**: No, madam: but I was born of honest parents, and merited—a better daughter.

**Marchioness**: Could you have had a better?

**Count**: Well! go on.

**Marchioness**: A better than Nanine?

**Count:** Prithee, go on.

**Peasant:** My daughter, I understood, was brought up here, and treated in the kindest manner; I thought myself happy, and blessed heaven for your goodness, and paternal care of her; I came to the neighboring village, full of hopes and fears; I own I trembled for her dangerous youth; and, by this lady's intimation, find I had but too much reason; it has shocked me to the soul; but I thought a hundred louis d'ors, besides diamonds, was a treasure too great to be fairly come by: she could never be mistress of them, but at the expense of her innocence: the bare suspicion makes me shudder; if it be so, I shall die with grief and shame: but I came as soon as possible, to give them you back again: they are yours, therefore, I beseech you, take them: if my daughter is to blame, punish me, but don't ruin her.

**Marchioness:** O my dear son, I cannot bear this; it overpowers me.

**Baroness:** What is all this? a dream? a trick?

**Count:** O what have I done?

**Peasant:** [Taking out the purse and the letter.] Here, sir, take them.

**Count:** I take them! no: they were given to her, and she has made a noble use of them: was it to you, then, the message was delivered? who brought it?

**Peasant:** Your gardener, sir, in whom Nanine ventured to confide.

**Count:** Was it directed to you?

**Peasant:** It was, I own it, sir.

**Count:** O grief! O tenderness! what excess of virtue in them both! but now your name?—O I am lost, distracted.

**Marchioness:** Ay, your name. What mystery is this?

**Peasant:** Philip Hombert de Gatine.

**Count:** O my father!

**Baroness:** What does he say?

**Count:** How day breaks in upon me! I have done wrong, and I must make amends for it: O if you knew how culpable I have been! I have injured the sublimest virtue. [He steps aside, and speaks to one of his servants.] away: fly.

**Baroness:** What is all this emotion for?

**Count:** My coach immediately.

**Marchioness:** Now, madam, you must be her protectress: when we have done such an injury, we should blush at nothing so much as an imperfect repentance; my son often has his whims, which people are too apt to mistake for unpardonable follies; but at bottom he has a generous soul, and is naturally good; I can do what I please with him: you, my daughter-in-law, are not so well-disposed.

**Baroness**: I shall grow out of all patience: how confused and thoughtful he looks! what strange scheme now is he meditating upon? well, sir, what do you intend to do?

**Marchioness**: Ay, for Nanine?

**Baroness**: Make her a handsome present, and satisfy her.

**Marchioness**: That will be the least we can do.

**Baroness**: But as to seeing her that I never will: she shall not come nigh the castle: do you hear me?

**Count**: Yes, I hear you.

**Marchioness**: [Aside.] What a heart of stone!

**Baroness**: Don't give my suspicions cause to break out, sir. Ha! you hesitate.

**Count**: [After a pause of some time.] No, madam, I am resolved.

**Baroness**: That respect at least is owing to me; nay, to both of us.

**Marchioness**: And can you be so cruel, son?

**Baroness**: What step do you propose to take?

**Count**: 'Tis taken already: you know my heart, madam, and the frankness of it: I must be plain with you: I had promised you my hand; but the design of our marriage was only to put an end to a tedious lawsuit between us, which I will now do immediately, by willingly resigning to you all those rights and pretensions which were the foundation of it: even the interest shall be yours; I give up everything, take, and enjoy it: if we cannot be man and wife, let us at least live as friends and relatives: let everything that gave mutual uneasiness be forgotten; there is no reason why, because we can't love, we should hate each other.

**Baroness**: Your falsehood is what I expected: but I renounce your presents, and yourself: yes, traitor, I see now who you mean to live with, and how low your passion sinks you: go, and be a slave to her, I leave you to your unworthy choice. [She goes out.]

## SCENE VII.

The Count, Marchioness, Philip Hombert.

**Count**: No, madam, 'tis not unworthy, my soul is not blinded by an idle passion: that virtue which it is my duty to reward ought to melt, but cannot debase me: what they call meanness in this old man constitutes his merit, and makes him truly noble: if I would be so, I must pay the price of it: where souls are thus ennobled by themselves, and distinguished by superior characters, we should pass over common rules: their birth, low as it is, when attended with such virtues, will make my family but more illustrious.

*Marchioness:* What are you talking about?

## SCENE VIII.

the count, marchioness, nanine, philip hombert.

*Count:* [To his mother.] Look at her, and guess.

*Marchioness:* [To Nanine.] My dearest child, come to my arms: but she is strangely clothed, and yet how handsome she looks, and modest too!

*Nanine:* [Pays her respects to the Marchioness, and then runs to her father.] O nature demands my first acknowledgments, my dear father!

*Philip Hombert:* O heaven! my daughter! O sir, you have made me amends for forty years' afflictions.

*Count:* Ay, but how must I repair the injury I have done to such exalted virtue! to come back in this dress, how mean it is, but she adorns it; Nanine does honor to everything: speak, my Nanine, can your goodness pardon the affront?

*Nanine:* Can you, sir, doubt my forgiveness of it? I never thought, after all your bounty to me, you could injure me.

*Count:* If you have indeed forgotten the wrong I did you, give me a proof of it: once more, and only once, I take upon me to command you; but this once you must swear—to obey me.

*Philip Hombert:* I am sure she owes it to you, and her gratitude—

*Nanine:* [To her father.] He need not doubt, sir, of my obedience.

*Count:* I shall depend on it: let me tell you then, that all your duty is not yet paid: I have seen you on your knees to my mother, and to your own father; one thing still remains for you, and that is, now, before them, to embrace—your husband.

*Nanine:* Who? I?

*Marchioness:* Are you in earnest? can it be?

*Philip Hombert:* O my child!

*Count:* [To his mother.] By your permission, madam.

*Marchioness:* My dear child, the family will be in a strange uproar about it.

*Count:* O when they see Nanine, they must approve.

*Philip Hombert:* What a stroke of fortune! O sir, I never thought you could descend thus low.

*Count:* You promised to obey, and I must have it so.

*Marchioness:* My son.

*Count:* My happiness, madam, depends on this important moment: interest alone, we know, has made a thousand marriages; we have seen the wisest men consult fortune and character only: her character is irreproachable; and as to fortune, she wants it not: justice and inclination shall do what avarice has so often done before: let me, then, madam, have your consent, and finish all.

**Nanine**: No, madam, you must not consent; indeed you must not; oppose his passion, oppose mine: let me entreat you, do: love has blinded him, do you, madam, remove the veil: let me live far from him, and at a distance only adore his virtues: you know my condition; you see my father: can I, ought I, ever to wish to call you mother?

**Marchioness**: Yes; you can, you ought: it is enough: I can hold out no longer: this last generosity has entirely subdued me: it tells me how much I ought to love: it is as singular, as extraordinary, as Nanine herself.

**Nanine**: Then, madam, I obey; my heart can no longer resist the power of love.

**Marchioness**: Let this happy day be the worthy recompense of virtue, but let it not be made a precedent.

### End

# The Prude

## Contents

Dramatis Personæ. . . . . . . . . . . . . . . . . . . . . . . . . . . . . . . . . . . . . . . . . 269
Act I. . . . . . . . . . . . . . . . . . . . . . . . . . . . . . . . . . . . . . . . . . . . . . . . . . . 269
Act II. . . . . . . . . . . . . . . . . . . . . . . . . . . . . . . . . . . . . . . . . . . . . . . . . . 280
Act III. . . . . . . . . . . . . . . . . . . . . . . . . . . . . . . . . . . . . . . . . . . . . . . . . 290
Act IV. . . . . . . . . . . . . . . . . . . . . . . . . . . . . . . . . . . . . . . . . . . . . . . . . 299
Act V. . . . . . . . . . . . . . . . . . . . . . . . . . . . . . . . . . . . . . . . . . . . . . . . . . 308

## Dramatis Personæ

Mme. de Dorfise, a Widow.
Mme. de Burlet, her Cousin.
Collette, Chambermaid to Dorfise.
Blandford, Captain of a Ship.
Darmin, his Friend.
Bartolin, a Cashier.
Mondor, a Coxcomb.
Adine, Niece to Darmin, and disguised like a young Turk.

This comedy is partly imitated from an English piece, called the Plain Dealer. It does not suit very well for the French stage; the manners are too rough and bold, though much less so than in the original. The English seem to take too much liberty, and the French too little.

## ACT I.

SCENE I.
Marseilles.
Darmin, Adine.

**Adine**: [Dressed like a Turk.] O my dear uncle, what a cruel voyage! what dangers have we run! and then my dress and appearance, too: still must I conceal under this turban my sex, my name, and the secret of my foolish heart.

**Darmin**: At last we are returned safe: in good truth, niece, I pity you; but, your father dying consul in Greece, both of us left, as we were after his death, without money or friends; your youth, beauty and accomplishments but so many dangerous advantages; and, to crown all our misfortunes, that wicked pasha desperately in love with you; what was to be done? you were obliged to disguise yourself, and make your escape as soon as possible.

**Adine**: Alas! I have yet other dangers to encounter.

**Darmin**: Dear girl, be composed, nor blush at what can't be prevented; embarking with me in such a hurry, and forced to disguise yourself in that manner, you could not with any decency resume your sex on board a ship before a hundred sailors, who were more to be feared than your old debauched pasha; but happily for us, everything has turned out well, and we are safely arrived at Marseilles, out of the reach of amorous pashas, near your friends and relatives, amongst Frenchmen, and good sort of people.

**Adine**: Blandford is certainly an honest man: but how dearly will his virtues cost me! that I should be forced to return with him!

**Darmin**: Your deceased father designed you for him: he had set his heart on that match when you were but a child.

**Adine**: There he was deceived.

**Darmin**: Blandford, my dear, when he is better acquainted with you, will do justice to your charms: he can never be long attached to a prude, who makes it her perpetual study to deceive and impose upon him.

**Adine**: They say she is handsome: he is constant in his nature, and will always love her.

**Darmin**: Constant! who is so, in love, child?

**Adine**: I am afraid of Dorfise.

**Darmin**: She has too much intrigue about her: her prudery, they say, has a little too much gallantry in it: her heart is false, and her tongue scandalous; never fear her, my girl, deceit can last only for a time.

**Adine**: Ay, but that time may be long, very long: the thought makes me miserable: Dorfise deceives him, and Dorfise has found the way to please.

**Darmin**: But, after all, niece, has Blandford really got so far into your heart?

**Adine**: He has, indeed; ever since that day, when the two Algerine vessels attacked us with such violence: O how I trembled for him! I think verily I was as much frightened for him as for you; I wished to be a man, indeed, that I might have defended him: don't you remember, uncle, it was Blandford alone who saved us when our ship was on fire? good heaven! how I admired his courage, and his virtues! they are deeply engraved in my heart, and never to be effaced.

**Darmin**: A grateful heart cannot but be prejudiced in favor of such distinguished virtue. I don't so much wonder at your choice: fine eyes, a noble demeanor, a good shape, and scarce thirty years of age, these are great recommendations to his—virtue: but then his strange humor and austerity can surely never be agreeable to you.

**Adine**: Why not? I am naturally serious myself, and perhaps in him may be fond even of my own faults.

**Darmin**: He hates the world.

**Adine**: They say he has reason.

**Darmin**: His temper is too easy and complying, he relies too much on others, and is too generous; and then his moroseness makes his freedom disagreeable.

**Adine**: The greatest fault he has, in my opinion, is his passion for Dorfise.

**Darmin**: That's too true; why, then, won't you endeavor to open his eyes, disabuse him, and shine in your true character?

**Adine**: How is it possible to shine in any character till we are able to please? alas! from the first day he took us both on board, I have been afraid he should discover me, and now I am on shore I have still the same apprehensions.

**Darmin**: I had intended to discover you to him myself.

**Adine**: For heaven's sake, don't; but join with me in my design upon him: sacrificed as I am to the adored Dorfise, I would wish to remain still unknown to him, and would have him continue a stranger to that victim which he offers up to love.

**Darmin**: What then is your design?

**Adine**: This very night to retire to a convent, and avoid the sight of an ungrateful man whom I cannot help loving.

**Darmin**: Indeed, niece, those who go to a convent in haste, generally live to repent it at leisure: I tell you, child, time will do all things: in the meanwhile, a more dreadful misfortune calls for our attention: the very instant that this new Du-Gué so nobly got off his ship, both his fortune and mine went to the bottom: we are both involved in the same calamity, and have come to Marseilles full of hope, but without a shilling! and must therefore look out for some immediate assistance: love, my dear niece, is not always the only thing to be thought of.

**Adine**: There, uncle, I differ from you; when you are in love, I think it is.

**Darmin**: Time will open your eyes: love, my dear, at your age is blind, but not at mine; and where there is no fortune, and nothing but grief and poverty with it, it has very few charms; only the rich and happy should be in love.

**Adine**: You think, then, my dear uncle, that now you are in distress you can have no mistress; and that your widow Burlet will forsake you as soon as she knows your circumstances.

**Darmin**: My distress perhaps may serve her for an excuse; such, my dear, is the custom of the world; but I have other cares to afflict me: I want money, and that's the most pressing calamity.

## SCENE II.
Blandford, Darmin, Adine.

**Blandford**: So! so! in the age we live in everything may be had of everybody but money: what a heap of close embraces, kisses, fulsome compliments, false oaths, joyous welcomes, have I received from this whole city! but no sooner were they acquainted with my distress than every soul forsook me: such is this world.

**Darmin**: It is indeed a base one: but your friends come in search of you?

**Blandford**: Friends? know you any such? I have looked for them, and have found a number of scoundrels of every rank and degree: I have found honest men, too, that live in the bosom of indolence and plenty, like their own marbles, hard, polished, and always wrapped up in themselves, and their own interests; but worthy hearts, elevated souls, who were not the slaves of fortune, such as take a generous pleasure in relieving the unhappy, these, Darmin, I have seldom, very seldom met with: there is naught but vice and corruption on every side: Mammon is the god of this world; and I wish with all my heart, that all mankind had sunk with our vessel, and was buried in the waves.

**Darmin**: Be so good as to except me from your general sentence.

**Adine**: The world, I do believe, is false: and yet I think there is in it still a heart worthy of you; a heart that can boast of courage with sensibility, and strength with softness; which would resent the unkind treatment you have met with, by loving you, if possible, but the more for it: tender in its vows, and constant in its attachment to you.

**Blandford**: Invaluable treasure! but where is it to be found?

**Adine**: In me.

**Blandford**: In thee! away, deceitful boy, am I in a condition, think you, to listen to such idle tales? prithee, young man, choose a fitter time to jest in: yes, even in this world, I know there are pure and uncorrupted hearts, who will cherish my misfortune, and pity my distress: even in this low condition I have the happiness to reflect, that Dorfise at least knows how to love and to distinguish virtue.

**Adine**: Dorfise then is the idol of your heart?

**Blandford**: She is.

**Adine**: You have tried and proved her then?

**Blandford**: I have.

**Darmin**: My late brother, before he went to Greece, if I remember aright, designed my niece for you.

**Blandford**: Your late brother, my friend, made a bad choice then: I have made a much better: I have determined in favor of that virtue which, banished from the world, hath taken up its residence in the breast of my Dorfise.

**Adine**: Merit like hers is rare indeed; I am astonished at it, but, great as it is, it cannot equal her happiness.

**Blandford**: This youth is of a noble nature, and I love him; he takes my part even against you.

**Darmin**: Not so much perhaps as you think: but pray tell me, how happened it that this Dorfise, with all her attachment and love for you, never wrote to you for a whole year?

**Blandford**: Would you have had her write to me through the air, or the post travel by sea? I have received large packets from her before now, letters written in such a style too—so much truth, so much good sense, nothing affected, embarrassed, or obscure, no false wit, nothing but the language of nature and the heart; such is the effect of real love.

**Darmin**: [To Adine.] You turn pale.

**Blandford**: [Looking earnestly at Adine.] What's the matter with you?

**Adine**: With me, sir? O sir, I have got a sad pain at my heart.

**Blandford**: [To Darmin.] His heart! and what a tone, too! a girl of his age would have more strength and courage: I love the lad, but am astonished at his effeminacy: he was never made for such a voyage; he's afraid of the sea, the enemy, and every wind that blows: I caught him one day sitting down to a looking-glass: he appears to be cut out for the gay world, to sit in a box at a playhouse and admire his fine form, which he seems to be mightily enamored with: 'tis a very Narcissus.

**Darmin**: He has beauty.

**Blandford**: Ay, but he should beware of vanity.

**Adine**: You need not fear, sir, 'tis not myself that I admire: I am more likely to hate myself, I assure you; I love nothing that resembles me.

**Blandford:** Dorfise, my friend, is after all the mistress of my fate: convinced as I have long been of her prudence, I gave her a promise of marriage; at parting I left everything I had in her possession: jewels, notes, contracts, ready money, all, thank heaven, have I frankly trusted to my dear Dorfise; and her I consigned to the virtue of my friend, M. Bartolin.

**Darmin:** What! Bartolin the cashier?

**Blandford:** The same; a good friend, who esteems me, and whom I love.

**Darmin:** [In an ironical tone.] To be sure you have made an excellent choice, and are extremely happy in a mistress and a friend: not at all prejudiced.

**Blandford:** Not in the least: I am impatient at their absence, and long to see them.

**Adine:** [Aside.] I can bear it no longer: I must go.

**Blandford:** You seem disordered.

**Adine:** Everyone has some misfortunes or other; mine are heavy indeed, they overpower me, but they will cease—with Blandford's. [She goes out.]

**Blandford:** I know not why, but this grief affects me.

**Darmin:** 'Tis an amiable youth, and seems wonderfully attached to you.

**Blandford:** Blandford's heart is not a bad one, and what fortune I have, howsoever small it be, shall be in common with us both; as soon as Dorfise returns me the money I left with her, your young Adine shall have a part of it: I wish his voice was a little more masculine, and his air more easy: but time and care must form the manners of youth: he is modest, sensible, and has just notions of right and wrong. I observed through the whole voyage, that he would blush at any indecent expression which my people made use of on board: I promise you I shall endeavor to be a father to him.

**Darmin:** That's not what he wants of you; but come, let us go immediately to Dorfise, at least we shall get your money of her.

**Blandford:** True; but that unlucky demon which always accompanies me, has contrived to keep her in the country still.

**Darmin:** Well, but the cashier—

**Blandford:** The cashier is there, too; but they will both come to town as soon as they know I am here.

**Darmin:** You are satisfied then that Mme. Dorfise is always devoted to your service.

**Blandford:** Why should she not be? if I keep my faith to her, surely she may do the same by me; I have not been so foolish, as, like you, to throw away my heart on a gay coquette.

Darmin: It may happen that I shall find myself despised, but that you know every man is liable to; I will own to you, her airy, trifling humor is very different from that of her wise cousin.

Blandford: But what will you do with a heart so—

Darmin: Nothing at all: I shall hold my tongue, till our two fair idols make their appearance at Marseilles: apropos, here comes our friend Mondor.

Blandford: Our friend? said you! he our friend?

Darmin: His head no doubt is a little of the lightest, but at the bottom he is a worthy character.

Blandford: Prithee, undeceive thyself, dear Darmin, and be assured that friendship requires a firmer mind than his; fools are incapable of love.

Darmin: But the wise man, does he love so much then? come, we may reap some advantage from this fool notwithstanding; as the case now stands with us, there will be no harm in borrowing his money.

## SCENE III.

Blandford, Darmin, Mondor.

Mondor: Morrow, morrow, my dears; so you are still in the land of the living: I'm glad of it, glad of it, with all my heart: good morrow to you; but pray, who is that pretty boy I saw in t'other room? whence comes he? did he come over with you? what is he, Turk, Greek, your son, your page, what do you do with him? where do you sup to-night, ha? boys, where do you throw your handkerchiefs? what! are you going post to Versailles to give an account of your battles? have you got ever a patron here?

Blandford: No.

Mondor: What, never made your bows at court?

Blandford: No: I made my bows at sea; my services are my patrons; the only artifices I make use of; I never was at court in my life.

Mondor: Then you never got anything.

Blandford: I never asked it; I wait till the master's eye in its own time shall find me out.

Mondor: Yes: and these fine sentiments will carry you, as they do everybody else, at their own time, to jail.

Darmin: We are pretty near it already, for our honor and glory has not left us a shilling.

Mondor: I am inclined to think so.

Darmin: Dear knight, let us fairly confess to you—

Mondor: In two words I must inform you—

**Darmin**: That our friend here has had a terrible loss—

**Mondor**: That I have made, my dear, a discovery—

**Darmin**: Of all his fortune—

**Mondor**: Of a famous beauty—

**Darmin**: Which he was carrying—

**Mondor**: To whom without vanity—

**Darmin**: By sea—

**Mondor**: After a good deal of mysterious conduct—

**Darmin**: In his ship—

**Mondor**: I have the happiness to be well with.

**Darmin**: This, sir, is a misfortune—

**Mondor**: O 'tis a most enchanting pleasure to conquer these excessive scruples, to get the better of that modesty, that fierce angry preceptor who is always thwarting and scolding at nature: I had once an inclination for Lady Burlet, for her gayety, and those pretty light airs she gives herself; but that was a foolish taste, as foolish as herself.

**Darmin**: I'm glad to hear it.

**Mondor**: O no, 'tis the prude I dote on: encouraged by the difficulty, I presented my apple to the beauty.

**Darmin**: Ay, sir, this prude, who has captivated your heart, this proud beauty is—

**Mondor**: Dorfise.

**Blandford**: [Laughing.] Dorfise! is it? O you know, I suppose, whom you are speaking to?

**Mondor**: To you, my friend.

**Blandford**: I pity thy folly, young man, and shall take care that, for the future, this lady shall never encourage such sparks as you.

**Mondor**: Very well, my dear: but let me tell you—your wise woman never complains when she is taken by a fool.

**Blandford**: Be so kind, however, my friend, as to play the fool no longer with her, for know, her virtues are destined to make me happy; she is mine, and has promised to marry me; she waits with impatience till we are united.

**Mondor**: [Laughing.] The pretty note that my friend, Blandford, has there! [To Darmin] you say he wants a few more in his distress; here, Darmin. [He is going to give him a pocketbook.]

**Blandford**: [Stopping Darmin.] Stay, take care, Darmin.

**Darmin**: Why, you would not—

**Blandford:** From him I would not—receive anything; when I do any man the favor to borrow of him, it shall be one whom I think worthy of it; it shall be a friend.

**Mondor:** And am not I your friend?

**Blandford:** No, sir: a friend indeed? an excellent friend who wants to run away with my wife; a friend who this very night perhaps would entertain twenty coxcombs at my expense: O I know them well; these fashionable friends, these friends of the world.

**Mondor:** That world, sir, which you grumble at, is better than all your ill-humor. Your servant, sir. I am going this moment to the fair Dorfise, to split my sides with laughing at your folly. [Is going off.]

**Blandford:** [Stopping him.] What say you, sir? Darmin, how is this? can Dorfise be here?

**Mondor:** Most assuredly.

**Blandford:** O heaven!

**Mondor:** And pray what is there in that so wonderful?

**Blandford:** In her own house?

**Mondor:** Yes, I tell you, at Marseilles; I met her just as I came in, returning in a violent hurry from the country.

**Blandford:** [Aside.] To meet me! thank heaven! now all my sorrows are past: come, I'll go, and see her.

**Mondor:** Done: with all my heart: the more fools there are, the more one laughs.

**Blandford:** [Going to the door.] I'll rap.

**Mondor:** Rap away.

**Collette:** [In the house.] Who's there?

**Blandford:** 'Tis I.

**Mondor:** 'Tis I myself.

SCENE IV.

Blandford, Darmin, Collette, Mondor.

**Collette:** [Coming out of the house.] Blandford! Darmin! amazing: lord, sir—

**Blandford:** Collette!

**Collette:** Bless me, sir, I thought you had been drowned long ago; you're welcome, sir.

**Blandford:** No, Collette; just heaven, propitious to my love, preserved me, that I might once more see thy dear mistress.

**Collette:** She is this moment gone out, sir.

**Darmin**: And her cousin, too?

**Collette**: Yes, sir, her cousin has gone along with her.

**Blandford**: But where, for heaven's sake, is she gone? where must I find her?

**Collette**: [Making a prudish curtsy.] At the—assembly.

**Blandford**: What assembly?

**Collette**: Lord, sir, you are mighty ignorant: you must know, sir, there are about twenty ladies of fashion most intimately connected to reform the age, to correct our foolish young women, to substitute in the room of that scandal which now prevails a prudent modesty and reserve, and Mme. Dorfise is at the head of the party.

**Blandford**: [To Darmin.] But how happens it, Darmin, that such a coxcomb as this should be suffered by so rigid, so severe a beauty?

**Darmin**: O prudes love coxcombs.

**Blandford**: Where does she go from the assembly?

**Collette**: That I can't tell: to do good in secret, I suppose.

**Blandford**: Secretly! that's the height of virtue; but when may I, in my turn, speak with her at home?

**Mondor**: That, sir, you must ask me; and I believe I may venture to grant it you: you may see her, sir, as you used to do.

**Blandford**: Your business, sir, is to respect her, and take care that you say nothing to her prejudice.

**Darmin**: And her cousin, too, pray where is she to be found? I was told they lived together.

**Collette**: They do so: but their tastes are different, and they are seldom together. Mme. de Burlet, with ten or a dozen young fellows, and as many pretty women, entertains herself every day, keeps a plentiful table, and goes forever to the comedy: afterwards they dance, or play; always at her house you will meet with good suppers, new songs, and bonsmots, old wines red and white, ice-cream, liquors, new ribbons, Saxon monkeys, rich bagatelles, invented by Hebert for the use of the fine ladies day and night, pleasures succeeding pleasures; scarce is there a moment left even to scandalize one another.

**Mondor**: Ay, this, my friend, is the way to live.

**Darmin**: But whither must I follow her?

**Collette**: Everywhere; for she runs about from morning to night, and sees everything; plays, balls, music, suppers; she is always employed: perhaps very late in the evening you may meet with her and her joyous companions at home, about supper-time.

**Blandford**: If, after what I have heard, you are fond of her, my friend, you must have as little understanding as herself; is it possible to love a woman, who has all the follies of her sex put together? to be sure, it will be worth your while to follow her chariot wheels, to dance after a coquette, and sigh and whine for a ridiculous creature who thinks of nothing but her pleasures.

**Darmin**: I may be mistaken, but I cannot help thinking that a love of pleasure, and the strictest honor, may be consistent with each other; and I am likewise of opinion, with all due deference to you be it spoken, that a prude, with all her severity of virtue, may do a great deal of good in public, and yet in secret is often good for—just nothing.

**Blandford**: Well, well! we shall be better judges by and by; you shall see my choice, and I yours.

**Mondor**: Ay, ay, by the time you return, my dears, the place will be taken.

**Blandford**: By whom, pray?

**Mondor**: By me.

**Blandford**: By you?

**Mondor**: I have made too good use of your absence to be afraid of your presence, I assure you: so fare you well.

SCENE V.
Blandford, Darmin.

**Blandford**: Well, what think you? can one be jealous of such a creature?

**Darmin**: O fools have fortune, you know: nothing more common.

**Blandford**: You can never imagine, surely—

**Darmin**: O yes: your sensible women are very fond of fools at times: but I must take my leave, to know my own fate, and see whether I am a happy or a forsaken lover. [He goes out.]

**Blandford**: [Alone.] Ay, ay, make haste, and get your dismissal: poor fellow! I pity him: how happy am I to have made choice of a woman worthy of my esteem! unfortunate as I have been, I have reason to bless the hour of my return: reason increases my passion: yes: I am resolved; I will leave the world, the whole ungrateful world, for one good and worthy woman. I have had enough of hopes and fears: the port at length appears, and there will I shelter myself: what is all the world to this? a foolish, ridiculous, fatal world! ought I not to detest it? there is not a friend remaining in it; not a creature, who at the bottom really cares a farthing for one: O 'tis a vile world: if there is any love or affection to be expected, it must be from a wife; all the difficulty is how to choose one. A coquette is a monster one would avoid, but a beautiful, a tender, and a sensible woman, is the noblest work of nature.

## ACT II.

**SCENE I.**
Dorfise, Mme. De Burlet, Mondor.

**Dorfise**: I must beg of you, M. Mondor, not to indulge yourself in this excessive familiarity: it is impossible for ears so chaste as mine to suffer such liberties.

**Mondor**: [Laughing.] And yet you like them: you rate me for my impertinence, but you listen to it: why, my dear, your hair is cut short on purpose, that you may hear the better.

**Dorfise**: Again?

**Mme. De Burlet**: Indeed I shall take his part: you are too rigid, and affect too much severity: liberty is not always licentiousness; there is nothing indecent, in my opinion, in little sallies of innocent mirth and gayety, which we may choose whether we will understand or not; but your outrageous virtue would shut up our mouths and our ears together.

**Dorfise**: I would indeed, cousin: and moreover, I would advise you to shut your doors, too, against some visitors whom I frequently see here; I have told you often enough, cousin, it will ruin your reputation: how can you suffer such a libertine crew? Cleon, that pretty fellow, who is very brilliant without a spark of wit, and is always laughing at the good things he would make you believe he has just said; Damon, who for twenty beauties that he is in love with, makes twenty madrigals as insipid as himself; and that Robin, who is always talking of himself, with the old pedant that makes every creature sick of him: then there's my cousin, too, that—

**Mondor**: Enough, enough, madam: let everybody speak in his turn; and since your ladyship shows so much good nature in speaking of the world, I will endeavor to convince you I have at least as much charity as yourself, and propose giving you in three words a picture of the whole city: to begin then with—

**Dorfise**: Stop thy licentious tongue: none should dare to chastise vice but persons of the strictest virtue; I cannot bear to hear libertines satirizing others who are much less culpable than themselves; for my part, what I say is from my regard to the honor of human nature, and disgust of the world, this vile world: how I do hate it!

**Mme. De Burlet**: For all that, cousin, it has some attractions.

**Dorfise**: For you, I believe it has, and to your ruin.

**Mme. De Burlet**: And has it none for you, cousin? do you really hate the world?

**Dorfise**: Horribly.

**Mme. De Burlet**: And all the pleasures of it?

**Dorfise**: Abominably.

**Mme. De Burlet**: Plays? balls?

**Mondor**: Music, dancing—

**Dorfise**: O my dear, they are all the devil's inventions.

**Mme. De Burlet**: But dress and finery? you must acknowledge—

**Dorfise**: All vanity! O how I regret every minute thrown away at my toilette! I hate to look at myself; and, of all things in nature, detest a looking-glass.

**Mme. De Burlet**: And yet, my dear rigid cousin, you seem tolerably well dressed.

**Dorfise**: Do I?

**Mondor**: Extremely well.

**Dorfise**: Plain, very plain.

**Mondor**: But with taste.

**Mme. De Burlet**: You may say what you please, but your wise ladyship loves to please.

**Dorfise**: I love to please? O heaven!

**Mme. De Burlet**: Come, come, be honest; have you not some small inclination to this young rattle? he's not ill made. [Pointing to Mondor.]

**Mondor**: O fie!

**Mme. De Burlet**: Young, rich, and handsome.

**Mondor**: Pooh, prithee.

**Dorfise**: O abominable! a handsome young man is my aversion; handsome and young! O fie, fie!

**Mondor**: Upon my soul, madam, I am concerned for both of us; the wicked woman to talk so: but pray, madam, this Blandford, who is come back without his ship, is he so rich, and young, and handsome?

**Dorfise**: Blandford? why, is he here?

**Mondor**: Certainly.

**Collette**: [Entering hastily.] O madam! I come to tell you—

**Dorfise**: [Whispering to Collette.] Hark'ee.

**Mme. De Burlet**: How's this?

**Dorfise:** [To Mondor.] I thought since he took his leave of me he had been cured of all his faults; to tell you the truth, I imagined he was dead long ago.

**Mondor:** No, madam, he is alive, I assure you: the pirate intends to sink me at once: he pretends to be a favorite of yours.

**Dorfise:** [Aside to Collette.] O Collette!

**Collette:** O madam!

**Dorfise:** [To Mondor.] Dear sir, can't you find out some means of sending him to sea again?

**Mondor:** O yes: with all my heart.

**Mme. De Burlet:** Pray, sir, is there any news of his intimate friend and confidant, Darmin? has he arrived?

**Mondor:** He has, madam: the captain it seems fell in with him at some port or other: they have had a battle at sea, and now are returned home without a stiver; Blandford has brought with him a little Greek, too, the handsomest, genteelest—

**Dorfise:** O yes: I believe I saw him just by my house: large black eyes?

**Mondor:** The same.

**Dorfise:** Penetrating, yet full of softness: rosy cheeks?

**Mondor:** He has so.

**Dorfise:** Fine hair, and teeth: something in his air that's noble and fine?

**Mondor:** The very paragon of nature.

**Dorfise:** If his morals are good; if he is well-born and discreet, I'll see him: you shall bring him to me—though he is young.

**Mme. De Burlet:** I must find out Darmin's lodging as soon as possible: here, la Fleur, go this minute and carry him these five hundred pounds, [she gives a purse to la Fleur] and tell him I expect Blandford and him to supper with me: our friends have long wished for his return, and none more than myself; never did I know a better creature, more honest, or ingenuous: I admire above all things his amiable complacency, and those social virtues that so strongly recommend him.

**Dorfise:** Blandford is not of his disposition: he is so serious.

**Mondor:** So full of spleen!

**Dorfise:** True, and so jealous!

**Mondor:** So affronting!

**Dorfise:** He is—

**Mondor:** Very true.

**Dorfise:** Let me speak, sir; I say he is—

**Mondor:** Yes, madam, I attend to you—he is—

**Dorfise:** He is in short a dangerous man.

**Mme. De Burlet:** They tell me he has fought nobly for his king and country, and distinguished himself greatly at sea.

**Dorfise:** That may be, cousin, but by land he is dreadfully troublesome.

**Mondor:** And besides he is—

**Dorfise:** True.

**Mondor:** O those sailors have all of them such horrid principles.

**Dorfise:** They have so.

**Mme. De Burlet:** But I have heard, cousin, that you formerly gave him some hopes—

**Dorfise:** Yes: but since that I have taken an antipathy to the whole world, and quitted it: I began with him; 'twas he and the world together that have made me so fearful.

## SCENE II.

Dorfise, Mme. De Burlet, Mondor, Collette.

**Collette:** Madam!

**Dorfise:** Well!

**Collette:** M. Blandford has come.

**Dorfise:** O heaven!

**Mme. De Burlet:** Is Darmin with him?

**Collette:** Yes, madam.

**Mme. De Burlet:** I am heartily glad of it.

**Dorfise:** And I'm heartily sorry; I must retire; I would fly from the whole world.

**Mondor:** With me, I hope.

**Dorfise:** No, sir, if you please, without you. [She goes out.]

## SCENE III.

Mme. De Burlet, Blandford, Darmin, Mondor, Adine.

**Darmin:** [To Mme. de Burlet.] Permit me, madam, at length on my knees—

**Mme. De Burlet:** [Running up to Darmin.] O my dear Darmin, come along, I've made an engagement for you to go to the ball when the comedy is over: we'll prate as we go along; my chariot's below. [To Blandford.] And you, M. Solemnity, will you come with us?

**Blandford:** No: I came here, madam, on a serious affair: away, ye train of triflers, go, and pretend to pleasures which you never enjoy; go, and be weary of one another as soon as you can: you and I [turning to Adine] will go in search of Dorfise.

## SCENE IV.
Blandford, Adine, Collette.

**Blandford**: Then we shall see a woman indeed; a woman submitting to every duty of life; a woman who for me has renounced the whole world; and who to her faithful passion joins the most scrupulous and rigid virtue: I hope you will endeavor to recommend yourself to her.

**Adine**: Of that, sir, you may assure yourself; I shall try to imitate her virtues; her example may be the best instruction to me.

**Blandford**: I'm glad to hear you think so: I'll introduce you to her: from this time forward I shall look upon you, Adine, as a son whom fortune has thrown in my way, to make amends for all her past unkindness; it is impossible to know without loving thee; your disposition is only too pliant and flexible; nothing therefore can be of more service to you than to keep company with a prudent and discreet woman, whose acquaintance will improve the goodness of your heart, and confirm you in your honesty, and love of justice, without depriving you at the same time of that sweetness and complacency which I own I find myself deficient in: a woman of sense and beauty, who has nothing trifling or ridiculous in her, is an excellent school for a young fellow at your time of life; it will form your mind, and direct your heart; her house is the temple of honor.

**Adine**: The sooner we visit it then the better; but her example is so uncommon, I fear I shall never be able to follow it.

**Blandford**: Why not?

**Adine**: Because I like yours better: there is something in your virtue, though the external appearance has too much severity in it, that charms me: it must, I am sure, be good at the bottom: you have always been my favorite, but for Dorfise—

**Blandford**: [Going towards the door of Dorfise's house.] You must not indeed flatter yourself that you can at once be able to imitate her; but in time you may: however, let me advise you to see Dorfise, and to avoid her cousin. [He is going in, Collette comes out, stops him, and shuts the door; he knocks at it.]

**Collette**: You must not go in, sir.

**Blandford**: Not I?

**Collette**: No, sir.

**Blandford**: How's this, Blandford refused admittance?

**Collette**: My mistress, sir, is retired to her apartment, and would be private.

**Blandford**: I admire her delicacy, but I must go in.
**Collette**: Pray hear me, sir.
**Blandford**: Not I: I will go in, and this minute too. [He goes in.]
**Collette**: Stay, sir.
**Adine**: I'll follow him and see the event of this strange interview.

SCENE V.
**Collette**: [Alone.] Now will he see her, and discover all: I'm frightened to death about it: 'twill be all over now with my poor mistress: what a foolish woman! to stipulate this secret marriage, and give herself to such a fellow as Bartolin: what will the malicious world say? well; women are strange creatures, that's the truth of it: nay, and so are the men too: what excessive weakness! to be sure my mistress is a fool; she deceives herself and everybody else; and half her time is employed in finding out artifices to hide her indiscretion, and repair her reputation. She follows her inclination, and then has recourse to intrigue and management, and yet she takes no care of the main point: this is a cursed adventure for us, and a most unfortunate return: how will Blandford take the injury she has done him? here have we no less than three husbands in the house, two of them promised, and the other, I believe, absolutely taken: a woman in such a case must be a little hampered.

SCENE VI.
Dorfise, Collette.
**Collette**: O madam, what's to be done?
**Dorfise**: Fear nothing; there are ways and means to dazzle people's eyes, to delay, and put off matters; men are easily managed, their weakness is our strength, and helps our designs against them: I have got myself out of the worst scrape: our disagreeable interview is over—and I have sent the good man—God speed him—into the country to his old crony Bartolin. who may lend him some money; at least I shall gain time by it, and that's enough.
**Collette**: But surely, madam, the deuce was in you to sign that plagued contract! what had you to do with Bartolin?
**Dorfise**: The devil, my dear, is full of spite, that's certain: that fellow persecuted me so: but we tempt, and are tempted, and the heart easily surrenders: you know we heard that Blandford would never come back again.
**Collette**: That he was dead.

**Dorfise**: I was left without any support, money or friends, and weak withal: all owing to the weakness of my sex, Collette; but our stars will prevail: 'tis often the lot of a beauty to marry a scab: my heart was severely attacked.

**Collette**: There are certain seasons very dangerous to a prude: but if you must sacrifice to love, you should have taken the chevalier, he is handsome.

**Dorfise**: O but I wanted a bit of intrigue and mystery, besides I am not fond of his character: but he is useful to me: he is my puffer, my emissary: he's a prate-apace you know, and can scatter reports about town for me that may be serviceable.

**Collette**: But Bartolin is such a villain.

**Dorfise**: Yes, but—

**Collette**: And for his wit, I'm sure there are no charms in that.

**Dorfise**: No: but—

**Collette**: But what?

**Dorfise**: Fate, whim, caprice, my unhappy circumstances, a little avarice withal, and then opportunity—in short, I surrendered, played the fool, and signed the contract. I kept, you know, Blandford's strong box, and after he was gone, gave away a little of his money for him—out of charity: who would ever have thought, that, after two years, he should be constant to his old flame, and come back again to look for his wife and his strong box?

**Collette**: Everybody here said he was dead, and now he is not; the fellow's a fool, and stands in his own light.

**Dorfise**: [Resuming the Prude.] Well, since the man's alive, I must give him his jewels back: let him take them: but Bartolin has got them to keep for me; he fancies they are mine, holds them fast, and is fond of them and as jealous as he is of me.

**Collette**: So I suppose.

**Dorfise**: Husbands, jewels, virtue, and character, how to reconcile you all, heaven knows!

## SCENE VII.

mondor, adine, dorfise.

**Mondor**: I must drive away this powerful rival, who gives himself such airs, and despises me; positively must.

**Adine**: [Coming in slowly.] What's this? I'll listen a little.

**Mondor**: In short, I must make myself happy, and punish his insolence: 'tis you, 'tis Dorfise alone whom I adore: let old Darmin enjoy his little coquette, they are not worth our notice: but Blandford, the severe and virtuous Blandford, there I own I could wish to triumph: he thinks you can refuse him nothing, because he is a man of honor and virtue: now to me these are the most disagreeable creatures in the universe; indeed, my queen, you'll soon be heartily tired of him.

**Dorfise:** [Prudishly, after looking steadfastly at Adine.] You are mistaken, sir: I have the highest respect and esteem for M. Blandford.

**Mondor:** There are those, madam, whom one may esteem, and yet laugh at, and make fools of: is it not so?

**Adine:** [Aside.] Amazing! she is constant and virtuous: doubtless she loves him: I am confounded: who would have thought it?

**Dorfise:** What is he talking of?

**Adine:** [Aside.] Dorfise is faithful, and, to complete my misery, she is handsome.

**Dorfise:** [To Mondor, after looking tenderly at Adine.] He says, I am handsome.

**Mondor:** There he's right: but he begins to be troublesome: hark'ee, child, I have something to say to this lady in private.

**Adine:** I will retire, sir.

**Dorfise:** [To Mondor.] I say, sir, you are greatly mistaken. [To Adine.] Stay you here, my dear. [To Mondor.] How dare you, sir, send him away? [To Adine.] Come hither, child: he's almost ready to weep; the sweet boy! he shall stay with me: Blandford brought him to me; and from the first moment I took a fancy to him: I like his disposition.

**Mondor:** O let his disposition alone, for heaven's sake, and attend to me: this Blandford, madam, I know you hate him: you have often told me he is brutal, jealous—

**Dorfise:** [Angrily.] Never, sir. [To Adine.] What age are you?

**Adine:** Eighteen, madam.

**Dorfise:** Such tender youth as thine requires the curb of wisdom to guide and direct it: vice is bewitching, temptations frequent, and example dangerous: a single glance may be your ruin; be upon your guard against women, nay, and against yourself, and dread the poisonous blast that withers the sweet flower of virtue.

**Mondor:** Prithee, Dorfise, let the boy's flower alone: what is it to you whether it be withered or not? mind me, my dear.

**Dorfise:** My God! his innocence is so engaging!

**Mondor:** 'Tis a mere child.

**Dorfise:** [Coming up to Adine.] What's your name, my dear, and whence come you?

**Adine:** My name, madam, is Adine; I was born in Greece: M. Blandford brought me over with Darmin.

**Dorfise:** 'Twas kindly done of him.

**Mondor:** What a ridiculous curiosity! here I am making strong love to you, and you all the while talking to a child.

**Dorfise:** [Softly.] Be quiet, you blockhead!

## SCENE VIII.

Dorfise, Mondor, Adine, Collette.

**Collette:** Madam.

**Dorfise:** Well!

**Collette:** They wait for you at the assembly.

**Dorfise:** Well: I shall be there presently.

**Mondor:** Hang your engagement: I tell you what, my dear; you and I will put an end to these prudish meetings, these conspiracies against love, taste, and gayety: upon my word, child, it does not become a beautiful young creature, as you are, to go about declaring against everything that's joyous, amongst a parcel of toothless old beldames, that meet together in their gloomy vaults to weep over the pleasures of the living: but I'll go and rout these immortal tattlers, and stop their clack with a hundred bon-mots.

**Dorfise:** For heaven's sake, don't go and expose me there, I desire you: positively you shall not.

**Mondor:** Positively I will, this minute, and tell them you are coming. [He goes out.]

**Dorfise:** The wild creature! [To Adine.]

Avoid, my dear, whatever you do, such fools as these: be prudent, and discreet: make my compliments to Blandford—what a piercing eye!

**Adine:** [Turning back.] Did you speak, madam?

**Dorfise:** That sweet complexion! that ingenuous look! so charming! so modest!—I hope I shall have the pleasure of seeing you often.

**Adine:** I shall pay my respects, madam, with the greatest pleasure: madam, your servant.

**Dorfise:** Adieu, my dear child.

**Adine:** I don't know what to think of it: I can't discover whether she deceives him or not; all I know is, I love him.

## SCENE IX.

Dorfise, Collette.

**Dorfise:** [Looking after Adine.] What said he? I love! love whom? perhaps the boy has fallen in love with me; he talks to himself, stops, and looks at me; I have certainly turned his brain.

**Collette:** He ogles you most wonderfully, and looks with such tenderness.

**Dorfise:** Is that my fault, Collette? how can I possibly help it?

**Collette:** Very true, madam: but danger approaches: I am terribly afraid of this Blandford's coming back again, and dread still more the savage resentment of Bartolin.

**Dorfise:** [Sighing.] This young Turk's mighty handsome! do you think he is a Turk? that an infidel can have such softness in his manner, so fine a figure? I fancy I could convert him.

**Collette:** I'll tell you what I fancy: that when it is discovered you are married to Bartolin, your reputation will be severely handled: Blandford will storm dreadfully, and your little Turk will be of no great service to you.

**Dorfise:** Never do you fear.

**Collette:** I have long, madam, relied on your prudence: but Bartolin is a jealous brute, and what's worse, he is—your husband: 'tis really a melancholy case, and indeed rather singular: the two rivals, I am afraid, will be very intractable.

**Dorfise:** O I can avoid them both: peace is the object of my wishes: it is my duty and my interest to foresee and prevent the ill consequences of a discovery; I have friends, men of merit and fortune.

**Collette:** Take their advice.

**Dorfise:** I intend to, immediately.

**Collette:** But whose?

**Dorfise:** Why, let me see—suppose I ask this stranger—this little—

**Collette:** Ask his advice? the advice of a beardless boy?

**Dorfise:** He seems to be very sensible, and if he is, why not consult him? let me tell you, young people are the best counsellors in things of this kind: he might throw some light on my affairs; besides, he is Blandford's friend, and I must talk with him.

**Collette:** O to be sure, madam, 'tis quite necessary.

**Dorfise:** And as one talks over such things better at table, it would not be amiss to ask him to dinner: what think you?

**Collette:** Softly there, madam: excuse me, but you who are so afraid of scandal—

**Dorfise**: I am afraid of nothing: I know what I am about: when once a reputation is established, we may be perfectly easy about it: all the party will defend us, and cry out on our side.

**Collette**: Ay, but the world will talk, madam.

**Dorfise**: Well! for once we'll submit to the wicked world: I'll give up this innocent dinner, and not sharpen their malicious tongues: I'll talk no more with Adine, never see him again; and yet, after all, what could they say of a child? but to chastity and virtue I will add the appearance of them also; will observe decency and decorum: I'll do it in my cousin's name, and beg her—

**Collette**: An excellent contrivance! a woman of the world has no reputation to lose; one may put her name to ten billets-doux; she may have as many lovers, as many assignations as she pleases: nobody's offended, nobody blushes, nobody's surprised: but if, perchance, a lady of honor makes a false step, it must be carefully concealed.

**Dorfise**: A false step! I make a false step! thank heaven! I have nothing to reproach myself with: to be sure, I have signed, but I am not yet absolute Mme. Bartolin: he has a claim, and that's all; and perhaps I may find a method to get rid of my master: I have an excellent design in my head: if this handsome Turk has any inclination to me, I am satisfied everything will go well; I am yet mistress of myself, and can terminate all happily: go you, and ask him to dinner: is there any harm in having an agreeable young fellow at one's table, and one that can give good advice, too?

**Collette**: O excellent advice! nothing can be more proper: let us immediately set about this charitable work.

# ACT III.

### SCENE I.
Dorfise, Collette.

**Dorfise**: Is it not he? how uneasy I am! hark! somebody knocks; he's come: Collette, hullo! Collette: 'tis he.

**Collette**: No, madam, 'tis the chevalier; that impertinent coxcomb, who runs in and out, skips, laughs, prates, and flutters about perpetually; he swears he will have a tête-à-tête with you; and at last, between jest and earnest, I have driven him away.

**Dorfise**: O send him to my cousin: I hate their insipid parties, their ridiculous prating and nonsense: dear Collette, preserve me from them.

**Collette**: Hush! hush! I hear somebody coming.

**Dorfise:** O 'tis my sweet Greek.
**Collette:** 'Tis he, I believe.

## SCENE II.
Dorfise, Adine.

**Dorfise:** Pray come in: good morrow to you, sir: how I tremble! pray, sir, be seated.

**Adine:** I'm quite confounded—I beg pardon, madam, I believe, another—

**Dorfise:** Be not alarmed, sir: I am that other: my cousin dines abroad to-day with Blandford: you must supply his place, and stay with me.

**Adine:** Supply his place, madam! who can do that? what passion can equal his, or who can exceed him in virtue, honor, and nobleness of soul?

**Dorfise:** You talk of him with warmth; your friendship has life and spirit in it: I admire you for it.

**Adine:** 'Tis a sincere regard, but an unhappy one.

**Dorfise:** Tenderness is to the last degree becoming in youth like thine; virtue is nothing, if it is not linked by the sacred bonds of friendship.

**Adine:** Alas! if a natural sensibility is the infallible mark of virtue, without vanity, I may boast some degree of worth and honesty.

**Dorfise:** A soul so noble deserves to be cultivated and improved; perhaps I was born to be the happy instrument; many a woman has long wished in vain to find a tender friend, lively, yet discreet, who possessed all the graces of youth without its flighty extravagance; and, if I am not deceived, in thee all those qualities are united: indeed they are: what lucky star conducted thee to Marseilles?

**Adine:** I was in Greece, and the brave Blandford brought me from thence; I have told you so twice already.

**Dorfise:** Suppose you have, I could hear it again and again: but tell me, why is that fair forehead wrapped up in a turban? are you really a Turk?

**Adine:** Greece is my country.

**Dorfise:** Who would have thought it? Is Greece in Turkey then? O how I should like to talk Greek with you! why you have all the sprightliness, all the natural ease of a true Frenchman: surely nature mistook when she made you a Greek: well, I bless Providence for throwing you thus amongst us.

**Adine:** Here I am, to my sorrow.

**Dorfise:** And canst thou be unhappy?

**Adine:** Indeed I am so: but 'tis the fault of my own heart.

**Dorfise**: Ay: 'tis the heart that does all the good and all the evil in this world: 'tis that which makes us both miserable: have you any engagement then?

**Adine**: I have, indeed: a base intriguing woman has betrayed me: her heart, like her face, is painted and disguised: she is bold, haughty, and full of artifice; more dangerous, because she hides her vices beneath the mask of virtue: how cruel is it that so false a heart should govern one who is but too honest!

**Dorfise**: Some faithless woman! let us be revenged on her: who is she? of what rank? what country? what is her name?

**Adine**: That I must not tell you.

**Dorfise**: Why so? I fear you have art, too, the art of concealment: O you have every talent to please and to delight, young and discreet, beautiful and sensible: but I will explain myself: if, to make you amends for all the injuries you have received, you should meet with a woman rich, amiable, admired, and esteemed; one who had a heart constant, firm, and hitherto untouched, such as is seldom to be met with in Turkey, and more seldom perhaps in this country; if such a one could be found, tell me, sweet youth, what think you? what would you say to her?

**Adine**: I would say—she meant but to deceive me.

**Dorfise**: Nay, that would be carrying your distrust too far: come, come, be more confident.

**Adine**: Forgive me, madam; but the unfortunate, you know, are always a little suspicious.

**Dorfise**: And what, for example, may your suspicions be whilst I am talking to and looking at you?

**Adine**: My suspicions are that you mean to try me.

**Dorfise**: O the malicious little rogue! how cunning he is with that air of innocence: 'tis love himself just out of his childhood: get you gone: I am in absolute danger: positively I'll see you no more.

**Adine**: Since 'tis your order, madam, I take my leave.

**Dorfise**: But you need not be in such a hurry to obey: come back, come back, I esteem you too much to be angry with you; but don't abuse my esteem, my sincere regard.

**Adine**: But you esteem Blandford: can one esteem two at the same time?

**Dorfise**: O no, never: the laws of reason and of love allow succession, but not division: you'll learn a great deal by living with me, child.

**Adine**: I have learned a great deal by what I see already.

**Dorfise**: When heaven, my dear, makes a fine woman, it always at the same time forms a man on purpose for her: we go in search of each other for a long time, and make twenty choices before we fix on the right; we are always looking as it were for our counterpart, and seldom, very seldom, meet with it—by a secret instinct we fly after true happiness; and she [looking tenderly at him] who finds you, need look no further.

**Adine**: If you knew what I really am, you would soon change your opinion of me.

**Dorfise**: Never.

**Adine**: If once you knew me, I'm sure you would think me unworthy, of your care: we should both be caught in the same snare.

**Dorfise**: Caught, my dear, what can you mean? we're interrupted: O 'tis you, Collette.

## SCENE III.

collette, dorfise, adine.

**Collette**: [In a violent flurry.] Ay, madam, I could not help it; but there's a more impertinent visitor still coming; M. Bartolin.

**Dorfise**: Indeed! I did not expect him till to-morrow: the villain has deceived me: returned already!

**Collette**: Ay, madam, and here's another unlucky accident: the chevalier, that king of coxcombs, not knowing the master of the house, is disputing with him in the street, and keeps him there in spite of his teeth.

**Dorfise**: So much the better.

**Collette**: No, madam, so much the worse: for this blunderer, not knowing whom he is talking to, laughs in his face, insists upon it that nobody shall come in here to-day; that everybody shall be excluded as well as himself; that he's an impertinent rascal, and that you were engaged in your own apartment in a sober tête-à-tête with a pretty young fellow. Bartolin swears in wrath that he'll break the door down: Mondor splits his sides with laughing, and the other bursts with spleen.

**Dorfise**: And I in the meantime am dying with fear. O Collette, what shall I do? at what hole shall we creep out?

**Adine**: What can this mystery be?

**Dorfise**: The mystery is, that we are both undone: Collette, where are you going?

**Adine**: What will become of me?

**Dorfise**: [To Collette.] Hark'ee: stay: what a time was this for him to return! [to Adine] you must hide yourself for tonight in this closet: you'll find a black sack there, wrap yourself up in it, and be quiet. My God! it is he, that's certain.

**Adine:** [Going into the closet.] O love, what do I suffer for thee!

**Dorfise:** Poor lad! he's desperately fond of me.

**Collette:** Hush! hush! here he comes, your dear spouse.

## SCENE IV.

Bartolin, Dorfise, Collette.

**Dorfise:** [Meeting Bartolin.] My dear sir, heaven be with you! how late you are: you made me so uneasy, I was ready to die with fretting.

**Bartolin:** Mondor told me quite another story.

**Dorfise:** It's all a lie, every syllable he says, a horrid lie: I think I ought to be believed first; you know I'm sincere: the fellow loves me to madness, and is piqued at my refusal of him: his eternal clack teases me to death: I will positively never see him again.

**Bartolin:** He seemed to me to talk rationally enough.

**Dorfise:** Don't believe a word he says.

**Bartolin:** Well, well, I shan't mind him: I only came to finish our affairs, and to take some necessaries here out of the closet.

**Dorfise:** [In a persuasive tone.] What are you doing there now? come, don't go into a body's closet.

**Bartolin:** Why not?

**Dorfise:** [After pausing a little.] Why, do you know, I had the same thought as you, and have just been putting my papers in order there, so I sent for our old advocate, and we were consulting together, when he was taken with a sudden weakness.

**Bartolin:** O nothing but old age, he's very old.

**Collette:** And so, sir, they took him in there to give him

**Bartolin:** Ay, I understand you.

**Dorfise:** He's retired a little, and has taken a dose of my syrup: I suppose by this time he has gone to sleep.

**Bartolin:** That he has not, I am sure, for I hear him walking about and coughing.

**Collette:** And would you go to disturb an advocate in the midst of his cough?

**Bartolin:** I don't like this: I'll go in.

**Dorfise:** Grant heaven he may find nothing there: hark! what do I hear! he cries out; murder! my poor advocate's killed to be sure, and I am undone: which way shall I fly? in what convent shall I hide my shame? where shall I drown myself?

**Bartolin:** [Returning, and holding Adine by the arm.] O ho! my dear spouse that is to be: your advocates are mighty pretty figures: you have made a good choice, picked him out from the whole bar: come, my old practitioner, you must disappear from this court, and harangue out the window: away with you.

**Dorfise:** My dear husband, do but hear me.

**Adine:** He her husband!

**Bartolin:** [To Adine.] Come, rascal! I must begin my revenge upon you, and curry you out of your insolence.

**Adine:** Alas! sir, on my knees I ask your pardon; indeed I have not merited your resentment: when you know me, you will lament my fate: I am not what I appear to be.

**Bartolin:** You appear, my friend, to be a scoundrel, a dangerous rival, and shall be punished: come along, sir.

**Adine:** Help, here, help! for heaven's sake, sir.

**Dorfise:** He's mad with passion: help, neighbors, help!

**Bartolin:** Hold your tongue.

**Dorfise, Collette, Adine:** Help, here, help!

**Bartolin:** [Thrusting out Adine.] Come, sir, get out of my house.

## SCENE V.
Dorfise, Collette.

**Dorfise:** What an unfortunate affair this is! he'll kill the poor boy, and me, too, perhaps.

**Collette:** To be sure, nothing but the devil could make you sign a contract with such a wretch as this.

**Dorfise:** The villain! go, Collette, this minute, to a justice, and get a warrant for him: charge him with—

**Collette:** With what, madam?

**Dorfise:** With everything.

**Collette:** Very well, madam: but which way are you going?

**Dorfise:** That I know not.

## SCENE VI.
Mme. De Burlet, Dorfise, Collette.

**Mme. De Burlet:** Why, cousin, cousin, what's the matter?

**Dorfise:** O cousin!

**Mme. De Burlet**: One would have thought you'd been robbed and murdered, or that your house had been on fire: what a roaring and a noise there is here, my dear!

**Dorfise**: O cousin, I'll tell you the affair; but, for heaven's sake, keep my secret.

**Mme. De Burlet**: I'm no keeper of secrets, cousin; but I can be as discreet as other folks upon occasion: what is this mighty affair of yours?

**Dorfise**: The affair's a very bad one, I assure you; in short—I am—

**Mme. De Burlet**: What?

**Dorfise**: Promised in marriage, cousin.

**Mme. De Burlet**: I know it, my dear—to Blandford: so much the better: I think it's a good match: I wish you happy, and intend to dance at your wedding.

**Dorfise**: O my dear, you're mistaken: Bartolin, who is now swearing below stairs, is the man.

**Mme. De Burlet**: Indeed! so much the worse: I don't approve of your choice; but if it is done, it can't be helped: is he absolutely your husband to all intents and purposes?

**Dorfise**: Not yet: the world is an utter stranger to it; but the contract has been made a great while.

**Mme. De Burlet**: O cancel it by all means.

**Dorfise**: It will set the wicked world talking: O cousin, I have been sadly treated. This vile man, you must know, found me with a young Turk, who was shut up in my closet; not with any bad design.

**Mme. De Burlet**: O no, to be sure! pray, cousin, is not this a little out of character for a prude?

**Dorfise**: Not at all: it is a little faux-pas, a small weakness only.

**Mme. De Burlet**: Well, I am glad you own so much: our faults are sometimes useful: this slip may soften your temper; perhaps for the future you will be less severe.

**Dorfise**: Severe or not, for heaven's sake, cousin, get me out of this scrape, and save me from the tongue of scandal, and the violence of Bartolin; if possible, deliver the poor lad, who is scarce eighteen. O, here comes my spouse.

### SCENE VII.

Bartolin, Dorfise, Mme. De Burlet.

**Mme. De Burlet**: What an uproar you are making here for nothing! only on a slight suspicion to put all her friends in such a taking: fie, M. Bartolin.

**Bartolin:** I ask pardon: indeed, ladies, I am ashamed, and sorry I conceived such suspicions; but appearances were strong against her: how indeed could I ever have imagined that this young fellow, for so I thought him, was only a girl in disguise?

**Dorfise:** [Aside.] An excellent come-off.

**Mme. De Burlet:** Mighty well indeed! so my lady here took a girl for a boy?

**Bartolin:** The poor child is in tears still: by my troth, I pitied her: but why could you not have told me who she was? why take a pleasure in trying my temper, and making me angry.

**Dorfise:** [Aside.] Droll enough this! he has played his part well, however, to persuade Bartolin he is a girl, and get off so well: 'twas a charming contrivance: the dear little rogue! but love is a great wit. [To Bartolin] Now thou abominable jealous wretch, answer me, how dare you thus affront my virtue? the poor little innocent confided in me; my cousin here knows how warmly I espoused her cause, and protected her honor: you ought to have had a loose coquette, a jilt, for your wife; you deserve no better, and I hope you'll meet with one: I'll expose you, sir, though I know it will cost me dear, but I am determined at all events to have the contract annulled.

**Bartolin:** I know upon these occasions women must cry: but prithee, my dear, don't cry so much: come, let us be friends; and let me desire you, madam, [to Mme.de Burlet] to say nothing about this affair: I have some very good reasons for concealing it.

**Dorfise:** [To Mme. de Burlet.] Be silent, dear cousin, and save me; on no account mention it to the good M. Blandford.

**Mme. De Burlet:** You may depend on it, I never will.

**Bartolin:** We shall be greatly obliged to you.

## SCENE VIII.

Dorfise, Mme. De Burlet, Bartolin, Collette.

**Collette:** M. Blandford is below, madam, and says he must come up.

**Dorfise:** O dreadful! this is my luck! always crossed—

**Bartolin:** But after all—

**Mme. De Burlet:** Nay, nay, after what you have seen, and being guilty of so much injustice as you have, you have no business to give yourself airs: try what you can do—to obey.

## SCENE IX.

Dorfise, Mme. De Burlet.

**Mme. De Burlet:** I'm glad to see this affair has turned out so well, however: to be sure your intended spouse is rather short-sighted: but between you and me, cousin, it was a strange choice this: and then to take a boy for a girl, at his age: well, husbands will be husbands still I find, always jealous, always laughed at, and led by the nose.

**Dorfise:** [Prudishly.] I don't understand this language, madam, nor have I deserved this treatment from you: surely you don't really believe that a young fellow was locked up in my closet?

**Mme. De Burlet:** Indeed but I do, my dear.

**Dorfise:** What! when my husband told you to the contrary?

**Mme. De Burlet:** Perhaps your spouse might be mistaken; he may have bad eyes: besides, cousin, did you not tell me yourself here in this very place, that a young fellow—

**Dorfise:** Ridiculous! what I, child, I tell you so? never: do you think I have lost my senses? indeed, cousin, you should take more care what you say: when once a woman's tongue has got a habit of talking thus lightly, and spreading scandalous stories, invented merely to calumniate and injure people, there is no end of it, but 'tis a hundred to one that she repents of it sometime in her life.

**Mme. De Burlet:** I calumniate, I scandalize you, cousin?

**Dorfise:** You, madam: I vow and swear—

**Mme. De Burlet:** Don't swear, cousin.

**Dorfise:** But I will.

**Mme. De Burlet:** Fie, my dear, fie: come, come, I shall believe no more of the story than I ought to believe: take a husband, cousin, two if you please; deceive them both as well as you can; make young fellows pass for girls; on the strength of your character govern twenty families, and be called a woman of virtue; with all my heart, it will give me no uneasiness, you are extremely welcome: nay, I admire your management and discretion: 'tis your pride and glory to deceive the world, and mine to divert myself with it, without descending to falsehood: I live for my pleasure: adieu, my dear, my worldly weakness bends in all humility to your profound wisdom: dear cousin, adieu.

### SCENE X.

Dorfise, Collette.

**Dorfise:** Now will that foolish creature go and pull me to pieces: my honor and my character are gone: the libertines will laugh at my expense: Dorfise will be the common butt of every satirist: my name will be hitched into a hundred rhymes, and furnish matter for every singsong in town: Blandford will believe the scandal, and Bartolin will cry for vengeance: how shall I stop the tongues of calumny? two husbands and a lover in one day! what a deal one has to go through to be a prude! would it not be better after all to fear nothing, to affect nothing, and be a plain woman of honor? well: one day or other I'll try to be one.

**Collette:** At least, madam, let us take care to appear as such; when we do all we can, you know, we have done enough; and she is not always a woman of virtue who wishes to be so.

## ACT IV.

### SCENE I.

Dorfise, Collette.

**Dorfise:** O Collette, I'm inevitably ruined: would I could see young Adine; he is so kind, and so sensible! he would tell me everything they do and say, and I might take my measures with him accordingly: my affairs would at least be more settled, and I should know what I have to depend on; what shall I do, Collette?

**Collette:** See him, and talk to him freely.

**Dorfise:** Right: towards evening: O Collette, if success would but crown this mysterious affair, if I could preserve my reputation, and keep my lover, if I could but keep one of them, I should be happy.

**Collette:** Ay, ay, one of them is enough, in conscience.

**Dorfise:** But have you taken care the chevalier shall be here presently; that he shall come privately; and, according to custom, let everybody know it?

**Collette:** O never fear, he'll be here I warrant you; he's always ready, and fancies you've a passion for him.

**Dorfise:** He may be of service: wise men in their designs, the better to compass their ends, always make use of fools.

### SCENE II.

Dorfise, Mondor, Collette.

**Dorfise:** My dear chevalier, come along: I have something to say to you.

**Mondor:** You know, madam, I am the lowest of your subjects, your humble slave, your chevalier: what must I do? tilt for you? fight for you? die for you? spite of all your cruelty, I am ready: speak, madam, and it is done.

**Dorfise:** And am I indeed so happy as to have charmed the agreeable Mondor? but do you love me as you ought to love me, with that pure and refined passion?

**Mondor**: I do; but prithee, my dear, don't be so formal; beauty is most engaging when it is easy and tractable: the excess of virtue is disgusting: in short, my dear, you want a little of my correction.

**Dorfise**: What think you of young Adine?

**Mondor**: Who, I? nothing at all? his figure makes me perfectly easy, I assure you: Mars and Hercules were never jealous of Adonis.

**Dorfise**: Well: I love your confidence, and shall reward it: the malicious world perhaps will tell you I am secretly engaged; but 'tis false; believe them not: a hundred lovers have ogled, and teased me, but I was born to be subdued by you, and you alone.

**Mondor**: That's more indeed than I could flatter myself with the hopes of.

**Dorfise**: To convince you of it, I promise to marry you as soon as ever you please: be prudent, and be happy.

**Mondor**: Happiness is enough for me, prudence we'll leave to another opportunity: but do not, my dear charmer, delay it: time, you know, is precious.

**Dorfise**: But then one thing I must insist on from you.

**Mondor**: I am your husband, madam, and you may command me.

**Dorfise**: You must take care that none of my troublesome visitors intrude on me to-night: the proud, peevish Blandford, my cousin, and her fool Darmin, with all their train of impertinent relations, must go somewhere else, for I positively will not be disturbed by them; then, chevalier, at midnight, and not before, I'll meet you in the arbor; bring your lawyer with you, and we'll sign and seal.

**Mondor**: Transporting thought! how I shall triumph over that fool Blandford! well, I will so laugh at, so ridicule the poor creature.

**Dorfise**: Be sure you don't forget to be at my window a little before midnight: away: be discreet.

**Mondor**: O if Blandford did but know this!

**Dorfise**: Away, begone, or we shall be surprised.

**Mondor**: Adieu, my dear wife.

**Dorfise**: Adieu.

**Mondor**: I go with rapture, to wait for the dear happy hour when prudery shall be sacrificed to love.

### SCENE III.

Dorfise, Collette.

**Collette**: Well, if I can guess at your design, hang me: 'tis a riddle to me.

**Dorfise**: I'll explain it to you: I've made Mondor promise to tell nothing, but I know very well he'll tell all, that's enough, his tale will justify me: Blandford will think everything mere calumny, and not know a word of the truth; to-day at least I shall be safe; and after to-morrow, if success crowns my designs, I shall be afraid of nobody.

**Collette**: Delightful! I'm glad to hear you say so, and yet you put me in a horrid fright: are you sure, ma'am, the plan is well laid? and that you won't, after all, fall into the snare yourself, which you laid for others? for heaven's sake, take care what you do.

**Dorfise**: O Collette, Collette, how strangely one slip brings on another! we are led aside from error to error, and from crime to crime, till our heads turn round, and we fall down the precipice: but I have one string still to my bow; I am sure of young Adine: the chevalier comes at twelve, but my little lover will be beforehand with him: let him be here at nine, Collette, do you hear me?

**Collette**: I'll take care of that, madam.

**Dorfise**: They take him for a girl, by his air, his voice, and his beardless chin; therefore, tell him I would have him dress himself in girl's clothes.

**Collette**: An excellent scheme! heaven prosper it!

**Dorfise**: The boy may serve, you know, to dispel one's melancholy: but the great point I would bring about is, to throw all the scandal upon my cousin, and to make Blandford believe that Adine came here upon her account: let him fall a dupe to his own credulity.

**Collette**: The fittest instrument you could have chosen: for he believes everything that's bad of her, and everything that's good of you: imagines he sees clearly, and at the same time is stark blind: I have taken care already to confirm him in the opinion that our little coquette is in love with the boy, and not you.

**Dorfise**: To be sure, lies are bad things; but they are mighty serviceable sometimes, and do a great deal of good.

SCENE IV.
Blandford, Dorfise.

**Blandford**: O tempora! O mores! dreadful corruption indeed! to desire him to visit her! the poor, simple, ingenuous youth, she wants to draw him into a passion for her, and employs all the little subtleties, all the snares which love makes use of to catch unwary hearts.

**Dorfise**: Well, but after all, M. Blandford, she may not have carried it so far as we imagine: I would not do her so much injury as to suppose it: one should not think evil of one's neighbor: to be sure, things were in a fair way, but you know our French coquettes.

**Blandford**: Yes, yes, I know them.

**Dorfise**: The moment a young man appears with an air of innocence and simplicity, they are after him.

**Blandford**: Yes; yes: vice, above all things, is fond of seducing virtue: but how, Dorfise, can you bear people of such character?

**Dorfise**: As patiently as I can, sir: but this is not all.

**Blandford**: Why, what, pray—

**Dorfise**: O sir, you have another tale to hear: do you know, these excellent contrivers would endeavor to persuade the world truly that the young fellow was brought in for me?

**Blandford**: For you?

**Dorfise**: Yes; they say I wanted to seduce him.

**Blandford**: Well, that to be sure is ridiculous to the last degree: for you!

**Dorfise**: Ay, for me, and that this pretty youth—

**Blandford**: That was really a fine invention.

**Dorfise**: A better than they think for. They have played me a great many such tricks: O M. Blandford, if you knew what I suffer! they'll tell you, too, I'm to be married to that fool, Mondor, and this very night.

**Blandford**: O my dear Dorfise! the more thou art wounded by the envenomed darts of slander and calumny, with the warmer zeal shall this heart, that adores thee, defend thy injured and unspotted virtue.

**Dorfise**: You are deceived, indeed you are.

**Blandford**: No, Dorfise: I think I know myself a little, and I would have laid my life on it I saw your cousin ogling Adine this very day: let me tell you, it requires sense and understanding to be honest: I never knew a fool with a good heart: virtue itself is nothing but good sense: I am sorry for Darmin, because I really love and esteem him; it was against my advice he ventured to embark in such a leaky vessel.

### SCENE V.

Blandford, Dorfise, Darmin, Mme. De Burlet.

**Mme. De Burlet**: What? always dismal and solemn, full of spleen and rancor, grumbling and growling at all mankind, that either don't hear you, or if they do, only laugh at your folly? dear virtuous fool, finish thy soliloquies, and come along with me: I have just bought a few trinkets, you shall have some of them: come, we're going to Mondor's, he's to treat us; I have ordered him to get music, to purge your melancholy humors; and after that, my dear, I'll take you by the hand, and dance with you till to-morrow morning, [to Dorfise] ay, and you shall dance too, Mme. Prim.

**Dorfise**: Prithee, hair-brains, hold thy tongue: such things would not become me; and besides, madam, you should remember—

**Mme. De Burlet**: None of your "besides" I beg you, madam: every thing is forgotten; my philosophy is, remember nothing.

**Dorfise**: [To Blandford.] You see now whether I was right or not: your servant, sir: she really grows too scandalous, I must be gone.

**Blandford**: O stay, madam.

**Dorfise**: No, sir: 'tis impossible: it hurts my soul, my honor—

**Mme. De Burlet**: My goodness! talk less of honor, madam, and regard it more. [Dorfise goes out.]

**Darmin**: [To Mme. de Burlet.] She seems out of humor: I fancy my friend, Blandford, begins to find her out.

**Mme. De Burlet**: O all the world must talk of it; but Darmin and I say nothing.

**Blandford**: I fancy not, indeed: you would hardly confess to me such folly and extravagance.

**Darmin**: No, sir; we would not make you so unhappy.

**Mme. De Burlet**: We know your humor too well, to make you still more miserable by reproaching you with your misfortunes.

**Blandford**: Go, go, hide yourselves both, and die with shame.

**Mme. De Burlet**: Why should we disturb at once the quiet of your whole life, by exposing Dorfise, and make you a common laughing-stock? no, sir; I own I am light and airy, free, and familiar, but have yet some goodness in me, and am no busybody: I should see you deceived a thousand times by your friend, and duped by your wife, hear your adventures chanted through every street, nay, sing them myself, before ever you should hear a word from me: to tell you the truth, the two great ends I have in view are peace and pleasure; I love myself, and therefore hate all idle reports and scandalous tales, true or false: live and be happy is my motto: and he, I think, is a great fool who makes himself miserable by the follies of others.

**Blandford**: Light, unthinking woman! it is not the affairs of others, it is your own, madam, that now call for your attention.

**Mme. De Burlet**: Mine, sir?

**Blandford:** Yes, madam: 'tis you who are to blame, and highly, too; you who seduced a virtuous youth, and then endeavored to lay the shameful intrigue on the innocent Dorfise.

**Mme. De Burlet:** O the scheme is excellent: it is more than I expected: and so it was I, who sometimes—

**Blandford:** Yes, madam, you yourself.

**Mme. De Burlet:** With Adine!

**Blandford:** Yes.

**Mme. De Burlet:** I am in love with him then?

**Blandford:** Most certainly.

**Mme. De Burlet:** And 'twas I that put him in the closet?

**Blandford:** It was: the thing was clear enough.

**Mme. De Burlet:** O mighty well! a lucky thought indeed! I admire the contrivance: O my dear madman, what a mixture thou art of honesty and folly! the very model of Don Quixote, brave, sensible, knowing, and virtuous, yet in one point an absolute fool; but for heaven's sake take care how you recover your senses: believe me, it would be the worst thing you ever did in your life: well, folly has its advantages: adieu: come, Darmin.

### SCENE VI.

Blandford, Darmin.

**Blandford:** Stay, Darmin, I have your honor and your interest at heart: I am angry, and I have reason to be so; in short, you must quit this artful woman, get out of the snare she has laid for you, despise her, or break with me.

**Darmin:** The alternative is a cruel one: I own to thee, I love my friend, and I love my mistress: but how can thy hard heart judge so uncharitably of all human kind: can't you see that this web of perfidy is woven by a base, designing woman? that she deceives you, and would lay the shame and ignominy on another?

**Blandford:** Dost thou not see, fool as thou art, that a vile, scandalous, abandoned wretch has chosen thee for her tool, her butt, her stalking horse, that, like an idiot, you bite at the hook; and that she is only trying to see how far she can exercise her tyranny over your easy heart?

**Darmin:** Easy as it is, let me entreat you, ask the only witness who is able to determine it: I have sent for young Adine, he will tell you the whole truth of the affair.

**Blandford:** O yes: I doubt not but the jade has tutored her young parrot well, and taught him his lesson: but let him come, let him endeavor to deceive me;

I shall not believe him: I see your intention, I see plainly enough, you want, by every artifice, to blacken and destroy my dear Dorfise, to draw me off to your niece, whose charms you have so often boasted: but you need not give yourself the trouble, for I shall never think of her.

**Darmin**: As you please for that: but indeed, Blandford, I pity your folly: to experience the falsehood of a perfidious woman may perhaps be many a poor man's fate, and must be borne; but really to lose one's money is a serious affair: this Bartolin, this noble friend of yours, has he refunded?

**Blandford**: What business is that of yours?

**Darmin**: I beg pardon, I thought it was; but I am mistaken: here comes Adine: I'll retire: let me inform you, if you distrust him, you are more in the wrong than you think for: he has a noble heart, and you may one day know he is not what perhaps he might appear to be.

### SCENE VII.
Blandford, Adine.

**Blandford**: So! I see they are all resolutely bent to lead me by the nose: Dorfise, thank heaven, is of another nature; she says nothing, but submits to her unhappy fate without appearing too deeply affected by it; too confident, or too timid; she avoids me, and hides herself in retirement; such is always the behavior of injured innocence. Now, young man, tell me the truth in every particular with sincerity; nature seems in you pure and uncorrupted; you know I love you; do not abuse my growing inclination to you, but consider that the happiness of my life is concerned in this affair.

**Adine**: Indeed, sir, I love you too well to abuse or to deceive you.

**Blandford**: Tell me then everything as it passed.

**Adine**: First then, I assure you, that Dorfise—

**Blandford**: Stop there, you mean her cousin, I'm sure you do.

**Adine**: I don't indeed, sir.

**Blandford**: Well, go on.

**Adine**: Dorfise then, I say, introduced me by a private door to her chamber.

**Blandford**: She did, but 'twas not for herself.

**Adine**: It was.

**Blandford**: No, child; 'twas Mme. de Burlet, you know it was.

**Adine**: I tell you, sir, Dorfise was positively in love with me.

**Blandford**: The little rascal!

**Adine**: The excess of her passion surprised and shocked me: I was far from being pleased with it: nay, I assure you, I was angry at her: I was incensed at her falsehood; and told her, if I had been like her, I should have been more faithful.

**Blandford**: The villain! how they have prepared him! well, what followed?

**Adine**: After this she grew loud and vehement, when on a sudden a violent knocking was heard, and who should come in but her husband.

**Blandford**: Her husband! O very well! what a ridiculous story! the chevalier, I suppose.

**Adine**: No: a real husband, I assure you; for he was extremely brutal, and extremely jealous: he threatened to murder her, called her false, perfidious, infamous, and abandoned: I expected to have been killed, too, for he was in a dreadful rage with me, though for what reason I know not: I was forced to fall on my knees and entreat him to spare my life; I'm sure I tremble yet at the thoughts of him.

**Blandford**: The little coward! but this husband, what was his name?

**Adine**: I don't know, indeed.

**Blandford**: A fine trick this!—what sort of a man was he? describe him to me.

**Adine**: He seemed to me, as far as the horrid fright I was in permitted me to observe him, a fellow of a very disagreeable aspect, fat and short, like a turnspit, flat-nosed, with a large chin, hunch-backed, a yellow-tanned complexion, gray eyebrows, and an eye that looked like—the devil.

**Blandford**: An excellent picture! how can I recollect him by all this? yellow, you say, tanned, gray, short and fat: who can it be? but you only mean, I see, to laugh at me.

**Adine**: Try, then, sir, and prove me: to-night, this very night, she has appointed again to meet me.

**Blandford**: Another appointment with Mme. de Burlet?

**Adine**: Still, sir, you will mistake the person.

**Blandford**: Not with Dorfise?

**Adine**: With her, indeed.

**Blandford**: With her?

**Adine**: With her, I tell you.

**Blandford**: Amazing! you confound me! an assignation with Dorfise this night?

**Adine**: This very night, sir; if you please, you may see me there: I am to go in girl's clothes, which she herself sent me; and to go in by a private door to your mistress, sir, your faithful, prudent, discreet mistress.

**Blandford:** This is too much; I cannot, will not bear it: whichever way I consider it, I fear she is disloyal: may I depend upon you?

**Adine:** My heart is too deeply concerned for your interest and happiness to be insincere: yours I know is truth itself: indeed, M. Blandford, I love, and am faithful to you.

**Blandford:** The little flatterer!

**Adine:** Can you doubt my honor?

**Blandford:** Away! I—

### SCENE VIII.
Blandford, Adine, Mondor.

**Mondor:** Come, come, you make the guests wait, and stop the course of pleasure: why, you never wanted mirth and good company more in your life: to be sure, your affairs go badly enough; you have lost your mistress, but never mind it: you should not have set up for my rival; I told you I should gain the victory, and so I have.

**Blandford:** What would you inform me of, friend?

**Mondor:** Nay, nothing of consequence, only that I'm going to be married to your mistress, that's all.

**Blandford:** O very well! I know that already.

**Mondor:** What! did you know that I was to carry the lawyer with me, and that—

**Blandford:** Yes, yes, I know it all, your whole plot, and I don't care a farthing about it: [Aside] This boy has not learned half his lesson; hark'ee, sir, [To Adine] this appointment and yours are a little incompatible: what say you to this, sir? does it strike you? either you endeavor to deceive me, or are deceived yourself: but you are young in the school of vice; a heart like thine, simple and inexperienced, is an excellent instrument in the hands of a villain: alas! thou camest here but to make me miserable.

**Adine:** This is too much, sir: take care lest your harsh temper, and ill-placed resentment, should destroy that pity which still pleads for you; 'tis that alone which keeps me here: but go, run headlong to your ruin; listen to nobody, suspect your best friend, and believe only those who abuse you; accuse and affront me; but learn to respect a heart that, with regard to you, was never a deceiver, or deceived.

**Mondor:** Hear you that, sir? but you are choked with spleen; even children laugh at you; prithee, learn to be wiser: come along with me, and drown all your cares in Greek wine: come away, boy.

### SCENE IX.
Blandford, Adine.

**Blandford**: Stay, Adine: thou hast moved me: thy concern alarms me: you know my humor, my folly, but you know my heart too; 'tis honest, and has only too much sensibility: you see how I am distressed; can you take a cruel pleasure in laughing at my misfortunes? tell me the truth, I conjure thee.

**Adine**: I know your heart is good, nor is mine less pure: never till this hour did I but once put on disguise; but with regard to Dorfise and yourself I have been honest and sincere: I own I lament in you that fatal passion which has blinded you, but 'tis passion I know that will seduce the wisest of us all; love alone can set everything right; that has taken away your sight, and that should restore it to you. [She goes out.]

**Blandford**: [Alone.] What can he mean? love alone should restore it; he once put on a disguise, and yet he is sincere! I don't understand it; certainly 'tis all a trick, a plot only to make a fool of me: Mondor, Darmin, her cousin, Bartolin, Adine, Dorfise, Collette, all the world in short conspires with my own foolish heart to make me miserable and ridiculous: this vile world, which I despise as it deserves, is nothing but a confused heap of folly and wickedness: but if in this tempest of the soul I must say whether I will be knave or fool, my choice is made, and I bless my lot: O heaven! let me be still a dupe, but O preserve my virtue!

# ACT V.

### SCENE I.
**Blandford**: [Alone.] What will become of me? where shall I fly for safety? my misfortunes follow one another without end: I go to sea; a pirate attacks and sinks my vessel: I come to land, and there I am told that an ungrateful woman, whom I adored, is a worse pirate still: a strong box, which I had left behind, is my only resource: a rascal promises to give it me back, and puts me off from time to time, and he perhaps may prove a third corsair: I am waiting for Adine, and he is not come yet; everybody provokes, and everybody avoids me: all perhaps the consequence of my unhappy temper which made me suspicious of every friend, and open to every enemy: if it be so, I am wrong; I own I am, and fortune has a right to sport thus with me: of what service is my melancholy virtue but to make me more sensible to my miseries, and more conscious of having deserved them? this boy, too, not come yet!

## SCENE II.

Blandford, Mme. De Burlet passing Across the Stage.

**Blandford**: [Stopping her.] Stay, madam, I beseech you stay, and calm, if possible, this tempest of my soul; for heaven's sake, one word with you: where are you running to?

**Mme. De Burlet**: To supper: to be merry: I'm in haste, sir.

**Blandford**: I know I affronted you, and you have reason to be angry; but forget and forgive.

**Mme. De Burlet**: [Smiling.] O I have forgiven you a great while ago: I'm not angry, I assure you.

**Blandford**: You are too good: will your gayety for once deign to interest itself in my distress?

**Mme. De Burlet**: Gay as I am, M. Blandford, I assure you, I have friendship, esteem, and pity for you.

**Blandford**: You are sorry, then, for my unhappy fate.

**Mme. De Burlet**: Your unhappy fate! yes: but more for your unhappy temper.

**Blandford**: You are honest, however, and truth you know, has always charms for me: but say, is Darmin a faithful friend, or does he deceive me?

**Mme. De Burlet**: Darmin loves you, and possesses all your virtues with more softness and complacency.

**Blandford**: And Bartolin?

**Mme. De Burlet**: You want me to answer for Bartolin, too, and for all the world, I suppose: excuse me; Bartolin, for aught I know, is an honest cashier; what reason have you to suspect him? he's your friend, and the friend of—Dorfise.

**Blandford**: Of Dorfise? but tell me freely; could Dorfise, could she entertain a passion for a boy, and in so short a time, too? and what is this lawyer that Mondor talks of? public report says he's to marry her.

**Mme. De Burlet**: Public reports should be despised.

**Blandford**: I am this moment come from her: she has sworn eternal truth to me: she has wept: love and grief were in her eyes: did they belie her heart? is she false? and is Adine—you laugh at me.

**Mme. De Burlet**: I laugh at your ridiculous figure: come, come, take courage, man: as for the boy, take my word for it, he'll never forsake you; 'tis impossible.

**Blandford**: You give me comfort: the coxcomb, Mondor, is not worth my care; Dorfise loves me, and I love her forever.

**Mme. De Burlet**: Forever? that's too much.

**Blandford:** Not where one is beloved; but then this Adine must be a base calumniator, must have a bad heart.

**Mme. De Burlet:** O no: be assured, he has a noble mind, candid, honest, and ingenuous, the happy favorite of indulgent nature.

**Blandford:** You mock me, madam.

**Mme. De Burlet:** Indeed I don't: 'tis truth.

**Blandford:** Now am I plunged again in darkness and uncertainty; you sport with my distress, and take pleasure in tormenting me: Dorfise, or he, has deeply injured me: one of them, you must allow, has been a traitor to me; is it not so?

**Mme. De Burlet:** [Laughing.] That may be.

**Blandford:** If it is, you see what reason I had—

**Mme. De Burlet:** And after all it may not be so: I accuse nobody.

**Blandford:** I'll be revenged.

**Mme. De Burlet:** Ridiculous! be less angry and more discreet: come, I'll tell you what; will you take the only sure method, one that I shall recommend to you?

**Blandford:** I will.

**Mme. De Burlet:** Then leave this dark mysterious affair to itself; make no bustle about it, but turn everything, as I do, into a jest; take your money from Bartolin, and live along with us without care or solicitate: never go too deeply into things, but float with me upon the surface; you know the world, and bear with it; the only way to enjoy is to skim lightly over it: you look upon me as a giddy creature, and so I am; but let me tell you, the only matter of importance in this life is to enjoy ourselves, and be happy.

### SCENE III.

**Blandford:** [Alone.] To be happy! good! excellent advice! would not one think now it were an easy thing; that one had only to wish for happiness, to possess it? would it were so! and why should it not be? why should I take so much pains to make myself unhappy? shall I suffer this boy, and Darmin, and Mondor to distract me thus? no: I'll follow this giddy girl's advice; she's gay, but honest and sincere: Dorfise loves me, and I am yet secure: for the future, I'll see nothing, listen to nothing: they wanted to alarm me with this Adine, to hoodwink, and then to lead me where they pleased; but I'm not to be caught in their snares: Darmin is wrapped up in that niece of his, and would fain palm her upon me; but I detest her: ha! what's this? [Adine appears in woman's clothes at the farther end of the stage.]

Yonder's that unhappy youth who has caused me so much uneasiness: he looks exactly like a girl: how genteel his air, and so easy, too, as if the clothes had been made for him! the face is too truly female.

## SCENE IV.
Blandford, Adine.

**Adine**: Well, sir, you see I'm dressed for my part, and now you will know the truth.

**Blandford**: I desire to know nothing more about it! I have heard enough; leave me, I beseech you; I have altered my sentiments, and hate this disguise; go, go, put on your own habit, and trouble yourself no more with this affair.

**Adine**: What say you, sir? at last then I perceive it is not in my power to change your unalterable heart, or to reverse your cruel fate; alas! you know not the weight of grief that hangs upon me, but ere long you will see the fatal effect of it: farewell! I leave you, sir, forever.

**Blandford**: What can this mean? he weeps! speak, I entreat thee, tell me, what interest hast thou in my happiness or misery?

**Adine**: My interest, sir, was yours: till this moment never knew I any other: but I have been to blame, I tried to serve you; 'tis not the first time.

**Blandford**: The innocence of his look, his modest confidence, his voice, his air, his open and ingenuous behavior, still plead for him—but the hour is past when this intrigue you told me of was to have taken place; I was to have been an eye-witness of it.

**Adine**: Hark! I hear a door opening: this is the place, and this the time, when you shall be convinced who it is that loves you.

**Blandford**: Just heaven! it is possible?

**Adine**: It is.

**Blandford**: Stay you here then: but 'tis all a trick, an artifice: Dorfise! no—

**Adine**: Hush! I hear a noise: it comes towards us: I'm frightened, 'tis so dark.

**Blandford**: Fear nothing.

**Adine**: Be silent: for I hear somebody coming: hush! away.

## SCENE V.
Adine, Blandford, on One Side of the Stage, Which Is Supposed to Be Quite Dark; dorfise on the Other, on Tiptoe.

**Dorfise**: I thought I heard my charmer's voice; how punctual he is! the dear boy.

**Adine**: Hush!

**Dorfise**: Hush, is it you?

**Adine**: Yes: 'tis I: still faithful to my love: 'tis I who come here to prove that I have deserved a better return for all my tenderness.

**Dorfise**: I cannot give thee a better: you must forgive me; I would not have made you wait so long, my dear, but Bartolin, whom I did not expect, is returned: in spite of all my care, he has got a fit of jealousy upon him.

**Adine**: Perhaps he is afraid of meeting Blandford here: he is a dangerous rival.

**Dorfise**: Very likely, indeed: O my dear, what with Blandford, and my vile husband, I'm dreadfully hampered: I don't know which I hate most: in short, I'm sure of nothing, but that I love you.

**Adine**: You hate Blandford then heartily?

**Dorfise**: I think I do: fear naturally begets aversion.

**Adine**: Well, but your other spouse—

**Dorfise**: O him I never think of.

**Blandford**: [Aside.] How I could wish now—

**Adine**: [Softly to Blandford.] Hush! hush!

**Dorfise**: I have been consulting, my dear, about the contract: it certainly might be set aside: I wish it were, and then I might have hopes of another match.

**Adine**: What, of marrying me?

**Dorfise**: I think the best way would be for us to part for a time, to avoid scandal; and then meet, and be united by a sacred and a lasting tie.

**Adine**: A lasting tie! come then: let us begone: but how are we to live?

**Dorfise**: Your prudent foresight charms me: I always admired your discretion: you must know, then, the fighting M. Blandford, a hero at sea, but an arrant blockhead at home, when he left Marseilles, to go after the pirates, most cordially and most affectionately consigned to me with his heart, his money and jewels also: as I was, like him, a novice in these affairs, I put them into the hands of my other husband; from him I must endeavor to recover them, and assist Blandford: the poor man is honest and should live: away: let us part immediately, and take care nobody follows us.

**Adine**: But what will the world say?

**Dorfise**: O never heed it: I was afraid of its scandal before I loved: but now I despise it: I'll be a slave to none but thee.

**Adine**: But me?

**Dorfise**: I'll go immediately and get this strong box: that you know will be very necessary to us both: stay here, I'll be back in an instant.

## SCENE VI.

Blandford, Adine.

**Adine:** Well, sir, what think you now?

**Blandford:** Never did I behold such base, such black ingratitude, such infernal falsehood; and yet, Adine, you see the force of powerful virtue, how its lively instinct speaks even in the most corrupted heart.

**Adine:** How, sir, in what?

**Blandford:** You see the perfidious wretch dared not rob me of all; she talked of assisting me.

**Adine:** [Ironically.] O yes, you are mightily obliged to her: have you not another strong box to intrust with this virtuous lady?

**Blandford:** Nay, do not laugh at me, Adine, nor plant such daggers in my heart.

**Adine:** I meant to heal and not to wound it: but can you yet admire her?

**Blandford:** No: she is loathsome: falsehood has robbed her of every charm.

**Adine:** If, sir, I free you from her snares, may I flatter myself, that while you detest her vices, you will not forget my honest service?

**Blandford:** No, generous youth! I look on you as my son and my deliverer, the guardian angel, whom heaven hath sent down to preserve me; the half of all I have will be but a poor reward for thy care and fidelity.

**Adine:** You must not know at present what reward I aspire to: but can your heart refuse the request which Darmin perhaps may ask of you?

**Blandford:** Ha! thou hast removed the veil: I see, I see it all; but who, what art thou? art thou indeed what thou resemblest?

**Adine:** [Smiling.] Whatever I am, for heaven's sake, be silent now: I hear Dorfise coming this way.

**Dorfise:** [With strong box.] I've got the box; propitious love has favored my design: here, my dear, take it: away: let us be gone: have you got it fast?

**Blandford:** [Taking it from her, and counterfeiting the voice of Adine.] Yes.

**Dorfise:** Come along then.

## SCENE VII.

blandford, dorfise, adine, bartolin with a sword in his hand, in the dark, he runs up to Adine.

**Bartolin:** Stop, villain, stop! art thou not satisfied with robbing me of my wife, but must run away with my money, too?

**Adine:** [To Blandford.] Help! murder! help!

**Blandford**: [Fighting with one hand, and holding out the box to Adine with the other.] Take the box.

### SCENE VIII.

Blandford, Dorfise, Adine, Bartolin, Darmin, Mme. De Burlet, Collette, Mondor with a Napkin and a Bottle in His Hand. Flambeaux.

**Mme. De Burlet**: What's the matter here! hui! hui! what! fighting, too?

**Mondor**: Hold, hold, gentlemen, what is all this noise about?

**Adine**: [To Blandford.] You're not wounded, sir, I hope?

**Dorfise**: [In confusion.] Ha!

**Mme. De Burlet**: What is the cause of this fray, gentlemen? pray inform us.

**Blandford**: [To Bartolin, after disarming him.] O nothing, madam; only this worthy gentleman, and trusty treasurer, this honest keeper of the strong box, had robbed me of my mistress and my fortune: by the assistance of this amiable youth, I have detected their infamous designs, and recovered my money: go, sir, I leave you to your miserable fate, to this virtuous lady: know, my friends, I have unmasked their treacherous hearts; this villain—

**Bartolin**: [Going off.] Your servant, sir.

**Mondor**: A ha! what comes of my assignation now?

**Blandford**: O, sir, they made a fool of you.

**Darmin**: And of you too, I think.

**Blandford**: They did so, indeed: I feel it yet.

**Mondor**: Treated you like an idiot.

**Blandford**: Dreadful, horrible! O prudery, how I detest thee!

**Mondor**: Well, come, let us think no more of prudes, wives, or women, but go in and drink about; that's my way of drowning misfortunes: the man that drinks is never melancholy.

**Mme. De Burlet**: I'm really sorry my cousin Dorfise should behave so foolishly: to be sure, it will set the world to talking, but it will be all over soon, and there's an end of it.

**Darmin**: Come, Blandford, banish sorrow, and for the future take care of a prude: but do you know this boy, who has restored to you your honor and fortune, and saved you from the dangerous precipice which your blind passion had led you to the brink of?

**Blandford**: [Looking at Adine.] But—

**Darmin**: 'Tis my niece.

**Blandford**: O heaven!

**Darmin:** The very woman whom I so often proposed to my deluded friend; who, deceived by a faithless wretch, despised and hated all but her.

**Blandford:** How could I injure, by an unkind refusal, so many charms! such beauty and such virtue!

**Adine:** You never would have known me, if chance and my own constancy had not removed the veil of black ingratitude, and saved you from yourself.

**Darmin:** You owe everything, your fortune, and your reason to her generous love: what, then, is she to hope for in return? what will you do to make her amends?

**Blandford:** [Kneeling to Adine.] Adore her!

**Mondor:** This turn of affairs is as agreeable as it is surprising: we shall all be gainers by the change: away.

### End

# Mérope

## Contents

Dramatis Personæ. . . . . . . . . . . . . . . . . . . . . . . . . . . . . . . . . . . . . . . . 316

A Letter to the Marquis Scipio Maffei, Author of the Italian Mérope, and Many Other Celebrated Performances. . . . . . . . . . . . . . . . . . . . . . . . . . . . 316

A Letter From M. de la Lindelle to M. De Voltaire. . . . . . . . . . . . . . . . . 326

The Answer of M. De Voltaire to M. de la Lindelle. . . . . . . . . . . . . . . . 329

Act I. . . . . . . . . . . . . . . . . . . . . . . . . . . . . . . . . . . . . . . . . . . . . . . . . . . 330

Act II. . . . . . . . . . . . . . . . . . . . . . . . . . . . . . . . . . . . . . . . . . . . . . . . . . 336

Act III. . . . . . . . . . . . . . . . . . . . . . . . . . . . . . . . . . . . . . . . . . . . . . . . . 343

Act IV. . . . . . . . . . . . . . . . . . . . . . . . . . . . . . . . . . . . . . . . . . . . . . . . . 349

Act V. . . . . . . . . . . . . . . . . . . . . . . . . . . . . . . . . . . . . . . . . . . . . . . . . . 354

## Dramatis Personæ

Mérope, Widow of Cresphontes, King of Messene.
Ægisthus, Son of Mérope.
Poliphontes, Tyrant of Messene.
Narbas, an old Man.
Euricles, Favorite of Mérope.
Erox, Favorite of Poliphontes.
Ismenia, Confidante of Mérope.

"Mérope," produced in 1743, is the greatest of Voltaire's tragedies and a perfect literary performance. Frederick the Great amused himself by turning it into the libretto of an opera. Its success was great and the author was called before the curtain, an honor until then unknown in France. The interest of the following correspondence justifies its length.

A Letter to the Marquis Scipio Maffei, Author of the Italian Mérope, and many other celebrated performances.

Sir:

The Greeks and Romans, to whom modern Italy, as well as all other nations, are indebted for almost everything, dedicated their works, without the ridiculous form of compliments, to their friends, who were masters of the art: by this claim I take the liberty of addressing to you the French "Mérope."

The Italians, who have been the restorers of almost all the fine arts, and the inventors of many, were the first, who, under the auspices of Leo X., revived tragedy; and you, sir, are the first who, in this age, when the Sophoclean art became enervated by love-intrigues, often foreign to the subject, and so often debased by idle buffooneries, that reflected dishonor on the taste of your ingenious countrymen, you, sir, were the first who had courage and genius enough to hazard a tragedy without gallantry, a tragedy worthy of Athens in its glory; wherein the maternal affection constitutes the whole intrigue, and the most tender interest arises from the purest virtue. France prides herself in her "Athalie"; it is indeed the masterpiece of our stage, perhaps of poetry itself: of all the pieces that are exhibited among us, it is the only one where love is not introduced: but at the same time we must allow, that it is supported by the pomp of religion, and that majesty of eloquence which appears in the prophets. You had not that resource, and yet you have so contrived, as to furnish out five acts, which it is so extremely difficult to fill up without episodes. I must own, your subject appeared to me much more interesting and tragical than that of "Athalie"; and even if our admirable Racine had worked up his masterpiece with more art, more poetry, and more sublimity than he has, yours, I am satisfied, would have drawn more tears from the audience.

The preceptor of Alexander—kings ought always to have such preceptors—the great Aristotle, that extensive genius, so just, and so deeply versed in all the learning of those times, Aristotle, in his art of poetry, has declared that the meeting of Mérope and her son was the most interesting circumstance of the whole Grecian theatre. This stroke was, in his opinion, infinitely superior to all the rest. Plutarch tells us, that the Greeks, who, of all the people in the world, had the quickest feeling, trembled with fear, lest the old man who was to stop the arm of Mérope, should not come in time enough. That piece, which was played in his time, and a few fragments of which are still extant, appeared to him the most affecting of all the tragedies of Euripides; but it was not the choice of his subject alone to which that poet owed his success, though in every species of the drama, a happy choice is, no doubt, of the greatest service.

France has seen several "Méropes," but none of them ever succeeded: the authors perhaps overloaded this simple subject with foreign ornaments: it was the naked "Venus" of Praxiteles which they wanted to cover with tinsel. It requires a great deal of time to teach men that everything which is great should be simple and natural. In 1641, when the French flag began to flourish, and even to raise itself above that of Greece, by the genius of P. Corneille, Cardinal Richelieu, who ambitiously sought for glory of every kind, and who had just then built a magnificent hall, for theatrical representations, in the Palais Royal, of which he had himself furnished the design, had a "Mérope" played there under the name of "Telephonte"; the plot of it is generally believed to have been entirely his own. There are about a hundred verses in it, supposed to be written by him; the rest was by Colletet, Bois-Roberts, Desmarets, and Chapelain; but all the power of Cardinal Richelieu could not impart to those writers that genius which they never possessed: his own was not indeed adapted to the stage, though he had a good taste; so that all he could do, or that could be expected from him, was to patronize and encourage the great Corneille.

Mr. Gilbert, resident of the celebrated Queen Christina, in 1643, gave us his "Mérope," which is at present as little known as the other. La Chapelle, of the French academy, author of a tragedy called "Cléopatre," which was played with some success, gave us another "Mérope" in 1683, and took care to insert a love episode: he complains withal in his preface, that the critics reproached him with too great a degree of the marvellous; but he was mistaken, it was not the marvellous that sank his performance, but in reality the want of genius, added to the coldness and insipidity of his versification; this is the great point, the capital fault, that condemns so many poems to oblivion.

The art of eloquence in verse is of all arts the most difficult and the most uncommon: there are a thousand geniuses to be found who can plan a work, and put it into verse after the common manner; but to treat it like a true poet, is a talent which is seldom bestowed on above two or three men on the face of the whole earth.

In December, 1701, M. de la Grange played his "Amasis," which is nothing more than the subject of "Mérope" under another name. Gallantry has its share in this performance likewise; and there is more of the marvellous in it than even in La Chapelle's: but it is more interesting, conducted with more art and genius, and written with more warmth and power; notwithstanding which, it met with no great success;

Et habent sua fata libelli.

Since that, however, it has been revived with great applause; and is one of those few pieces which generally give pleasure in the representation.

Before and after "Amasis" we have had several tragedies on subjects very nearly resembling this, wherein a mother is going to avenge the death of her son on the son himself, and discovers him just at the instant when she was about to kill him. We frequently saw on our stage that striking but rarely probable situation, wherein a person comes with a poniard in his hand ready to destroy his enemy, and another arrives at the same instant, and snatches it from him. This incident recommended, at least for a time, the "Camma" of Thomas Corneille.

But amongst all the tragedies on this subject, which I have here enumerated, there is not one of them but is filled with some episode of love, or rather gallantry; for everything must give way to the reigning taste. But you must not believe, sir, that this unhappy custom of loading our tragedies with ridiculous love-intrigues was owing to Racine; a crime, which, in Italy, I know he is generally reproached with: on the contrary, he did everything in his power to reform the public taste in this particular: the passion of love is never brought in by him as a mere episode; it is the foundation or ground-plot of all his pieces, and forms the principal interest: it is certainly of all the passions the most truly theatrical, the most fruitful in sentiments, and admits of the greatest variety: it ought, therefore, no doubt, to be the soul of a dramatic performance, or entirely to be banished from it: if love is not tragical, it is insipid; and when it is tragical, it should reign alone; it was never made for a second place. It was Rotrou, or rather we must own, the great Corneille himself, who, in his creation of the stage, at the same time disfigured and disgraced it, by those ridiculous intrigues, bespoken, as it were, and made on purpose, those affairs of gallantry, which not being true passions, were unworthy of the stage; if you would know the reason why Corneille's tragedies are so seldom played, the reason is plain enough: it is because, in his "Otho."

"Otho makes a compliment to his mistress more like a man of wit than a real lover: he follows step by step the effort of his memory, which it is much more easy to admire than to believe. Camille herself seemed to be of his opinion; she would have liked much better a discourse less studied.—Tell me then, when Otho made love to Camille, was he contented, or was she kind?"

It is because in, "Pompey," Cleopatra—a useless character—says that Cæsar "sighs for her," and in a plaintive style calls himself "her captive, even in the field of victory."

It is because Cæsar asks Antony if he has seen this "adorable queen": to which Antony replies, "Yes, my lord, I have seen her, she is incomparable."

It is because, in "Sertorius," old Sertorius falls in love, not only because he likes the lady, but with a political view, and cries out: "I love: but it suits my age so ill to be in love, that I even conceal it from the fair one who has charmed me, as I know that the deep and yellow wrinkles on my forehead can have no great power in captivating the senses."

It is because, in "Œdipus," Theseus begins by saying to Dirce, "Whatever dreadful havoc the plague may make here, absence to true lovers is far more dreadful."

In a word, it is because such love as this will never make us shed tears; and when that passion does not affect us, it must be quite insipid.

I have said no more here, sir, than what all good judges, and men of taste, say to one another every day; what you have often heard at my house; in short, what everybody thinks, but none dare to publish: you know well enough the nature of mankind: half the world write in opposition to their own opinions, for fear of shocking received prejudices and vulgar errors. With regard to myself, who have never mixed any political reserve with my sentiments on literature, I speak the truth boldly, and will add, that I respect Corneille more, and have a higher opinion of the real merit of this great father of the stage, than those who praise him indiscriminately, and are blind to all his faults.

A "Mérope" was exhibited at London in 1731: who would have thought a love-intrigue could ever have been thought of at that time? But ever since the reign of Charles II. love has taken possession of the English stage; though there is not a nation upon earth by whom that passion is so ill painted; but the intrigue so absurdly brought in, and so badly treated, is the least fault of the English "Mérope." The young Ægisthus, delivered out of prison by a maid of honor, who is in love with him, is brought before the queen, who presents him with a bowl of poison, and a dagger, and speaks thus to him: "If you don't swallow the poison, this dagger shall put an end to your mistress' life." The young man drinks the poison, and is carried off in the agonies of death: he comes back in the fifth act coldly to inform Mérope that he is her son, and that he has slain the tyrant. Mérope asks him how this miracle was performed: to which he replies, that a friend of the maid of honor had put poppy-water, instead of poison, into the cup. "I was only asleep," says he, "when they thought me dead; I learned, when I awaked, that I was your son, and immediately killed the tyrant." Thus ends the tragedy; no doubt but it met with a bad reception: but is it not strange that it should ever have been represented? Is it not a proof that the English stage is not yet refined? It seems as if the same cause that deprives the English of any excellency in, or genius for, music and painting, takes from them also all perfection in tragedy. This island, which has produced the finest philosophers in the world, is not equally productive of the fine arts; and if the English do not seriously apply themselves to the study of those precepts which were given them by their excellent countrymen, Addison and Pope, they will never come near to other nations in point of taste and literature.

But whilst the subject of "Mérope" has been thus disgraced and disfigured in one part of Europe, it has met with better fate in Italy, where it has for a long time been treated in the true taste of the ancients. In this sixteenth century, which will be famous throughout all ages, the Count de Torelli gave us his

"Mérope" with choruses. If in La Chapelle's tragedy we find all the faults of the French stage, such as useless intrigues, episodes, and a romantic air; and in the English author the highest degree of indecency, barbarism, and absurdity; we likewise meet in the Italian with all the faults of the Greek theatre, such as the want of action, and declamation. You, sir, have avoided all the rocks which they split upon; you, who have done honor to your country, by complete models of more than one kind, you have given us in your "Mérope" an example of a tragedy that is at once both simple and interesting.

The moment I read it I was struck with it; my love to my own country has never shut my eyes against the merit of foreigners. On the other hand, the more regard I have for it, the more I endeavor to enrich it, by the addition of treasures that are not of its own growth. The desire which I had of translating your "Mérope," was increased by the honor of a personal acquaintance with you at Paris, in the year 1733. By loving the author, I became still more enamored with his work; but when I sat down to it, I found it was impossible to bring it on the French stage. We are grown excessively delicate: like the Sybarites of old, we are so immersed in luxury, that we cannot bear that rustic simplicity, and that description of a country life, which you have imitated from the Greek theatre. I am afraid our audiences would not suffer young Ægisthus to make a present of his ring to the man that stops him. I could not have ventured to seize upon a hero, and take him for a robber; though, at the same time, the circumstances he is in authorize the mistake. Our manners, which probably admit of many things which yours do not, would not permit us to represent the tyrant, the murderer of Mérope's husband and children, pretending, after fifteen years, to be in love with her; nor could I even have dared to make the queen say to him, "Why did not you talk to me of love before, when the bloom of youth was yet on my face?" Conversations of this kind are natural; but our pit, which at some times is so indulgent, and at others so nice and delicate, would think them perhaps too familiar, and might even discover coquetry, where, in reality, there might be nothing but what was just and proper. Our stage would by no means have suffered Mérope to bind her son to a pillar, nor to run after him with a javelin, and an axe in her hand, nor have permitted the young man to run away from her twice, and beg his life of the tyrant: much less could we have suffered the confidante of Mérope to have persuaded Ægisthus to go to sleep on the stage, merely to give the queen an opportunity of coming there to assassinate him: not but all this is natural: but you must pardon us for expecting that nature should always be presented to us with some strokes of art; strokes that are extremely different at Paris from those which we meet with at Verona.

To give you a proper idea of the different taste and judgment of polite and cultivated nations, with regard to the same arts, permit me here to quote a few passages from your own celebrated performance, which seem dictated by pure nature. The person who stops young Cresphontes, and takes the ring from him, says:

Or dunque in tuo paese i servi
Han di coteste gemme? un bel pacse
Sia questo tuo, nel nostro una tal gemma
Ad un dito real non sconverebbe.

I will take the liberty to translate this into blank verse, in which your tragedy is written, as I have not time at present to work it into rhyme.

Have slaves such precious jewels where thou livest?
Sure 'tis a noble country; for, with us,
Such rings might well adorn a royal hand.

The tyrant's confidant tells him, when speaking of the queen, who refuses, after twenty years, to marry the known murderer of her family:

La donna, come sai, ricusa e brama
Women, we know, refuse when most they love.

The queen's waiting-woman answers the tyrant, who presses her to use her influence in his favor, thus:

—dissimulato in vano
Soffre di febre assalto; alquanti giorni
Donare e forza a rinfrancar suoi spiriti.

The queen, sir has a fever, 'tis in vain
To hide it, and her spirits are oppressed;
She must have time to recollect them

In your fourth act, old Polydore asks one of Mérope's courtiers who he is? To which he replies, "I am Eurises, the son of Nicander." Polydore then, speaking of Nicander, talks in the style of Homer's Nestor.

—Egli cra humano
Eliberal, quando appariva, tutti
Faceangli honor; io mi ricordo ancora
Diquanto ei festeggio con bella pompa
Le sue nozze con Silvia, ch'era figlia
D'Olimpia e di Glicon fratel d'Ipparcho.
Ju dunque sir quel fanciullin che in corte
Silvia condur solea quasi per pompa;
Parmi' l'altir hieri: O quanto siete presti,
Quanto voi v'affrettate, O giovinetti,

A farvi adulti ed a gridar tacendo
Che noi diam loco!
The most humane, most generous of mankind,
Where'er he went, respected and beloved:
O I remember well the feast he gave
When to his Sylvia wedded, the fair daughter
Of Glycon, brother of the brave Hipparchus,
And chaste Olympia: and art thou that infant
Whom Sylvia to the court so often brought
And fondled in her arms? alas! methinks
It was but yesterday: how quickly youth
Shoots up, and tells us we must quit the scene!

In another place the same old man, being invited to the ceremony of the queen's marriage, says:

—Oh curioso
Punto io non son, passo stagione. Assai
Veduti ho sacrificii; io mi recordo
Di quello ancora quando il re Cresphonte
Incomincio a regnar. Quella fu pompa.
Ora piu non si fanno a questi tempi
Di cotai sacrificii. Piu di cento
Fur le beste sivenate i sacerdoti
Risplendean tutti, ed ove ti volgessi
Altro non si vedea che argento ed oro.

My time is past, and curiosity
Is now no more: already I have seen
Enough of nuptial rites, enough of pomp
And sacrifice: I still remember well
The great solemnity, when King Cresphontes
Began his reign: O 'twas a noble sight!
We cannot boast of such in these our days:
A hundred beasts were offered up, the priests
In all their splendor shone, and naught was seen
But gold and silver.—

All these strokes are natural, all agreeable to the characters and manners represented: such familiar dialogues would, no doubt, have been well received at Athens; but Paris and our pit expect a simplicity of another kind. We may, perhaps, even boast of a more refined taste than Athens itself, where, though the principal city of all Greece, it does not appear to me that they ever represented any theatrical pieces except on the four solemn festivals; whereas at Paris there is always more than one every day in the year. At Athens the number of citizens was computed at only ten thousand, and Paris has nearly eight hundred thousand inhabitants; among whom, I suppose, we may reckon thirty thousand judges of dramatic performances, who really do pass their judgments almost every day of their lives.

In your tragedy you took the liberty to translate that elegant and simple comparison from Virgil.

Qualis populea maerens Philomela sub umbra
Amissos queritur faetus.

But if I were to take the same in mine, they would say it was fitter for an epic poem: such a rigid master have we to please in what we call the public:

Nescis, heu! nescis nostra fastidia Romae:
Et pueri nasum Rhinocerontis habent.

The English have a custom of finishing almost all their acts with a simile; but we expect that, in a tragedy, the hero should talk, and not the poet. Our audience is of opinion that in an important crisis of affairs, in a council, in a violent passion, or a pressing danger, princes and ministers should never make poetical comparisons.

How could I ever venture to make the under characters talk together for a long time? With you those conversations serve to prepare interesting scenes between the principal actors: they are like the avenues to a fine palace: but our spectators are for coming into it at once. We must therefore comply with the national taste, which is, perhaps, grown more difficult, from having been cloyed, as it were, with such a variety of fine performances: and yet among these recitals, which our excessive severity condemns, how many beauties do I regret the loss of! How does simple nature delight me, though beneath a form that appears strange to us!

I have here, sir, given you some of those reasons which prevailed on me not to follow what I so much admired. I was obliged, not without regret, to write a new "Mérope"; I have done it in a different manner, but I am far from thinking that I have therefore done it better. I look upon myself, with regard to you, as a traveller to whom an eastern monarch had made a present of some very rich stuffs: the king would certainly permit this traveller to wear them according to the fashion of his own country.

My "Mérope" was finished in the beginning of the year 1736, pretty nearly as it now stands; studies of another kind prevented me from bringing it on the stage: but what weighed most with me was, the hazard which I ran in producing it, after several successful pieces on almost the same subject, though under different names. At length, however, I ventured to produce it, and the public gave me a convincing proof that they could condescend to see the same matter worked up in a different manner. That happened to our stage which we see every day in a gallery of pictures, where there are many of them on exactly the same subject. The judges are pleased by the observation of these different manners, and everyone marks down and enjoys, according to his own taste, the character of every painter. This is a kind of happy concurrence, which, at the same time that it contributes towards the perfection of the Art, gives the public a better insight into it. If the French "Mérope" has met with the same success as the Italian, it is to you, sir, I am indebted for it; to that simplicity in your performance which I have taken for my model, and which I was always an admirer of. Though I walked in a different path, you were always my guide. I could have wished, after the examples of the Italians and English, to employ the happy facility of blank verse, and have often called to mind this passage of "Rucellai":

Tu sai purche l' imagine della voce
Che risponde da i sassi, dove l' echo alberga.
Sempre nemica fu del nostro regno,
E fu inventrice delle prime rime.

But I am satisfied, as I have long since declared, that such an attempt would never succeed in France, and it would be rather a mark of weakness than good sense, to endeavor to shake off a yoke which so many authors have borne, whose works will last as long as the nation itself. Our poetry has none of those liberties which yours has; and this is perhaps one of the reasons why the Italians got the start of us, by three or four centuries, in this most difficult and most delightful art.

As I have endeavored to imitate you in tragedy, I should be glad to follow your example in other branches of literature, for which you are so eminently distinguished: I could wish to form my taste by yours in the science of history; I do not mean the empty, barren knowledge of dates and facts, that only informs us at what period of time a man died, who perhaps was a useless or a pernicious member of society; the science of lexicography, that loads the memory without improving the mind; I mean that history of the human heart which teaches us men and manners, which leads us from error to error, and from prejudice to prejudice, into the effects of the various passions and affections that agitate mankind: which shows us all the evils that ignorance, or knowledge misapplied, has produced in the world; and which, above all, gives us a clue to the progress of the arts, and follows them through the dangers of so many contending powers, and the ruin of so many empires.

It is this which makes history delightful; and it becomes still more so to me, by the place which you will possess amongst those who have pleased and instructed mankind. It will raise the emulation of posterity, to hear that your country has bestowed on you the most signal honors, that Verona has raised a statue, with this inscription, "To the Marquis Scipio Maffei in his lifetime"—an inscription as beautiful in its kind as that at Montpellier to Louis XIV. after his death.

Deign, sir, to accept, with the respects of your fellow-citizens, those of a stranger, who esteems and honors you as much as if he had been born at Verona.

A Letter from M. de la Lindelle to M. de Voltaire.

Sir:

You had the politeness to dedicate your tragedy of "Mérope" to M. Maffei, and have served the cause of literature both in Italy and France, by pointing out, from the perfect knowledge which you have of the theatre, the different rules and conduct of the Italian and French stages. The partial attachment which you have to everything that comes from Italy, added to your particular regard for M. Maffei, would not permit you to censure the real faults of that excellent writer; but as I have myself nothing in view but truth, and the advancement of the arts, I shall not be afraid to speak the sentiments of the judicious public, and which I am satisfied must be yours also.

The Abbé Desfontaines had already remarked some palpable errors in the "Mérope" of M. Maffei; but, according to his usual manner, with more rudeness than justice, he has mingled a few good criticisms with many bad ones. This satirist, so universally decried, had neither knowledge enough of the Italian tongue, nor taste enough to form an equitable judgment.

This, then, is the opinion of the most judicious amongst those literati whom I have consulted, both in France and on the other side of the Alps. "Mérope" appears to every one of them, past dispute, the most interesting and truly tragic subject that was ever brought on the stage, infinitely beyond that of "Athalie"; because Athalie does not want to assassinate the young king, but is deceived by the High-Priest, who seeks revenge on her for her former crimes: whereas in Mérope we see a mother, who, in avenging her son, is on the point of murdering that very son himself, her only desire, and her only hope: the interest of "Mérope" therefore affects us in a very different manner from that of "Athalie": but it seems as if M. Maffei was satisfied with what the subject naturally suggested to him, without making use of any theatrical art in the conduct of it.

1. The scenes in many places are not linked together, and the stage is left void; a fault which, in the present age, is looked upon as unpardonable, even in the lowest class of dramatic writers.

2. The actors frequently come in and go out without reason; a fault no less considerable.

3. There is no probability, no dignity, no decorum, no art in the dialogue: in the very first scene we see a tyrant reasoning in the calmest manner with Mérope, whose husband and children he had murdered, and making love to her: this would have been hissed at Paris, even by the poorest judges.

4. While the tyrant is thus ridiculously making love to the old queen, word is brought that they have found a young man who had committed murder; but it does not appear through the whole course of the play who it was he had killed: he pretends it was a thief, who wanted to steal his clothes. How low, little and poor is this! It would not be borne in a farce at a country fair.

5. The captain of the guard, provost, or whatever you call him, examines the murderer, who has a fine ring upon his finger: this scene is quite low comedy, and the style is agreeable to it, and worthy of the scene.

6. The mother immediately supposes that the robber, who was killed, is her son. It is pardonable, no doubt, in a mother to fear everything; but a queen who is a mother should have required better proofs.

7. In the midst of all these fears, the tyrant Poliphontes reasons with Mérope's waiting-woman about his pretended passion. These cold and indecent scenes, which are only brought in to fill up the act, would never be suffered on a regular stage. You have only, sir, modestly taken notice of one of these scenes, where Mérope's woman desires the tyrant not to hasten the nuptials; because, she says, her mistress has "an attack of a fever": but I, sir, will boldly aver, in the name of all the critics, that such a conversation, and such an answer, are only fit for Harlequin's theatre.

8. I will add, moreover, that when the queen, imagining her son to be dead, tells us she longs to pull the heart out of the murderer's breast, and tear it with her teeth, she talks more like a cannibal than an afflicted mother; and that decency should be preserved in everything.

9. Ægisthus, who was brought in as a robber, and who had said that he had himself been attacked, is taken for a thief a second time, and carried before the queen, in spite of the king, who notwithstanding undertakes to defend him. The queen binds him to a pillar, is going to kill him with a dart; but before she throws it, asks him some questions. Ægisthus tells her, that his father is an old man, upon which the queen immediately relents. Is not this an excellent reason for changing her mind, and imagining that Ægisthus might be her own son? a

most indisputable mark to be sure: is it so very extraordinary that a young man should have an old father? Maffei has added this absurdity, this deficiency of art and genius, to another even more ridiculous, which he had made in his first edition. Ægisthus says to the queen, "O Polydore, my father." This Polydore was the very man to whom Mérope had entrusted the care of Ægisthus. At hearing the name of Polydore, the queen could no longer doubt that Ægisthus was her son: thus the piece was entirely at an end. This error was removed; but removed, we see, only to make room for a greater.

10. While the queen is thus ridiculously, and without any reason, in suspense, occasioned by the mention of an old man, the tyrant comes in, and takes Ægisthus under his protection. The young man, who should have been represented as a hero, thanks the king for his life, with a base and mean submission that is disgusting, and entirely degrades the character of Ægisthus.

11. At length Mérope and the tyrant are left together: Mérope exhausts her resentment in reproaches without end. Nothing can be more cold and lifeless than these scenes, full of declamation, that have no plot, interest, or contrasted passion in them; they are schoolboy scenes: everything in a play, that is without action, is useless.

12. There is so little art in this piece that the author is always forced to employ confidants to fill up the stage. The fourth act begins with another cold and useless scene between the tyrant and the queen's waiting-woman, who, a little afterwards, lights, we know not how, on young Ægisthus, and persuades him to rest himself in the porch, merely to give the queen a fair opportunity of despatching him when he falls asleep; which he does according to promise. An excellent plot this! and then the queen comes a second time, with an axe in her hand, in order to kill the young man, who is gone to sleep for that purpose. This circumstance, twice repeated, is surely the height of barrenness, as the young man's sleep is the height of ridicule. M. Maffei thinks there is genius and variety in this repetition, because the queen comes in the first time with a dart, and the second with an axe. What a strange effect of fancy!

13. At last old Polydore comes in apropos, and prevents the queen from striking the blow. One would naturally imagine that this happy instant must produce a thousand affecting incidents between the mother and son; but we meet with nothing of this kind: Ægisthus flies off, and sees no more of his mother: he has not so much as one scene with her. This betrays a want of genius that is insupportable. Mérope asks the old man what recompense he demands; and the old fool begs her to make him young again. In this manner the queen employs her time, which doubtless she should have spent in running after her son: all this is low, ill-placed, and ridiculous to the last degree.

14. In the course of this piece the tyrant is always for espousing Mérope; and, to compass his end, he bids her agents tell her, that he will murder all her servants, if she does not consent to give him her hand. What a ridiculous idea, and how extravagant a tyrant! Could not M. Maffei have found out a more specious pretext to save the honor of a queen, who had meanness enough to marry the murderer of her whole family?

15. Another childish college trick: the tyrant says to his confidant, "I know the art of reigning; I'll put the bold and rebellious to death; give the reins to all kinds of vice; invite my subjects to commit the most atrocious crimes, and pardon the most guilty; expose the good to the fury of the wicked." Did ever man pronounce such vile stuff? This declamation of a regent of sixteen, does it not give us a fine idea of a man who knows how to govern? Racine was condemned for having made Mathan—in his "Athalie"—say too much against himself; and yet Mathan talks reasonably: but here it is to the last degree absurd to pretend, that throwing everything into confusion is the art of ruling well; it is rather the art of dethroning himself. One cannot read anything so ridiculous without laughing at it. M. Maffei is a strange politician.

In a word, sir, this work of Maffei is a fine subject, but a very bad performance. Everybody at Paris agrees that it would not go through one representation; and the sensible men in Italy have a very poor opinion of it. It is in vain the author has taken so much pains in his travels, to engage the worst writers he could pick up to translate his tragedy: it was much easier for him to pay a translator, than to make his piece a good one.

The Answer of M. de Voltaire to M. de la Lindelle.

Sir:

The letter which you did me the honor to write to me entitles you to the name of "Hypercritic," which was given to the famous Scaliger; you are truly a most redoubtable adversary; if you treat M. Maffei in this manner, what am I to expect from you? I acknowledge that, in many points, you have too much reason on your side. You have taken a great deal of pains to rake together a heap of brambles and briars; but why would you not enjoy the pleasure of gathering a few flowers? There are certainly many in M. Maffei; and which, I dare affirm, will flourish forever. Such are the scenes between the mother and son, and the narration of the catastrophe. I can't help thinking that these strokes are affecting and pathetic. You say, the subject alone makes all the beauty; but was it not the same subject in other authors who have treated Mérope? Why, with the same assistance, had they not the same success? Does not this single argument prove, that M. Maffei owes as much to his genius as to his subject?

To be plain with you, I think M. Maffei has shown more art than myself, in the manner by which he has contrived to make Mérope think that her son is the murderer of her son. I could not bring myself to make use of the ring as he did; because, after the royal ring that Boilieu laughs at in his satires, this circumstance would always appear too trifling on our stage. We must conform to the fashions of our own age and nation; and, for the same reason, we ought not lightly to condemn those of foreigners.

Neither M. Maffei nor I have sufficiently explained the motives that should so strongly incline Poliphontes to espouse the queen. This is, perhaps, a fault inherent in the subject; but I must own I think this fault very inconsiderable, when the circumstances it produces are so interesting. The grand point is to affect and draw tears from the spectators. Tears were shed both at Verona and at Paris. This is the best answer that can be made to the critics. It is impossible to be perfect; but how meritorious is it to move an audience, in spite of all our imperfections! Most certain it is, that in Italy many things are passed over, which would not be pardoned in France: first, because taste, decorum, and the stage itself, are not the same in both; secondly, because the Italians, having no city where they represent dramatic pieces every day, cannot possibly be so used to things of this kind as ourselves. Opera, that splendid monster, has driven Melpomene from among them; and there are so many of the Castrati there, that no room is left for Roscius and Æsopus: but if ever the Italians should have a regular theatre, I believe they would soon get beyond us: their stages are more extensive, their language more tractable, their blank verses easier to be made, their nation possessed of more sensibility; but they want encouragement, peace, and plenty.

# ACT I.

### SCENE I.
Scene at Messene, in the Palace of Mérope.
Ismenia, Mérope.

**Ismenia**: Let not, great queen, thy soul forever dwell On images of horror and despair; The storm is past, and brighter days succeed: Long hast thou tasted heaven's severest wrath, Enjoy its bounties now: the gods, thou seest, Have blessed our land with victory and peace; And proud Messene, after fifteen years Of foul division and intestine wars, Now from her ruins lifts her towering front, Superior to misfortune: now no more Shalt thou behold her angry chiefs support Their jarring interests, and in guilt alone United, spread destruction, blood and slaughter, O'er half thy kingdom, and dispute the throne Of good Cresphontes: but the ministers Of heaven, the guardians of our sacred laws, The rulers, and the people, soon shall meet, Free in their choice, to fix the power supreme: If virtue gives the diadem, 'tis thine: Thine by irrevocable right: to thee, The widow of Cresphontes, from our kings Descended, must devolve Messene's throne: Thou, whom misfortunes and firm constancy Have made but more illustrious, and more dear; Thou, to whom every heart in secret tied—

Mérope: No news of Narbas! shall I never see My child again?

Ismenia: Despair not, madam: slaves Have been despatched on every side; the paths Of Elis all are open to their search: Doubtless the object of your fears is placed In faithful hands, who will restore to you Their sacred trust.

Mérope: Immortal gods! who see My bitter griefs, will ye restore my son? Is my Ægisthus living? have you saved My wretched infant? O preserve him still, And shield him from the cruel murderer's hand! He is your son, the pure, the spotless blood Of your Alcides. Will you not protect The dear, dear image of the best of men, The best of kings, whose ashes I adore?

Ismenia: But wherefore must this tender passion turn Thy soul aside from every other purpose?

Mérope: I am a mother: canst thou wonder yet?

Ismenia: A mother's fondness should not thus efface The duty of a queen, your character, And noble rank; though in his infant years You loved this son, yet little have you seen Or known of him.

Mérope: Not seen him, my Ismenia? O he is always present to my heart, Time has no power to loose such bonds as these; His danger still awakens all my fears, And doubles my affection: once I've heard From Narbas, and but once these four years past, And that alas! but made me more unhappy. "Ægisthus," then he told me, "well deserves A better fate; he's worthy of his mother. And of the gods, his great progenitors: Exposed to every ill, his virtue braves, And will surmount them: hope for everything From him, but be aware of Poliphontes."

Ismenia: Prevent him then, and take the reins of empire In your own hands.

Mérope: That empire is my son's: Perdition on the cruel step-mother, The lover of herself, the savage heart, That could enjoy the pleasures of a throne, And disinherit her own blood! O no: Ismenia, If my Ægisthus lives not, what is empire. Or what is life to me! I should renounce them. I should have died when my unhappy lord Was basely slain, by men and gods betrayed. O perfidy! O guilt! O fatal day! O death! forever present to my sight! Methinks even now I hear the dismal shrieks, I hear them cry, "O save the king, his wife, His sons;" I see the walls all stained with blood, The flaming palace, helpless women crushed Beneath the smoking ruins, fear and tumult On every side, arms, torches, death, and horror: Then, rolled in dust, and bathing in his blood, Cresphontes pressed me to his arms, upraised His dying eyes, and took his last farewell; Whilst his two hapless babes, the tender fruits Of our first love, thrown on the bleeding bosom Of their dead father, lifted up the hands Of innocence, and begged me to protect them Against the barbarous murderers: Ægisthus Alone escaped: some god defended him. O thou who didst protect his infancy Watch o'er and guard him, bring him to my eyes; O let him from inglorious solitude Rise to the rank of his great ancestors! I've borne his absence long, and groaned in chains These fifteen years: now let Ægisthus reign Instead of Mérope: for all my pains And sorrows past, be that the great reward.

SCENE II.
Mérope, Ismenia, Euricles.
**Mérope**: Well! what of Narbas, and my son?
**Euricles**: [Confused] I stand before thee; all our cares are vain; We've searched the banks of Peneus, and the fields Of fair Olympia, even to the walls Of proud Salmoneus, but no Narbas there Is to be found or heard of, not a trace Remaining of him.
**Mérope**: Narbas is no more, And all is lost.
**Ismenia**: Whatever thy fears suggest Thou still believest; and yet who knows but now, Even whilst we speak, the happy Narbas comes To crown thy wishes, and restore thy son.
**Euricles**: Perhaps his love, tempered with fair discretion, Which long concealed Ægisthus from the eyes Of men, may hide his purposed journey from thee: He dreads the murderer's hand, and still protects him From those who slew Cresphontes: we must strive By artful methods to elude the rage That cannot be opposed: I have secured Their passage hither, and have placed some friends Of most approved valor, whose sharp eyes Will look abroad, and safe conduct them to thee.
**Mérope**: I've placed my surest confidence in thee.
**Euricles**: But what alas! can all my watchfulness And faithful cares avail thee, when the people Already meet to rob thee of thy right, And place another on Messene's throne? Injustice triumphs, and the shameless crowd, In proud contempt of sacred laws, incline To Poliphontes.
**Mérope**: Am I fallen so low: And shall my son return to be a slave? To see a subject raised to the high rank Of his great ancestors, the blood of Jove Debased, degraded, forced to own a master. Have I no friend, no kind protector left?

Ungrateful subjects! have you no regard, No reverence for the memory of Cresphontes? Have you so soon forgot his glorious deeds, His goodness to you?

**Euricles:** Still his name is dear, Still they regret him, still they weep his fate, And pity thine: but power intimidates, And makes them dread the wrath of Poliphontes.

**Mérope:** Thus, by my people still oppressed, I see Justice give way to faction, interest still, The arbiter of fate, sells needy virtue To powerful guilt; the weak must to the strong Forever yield: but let us hence, and strive To fire once more their coward hearts to rage And fierce resentment, for the injured blood Of Hercules: excite the people's love; Flatter their hopes; O tell them, Euricles, Their master is returned.

**Euricles:** I've said too much Already; Poliphontes is alarmed: He dreads your son; he dreads your very tears: Restless ambition, that holds nothing dear Or sacred but itself, has filled his soul With bitterness and pride: because he drove The ruffian slaves from Pylos and Amphrysa, And saved Messene from a band of robbers, He claims it as his conquest: for himself Alone he acts, and would enslave us all: He looks towards the crown, and to attain it Would throw down every fence, break every law, Spill any blood that shall oppose him: they Who killed thy husband were not more revengeful, More bloody, than the cruel Poliphontes.

**Mérope:** I am entangled in some fatal snare On every side, danger and guilt surround me: This Poliphontes, this ambitious subject, Whose crimes—

**Euricles:** He's here: you must dissemble.

## SCENE III.

Mérope, Poliphontes, Erox.

**Euricles:** Madam, At length I come to lay my heart before you: I've served the state, and my successful toils Have opened me a passage to the throne: The assembled chiefs awhile suspend their choice, But soon must fix it, or on Mérope, Or Poliphontes: the unhappy feuds That laid Messene waste, and filled the land With blood and slaughter, all are buried now In peaceful harmony, and we alone Remain to part the fair inheritance. We should support each other's mutual claim; Our common interest, and our common foes, Love for our country, reason, duty, all Conspire to join us, all unite to say The warrior who avenged thy husband, he Who saved thy kingdom, may aspire to thee. I know these hoary locks, and wrinkled brow, Have little charms to please a youthful fair one. Thou'rt in the bloom of spring, and mayest despise The winter of my days; but statesmen heed not Such fond objections: let the royal wreath Hide these gray hairs, a sceptre and a queen Will recompense my toils: nor think me rash, Or vain, you are the daughter of a king, I know you are, but your Messene wants A master now; therefore remember, madam, If you would keep your right, you must—divide it.

**Mérope**: Heaven, that afflicts me with its bitterest woes, Prepared me not for this, this cruel insult: How darest thou ask it? wert thou not the subject Of great Cresphontes? thinkest thou I will e'er Betray the memory of my dearest lord, To share with thee his son's inheritance, Trust to thy hands his kingdom and his mother? Thinkest thou the royal wreath was made to bind A soldier's brows?

**Euricles**: That soldier has a right To rule the kingdom which his arm defended. What was the first that bore the name of king, But a successful soldier? he who serves His country well requires not ancestry To make him noble: the inglorious blood, Which I received from him who gave me life, I shed already in my country's cause, It flowed for thee; and, spite of thy proud scorn, I must at least be equal to the kings I have subdued: but, to be brief with you, The throne will soon be mine, and Mérope May share it with me, if her pride will deign To accept it: I've a powerful party, madam.

**Mérope**: A party! wretch, to trample on our laws: Is there a party which thou darest support Against the king's, against the royal race? Is this thy faith, thy solemn vows, thy oath, Sworn to Cresphontes, and to me; the love, The honor due to his illustrious shade, His wretched widow, and his hapless son; The gods he sprang from, and the throne they gave?

**Euricles**: 'Tis doubtful whether yet your son survives; But grant that, from the mansions of the dead, He should return, and in the face of heaven Demand his throne, believe me when I say He would demand in vain; Messene wants A master worthy of her, one well proved, A king who could defend her: he alone Should wield the sceptre who can best avenge His country's cause: Ægisthus is a child, Yet unexperienced in the ways of men, And therefore little will his birth avail him; Naught hath he done for us, and naught deserved: He cannot purchase at so cheap a rate Messene's throne, the right of power supreme Defends no more the gift of nature, here From son to son; it is the price of toil, Of labor, and of blood; 'tis virtue's meed, Which I shall claim: have you so soon forgot The savage sons of Pylos and Amphrysa, Those lawless plunderers? Think on your Cresphontes, And your defenceless children whom they slew: Who saved your country then? Who stopped their fury? Who put your foes to flight, and chased them hence? Did not this arm avenge that murdered lord Whom yet you weep? these, madam, are my rights, The rights of valor: this is all my rank, This all my title, and let heaven decide it. If thy Ægisthus comes, by me perhaps

He may be taught to live, by me to reign: Then shall he see how Poliphontes guides The reins of empire. I esteem the blood Of great Alcides, but I fear it not; I look beyond Alcides' race, and fain Would imitate the god from whom he sprung: I would defend the mother, serve the son; Be an example to him, and a father.

**Mérope:** O, sir, no more of your affected cares; Your generous offers, meant but to insult My hapless son; if you would wish to tread In great Alcides' steps, reserve the crown For his descendant: know, that demi-god Was the avenger of wronged innocence; No ravisher, no tyrant; take thou care, And with his valor imitate his justice; Protect the guiltless, and defend your king, Else shalt thou prove a worthless successor. If thou wouldst gain the mother, seek the son; Go, bring him to me; bring your master here, And then perhaps I may descend to you: But I will never be the vile accomplice, Or the reward, of guilt like thine.

**SCENE IV.**
Poliphontes, Erox.

**Erox:** My lord, Did you expect to move her? Does the throne Depend on her capricious will? Must she Conduct you to it?

**Euricles:** 'Twixt that throne and me, Erox, I see a dreadful precipice I must o'erleap, or perish: Mérope Expects Ægisthus; and the fickle crowd, If he returns, perhaps may bend towards him. In vain his father's and his brothers' blood, Have opened wide my passage to the throne; In vain hath fortune cast her friendly veil O'er all my crimes; in vain have I oppressed The blood of kings, whilst the deluded people Adored me as their friend, if yet there lives A hateful offspring of Alcides' race: If this lamented son should e'er again Behold Messene, fifteen years of toil At once are lost, and all my hopes o'erthrown; All the fond prejudice of birth and blood Will soon revive the memory of Cresphontes, A hundred kings for his proud ancestors, The boasted honor of a race divine, A mother's tears, her sorrows, her despair, All will conspire to shake my feeble power: Ægisthus is a foe I must subdue: I would have crushed the serpent in his shell, But that the diligent and subtle Narbas Conveyed him hence, e'er since that time concealed In some far distant land, he hath escaped My narrowest search, and baffled all my care: I stopped his couriers, broke the intelligence 'Twixt him and Mérope; but fortune oft Deserts us: from the silence of oblivion Sometimes a secret may spring forth; and heaven, By slow and solemn steps, may bring down vengeance.

**Erox:** Depend, undaunted, on thy prosperous fate; Prudence, thy guardian god, shall still protect thee: Thy orders are obeyed; the soldiers watch Each avenue of Elis and Messene: If Narbas brings Ægisthus here, they both Must die.

**Euricles:** But say, canst thou depend on those Whom thou hast placed to intercept them?

**Erox:** Yes: None of them know whose blood is to be shed, Or the king's name whom they must sacrifice. Narbas is painted to them as a traitor, A guilty vagabond, that seeks some place Of refuge; and the other, as a slave, A murderer, to be yielded up to justice.

**Euricles:** It must be so: this crime and I have done; And yet, when I have rid me of the son, I must possess the mother: 'twill be useful: I shall not then be branded with the name Of a usurper; she will bring with her A noble portion in the people's love: I know their hearts are not inclined to me; With fears dejected, or inflamed with hope, Still in extremes, the giddy multitude Tumultuous rove, and interest only binds them, That makes them mine. Erox, thy fate depends On my success; thou art my best support: Go, and unite them; bribe the sordid wretch With gold to serve me, let the subtle courtier Expect my favors; raise the coward soul, Inspire the valiant, and caress the bold; Persuade and promise, threaten and implore: Thus far this sword hath brought me on my way; But what by courage was begun, by art We must complete; that many-headed monster, The people, must be soothed by flattery's power: I'm feared already, but I would be loved.

# ACT II.

SCENE I.

Mérope, Euricles, Ismenia.

**Mérope:** Hast thou heard nothing of my dear Ægisthus? No news from Elis' frontiers? O, too well I know the cause of this ill-boding silence!

**Euricles:** In all our search we have discovered naught, Save a young stranger, reeking with the blood Of one whom he had murdered: we have chained, And brought him hither.

**Mérope:** Ha! a murderer, A stranger too! Whom, thinkest thou, he has slain? My blood runs cold.

**Euricles:** The mere effect of love And tenderness: each little circumstance Alarms a soul like thine, that ever dwells On one sad object; 'tis the voice of nature, And will be heard; but let not this disturb thee, A common accident: our borders long Have been infested with these ruffian slaves, The baneful fruit of our intestine broils; Justice hath lost her power; our husbandmen Call on the gods for vengeance, and lament The blood of half their fellow-citizens, Slain by each other's hand: but, be composed, These terrors are not thine.

**Mérope:** Who is this stranger? Answer me, tell me.

**Euricles:** Some poor nameless wretch, Such he appears; brought up to infamy, To guilt, and sorrow.

**Mérope:** Well, no matter who, Or what he is; let him be brought before me. Important truths are often brought to light By meanest instruments. Perhaps my soul Is too much moved; pity a woman's weakness, Pity a mother, who has all to fear, And nothing to neglect: let him appear; I'll see, and question him.

**Euricles:** Your orders, madam, Shall be obeyed. [To Ismenia.] Tell them to bring him here, Before the queen.

**Mérope:** I know my cares are vain; But grief overpowers, and hurries me to act Perhaps imprudent; but you know I've cause For my despair; they have dethroned my son, And would insult the mother: Poliphontes Hath taken advantage of my helpless state, And dared to offer me his hand.

**Euricles:** Thy woes Are greater even than thou thinkest they are. I know this marriage would debase thy honor, And yet I see it must be so; thy fate Hath bound thee to it by the cruel tie Of dire necessity: I know it wears A dreadful aspect, yet perchance may prove The only means of placing on the throne Its rightful master, so the assembled chiefs And soldiers think; they with—

**Mérope:** My son would ne'er Consent to that: no: poverty and exile, With all their pains, were far less dreadful to him Than these base nuptials.

**Euricles:** If to assert his rights Alone sufficed to seat him on the throne, Doubtless his pride would spurn the shameful bond: But if his soul is by misfortune taught To know itself, if prudence guides his steps, If his own interest, if his friends' advice, And above all, necessity, the first Of human laws, have any influence o'er him, He would perceive, that his unhappy mother Could not bestow on him a dearer mark Of her affection.

**Mérope:** Ha! what sayest thou?

**Euricles:** Truth, Unwelcome truth, which nothing but my zeal, And your misfortunes, should have wrested from me.

**Mérope:** Wouldst thou persuade me then, that interest e'er Can get the better of my fixed aversion For Poliphontes, you who painted him In blackest colors to me?

**Euricles:** I described him Even as he is, most dangerous and bold; I know his rashness, and I know his power; Naught can resist him, he's without an heir. Remember that: you say, you love Ægisthus.

**Mérope**: I do; and 'tis that love which makes the tyrant Still more detested: wherefore talkest thou thus Of marriage and of empire? speak to me Of my dear son; and tell me if he lives; Inform me, Euricles.

**Euricles**: Behold the stranger Whom you desired to question; see, he comes.

## SCENE II.

Mérope, Euricles, Ægisthus in Chains, Ismenia, Guards.

**Ægisthusin**: [At the bottom of the stage. To Ismenia.] Is that the great unfortunate, the queen, Whose glory and whose sorrows reached even me Amidst the desert wild where I was hid?

**Ismenia**: 'Tis she.

**Ægisthusin**: Thou great creator of mankind! Thou, who didst form those matchless charms, look down And guard thy image: virtue on a throne Is sure the first and fairest work of heaven.

**Mérope**: Is that the murderer? Can such features hide A cruel heart? Come near, unhappy youth, Be not alarmed, but answer me; whose blood Is on thy hands?

**Ægisthusin**: O, queen, forgive me; fear, Respect, and grief, bind up my trembling lips. [Turning to Euricles.] I cannot speak; her presence shakes my soul With terror and amazement.

**Mérope**: Tell me whom Thy arm has slain.

**Ægisthusin**: Some bold presumptuous youth, Whom fate condemned to fall the wretched victim Of his own rashness.

**Mérope**: Ha! a youth! my blood Runs cold within me: didst thou know him?

**Ægisthusin**: No: Messene's walls, her fields, and citizens, Are new to me.

**Mérope**: And did this unknown youth Attack thee then? 'twas in thy own defence?

**Ægisthusin**: Heaven is my witness, I am innocent. Just on the borders of Pamisus, where A temple stands, sacred to Hercules, Thy great progenitor, I offered up To the avenger of wronged innocence My humble prayers for thee; I had no victims, No precious gifts to lay before him; all I had to give him, was a spotless heart, And simple vows, the poor man's hecatomb: It seemed as if the god received my homage With kind affection, for I felt my heart By more than common resolution fired: Two men, both armed, and both unknown, surprised me; One in the bloom of youth, the other sunk Into the vale of years: "What brings thee here?" They cried, "and wherefore for Alcides' race Art thou a suppliant?" At this word they raised The dagger to my breast: but heaven preserved me. Pierced o'er with wounds, the youngest of them fell Dead at my feet; the other basely fled, Like an assassin: knowing not what blood I might have shed, and doubtful of my fate, I threw the bloody corpse into the sea, And fled; your soldiers stopped me; at the name Of Mérope, I yielded up my arms, And they have brought me hither.

**Euricles:** Why these tears, My royal mistress?

**Mérope:** Shall I own it to thee? I melted with compassion, as he told His melancholy tale; I know not why, But my heart sympathized with his distress: It cannot be, I blush to think it, yet Methought I traced the features of Cresphontes: Cruel remembrance! wherefore am I mocked With such deceitful images as these, Such fond delusions?

**Euricles:** Do not then embrace Such vain suspicions, he's not that barbarian, That vile impostor, which we thought him.

**Mérope:** No: Heaven hath imprinted on his open front The marks of candor, and of honesty. Where wert thou born?

**Ægisthusin:** In Elis.

**Mérope:** Ha! in Elis! In Elis! sayst thou? Knowst thou aught of Narbas, Or of Ægisthus? Never hath that name Yet reached thine ear? What rank, condition, friends, Who was thy father?

**Ægisthusin:** Polycletes, madam, A poor old man: to Narbas, or Ægisthus, Of whom thou speakest, I am a stranger.

**Mérope:** Gods! Why mock ye thus a poor unhappy mortal? A little dawn of hope just gleamed upon me, And now my eyes are plunged in deepest night: Say, what rank did thy parents hold in Greece?

**Ægisthusin:** If virtue made nobility, old Sirris And Polycletes, from whose blood I sprang, Are not to be despised: their lot indeed Was humble, but their exemplary virtues Made even poverty respectable: Clothed in his rustic garb, my honest father Obeys the laws, does all the good he can, And only fears the gods.

**Mérope:** [Aside.] How strangely he affects me! every word Has some new charm: [Turning to Ægisthus.] But wherefore left you then The good old man? It must be dreadful to him To lose a son like thee.

**Ægisthusin:** A fond desire Of glory led me hither: I had heard Of your Messene's troubles, and your own: Oft had I heard of the illustrious queen, Whose virtues merited a better fate; The sad recital moved my soul; ashamed To spend at Elis my inglorious days, I longed to brave the terrors of the field Beneath thy banners: this was my design, And this alone: an idle thirst of fame Misled my steps, and in their helpless age Persuaded me to leave my wretched parents: 'Tis my first fault, and I have suffered for it: Heaven hath avenged their cause, and I am fallen Into a fatal snare.

**Mérope:** 'Tis plain he is not, Cannot be guilty; falsehood never dwells With such ingenuous, sweet simplicity: Heaven has conducted here this hapless youth, And I will stretch the hand of mercy to him: It is enough for me he is a man, And most unfortunate; my son perhaps Even now laments his more distressful fate: O he recalls Ægisthus to my thoughts: Their age the same; perhaps Ægisthus now Wanders like him from clime to clime, unknown, Unpitied, suffers all the bitter woes And cruel scorn that waits on penury: Misery like this will bend the firmest soul, And wither all its virtues: lot severe For a king's offspring, and the blood of gods! O if at least—

## SCENE III.
Mérope, Ægisthus, Euricles, Ismenia.

**Ismenia:** Hark! madam, heard you not Their loud tumultuous cries? You know not what—

**Mérope:** Whence are thy fears?

**Ismenia:** 'Tis Poliphontes' triumph: The wavering people flatter his ambition, And give their voices for him; he is chosen Messene's king: 'tis done.

**Ægisthusin:** I thought the gods Had on the throne of her great ancestors Placed Mérope: O heaven! the greater still Our rank on earth, the more have we to fear: A poor abandoned exile, like myself, Is less to be lamented than a queen: But we have all our sorrows. [Ægisthus is led off.]

**Euricles:** [To Mérope.] I foretold it: You were to blame to scorn his proffered hand, And brave his power.

**Mérope:** I see the precipice That opens wide its horrid gulf before me; But men and gods deceived me; I expected Justice from both, and both refused to grant it.

**Euricles:** I will assemble yet our little force Of trusty friends, to anchor our poor bark, And save it from the fury of the storm; To shield thee from the insults of a tyrant, And the mad rage of an ungrateful people.

## SCENE IV.
Mérope, Ismenia.

**Ismenia:** 'Tis not the people's fault; they love you still, And would preserve the honor of your crown: They wish to see you joined to Poliphontes, That from your hand he then might seem to hold The sovereign power.

**Mérope:** They give me to a tyrant, Betray Ægisthus, and enslave his mother.

**Ismenia:** They call you to the throne of your forefathers: Obey their voice; it is the voice of heaven.

**Mérope**: And wouldst thou have me purchase empty honors With infamy and shame?

### SCENE V.
Mérope, Euricles, Ismenia.

**Euricles**: O queen, I tremble To stand before thee: now prepare thy heart For the most dreadful stroke; call forth thy courage To bear the news.

**Mérope**: I have no courage left, 'Tis worn out by misfortune; but no matter. Proceed, inform me.

**Euricles**: All is past; and fate— I can no more.

**Mérope**: Go on: my son—

**Euricles**: He's dead: It is too true: the dreadful news hath shocked Your friends, and froze their active zeal.

**Mérope**: My son, Ægisthus, dead!

**Ismenia**: O gods!

**Euricles**: Some base assassins Had in his passage laid the snares of death; The horrid crime is done.

**Mérope**: O hateful day! Why shines the sun on such a wretch as I? He's lost; he's gone: what cruel hand destroyed him! Who shed his blood, the last of my sad race?

**Euricles**: It was that stranger, that abandoned slave, Whose persecuted virtue you admired, For whom such pity rose in your kind breast; Even he whom you protected.

**Mérope**: Can it be! Was he that monster?

**Euricles**: We have certain proofs, And have discovered two of his companions, Who, lurking here, were still in search of Narbas, Who had escaped them: he who slew Ægisthus Had taken from your son these precious spoils, [The armor is shown at a distance at the farther end of the stage.] The armor which old Narbas bore from hence. The traitor, that he might not be discovered, Had thrown aside these bloody witnesses.

**Mérope**: What hast thou told me? O these trembling hands Did on Cresphontes put that very armor When first he went to battle. Ye dear relics, O to what hands were ye delivered! monster, To seize this sacred armor.

**Euricles**: 'Tis the same Ægisthus did bring hither.

**Mérope**: Now behold it Stained with his blood! but in Alcides' temple Did they not see a poor old man?

**Euricles**: 'Twas Narbas: So Poliphontes owns.

**Mérope:** O dreadful truth! The villain, to conceal his crime, hath cast His body to the waves, and buried him In the rude ocean: O I see it all, All my sad fate: O my unhappy son!

**Euricles:** Would you not have the traitor brought before you, And questioned here?

## SCENE VI.

Mérope, Euricles, Ismenia, Erox, Guards.

**Erox:** Permit me in the name Of Poliphontes, my rejected master. Perhaps rejected but because unknown, To offer you, in this distressful hour, His best assistance: he already knows Ægisthus is no more, and bears a part In your misfortunes.

**Mérope:** That I know he does, A joyful part, and reaps the fruits of them, The throne of my Cresphontes, and Ægisthus.

**Erox:** That throne he wishes but to share with you, And throw his sceptre at thy feet; the crown He hopes will make him worthy of thy hand: But to my hands the murderer must be given, For sacred is the power of punishment, 'Tis a king's duty; he alone must wield The sword of justice, the throne's best support, That to his people and to you he owes; Midst hymen rites the murderer's blood shall flow, A great sacrifice.

**Mérope:** My hand alone Shall strike the fatal blow: though Poliphontes Reigns o'er Messene, he must leave to me The work of vengeance: let him keep my kingdom, But yield to me the right of punishment: On that condition, and on that alone, I will be his: go, and prepare the rites: This hand, fresh bleeding from the traitor's bosom, Shall at the altar join with Poliphontes

**Erox:** Doubtless, the king, whose sympathetic heart Feels for your woes, will readily consent.

## SCENE VII.

Mérope, Euricles, Ismenia.

**Mérope:** O Euricles, this vile detested marriage. Whate'er I promised, ne'er will come to pass: This arm shall pierce the savage murderer's breast, And instant turn the dagger to my own.

**Euricles:** O! madam, let me by the gods conjure you—

**Mérope:** They have oppressed me sorely; I have been Too long the object of their wrath divine: They have deprived me of my dearest child, And at their altars shall I ask a husband? Shall I conduct a stranger to the throne Of my forefathers? Wouldst thou have me join The hymeneal to the funeral torch?

Shall Mérope still raise her weeping eyes To heaven, that shines no more on my Ægisthus? Shall she wear out her melancholy days Beneath a hateful tyrant, and expect In tears and anguish an old age of sorrow? When all is lost, and not even hope remains, To live is shameful, and to die, our duty.

# ACT III.

### SCENE I.
**Narbas:** O grief! O horror! O the weight of age! The youthful hero's warm imprudent ardor Was not to be restrained; his courage burst The inglorious chains of vile obscurity, And he is lost to me, perhaps forever. How shall I dare to see my royal mistress! Unhappy Narbas! hither art thou come Without Ægisthus; Poliphontes reigns, That subtle, proud artificer of fraud, That savage murderer, who pursued us still From clime to clime, and laid the snares of death On every side, fixed on the sacred throne, Which by his crimes so oft he hath profaned, The proud usurper sits, and smiles secure: Hide me, ye gods, from his all-piercing eye, And save Ægisthus from the tyrant's sword: O guide me, heaven, to his unhappy mother, And let me perish at her feet! Once more I see the palace, where the best of kings Was basely slain, and his defenceless child Saved in these arms; and after fifteen years Shall I return to fill a mother's heart With anguish? Who will lead me to the queen? No friend appears to guide me: but behold, Near yonder tomb I see a weeping crowd, And hear their loud laments! Within these walls Forever dwells some persecuting god.

### SCENE II.
Narbas, Ismenia.
[At the farther end of the stage several of the queen's attendants, near the tomb of Cresphontes.]

**Ismenia:** What bold intruder presses thus unknown To the queen's presence, and disturbs the peace Of her retirement? comes he from the tyrant, A spy upon our griefs, to count the tears Of the afflicted?

**Narbas:** Whosoe'er thou art, Excuse the boldness of a poor old man; Forgive the intrusion; I would see the queen, Perhaps may serve her.

**Ismenia:** What a time is this Which thou hast chosen to interrupt her griefs! Respect a mother's bitter sorrows; hence, Unhappy stranger, nor offend her sight.

**Narbas:** O, in the name of the avenging gods, Have pity on my age, my misfortunes: I am no stranger here: O, if you serve And love the queen, forgive the tears that long Have flowed for her, and trust a heart that feels For Mérope as deeply as thy own. What tomb is that where you so late did join Your griefs?

**Ismenia**: The tomb of an illustrious hero, A wretched father, and a hapless king, The tomb of great Cresphontes.

**Narbas**: [Going towards the tomb My loved master!] Ye honored ashes!

**Ismenia**: But Cresphontes' wife Is more to be lamented still.

**Narbas**: What worse Could happen to her?

**Ismenia**: A most dreadful stroke; Her son is slain.

**Narbas**: Her son! Ægisthus! gods! And is Ægisthus dead?

**Ismenia**: All know it here Too well

**Narbas**: Her son?

**Ismenia**: A barbarous assassin Did slay him at Messene's gates.

**Narbas**: O death, I did foretell thee: horror and despair! Is the queen sure, and art thou not deceived?

**Ismenia**: O 'tis too plain; we have undoubted proofs; It must be so: he is no more.

**Narbas**: Is this The fruit of all my care?

**Ismenia**: The wretched queen, Abandoned to despair, will scarce survive him: She lived but for her child, and now the ties Are loosed that bound her to this hated life: But, ere she dies, with her own hand she waits To pierce the murderer's heart, and be revenged; Ev'n at Cresphontes' tomb his blood shall flow. Soon will the victim, by the king's permission, Be hither brought, to perish at her feet: But Mérope is lost in grief, and therefore Would wish to be alone: you must retire.

**Narbas**: If it be so, why should I seek the queen? I will but visit yonder tomb, and die.

### SCENE III.
**Ismenia**: [Alone.] This old man seems most worthy: how he wept! Whilst the unfeeling slaves around us seem, Like their proud master, but to mock our sorrows: What interest could he have? yet tranquil pity Doth seldom shed so many tears; methought He mourned the lost Ægisthus like a father: He must be sought—but here's a dreadful sight.

### SCENE IV.
Mérope, Ismenia, Euricles, Ægisthusin Chains, Guards, Sacrificers.

Mérope: [Near the tomb.] Bring forth that horrid victim to my sight; I must invent some new unheard of torment, That may be equal to his crime; alas! Not to my grief, that were impossible.

Ægisthusin: Dear have I bought thy momentary kindness, Guardians of innocence, protect me now!

Euricles: Before the traitor suffers, let him name His vile accomplices.

Mérope: [Coming forward.] He must; he shall: Say, monster, what induced thee to a crime So horrible to nature! How had I E'er injured thee?

Ægisthusin: Now bear me witness, gods, You who avenge the perjuries of men, If e'er my lips knew fraud or base imposture; I told thee naught but simple truth: thy heart, Fierce as it was, relented at my tale, And you stretched forth a kind, protecting hand; So soon is justice weary of her talk? Unwitting I have shed some precious blood: Whose was it, tell me, what new interest sways thee?

Mérope: What interest? barbarian!

Ægisthusin: O'er her cheek A deadly paleness spreads: it wounds my soul To see her thus. O I would spill my blood A thousand times to save her.

Mérope: Subtle villain! How artfully dissembled is that grief! He kills me, and yet seems to weep my fate. [She falls back into the arms of Ismenia.]

Euricles: Madam, avenge yourself, avenge the laws, The cause of nature, and the blood of kings.

Ægisthusin: Is this the royal justice of a court? Ye praise and flatter first, and then condemn me. Why did I leave my peaceful solitude! O good old man, what will thy sorrows be, And thou, unhappy mother, whose dear voice So oft foretold—

Mérope: Barbarian, and hast thou A mother? I had been a mother yet But for thy rage, thou hast destroyed my son.

Ægisthusin: If I am thus unhappy, if he was Indeed thy son, I ought to suffer for it; But though my hand was guilty, yet my heart Was innocent: heaven knows I would have given This day my life to save or his or thine.

Mérope: Didst thou take this armor from him?

Ægisthusin: No: It is my own.

Mérope: What sayest thou?

Ægisthusin: Yes; I swear By thee, by him, by all thy ancestors, My father gave to me that precious gift.

Mérope: Thy father! where? in Elis: how he moves me! What was his name? speak, answer.

Ægisthusin: Polycletes: I've told thee so already.

**Mérope**: O thou rivest My heart: what foolish pity stopped my vengeance? It is too much: assist me, friends, bring here The monster, the perfidious— [Lifting up the dagger.] O ye manes Of my dear son, this bloody arm—

**Narbas**: [Entering on a sudden.] O gods! What wouldst thou do?

**Mérope**: Who calls?

**Narbas**: Stop: stop—alas! If I but name his mother, he's undone.

**Mérope**: Die, traitor.

**Narbas**: Stop.

**Ægisthusin**: [Turning towards Narbas.] My father!

**Mérope**: Ha! his father!

**Ægisthusin**: [To Narbas.] What do I see? and whither wert thou going? Camest thou to be a witness of my death?

**Narbas**: O, madam, go no further: Euricles, Remove the victim, let me speak to thee.

**Euricles**: [Takes away Ægisthus, and shuts up the lower part of the scene.] O heaven!

**Mérope**: [Coming forward.] Thou makest me tremble: I was going To avenge my son.

**Narbas**: [Kneeling down.] To sacrifice—Ægisthus.

**Mérope**: Ægisthus! ha!

**Narbas**: 'Twas he, whom thy rash arm Had well nigh slain; believe me, 'twas Ægisthus.

**Mérope**: And lives he then?

**Narbas**: 'Tis he, it is your son.

**Mérope**: [Fainting in the arms of Ismenia.] I die!

**Ismenia**: Good heaven!

**Narbas**: [To Ismenia.] Recall her fleeting spirit; This sudden transport of tumultuous joy, Mixed with anxiety and tender fears, May quite o'erpower her.

**Mérope**: [Coming to herself.] Narbas, is it you? Or do I dream? is it my son? where is he? Let him come hither.

**Narbas**: No: refrain your love, Restrain your tenderness. [To Ismenia.] O keep the secret; The safety of the queen, and of Ægisthus, Depend on that.

**Mérope**: Alas! and must fresh danger Embitter my new joys? O dear Ægisthus, What cruel god still keeps thee from thy mother? Was he restored but to afflict me more?

**Narbas**: You knew him not, and would have slain your son: If his arrival here be once discovered, And you acknowledge him, he's lost forever. Dissemble, therefore, for thou knowest that guilt Reigns in Messene: thou art watched; be cautious.

SCENE V.
Mérope, Euricles, Narbas, Ismenia.
**Euricles**: 'Tis the king's order, madam, that we seize—
**Mérope**: Whom?
**Euricles**: The young stranger, whom thou had'st condemned To death.
**Mérope**: [With transport.] That stranger is my child, my son: They would destroy him, Narbas, let us fly—
**Narbas**: No: stay.
**Mérope**: It is my son; they'll have him from me, My dear Ægisthus: why is this?
**Euricles**: The king Would question him before he dies.
**Mérope**: Indeed! And knows he then I am his mother?
**Euricles**: No: 'Tis yet a secret to them all.
**Mérope**: We'll fly To Poliphontes, and implore his aid.
**Narbas**: Fear Poliphontes, and implore the gods.
**Euricles**: Howe'er Ægisthus may alarm the tyrant, Thy promised nupitals make his pardon sure: Bound to each other in eternal bonds, Thy son will soon be his; though jealousy May now subsist, it must be lost in love When he's your husband.
**Narbas**: He your husband, gods! I'm thunderstruck.
**Mérope**: I will no longer bear Such anguish, let me hence.
**Narbas**: Thou shalt not go: Unhappy mother! thou shalt ne'er submit To these detested nuptials.
**Euricles**: She is forced To wed him, that she may avenge Cresphontes.
**Narbas**: He was his murderer.
**Mérope**: He! that traitor!
**Narbas**: Yes: By Poliphontes thy Ægisthus fell, His father, and his brothers: I beheld The tyrant weltering in Cresphontes' blood.
**Mérope**: O gods!
**Narbas**: I saw him glorying in his crimes; Saw him admit the foe, and through the palace Spread fire and slaughter; yet appeared to those Who knew him not, the avenger of that king Whom he had slain: I pierced the savage crowd, And in my feeble arms upraised your son, And bore him thence; the pitying gods protected His helpless innocence: these fifteen years, From place to place I led him, changed my name To Polycletes, hid him from the foe, And now at last it

seems have brought him hither, To see a tyrant on Messene's throne, And Mérope the wife of Poliphontes.

**Mérope:** Thy tale has harrowed up my soul.

**Euricles:** He comes: 'Tis Poliphontes.

**Mérope:** Is it possible? Away, good Narbas, hide thee from his rage.

**Narbas:** Now, if Ægisthus e'er was dear to thee, Dissemble with the tyrant.

**Euricles:** We must hide This secret in the bottom of our hearts, A word may ruin all.

**Mérope:** [To Euricles.] Go thou and guard That precious treasure well.

**Euricles:** O doubt it not.

**Mérope:** My hopes depend on thee: he is my son Remember, and thy king.—The monster comes.

## SCENE VI.

Mérope, Poliphontes, Erox, Ismenia, Attendants.

**Euricles:** The altar is prepared, the throne awaits you, Our interests soon will with our hearts be joined: As king, and husband, 'tis my duty now Both to defend and to avenge you, madam: Two of the traitors I have seized already, Who shall repay the murder with their blood: But, spite of all my care, the tardy vengeance Hath seconded but ill my purposes: You told me you would wish yourself to slay The murderer, and I gave him to your justice.

**Mérope:** O that I might be my own great avenger!

**Euricles:** 'Tis a king's duty, and shall be my care.

**Mérope:** Thine, saidst thou?

**Euricles:** Wherefore is the sacrifice Delayed? dost thou no longer love thy son?

**Mérope:** May all his foes meet with their due reward! But if this murderer has accomplices, By him perhaps I may hereafter learn Who killed my dear Cresphontes: they who slew The father would forever persecute The mother and the son: O if I e'er—

**Euricles:** I too could wish to be informed of that, And therefore I have taken him to my care.

**Mérope:** To thine?

**Euricles:** Yes, madam, and I hope to draw The secret from him.

**Mérope:** But you must not keep This murderer: I must have him; nay, you promised, You know you did— [Aside.] O cruel fate! my son! What art thou doomed to? [To Poliphontes.] Pity me, my lord!

**Euricles:** Whence is this sudden transport? he shall die.

**Mérope:** Who? he?

**Euricles:** His death shall satisfy thy soul.

**Mérope:** Ay: but I want to see, to speak to him.

**Euricles:** These starts of passion, and these sudden transports Of rage and tenderness, that face of horror, Might give me cause perhaps of just suspicion; And, to be plain with you, some strange disgust, Some groundless fears, some new alarm, hath raised This tempest in your soul; what have you heard From that old man who went so lately hence? Why doth he shun me? what am I to think? Who is he?

**Mérope:** O my lord! so lately crowned Do fears and jealousies already wait Around your throne?

**Euricles:** Why wilt not thou partake it? Then should I bid adieu to all my fears: The altar waits, prepared for Mérope And Poliphontes.

**Mérope:** Thou hast gained the throne, The gods have given it thee, and now thou wantest Cresphontes' wife to make his kingdom sure. This crime alone—

**Ismenia:** O stop—

**Mérope:** My lord, forgive me; I am a wretched mother; I have lost My all; the gods, the cruel gods have robbed me Of every bliss: O give me, give me back The murderer of my son!

**Euricles:** This hand shall shed The traitor's blood: come, madam, follow me.

**Mérope:** O gracious heaven! in pity to my woes, Preserve a mother, and conceal her weakness!

## ACT IV.

SCENE I.

**Euricles:** I almost thought she had discovered something Touching her husband's murder, for she frowned Indignant on me; but I want her hand, And not her heart; the crowd will have it so; We must not disoblige them; by this marriage I shall secure them both: I look on her But as a slave that's useful to my purpose, Chained to my chariot wheels to grace my triumph, And little heed her hatred or her love. But thou hast talked to this young murderer, What thinkest thou of him?

**Erox:** He's immovable, Simple in speech, but of undaunted courage, He braves his fate: I little thought to find In one of his low birth a soul so great; I own, my lord, I cannot but admire him.

**Euricles:** Who is he?

**Erox:** That I know not; but most certain He is not one of those whom we employed To watch for Narbas.

**Euricles**: Art thou sure of that? The leader of that band I have myself Despatched, and prudent buried in his blood The dangerous secret; but this young unknown Alarms me: is it certain he destroyed Ægisthus? has propitious fate, that still Prevented all my wishes, been thus kind?

**Erox**: Mérope's tears, her sorrow, and despair, Are the best proofs; but all I see confirms Thy happiness, and fortune hath done more Than all our cares.

**Euricles**: Fortune doth often reach What wisdom cannot: but I know too well My danger, and the number of my foes, To leave that fortune to decide my fate: Whoe'er this stranger be, he must not live, His death shall purchase me this haughty queen, And make the crown sit firmer on my head. The people then, subjected to my power, Will think at last their prince is dead, and know That I avenged him: but, inform me, who Is this old man that shuns me thus? there seems Some mystery in his conduct; Mérope, Thou tellest me, would have slain the murderer, But that this old man did prevent her; what Could move him to it?

**Erox**: He's the young man's father, And came to implore his pardon.

**Euricles**: Ha! his pardon! I'll see, and talk with him; but he avoids me, And therefore I suspect him; but I'll know This secret: what could be the queen's strange purpose, In thus deferring what so ardently She seemed to wish for? all her rage was changed To tenderest pity: through her griefs methought A ray of joy broke forth.

**Erox**: What is her joy, Her pity, or her vengeance, now to thee?

**Euricles**: It doth concern me nearly; I have cause For many fears; but she approaches:—bring That stranger to me.

## SCENE II.

Poliphontes, Erox, Ægisthus, Euricles, Mérope, Ismenia, Guards.

**Mérope**: Fulfil your word, sir, and avenge me; give The victim to my hands, and mine alone.

**Euricles**: You see I mean to keep it: he's before you: Revenge yourself, and shed the traitor's blood; Then, madam, with your leave, we'll to the altar.

**Mérope**: O gods!

**Ægisthus**in: [To Poliphontes.] Am I then to be made the purchase Of the queen's favor? my poor life indeed Is but of little moment, and I die Contented; but I am a stranger here, A helpless, innocent, unhappy stranger; If heaven has made thee king, thou shouldst protect me: I've slain a man, 'twas in my own defence; The queen demands my life; she is a mother, Therefore I pity her, and bless the hand Raised to destroy me: I accuse none here But thee, thou tyrant.

## Voltaire

**Euricles:** Hence, abandoned villain; Darest thou insult—

**Mérope:** O pardon his rash youth, Brought up in solitude, and far removed From courts, he knows not the respect that's due To majesty.

**Euricles:** Amazing! justified By you!

**Mérope:** By me, my lord?

**Euricles:** Yes, madam, you. Is this the murderer of your son?

**Mérope:** My child, My son, the last of a long line of kings, Beneath a vile assassin's hand—

**Ismenia:** O heaven! What wouldst thou do?

**Euricles:** Thine eyes are fixed upon him With tenderness and joy; thy tears too flow, Though thou wouldst hide them from me.

**Mérope:** No: 'tis false: I would not, cannot hide them: well thou knowest I've too much cause to weep.

**Euricles:** Dry up your tears; He dies this moment: soldiers, do your office.

**Mérope:** [Coming forward.] O spare him, spare him.

**Ægisthusin:** Ha! she pities me.

**Euricles:** Despatch him.

**Mérope:** O he is—

**Euricles:** Strike.

**Mérope:** Stay, barbarian, He is—my son.

**Ægisthusin:** Am I thy son?

**Mérope:** [Embracing him.] Thou art: And heaven, that snatched thee from this wretched bosom, Which now too late hath opened my longing eyes, Restores thee to a weeping mother's arms But to destroy us both.

**Ægisthusin:** What miracle Is this, ye gods?

**Euricles:** A vile imposture: thou His mother? thou, who didst demand his death?

**Ægisthusin:** O if I die the son of Mérope I die contented, and absolve my fate.

**Mérope:** I am thy mother, and my love of thee Betrayed us both; we are undone, Ægisthus; Yes, Poliphontes, the important secret At length is thine; before thee stands my son, Cresphontes' heir; thy master, and thy king; The offspring of the gods, thy captive now; I have deceived thee, and I glory in it; 'Twas for my child: but nature has no power O'er tyrants' hearts, that still rejoice in blood: I tell thee, 'tis my son, 'tis my Ægisthus.

**Euricles:** Ha! can it be?

**Ægisthusin:** It is; it must be so; Her tears confirm it: yes, I am the son Of Mérope, my heart assures me of it: And, hadst thou not disarmed me, with this hand I would chastise thee, traitor.

**Euricles:** 'Tis too much; I'll bear no more: away with him.

**Mérope:** [Falling on her knees.] Behold Thus low on earth the wretched Mérope Falls at your feet, and bathes them with her tears: Doth not this humble posture speak my griefs, And say I am a mother? O I tremble When I look back on the dire precipice I have escaped, the murder of my son; Still I lament the involuntary crime Didst thou not say thou wouldst protect his youth, And be a father to him? and yet now Thou wouldst destroy him: O have pity on him: Some guilty hand bereaved him of a father; O save the son, defend the royal race, The seed of gods: defenceless and alone He stands before thee: trample not on him, Who is unable to resist thy power; Let him but live, and I am satisfied; Save but my child, and all shall be forgotten: O he would make me happy even in woe; My husband and my children all would live Once more in my Ægisthus: O behold, His royal ancestors with me implore thee To spare the noble youth, and save thy king.

**Ægisthusin:** Rise, madam, rise, or I shall never believe Cresphontes was my father; 'tis beneath His queen, beneath the mother of Ægisthus To supplicate a tyrant; my fierce heart Will never stoop so low: undaunted long I braved the meanness of my former fortune, Nor am I dazzled by the splendid lustre Of these new honors; but I feel myself Of royal blood, and know I am thy son. Great Hercules, like me, began his days In misery and sorrow; but the gods Conducted him to immortality, Because, like me, he rose superior to them: To me his blood descends; O let me add His courage, and his virtues; let me die Worthy of thee; be that my heritage! Cease then thy prayers, nor thus disgrace the blood Of those immortal powers from whom I sprang.

**Euricles:** [To Mérope.] Trust me, I bear a part in your misfortunes, Feel for your griefs, and pity your distress; I love his courage, and esteem his virtue; He seems well worthy of the royal birth Which he assumes; but truths of such importance Demand more ample proofs; I take him therefore Beneath my care, and, if he is thy son, I shall adopt him mine.

**Ægisthusin:** Thou, thou adopt me?

**Mérope:** Alas! my child!

**Euricles:** His fate depends on thee: It is not long since, to secure his death. Thou didst consent to marry Poliphontes; Now thou wouldst save him, shall not love do more Than vengeance?

**Mérope:** Ha! barbarian!

**Euricles:** Madam, know His life, or death, depends on thy resolve: I know your love, your tenderness, too well, To think you will expose to my just wrath So dear an object by a harsh refusal.

**Mérope:** My lord, at least let me be free, and deign—

**Euricles:** He is your son, or he's a traitor, madam; I must be yours before I can protect him, Or be revenged on both; a word from you Decides his fate, or punishment, or pardon; Or as his mother I shall look upon you As his accomplice; therefore make your choice: I will receive your answer at the temple Before the attesting gods. [To the soldiers.] Guard well your prisoner: Come, follow me: [Turning to Mérope.] I shall expect you, madam; Be quick in your resolve; confirm his birth By giving me your hand; your answer only Saves or condemns him; and as you determine He is my victim, madam, or—my son.

**Mérope:** O grant me but the pleasure to behold him; Restore him to my love, to my despair.

**Euricles:** You'll see him at the temple.

**Ægisthusin:** [As the guards are carrying him off.] O great queen, I dare not call thee by the sacred name Of mother, do not, I beseech thee, aught Unworthy of thyself, or of Ægisthus; For, if I am thy son, thy son shall die As a king ought.

### SCENE III.

**Mérope:** [Alone.] Ye cruel spoilers, why Will you thus tear him from me? O he's gone, I've lost him now forever; wherefore, heaven, Didst thou restore him to a mother's vows, Or why preserve him in a foreign land, To fall at last a wretched sacrifice, A victim to the murderer of his father? O save him, hide him in the desert's gloom; Direct his steps, and shield him from the tyrant!

### SCENE IV.

mérope, narbas, **Euricles:** Mérope, O Narbas, knowest thou the unhappy fate To which I am doomed?

**Narbas:** Well I know the king Must die; I know Ægisthus is in chains.

**Mérope:** And I destroyed him.

**Narbas:** You?

**Mérope:** Discovered all: But thinkest thou, Narbas, ever mother yet Could see a child, as I did, and be silent? But it is past: and now I must repair My weakness with my crimes.

**Narbas:** What crimes?

### SCENE V.

Mérope, Narbas, Euricles, Ismenia.

**Ismenia:** O madam, Now call forth all the vigor of your soul, The hour of trial comes: the fickle crowd, Still fond of novelty, with ardent zeal, Press forward to behold the expected nuptials; Each circumstance conspires to serve the tyrant: Already the bribed priest has made his god Declare for Poliphontes: "He received Your vows, Messene was a witness to them, And heaven will see the contract is fulfilled:" Thus spoke the holy seer; the people answered With acclamations loud, and songs of joy; They little know the grief that wrings thy heart; But thank the gods for these detested nuptials, And bless the tyrant for his cruelty.

**Mérope:** And are my sorrows made the public joy?

**Narbas:** O these are dreadful means to save thy son.

**Mérope:** They are indeed: thou shudderest at the thought: It is a crime.

**Narbas:** But to destroy thy child Were still more horrible.

**Mérope:** Away: despair Has given me courage, and restored my virtue: Let's to the temple; there I'll show the people My dear Ægisthus; 'twixt myself and the altar Will place my son; the gods will see him there; They will defend him, for from them he sprang: Too long already persecuting heaven Hath scourged his helpless innocence; and now It will avenge him: O I will set forth His savage murderer in the blackest colors, Till vengeance shall inspire each honest heart With tenfold rage: now dread a mother's cries, Ye cruel tyrants, for they will be heard: They come; alas! I tremble yet, despair And horror seize me: hark, they call, my son Is dying: see the cruel murderer plants A dagger in his breast: a moment more And he is lost: ye savage ministers [Turning to the sacrificers.] Of the base tyrant, you must drag the victim Up to the altar; can you, must you do it? O vengeance, duty, tenderness, and love, And thou great nature, what will ye ordain, What will ye do with an unhappy queen, Abandoned to despair?

# ACT V.

SCENE I.

Ægisthus, Narbas, Euricles.

**Narbas:** Our fate is yet uncertain, whilst the tyrant Still keeps us in the palace; all my fears Are for Ægisthus: O my king, my son, Let me still call thee by that tender name, O live, disarm the tyrant's rage, preserve A life so dear, so precious to Messene, So valued by thy faithful Narbas!

**Euricles:** Think On the poor queen, who, for thy sake alone A humble suppliant, sprinkles with her tears The tyrant's murderous hand.

**Ægisthusin:** I'm scarce awakened From my long dream, I seem as one new-born; A wandering stranger in a world unknown; New thoughts inspire, new day breaks in upon me; The son of Mérope, and great Cresphontes; And yet his murderer triumphs; he commands, And I obey; the blood of Hercules A captive and in chains!

**Narbas**: O would to heaven The grandson of Alcides still remained Unknown in Elis!

**Ægisthusin**: Is it not most strange, Young as I am, that I should know already, By sad experience, every human woe? Horror and shame, and banishment, and death, Since my first dawn of life, have pressed upon me: A persecuted wretch I wandered long From clime to clime, hid in the desert's gloom, I languished there in vile obscurity: Yet, bear me witness, heaven, midst all my woes Nor murmured nor complained: though proud ambition Devoured my soul, I learned the humble virtues That suited best my hard and low condition: Still I respected, still obeyed thee, Narbas, And loved thee as a father; nor would e'er Have wished to find another, but high heaven Would change my fate to make me but more wretched: I am Cresphontes' son, yet can't avenge him; I've found a mother, and a tyrant now Will snatch her from me; soon she must be his: O I could curse the hour that gave me birth, And the kind succor which thy goodness lent me: O why didst thou hold back the uplifted hand Of a mistaken mother? But for thee I had fulfilled my fate, and all my woes Had ended with my life.

**Narbas**: We are undone, The tyrant comes.

## SCENE II.

poliphontes, ægisthus, narbas, euricles, Guards.

**Euricles**: [To Narbas and the rest.] Retire: and thou, rash youth, Whose tender years demand my pity, list, And mark me well; for the last time I come To give thee here thy choice of life or death, Thy present and thy future happiness, Thy very being hangs upon my will: I can advance thee to the highest rank, Or shut thee in a dungeon, kill or save thee: Removed from courts, and bred in solitude, Thou art not fit to govern; let me guide In wisdom's ways thy inexperienced youth; Assume not in thy humble state a pride Which thou mistakest for virtue: if thy birth Be mean and lowly, bend to thy condition; If happier fate hath given thee to descend From royal blood, and thou wert born a prince, Make thyself worthy of thy noble rank, And learn of me to rule: the queen, thou seest, Has set thee an example; she obeys, And meets me at the temple; follow her, Tread in my steps, attend us to the altar, And swear eternal homage to thy king, To Poliphontes: if thou fearest the gods, Call them to witness thy obedience; haste, The gates of glory open to receive, And not to enter may be fatal to thee: Determine therefore now, and answer me.

**Ægisthusin:** How can I answer when thou hast disarmed me? Thy words, I own, astonish and confound; But give me back that weapon which thy fears Have wrested from me; give me my good sword, And I will answer as I ought; will show thee, Perfidious as thou art, which is the slave, And which the master, whether Poliphontes Was born to rule o'er princes, or Ægisthus To scourge oppressors.

**Euricles:** Impotence and rashness! My kind indulgence makes thee insolent: Thou thinkest I'll not demean myself so far To punish an unknown rebellious slave; But mercy, thus abused, will change to wrath: I give thee but a moment to determine, And shall expect thee at the altar; there To die or to obey: guards, bring him to me: Narbas, to you and Euricles I leave The haughty rebel; you shall answer for him: I know your hatred of me, and I know Your weakness, too, but trust to your experience, You will advise him for the best; meantime Remember, whether he's the son of Narbas Or Mérope, he must obey, or die.

## SCENE III.

Ægisthus, Narbas, Euricles.

**Ægisthusin:** I'll listen to no counsel but the voice Of vengeance; O inspire me, Hercules, O from thy seat of endless bliss look down On thy Ægisthus, animate his soul, And guide his footsteps! Poliphontes calls, I will attend him; let us to the altar.

**Narbas:** Wilt thou then die?

**Euricles:** We must not follow thee: Let us collect our few remaining friends, And strive—

**Ægisthusin:** Away: another time my soul Would listen to your kind advice, for well I know ye love me; but no counsellors Must now be heard save all-directing heaven And my own heart: the irresolute alone Is swayed by others, but the blood of heroes Will guide itself: away, the die is cast. What do I see? O gracious heaven! my mother!

## SCENE IV.

Mérope, Ægisthus, Narbas, Euricles, Attendants.

**Mérope:** Once more, Ægisthus, by the tyrant's order, We meet together; he has sent me to thee: Think not that, after these detested nuptials, I mean to live; but for thy sake, my son, I have submitted to this shameful bondage: For thee alone I fear; for thee I bear This load of infamy: O live, Ægisthus, Let me entreat thee, live; ere thou canst rule Thou must obey, and servitude must open The path to vengeance; thou contemnest my weakness, I know thou dost; but O the more I love The more I fear. O my dear child—

**Ægisthusin:** Be bold, And follow me.

**Mérope:** Alas! what wouldst thou do? Why, ye just gods, why was he made too virtuous?

**Ægisthusin:** Seest thou my father's tomb? dost thou not hear His voice? art thou a mother and a queen? O if thou art, come on.

**Mérope:** Methinks some god Inspires thy soul, and raises thee above The race of mortals: now I see the blood Of great Alcides flows through every vein, And animates Ægisthus: O my son, Give me a portion of thy noble fire, And raise this drooping heart!

**Ægisthusin:** Hast thou no friends Within this fatal temple?

**Mérope:** Once I had A crowd of followers when I was a queen, But now their virtue sinks beneath the weight Of my misfortunes, and they bend their necks To this new yoke: they hate the tyrant, yet Have crowned him; love their queen, and yet desert her.

**Ægisthusin:** By all art thou abandoned; at the altar Waits Poliphontes for thee?

**Mérope:** Yes.

**Ægisthusin:** His soldiers, Do they attend him?

**Mérope:** No: he is surrounded By that ungrateful faithless crowd that once Encircled Mérope, by them upled To the altar, I will force for thee alone A passage.

**Ægisthusin:** And alone I'll follow thee: There shall I meet my ancestors divine; The gods who punish murderers will be there.

**Mérope:** Alas! these fifteen years they have contemned thee.

**Ægisthusin:** They did it but to try me.

**Mérope:** What's thy purpose?

**Ægisthusin:** No matter what; let us begone: farewell My mournful friends, at least ye soon shall know The son of Mérope deserved your care. [To Narbas, embracing him.] Narbas, believe me, thou shalt never blush To own me for thy son.

### SCENE V.

**Narbas:** What means Ægisthus? Alas! my cares are fruitless all and vain: I hoped the sure slow-moving hand of time Would justify the ways of heaven, and place The wronged Ægisthus on Messene's throne; But guilt still triumphs, and my hopes are vanished; His courage will destroy him; death awaits His disobedience. [A noise within.]

**Euricles:** Hark! they shout.

**Narbas:** Alas! It is the fatal signal.

**Euricles:** Let us listen.

**Narbas:** I tremble.

**Euricles:** Doubtless, at the very moment When Poliphontes was to wed the queen, She has dissolved the shameful bonds by death, For so her rage had purposed.

**Narbas:** Then Ægisthus Must perish too, she should have lived for him.

**Euricles:** The noise increases, like the rolling thunder Onward it comes, and every moment grows More dreadful.

**Narbas:** Hark! I hear on every side The trumpets sound, the groans of dying men, And clash of swords; they force the palace.

**Euricles:** See Yon bloody squadron; look, it is dispersed; They fly.

**Narbas:** Perhaps to serve the tyrant's cause.

**Euricles:** Far as my eyes can reach I see them still Engaged in fight.

**Narbas:** Whose blood will there be shed? Surely I heard the name of Mérope, And of Ægisthus.

**Euricles:** Thanks to heaven, the ways Are open, I will hence, and know my fate. [He goes out.]

**Narbas:** I'll follow thee, but not with equal steps, For I am old and feeble: O ye gods! Restore my strength, give to this nerveless arm Its former vigor; let me save my king, Or yield up the poor remnant of my days, And die in his defence.

### SCENE VI.

Narbas, Ismenia.

[A crowd of people.]

**Narbas:** Who's there? Ismenia? Bloody and pale! O horrid spectacle! Art thou indeed Ismenia?

**Ismenia:** O my voice, My breath is lost; let me recover them, And I will tell thee all.

**Narbas:** My son— The queen—do they yet live?

**Ismenia:** I'm scarce myself; Half dead with fear; the crowd has borne me hither.

**Narbas:** How does Ægisthus?

**Ismenia:** O he is indeed The son of gods; a stroke so terrible, So noble! never did the unconquered courage Of great Alcides with a deed so bold Astonish mortals.

**Narbas:** O my son, my king, The work of my own hands, the gallant hero!

**Ismenia:** Crowned with fresh flowers the victim was prepared, And Hymen's torches round the altar blazed, When Poliphontes, wrapped in gloomy silence,

Stretched forth his eager hand; the priest pronounced The solemn words; amidst her weeping maids Stood fixed in grief the wretched Mérope; Slow she advanced, and trembling in these arms, Instead of Hymen, called on death; the people Were silent all; when from the holy threshold, A more than mortal form, a youthful hero Stepped forth, and sudden darted to the altar; It was Ægisthus; there undaunted seized The axe that for the holy festival Had been prepared; then with the lightning's speed He ran, and felled the tyrant; "Die," he cried, "Usurper, die; now take your victim, gods." Erox, the monster's vile accomplice, saw His master weltering in his blood, upraised His hand for vengeance; but Ægisthus smote The slave, and laid him at the tyrant's feet: Meantime, recovered, Poliphontes rose And fought; I saw Ægisthus wounded; saw The fierce encounter: the guards ran to part them; When Mérope, such power has mighty love, Pierced through opposing multitudes, and cried, "Stop, ye inhuman murderers, 'tis my son, 'Tis my Ægisthus, turn your rage on me, And plant your daggers in the breast of her Who bore him, of his mother, and your queen:" Her shrieks alarmed the crowd, and a firm band Of faithful friends secured her from the rage Of the rude soldiers; then might you behold The broken altars, and the sacred ruins: On every side, confusion, war, and slaughter Triumphant reigned; brothers on brothers rose, Children were butchered in their mothers' arms, Friends murdered friends, the dying and the dead Together lay, and o'er their bodies trampled The flying crowd; with groans the temple rung. Amidst the uproar of contending legions I lost Ægisthus and the queen, and fled: In vain I asked each passing stranger whither They bent their way; their answers but increased My terrors; still they cry, he falls, he's dead, He conquers; all is darkness and confusion: I ran, I flew, and by the timely aid Of these kind friends have reached this place of safety: But still I know not whether yet the queen And great Ægisthus are preserved; my heart Is full of terrors.

**Narbas**: Thou great arbiter Of all that's mortal, providence divine, Complete thy glorious work, protect the good, Support the innocent, reward the wretched, Preserve my son, and I shall die in peace! Ha! midst you crowd do I behold the queen?

### SCENE VII.
Mérope, Ismenia, Narbas, People, Soldiers.
[At the farther part of the stage is exposed the corpse of Poliphontes, covered with a bloody robe.]

**Mérope**: Priests, warriors, friends, my fellow-citizens, Attend, and hear me in the name of heaven. Once more I swear, Ægisthus is your king, The scourge of guilt, the avenger of his father, And yonder bleeding corpse, a hated monster, The foe of gods and men, who slew my husband, My dear Cresphontes, and his helpless children, Oppressed Messene, and usurped my kingdom, Yet dared to offer me his savage hand, Still reeking with the blood of half my race. [Meeting Ægisthus, who enters with the axe in his hand.] But here behold Messene's royal heir, My only hope, your queen's illustrious son, Who conquered Poliphontes: see, my friends, This good old man, [Pointing to Narbas.] Who saved him from the tyrant, And brought him here: the gods have done the rest.

**Narbas**: I call those gods to witness, 'tis your king; He fought for them, and they protected him.

**Ægisthusin**: O hear a mother pleading for her son, And know me for your king! I have avenged A father, I have conquered but for you.

**Mérope**: If still ye doubt, look on his glorious wounds: Who, but the great descendant of Alcides, Could save Messene thus, and scourge a tyrant? He will support his subjects, and avenge An injured people: hark! the voice of heaven Confirms your choice, and speaks to you in thunder; It cries aloud, "Ægisthus is my son."

## SCENE VIII.

Mérope, Ægisthus, Ismenia, Narbas, Euricles, People.

**Euricles**: O madam, show yourself to the pleased people, The king's return has fixed their wavering minds, And every heart is ours: the impatient crowd Sheds tears of joy, and blesses your noble son: Forever will they hold this glorious day In sweet remembrance; ardently they long To see their youthful sovereign, to behold His faithful Narbas, and adore their queen: The name of Poliphontes is detested; Thine and the king's the praise of every tongue. O haste, enjoy thy victory and thy fame; Enjoy a nobler prize, thy people's love.

**Ægisthusin**: To heaven ascribe the glory, not to me; Thence comes our happiness, and thence our virtue: While Mérope survives, I will not mount Messene's throne, my joy shall be to place A mother there; and thou, my dearest Narbas, Shall be my friend, my guide, my father still.

End

# Olympia

## Contents

Act I. .................................................... 361

Act II. ................................................... 367

Act III. .................................................. 373

Act IV. .................................................. 380

Act V. ................................................... 386

## ACT I.

**SCENE I.**
Cassander, Sosthenes.

**Cassander**: —Yet it is too soon. When I possess the crown, your faithful eyes Shall be the witnesses of all my deeds. Stay in this porch, the priestesses to-day Present Olympia to the powers divine: This day in secret she must expiate, Sins which are even to herself unknown. This day a better life I shall begin. O! dear Olympia, may you never know The heinous crime that's hardly yet effaced, To whom your birth you owe, what blood I've shed.

**Sosthenes**: Can then my lord, a girl in infancy. Stolen on Euphrates' banks, and by your sire Condemned to slavery, in your royal breast Raise such a conflict?—

**Cassander**: —Sosthenes, respect A slave to whom the world should homage pay: The wrongs of fate I labor to repair. My father had his reasons to conceal The noble blood to which she owed her birth. What do I say? O cruel memory! He set her down amongst the victims doomed To bleed, that he might unmolested reign. . . . . Although in cruelty and carnage bred I pitied her, and turned my father's heart; I who the mother stabbed, the daughter saved, My frenzy and my crime she never knew. Olympia, may thy error ever last, Though as a benefactor thou dost love Cassander, quickly he would have thy hate Wert thou to know what blood his hands have shed.

**Sosthenes**: I don't into those secrets strive to pry. Of your true interest I speak alone. Of all the several monarchs who pretend To Alexander's throne, Antigones, And he alone, is to your cause a friend.

**Cassander**: His friendship I have always held most dear. I will to him be faithful—

**Sosthenes:** —He to you Equal fidelity and friendship owes, But since we've seen him enter first these walls, His heart by secret jealousy seems filled, And from your love he seems to be estranged.

**Cassander:** What matters it? Oh, ever honored shades Of Alexander and Statira—Dust Of a famed hero, of a demi-god, By my remorse you are enough avenged. Olympia from their shades appeased obtain The peace for which my heart so long has sighed; Let your bright virtues all my fears dispel, Be my defence and heaven propitiate; But to this porch, just opened ere the day, I see Antigones the king advance.

### SCENE II.
Cassander, Sosthenes, Antigones, Hermas.

**Antigones:** [To Hermas behind.] I must this secret know, it importunes me. Even in his heart I'll read what he conceals. Depart, but be at hand—

**Cassander:** When scarce the sun Darts his first rays, what cause can bring you here?

**Antigones:** Your interests, Cassander, since the gods By penitence you have propitious made, The earth between us we must strive to share. No more war's horrors Ephesus dismay; Your secret mysteries which awe inspire Have banished discord and calamities. Monarchs' contentions are awhile composed, But this repose is short, and soon our climes By flames and by the sword will be laid waste; The sword's not sheathed nor flames extinguished yet. Antipater's no more, your courage, cares, His undertaking doubtless will complete, The brave Antipater had never borne To see Seleucus and the Lagides, And treacherous Antiochus, insult The tomb of Alexander, boldly seize His conquests and his great successors brave.

**Cassander:** Would to the gods that Alexander could From heaven's height this daring man behold; Would he were still alive—

**Antigones:** Your words surprise; Can you then Alexander's loss regret? What can to such a strange remorse give rise! Of Alexander's death you're innocent.

**Cassander:** Alas! I caused his death—

**Antigones:** —He justly fell. That victim loudly all the Grecians claimed. Long was the world of his ambition tired. The poison that he drank from Athens came, Perdiccas cast it in the sparkling bowl; The bowl your father put into your hand, But never intimated the design. You then were young, you at the banquet served, The banquet where the haughty tyrant died.

**Cassander:** The impious parricide excuse no more.

**Antigones:** Can you then abjectly thus deify The murderer of Clitus, whose fell rage Destroyed Parmenio, and who, madly vain, Dishonoring his mother durst aspire To be a god, and adoration claimed? 'Tis he deserves the name of parricide; And when at Babylon we cut him off, When fate o'ertook him in the poisoned bowl, We mortals and the gods at once revenged.

**Cassander:** Although he had his faults, you still must own He was a hero and our lawful king.

**Antigones:** A hero!—

**Cassander:** —Doubtless he deserves the name.

**Antigones:** It was our valor, 'twas our arms, our blood, To which the ungrateful wretch his conquests owed.

**Cassander:** Ye tutelary gods! Who could be more ungrateful than our sires? All to that rank exalted strove to rise. But wherefore were his wife and children slain? Who can relate the horrors of that day?

**Antigones:** This late repentance fills me with surprise. Jealous and quite suspicious of his friends He had become a Persian, and espoused A daughter of Darius; we were slaves. Do you then wish that, furious for revenge, Statira had his subjects roused to arms, And to his shade had sacrificed us all? She armed them all, Antipater himself That day with difficulty escaped her rage. A father's life you saved—

**Cassander:** —'Tis true, but still This hand the wife of Alexander slew.

**Antigones:** It is the fate of combats, our success Should not be followed by regret and tears.

**Cassander:** After the fatal stroke I wept I own, And, stained with that august but hapless blood, Astonished at myself and mad with grief For what my father forced me to commit, I long have groaned in secret—

**Antigones:** —But declare Wherefore to-day you feel these pangs of grief. A friend should to a friend his heart disclose, You still dissemble—

**Cassander:** Friend, what can I say? Depend upon it there's a time the heart To virtue's paths by instinct's force returns; And when the memory of former guilt With terror harrows up the frighted soul—

**Antigones:** Of murders expiated think no more, But let us to our interests still attend. If your soul must be ruffled by remorse, Repent that you've abandoned Asia's plains To insolent Antiochus's sway. May my brave warriors and your valiant Greeks Again with terror shake Euphrates' shores: Of all these upstart kings, elate with pride, Not one is worthy of the name, not one Like us has served Darius' conqueror. Our chiefs are all cut off—

**Cassander:** —Perhaps the gods Have sacrificed them to their monarch's shade.

**Antigones:** We who still live should labor to restore The few who have survived the general wreck. The victor dying, to the worthiest left His host, who saves it is the man he meant. My fortune and your own at once secure, The strongest all men must the worthiest own. The fallen powers of Greece let's raise again: Let discord from our councils be removed, Lest to these tyrants we should fall a prey; They were not born to vie with men like us. Say, will you second me?—

**Cassander:** —My friend, I swear I'm ready to assert our common cause. Unworthy hands have Asia's sceptre seized, Nile and the Euphrates both are tyrannized; I'll fight for you, for Greece and for myself.

**Antigones:** Interest your promise dictates; both I trust, But much more in your friendship I confide, That secret tie by which we both are bound. But of your friendship I require a proof: Do not refuse it.

**Cassander:** By your doubt I'm wronged. If what you ask is in my power, your will I as a sacred order shall obey.

**Antigones:** Perhaps you will consider with surprise The trifle which in friendship's name I ask; 'Tis but a slave—.

**Cassander:** —All mine you may command, They're prostrate at your feet, choose which you will.

**Antigones:** A foreign damsel, suffer me to ask, In Babylon made captive by your sire. She's yours by lot, I claim her as the prize Of labors which for you I've undergone. Your father used her hardly I am told, But in my court she'll meet with due respect. Her name's Olympia—

**Cassander:** Olympia!

**Antigones:** That's the fair one's name.

**Cassander:** How unexpectedly he wounds my heart! Must I resign Olympia?

**Antigones:** Hear me, friend, I hope I shall Cassander grateful find; In trifles a refusal may offend, And sure you do not mean to injure me.

**Cassander:** No, you shall soon the youthful slave behold: You shall yourself decide if 'twould be fit That I should give her up at your request: To this shrine none profane can find access. Under the inspection of the powers divine, Olympia 'midst the priestesses remains. The gates will open at the proper time Within this porch, to which access is free; My coming wait, and all complaint suspend. New mysteries may strike you with surprise; You quickly may determine whether kings Can to Olympia now have any claim. [He enters the temple again, and Sosthenes goes out.]

### SCENE III.

Antigones and Hermas in the Porch.

**Hermas:** My lord, you move my wonder, whilst alarms Disturb all Asia, and a hundred kings For power supreme in fields of blood contend; When fortune Alexander's wide domains Prepares amongst the valiant to divide. Whilst greatly you to sovereign sway lay claim, Can a slave be the object of your wish?

**Antigones:** Your wonder's just; but reasons, which to none I dare disclose, to this pursuit excite. Perhaps this slave may of importance prove To Asia's kings;

to all men who aspire; To him who in his bosom bears a heart Which nobly aims at Alexander's throne. Strangest conjectures long my soul has framed Upon the slave's adventures, and her name. I sought for information; oft my eyes Have gazed upon her from these ramparts' height. The time and place to which she owes her birth, The great respect which even a master shows her, Cassander's sorrow and obscure discourse, With fresh suspicions have my soul inspired; The mystery dark, I think, I can see through.

**Hermas**: He loves her, I am told; and, with the care Of a kind father, educates her youth.

**Antigones**: We'll know the truth, but see, the temple opens And shows the sacred altar decked with flowers. The priestesses are ranged on either side; The high priest sits within the sacred shrine, Cassander and Olympia now advance.

### SCENE IV.

The three doors of the temple are opened. The inside of the temple is discovered. The priests advance slowly on one side, and the priestesses on the other. They are all clothed in white raiment, with blue girdles, the ends of which touch the ground. Cassander and Olympia lay their hands on the altar. Antigones and Hermas stand in the porch.

**Cassander**: Oh God of kings and gods, eternal mind Who in these sacred mysteries stand revealed; Who dost the wicked punish, and the just Support, with whom remorse atones for crimes: Great God confirm the vows which here I make. Olympia, heavenly fair! those vows receive; To you my throne, my life I dedicate. A love as pure, as holy as the fire Of Vesta, which ne'er dies, I promise here, To heaven devoted, priestesses august, Receive the vows and promises I make; Bear them in clouds of incense to the throne Of listening gods, and may they still avert The punishment that's due to crimes like mine.

**Olympia**: Protect, O gods! in whom I put my trust, The master who supplied a father's care; Let my kind lover and my husband still Be dear to you, and worthy of your care. My heart is to you known, his rank, his crown Are the least gifts which on me he bestows: 'Tis yours to answer for my ardent flame, Who here bear witness to its purity. May I from him to please you learn, and may Your justice doom me to the infernal shades, If faithless to your laws I e'er forget My former state, and what I owe to him.

**Cassander**: Let's to the shrine return, where bliss invites. The solemn pomp you priestesses prepare, The pomp from which my happiness I date; Sanctify both my passion and my life, I've at the temple seen the gods, in her I see them; may they hate me if I am false. Antigones, you hear what I have said, Sufficient answer have I now returned? Acknowledge now that you should cease to claim Cassander's slave; know even my throne itself, And all my grandeur, are below her worth. Whatever friendship may unite our hearts, You cannot such a sacrifice expect. [They enter the temple again, and the doors are shut.]

SCENE V.
Antigones, Hermas.

**Antigones**: I doubt no more, I have discovered all. He braved me, but his ruin is at hand. He's ardent and impetuous, and prone Sometimes to serve the gods, sometimes offend; The world has many characters like his, Made up of passion and religious zeal. With headlong passion, tenderness they mix, They oft repent, and all things undertake. He says he weds a slave, ah, never think That love could make him so debase himself. That slave is of a race himself respects, His secret machinations I surmise. He thinks in virtue of Olympia's rights He one day may become supreme of kings. Had love alone been master of his breast, He had not from me kept it thus concealed. His friendship weak, you'll quickly see give place To rancor and inveterate enmity.

**Hermas**: Perhaps to his infatuated heart, Designs too deep for lovers you ascribe; Our actions oft, even in our great concerns, Are but effects which from our passions spring. Their power tyrannic, we in vain disguise, The weak is oft a politician deemed; Cassander's not the first king who has stooped To love a slave, and raise her to his bed. Heroes have often, by their flames subdued, Yielded to women, whilst they monarchs braved.

**Antigones**: What you have said is just, you reason right, But all I see, suspicion has confirmed. Shall I avow the truth? Olympia's charms Have jealousy excited in my soul: My secret sentiments too plain you see. Perhaps love mingles with these great concerns. More than I thought, their marriage grieves my soul. Cassander's not the only man that's weak.

**Hermas**: But he relied upon you. Can then kings Never be to the laws of friendship true? Nor your alliance, nor your fellowship In arms, the dangers which you both have shared, Nor oaths redoubled, nor united cares, Can save you from the woes that discord brings. Is then true friendship banished from the earth?

**Antigones**: I know to friendship Greece has temples raised, To interest none, though interest's there adored. At once with love and with ambition blind Cassander hides from me Olympia's birth. Cassander views me with a jealous eye: He's in the right; perhaps this very day The object of his wishes will be mine. [The initiated, the priests and the priestesses pass over the stage in procession, with garlands of flowers in their hands.]

**Hermas**: He has received her hand, the sacred shrine Already sees their nuptial pomp prepared: The initiated, followed by the priests, With garlands in their hands, attend in crowds, Over the rites love's sacred power presides.

**Antigones**: His conquest may be ravished from him soon: I shall on your fidelity rely. Gods, laws, and people, will for me declare. Let us a moment fly these odious pomps, And take the measures my designs require; Let us pollute this sanctuary o'er, Not with the blood of bulls, but human gore.

# ACT II.

### SCENE I.

The three doors of the temple are opened. Though this scene and many others, are supposed to pass in the innermost part of the temple, as theatres are not built in a manner favorable to the voice, the performers are obliged to advance forward towards the porch, but the three doors of the temple are open, to show that they are supposed to be in the temple.

The Hierophants, the Priests, and the Priestesses.

**The Hierophants**: What in these sacred days, this shrine august, When God consoles the just, and sins forgives, Shall one of all the priestesses presume To interrupt the rites, and disobey? Must Arzane from duty be exempt?

**One of the Priestesses**: Arzane bent on silence in retreat, Bathes with her tears the statues of the gods; She hides herself, my lord, from every eye; A prey to grief, and weakened by her woes, And wishes death may end her misery.

**The Hierophants**: Her woes we pity, but she must obey; Let her a moment at the rites attend. Since she has lain concealed in her retreat, First on this day her presence is required. Bid her approach, the sacred will of heaven [The inferior priestess goes in quest of Arzane.] Calls to the altar, and won't brook delay. Adorned by her with wreaths of gayest flowers, Olympia must before the gods be led. Initiated in our sacred rites, Cassander must be purified by her; Our mysteries soon must be complete, and all The orders of the gods must be obeyed; They never vary, are forever fixed, Nor like the changeful laws of humankind.

### SCENE II.

The Hierophants, the Priests and Priestesses, Statira.

**The Hierophants**: [To Statira.] You must not duty's sacred call neglect, Nor your most holy ministry decline. Since in this blest asylum first you made The vow, which never more can be recalled; Upon this day first by the gods you're chosen Their laws to Asia's victors to declare. Be worthy of the god you represent.

**Statira**: [Covered with a veil which does not conceal her features.] Oh heavens, why after fifteen years that here, Within deep solitudes and silent walls,

Remote from mankind, fate has buried me; Why do you force me from obscurity? Why do you bring me to the light and woe? [To the Hierophants.] My lord, when to this temple I repaired, 'Twas but to weep, and die in secret here. You know that was my purpose—

**The Hierophants**: —Other laws The will of heaven prescribes you on this day, And since at nuptials now you first preside, Your name, your rank no longer must be hid. You must declare them—

**Statira**: —Sir, what matter these? The blood of beggars and the blood of kings, Are they not equal in the sight of heaven? By heaven we're better known than by ourselves, Great names might formerly have dazzled me; They're all forgotten in the silent tomb, Let them be ever blotted from my mind.

**The Hierophants**: Vain glory and ambition we renounce. In this point we're agreed, but still the gods Exact a full confession of the truth. Say all, you shudder—

**Statira**: —So you will yourself. [To the Priests and Priestesses.] You, who on heaven's high majesty attend, Who share my fate, whose lives are passed in prayer, Religiously my secret ever keep.

**The Hierophants**: We swear it solemnly.

**Statira**: —Ere I proceed, Say, is Cassander, that blood-thirsty man, Admitted to your sacred mysteries?

**The Hierophants**: Madam, he is—

**Statira**: —Are then his crimes atoned?

**The Hierophants**: Of mercy every mortal stands in need. If innocence alone could heaven approach, Who in this temple would the gods adore? All human virtue from repentance springs. Such is the eternal order of the gods. Mortals are guilty, but heaven pardons all.

**Statira**: If you then knew the barbarous, horrid deeds Which make him sue for grace and vengeance dread, If you knew that by him his master fell, A master dear to heaven, and if you knew What blood he shed within these flaming walls, When even in dying Alexander's eyes, He gored the bosom of his weeping queen, And threw her dying on her husband's corpse, You'll still be more surprised when I've revealed Secrets as yet unknown to human kind. That wife who once on glory's summit sat, Whose memory bleeding Persia honors still, Darius' daughter, Alexander's wife, She's here before you, ask her nothing more. [The priests and priestesses lift up their hands and bend their bodies.]

**The Hierophants**: What have I heard, you gods whom crimes offend, How do you strike your images on earth? Statira in this temple, give me leave Respect profoundest—

**Statira**: —Rise, thou reverend priest, No longer am I mistress of the world, Only respect the anguish of my mind. In me of human greatness see the fate.

What my sire found the moment of his death, I found in Babylon when drenched in blood Darius, king of kings of throne deprived, A fugitive in deserts, quite forlorn, By his own treacherous followers was slain, A stranger, wretched outcast of the earth, Consoled his misery in his dying hour, See you that woman to my court a stranger. [Showing the inferior priestess.] Her hand, her hand alone preserved my life. 'Twas she that brought me from the slaughtered heap Where my base friends had left me to expire; She is of Ephesus; my steps she led To this asylum on my realm's confines. I saw my spoils by numerous plunderers torn, The field strewed o'er with dying and the dead, All Alexander's soldiers raised to kings, And public robberies called great exploits. The world I hated and its various woes; I left it, and lived here interred alive. I own I mourn a daughter much beloved, Torn from me whilst I weltered in my gore. This stranger here is all my family. My husband, daughter, and Darius lost, Heaven's my resource alone—

**The Hierophants:** —Be heaven your prop. From the throne which you lost to heaven you rise, God's temple is your court, be happy there. Your grandeur though august was dangerous, The throne was terrible, forget it quite And look upon it with a pitying eye.

**Statira:** This temple, sir, sometimes has calmed my griefs, But you may well conceive how much I'm shocked At seeing by Cassander the same gods Implored whom I've invoked against his head.

**The Hierophants:** This, I acknowledge, needs must give you pain: But our law speaks to you and must be heard. You have embraced it.—

**Statira:** —Could I ever think It would so horrid an injunction lay? The torch of my sad days grows pale and dim, And these last moments which high heaven bestows What purpose serve they?—

**The Hierophants:** —You'll perhaps forgive, You have yourself traced out your great career. Proceed in it and never look behind. Shades when unbound from cumbrous, fleshly chains, Taste lasting rest, and are from passion free. A new day gives them light, a cloudless day; They live for heaven, their lot is like to ours. Soon on our hearts a blest retreat bestows Oblivion of our enemies and griefs.

**Statira:** I'm priestess now, 'tis true, though once a queen, My duty's harsh, oh! with my weakness bear. What must I do?—

**The Hierophants:** —Olympia on her knees Will soon appear before you, then 'tis yours To bless the marriage of the illustrious pair.

**Statira:** I'll reconcile her to a life of woe, That is the lot of mortals.—

**The Hierophants:** —The incense, The water for ablution, and the gifts Offered up to the gods, your royal hands Shall bear, and at their sacred shrine present.

**Statira:** For whom should I present them, wretch—must then My life be filled with horror to its close? In my retreat I thought to 'scape from woe, Oh fruitless hope! woe everywhere abounds: Let me obey the law which I have made.

**The Hierophants:** Farewell, I both lament you and admire. Behold, she comes. [Exit.]

### SCENE III.

Statira and Olympia.

**Statira:** [The stage shakes.] Dark and awful cells, You shake, a horrid murmur strikes my ear: The temple quakes, must nature then be moved When she appears, must all my senses fail, And the same trouble and confusion feel?

**Olympia:** [Terrified.] Ah madam!

**Statira:** Young, tender victim to the nupital law, Approach. These frightful omens crime denote, Such charms as yours for virtue's self seem made.

**Olympia:** My sinking courage, oh just gods support! Oh you, the confidant of their decrees, Deign to direct my innocence and youth. I claim your care, my terror dissipate.

**Statira:** Alas, mine yours exceeds, embrace me, daughter, Do you then know your husband's history, Or do you know your country or your birth?

**Olympia:** Of humble birth, I never did expect My present rank, to which I have no right. Cassander, madam's king, he deigned in Greece To educate me at his father's court. Since I've been near his person, I have seen In him the greatest of all human kind. The husband's dear, the master is revered; Thus have I all my sentiments made known.

**Statira:** How easily a youthful heart's deceived! How much I love your candid innocence! Cassander, then, has taken charge of you. Do you not from some king derive your birth?

**Olympia:** Can none love virtue or obey its laws, But such as from a kingly race descend?

**Statira:** I think not so, guilt dwells too near the throne.

**Olympia:** I was a slave, no more.—

**Statira:** —I'm much surprised Upon your front august, and in your eyes, In every noble feature of your face We read the virtues of a royal mind. Could you be then a slave?

**Olympia:** —Antipater Seized on my infancy by chance of war. All to his son I owe.—

**Statira:** —Your first days thus Have felt misfortunes, which at length have ceased; My woes have been as lasting as my life. Say where and when you were by fate involved In ills which brought you to captivity?

Olympia: I'm told a king, the world's victorious lord Was slain, and rivals for his empire strove; That whilst it was by fierce contentions torn, In Babylon Cassander saved my life, When it was threatened by the murderous blade.

Statira: In days made sad by Alexander's death, Were you then captive of Antipater, And did you by Cassander's favors live?

Olympia: I never could learn more. Misfortunes past Felicity has banished from my thought.

Statira: Captive at Babylon; eternal powers Do you then make of mortals' woes your sport? The time, the place, her age, have in my soul At once roused joy, grief, tenderness, and dread. Am I not then deceived? Upon her face My valiant husband's image is impressed. . . . .

Olympia: What say you?—

Statira: —Heavens! such looks the hero cast, When mild and from the bloody field retired! He raised my family, which scarce had escaped The insatiate fury of the murderous blade! When he raised all my fallen family To their first rank, and when his hand touched mine! Illusion dear! enchanting hope! but vain. Can it be possible! List, princess, list, Pity the agitation of my soul! Have you no memory of a mother left!

Olympia: Those who have had it in their power to tell Of the transactions of my infancy, Informed me that I, in those days of slaughter, Was even, when in my cradle, made a slave. A mother's fondness ne'er to me was known. I know not who I am, from whom I'm sprung. Alas, you sigh, you weep; my trickling tears I mix with yours, and in them I find charms. With faint embrace your languid arms clasp me; Your organs fail; you strive to speak, in vain. Speak to me.—

Statira: My utterance fails, I sink, I'm overwhelmed; The trouble which I feel will end my days.

SCENE IV.

statira, olympia, the hierophants. **The Hierophants**: Priestess of heaven, and queen of human race, Say what new change has happened in your fate? What must we do? What art thou now to hear?

Statira: Misfortunes, but I'm now prepared for all.

**The Hierophants**: The greatest good is ever dashed with grief; No bliss is pure. Antigones's rage, The troops, the citizens that rise in arms, The general voice, by ardent zeal inspired, All these things prove the object you behold, Like you long buried in obscurity. The object which your hands should to Cassander This day have given, Olympia—

Statira: —What means this!

**The Hierophants**: Is daughter of the late victorious king.

**Statira**: [Running to embrace Olympia.] My torn heart had told me this before. My child! my daughter! dear, but fatal names; Do I then press you in a close embrace, When by your marriage thus you wound my soul!

**Olympia**: Does then to be my mother make you grieve?

**Statira**: No, I thank heaven, whose anger long I felt, Nature pleads loudly, joy pours on my soul; But heaven deprives me of the promised bliss. You are to wed Cassander.—

**Olympia**: If from you Olympia is descended, if the love A parent bears a child inspires your heart, Cassander surely never could offend.

**The Hierophants**: You are descended from her, doubt it not; Cassander owns and will attest the truth. With him united, may you both find means To make two hostile races live in peace.

**Olympia**: Is he your foe then, am I so accursed?

**Statira**: The villain poisoned your victorious sire; He plunged his dagger in your mother's breast, Even in her breast whose hapless womb first bore you; He plunged the steel which oft had princes pierced: Even to this temple he pursues my steps; The gods he braves, pretending to appease: He tears you from your weeping mother's arms, And can you ask me why I hate this man?

**Olympia**: Does then the conqueror's family survive? Are you his widow; is he then my sire? Have I my mother's assassin espoused? Am I become an object of your wrath, And is this marriage then a horrid crime?

**The Hierophants**: Hope in the gods—

**Olympia**: Ah, if their ruthless hate To my soul's wishes can no hopes afford; Opening my eyes a pit they opened before me. Knowing myself too well I know my fate. My great misfortune is to know my birth, Before the altar where you joined our hands I should have fallen, and at your feet expired.

SCENE V.
Statira, Olympia, the Hierophants, and a Priest.

**The Priest**: The temple's threatened, all our mysteries Quickly will be profaned by impious hands; The two contending kings dispute the right There to command where gods alone should sway. Groans heard within these vaults foreboded this, In sign of this the ground shook under us. The gods denounce some change to mortal man, The earth offends them; they must be appeased. The furious people whom fell discord fires Run headlong to this temple's sacred porch; Two rival factions Ephesus divide. Like other nations we shall be at strife; Morals, peace, sanctity, shall all give way; Kings shall prevail and we shall have a Lord.

**The Hierophants**: Ah may they bear from Ephesus their crimes, And leave one place of refuge to the earth: Oh royal mother sprung from royal race,

Olympia, shall I say Cassander's wife? Before these altars you'll protection find. To daring kings I shall present myself. I know how much respect is due to crowns, But more by far is due to Heaven that gives them. Let them keep fair with Heaven if they would reign: We have not arms or soldiers, it is true, Our power we only from our laws derive. God's my support, his temple's my defence, Should tyranny once dare to make approach. My bloody corpse awhile shall bar its way. [The Hierophants go out with the inferior priest.]

### SCENE VI.
Statira, Olympia.

**Statira:** Oh fate! oh God of altars and of thrones! Oppose Cassander, shield Antigones I must, my daughter, in my close of life Aid only from my enemies expect, And look for vengeance in my misery From the usurpers of your father's throne; From my own subjects who with jealous rage Contend for states of which I was possessed! They're now my masters; once they were my slaves. Oh noble race of Cyrus the renowned, How from thy ancient glory art thou fallen! So vain is greatness, thou art known no more.

**Olympia:** Mother, I follow you, in this sad day Render me worthy of your glorious name; To do my duty's all I hope for now.

**Statira:** Sprung from a king who over kings has reigned, Do that and equal glory thou hast gained.

# ACT III.

### SCENE I.
(The Temple is shut.)
Cassander, Sosthenes.

**Cassander:** [Within the porch.] The truth prevails, no more can I suppress The fatal secret by my sire concealed: Forced to the public voice at length to yield To a king's daughter I have justice done; Should I then longer injure royal blood By cruel silence keeping it concealed? Already I've incurred enough of guilt.

**Sosthenes:** A jealous rival of Olympia's name Avails himself intent upon your ruin; The people he excites, the town's alarmed. Antigones religious zeal contemns, And yet has blown its fire to tenfold rage. 'Tis thought a shocking crime in you to wed The daughter, you who had the mother slain.

**Cassander:** Ye gods, the keen reproaches of my heart Torture me more than all the Ephesians say. The hearts of all the citizens I've calmed, Yet still my own is by the furies torn Victim of love and of my cruelty. I would have had her all things owe to me, Not know a fate replete with horrors dire. Her sire's dominions to her I restored. Transmitted from Antipater to me. Blest in the favors on my love conferred, I was to calm tranquillity restored, I had repaired all wrongs, and justice done. My heart indeed was conscious of no crime; I killed Statira by the chance of war, Even whilst I strove to save a father's life. 'Twas in the heat of slaughter and of rage When duty to excess my valor drove; 'Twas in the blindness which a sable cloud Of horror shed upon my darkened eyes; I shuddered to think on it e'er I felt The fatal passion which enslaved my soul, I thought myself acquitted in the sight Of God and of the world, not in my own. Nor in Olympia's, that's what racks my soul: Despair lies that way: she must either choose To seal my pardon or to pierce my heart, This heart that burns with love's consuming fire.

**Sosthenes**: 'Tis said, Olympia to this temple brought Can here retract the faith which she has sworn.

**Cassander**: I know it, Sosthenes, and if this law Should be abused by her my soul adores, Woe to my rival and the temple too; Though I am here a model of true zeal, The temple I'd a scene of vengeance make. But let me banish far this terror vain; I am beloved, her heart was ever mine; The god of love shall undertake my cause: To her upon the wings of love I fly.

SCENE II.

Cassander, Sosthenes, the Hierophants.

[Coming out of the Temple.]

**Cassander**: Interpreter of heaven and minister Of clemency, I in this solemn day Have from your temple banished war's alarms: I have not fought against Antigones. Days to peace consecrated I revered; That peace to my distracted soul restore. My rites are numerous, I'll defend them all; Let us conclude this marriage. But first say What does the daughter of the conqueror?

**The Hierophants**: My lord, Olympia duties now fulfils, Duties most sacred, to her heart most dear.

**Cassander**: Mine shares them. Where's the priestess whose kind hand Is to present the bride and bless our loves?

**The Hierophants**: She'll bring her quickly, may such glorious ties Not end in the destruction of you both.

**Cassander**: Alas! upon this very day the woes I long groaned under seemed to have an end. For the first time a moment of repose Seemed to becalm the troubles of my soul

**The Hierophants**: Perhaps Olympia's woe surpasses yours.

**Cassander**: What do you say? can she have aught to fear?

**The Hierophantes**: [Going.] Too soon you'll know it—

**Cassander**: Stay, explain yourself. Do you espouse Antigones's cause?

**The Hierophants**: Forbid it, Heaven, that I should pass the bounds Which to my zeal my duty has prescribed. The din of factions, the intrigues of courts, The passions that distract the human soul Have never troubled our obscure retreats; We lift pure hands unto the God we serve. Contests of kings too much to discord prone We learn but with intention to compose: And of their greatness we should never hear Did they not often need our friendly prayers. I go, my lord, to invoke the immortal gods For you, Olympia, and for many more.

**Cassander**: Olympia!

**The Hierophants**: This moment to the temple she returns. Try if she still will own you for her lord. I leave you. [He goes out, and the temple opens.]

## SCENE III.

Cassander, Sosthenes, Statira, Olympia.

**Cassander**: By heaven she trembles! and I quake all o'er; You cast upon the ground your streaming eyes! You turn aside that face where nature's hand With the most strong expression traced at once The noblest and the tenderest of souls!

**Olympia**: [Throwing herself into her mother's arms.] Ah cruel man! ah madam!

**Cassander**: Speak, explain This agitation. Wherefore do you fly me? Whose arms do you run into? What means this? Why must my anxious soul be thus alarmed? Who is't attends and bathes you with her tears?

**Statira**: [Unveiling and turning towards Cassander.] Hast thou forgot me?—

**Cassander**: —At that voice, those looks My blood runs cold. Where am I? What means this?

**Statira**: That thou'rt a villain—

**Cassander**: Is Statira here?

**Statira**: Behold, thou wretch, the widow of thy lord, Olympia's mother.—

**Cassander**: Oh you bolts of Jove, Against my guilty head point all your rage.

**Statira**: Thou shouldst have sooner for destruction prayed, Eternal enemy of me and mine, If 'twas the will of heaven that both my throne And husband to thy rage should owe their fall, If amidst carnage, in that day of crimes Thy cowardice and cruelty was such, That thou couldst pierce a woman's breast, and plunge Her body in the flood of gore she shed, Leave me what of that hapless blood remains. Must you be ever fatal to my peace? Tear not my daughter from my heart, my arms, Deprive me not of her whom heaven restores, Respect the place of refuge which I've chosen, That from earth's tyrants I might live retired. Monster to crimes inured, cease, cease at length In sacred tombs to persecute the dead.

**Cassander:** Less dread the voice of thunder would inspire; I dare not prostrate kiss the ground before you; I own I am made unworthy by my crimes, If in excuse war's horrors I should urge, If I should say I was imposed upon When the illustrious hero was cut off; That I to serve my sire took arms against you, I should not pacify your angry soul. You'll no excuse admit, though I might say I saved your daughter whom my soul adores; That at your feet I lay my crown and realms. All makes against me, no defence you'll hear, Soon to my wretched life I'll put an end, A life whose punishment outweighs its guilt, If your own child, spite of herself and me, Did not attach me to detested life. Your daughter I brought up with tender care, And to her friends' and father's place supplied; She has my every wish, my heart; the gods Perhaps have made us in this temple meet, That we by Hymen's sacred ties might change, The horrors of our destiny to bliss.

**Statira:** Heavens! what a match. Could you the villain wed Who slew your sire, and would have murdered me?

**Olympia:** No, no, extinguished ever be the torch, The guilty torch of nuptials so accursed: Blot from my heart the shocking memory Of those dire bands which were to join our hands. My soul prefers, you'll wonder at the choice, Your ashes to the sceptre he bestows. I must not hesitate; in your kind arms, Let me forget his love, and all his crimes. Your daughter loving him partook his guilt. Forgive me, my dire sacrifice accept: Think not his villainies involve my heart, But keep me, keep me ever from his sight.

**Statira:** Thou showest a spirit worthy of thy race, These sentiments revive my drooping soul. Eternal gods, could you have then decreed That with these hands I should Olympia give To the most barbarous of the human race? Can you exact it of me? Such a deed The priestess and the mother both disclaim. You pitied me, it was not your design That I so dire a duty should perform .... Villain, no more the altar and the throne Insult, the walls of Babylon you stained With this heart's blood, but I would rather see That blood shed now by such a parricide, Than see my foe, my subject—see Cassander Presume audaciously to proffer love To Alexander's daughter, and to mine.

**Cassander:** Still with more rigor I condemn myself; But then I love, to frantic love give way. Olympia's mine; who was her sire I know; Like him I am a king, I have the right, I have the power, in fine, Olympia's mine. Her fate and mine are not to be disjoined. Neither her fears nor you, the gods, my crimes, Nor aught shall break a tie so sanctified; The gods did not my penitence reject. When they united us they pardoned all. But if you'd rob me of my charming bride, Whose hand I have received and plighted faith, This blood you first must shed, pluck out this heart Which beats for her alone, which you detest. No privilege your altars shall protect, Who murdered now shall sacrilege commit. I'll from this temple, from your very arms, From the unpitying gods bear off my wife. I seek for death, 'tis my desire, my wish. But I'll the husband of Olympia die. In spite of you I'll carry to the grave The tenderest love, and most illustrious name, And grief for an involuntary crime, Which will the manes of her sire appease. [Exit Cassander with Sosthenes.]

SCENE IV.
Statira, Olympia.
**Statira**: What horrid blasphemies have reached my ear? Daughter, how dearly for thy life I pay! The horrors which I feel you suffer, too, My grief I in your eyes conspicuous read; Our hearts still sympathize. Your kind embraces And deep-fetched sighs console my wounded soul; Because you share my griefs, I feel them less; In you I find a shelter from the storm. I brave my fate since you possess a heart Worthy of Alexander and of me.

**Olympia**: Heaven knows my heart was ne'er by nature formed To copy after yours, to be inspired By such high sentiments, such swelling virtues. O widow of famed Alexander, sprung From famed Darius, wherefore being torn From thy maternal arms, was I brought up By this Cassander, thy most mortal foe? Why on Olympia did your assassin Unasked new favors every day confer? Why did he not with cruel hand oppress me? Too dangerous favors! why was I beloved? Heavens, who do I behold in this retreat! [Antigones advances.]

SCENE V.
Statira, Olympia, Antigones.
**Antigones**: —Retire not queen. You see a king by Alexander taught. His widow I respect and will defend. You from that altar's foot again might rise To the high rank which you possessed before; Replace your daughter there, and vengeance take Of that proud ravisher who injures both. Your story's known, and every heart is yours; All men are weary of those tyrants' yoke, Who at your husband's death the empire seized. Your name this revolution will support; As your defender will you own me here?

**Statira**: Yes, if 'tis pity that directs your heart, And if this friendly offer is sincere.

**Antigones**: I will not suffer an audacious youth To gain a double right to Cyrus' throne, When of your virtuous daughter's hand possessed. He is unworthy, and I cannot doubt But you will never grant him your consent. I have not to the priest explained myself: Though I came hither as a worshipper, Who to the gods for clemency applies, I come before you with fierce vengeance armed. The widow of the conqueror may forget Her greatness, but the honor of her race She never can forget or overlook.

**Statira**: I'm weary both of life and of the throne; One's taken from me, the other near an end. If from an impious ravisher you snatch The only comfort heaven has left my woe: If you protect her and avenge her sire, I'll own you as my tutelary god. Oh! sir, whilst on life's utmost verge I stand, Preserve my daughter from the dangerous crime Of marrying him whose bloody malice strove Her hapless mother to deprive of life.

**Antigones**: Say worthy offspring of the conqueror, Dost thou accept the offer which I make?

**Olympia**: Cassander I should hate.—

**Antigones**: —You then must grant The prize, the noble prize I come to ask. Against my all I will assert your cause, Since I deserve you be my recompense. 'Tis this I ask, all other prize I scorn, Such worth should never be Cassander's lot; Speak: the unequalled glory I will owe To this right arm, the queen, and to yourself.

**Statira**: Decide.—

**Olympia**: —My scattered spirits let me first Awhile recover. Scarce my eyes are opened, Trembling and terrified from slavery, I to this temple's hallowed cells retire, Sprung from Statira and a demi-god; A mother in this shrine august I find Divested of her name, her rank, her all, And hardly from a dream of death awakened. I as a benefactor wed the man Whose dagger had my mother's bosom gored. While thus disasters compass me about, Your arm you offer to avenge my cause. What answer can I make? . . . At such a time [Embracing her mother.] 'Tis here that my first duties are required. Judge if the torch of Hymen's e'er was made To yield its light amidst this gloom of woe: See in one day how I'm with ills o'erwhelmed, And think not I can listen now to love.

**Statira**: I'll answer for her, heaven decrees her to you. Perhaps in former times the majesty— Or call it pride—of my imperial throne, My daughter to a subject had denied, But you deserve her since you would defend, 'Twas you that Alexander meant his heir. He named the worthiest, you the worthiest prove. His throne you have a right to, who support. May the unceasing favor of the gods Second you, may their power to empire raise. Both Alexander and his queen interred He in his tomb, and I within these walls, Will see you on our throne without regret: And may henceforth the fates, grown less severe, Oppose for you that strange fatality, Which oft has overwhelmed that throne in blood.

**Antigones**: It shall be raised by fair Olympia's hand. To Asia's people show yourself and her. Quit this asylum. All things I'll prepare Your husband to avenge, and fill his place. [Exit Antigones.]

SCENE VI.
Statira, Olympia.

*Statira*: By your means, daughter, I the barrier break That keeps me distant from all human kind; Again I enter this degenerate world My husband to avenge, and break thy chains. New strength the gods will to a mother give, And soon thou shalt be set at liberty. Help me to keep my word, by a new oath Help me to wipe away the former's guilt.

**Olympia**: Alas!

*Statira*: You groan!

**Olympia**: Must then this fatal day Twice light up Hymen's inauspicious torch?

*Statira*: What dost thou say?

**Olympia**: —Permit me, this first time, My thoughts to utter with a trembling voice. So much I love thee, mother, I would shed The blood which from thee I derive, if so The gods would, by new added years, protract Thy life, or render it completely blessed.

*Statira*: Dearest Olympia!

**Olympia**: Shall I tell those gods I ask no throne except this calm retreat? In it you'll see me lead my life resigned And look with scorn on crowns forgot by you. Thinkest thou my father, in the silent tomb, Desires his foe should perish by our hands? Amidst the horrors of the fight, let kings Destroy each other, and avenge his death: But we, the victims of so many ills, Shall we, with feeble hands, assist their rage? Shall we a fruitless murder undertake? Tears are our portion, crimes for them were made.

*Statira*: Our portion tears! For whom thus dost thou weep? Is Alexander's daughter by the gods Restored me? Heavens, is it her whose voice I hear!

**Olympia**: Mother!

*Statira*: Ye angry gods!

**Olympia**: Cassander! . . .

*Statira*: Explain yourself, my soul is shocked to hear you.

**Olympia**: I cannot speak—

*Statira*: —You wound me to the heart. End this anxiety, I charge thee, speak.

**Olympia**: Madam, too well I see I give you pain, But whom I love I never will deceive. Although forever I am resolved to shun My guilty husband, I must love him still.

*Statira*: Oh words accursed! ah, daughter since you love This cruel husband, you will never fly him. Thus Alexander you betray and me! Ye gods, I saw my sire and husband die: My daughter from me torn, your cruel will Restores to make me perish by her fault.

**Olympia**: Thus prostrate falling—

*Statira*: —Daughter ever dear, But cruel and unnatural—

**Olympia**: Alas! Oppressed with woe I bathe your knees with tears. Mother forgive me.—

**Statira:** —So I will and die.

**Olympia:** Be calm and hear me—

**Statira:** —What have you to say?

**Olympia:** I swear by heaven, by my own name, by you, By nature, I the punishment will bear Of my own guilt. This hand to-day should shed My blood ere I'd consent to be his wife. You know my heart, I've told you that I love; By this confession and my weakness judge If my heart's yours, if love for you prevails Over that love which has subdued my senses. Consider not my sex or tender age, Courage from my great parents I derive. I might offend them, I cannot betray; You'll know Olympia, when you see her die.

**Statira:** Dear, but inhuman daughter, can you die, And yet not hate the assassin of your sire!

**Olympia:** Tear out my heart, examine it, you'll find, Though dear, my husband reigned not there like you. The blood which animates it then you'll know; Your daughter sacrifice.—

**Statira:** —I know your heart. I pity you, my child, and don't condemn. Your courage and your duty give me hope, I pity even the love that injures me. You tear my heart, yet you affect it too. Console your mother whilst you cause her death. Alas! I am wretched, but you're not to blame.

**Olympia:** Which bears, oh heavens, of woe the greatest weight! Which has most reason, to complain, of fate!

# ACT IV.

SCENE I.
Antigones, Hermas.
[In the porch.]

**Hermas:** You warned me well; the holy place profaned, Will soon of strife and slaughter be the scene. Your soldiers guard our passage near the shrine, Cassander mad with love, with grief, and rage, Daring the gods whom he before invoked, Advances towards you by another path. The signal's given, but in this enterprise The people doubt whose cause they should espouse. [Going out.]

**Antigones:** I'll soon unite them.

SCENE II.
Antigones, Hermas, Cassander, Sosthenes.

**Cassander:** [Stopping Antigones.] —Stay unworthy friend, False ally, and detested enemy, How durst thou claim what heaven bestows on me?

**Antigones:** I do—should that in thee excite surprise? The conqueror's daughter has sufficient right To make the sons of Asia rise in arms, And haughty tyrants tremble on their thrones. Her portion's Babylon, but she may claim The empire's wide extent in right of birth. I, to possess them both, aspire, and know Thy tears, thy expiations and thy grief, The piercing eyes of nations cannot blind. Think not Olympia's love still prone to doubt, If thou art guilty of her father's death. In her opinion you are now condemned. Your heart, enslaved and tyrannized by love, Seduced Olympia, and you hid her birth. You thought to bury in oblivion's night The fatal secret which to me is known. Her love you owe to baseness and deceit. But time at length her eyes has opened, and now Cassander his pretensions must forego. What, were thy hopes presumptuous? Didst thou think By her right, to become the king of kings? . . . By arms I may defend Statira's cause, But would you our alliance still preserve? In your new kingdom would you reign in peace, Regain my friendship, on my arm depend?

**Cassander**: Proceed.—

**Antigones**: Olympia yield, and we are friends: For you I'll spill my blood; if you refuse I'll henceforth be the greatest of your foes. Maturely weigh your interests, and choose.

**Cassander**: My choice is easy, and I hither came To make to you an offer that may please. You know nor law nor pity, nor remorse; Friendship to violate, to you is sport. The gods I feared, you heavenly justice mock; The fruit of all your crimes you now enjoy; You shall not long.—

**Antigones**: —What mean these swelling words?

**Cassander**: If your fierce soul of virtue is not void, Let us not to our soldiers have recourse Our rage to second, and our anger serve. Our people should not in our quarrels bleed, They should not in our contests be involved. You, if you're bold enough, alone should brave My courage, and my single arm oppose: I was not to the commerce of the gods Admitted in their sight to slay my friend; 'Tis an unheard-of crime prepared by you: Come, we were born to act this bloody part. Come on, decide both of my fate and yours, Pour out your blood, or glut yourself with mine.

**Antigones**: With joy the combat I accept; be sure Olympia weds the man by whom thou art slain. [They draw.]

### SCENE III.

The Hierophants come precipitately from the temple with the priests and the initiated, who, with a multitude of the populace, part Cassander and Antigones, and disarm them.

**The Hierophants**: Hold your audacious hands, you men profane! Respect our god, respect his sacred rites! Haste, priests and people, part these barbarous men: Banish fierce discord from this sacred shrine. Your crimes atone—swords quickly disappear— Ye gods grant pardon—monarchs heaven obey.

**Cassander**: To you and heaven I yield.—

**Antigones**: —I still persist, I call to witness Alexander's shade, I call to witness the avenging gods, That whilst I live, Olympia, my beloved, Ne'er shall be folded in my rival's arms. The impious match on Ephesus would bring Shame, and make Asia's sons with horror shrink.

**Cassander**: It would, no doubt, had it been made by you.

**The Hierophants**: With spirit calmer, and with heart less fierce. Yield to the law obedience and respect. All men it binds, by all should be fulfilled. The poor man's hut, the haughty monarch's throne, Alike subjected hear the voice of law; The weak she aids, transgressors she restrains, And her power sets the blameless victim free. Whene'er a husband of whatever rank Has chanced the parents of his wife to slay, Though he be by our mysteries purified, By Vesta's fire, and by her healthful stream, And by repentance more essential still, His wife that day may new engagements form. She may, without offence, except she choose To imitate the gods and pardon him. As still Statira lives, you well may think That she will of her daughter's fate dispose. A mother's woes, a mother's rights respect; The law of nations, and the character Which nature gives, and nothing can efface. Her voice august Olympia must obey. All your attempts are vain since you must wait, The widow's and her daughter's final will. [Exit with his followers.]

**Antigones**: I to these terms subscribe, she's surely mine. [Exit Antigones with Hermas.]

## SCENE IV.

Cassander, Sosthenes

[In the porch.]

**Cassander**: You shall not find her treacherous, cruel man. Let us remove her from this fatal shrine, And disappoint this daring villain's hopes, He laughs at my remorse, insults my grief, And would with calm serenity and joy Concealed, destroy my peace and tear my heart.

**Sosthenes**: Statira he seduces, sir, the deed He justifies by laws he violates, And by the gods his impious soul contemns.

**Cassander**: Let's take her from the gods whom I have served, Those cruel gods by whom I am betrayed. I'd gladly die, the thunderer's stroke I'd bless; But that my wife should in this fatal day Pass from Cassander's to his rival's hand: Ere that I bear, this temple shall be laid In ashes, oh ye gods, you pardoned me! My soul grown calm with blessed tranquillity, Gave itself up to that delusive hope, Ye gods, you snatch Olympia from my arms, Thus do you pardon expiated crimes?

**Sosthenes**: You have not lost the fair; her tender heart To you obedient and devoted still Cannot so soon the man she loved forget; Changes so quick are to the heart unknown. By loving you she breaks not nature's law; The wounds which you in fight at random dealt Have, I will grant you, shed most precious blood! The gods permitted that calamity. You are not guilty of her father's death. Your tears have for her mother's blood atoned; Her woes are past, your favors present still.

**Cassander**: The anguish of my soul you sooth in vain: Statira's blood and Alexander's ghost Cry from the ground and fill my soul with dread She is their daughter, and may justly hate Her hapless husband with relentless rage; Olympia hates me, she whom I prefer To Cyrus' throne, to all the thrones on earth. Those expiations, secret mysteries By kings neglected, sought with care by me, She was their object, and my guilty soul Approached the gods her presence to enjoy.

**Sosthenes**: [Seeing Olympia.] Alas! behold her to her griefs a prey, She clasps the altar, bathes it with her tears.

**Cassander**: 'Tis time to take her from this shrine by force: Go, lose no time, but everything prepare. [Exit Sosthenes.]

cassander, olympia.

**Olympia**: [Reclined upon the altar without seeing Cassander.] How my heart rises in my throbbing breast! How in despair 'tis plunged! how self-condemned! [Seeing Cassander.] What do I see?—

**Cassander**: Your husband plunged in woe.

**Olympia**: Cassander, to that name no more pretend, That you should be my husband's not in fate.

**Cassander**: I own myself unworthy of such bliss. I know the crimes which cruel destiny For both our ruin made my hand commit. Thinking to expiate I've their measure filled. My presence hurts you and my love insults. Howe'er, vouchsafe to answer: has my aid From war and from destruction saved your youth?

**Olympia**: Why did you save it?—

**Cassander**: Even in infancy Was not your innocence by me revered? Did I not idolize you?—

**Olympia**: That's my grief.

**Cassander**: After acknowledging the purest flame, Free in your choice and mistress of yourself, Did you not in the presence of the gods Before this shrine receive my solemn vows?

**Olympia**: It is too true. May pitying Heaven avert The punishment I have thereby incurred

**Cassander**: I had your heart, Olympia.—

**Olympia**: Do not add To my distress by such a keen reproach. My youth 'twas easy for you to seduce; My ignorance and weakness you deceived: Your guilt's by this enhanced, fly hence. To hear Your conversation is in me a crime.

**Cassander**: Beware how you a greater crime commit In listening to a treacherous villain's vows. If for Antigones—

**Olympia**: Cease, wretched man, My soul rejects his vows as well as yours. Since I was once deluded and this hand Was joined to thine stained with my parents' blood, No mortal to my heart shall e'er lay claim: Marriage, the world, and life alike I hate. Since now my soul is mistress of her choice, I without hesitation choose these tombs Which hide my mother, for my last retreat; I this asylum choose whose God alone My heart by thee deceived shall now possess. These altars I embrace, all thrones detest, All Asia's thrones, but far above the rest That which by proud Antigones is filled. See me no more, go, let me mourn alone That promised love which now I must abhor.

**Cassander**: If then your heart my rival's love rejects, You can't deprive me of a ray of hope; And when your virtue a new husband shuns, I think a favor is conferred on me. Although I with your parents' blood am stained, My soul, my being must depend on you; Wife ever dear, whose virtues turned aside The thunders aimed at my devoted head, Still o'er my soul maintained a sovereign sway And should your mother's rigor have disarmed.

**Olympia**: My mother! can your tongue pronounce her name! Ah, if repentance, pity or soft love Have any influence upon your heart, Fly from the places she inhabits, fly The altars I embrace.—

**Cassander**: No, without you I cannot go, you must my steps attend. [He takes her by the hand.] Come, dearest wife.—

**Olympia**: [Pulling back her hand.] Then like my mother treat me, This bosom, to its duty faithful, pierce: A surer dagger plunge in this sad heart, To shed my blood that cruel hand was formed. Strike here.—

**Cassander**: Your vengeance carries you too far. My cruelty and violence were less. Heaven pardons man, you how to punish know: But your ingratitude exceeds all bounds When thus a benefactor feels your hate.

**Olympia**: Have you not by your deeds incurred my hate? Cassander, had thy fierce, thy bloody hand, Which with the murderous steel my mother gored, Stabbed me alone and shed no other blood, I could have pardoned thee and loved thee still. Fly, cruel man, fate wills that we should part.

**Cassander**: No, destiny itself can't separate Our fates, did you Cassander more detest; Had you even married me to pierce my heart, You must my steps attend; 'tis fate's decree. Let me still love you as a punishment: I swear by you it never will have end: Punish, detest your husband, don't forsake.

## SCENE VI.
Cassander, Olympia, Sosthenes.

**Sosthenes**: Appear, or soon Antigones prevails: The gate he blocks, your warriors he harangues, Your friends assembled near the sacred shrine He strives to gain, and their fidelity Seems to be shaken by his daring words: He on Olympia calls, and on her sire; Tremble both for your love and for your life; Come.—

**Cassander**: Is it thus you sacrifice me then To a detested rival? I in quest Of death will go, since you my death desire.

**Olympia**: Alas! Olympia cannot wish thy death. Live distant from her.—

**Cassander**: Without thee the light Of heaven is odious to my eyes, and life An object full of horror; if I escape Death's rage, I to this temple will return And force thee hence, or with the vital drops That warm my heart the sacred pavement stain. [Exit with Sosthenes.]

## SCENE VII.
**Olympia**: [Alone.]

Ah, wretch! 'tis he that causes my alarms! Wherefore, Cassander, should I weep for you? Is it so hard our duty to perform? The blood from whence I sprung shall o'er my mind Rule with despotic sway. By nature's voice I'll be directed, by her power I swear To sacrifice my sentiments to you. Far different oaths I at this altar made, Gods, you received them, and your clemency Approved the passion which inspired my soul. My state your power has changed, then change my heart, Give me a virtue suited to my woe. Pity a soul by ruthless passion torn, Which must its nature or its faith forego. Whilst yet obscure, I lived in perfect bliss, The world forgetting in captivity; Both to my parents and myself unknown. Ruin to my illustrious name I owe, At least I'll strive to merit it. Cassander I must forsake, must fly thee; can I hate? How little power has woman o'er her heart! Weeping, I tear the wound that rankles there, And whilst my hand, with trembling, seeks the dart, I plunge it deeper, make the wound more wide.

## SCENE VIII.
Olympia, the Hierophants, Attendants.

**Olympia**: Pontiff, where go you? Oh! protect the weak: You tremble, and your eyes with tears o'erflow.

**The Hierophants**: I grieve, unhappy Princess! at your lot.

**Olympia**: Since I am forlorn, afford me then thy aid.

**The Hierophants**: With resignation to their heavenly will Expect protection from the gods alone.

**Olympia:** Alas! what words are these!—

**The Hierophants:** —O daughter dear! The widow of great Alexander.—

**Olympia:** —Gods! Has aught befallen my mother? quickly speak.

**The Hierophants:** All's lost, both kings roused up to furious rage, Trampling on law, and armed against the gods, Within this temple's consecrated porch, Their troops spurred on to murder and to rage. Blood flowed on every side, with sword in hand, To you Cassander cut himself a path. I marched against him, having no defence But laws neglected and offended gods. Your mother in despair his fury met— She thought him master of the shrine and you. Tired of such horrors, tired of such black deeds, She seized the knife with which we victims slay, And plunged it in those loins wherein you found The source of life and of calamity.

**Olympia:** I die! Support me—is she yet alive?

**The Hierophants:** Cassander's with her, he laments her fate, And even presumes to offer her relief, To second those whose virtuous hands assist her. He raves, himself he blames, throws down his arms, Her feet embraces, bathes them with his tears. Hearing his cries, her dying eyes she opes, And looks upon him as a monster fierce Come to deprive her of life's poor remains, By the same hand which she had escaped before; She makes an effort weak to raise herself, Then falls again and gasps for her last breath: Cassander and the light she hates alike, Then opening with regret her half-closed eyes, Go, says she to me, hapless minister Of a sad shrine profaned with human gore, Console Olympia, she her mother loves, Tell her it is my pleasure that she wed Antigones, he will avenge my death.

**Olympia:** I'll go and near her die; now hear me gods, Accompany my steps and close my eyes.

**The Hierophants:** Intrepid courage to your ills oppose.

**Olympia:** Perhaps I soon may show to proud mankind, That courage may inspire the female mind.

# ACT V.

SCENE I.

Antigones, Hermas.

**Hermas:** [In the porch.] Vengeance is vain, compassion now should speak, A hapless rival is not worth your hate. Fly from this dire abode; Olympia, sir, Is lost both to Cassander and yourself.

**Antigones:** Is then Statira dead?—

**Hermas:** —Cassander's fate Has made him fatal to the conqueror's race. Statira sinking with a load of woe, Expires with horror in her daughter's arms. Tender Olympia stretched upon the corpse, Seems scarcely to retain the breath of life. The priests and priestesses dissolved in tears, Increase their griefs by mixing them with hers. With cries and groans the temple's vaults resound, A funeral pile's prepared, and all the pomp With which man's vanity adorns the dead. 'Tis said Olympia in this solitude Will dwell where once her mother lived retired; And that renouncing marriage and the world, She'll dedicate to heaven her future life, And that she'll in eternal silence weep Her family, her mother, and her birth.

**Antigones:** No, no, her duty's law she must obey, My right to her admits of no dispute. Statira gives her to me, and her will When at the point of death's a law divine. Frantic Cassander and his fatal love Statira's daughter must with horror fill.

**Hermas:** Sir, can you think it?

**Antigones:** She herself declares That her sad heart disclaims this barbarous man. Should he persist in his audacious love. He shall with life for his presumption pay.

**Hermas:** Would you mix blood with tears, and with the flames Of the sad pile where burns the royal corpse? Your awe-struck soldiers will with horror start From such an object, they'll not follow you.

**Antigones:** No, I will not disturb the funeral rites; This I have sworn; Cassander will revere them, Awhile Olympia shall my rage suspend, But when the funeral's o'er I'll give it scope. [The temple opens.]

SCENE II.

Antigones, Hermas, the Hierophants, the Priests.

[Advancing slowly olympia in mourning, and supported by the priestesses.]

**Hermas:** Olympia scarce alive, is this way led. I see the pontiff of the sacred shrine, Who following bathes her tracks with floods of tears. The priestesses support her in their arms.

**Antigones:** I own these objects in the hardest heart Would raise emotion. Madam, give me leave [To Olympia] To mix with yours my sorrows, and to swear That I'll avenge the wrongs you have sustained. The wretch by whom you twice a mother lost, A hope presumptuous madly entertains, But know his punishment is not far off. To your afflictions add not trembling fear: But all his rash attempts defy secure.

**Olympia:** Ah! speak not now of vengeance and of blood, Statira's dead, I'm dead to human kind.

**Antigones:** Her loss I mourn, and I pity you, Her sacred will I justly might allege, Dear to my hopes, and by yourself revered; But I know what is in this juncture due, Both to her shade, her daughter, and your grief. Madam, consult yourself, her will obey. [Exit with Hermas.]

SCENE III.
Olympia, the Hierophants, Priests, Priestesses.

**Olympia:** You who alone compassionate my woes, Priest of a God of mildness and of peace, Can I not forever dedicate my woe To this sad shrine bathed with my mother's tears? Sure, sir, you cannot have so hard a heart To shut this place of refuge from my grief? 'Tis all that's claimed by one of royal race, Do not refuse this poor inheritance.

**The Hierophants:** I mourn your fate, but how can I assist you? Your mother dying has your husband named You yourself heard her her last will declare, Whilst with our hands we closed her dying eyes. And if you will not her commands obey, Cassander still may claim you as his right.

**Olympia:** 'Tis true, I to my dying mother swore Ne'er to receive Cassander's bloody hand, My oath I'll keep.—

**The Hierophants:** —You freedom still enjoy, The gods alone can of your hand dispose. Things soon will change; you now, Olympia, may Determine and dispose your future life. Indeed it fits not that the self-same day Should light the funeral pile and hymen's torch. Such marriage would be shocking, but a word Suffices, and that word I want to hear. In this extremity your heart should know What to your royal race is justly due.

**Olympia:** Sir, I have told you any nuptial tie Is hateful to my heart, and should be to yours. A mother's injured shade I'll not betray: A husband I forsake, that should suffice. Both from the throne and marriage let me fly.

**The Hierophants:** Antigones or else Cassander choose. Those armed rivals, jealous as they're proud, Are forced by your decision to abide. You with a word confusion may prevent, And slaughter which would quickly rage again; Were not men filled with reverence and respect By all that funeral pomp, that pile, those altars, Those duties, and those honors which awhile To serious contemplation souls dispose. Piety lasts not long amongst the great; Their rage I hardly could awhile suspend; To-morrow blood will Ephesus o'erflow. Princess, decide, and all will be appeased: The people ever to the law adhere. When you have spoken they'll support your choice; If not, with sword in hand within this shrine, Cassander will your plighted faith require; What he possessed he has a right to claim, Though with just horror he inspires your soul.

*Olympia*: Enough, your apprehensions I conceive, My soul shall never to complaint give way: To fate I yield, you all its rigor know..... My choice already in my heart is made: I have resolved.—

*The Hierophants*: —Then shall Antigones Be happy, and your plighted faith receive?

*Olympia*: Howe'er that be, this juncture, Sir, ill suits With such engagements; you yourself must own The fatal day on which a mother died, Should quite engross a daughter's every thought... Must you not bear her to the funeral pile?

*The Hierophants*: 'Tis ours that mournful duty to perform: All that remains of her an urn shall hold; Her ashes to deposit be your care.

*Olympia*: Alas! her guilty daughter caused her death, Something that daughter owes her injured shade.

*The Hierophants*: All things I'll now prepare.—

*Olympia*: —Say, do your laws Permit me to behold her on the pile? May I approach the funeral pomp, and shed Tears on her body while the flames ascend?

*The Hierophants*: It is your duty, we partake your grief. You've naught to dread, those armed rivals now Will not presume your sorrows to disturb. Present perfumes, your veils and locks of hair, And a libation, offering sad, but pure. [The priestesses lay these offerings on the altar.]

*Olympia*: [To the Hierophants.] This is the only favor I require. [To the inferior priestess. You who attended her in this abode Of death, and shared the horrors of her fate, Return and give me notice when the fire Is ready to consume those loved remains: Since 'tis permitted, let my last farewell Her manes satisfy.—

*Priestess*: I shall obey. [Exit.]

*Olympia*: [To the Hierophants.] Go, holy priest, the sacred pile erect, Prepare the wreaths of cypress and the urn: Bid the two rivals to the pile repair, I in their presence will explain myself Before my mother's corpse, and in the sight Of holy priestesses, who to my woes And to my promises can witness bear, My sentiments, my choice shall be declared; You must approve them, though perhaps you'll grieve.

*The Hierophants*: You still are mistress of your destiny: This day expired, your freedom will be o'er. [Exit with the priests.]

SCENE IV.

*Olympia*: [At the front of the stage, the priestesses in a semi-circle at the bottom.] Oh thou who to my shame dost still enslave My heart, which has deliberately made choice; Who o'er Statira dead dost triumph still, O'er Alexander and their hapless race! O'er earth and heaven against thee both conspired. Reign, hapless lover, o'er my tortured sense: If you still love me, which I scarce can wish, Your fatal victory will cost you dear.

### SCENE V.
Olympia, Cassander, the Priestesses.

**Cassander**: Your wishes to fulfil, I hither come; This fatal pile shall with my blood be stained. Accept my death; the only hope I've left Is that your pity, not you vengeance, asks it.

**Olympia**: Cassander!

**Cassander**: Dearest wife!

**Olympia**: Ah, cruel man!

**Cassander**: No pardon for this criminal remains, The hapless slave of cruel destiny; To be a parricide was still my fate: Still I am thy husband: Spite of all my crimes, My soul Olympia idolizes still. Although you hate me, Hymen's rites respect: You have no tie on earth except to me: 'Tis death alone can separate our fates; I must, in dying, see you and adore. [He throws himself at her feet.] Wreak vengeance on my guilty head, my crimes Severely punish, but forsake me not. Hymen's more sacred are than nature's ties.

**Olympia**: Rise, rise, the funeral rites profane no more, No more profane the ashes of the dead. Whilst on the dreadful pile the flames consume My mother's body, don't pollute the gifts Which here I at the funeral pile present: Do not approach, but at a distance hear me.

### SCENE VI.
Olympia, Cassander, Antigones and the Priestesses.

**Antigones**: Your virtue cannot still decline a choice: Her will Statira at her death explained: This day of terror filled my soul with awe, And I the dead respected; else this arm, This vengeful arm had plunged the shrine in blood: And, in obedience to your orders, now I come as to my rival's judge and mine: From apprehensions free, pronounce our doom. I hope you will a just distinction make Between the man by whom your mother bled, And him who strove her murder to avenge. Nature has sacred rites; Statira, placed By Alexander, looks on you from heaven. Within this darksome shrine you're buried now, But heaven and earth attentive mark your deeds: Between us two Olympia must decide.

**Olympia**: I shall, but you must treat me with respect. You see these preparations and these gifts, Which to the infernal gods I must present; And you, like furious rivals, choose this time, Midst tombs, to talk of marriage and of love! You soldiers of the potent king, my sire, Who, by his death, are kings become yourselves, If I am dear to you, I charge you swear You'll not oppose my duties or my choice.

**Cassander:** I swear it solemnly, and you shall find That I respect you as I scorn that traitor.

**Antigones:** I swear it too, for sure I am, your heart Must from my barbarous rival shocked recoil. Declare yourself.—

**Olympia:** Think then what e'er befalls, That Alexander's present, that he hears us.

**Antigones:** Decide before him.—

**Cassander:** —I your pleasure wait.

**Olympia:** Then know the heart which thus you persecute, And judge what resolution I should take. Whatever choice I make, must fatal prove; The grief that racks my soul too well you know, Know likewise that I have deserved it all. My parents I betrayed, who might have known I caused the death of her who gave me birth: I found a mother in this dire abode, I quickly lost her, in these arms she died. To her sad daughter, dying thus she spoke, "Marry Antigones, I die content." Then she was seized with agonies, and I Her death to hasten, her desire opposed.

**Antigones:** Thus do you brave me and insult my love, Your mother injure, nature's laws betray.

**Olympia:** Her shade I injure not, nor injure you; I justice do to all and to myself. . . . . Cassander, first to you my faith I gave: Think you the gods our union could approve? Decide this point yourself: you know your crimes, I will not now reproach you with your guilt. Repair it when you can.—

**Cassander:** —I can't appease you! I can't assuage the horror I inspire, My heart you soon shall know: your promise keep. [The temple opens, and the pile is seen in flames.]

**SCENE the Last.**[†]
Olympia, Cassander, Antigones, the Hierophants, Priests, Priestesses.
The Inferior Priestess: Princess, 'tis time.—

**Olympia:** [To Cassander.] Behold you flaming pile. Now mourn, Cassander, your unhappy fate. Those royal ashes and that pile remark; Remember Alexander and my chains! Behold his widow! Tell me how to act.

**Cassander:** Exterminate me.—

**Olympia:** —You pronounce your doom. . . . . To mine bear witness. Oh thou sacred shade, [She mounts the steps before the altar, which is near the funeral pile. The priestesses present her the offerings.] Shade of my mother! I this duty pay To thee, who justly may be still incensed; Perhaps these gifts your manes may appease, They may prove worthy of my sire and you. [To Cassander.] Thou husband of Olympia, who by fate Wert ne'er intended for her; who preserved My life, by whom I both my parents lost; Thou who so loved me, and for whom my soul Felt all the weakness of a tender love; Thou thinkest my guilty passion from my breast Is banished; know that I adore thee still, And will upon myself that guilt revenge. Oh ever-honored ashes of Statira, The body of Olympia now receive! [She stabs herself, and throws herself into the pile.] All present cry out, Oh heavens!

**Cassander**: [Running to the pile.] Olympia!

**Priests**: Heavens!

**Antigones**: [Running also to the pile.] Oh, frenzy strange!

**Cassander**: She's now no more, our efforts all are vain. [Returning to the porch.] Gods, are you satisfied? My hands accursed, A royal pair have of their lives deprived. Still dost thou envy me, Antigones? Canst thou, unmoved, this shocking death behold, And thinkest thou still Cassander's fate is blessed? If my felicity provokes thy rage, Share it, this dagger take and do like me. [Stabs himself.]

**The Hierophants**: Oh, holy shrine! Just, but vindictive gods, In courts profane were e'er such horrors seen!

**Antigones**: Thus Alexander and his family, Successors, assassins, are all destroyed! Gods! since the world must ever feel your rage, Why into being did you mortals call? What were Statira's or Olympia's crimes? To what am I reserved in future times!

†The Hierophants, the priests and the priestesses, all show their astonishment and consternation.

**End**

# The Orphan of China

## Contents

Dramatis Personæ . . . . . . . . . . . . . . . . . . . . . . . . . . . . . . . . . . . . . . 393

Act I. . . . . . . . . . . . . . . . . . . . . . . . . . . . . . . . . . . . . . . . . . . . . . . . . 397

Act II. . . . . . . . . . . . . . . . . . . . . . . . . . . . . . . . . . . . . . . . . . . . . . . . 402

Act III. . . . . . . . . . . . . . . . . . . . . . . . . . . . . . . . . . . . . . . . . . . . . . . 406

Act IV. . . . . . . . . . . . . . . . . . . . . . . . . . . . . . . . . . . . . . . . . . . . . . . 411

Act V. . . . . . . . . . . . . . . . . . . . . . . . . . . . . . . . . . . . . . . . . . . . . . . . 415

## Dramatis Personæ

Genghis Khan, Emperor of the Tartars.
Octar, Officers under Genghis Khan.
Osman, Officers under Genghis Khan.
Zamti, a learned Mandarin.
Idame, wife of Zamti.
Asseli, friend to Idame.
Etan, friend to Zamti.

This piece was produced in Paris, 1755, when the author was in exile.

To the most noble Duke of Richelieu, Marshal and Peer of France, First Gentleman of the Chamber to his Majesty, Governor of Languedoc, and Member of the Academy of Sciences.

My Lord, I would have presented you with a piece of fine marble; but, instead of it, can only offer you a few Chinese figures. This little performance is not indeed worthy of your acceptance; there is no hero in this piece, who has united all parties in his favor, and rendered himself universally agreeable, by the force of superior talents, or supported a falling kingdom, or made the noble attempt to overthrow an English colony with four cannons only. I know better than anybody else the insignificance of my own works; but everything may be forgiven to an attachment of forty years' standing. The world, indeed, will say, that, retired as I am to the foot of the Alps, covered with eternal snows, and where I ought to be nothing but a philosopher, I had still vanity enough to let it be known, that France's brightest ornament on the banks of the Seine has not forgotten me. I have consulted my own heart alone, which has always guided me, inspired every word, and directed every action. You know it has sometimes deceived me; but not after such long and convincing proofs. If this tragedy should survive its author, permit it to inform posterity, that he who wrote it was honored with your friendship; that your uncle laid the foundation of the fine arts in France, and that you supported them in their decline.

I took the first hint of this tragedy some time since from reading the "Orphan of Tchao," a Chinese tragedy, translated by Father Bremare, an account of which is given in Du Halde's history. This piece was written in the fourteenth century, and under the dynasty of Genghis Khan; an additional proof, that the Tartar conquerors did not change the manners of the conquered nation; on the other hand, they protected and encouraged all the arts established in China, and adopted their laws: an extraordinary instance of the natural superiority which reason and genius have over blind force and barbarism. Twice have the Tartars acted in this manner; for when they had once more subdued this great empire, the beginning of last century, they submitted a second time to the wisdom of the conquered, and the two nations formed but one people, governed by the most ancient laws in the world; a most remarkable event, the illustration of which was the principal end of this performance.

The Chinese tragedy, which they call "The Orphan," was taken out of an immense collection of the theatrical performances of that nation, which has cultivated this art for about three thousand years before it was invented by the Greeks, the art of making living portraits of the actions of men, establishing schools of morality, and teaching virtue in dialogue and representation. For a long time dramatic poetry was held in esteem only in that vast country of China, separated from and unknown to the rest of the world, and in the city of Athens. Rome was unacquainted with it till above four hundred years afterwards. If you look for it among the Persians, or Indians, who pass for an inventive people, you will not find it there; it has never yet reached them. Asia was contented with the fables of Palpay and Lokman, which contain all their morality, and have instructed by their allegories every age and nation.

One would have imagined, that from making animals speak, there was but one step to make men speak also, to introduce them on the stage, and to form the dramatic art; and yet this ingenious people never thought of it: from whence we may infer, that the Chinese, Greeks, and Romans are the only ancient nations, who were acquainted with the true spirit of society. Nothing indeed renders men more sociable, polishes their manners, or improves their reason more than the assembling them together for the mutual enjoyment of intellectual pleasure. Scarce had Peter the Great polished Russia before theatres were established there. The more Germany improves, the more of our dramatic representations has it adopted. Those few places where they were not received in the last age are never ranked amongst the civilized countries.

The "Orphan of Tchao" is a valuable monument of antiquity, and gives us more insight into the manners of China than all the histories which ever were, or ever will be written of that vast empire. 'Tis true, indeed, it is extremely barbarous, when compared with the excellent performances of our times; but, notwithstanding, is a masterpiece, when placed in competition with the pieces written by our authors in the fourteenth century. Our "Troubadours," "Bazoche," the company of "Children Without Care," and "The Foolish Mother," all of them fall short of the Chinese author. It is remarkable also, that this piece is written in the language of the Mandarins, which has never changed, whilst we can scarce understand the language that was spoken in the time of Louis XII. and Charles VIII.

One can only compare the "Orphan of Tchao" to the English and Spanish tragedies of the sixteenth century, which still please beyond sea, and on the other side of the Pyrenees. The action lasts five and twenty years, as in some of the monstrous farces of Shakespeare and Lope de Vega, which are called tragedies, though they are nothing but a heap of incredible stories. The enemy of the house of Tchao wants to destroy the head of it; and for that purpose lets loose on him a great dog, whom he imagines endowed with the power of discovering guilt by instinct, as James Aimar amongst us was said to have found out thieves by his wand: at last he forges an order from the emperor, and sends his enemy Tchao a rope, a dagger, and some poison. Tchao sings, according to the custom of his country, and very deliberately cuts his own throat, in consequence of that obedience, which every man owes to the divine right of the emperor of China. The persecutor puts to death three hundred persons of the family of Tchao. The prince's widow is brought to bed of the orphan. The infant is saved from the rage of the tyrant, who had exterminated the whole family, and would have destroyed the only remaining branch of it: the tyrant orders all the children in all the towns round about to be destroyed, in hopes that the orphan might perish amongst the rest in the general slaughter.

We fancy we are reading the Arabian Night's Entertainment put into scenes; and yet, in spite of all these marvellous and improbable things, it is extremely interesting: though there is such a multiplicity of events, all is clear and simple; a merit which must recommend it to every age and nation, and which is greatly wanting in our modern performances. The Chinese piece is indeed very deficient with regard to all other beauties: there is no unity of time or action, no picture of the manners; no sentiment, eloquence, reason or passion in it; and yet, as I said before, the work is superior to anything we could produce in former ages.

How comes it to pass, that the Chinese, who in the fourteenth century, and a long time before, could boast of better dramatic performances than any European nation, still remain, as it were, in the infancy of this art, while we, in process of time, and by dint of pains and assiduity, have been able to produce about a dozen pieces, which, if they are not absolutely perfect, are at least much above anything the rest of the world could ever pretend to of this kind. The Chinese, as well as the rest of the Asiatics, have stopped at the first elements of poetry, eloquence, natural philosophy, astronomy, and painting; all practised by them so long before they were known to us. They began in everything much sooner than us, but made no progress afterwards; like the ancient Egyptians, who first taught the Greeks, and became at last so ignorant, as not even to be capable of receiving instruction from them.

These people, whom we take so much pains and go so far to visit; from whom, with the utmost difficulty, we have obtained permission to carry the riches of Europe, and to instruct them, do not to this day know how much we are their superiors; they are not even far enough advanced in knowledge to venture to imitate us, and don't so much as know whether we have any history or not.

The celebrated Metastasio has made choice of pretty nearly the same subject as myself for one of his dramatic poems, an orphan escaped from the destruction of his family, and has drawn his plot from a dynasty nine hundred years before our era.

The Chinese tragedy of the "Orphan of Tchao" differs in many respects; and I have chosen one that is not much like either of them, except in the name, as I have confined my plan to the grand epoch of Genghis Khan. I have endeavored to describe the manners of the Tartars and Chinese: the most interesting events are nothing when they do not paint the manners; and this painting, which is one of the greatest secrets of the art, is no more than an idle amusement, when it does not tend to inspire notions of honor and virtue.

I will venture to say, that from the "Henriade" to the publication of "Zaïre," and this tragedy, be it good or bad, such is the principle by which I have always been governed; and that in my history of the age of Louis XIV., I have celebrated both my king and country, without flattery to either. In labors of this kind I have spent above forty years of my life. But observe the following words of a Chinese author, translated into Spanish by the famous Navarrete.

"When you compose any work, show it only to your friends; dread the public, and your brother writers; for they will play false with you, abuse everything you do, and impute to you what you never did: calumny with her hundred trumpets, will sound them all to your destruction; whilst truth, who is dumb, shall remain with you. The celebrated Ming was accused of hating Tien and Li, and the

Emperor Vang: when the old man died, they found amongst his papers a panegyric on Vang, a hymn to Tien, another to Li, etc."

Voltaire.

# ACT I

### SCENE I

Scene a Mandarin's palace near the court, in the city of Cambalu, now called Pekin.

Idame, Asseli

**Idame:** O Asseli, amidst this scene of horror, Whilst desolation rages through the land, And the proud Tartar threatens instant ruin To this devoted palace, must thy friend Experience new calamities?

**Asseli:** Alas! We all partake the general ruin; all Must with the public sorrows mix our own: Who doth not tremble for a father's life, A husband's, son's, or brother's? even within These sacred walls, where dwells the holy band, The ministers of heaven, the interpreters Of China's laws, with helpless infancy, And feeble age; even here we are not safe: Who knows how far the cruel conqueror May urge his triumphs, whilst the thunder breaks On every side, and soon may burst upon us?

**Idame:** Who is this great destroyer, this dire scourge Of Catai's sinking empire?

**Asseli:** He is called The king of kings, the fiery Genghis Khan, Who lays the fertile fields of Asia waste, And makes it but a monument of ruin: Already Octar, his successful chief, Has stormed the palace; this once powerful empire, The mistress of the world, is bathed in blood!

**Idame:** Knowest thou, my friend, that this destructive tyrant, Whom now we tremble at, who proudly thus Treads on the necks of kings, is yet no more Than a wild Scythian soldier; bred to arms And practised in the trade of blood; who long Had wandered o'er the neighboring deserts, there Formed a rude band of lawless rioters, And fought his way to glory; now successful, And now oppressed, at length by fortune led Hither he came for refuge: Asseli, I think thou must remember him, his name Was Temugin

**Asseli:** Ha! he who once addressed His vows to thee! thy angry father then Rejected him with scorn; though now his name Is grown so terrible

**Idame:** It is the same: Methought even then I saw the rising dawn Of future glory: I remember well, Even when he came a beggar to the palace, And craved protection, he behaved like one Born to command: he loved me; and I own My foolish heart had well nigh listened to him: Perhaps it soothed the woman's vanity To hold this lion in my toils; perhaps I hoped in time to soften his rude soul, And bend his savage fierceness to the ways Of social life: he might have served the state Which now he would destroy: our proud refusal Incensed the hero, fatal may it prove To this unhappy kingdom: well thou knowest Our pride and jealousy: the ancient laws Of this imperial city; our religion, Our interest and our glory, all forbid Alliance with the nations: for myself, The noble Zamti merited my love, And heaven hath joined me to him by the ties Of holy marriage: who would e'er have thought This poor despised abandoned Scythian thus Should triumph over us? I refused his hand; I am a wife and mother; how that thought Alarms me! he is fiery and revengeful; A Scythian never pardons: cruel fate! And will this valiant nation tamely yield Its neck to slavery, and be led like sheep To slaughter?

**Asseli**: 'Tis reported the Koreans Have raised an army, but we know not yet If it be true

**Idame**: This sad uncertainty But doubles our distress: heaven only knows What we must suffer, if the emperor Has found a place of refuge, if the queen Is fallen beneath the tyrant's power, if yet They live; alas! the last surviving pledge Of their unhappy nuptials, the dear infant Entrusted to our care! I tremble for him Perhaps my Zamti's sacred character And holy office may subdue the hearts Of these proud conquerors; savage as they are, And thirsting for the blood of half mankind, They yet believe there is a power above That rules o'er all; nature in every breast Hath wisely stamped the image of its God: I talk of hope, but have a thousand fears That wring my heart

### SCENE II
Idame, Zamti, Asseli

**Asseli**: O my unhappy lord, Speak, what must be our fate? is it determined? What hast thou seen?

**Zamti**: I tremble to repeat it: We are undone: our empire is no more; A prey to robbers: what hath it availed us That we have trod in the fair paths of virtue? Long time secure within the arms of peace We shone illustrious in the rolls of time, And gave a bright example to mankind: From us the world received its laws; but vain Is human worth when lawless power prevails: I saw the northern hive rush in upon us, And force their passage through a sea of blood; Where'er they passed they spread destruction round them: At length they seized the palace, where the best Of sovereigns and of men, with calm composure And resignation yielded to his fate: The wretched queen lay fainting in his arms: Those of their numerous sons, whom lusty manhood Had sent to battle, were already slain: The rest, who naught could give him but their tears, Hung at his knees and wept; by secret paths I found an entrance to the palace; there Did

I behold the cruel tyrants bind In ignominious chains the conquered king, His children, and his wife

**Idame:** Unhappy monarch! O what a change is this! relentless heaven!

**Zamti:** The wretched captive turned his eyes towards me, And in the sacred language, to the Tartar And to the multitude unknown, cried out, "Preserve my last and only hope—my son." From my full heart I promised, swore to act As he directed me, then fled to thee Whether the tyrants, busied in their search Of plunder, thought not of me, or the symbol Which here I wear of the divinity Struck their rude souls with reverential awe, Or whether heaven in kind compassion meant To save my precious charge, and cast a cloud O'er their deluded eyes, I know not what Drew their attention, but they let me pass

**Idame:** We yet may save him, he shall go with me, And with my son; old Etan shall conduct us: In some lone wood, or solitary cave, We may conceal him till the search is past: Thank heaven they have not reached us yet

**Zamti:** Alas! No place is sacred, no asylum's left For the dear royal infant: I expect The brave Koreans, but they'll come too late: But let us seize the favorable hour, And lodge our precious pledge in safety

### SCENE III

Zamti, Idame, Asseli, Etan

**Zamti:** Etan, Thou seemest disordered: what's the news?

**Idame:** My lord, We must away; the Scythian has prevailed, And all is lost

**Etan:** You are observed, and flight Is now impossible: a guard is placed Around us: all obey the conqueror, And tremble at his power: the emperor's loss Fills every heart with terror

**Zamti:** Is he dead?

**Idame:** O heaven!

**Etan:** It was indeed a dreadful sight: Himself, his queen, his children, butchered all; A race divine, respected, loved, adored; Their headless trunks exposed to the derision Of their proud conqueror, whilst their trembling subjects Submissive bend beneath the yoke, nor dare To shed a tear o'er those whom long they loved At length our haughty lord, grown tired of conquest, And satiated with blood, proclaimed to all The terms of life, eternal slavery This northern tyrant, whom the wrath of heaven Hath sent for our destruction, once contemned And spurned at by our court, returns to glut His vengeance on us: these wild sons of rapine, Who live in tents, in chariots, and in fields, Will never brook confinement 'midst the walls Of this close city: they detest our arts, Our customs, and our laws; and therefore mean To change them all; to make this splendid seat Of empire one vast desert, like their own

**Idame:** I know the conqueror comes to sate his vengeance On this unhappy kingdom: whilst I lived Unnoticed and obscure, I might have hope Of safety; but that hope is now no more: The night is past that hid me from the eye Of persecution, and I must be wretched Thrice happy those, who to a tyrant master Are still unknown

**Zamti:** Who knows but gracious heaven May interpose and save the royal infant: 'Tis our first duty to preserve the charge Committed to our care, and guard him well What comes this Tartar for?

**Idame:** O heaven! defend us,

### SCENE IV

**Octar:** Hear, slaves; and let your answer be—obedience: An infant yet remains, of royal race, Amongst you: in the conqueror's name I here Command you to deliver him—to me I shall expect him here: begone; delay Were dangerous: bring him instantly, or know, Destruction waits on all, but first on you The day's far spent; ere night he must be found: Remember, and obey

### SCENE V

Zamti, Idame

**Idame:** O dreadful message! For what are we reserved? Alas! my lord, Ne'er till this day of blood did crimes like this Affright my soul: you answer not, but send Your fruitless sighs to heaven. Sweet innocent, Must we then give thee up a sacrifice To brutal rage?

**Zamti:** I've promised, sworn to save him

**Idame:** What can thy oaths, thy promises avail? Thou canst not keep them; every hope is lost

**Zamti:** And wouldst thou have me sacrifice the son Of my loved sovereign?

**Idame:** O I cannot bear To think of it; my eyes are bathed in tears O were I not a mother, would kind heaven But grant me now to shorten my sad days, Then would I say to Zamti, come, my lord, We'll die together; all is lost to us, And we will perish with our country

**Zamti:** Who That sees the wretched fate of Cathay's kings Would wish to live? what is this phantom death, That thus appalls mankind? the wretch's hope, The villain's terror, and the brave man's scorn: Without reluctance, and without regret, The wise expect and meet him as a friend

**Idame:** What secret purpose labors in your breast? Your cheek is pale, your eyes are filled with tears; My sympathizing heart feels all your sorrows, And would relieve them; what have you resolved?

**Zamti:** To keep my oath; therefore away, and watch  The royal infant: I shall follow you

**Idame:** Alas! a woman's tears can ne'er defend him

## SCENE VI
Zamti, Etan

**Zamti:** Vain is your care, your kind compassion vain,  For he must die; the nation's weal demands it  Think rather how thou mayest preserve thy country

**Zamti:** Yes, I will make the dreadful sacrifice  Etan, I know thou holdest this empire dear;  Yes, thou adorest the God of heaven and earth,  As worshipped by our ancestors; that God  Our bonzes know not, and our tyrants scorn

**Etan:** In him I trust, on him alone rely  For my own comfort, and my country's safety

**Zamti:** Swear then by him, and his all-ruling power,  That thou wilt bury in eternal silence  The solemn secret that I mean to pour  Into thy faithful bosom: swear, thy hand  Shall still be ready to perform whate'er  Thy duty and thy God by me command

**Etan:** I swear; and may the miseries that have fallen  On this unhappy kingdom light on me,  If ever I am false in word or deed!

**Zamti:** I cannot now recede: then mark me, Etan

**Etan:** Alas! thou weepest: amidst the general ruin  Can there be cause for added grief?

**Zamti:** The doom  Is past, my friend, and cannot be reversed

**Etan:** I know it cannot; but a stranger's son—

**Zamti:** A stranger! he, my king!

**Etan:** When I remember  He is our emperor's child, I shudder at it:  What's to be done?

**Zamti:** My path thou seest, is here  Prescribed, and every action noted down  By our new tyrants; thou mayest act with freedom,  Because unknown and unobserved: thou knowest  The orphan's place of refuge: for a time  We may conceal him 'midst the secret tombs  Of our great ancestors; then shelter him  Beneath Korea's chief; he will protect  The royal infant: leave the rest to me

**Etan:** And how will you appear without him, how  Appease the conqueror?

**Zamti:** I have wherewithal  To glut his vengeance

**Etan:** You, my lord?

**Zamti:** O nature! O cruel duty!

**Etan:** How—

**Zamti:** I have a son,  An only child, now in his cradle—go  And seize him

**Etan:** Ha! your son!

**Zamti:** To save—my king  Away, and let him—but I can no more

**Etan:** Alas! my lord, what a command is this! I never can obey it

**Zamti:** Think on Zamti; Think on his love, his weakness, his misfortunes, Thy duty, and—thy oath

**Etan:** 'Twas rash and vain: Thou didst extort it from me: I admire Thy generous purpose; but if as a friend I might be heard—

**Zamti:** No more; I've heard too much Already: what is all that thou couldst say To what a father feels? When nature's silenced, Friendship should urge no longer

**Etan:** I obey

**Zamti:** Leave me for pity's sake

### SCENE VIII

**Zamti:** [Alone.] Is nature silent? O wretched father! still thou hearest that voice So fatal and so dear: O drown it, heaven, In sweet oblivion; do not let my wife And her dear babe distract this heart; O heal My wounded heart: but man is far too weak To conquer nature: let thy aid divine Support me, and assist my feeble virtue!

# ACT II

### SCENE I

**Zamti:** [Alone.] This tardy Etan, wherefore comes he not To tell me—what I dread to hear? perhaps Ere this the dreadful sacrifice is past: I had not power to offer it myself O my dear child, how shall I ask my friend The horrid question, how conceal my grief?

### SCENE II

Zamti, Etan

**Zamti:** I see 'tis done; I know it by thy tears; They speak too plainly

**Etan:** Thy unhappy son—

**Zamti:** No more of that: speak of our empire's hope, The royal infant; is he safe?

**Etan:** He is: Within the tombs of his great ancestors Concealed from every eye; to you he owes A life begun in misery, perhaps A fatal gift

**Zamti:** It is enough, he lives O you, to whom I pay this cruel duty, Forgive a father's tears

**Etan:** Alas! my lord, You must not give away to sorrow here: 'Tis dangerous even to weep

**Zamti:** And whither, Etan, Must I transport my griefs? how bear the cries, The bitter anguish, the despair, the rage, The execrations of a frantic mother? May we not yet deceive her for a time?

**Etan:** We seized him in her absence, and I flew To guard the orphan king

**Zamti:** A while, my friend, We might impose on her credulity Couldst thou not say we had delivered up The royal orphan, and concealed her son In safety? Truth is often most destructive, And still we love it, though it makes us wretched Come, Etan, let us home—O heaven! she's here! Observe her, what despair and terror dwell On her pale cheek!

## SCENE III
Zamti, Idame

**Idame:** Barbarian, can it be? Could Zamti e'er command it? could he offer The dreadful sacrifice? I'll not believe it: Thou couldst not be more cruel than the laws Of our proud conquerors, or the Tartar's sword Alas! thou weepest

**Zamti:** Thou too must weep with Zamti But thou must join with him to save thy king

**Idame:** What! sacrifice my child!

**Zamti:** It must be so: Thou wert a subject ere thou wert a mother

**Idame:** Has nature then lost all her influence o'er A father's heart?

**Zamti:** She has too much; but ne'er Shall thwart my duty

**Idame:** 'Tis a barbarous virtue, And I abhor it: I have seen, like thee, Our empire lost, and wept our sovereign's fate; But why pour forth an infant's guiltless blood, Yet undemanded; why revere as gods Your sleeping kings, that moulder in the tomb? Hath Zamti sworn to them that he would kill His darling child? alas! the rich and poor, The monarch and the slave, are equal all By nature; all alike to sorrow born, Each has his share; and in the general wreck, All duty bids us is—to save our own O had I fallen into the snare, and staid A moment longer with the royal orphan, My child had fallen into the cruel hands Of ruffians; but I would have perished with him Nature and love recalled me, and I snatched My lovely infant from the ravishers, Preserved the son and mother; saved even thee, Thou barbarous father

**Zamti:** Doth my son then live?

**Idame:** He doth; and thou shouldst bend to gracious heaven For goodness thus unmerited: repent, And be a father

**Zamti:** O almighty power, Forgive the joy that, spite of all my firmness, Thus mingles with my tears: alas! my love, Vain are our hopes of happiness, and vain Thy fond endeavors to prolong the life Of our dear infant; these inhuman tyrants Will force him from us; he must yield to fate

**Idame:** But hear me, dearest Zamti.

**Zamti**: He must die

**Idame**: Barbarian, stay, and tremble at the rage  Of an afflicted desperate mother

**Zamti**: I Shall do my duty, you may give up yours,  And sacrifice your husband to the foe: This is a day of blood; let Zamti join  His murdered king, and perish with his country

**Idame**: What is your country, what your king to me? The name of subject is not half so sacred  As husband or as father. Love and nature  Are heaven's first great unalterable laws,  And cannot be reversed: the rest are all  From mortal man, and may be changed at pleasure  Would I could save the royal heir, but not  By the much dearer blood of Zamti's son! Pity a wretched mother; on my knees I beg thee, cruel Zamti: O remember  For whom I slighted this proud conqueror,  This mighty warrior; was it not for thee? And wilt thou not protect my son, not hear  The voice of nature pleading for thy child?

**Zamti**: It is too much: thou dost abuse the power  Which love has given thee o'er thy Zamti's heart: Couldst thou but see—

**Idame**: I own, my lord, I feel  A mother's weakness, and a mother's sorrows; Yet may I boast a heart as firm as thine; Away, and lead me on to death: I'm ready  To perish for my son

**Zamti**: I know thy virtues

## SCENE IV

Zamti, Idame, Octar

**Octar**: Where are these traitors? why are my commands  Thus disobeyed? what have ye done with him,  The orphan prince? guards, bring him to our presence,  The emperor approaches; let him see  The victim at his feet: you, soldiers, watch  These rebels

**Zamti**: I obey, my lord, the orphan  Shall be delivered up

**Idame**: 'Tis false; he shall not: I'll sooner lose my life than part with him

**Octar**: Guards, take this woman hence: the emperor comes

## SCENE V

Genghis, Octar, Osman

**Genghis**: At length, my friends, 'tis time to sheathe the sword,  And let the vanquished breathe; I've spread destruction  And terror through the land, but I will give  The nation peace: the royal infant's death  Shall satisfy my wrath; with him shall rot  The seeds of foul rebellion; all the plots,  Feuds and divisions, fears and jealousies,  That whilst the phantom of a royal heir  Subsists, must disunite us, he alone  Of all the hated race remains, and he  Shall follow them: henceforth we will not raze  Their boasted works, their monuments of art,

Their sacred laws; for sacred they esteem  The musty rolls, which superstition taught  Their ancestors to worship: be it so,  The error may be useful, it employs  The people, and may make them more obedient [To Octar] Octar, to thee I shall commit the power,  To bear my standard to the western world [To another officer]  Rule thou in conquered India, and interpret  Thy sovereign's great decrees; from Samarcand  To Tanais' borders, I shall send my sons  Away—stay, Octar

### SCENE VI
Genghis, Octar

**Genghis**: Couldst thou e'er have thought  Fortune would raise me to this height of glory?  That I should reign supreme, and triumph here,  Even in this palace, where disgraced and wretched  I sought in vain for refuge, and was treated  With insolence and scorn: the proud possessors  Of this unconquered empire then disdained  A Scythian, and a haughty fair refused  That hand which now directs the fate of millions

**Octar**: Amidst this scene of glory, how, my lord,  Can thoughts like these disturb you?

**Genghis**: Still the wrongs  I suffered in adversity oppress me:  I own the weakness of my foolish heart,  And hoped to find that happiness in love,  Which glory, wealth, and empire, cannot give  It hurts my pride to think how I was spurned  By that contemptuous woman; she shall know,  At least, and see the object of her scorn  To have her mourn the honors that she lost  In losing Genghis will be some revenge

**Octar**: The shouts of victory, and the voice of fame,  Have been so long familiar to my ears,  That I have little relish for the plaints  Of whining love

**Genghis**: Nor has thy friend indulged  That fatal passion since her proud refusal:  I own the fair Idame won my heart,  By charms unknown before: our barren deserts  Could never produce a face like hers, a mind  So formed to please; her every motion fired  My captive soul, but her imprudent scorn  Restored my freedom; nobler objects claim  A monarch's care; I'll think no more of her,  Let her repent at leisure of her pride  Octar, I charge thee, talk not of Idame.

**Octar**: You have, indeed, affairs of greater moment  That call for your attention

**Genghis**: Then farewell  To love, and all its follies

### SCENE VII
Genghis, Octar, Osman

**Osman:** O my lord, The victim was prepared, the guard was ranged On every side, when (wonderful to tell!) A strange event perplexed us all.—A woman Of frantic mien, with wild dishevelled hair, And bathed in tears, rushed in upon us; "stop," Aloud she cried, "inhuman ruffians, stop, It is my son, you've been deceived; 'tis not The emperor's child, but mine:" her eyes, her voice, Her fury, her despair, her every gesture, Was nature's language all, and spoke the mother: When lo! her husband came, with downcast eyes And gloomy aspect; sullenly he cried, "This is the royal orphan, this the blood, Which you demanded, take it:" as he spake, Fast flowed his tears. The wretched matron, pale And motionless awhile, as struck with death, Fell prostrate; then, long as her faltering voice Could utter the imperfect sound, cried out, "Give me my son:" her sorrows were sincere, Never was grief more bitter, doubts arose Amongst us, and I came to know your orders

**Genghis:** If 'tis the work of art, I will explore The mystery soon, and woe to the deceivers: Think they to cast a veil before my eyes, And mock their sovereign? let them if they dare

**Octar:** My lord, this woman never can deceive us; The emperor's son was placed beneath her care; A master's child might easily attract The faithful servant's love, and danger make The charge more precious still; the ties of nature Are not more strong than those of fantasy: But we shall soon unravel it

**Genghis:** Who is This woman?

**Octar:** Wife of a proud Mandarin: One of those lettered sages who defy The power of kings; a numerous band! but now, Thank heaven, reduced by thy victorious arms To slavery: Zamti is the traitor's name Who watches o'er the victim

**Genghis:** Go, my Octar, Interrogate this guilty pair, and learn, If possible, the truth: let all our guards Be ready at their posts: they talk, it seems, Of a surprise that the Koreans mean To march against us on the river's bank: An army hath been seen: we soon shall know What bold adventurers are so fond of death, To court destruction from the sons of war, And force them to depopulate the world

# ACT III

**SCENE I**
Genghis, Octar, Osman, Attendants

**Genghis**: What say the captives, is the fraud discovered, And vengeance taken on these vile impostors? Have they delivered up the orphan prince To Octar?

**Osman**: Prayers, and threats, and torments, all Are vain: the undaunted Zamti still persists In his first answer: on his open brows Are engraved the marks of truth: the mournful fair one, Whose grief but adds new lustre to her charms, With tears incessant and heart-rending sighs, Moves every heart: spite of ourselves we wept Her wretched fate: ne'er did my eyes behold A sweeter mourner: she entreats to see And speak with you; the conqueror of kings, She hopes, will hear the wretched, and in wrath Remember mercy; that he will protect A guiltless child, and show mankind his goodness Is like his power, unlimited. 'Twas thus, My lord, she spoke of you, and I have promised She shall have audience

**Genghis**: [To one of the attendants] Bid her enter now, We shall unravel this deep mystery; But let her not imagine a few sighs, And bidden tears, can e'er impose on me: I have experienced all these female arts, But I defy them now: let her be careful, Her life depends on her sincerity

**Osman**: My lord, she comes

**Genghis**: What do I see? O heaven! It cannot be Idame, sure my senses—

## SCENE II

Genghis, Idame, Octar, Osman, Guards

**Idame**: My lord, I came not to solicit pardon, My forfeit life is yours, I ask not for it: Why should I wish for years of added woe? But spare a guiltless infant

**Genghis**: Rise, Idame, Fate conquers all, it has deceived us both If heaven hath raised a poor inhabitant Of Scythia, once the object of your scorn, To power, and splendor, you have naught to fear: The emperor never will avenge the wrongs Of Temugin; but public good demands The royal victim; 'tis a sacrifice Which must be made: for your own son, myself Will be his guard: I promise to protect him

**Idame**: Then I am happy

**Genghis**: But inform me, madam, What is this fraud, this mystery between you? For I must know it all

**Idame**: O spare the wretched

**Genghis**: Have I not cause to hate this Zamti? **Idame**: You, My lord?

**Genghis**: I've said too much

**Idame**: Restore my child, You've promised it

**Genghis**: His pardon must depend On you alone: you know I have been injured, My favors scorned, my orders disobeyed: Who is this Zamti, this respected lord, This husband? in that name alone comprised Is every guilt: what charms has he to boast Who braves me thus?

**Idame**: He was my only comfort, My joy, my happiness, the best of men; He served his God, his country, and his king

**Genghis**: How long, Idame, have you been united?

**Idame**: Ever since the fatal time, when wayward fortune Espoused thy cause, and gave a tyrant power To scourge mankind

**Genghis**: I understand you, madam, E'er since the time you mean, when I was scorned By a proud beauty, when this country first Deserved the chains which it was doomed to wear

### SCENE III

Genghis, Octar, Osman
[On one side of the stage Idame, and Zamti On the other, Guards.]

**Genghis**: What sayest thou, slave? hast thou delivered up The emperor's son?

**Zamti**: I have, my lord, 'tis done: I have fulfilled my duty

**Genghis**: Well thou knowest Nor fraud, nor insolence escape my vengeance: If thou hast dared to hide him from my wrath, He must be found, his death shall follow thine [To the guards] Seize and destroy that infant

**Zamti**: Wretched father! **Idame**: Stay, cruel tyrant, stay, is this your pity, Is this your promise?

**Genghis**: I have been deceived; Explain the mystery, madam, or he dies

**Idame**: I'll tell thee all; and if it be a crime To follow nature, and obey her laws, If still thy cruel spirit thirsts for blood, Let all your anger light on me, but spare The noble Zamti: to our mutual care The emperor entrusted his dear son: Thou knowest too well what scenes of horrid slaughter Followed thy cruel victory, and marked Thy steps with blood; that might have satisfied A less inhuman conqueror: when thy slaves Demanded our last hope, the royal heir, My generous Zamti, faithful to his king, To duty gave up all, and sacrificed His son, nor listened to the powerful voice Of nature; I admired that patriot firmness I had not strength to imitate: alas! I am a mother, how could I consent To my child's death? my terrors, my despair, My rage, my anguish, all too plainly spoke What Zamti strove to hide: behold, my lord, The wretched father, he deserves your pity: So does my guiltless infant: punish me, And me alone: forgive me, dearest Zamti, Forgive a mother's tenderness, forgive A wife that loves thee and would save thy son

**Zamti**: I have forgiven thee, and, thank heaven, my king, The royal infant's safe

**Genghis:** 'Tis false; begone, And find him, traitor, or thou diest; atone For thy past crimes

**Zamti:** The crime were to obey A tyrant, but my royal master's voice Cries from the tomb, and bids me tell thee, Genghis, Thou art my conqueror, but not my king: Were Zamti born thy subject, he had been Most faithful to thee: I have sacrificed My son, and thinkest thou I can fear to die?

**Genghis:** [To the guard] Away with him

**Idame:** O stay

**Genghis:** I'll hear no more

**Idame:** I have deserved thy anger, I alone Should feel thy vengeance: thou hast slain my king, And now my husband and my child must fall By thy destructive hand: inhuman tyrant, When will thy wrath be satisfied?

**Genghis:** Away: Follow thy guilty husband: darest thou plead For mercy, thou reproach me?

**Idame:** Then all hope Is lost

**Genghis:** If ever I think of clemency, It must not be till ample reparation Is made for all my wrongs: you understand me

## SCENE IV
Genghis, Octar

**Genghis:** What means this fluttering heart, and wherefore thus Steals from my breast the involuntary sigh? Some power divine protects her: O my Octar, What secret charms have innocence and beauty, That proud authority should thus submit To own their influence? I have lost myself And want a friend; O lend me thy kind counsel

**Octar:** Since I must speak, I'll speak with freedom; know then This dangerous branch of a detested race Must be cut off, or we are not secure In our new conquest; victory's best guard Is rigor; by severity alone Your power can be established. Time, my lord, Will bring back order and tranquillity; The people by degrees forget their wrongs, Or pardon them: you then may reign in peace

**Genghis:** And can it be Idame, that proud beauty, Given to another, to my mortal foe! **Octar:** She merits not your pity, but your hate; I cannot, must not think you ever loved her; 'Twas but a short and momentary flame, That sparkled and expired; her cruel scorn, Her proud refusal, and the hand of time, Have quite extinguished it; she is no more To Genghis now than the ignoble wife, Of an abandoned traitor

**Genghis:** He shall die; A slave! a rival!

**Octar:** Wherefore lives he yet? Strike, and revenge thyself

**Genghis**: I know not why, But my fond heart still trembles at the thought Of injuring her: subdued by beauty's tears I dare not hurt a rival and a slave; Even in the husband I respect the wife: Is love indeed so great a conqueror, And must I grace his triumphs?

**Octar**: All I know, And all I wish for, is to follow thee, The rattling chariot, and the sounding bow, The fiery coursers, and the din of arms: These are my passions, these the joys of Octar: I am a stranger to the sighs of love, And think them far beneath the royal soul Of Genghis; they debase a character So great as thine

**Genghis**: I know my power, I know That I could make her mine: but what avails The fairest form without the conquered heart? Where is the joy to press within our arms A trembling slave? to see her beauteous eyes Forever bathed in tears, and her full heart Oppressed with sorrow? 'tis a barbarous triumph: The savage herd, that through the forest roam, Enjoy more peace, and boast a purer love: The fair Idame has some secret power That charms me more than victory and empire: I thought I could have driven her from my heart, But she returns, and triumphs

### SCENE V
Genghis, Octar, Osman

**Genghis**: Well: what says she?

**Osman**: That she will perish with her husband rather Than tell the place where, hid from every eye, The orphan lies concealed; the tender husband Supports her in his arms; with added courage Inspires her soul, and teaches her to die They wish to be united in the grave; The people throng around, and every eye Is wet with tears, lamenting their sad fate

**Genghis**: And does Idame talk of death from me? Fly, Osman, fly, tell her I hold her life As sacred as my own: away

### SCENE VI
Genghis, Octar

**Octar**: This infant, Concerning him, my lord—what's to be done?
**Genghis**: Nothing
**Octar**: You gave commands he should be torn Even from Idame's bosom
**Genghis**: We must think Of that hereafter
**Octar**: What if they should hide—
**Genghis**: He cannot escape us
**Octar**: Still they may deceive you
**Genghis**: Idame is incapable of fraud
**Octar**: And would you then preserve the royal race?

**Genghis**: I would preserve Idame; for the rest 'Tis equal all, dispose it as thou wilt Go, bring her hither—stay—my Octar—try If thou canst soften this rebellious slave, This Zamti, and persuade him to obey me We will not heed this infant; he shall make me A nobler sacrifice

**Octar**: Who, he, my lord?

**Genghis**: Ay, he

**Octar**: What hopest thou?

**Genghis**: To subdue Idame, To see her, to adore her, to be loved By that ungrateful fair one; or to take My full revenge, to punish her, and die

# ACT IV

### SCENE I

**Genghis**: [A troop of Tartar soldiers] Are these my promised joys? is this the fruit Of all my labors? where's the liberty, The rest I hoped for? I but feel the weight Without the joys of power: I want Idame, And, instead of her, a crowd of busy slaves Are ever thronging round me [To his attendants] Hence, away, And guard the city walls; these proud Koreans May think to find us unprepared; already, It seems, they have proclaimed their orphan king; But I'll be duped no longer; he shall die I am distracted with a thousand cares, Dangers, and plots, and foes on every side; Intruding rivals, and a wayward people, Oppress me: when I was a poor unknown I was more happy

### SCENE II

Octar, Genghis

**Genghis**: Well, my friend, you've seen This proud presumptuous Mandarin: what says he?

**Octar**: He is inflexible; nor threats alarm Nor promises allure him; still he talks Of duty and of virtue, as if we Were vanquished slaves, and he the conqueror I blush to think how we demeaned ourselves, By talking to a wretch, whom by a word We might destroy: let the ungrateful pair Perish together; mutual is their crime, And mutual be their punishment

**Genghis**: 'Tis strange, That sentiments like these, to us unknown, Should rise in mortal breasts: without a groan, A murmur, or complaint, a father breaks The ties of nature, and would sacrifice His child to please the manes of his sovereign, And the fond wife would die to save her lord The more I see, the more must I admire This wondrous people, great in arts and arms, In learning and in manners great; their kings On wisdom's basis founded all their power; They gave the nations law, by virtue reigned, And governed without conquest;

naught hath heaven Bestowed on us but force; our only art Is cruel war; our business to destroy What have I gained by all my victories, By all my guilty laurels stained with blood? The tears, the sighs, the curses of mankind Perhaps, my friend, there is a nobler fame, And worthier of our search: my heart in secret Is jealous of their virtues; I would wish, All conqueror as I am, to imitate The vanquished

**Octar**: Can you then admire their weakness? What are their boasted arts, the puny offspring Of luxury and vice, that cannot save them From slavery and death? the strong and brave Are born to rule, the feeble to obey: Labor and courage conquer all; but you Tamely submit, a voluntary slave: And must the brave companions of your toil Behold their honor stained, their glory lost, Their king dependent on a woman's smile? Their honest hearts with indignation glow; By me they speak, by me reproach thee, Genghis: Excuse a friend, a fellow soldier, grown Old in thy service; one who cannot bear This amorous sickness of the soul, and longs To guide thy footsteps to the paths of glory

**Genghis**: Go, fetch Idame

**Octar**: What, my lord—

**Genghis**: Obey: Nor dare to murmur; 'tis a subject's part To reverence even the weakness of his master

### SCENE III

**Genghis**: [Alone.] 'Tis not in mortals to resist their fate; She must be mine; what's victory without her? I have made thousands wretched, and am now Myself unhappy: 'midst the venal crowd Of slaves that court my favor, is there one That can relieve the anguish of my soul, Or fill my heart with real bliss? I wanted Some happy error, some delusive joy, To mitigate the sorrows of a king, And lessen the oppressive weight of empire; But Octar, who should heal, hath probed my wounds Too deeply; I have none but monsters round me, Blood-thirsty slaves, unfeeling, merciless, And cruel, disciplined to blood and slaughter: O for a few soft hours of gentle love To brighten this dark scene! they shall not judge, Shall not arraign the conduct of their king: Where is Idame?—ha! she comes

### SCENE IV

Genghis, Idame

**Idame**: My lord, 'Tis cruel to insult a friendless woman, And add fresh weight to her calamities

**Genghis**: Be not alarmed; your husband yet may live; My vengeance is suspended for a while, And for thy sake I will be merciful: Perhaps it was decreed by heaven Idame Should be reserved to captivate her master, To bend the stubborn fierceness of his nature, And soften his rude heart: you understand me; My laws permit divorce: embrace the offer, And make the sovereign of the world your own I know you love me not, but think what joys Surround a throne; think how thy country's good, Her welfare, and her happiness depend On thy resolve: I know it moves thy wonder To see a haughty conqueror at thy feet: Forget my power, forget my cruelty, Weigh your own interest well, and speak my fate

**Idame**: I am indeed surprised, and so perhaps Will Genghis be when I shall answer him: There was a time, my lord, you well remember, When he who holds the subject world in awe, This terror of the nations, was no more Than a poor soldier, friendless and unknown; He offered me the pure unspotted heart Of Temugin, and I with pleasure then Would have received it

**Genghis**: Ha! couldst thou have loved me?

**Idame**: Perhaps I might; but those to whom I owe My first obedience doomed me to another: Thou knowest the power of parents o'er their children; They are the image of that God we serve, And next to them should be obeyed: this empire Was founded on paternal right, on justice, Honor, and public faith, and holy marriage; And if it be the sacred will of heaven That it must fall a sacrifice to thee, And thy successful crimes, the enlivening spirit That long supported it shall never perish: Your fate has changed; Idame's never can

**Genghis**: Couldst thou have loved me then?

**Idame**: I could, my lord, And therefore never must hereafter think On Genghis; I am bound in sacred bonds To Zamti; nay, I'll tell thee more; I love him, Prefer him to the splendor of a throne, And all the honors thou canst lavish on me: Think not it soothes my vanity to spurn A conqueror, all I wish is to fulfil My duty, and do justice to myself: Bestow your favors on some grateful heart, Worthier than mine, that will with joy receive them: May I implore you to conceal from Zamti These proffered terms? 'twould wound his soul to think My truth to him had ever thus been questioned

**Genghis**: He knows what I expect, and will obey If he desires to live

**Idame**: He never will: Though cruel torments should extort from him A feigned submission, my firm constancy Would soon recall him to the paths of duty, Of honor, truth, and virtue

**Genghis**: Can it be, When this ungenerous husband would have given Thy son to death?

**Idame**: He did: he loved his country: It was a noble crime, and I forgive him: He acted like a hero, and Idame Like the fond mother: even if I had hated I would not have been false to him

**Genghis**: Amazing! Resistance but inflames my passion for thee, And the more injured, I but love thee more: Yet know, I have a soul that's capable Of rage as well as tenderness

**Idame**: I know Thou art the master here, and life or death Depend on thee: but tremble at the laws

**Genghis**: The laws! they are no more, or in my will Alone are to be found; your laws already Have been too fatal to me; they prevented That happy union which my soul desired, And bound thee to another; but they are void, And stand dissolved by my superior power: Obey me, madam, I have given my orders, And I expect your husband should deliver Into my hands the emperor and Idame: Remember, Zamti's life depends on you: Let prudence teach you to disarm the wrath Of an offended king, who, blushing, owns His foolish fondness for a worthless woman

SCENE V

Idame, Asseli

**Idame**: Thou seest my wretched fate; the tyrant leaves me The cruel choice of infamy or death O, Zamti, I must yield thee to thy fate

**Asseli**: Rather exert the power which beauty gives thee O'er the proud Scythian, you have found the art To please him

**Idame**: Would I had not! that, alas! But makes me more unhappy

**Asseli**: You alone Might soften all the rigor of our fate; For you already his relenting soul Withheld its fierceness; you subdued his rage; Zamti still lives, his rival, and his foe: This bloody conqueror stands in awe of thee, And dare not hurt him: here he first beheld Thy lovely form, here paid his guiltless vows

**Idame**: No more: it were a crime to think of them

SCENE VI

Zamti, Idame, Asseli

**Idame**: Zamti! what brought thee hither? what kind power Hath thus restored thee to my arms?

**Zamti**: The tyrant Hath given me this short respite; by his orders I came to seek thee

**Idame**: Hast thou heard, my Zamti, The shameful terms proposed to save thy life, And the dear Orphan's?

**Zamti**: Mine's not worth thy care: What is the loss of one unhappy being Amidst the general ruin? O Idame, Remember my first duty is to save My king; whate'er we boast, whate'er we love, To him we owe it all, except our honor, That only good which we can call our own I have concealed the Orphan 'midst the tombs Of his great ancestors, unless we soon Fly to relieve him, he must perish there   Korea's generous prince in vain expects him:   Etan, our faithful servant, is in chains;   Thou art our only hope; preserve the life   Of thy dear infant, and thy husband's honor

**Idame**: What wouldst thou have me do?

**Zamti**: Forget me, live   But for thy country, give up all to that, And that alone; heaven points out the fair path   Of glory to thee, and a husband's death, For Zamti soon must die, shall leave thee free   To act as best may serve the common cause:   Enslave the Tartar, make him all thy own;   And yet to leave thee to that proud usurper   Will make the pangs of death more bitter to me:   It is a dreadful sacrifice, but duty   Spreads sweet content o'er all that she inspires: Idame, be a mother to thy king,   And reign; remember, 'tis my last command, Preserve thy sovereign, and be happy

**Idame**: Stay,   Thou knowest me not: thinkest thou I'll ever purchase   Those shameful honors with my Zamti's blood?   O thou art doubly guilty; love and nature   Cry out against thee! barbarous to thy son, And still more cruel to thy wife.   O Zamti,   Heaven points us out a nobler way to death   The tyrant, whether from contempt or love   I know not, leaves me at full liberty;   I am not watched, or guarded here;   I know   Each secret path and avenue that leads   To the dark tombs where thou hast hid the king;   Thither I'll fly, and to Korea's chief   Bear the rich prize, the nation's only hope,   The royal infant, as a gift from heaven: I know 'twill be in vain, and we must die;   But we shall die with glory; we shall leave   Behind us names that, worthy of remembrance,   shall shine forever in the rolls of time   Now, Zamti, have I followed thy example?

**Zamti**: Thou gracious God, who hast inspired, support her!   I blush, my love, at thy superior virtue;   Heaven grant thee power to save thy king and country!

# ACT V

### SCENE I
Idame, Asseli

**Asseli**: All then is lost; twice in one fatal day   Have I beheld thee made a slave:   alas!   What could a helpless woman unsupported   Against a mighty conqueror?

**Idame**: I have done   What duty bade me, carried in my arms   The royal infant; for a while his presence   Inspired our troops, but Genghis came, and death   Followed his steps, the savage herd prevailed,   And bore down all before them;   I was made   Once more a captive

**Asseli**: Zamti then must perish,   And share his master's fate

**Idame:** They both must die: Perhaps some cruel torments, worse than death, Already are prepared; my son perhaps Must follow them: to triumph o'er my grief, And aggravate my sorrows, the proud tyrant Called me before him: how his looks appalled My shrinking soul, when thrice he lifted up His bloody hand against the wretched infants! Trembling I stepped between, and at his feet Fell prostrate; rudely then he pushed me from him, And turned aside; the savage guards around Seemed waiting for his orders to despatch me

**Asseli:** He cannot, dare not do it: still, thou seest, Zamti is spared, the orphan king still lives; Let but Idame sue to him for pardon, And all will be forgiven

**Idame:** O no; his love Is turned to rage; he smiled at my distress, Laughed at my tears, and vowed eternal hatred

**Asseli:** And yet you may subdue him; the fierce lion Roars in the toils, and bites his chain; he would not Thus talk of hatred if he did not love

**Idame:** Whether he loves or hates, 'tis time to end This wretched being

**Asseli:** What have you resolved?

**Idame:** When heaven hath poured out all its wrath upon us, And filled up the sad measure of our woes, It gives us courage to support our griefs, And suits our strength to our calamities: I feel new force, new vigor in my heart, 'Midst all my sorrows; henceforth I defy The tyrant, and am mistress of my fate

**Asseli:** But can you leave your child, the dear loved object Of all your hopes and fears?

**Idame:** There Asseli, You pierce my heart: O dreadful sacrifice! I have done all to save him: the usurper Will not descend so low as to destroy A helpless infant; for his mother's sake, Whom once he loved, perhaps may spare my child; That pleasing hope at least will soothe my soul In the dark hour of death: he will relent When I am gone, nor carry his fierce wrath Beyond the grave, to persecute my son

SCENE II
Idame, Asseli, Octar

**Octar:** Madam, you must attend the emperor [To the guards] Guard you these infants; watch the door, that none May pass this way [To Asseli] You, madam, may retire

**Idame:** The emperor send for me?—but I obey Could I have seen my Zamti first! perhaps It is a vain request: does pity never Dwell in a Tartar's breast? might I implore Your friendship to assist me?

**Octar:** No: when once The royal word is passed, to offer counsel Is little less than treason: you had kings Indeed of old who gave up all their rights, And let their subjects rule; but manners change With times; we listen not to idle prayers, Nor yield to woman's tears; by arms alone We rule the subject world: therefore obey, And wait the emperor's commands

SCENE III
**Idame**: [Alone.] Thou God Of the afflicted, who beholdest my wrongs, Support me now, inspire me with a portion Of my dear Zamti's courage

SCENE IV
Genghis Khan, Idame
**Genghis**: Genghis comes Once more to humble thy proud soul; to show thee Thy foul ingratitude, thy base return For all my kindness to thee; yet thou knowest not How guilty thou hast been; thou knowest not yet Thy danger, nor the anguish of my soul; Thou whom I loved and whom I ought to hate, To punish, to destroy

**Idame**: Then punish me, And me alone; 'tis all I ask of Genghis: Finish a life of misery, satiate here Thy thirst of blood: Idame hath been faithful, That is a crime thou never canst forgive: Strike then, and be revenged

**Genghis**: Thou knowest I cannot; Thou knowest I am more wretched than thyself; But I'm resolved: the Orphan, and thy son, Are in my power: for Zamti, he has long Deserved to die; the rebel braves my wrath, And yet I spare him; if you wish his life You must forget him; death will break the chain That binds you; then I might with justice seize And make you mine; but know, this proud barbarian, This Scythian tyrant, whom you treat with scorn, Is not unworthy of Idame's love: Abjure your marriage, and I'll raise your child To equal rank and splendor with my own: The orphan shall be safe, your husband spared; Their lives, their welfare, and their happiness, The happiness of Genghis, all depend On thee, Idame; for I love thee still: But think not I will bear thy cruel insults, Thy tyrant scorn, and all the pride of beauty: My soul, thou knowest, is violent; take heed, Provoke it not, least vengeance fall upon thee Speak the decisive word that must determine The fate of Genghis, and his empire; say, Or must I love or hate Idame?

**Idame**: Neither: Your hatred were unjust, your love most guilty, And most unworthy of us both: I ask Your justice; I demand it; 'tis a debt Which a king owes to all: if you have lost, I would restore it to you, and, in secret, I know your conscience justifies Idame.

**Genghis**: Then hatred is your choice; 'tis well; henceforth Expect the vengeance of an injured monarch: Your prince, your husband, and your son shall pay For proud Idame's scorn, and with their blood Atone for her ingratitude: their doom Was sealed by thee, thou art their murderer

**Idame**: Barbarous, inhuman Genghis

**Genghis:** So I am, Thanks to thy kind regard! you might have had A tender love, but you chose a master Proud, merciless, and savage, one whose hatred Is equal to thy own

**Idame:** He is my king; As such I reverence him: this single boon, Low on my knees entreat

**Genghis:** Idame, rise; Speak, I attend: perhaps some kinder thoughts—

**Idame:** Might Zamti be permitted for a while To visit me in secret?

**Genghis:** What?

**Idame:** My lord, But for a moment, 'tis my last request; Perhaps it may be better for us both

**Genghis:** 'Tis strange: but be it so: perhaps the slave, Taught by calamity, that best of masters, No longer will desire the fatal honor Of being rival to a conqueror: On you his fate depends; divorce, or death: Give him the choice [To Octar] Watch here [To the guards] Guards, follow me: Still am I wavering, still unhappy; still Is Genghis doomed to be the slave of love [Exit]

**Idame:** [Alone] Once more Idame lives; methinks I feel New strength and vigor shoot through every vein: Now, Genghis, I defy thee!

## SCENE V
Zamti, Idame

**Idame:** O my Zamti, Dearer to me than all those conquerors, Whom servile mortals flatter into gods; My other deity, to whom in vain I never sue: alas, my love, too well Thou knowest our fate; the dreadful hour is come

**Zamti:** I know it is

**Idame:** In vain thy patriot care Strove to preserve the orphan king

**Zamti:** That hope Is lost; we'll think no more on it: thou hast done Thy every duty, and I die content

**Idame:** What will become of our dear child? forgive A mother, Zamti; I have shown some courage, And therefore thou wilt pardon me

**Zamti:** The kings Of Cathay are no more; the nobles held In ignominious chains; they most deserve Our pity, who are still condemned to live

**Idame:** O they have doomed thee to a shameful death

**Zamti:** 'Tis what I've long expected

**Idame:** Hear me then; Is there no path to death but from the palace? Bulls bleed at the altar; criminals are dragged To punishment; but generous minds are masters Of their own fate: why meet it from the hands Of Genghis? were we born dependent thus On others' wills? no; let us imitate Our bolder neighbors, live with ease, and die When life grows burdensome: wrongs unrevenged To them are insupportable, and death More welcome far than infamy: they wait not For a proud tyrant's nod, but meet their fate: We've taught these islanders some useful arts, And wherefore deign we not to learn from them Some necessary virtues?—let us die

**Zamti:** Yes: I approve thy noble resolution, And think, extremity of sorrow mocks The power of laws; but wretched slaves, disarmed As we are, and bowed down beneath our tyrants, Must wait the blow

**Idame:** [Drawing out a poniard] Strike, Zamti, and be free

**Zamti:** O heaven!

**Idame:** Strike here, my Zamti, this weak arm Perhaps might err; thy firmer hand will best Direct the fatal stroke; now sacrifice A faithful wife, and let her husband fall Beside her: yes, my love, we'll die together; With jealous eye the tyrant shall behold us Expiring in each other's arms

**Zamti:** Thank heaven! Thy virtue never fails; this is the last The dearest mark of my Idame's love; Receive my last farewell; give me the dagger: Now turn aside

**Idame:** There, take it [Gives him the dagger] Kill me first; Thou tremblest

**Zamti:** O I cannot

**Idame:** Strike, my lord

**Zamti:** I shudder at the thought

**Idame:** O cruel Zamti, Strike here, and then—

**Zamti:** I will—now follow me [Attempts to stab himself

**Idame:** [Laying hold of his arm] You must not—here, my lord—

SCENE VI

Genghis, Octar, Idame

**Zamti:** Guards

**Genghis:** O heaven! disarm him [Guards disarm him What would ye do?

**Idame:** We would have freed ourselves From misery and thee

**Zamti:** Thou wilt not envy us The privilege to die

**Genghis:** Indeed I will: O power supreme, thou witness of my wrongs And of my weakness, thou who hast subdued So many kings for me, shall I at last Be worthy of thy goodness?—Zamti, thou Still triumphest o'er me; she whom I adored, Thy wife, had rather die by thy loved hand Than live with Genghis: but ye both shall learn To bear my yoke, perhaps yet more

**Idame:** What sayest thou?

**Zamti:** For what new scene of inhumanity Are we reserved?

**Idame:** Why is our fate concealed?

**Genghis:** Be not impatient; ye shall know it soon Ye've done me ample justice, be it mine Now to return it: I admire you both; You have subdued me, and I blush to sit On Cathay's throne, whilst there are souls like yours So much above me; vainly have I tried By glorious deeds to build myself a name

Among the nations; you have humbled me, And I would equal you: I did not know That mortals could be masters of themselves; That greatest glory I have learned from you: I am not what I was; to you I owe The wondrous change; I come to reunite, To save, and to protect you: watch, Idame, Your prince's tender years; to thee I give The precious charge, by right of conquest mine; Hereafter I will be a father to him: At length you may confide in Genghis; once I was a conqueror, now I am a king [To Zamti  Zamti, be thou our law's interpreter, And make the world as good and pure as thou art; Teach reason, justice, and morality, And let the conquered rule the conquerors; Let wisdom reign, and still direct our valor; Let prudence triumph over strength; her king Will set the example, and your conqueror Henceforth shall be obedient to your law

**Idame**: What do I hear?

**Zamti**: Thou art indeed our king, And we shall bless thy sway

**Idame**: What could inspire This great design, and work this change?

**Genghis**: Thy virtues

**End.**

# Mahomet

## Contents

Dramatis Personæ............................. 421

A Letter to His Majesty the King of Prussia................. 421

A Letter From M. De Voltaire to Pope Benedict XIV............. 425

The Answer of Pope Benedict........................ 426

A Letter of Thanks From M. De Voltaire to the Pope............. 426

Act I. ........................................ 427

Act II......................................... 433

Act III........................................ 440

Act IV........................................ 446

Act V......................................... 452

## Dramatis Personæ

Mahomet.
Zopir, Sheik of Mecca.
Omar, General and second in command to Mahomet.
Seid, Slave to Mahomet.
Palmira, Slave to Mahomet.
Phanor, Senator of Mecca.
Company of Meccans.
Company of Mussulmans.

This powerful work was read by Voltaire to Frederick of Prussia in 1740, to the king's great delight. The following correspondence has peculiar interest. In his "Life of Voltaire" James Parton says: "The great lesson of the play is that the founders of false religions at once despise and practise upon the docile credulity of men. When I remember that this powerful exhibition of executive force triumphing over credulity and weakness was vividly stamped upon the susceptible brain of Frederick by Voltaire's impassioned declamation, at the very time he was revolving his Silesian project, I am inclined to the conjecture that it may have been the deciding influence upon the king's mind." The play was withdrawn after the fourth representation, under pressure of Church authorities who professed to see in it a "bloody satire against the Christian religion." This letter preserves the original characteristics.

To His Majesty the King of Prussia.

Rotterdam, January 20, 1742.

Sir:

I am at present, like the pilgrims of Mecca, turning their eyes perpetually towards that city after leaving it, as I do mine towards the court of Prussia. My heart, deeply penetrated with the sense of your majesty's goodness, knows no grief but that which arises from my incapacity of being always with you. I have taken the liberty to send your majesty a fresh copy of "Mahomet," the sketch of which you have seen some time ago. This is a tribute which I pay to the lover of arts, the sensible critic, and above all, to the philosopher much more than to the sovereign. Your majesty knows by what motive I was inspired in the composition of that work. The love of mankind, and the hatred of fanaticism, two virtues that adorn your throne, guided my pen: I have ever been of opinion, that tragedy should correct, as well as move the heart. Of what consequence or importance to mankind are the passions or misfortunes of any of the heroes of antiquity, if they do not convey some instruction to us? It is universally acknowledged, that the comedy of "Tartuffe," a piece hitherto unequalled, did a great deal of good in the world, by showing hypocrisy in its proper light; and why therefore should we not endeavor in a tragedy to expose that species of imposture which sets to work the hypocrisy of some, and the madness of others? Why may we not go back to the histories of those ancient ruffians, the illustrious founders of superstition and fanaticism, who first carried the sword to the altar to sacrifice all those who refused to embrace their doctrines?

They who tell us that these days of wickedness are past, that we shall never see any more Barcochebas, Mahomets, Johns of Leyden, etc., and that the flames of religious war are totally extinguished, in my opinion, pay too high a compliment to human nature. The same poison still subsists, though it does not appear so openly—some symptoms of this plague break out from time to time—enough to infect the earth: have not we in our own age seen the prophets of Cévennes killing in the name of God those of their sect, who were not sufficiently pliant to their purposes?

The action I have described is terrible; I do not know whether horror was ever carried farther on any stage. A young man born with virtuous inclinations, seduced by fanaticism, assassinates an old man who loves him; and whilst he imagines he is serving God, is, without knowing it, guilty of parricide: the murder is committed by the order of an impostor, who promises him a reward, which proves to be incest. This, I acknowledge, is full of horror; but your majesty is thoroughly sensible, that tragedy should not consist merely of love, jealousy, and marriage: even our histories abound in actions much more horrible than that which I have invented. Seid does not know that the person whom he assassinates is his father, and when he has committed the crime, feels the deepest remorse for it; but Mézeray tells us, that at Milan a father killed his son with his own hand on account of religion, and was not in the least sorry for it. The story of the two brothers Diaz is well known; one of them was at Rome and the other in Germany, in the beginning of the commotions raised by Luther: Bartholomew Diaz, hearing that his brother embraced the opinion of Luther at Frankfort, left Rome on purpose to assassinate him, and accordingly did so. Herrera, a Spanish author, tells us, that Bartholomew Diaz ran a great hazard in doing this, but nothing intimidates a man of honor guided by honesty. Herrera, we see, brought up in that holy religion which is an enemy to cruelty, a religion which teaches long-suffering and not revenge, was persuaded that honesty might make a man an assassin and a parricide: ought we not to rise up on all sides against such infernal maxims? These put the poniard into the hand of that monster who deprived France of Henry the Great: these placed the picture of James Clement on the altar, and his name amongst the saints: these took away the life of William, prince of Orange, founder of the liberty and prosperity of his country. Salcede shot at and wounded him in the forehead with a pistol; and Strada tells us, that Salcede would not dare to undertake that enterprise till he had purified his soul by confession at the feet of a Dominican, and fortified it by the holy sacrament. Herrera has something more horrible, and more ridiculous concerning it. "He stood firm," says he, "after the example of our Saviour, Jesus Christ, and His saints." Balthasar Girard, who afterwards took away the life of that great man, behaved in the same manner as Salcede.

I have remarked, that all those who voluntarily committed such crimes were young men like Seid. Balthasar Girard was about twenty years old, and the four Spaniards who had bound themselves by oath with him to kill the prince, were of the same age. The monster who killed Henry III., was but four-and-twenty, and Poltrot, who assassinated the great Duke of Guise only twenty-five: this is the age of seduction and madness. In England I was once a witness to how far the power of fanaticism could work on a weak and youthful imagination: a boy of sixteen, whose name was Shepherd, engaged to assassinate King George I., your majesty's grandfather by the mother's side. What could prompt him to such madness? the only reason to be assigned was, that Shepherd was not of the same religion with the king. They took pity on his youth, offered him his pardon, and for a long time endeavored to bring him to repentance; but he always persisted in saying, it was better to obey God than man; and if they let him go, the first use he made of his liberty should be to kill the king: so that they were obliged at last to execute him as a monster, whom they despaired of bringing to any sense of reason.

I will venture to affirm that all who have seen anything of mankind must have remarked how easily nature is sometimes sacrificed to superstition: how many fathers have detested and disinherited their children! how many brothers have persecuted brothers on this destructive principle! I have myself seen instances of it in more than one family.

If superstition does not always signalize itself in those glaring crimes which history transmits to us, in society it does every day all the mischief it possibly can: disunites friends, separates kindred and relations, destroys the wise and worthy by the hands of fools and enthusiasts: it does not indeed every day poison a Socrates, but it banishes Descartes from a city which ought to be the asylum of liberty, and gives Jurieu, who acted the part of a prophet, credit enough to impoverish the wise philosopher Bayle: it banished the successor of the great Leibnitz, and deprives a noble assembly of young men that crowded to his lectures, of pleasure and improvement: and to re-establish him heaven must raise up amongst us a royal philosopher, that true miracle which is so rarely to be seen. In vain does human reason advance towards perfection, by means of that philosophy which of late has made so great a progress in Europe: in vain do you, most noble prince, both inspire and practise this humane philosophy: whilst in the same age wherein reason raises her throne on one side, the most absurd fanaticism adorns her altars on the other.

It may perhaps be objected to me, that, out of my too abundant zeal, I have made Mahomet in this tragedy guilty of a crime which in reality he was not capable of committing. The count de Boulainvilliers, some time since, wrote the life of this prophet, whom he endeavored to represent as a great man, appointed by Providence to punish the Christian world, and change the face of at least one-half of the globe. Mr. Sale likewise, who has given us an excellent translation of the Koran into English, would persuade us to look upon Mahomet as a Numa or a Theseus. I will readily acknowledge, that we ought to respect him, if born a legitimate prince, or called to government by the voice of the people, he had instituted useful and peaceful laws like Numa, or like Theseus defended his countrymen: but for a driver of camels to stir up a faction in his village; to associate himself with a set of wretched Koreish, and persuade them that he had an interview with the angel Gabriel; to boast that he was carried up to heaven, and there received part of that unintelligible book which contradicts common sense in every page; that in order to procure respect for this ridiculous performance he should carry fire and sword into his country, murder fathers, and ravish their daughters, and after all give those whom he conquered the choice of his religion or death; this is surely what no man will pretend to vindicate, unless he was born a Turk, and superstition had totally extinguished in him the light of nature.

Mahomet, I know, did not actually commit that particular crime which is the subject of this tragedy: history only informs us, that he took away the wife of Seid, one of his followers, and persecuted Abusophan, whom I call Zopir; but what is not that man capable of, who, in the name of God, makes war against his country? It was not my design merely to represent a real fact, but real manners and characters, to make men think as they naturally must in their circumstances; but above all it was my intention to show the horrid schemes which villainy can invent, and fanaticism put in practice. Mahomet is here no more than Tartuffe in arms.

Upon the whole I shall think myself amply rewarded for my labor, if any one of those weak mortals, who are ever ready to receive the impressions of a madness foreign to their nature, should learn from this piece to guard themselves against such fatal delusions; if, after being shocked at the dreadful consequences of Seid's obedience, he should say to himself, why must I blindly follow the blind who cry out to me, hate, persecute all who are rash enough not to be of the same opinion with ourselves, even in things and matters we do not understand? what infinite service would it be to mankind to eradicate such false sentiments! A spirit of indulgence would make us all brothers; a spirit of persecution can create nothing but monsters. This I know is your majesty's opinion: to live with such a prince, and such a philosopher, would be my greatest happiness; my sincere attachment can only be equalled by my regret; but if other duties draw me away, they can never blot out the respect I owe to a prince, who talks and thinks like a man, who despises that specious gravity which is always a cover for meanness and ignorance: a prince who converses with freedom, because he is not afraid of being known; who is still eager to be instructed, and at the same time capable himself of instructing the most learned and the most sagacious.

I shall, whilst I have life, remain with the most profound respect, and deepest sense of gratitude, your majesty's,

Voltaire.

A Letter from M. de Voltaire to Pope Benedict XIV.

Most blessed Father—

Your holiness will pardon the liberty taken by one of the lowest of the faithful, though a zealous admirer of virtue, of submitting to the head of the true religion this performance, written in opposition to the founder of a false and barbarous sect. To whom could I with more propriety inscribe a satire on the cruelty and errors of a false prophet, than to the vicar and representative of a God of truth and mercy? Your holiness will therefore give me leave to lay at your feet both the piece and the author of it, and humbly to request your protection of the one, and your benediction upon the other; in hopes of which, with the profoundest reverence, I kiss your sacred feet.

Paris, August 17, 1745.

Voltaire.

The Answer of Pope Benedict XIV. to M. de Voltaire.

Benedictus P. P. dilecto filio salutem & Apostolicam Benedictionem.

This day sevennight I was favored with your excellent tragedy of Mahomet, which I have read with great pleasure: Cardinal Passionei has likewise presented me with your fine poem of Fontenoy. Signor Leprotti this day repeated to me your distich made on my retreat. Yesterday morning Cardinal Valenti gave me your letter of the 17th of August. Many are the obligations which you have conferred on me, for which I am greatly indebted to you, for all and every one of them; and I assure you that I have the highest esteem for your merit, which is so universally acknowledged.

The distich has been published at Rome, and objected to by one of the literati, who, in a public conversation, affirmed that there was a mistake in it with regard to the word hic, which is made short, whereas it ought to be always long. To which I replied, that it may be either long or short; Virgil having made it short in this verse,

Solus hic inflexit sensus, animumque labantem.

And long in another,

Hic finis Priami fatorum, hic exitus illum.

The answer I think was pretty full and convincing, considering that I have not looked into Virgil these fifty years. The cause, however, is properly yours; to your honor and sincerity, therefore, of which I have the highest opinion, I shall leave it to be defended against your opposers and mine, and here give you my apostolical benediction. Datum Romæ apud sanctam Mariam majorem die 19 Sept. Pontificatus nostri anno sexto.

A Letter of Thanks from M. de Voltaire to the Pope.

The features of your excellency are not better expressed on the medal you were so kind as to send me, than are the features of your mind in the letter which you honored me with: permit me to lay at your feet my sincerest acknowledgments: in points of literature, as well as in matters of more importance, your infallibility is not to be disputed: your excellency is much better versed in the Latin tongue than the Frenchman whom you condescended to correct: I am indeed astonished how you could so readily appeal to Virgil: the popes were always ranked amongst the most learned sovereigns, but amongst them I believe there never was one in whom so much learning and taste united.

Agnosco rerum dominos, gentemque togatam.

If the Frenchman who found fault with the word hic had known as much of Virgil as your excellency, he might have recollected a verse where hic is both long and short.

Hic vir hic est tibi quem promitti sæpius audis.

I cannot help considering this verse as a happy presage of the favors conferred on me by your excellency. Thus might Rome cry out when Benedict XIV. was raised to the papacy: with the utmost respect and gratitude I kiss your sacred feet, etc.

Voltaire.

## ACT I.

Scene, Mecca.

SCENE I.

Zopir, Phanor.

**Zopir**: Thinkest thou thy friend will ever bend the knee To this proud hypocrite; shall I fall down And worship, I who banished him from Mecca? No: punish me, just heaven, as I deserve, If e'er this hand, the friend of innocence And freedom, stoop to cherish foul rebellion, Or aid imposture to deceive mankind!

**Phanor**: Thy zeal is noble, and becomes the chief Of Ishmael's sacred senate, but may prove Destructive to the cause it means to serve: Thy ardor cannot check the rapid power Of Mahomet, and but provokes his vengeance: There was a time when you might safely draw The sword of justice, to defend the rights Of Mecca, and prevent the flames of war From spreading o'er the land; then Mahomet Was but a bold and factious citizen, But now he is a conqueror, and a king; Mecca's impostor at Medina shines A holy prophet; nations bend before him, And learn to worship crimes which we abhor. Even here, a band of wild enthusiasts, drunk With furious zeal, support his fond delusions, His idle tales, and fancied miracles: These spread sedition through the gaping throng, Invite his forces, and believe a God Inspires and renders him invincible. The lovers of their country think with you, But wisest counsels are not always followed; False zeal, and fear, and love of novelty Alarm the crowd; already half our city Is left unpeopled; Mecca cries aloud To thee her father, and demands a peace.

**Zopir**: Peace with a traitor! coward nation, what Can you expect but slavery from a tyrant! Go, bend your supple knees, and prostrate fall Before the idol whose oppressive hand Shall crush you all: for me, I hate the traitor; This heart's too deeply wounded to forgive: The savage murderer robbed me of a wife And two dear children: nor is his resentment Less fierce than mine; I forced his camp, pursued The coward to his tent, and slew his son: The torch of hatred is lit up between us, And time can never extinguish it.

**Phanor**: I hope It never will; yet thou shouldst hide the flame, And sacrifice thy griefs to public good: What if he lay this noble city waste, Will that avenge thee, will that serve thy cause? Thou hast lost all, son, brother, daughter, wife. Mecca alone remains to give thee comfort, Do not lose that, do not destroy thy country.

**Zopir**: Kingdoms are lost by cowardice alone.

**Phanor**: As oft perhaps by obstinate resistance.

**Zopir**: Then let us perish, if it be our fate.

**Phanor**: When thou art almost in the harbor, thus To brave the storm is false and fatal courage: Kind heaven, thou seest, points out to thee the means To soften this proud tyrant; fair Palmira, Thy beauteous captive, brought up in the camp Of this destructive conqueror, was sent By gracious heaven, the messenger of peace, Thy guardian angel, to appease the wrath Of Mahomet; already by his herald He has demanded her.

**Zopir**: And wouldst thou have me Give up so fair a prize to this barbarian? What! whilst the tyrant spreads destruction round him, Unpeoples kingdoms, and destroys mankind, Shall beauty's charms be sacrificed to bribe A madman's frenzy? I should envy him That lovely fair one more than all his glory; Not that I feel the stings of wild desire, Or, in the evening of my days, indulge, Old as I am, a shameless passion for her; But, whether objects born like her to please, Spite of ourselves, demand our tenderest pity, Or that perhaps a childless father hopes To find in her another daughter, why I know not, but for that unhappy maid Still am I anxious; be it weakness in me, Or reason's powerful voice, I cannot bear To see her in the hands of Mahomet; Would I could mould her to my wishes, form Her willing mind, and make her hate the tyrant As I do! She has sent to speak with me Here in the sacred porch—and lo! she comes: On her fair cheek the blush of modesty And candor speaks the virtues of her heart.

## SCENE II.

Zopir, Palmira.

**Zopir**: Hail, lovely maid! the chance of cruel war Hath made thee Zopir's captive, but thou art not Amongst barbarians; all with me revere Palmira's virtues, and lament her fate, Whilst youth with innocence and beauty plead Thy cause; whatever thou askest in Zopir's power, Thou shalt not ask in vain: my life declines Towards its period, and if my last hours Can give Palmira joy, I shall esteem them The best, the happiest I have ever known.

**Palmira**: These two months past, my lord, your prisoner here, Scarce have I felt the yoke of slavery; Your generous hand, still raised to soothe affliction,

Hath wiped the tears of sorrow from my eyes, And softened all the rigor of my fate: Forgive me, if emboldened by your goodness I ask for more, and centre every hope Of future happiness on you alone; Forgive me, if to Mahomet's request I join Palmira's, and implore that freedom He hath already asked: O listen to him, And let me say, that after heaven and him I am indebted most to generous Zopir.

*Zopir*: Has then oppression such enticing charms That thou shouldst wish and beg to be the slave Of Mahomet, to hear the clash of arms, With him to live in deserts, and in caves, And wander o'er his ever shifting country?

*Palmira*: Where'er the mind with ease and pleasure dwells, There is our home, and there our native country: He formed my soul; to Mahomet I owe The kind instruction of my earlier years; Taught by the happy partners of his bed, Who still adoring and adored by him Send up their prayers to heaven for his dear safety, I lived in peace and joy! for ne'er did woe Pollute that seat of bliss till the sad hour Of my misfortune, when wide-wasting war Rushed in upon us and enslaved Palmira: Pity, my lord, a heart oppressed with grief, That sighs for objects far, far distant from her.

*Zopir*: I understand you, madam; you expect The tyrant's hand, and hope to share his throne.

*Palmira*: I honor him, my lord; my trembling soul Looks up to Mahomet with holy fear As to a god; but never did this heart E'er cherish the vain hope that he would deign To wed Palmira: No: such splendor ill Would suit my humble state.

*Zopir*: Whoe'er thou art, He was not born, I trust, to be thy husband, No, nor thy master; much I err, or thou Springest from a race designed by heaven to check This haughty Arab, and give laws to him Who thus assumes the majesty of kings.

*Palmira*: Alas! we know not what it is to boast Of birth or fortune; from our infant years Without or parents, friends, or country, doomed To slavery; here resigned to our hard fate, Strangers to all but to that God we serve, We live content in humble poverty.

*Zopir*: And can ye be content? and are ye strangers, Without a father, and without a home? I am a childless, poor, forlorn, old man; You might have been the comfort of my age: To form a plan of future happiness For you, had softened my own wretchedness, And made me some amends for all my wrongs: But you abhor my country and my law.

*Palmira*: I am not mistress of myself, and how Can I be thine? I pity thy misfortunes, And bless thee for thy goodness to Palmira; But Mahomet has been a father to me.

*Zopir*: A father! ye just gods! the vile impostor!

**Palmira**: Can he deserve that name, the holy prophet, The great ambassador of heaven, sent down To interpret its high will?

**Zopir**: Deluded mortals! How blind ye are, to follow this proud madman, This happy robber, whom my justice spared, And raise him from the scaffold to a throne!

**Palmira**: My lord, I shudder at your imprecations; Though I am bound by honor and the ties Of gratitude to love thee for thy bounties, This blasphemy against my kind protector Cancels the bond, and fills my soul with horror. O superstition, how thy savage power Deprives at once the best and tenderest hearts Of their humanity!

**Zopir**: Alas! Palmira, Spite of myself, I feel for thy misfortunes, Pity thy weakness, and lament thy fate.

**Palmira**: You will not grant me then—

**Zopir**: I cannot yield thee To him who has deceived thy easy heart, To a base tyrant; No: thou art a treasure Too precious to be parted with, and makest This hypocrite but more detested.

SCENE III.

Zopir, Palmira, Phanor.

**Zopir**: Phanor, What wouldst thou?

**Phanor**: At the city gate that leads To Moad's fertile plain, the valiant Omar Is just arrived.

**Zopir**: Indeed; the tyrant's friend, The fierce, vindictive Omar, his new convert, Who had so long opposed him, and still fought For us!

**Phanor**: Perhaps he yet may serve his country, Already he hath offered terms of peace; Our chiefs have parleyed with him, he demands An hostage, and I hear they've granted him The noble Seid.

**Palmira**: Seid? gracious heaven!

**Phanor**: Behold! my lord, he comes.

**Zopir**: Ha! Omar here! There's no retreating now, he must be heard; Palmira, you may leave us.—O ye gods Of my forefathers, you who have protected The sons of Ishmael these three thousand years, And thou, O Sun, with all those sacred lights That glitter round us, witness to my truth, Aid and support me in the glorious conflict With proud iniquity!

SCENE IV.

Zopir, Omar, Phanor, Attendants.

**Zopir**: At length, it seems, Omar returns, after a three years' absence, To visit that loved country which his hand So long defended, and his honest heart Has now betrayed: deserter of our gods, Deserter of our laws, how darest thou thus

Approach these sacred walls to persecute And to oppress; a public robber's slave; What is thy errand? wherefore comest thou hither?

**Omar:** To pardon thee: by me our holy prophet, In pity to thy age, thy well-known valor, And past misfortunes, offers thee his hand: Omar is come to bring thee terms of peace.

**Zopir:** And shall a factious rebel offer peace Who should have sued for pardon? gracious gods! Will ye permit him to usurp your power, And suffer Mahomet to rule mankind? Dost thou not blush, vile minion as thou art, To serve a traitor? hast thou not beheld him Friendless and poor, an humble citizen, And ranking with the meanest of the throng? How little then in fortune or in fame!

**Omar:** Thus low and grovelling souls like thine pretend To judge of merit, whilst in fortune's scale Ye weigh the worth of men: proud, empty being, Dost thou not know that the poor worm which crawls Low on the earth, and the imperial eagle That soars to heaven, in the all-seeing eye Of their eternal Maker are the same, And shrink to nothing? men are equal all; From virtue only true distinction springs, And not from birth: there are exalted spirits Who claim respect and honor from themselves And not their ancestors: these, these, my lord, Are heaven's peculiar care, and such is he Whom I obey, and who alone deserves To be a master; all mankind like me Shall one day fall before the conqueror's feet, And future ages follow my example.

**Zopir:** Omar, I know thee well; thy artful hand In vain hath drawn the visionary portrait; Thou mayest deceive the multitude, but know, What Mecca worships Zopir can despise: Be honest then, and with the impartial eye Of reason look on Mahomet; behold him But as a mortal, and consider well By what base arts the vile impostor rose, A camel-driver, a poor abject slave, Who first deceived a fond, believing woman, And now supported by an idle dream Draws in the weak and credulous multitude: Condemned to exile, I chastised the rebel Too lightly, and his insolence returns With double force to punish my indulgence. He fled with Fatima from cave to cave, And suffered chains, contempt and banishment; Meantime the fury which he called divine Spread like a subtle poison through the crowd; Medina was infected: Omar then, To reason's voice attentive, would have stopped The impetuous torrent; he had courage then And virtue to attack the proud usurper, Though now he crouches to him like a slave. If thy proud master be indeed a prophet, How didst thou dare to punish him? or why, If an impostor, wilt thou dare to serve him?

**Omar:** I punished him because I knew him not; But now, the veil of ignorance removed, I see him as he is; behold him born To change the astonished world, and rule mankind: When I beheld him rise in awful pomp, Intrepid, eloquent, by all admired, By all adored; beheld him speak and act,

Punish and pardon like a god, I lent My little aid, and joined the conqueror. Altars, thou knowest, and thrones were our reward; Once I was blind, like thee, but, thanks to heaven! My eyes are opened now; would, Zopir, thine Were open, too! let me entreat thee, change, As I have done; no longer boast thy zeal And cruel hatred, nor blaspheme our God, But fall submissive at the hero's feet Whom thou hast injured; kiss the hand that bears The angry lightning, lest it fall upon thee. Omar is now the second of mankind; A place of honor yet remains for thee, If prudent thou wilt yield, and own a master: What we have been thou knowest, and what we are: The multitude are ever weak and blind, Made for our use, born but to serve the great, But to admire, believe us, and obey: Reign then with us, partake the feast of grandeur, No longer deign to imitate the crowd, But henceforth make them tremble.

**Zopir**: Tremble thou, And Mahomet, with all thy hateful train: Thinkest thou that Mecca's faithful chief will fall At an impostor's feet, and crown a rebel? I am no stranger to his specious worth; His courage and his conduct have my praise; Were he but virtuous I like thee should love him; But as he is I hate the tyrant: hence, Nor talk to me of his deceitful mercy, His clemency and goodness; all his aim Is cruelty and vengeance: with this hand I slew his darling son; I banished him: My hatred is inflexible, and so Is Mahomet's resentment: if he e'er Re-enters Mecca, he must cut his way Through Zopir's blood, for he is deeply stained With crimes that justice never can forgive.

**Omar**: To show thee Mahomet is merciful, That he can pardon though thou canst not, here I offer thee the third of all our spoils Which we have taken from tributary kings; Name your conditions, and the terms of peace; Set your own terms on fair Palmira; take Our treasures, and be happy.

**Zopir**: Thinkest thou Zopir Will basely sell his honor and his country, Will blast his name with infamy for wealth, The foul reward of guilt, or that Palmira Will ever own a tyrant for her master? She is too virtuous e'er to be the slave Of Mahomet, nor will I suffer her To fall a sacrifice to base impostors Who would subvert the laws, and undermine The safety and the virtue of mankind.

**Omar**: Implacably severe; thou talkest to Omar As if he were a criminal, and thou His judge; but henceforth I would have thee act A better part, and treat me as a friend, As the ambassador of Mahomet, A conqueror and a king.

**Zopir**: A king! who made, Who crowned him?

**Omar**: Victory: respect his glory, And tremble at his power: amidst his conquests The hero offers peace; our swords are still Unsheathed, and woe to this rebellious city If she submits not: think what blood must flow, The blood of half our fellow-citizens; Consider, Zopir, Mahomet is here, And even now requests to speak with thee.

**Zopir**: Ha! Mahomet!

**Omar**: Yes, he conjures thee.

**Zopir**: Traitor! Were I the sole despotic ruler here He should be answered soon—by chastisement.

**Omar**: I pity, Zopir, thy pretended virtue; But since the senate insolently claim Divided empire with thee, to the senate Let us begone; Omar will meet thee there.

**Zopir**: I'll follow thee: we then shall see who best Can plead his cause: I will defend my gods, My country, and her laws; thy impious voice Shall bellow for thy vengeful deity, Thy persecuting god, and his false prophet. [Turning to Phanor.] Haste, Phanor, and with me repulse the traitor; Who spares a villain is a villain:—come, Let us, my friend, unite to crush his pride, Subvert his wily purposes, destroy him, Or perish in the attempt: If Mecca listens To Zopir's councils, I shall free my country From a proud tyrant's power, and save mankind.

# ACT II

SCENE I.
Seid, Palmira.

**Palmira**: Welcome, my Seid, do I see thee here Once more in safety? what propitious god Conducted thee? at length Palmira's woes Shall have an end, and we may yet be happy.

**Seid**: Thou sweetest charmer, balm of every woe, Dear object of my wishes and my tears, O since that day of blood when flushed with conquest The fierce barbarian snatched thee from my arms, When midst a heap of slaughtered friends I lay Expiring on the ground, and called on death, But called in vain, to end my hated being, What have I suffered for my dear Palmira! How have I cursed the tardy hours that long Withheld my vengeance! my distracted soul's Impatience thirsted for the bloody field, That with these hands I might lay waste this seat Of slavery, where Palmira mourned so long In sad captivity; but thanks to heaven! Our holy prophet, whose deep purposes Are far beyond the ken of human wisdom, Hath hither sent his chosen servant Omar; I flew to meet him, they required a hostage; I gave my faith, and they received it; firm In my resolve to live or die for thee.

**Palmira**: Seid, the very moment ere thou camest To calm my fears, and save me from despair, Was I entreating the proud ravisher; Thou knowest, I cried, the only good on earth I prized is left behind, restore it to me: Then clasped his knees, fell at the tyrant's feet, And bathed them with my tears, but all in vain: How his unkind refusal shocked my soul! My eyes grew dim, and motionless I stood As one deprived of life; no succor nigh, No ray of hope was left, when Seid came To ease my troubled heart, and bring me comfort.

**Seid**: Who could behold unmoved Palmira's woes?

**Palmira**: The cruel Zopir; not insensible He seemed to my misfortunes, yet at last Unkindly told me, I must never hope To leave these walls, for naught should tear me from him.

**Seid**: 'Tis false; for Mahomet, my royal master, With the victorious Omar, and forgive me, If to these noble friends I proudly add The name of Seid, these shall set thee free, Dry up thy tears, and make Palmira happy: The God of Mahomet, our great protector, That God whose sacred standard I have borne; He who destroyed Medina's haughty ramparts Shall lay rebellious Mecca at our feet; Omar is here, and the glad people look With eyes of friendship on him; in the name Of Mahomet he comes, and meditates Some noble purpose.

**Palmira**: Mahomet indeed Might free us, and unite two hearts long since Devoted to his cause; but he, alas! Is far removed, and we abandoned captives.

## SCENE II.

palmira, seid, omar.

**Omar**: Despair not; heaven perhaps may yet reward you, For Mahomet and liberty are nigh.

**Seid**: Is he then come?

**Palmira**: Our friend and father?

**Omar**: Yes. I met the council, and by Mahomet Inspired, addressed them thus: "Within these walls, Even here," I cried, "the favorite of heaven, Our holy prophet, first drew breath; the great, The mighty conqueror, the support of kings; And will ye not permit him but to rank As friend and fellow-citizen? he comes not To ruin or enslave, but to protect, To teach you and to save, to fix his power, And hold dominion o'er the conquered heart." I spoke; the hoary sages smiled applause, And all inclined to favor us; but Zopir, Still resolute and still inflexible, Declared, the people should be called together, And give their general voice: the people met, Again I spoke, addressed the citizens, Exhorted, threatened, practised every art To win their favor, and at length prevailed; The gates are opened to great Mahomet, Who after fifteen years of cruel exile Returns to bless once more his native land; With him the gallant Ali, brave Hercides, And Ammon the invincible, besides A numerous train of chosen followers: The people throng around him; some with looks Of hatred, some with smiles of cordial love; Some bless the hero, and some curse the tyrant: Some threaten and blaspheme, whilst others fall Beneath his feet, embrace and worship him; Meantime the names of God, of peace, and freedom, Are echoed through the all-believing crowd; Whilst Zopir's dying party bellows forth In idle threats its impotent revenge: Amidst their cries, unruffled and serene, In triumph walks the god-like Mahomet, Bearing the olive in his hand; already Peace is proclaimed, and see! the conqueror comes.

SCENE III.
Mahomet, Omar, Hercides, Seid, Palmira, Attendants.
**Mahomet**: My friends, and fellow-laborers, valiant Ali, Morad, and Ammon, and Hercides, hence To your great work, and in my name instruct The people, lead them to the paths of truth, Promise and threaten; let my God alone Be worshipped, and let those who will not love Be taught to fear him.—Seid, art thou here?
**Seid**: My ever-honored father, and my king, Led by that power divine who guided thee To Mecca's walls, preventing your commands I came, prepared to live or die with thee.
**Mahomet**: You should have waited for my orders; he Who goes beyond his duty knows it not; I am heaven's minister, and thou art mine; Learn then of me to serve and to obey.
**Palmira**: Forgive, my lord, a youth's impatient ardor: Brought up together from our infant years, The same our fortunes, and our thoughts the same: Alas! my life has been a life of sorrow; Long have I languished in captivity, Far from my friends, from Seid, and from thee; And now at last, when I beheld a ray Of comfort shining on me, thy unkindness Blasts my fair hopes, and darkens all the scene.
**Mahomet**: Palmira, 'tis enough: I know thy virtues; Let naught disturb thee: spite of all my cares, Glory, and empire, and the weight of war, I will remember thee; Palmira still Lives in my heart, and shares it with mankind: Seid shall join our troops; thou, gentle maid, Mayest serve thy God in peace: fear naught but Zopir.

SCENE IV.
Mahomet, Omar.
**Mahomet**: Brave Omar, stay, for in thy faithful bosom Will I repose the secrets of my soul: The lingering progress of a doubtful siege May stop our rapid course; we must not give These weak deluded mortals too much time To pry into our actions; prejudice Rules o'er the vulgar with despotic sway. Thou knowest there is a tale which I have spread And they believe, that universal empire Awaits the prophet, who to Mecca's walls Shall lead his conquering bands, and bring her peace. 'Tis mine to mark the errors of mankind, And to

avail me of them; but whilst thus I try each art to soothe this fickle people, What thinks my friend of Seid and Palmira?

**Omar**: I think most nobly of them, that amidst Those few staunch followers who own no God, No faith but thine, who love thee as their father, Their friend, and benefactor, none obey Or serve thee with an humbler, better mind; They are most faithful.

**Mahomet**: Omar, thou art deceived; They are my worst of foes, they love each other.

**Omar**: And can you blame their tenderness?

**Mahomet**: My friend, I'll tell thee all my weakness.

**Omar**: How, my lord!

**Mahomet**: Thou knowest the reigning passion of my soul; Whilst proud ambition and the cares of empire Weighed heavy on me, Mahomet's hard life Has been a conflict with opposing Nature, Whom I have vanquished by austerity, And self-denial; have banished from me That baleful poison which unnerves mankind, Which only serves to fire them into madness, And brutal follies; on the burning sand Or desert rocks I brave the inclement sky, And bear the seasons' rough vicissitude: Love is my only solace, the dear object Of all my toils, the idol I adore, The god of Mahomet, the powerful rival Of my ambition: know, midst all my queens, Palmira reigns sole mistress of my heart: Think then what pangs of jealousy thy friend Must feel when she expressed her fatal passion For Seid.

**Omar**: But thou art revenged.

**Mahomet**: Judge thou If soon I ought not to take vengeance on them: That thou mayest hate my rival more, I'll tell thee Who Seid and Palmira are—the children Of him whom I abhor, my deadliest foe.

**Omar**: Ha! Zopir!

**Mahomet**: Is their father: fifteen years Are past since brave Hercides to my care Gave up their infant years; they know not yet Or who or what they are; I brought them up Together; I indulged their lawless passion, And added fuel to the guilty flame. Methinks it is as if the hand of heaven Had meant in them to centre every crime. But I must—Ha! their father comes this way, His eyes are full of bitterness and wrath Against me—now be vigilant, my Omar, Hercides must be careful to possess This most important pass; return, and tell me Whether 'tis most expedient to declare Against him, or retreat: away.

SCENE V.

Zopir, Mahomet.

**Zopir**: Hard fate! Unhappy Zopir! thus compelled to meet My worst of foes, the foe of all mankind!

**Mahomet:** Since 'tis the will of heaven that Mahomet And Zopir should at length unite, approach Without a blush, and fearless tell thy tale.

**Zopir:** I blush for thee alone, whose baneful arts Have drawn thy country to the brink of ruin; Who in the bosom of fair peace wouldst wage Intestine war, loosen the sacred bonds Of friendship, and destroy our happiness; Beneath the veil of proffered terms thou meanest But to betray, whilst discord stalks before thee: Thou vile assemblage of hypocrisy And insolence, abhorred tyrant! thus Do the chosen ministers of heaven dispense Its sacred blessings, and announce their God?

**Mahomet:** Wert thou not Zopir, I would answer thee As thou deservest, in thunder, by the voice Of that offended Being thou deridest: Armed with the hallowed Koran I would teach thee To tremble and obey in humble silence: And with the subject world to kneel before me; But I will talk to thee without disguise, As man to man should speak, and friend to friend: I have ambition, Zopir; where's the man Who has it not? but never citizen, Or chief, or priest, or king projected aught So noble as the plan of Mahomet; In acts or arms hath every nation shone Superior in its turn; Arabia now Steps forth; that generous people, long unknown And unrespected, saw her glories sunk, Her honors lost; but, lo! the hour is come When she shall rise to victory and renown; The world lies desolate from pole to pole; India's slaves, and bleeding Persia mourns Her slaughtered sons; whilst Egypt hangs the head Dejected; from the walls of Constantine Splendor is fled; the Roman Empire torn By discord, sees its scattered members spread On every side inglorious;—let us raise Arabia on the ruins of mankind: The blind and tottering universe demands Another worship, and another God. Crete had her Minos, Egypt her Osiris, To Asia Zoroaster gave his laws, And Numa was in Italy adored: O'er savage nations where nor monarchs ruled Nor manners softened, nor religion taught, Hath many a sage his fruitless maxims spread; Beneath a nobler yoke I mean to bend The prostrate world, and change their feeble laws, Abolish their false worship, pull down Their powerless gods, and on my purer faith Found universal empire: say not, Zopir, That Mahomet betrays his country, no: I mean but to destroy its weak supports, And, banishing idolatry, unite it Beneath one king, one prophet, and one God; I shall subdue it but to make it glorious.

**Zopir:** Is this thy purpose then, and darest thou thus Avow it? canst thou change the hearts of men, And make them think like thee? are war and slaughter The harbingers of wisdom and of peace; Can he who ravages instruct mankind? If in the night of ignorance and error We long have wandered, must thy dreadful torch Enlighten us? What right hast thou to empire?

**Mahomet:** That right which firm, exalted spirits claim O'er vulgar minds.

**Zopir**: Thus every bold impostor May forge new fetters, and enslave mankind: He has a right, it seems, to cheat the world If he can do it with an air of grandeur.

**Mahomet**: I know your people well; I know they want A leader; my religion, true or false, Is needful to them: what have all your gods And all your idols done? what laurels grow Beneath their altars? your low, grovelling sect Debases man, unnerves his active soul, And makes it heavy, phlegmatic, and mean; Whilst mine exalts it, gives it strength and courage: My law forms heroes.

**Zopir**: Rather call them robbers: Away; nor bring thy hateful lessons here; Go to the school of tyrants, boast thy frauds To lost Medina, where thou reignest supreme, Where blinded bigots bend beneath thy power, And thou beholdest thy equals at thy feet.

**Mahomet**: My equals! Mahomet has none; long since I passed them all; Medina is my own, And Mecca trembles at me; if thou holdest Thy safety dear, receive the peace I offer.

**Zopir**: Thou talkest of peace, but 'tis not in thy heart; I'm not to be deceived.

**Mahomet**: I would not have thee; The weak deceive, the powerful command: To-morrow I shall force thee to submit; To-day, observe, I would have been thy friend.

**Zopir**: Can we be friends? can Mahomet and Zopir E'er be united? say, what god shall work A miracle like that?

**Mahomet**: I'll tell thee one, A powerful God, one that is always heard, By me he speaks to thee.

**Zopir**: Who is it? name him.

**Mahomet**: Interest, thy own dear interest.

**Zopir**: Sooner heaven And hell shall be united; interest May be the god of Mahomet, but mine Is—justice: what shall join them to each other? Where is the cement that must bind our friendship? Is it that son I slew, or the warm blood Of Zopir's house which thou has shed?

**Mahomet**: It is Thy blood, thy son's—for now I will unveil A secret to thee, known to none but me: Thou weepest thy children dead; they both are—living.

**Zopir**: What sayest thou? living? unexpected bliss! My children living?

**Mahomet**: Yes; and both—my prisoners.

**Zopir**: My children slaves to thee? impossible!

**Mahomet**: My bounty nourished them.

**Zopir**: And couldst thou spare A child of Zopir's?

**Mahomet**: For their father's faults I would not punish them.

**Zopir**: But tell me, say, For what are they reserved?

**Mahomet**: Their life or death Depend on me: speak but the word, and thou Art master of their fate.

**Zopir**: O name the price And thou shalt have it; must I give my blood, Or must I bear their chains, and be the slave Of Mahomet?

**Mahomet**: I ask not either of thee: Lend me thy aid but to subdue the world; Surrender Mecca to me, and give up Your temple, bid the astonished people read My sacred Koran; be thou my vassal, And fall before me, then will I restore Thy son, perhaps hereafter may reward thee With honors, and contract a closer tie With Zopir.

**Zopir**: Mahomet, thou seest in me A tender father: after fifteen years Of cruel absence, to behold my children, To die in their embraces, were the first And fairest blessings that my soul could wish for; But if to thee I must betray my country, Or sacrifice my children, know, proud tyrant, The choice is made already—fare thee well.

**Mahomet**: Inexorable dotard! but henceforth I will be more implacable, more cruel Even than thyself.

SCENE VI.
Mahomet, Omar.

**Omar**: And so indeed thou must be, Or all is lost: already I have bought Their secret counsels: Mahomet, to-morrow The truce expires, and Zopir reassumes His power; thy life's in danger: half the senate Are leagued against thee: those who dare not fight May hire the dark assassin to destroy thee; May screen their guilt beneath the mask of justice, And call the murder legal punishment.

**Mahomet**: First they shall feel my vengeance: persecution, Thou knowest, has ever been my best support. Zopir must die.

**Omar**: 'Tis well resolved: his fate Will teach the rest obedience: lose no time.

**Mahomet**: Yet, spite of my resentment, I must hide The murderous hand that deals the blow, to 'scape Suspicion's watchful eye, and not incense The multitude.

**Omar**: They are not worth our care.

**Mahomet**: And yet they must be pleased: I want an arm That will strike boldly.

**Omar**: Seid is the man; I'll answer for him.

**Mahomet**: Seid?

**Omar**: Ay: the best, The fittest instrument to serve our purpose: As Zopir's hostage he may find occasion To speak with him, and soon avenge his master. Thy other favorites are too wise, too prudent For such a dangerous enterprise; old age Takes off the bandage of credulity From mortal eyes; but the young, simple heart, The willing slave to its own fond opinions, And void of guile, will act as we direct it: Youth is the proper period for delusion. Seid, thou knowest, is superstitious, bold, And violent, but easy to be led; Like a tame lion, to his keeper's voice Obedient.

**Mahomet:** What! the brother of Palmira?

**Omar:** Ay; Seid, the fierce son of thy proud foe, The incestuous rival of great Mahomet, His master's rival.

**Mahomet:** I detest him, Omar, Abhor his very name; my murdered son Cries out for vengeance on him; but thou knowest The object of my love, and whence she sprung: Thou seest I am oppressed on every side; I would have altars, victims, and a throne; I would have Zopir's blood, and Seid's too: I must consult my interest, my revenge, My honor, and my love, that fatal passion, Which, spite of my resentment, holds this heart In shameful chains: I must consult religion, All powerful motive, and necessity That throws a veil o'er every crime: away.

# ACT III.

### SCENE I.
Seid, Palmira.

**Palmira:** O Seid, keep me not in dread suspense, What is this secret sacrifice? what blood Hath heaven demanded?

**Seid:** The eternal power Deigns to accept my service, calls on me To execute its purposes divine; To him this heart's devoted, and for him This arm shall rise in vengeance; I am bound To Omar and to Mahomet, have sworn To perish in the glorious cause of heaven: My next and dearest care shall be Palmira.

**Palmira:** Why was not I a witness to thy oath? Had I been with thee, I had been less wretched; But doubts distract me: Omar talks of treason, Of blood that soon must flow; the senate's rage, And Zopir's dark intrigues: the flames of war Once more are kindled, and the sword is drawn Heaven only knows when to be sheathed again: So says our prophet, he who cannot lie, Cannot deceive us: O I fear for Seid, Fear all from Zopir.

**Seid:** Can he have a heart So base and so perfidious? but this morning, When as a hostage I appeared before him, I thought him noble, generous, and humane; Some power invincible in secret worked, And won me to him; whether the respect Due to his name, or specious form external Concealed the blackness of his heart I know not; Whether thy presence filled my raptured soul With joy that drove out every painful sense, And would not let me think of aught but thee: Whate'er the cause, methought I was most happy When nearest him: that he should thus seduce My easy heart makes me detest him more; And yet how hard it is to look on those With eyes of hatred whom we wish to love!

*Palmira*: By every bond hath heaven united us, And Seid and Palmira are the same: Were I not bound to thee, and to that faith Which Mahomet inspires, I too had pleaded The cause of Zopir; but religion, love, And nature, all forbid it.

*Seid*: Think no more Of vain remorse, but listen to the voice Of heaven, the God we serve will be propitious: Our holy prophet who protects his children Will bless our faithful love: for thy dear sake I hazard all. Farewell.

SCENE II.

*Palmira*: [Alone.] Some dark presage Of future misery hangs o'er me still: That love which made my happiness, this day, So often wished for, is a day of horror: What is this dreadful oath, this solemn compact Which Seid talks of? I've a thousand fears Upon me when I think of Zopir: oft As I invoke great Mahomet, I feel A secret dread, and tremble as I worship: O save me, heaven! fearful I obey, And blind I follow: O direct my steps Aright, and deign to wash my tears away!

SCENE III.

mahomet, palmira.

*Palmira*: Propitious heaven hath heard my prayers; he comes, The prophet comes. O gracious Mahomet, My Seid—

*Mahomet*: What of him? thou seemest disturbed; What should Palmira fear when I am with her!

*Palmira*: Have I not cause when Mahomet himself Seems touched with grief?

*Mahomet*: Perhaps it is for thee: Darest thou, imprudent maid, avow a passion Ere I approved it: is the heart I formed Turned rebel to its master, to my laws Unfaithful? O ingratitude!

*Palmira*: My lord, Behold me at your feet, and pity me: Didst thou not once propitious smile upon us, And give thy sanction to our growing love? Thou knowest the virtuous passion that unites us Is but a chain that binds us more to thee.

*Mahomet*: The bonds that folly and imprudence knit Are dangerous; guilt doth sometimes follow close The steps of innocence: our hearts deceive us, And love, with all his store of dear delights, May cost us tears, and dip his shafts in blood.

*Palmira*: Nor would I murmur if it flowed for Seid.

*Mahomet*: Are you indeed so fond?

*Palmira*: E'er since the day When good Hercides to thy sacred power Consigned us both, unconquerable instinct, Still growing with our years, united us In tender friendship; 'twas the work of heaven That guides our every action, and o'errules The fate of mortals; so thy doctrines teach: God cannot change, nor gracious heaven condemn That love itself inspired: what once was right Is always so; canst thou then blame Palmira?

**Mahomet**: I can, and must; nay, thou wilt tremble more When I reveal the horrid secret to thee. Attend, rash maid, and let me teach thy soul What to avoid, and what to follow: listen To me alone.

**Palmira**: To thee alone Palmira Will listen ever, the obedient slave Of Mahomet; this heart can never lose Its veneration for thy sacred name.

**Mahomet**: That veneration in excess may lead To foul ingratitude.

**Palmira**: When I forget Thy goodness, then may Seid punish me!

**Mahomet**: Seid!

**Palmira**: O why, my lord, that cruel frown, And look severe?

**Mahomet**: Be not alarmed; I meant But to explore the secrets of thy heart, And try if thou wert worthy to be saved: Be confident, and rest on my protection; On your obedience will depend your fate; If ye expect a blessing at my hands, Be careful to deserve it, and whate'er The will of heaven determines touching Seid, Be thou his guide, direct him in the paths Of duty, and religion; let him keep His promise, and be worthy of Palmira.

**Palmira**: O he will keep it; doubt him not, my lord, I'll answer for his heart as for my own; Seid adores thee, worships Mahomet More than he loves Palmira; thou art all To him, his friend, his father, and his king: I'll fly, and urge him to his duty.

## SCENE IV.

**Mahomet**: [Alone.] Well: Spite of myself I must, it seems, be made A confidant; the simple girl betrayed Her guilty flame, and innocently plunged The dagger in my heart: unhappy race! Father and children, all my foes, all doomed To make me wretched! but ye soon shall prove That dreadful is my hatred—and my love.

## SCENE V.

Mahomet, Omar.

**Omar**: At length the hour is come, to seize Palmira, To conquer Mecca, and to punish Zopir; His death alone can prop our feeble cause, And humble these proud citizens: brave Seid Can best avenge thee; he has free access To Zopir: yonder gloomy passage leads To his abode; there the rebellious chief His idle vows and flattering incense pours Before his fancied deities; there Seid, Full of the law divine by thee inspired, Shall sacrifice the traitor to the God Of Mahomet.

**Mahomet**: He shall: that youth was born For crimes of deepest dye: he shall be first My useful slave, my instrument, and then The victim of my rage; it must be so: My safety, my resentment, and my love, My holy faith, and the decrees of fate Irrevocable, all require it of me: But thinkest thou, Omar, he hath all the warmth Of wild fanaticism?

**Omar**: I know he has, And suits our purpose well; Palmira, too, Will urge him on; religion, love, resentment Will blind his headstrong youth, and hurry him To madness.

**Mahomet**: Hast thou bound him by an oath?

**Omar**: O yes; in all the gloomy pomp of rites Nocturnal, oaths, and altars, we have fixed His superstitious soul, placed in his hand The sacred sword, and fired him with the rage Of fierce enthusiasm—but behold him.

SCENE VI.
Mahomet, Omar, Seid.

**Mahomet**: Child Of heaven, decreed to execute the laws Of an offended God, now hear by me His sacred will: thou must avenge his cause.

**Seid**: O thou, to whom my soul devoted bends In humblest adoration, king, and prophet, Sovereign, acknowledged by the voice of heaven, O'er prostrate nations—I am wholly thine: But O enlighten my dark mind! O say, How can weak man avenge his God?

**Mahomet**: Oft-times Doth he make use of feeble hands like thine To punish impious mortals, and assert His power divine.

**Seid**: Will he, whose perfect image Is seen in Mahomet, thus condescend To honor Seid?

**Mahomet**: Do as he ordains; That is the highest honor man can boast, Blindly to execute his great decree: Be thankful for the choice, and strike the blow: The angel of destruction shall assist, The God of armies shall protect thee.

**Seid**: Speak; What tyrant must be slain? what blood must flow?

**Mahomet**: The murderer's blood whom Mahomet abhors, Who persecutes our faith, and spurns our God, Who slew my son; the worst of all my foes, The cruel Zopir.

**Seid**: Ha! must Zopir fall?

**Mahomet**: And dost thou pause? presumptuous youth! 'tis impious But to deliberate: far from Mahomet Be all who for themselves shall dare to judge Audacious; those who reason are not oft Prone to believe; thy part is to obey. Have I not told thee what the will of heaven Determines? if it be decreed that Mecca, Spite of her crimes and base idolatry, Shall be the promised temple, the chosen seat Of empire, where I am appointed king, And pontiff, knowest thou why our Mecca boasts These honors? knowest thou holy Abram here Was born, that here his sacred ashes rest? He who, obedient to the voice of God, Stifled the cries of nature, and gave up His darling child: the same all-powerful Being

Requires of thee a sacrifice; to thee He calls for blood; and darest thou hesitate When God commands? hence, vile idolater, Unworthy Mussulman, away, and seek Another master; go, and love Palmira; But thou despisest her, and bravest the wrath Of angry heaven; away, forsake thy lord, And serve his deadliest foes.

    **Seid**: It is the voice Of God that speaks in Mahomet:—command, And I obey.

    **Mahomet**: Strike, then, and by the blood Of Zopir merit life eternal.—Omar, Attend and watch him well.

### SCENE VII.

    **Seid**: [Alone.] To sacrifice A poor, defenceless, weak old man!—no matter: How many victims at the altar fall As helpless! yet their blood in grateful streams Rises to heaven: God hath appointed me; Seid hath sworn, and Seid shall perform His sacred promise:—O assist me now, Illustrious spirits, you who have destroyed The tyrants of the earth, O join your rage To mine, O guide this trembling hand, and thou Exterminating angel who defendest The cause of Mahomet, inspire this heart With all thy fierceness!—ha! what do I see?

### SCENE VIII.

Zopir, Seid.

    **Zopir**: Seid, thou seemest disturbed; unhappy youth! Why art thou ranked amongst my foes? my heart Feels for thy woes, and trembles at thy danger; Horrors on horrors crowd on every side; My house may be a shelter from the storm. Accept it, thou art welcome, for thy life Is dear to Zopir.

    **Seid**: Gracious heaven! wilt thou Protect me thus? will Zopir guard his foe? What do I hear! O duty, conscience, virtue! O Mahomet, this rives my heart.

    **Zopir**: Perhaps Thou art surprised to find that I can pity An enemy, and wish for Seid's welfare; I am a man like thee; that tie alone Demands at least a sympathetic tear For innocence afflicted: gracious gods, Drive from this earth those base and savage men, Who shed with joy their fellow-creatures' blood.

    **Seid**: O glorious sentiments! and can there be Such virtue in an infidel?

    **Zopir**: Thou knowest But little of that virtue, thus to stand Astonished at it! O mistaken youth, In what a maze of errors art thou lost! Bound by a tyrant's savage laws, thou thinkest Virtue resides in Mussulmans alone; Thy master rules thee with a rod of iron, And shackles thy free soul in shameful bonds; Zopir thou hatest, alas! thou knowest him not: I pardon thee because thou art the slave Of Mahomet; but how canst thou believe A God who teaches hatred, and delights In discord?

    **Seid**: O I never can obey him! I know, and feel I cannot hate thee, Zopir.

    **Zopir**: Alas! the more I talk to him, the more He gains upon me; his ingenuous look, His youth, his candor, all conspire to charm me; How could a follower of this vile impostor Thus win my heart! who gave thee birth? what art thou?

**Seid**: A wretched orphan; all I have on earth Is a kind master, whom I never yet Have disobeyed; howe'er my love for thee May tempt me to betray him.

**Zopir**: Knowest thou not Thy parents then?

**Seid**: His camp was the first object My eyes beheld; his temple is my country; I know no other; and amidst the crowd Of yearly tributes to our holy prophet, None e'er was treated with more tenderness Than Seid was.

**Zopir**: I love his gratitude: Thy kind return for benefits received Merits my praise:—O why did heaven employ The hand of Mahomet in such an office? He was thy father, and Palmira's, too; Why dost thou sigh? why dost thou tremble thus? Why turn thee from me? sure some dreadful thought Hangs on thy mind.

**Seid**: It must be so: the times Are full of terror.

**Zopir**: If thou feelest remorse Thy heart is guiltless; murder is abroad, Let me preserve thy life.

**Seid**: O gracious heaven! And can I have a thought of taking thine? Palmira! O my oath! O God of vengeance!

**Zopir**: For the last time remember I entreat thee To follow me; away, thy fate depends Upon this moment.

### SCENE IX.
Zopir, Seid, Omar.

**Omar**: [Entering hastily.] Traitor, Mahomet Expects thee.

**Seid**: O I know not where or what I am; destruction, ruin and despair On every side await me: whither now Shall wretched Seid fly?

**Omar**: To him whom God Hath chosen, thy injured king, and master.

**Seid**: Yes: And there abjure the dreadful oath I made.

### SCENE X.
**Zopir**: [Alone.] The desperate youth is gone—I know not why, But my heart beats for his distress; his looks, His pity, his remorse, his every action Affect me deeply: I must follow him.

### SCENE XI.
Zopir, Phanor.

**Phanor**: This letter, sir, was by an Arab given In secret to me.

**Zopir**: From Hercides! gods, What do I read? will heaven in tenderest pity At length repay me for a life of sorrows? Hercides begs to see me—he who snatched From this fond bosom my two helpless children; They yet are living, so this paper tells me, Slaves to the tyrant—Seid and Palmira Are orphans both, and know not whence they sprang, Perhaps my children—O delusive hope, Why wilt thou flatter me? it cannot be; Fain would I credit thee, thou sweet deceiver: I fly to meet and to embrace my children; Yes; I will see Hercides: let him come At midnight to me, to this holy altar, Where I so often have invoked the gods, At last, perhaps, propitious to my vows: O ye immortal powers, restore my children, Give back to virtue's paths two generous hearts Corrupted by an impious, vile usurper! If Seid and Palmira are not mine, If such is my hard fate, I will adopt The noble pair, and be their father still.

# ACT IV.

**SCENE I.**
Mahomet, Omar.
**Omar**: My lord, our secret is discovered; Seid Has told Hercides; we are on the verge Of ruin, yet I know he will obey.
**Mahomet**: Revealed it, sayest thou?
**Omar**: Yes: Hercides loves him With tenderness.
**Mahomet**: Indeed! What said he to it?
**Omar**: He stood aghast and seemed to pity Zopir.
**Mahomet**: He's weak, and therefore not to be entrusted; Fools ever will be traitors; but no matter, Let him take heed; a method may be found To rid us of such dangerous witnesses: Say, Omar, have my orders been obeyed?
**Omar**: They have, my lord.
**Mahomet**: 'Tis well: remember, Omar, In one important hour or Mahomet Or Zopir is no more; if Zopir dies, The credulous people will adore that God Who thus declared for me, and saved his prophet: Be this our first great object; that once done, Take care of Seid; art thou sure the poison Will do its office?
**Omar**: Fear it not, my lord.
**Mahomet**: O we must work in secret, the dark shades Of death must hide our purpose—while we shed Old Zopir's blood, be sure you keep Palmira In deepest ignorance; she must not know The secret of her birth: her bliss and mine Depend upon it; well thou knowest, my triumphs From error's fruitful source incessant flow: The ties of blood, and all their boasted power Are mere delusions: what are nature's bonds? Nothing but habit, the mere force of custom: Palmira knows no duty but obedience To me; I am her lord, her king, her father, Perhaps may add the name of husband to them: Her little heart will beat with proud ambition To captivate her master—but the hour Approaches that must rid me of my foe, The hated Zopir: Seid is prepared— And see, he comes: let us retire.

**Omar**: Observe His wild demeanor; rage and fierce resentment Possess his soul.

## SCENE II.
Mahomet, Omar, Retired to One Side of the Stage; Seid at the Farther End.
**Seid**: This dreadful duty then Must be fulfilled.
**Mahomet**: [To Omar.] Let us begone, in search Of other means to make our power secure. [Exit with Omar.]
**Seid**: [Alone.] I could not answer: one reproachful word From Mahomet sufficed: I stood abashed, But not convinced: if heaven requires it of me, I must obey; but it will cost me dear.

## SCENE III.
Seid, Palmira.
**Seid**: Palmira, art thou here? what fatal cause Hath led thee to this seat of horror?
**Palmira**: Fear And love directed me to find thee, Seid, To ask thee what dread sacrifice thou meanest To offer here; do heaven and Mahomet Demand it of thee, must it be? O speak.
**Seid**: Palmira, thou commandest my every thought And every action; all depend on thee: Direct them as thou wilt, inform my soul, And guide my hand: be thou my guardian god, Explain the will of heaven which yet I know not; Why am I chosen to be its instrument Of vengeance? are the prophet's dread commands Irrevocable?
**Palmira**: Seid, we must yield in silence, Nor dare to question his decrees; he hears Our secret sighs, nor are our sorrows hid From Mahomet's all-seeing eye: to doubt Is profanation of the deity. His God is God alone; he could not else Be thus victorious, thus invincible.
**Seid**: He must be Seid's God who is Palmira's: Yet cannot my astonished soul conceive A being, tender, merciful, and kind, Commanding murder; then again I think To doubt is guilt: the priest without remorse Destroys the victim: by the voice of heaven I know that Zopir was condemned, I know That Seid was predestined to support The law divine: so Mahomet ordained, And I obey him; fired with holy zeal I go to slay the enemy of God; And yet methinks another deity Draws back my arm, and bids me spare the victim: Religion lost her power when I beheld The wretched Zopir; duty urged in vain Her cruel plea, exhorting me to murder; With joy I listened to the plaintive voice Of soft humanity: but Mahomet— How awful! how majestic! who can bear His wrath? his frowns reproached my shameful weakness; Religion is a dreadful power: alas! Palmira, I am lost in doubts and fears, Discordant passions tear this feeble heart: I must

be impious, must desert my faith, Or be a murderer: Seid was not formed For an assassin; but 'tis heaven's command, And I have promised to avenge its cause: The tears of grief and rage united flow, Contending duties raise a storm within, And thou alone, Palmira, must appease it; Fix my uncertain heart, and give it peace: Alas! without this dreadful sacrifice, The tie that binds us is forever broke; This only can secure thee.

Palmira: Am I then The price of blood, of Zopir's blood?

Seid: So heaven And Mahomet decree.

Palmira: Love ne'er was meant To make us cruel, barbarous, and inhuman.

Seid: To Zopir's murderer, and to him alone, Palmira must be given.

Palmira: O hard condition!

Seid: But 'tis the will of Mahomet and heaven.

Palmira: Alas!

Seid: Thou knowest the dreadful curse that waits On disobedience—everlasting pain.

Palmira: If thou must be the instrument of vengeance, If at thy hands the blood which thou hast promised Shall be required—

Seid: What's to be done?

Palmira: I tremble To think of it—yet—

Seid: It must be so then: thou Hast fixed his doom; Palmira has consented.

Palmira: Did I consent?

Seid: Thou didst.

Palmira: Detested thought! What have I said?

Seid: By thee the voice of heaven Speaks its last dread command, and I obey: Yon fatal altar is the chosen seat Of Zopir's worship, there he bends the knee To his false gods; retire, my sweet Palmira.

Palmira: I cannot leave thee.

Seid: Thou must not be witness To such a deed of horror: these, Palmira, Are dreadful moments: fly to yonder grove, Thou wilt be near the prophet there: away.

Palmira: Zopir must die then?

Seid: Yes: this fatal hand Must drag him to the earth, there murder him, And bathe yon ruined altar in his blood.

Palmira: Die by thy hand! I shudder at the thought: But see! he comes; just heaven! [The farther part of the stage opens, and discovers an altar.]

SCENE IV.

Seid, Palmira, on One Side; zopir, standing near the Altar.

Zopir: Ye guardian gods Of Mecca, threatened by an impious sect Of vile impostors, now assert your power, And let your Zopir's prayers, perhaps the last

He e'er shall make, be heard! the feeble bonds Of our short peace are broken, and fierce war Vindictive rages; O if ye support The cause of this usurper—

Seid: [Aside to Palmira.] Hear, Palmira, How he blasphemes!

Zopir: May death be Zopir's lot! I wish for naught on earth but to behold, In my last hour, and to embrace my children, To die in their loved arms, if yet they live, If they are here, for something whispers me That I shall see them still.

Palmira: [Aside to Seid.] His children, said he?

Zopir: O I should die with pleasure at the sight: Watch over and protect them, ye kind gods, O let them think like me, but not like me Be wretched!

Seid: See! he prays to his false gods: This is the time to end him. [Draws his sword.]

Palmira: Do not, Seid.

Seid: To serve my God, to please and merit thee, This sword, devoted to the cause of heaven, Is drawn, and shall destroy its deadliest foe: Yon dreary walk invites me to the deed, Methinks the path is bloody, wandering ghosts Glide through the shade, and beckon me away.

Palmira: What sayest thou, Seid?

Seid: Ministers of death, I follow you; conduct me to the altar, And guide my trembling hand!

Palmira: It must not be; 'Tis horrible: O stop, my Seid.

Seid: No: The hour is come, and see! the altar shakes.

Palmira: 'Tis heaven's assent, and we must doubt no more.

Seid: Means it to urge me on, or to restrain? Our prophet will reproach me for this weakness: Palmira!

Palmira: Well!

Seid: Address thyself to heaven: I go to do the deed. [He goes behind the altar where Zopir is retired.]

Palmira: [Alone.]

O dreadful moment! What do I feel within! my blood runs cold: And yet if heaven demands the sacrifice, Am I to judge, to ask, or to complain? Where is the heart that knows itself, that knows Its innocence or guilt? We must obey: But hark! methought I heard the plaintive voice Of death; the deed is done—alas! my Seid.

Seid: [Returns looking wildly around] What voice was that? where am I? where's Palmira? I cannot see Palmira; O she's gone, She's lost forever.

Palmira: Art thou blind to her Who only lives for thee?

Seid: Where are we?

Palmira: Speak, My Seid, is the dreadful sacrifice Performed, and thy sad promise all fulfilled?

Seid: What sayest thou?

**Palmira:** Zopir? is he dead?

**Seid:** Who? Zopir?

**Palmira:** Good heaven, preserve his senses!—come, my Seid, Let us be gone.

**Seid:** How will these tottering limbs Support me!—I recover—is it you, Palmira?

**Palmira:** Yes: what hast thou done?

**Seid:** Obeyed The voice of heaven, seized with this desperate hand His silver hairs, and dragged him to the earth: 'Twas thy command: O God! thou couldst not bid me Commit a crime! trembling and pale a while I stood aghast, then drew this sacred sword, And plunged it in his bosom: what a look Of tenderness and love the poor old man Cast on his murderer! a scene so mournful Ne'er did these eyes behold: my heart retains And will forever keep the sad idea: Would I were dead like him!

**Palmira:** Let us repair To Mahomet, the prophet will protect us; Here you're in danger; follow me.

**Seid:** I cannot: Palmira, pity me.

**Palmira:** What mournful thought Can thus depress thee?

**Seid:** O if thou hadst seen His tender looks, when from his bleeding side He drew the fatal weapon forth, and cried: "Dear Seid, poor unhappy Seid!" Oh, That voice, those looks, and Zopir at my feet Weltering in blood, are still before my eyes: What have we done?

**Palmira:** I tremble for thy life: O in the name of all the sacred ties That bind us, fly, and save thyself.

**Seid:** Away, And leave me: why did thy ill-fated love Command this dreadful sacrifice, Palmira? Without thy cruel order heaven itself Had never been obeyed.

**Palmira:** Unkind reproach! Couldst thou but know what thy Palmira suffers How wouldst thou pity her!

**Seid:** What dreadful object Is that before us? [Zopir rises up slowly from behind the altar, and leans upon it.]

**Palmira:** 'Tis the murdered Zopir; Bloody and pale he drags his mangled limbs Towards us.

**Seid:** Wilt thou go to him?

**Palmira:** I must; For pity and remorse distract my soul, And draw me to him.

**Zopir:** [Comes forward leaning on Palmira.] Gentle maid, support me! [He sits down.] Ungrateful Seid, thou hast slain me; now Thou weepest; alas! too late.

## SCENE V.

Zopir, Seid, Palmira, Phanor.

**Phanor:** O dreadful sight! What's here?

**Zopir:** I wish I could have seen my friend Hercides—Phanor, art thou there?—behold My murderer. [Points to Seid.]

**Phanor**: O guilt! accursed deed! Unhappy Seid, look upon—thy father.
**Seid**: Who?
**Palmira**: He?
**Seid**: My father?
**Zopir**: Gracious heaven!
**Phanor**: Hercides In his last moments took me in his arms, And weeping cried: "If there be time, O haste Prevent a parricide, and stop the arm Of Seid;" in my breast the tyrant lodged The dreadful secret; now I suffer for it, And die by Mahomet's detested hand: Haste, Phanor, fly, inform the hapless Zopir, That Seid and Palmira are—his children.
**Seid**: Palmira!
**Palmira**: Thou my brother?
**Zopir**: O ye gods! O nature, thou hast not deceived me then, When thou didst plead for them! unhappy Seid, What could have urged thee to so foul a deed?
**Seid**: [Kneeling.] My gratitude, my duty, my religion, All that mankind hold sacred, urged me on To do the worst of actions:—give me back That fatal weapon.
**Palmira**: [Laying hold of Seid's arm.] Plunge it in my breast; I was the cause of my dear father's murder; And incest is the price of parricide:
**Seid**: Strike both: heaven hath not punishment enough For crimes like ours.
**Zopir**: [Embracing them.] Let me embrace my children: The gods have poured into my cup of sorrow A draught of sweetest happiness: I die, Contented, and resign me to my fate: But you must live, my children; you, my Seid, And you, Palmira, by the sacred name Of nature, by thy dying father's blood, Fast flowing from the wound which thou hast made, Let me entreat you, live; revenge yourselves, Avenge the injured Zopir, but preserve Your gracious lives; the great, the important hour Approaches, that must change the mournful scene: The offended people, ere to-morrow's dawn, Will rise in arms and punish the usurper; My blood will add fresh fuel to their rage; Let us await the issue.
**Seid**: O I fly To sacrifice the monster, to take vengeance For a dear father's life, or lose my own.

## SCENE VI.

Zopir, Seid, Palmira, Omar, Attendants.

**Omar**: Guards, seize the murderer; Mahomet is come To punish guilt, and execute the laws.
**Zopir**: What do I hear?
**Seid**: Did Mahomet command thee To punish Seid?
**Palmira**: Execrable tyrant! Was not the murder done by thy command?
**Omar**: 'Twas not commanded.

**Seid:** Well have I deserved This just reward of my credulity.

**Omar:** Soldiers, obey.

**Palmira:** O stop, ye shall not—

**Omar:** Madam, If Seid's life is dear to you, submit With patience, lest the prophet's anger fall Like thunder on your head; if you obey, Great Mahomet is able to protect you: Guards, lead her to the king.

**Palmira:** O take me, death, From this sad scene of never-ending woe! [Seid and Palmira are carried off.]

**Zopir:** [To Phanor.] They're gone, they're lost: O most unhappy father, The wound which Seid gave is not so deep, So painful as this parting.

**Phanor:** See, my lord, The day appears, and the armed multitudes Press onward to defend the cause of Zopir.

**Zopir:** Support me, Phanor: yet thy friend may live To punish this vile hypocrite; at least In death may serve my dear—my cruel—children.

# ACT V.

### SCENE I.

Mahomet, Omar, Guards at a Distance.

**Omar:** Zopir's approaching death alarms the people, We have endeavored to appease their clamors, And disavowed all knowledge of the deed; To some, we called it the avenging hand Of heaven that favors thus its prophet's cause: With others, we lament his fall, and boast Thy awful justice that will soon avenge it. The crowd attentive listen to thy praise, And all the danger of the storm is o'er; If aught remains of busy faction's rage It is but as the tossing of the waves After the tempest, when the vault of heaven Is placid and serene.

**Mahomet:** Be it our care To keep it so: where are my valiant bands?

**Omar:** All ready; Osman in the dead of night By secret paths conducted them to Mecca.

**Mahomet:** 'Tis strange that men must either be deceived Or forced into obedience: Seid knows not It is a father's blood that he has shed?

**Omar:** Who could inform him of it? he alone Who knew the secret is no more; Hercides Is gone, and Seid soon shall follow him; For know, he has already drunk the poison; His crime was punished ere it was committed: Even whilst he dragged his father to the altar Death lurked within his veins; he cannot live: Palmira, too, is safe; she may be useful: I've given her hopes of Seid's pardon: that May win her to our cause; she dare not murmur, Besides, her heart is flexible and soft, Formed to obey, to worship Mahomet, And make him soon the happiest of mankind: Trembling and pale, behold! they bring her to thee.

**Mahomet**: Collect my forces, Omar, and return.

## SCENE II.
Mahomet, Palmira, Guards.

**Palmira**: O heaven! where am I? gracious God!

**Mahomet**: Palmira, Be not alarmed; already I have fixed Thy fate and Mecca's: know, the great event That fills thy soul with horror is a mystery 'Twixt heaven and me that's not to be revealed: But thou art free, and happy: think no more Of Seid, nor lament him; leave to me The fate of men; be thankful for thy own: Thou knowest that Mahomet hath loved thee long, That I have ever been a father to thee; Perhaps a nobler fate, and fairer title May grace thee still, if thou deservest it; therefore Blot from thy memory the name of Seid, And let thy soul aspire to greater blessings Than it could dare to hope for; let thy heart Be my last noblest victory, and join The conquered world to own me for its master.

**Palmira**: What joys, what blessings, or what happiness Can I expect from thee, thou vile impostor? Thou bloody savage! This alone was wanting, This cruel insult to complete my woes: Eternal Father, look upon this king, This holy prophet, this all-powerful god Whom I adored: thou monster, to betray Two guiltless hearts into the crying sin Of parricide; thou infamous seducer Of my unguarded youth, how darest thou think, Stained as thou art with my dear father's blood, To gain Palmira's heart? but know, proud tyrant, Thou art not yet invincible: the veil Is off that hid thee, and the hand of vengeance Upraised to scourge thy guilt: dost thou not hear The maddening multitude already armed In the defence of injured innocence? From death's dark shades my murdered father comes To lead them on: O that these feeble hands Could tear thee piece-meal, thee and all thy train! Would I could see them weltering in their blood; See Mecca, and Medina, Asia, all Combined against thee! that the credulous world Would shake off thy vile chains, and thy religion Become the jest and scorn of all mankind To after ages! may that hell, whose threats Thou hast so often denounced 'gainst all who dared To doubt thy false divinity, now open Her fiery gates, and be thy just reward! These are the thanks I owe thee for thy bounties, And these the prayers I made for Mahomet.

**Mahomet**: I see I am betrayed; but be it so: Whoe'er thou art, learn henceforth to obey; For know, my heart—

## SCENE III.
Mahomet, Palmira, Omar, Ali, Attendants.

**Omar**: The secret is revealed; Hercides told it in his dying moments: The people all enraged have forced the prison: They're up in arms, and bearing on their shoulders The bloody corpse of their unhappy chief, Lament his fate, and cry aloud for vengeance: All is confusion: Seid at their head Excites them to rebellion, and cries out, "I am a parricide;" with rage and grief He seems distracted; with one voice the crowd Unite to curse the prophet and his God: Even those who promised to admit our forces Within the walls of Mecca, have conspired With them to raise their desperate arms against thee; And naught is heard but cries of death and vengeance.

**Palmira**: Just heaven pursue him, and defend the cause Of innocence!

**Mahomet**: [To Omar.] Well, what have we to fear?

**Omar**: Omar, my lord, with your few faithful friends, Despising danger, are prepared to brave The furious storm, and perish at your feet.

**Mahomet**: Alone I will defend you all; come near: Behold, and say I act like Mahomet.

### SCENE IV.

Mahomet, Omar, and His Party One Side, Seid, and the People on the Other Palmira in the Middle.

**Seid**: Avenge my father, seize the traitor.

**Mahomet**: People, Born to obey me, listen to your master.

**Seid**: Hear not the monster; follow me: [He comes forward a little, and then staggers.] O heaven! What sudden darkness spreads o'er my dim eyes? Now strike, my friends—O I am dying.

**Mahomet**: Ha! Then all is well.

**Palmira**: My brother, canst thou shed No blood but Zopir's?

**Seid**: Yes: come on—I cannot; Some god unnerves me. [He faints.]

**Mahomet**: Hence let every foe Of Mahomet be taught to fear and tremble: Know, ye proud infidels, this hand alone Hath power to crush you all, to me the God Of nature delegates his sovereign power: Acknowledge then his prophet, and his laws, 'Twixt Mahomet and Seid let that God Decide the contest, which of us forever Is guilty, now, this moment let him perish!

**Palmira**: My brother—Seid—can this monster boast Such power? the people stand astonished at him, And tremble at his voice; and wilt thou yield To Mahomet?

**Seid**: [Supported by his attendants.] Alas! the hand of heaven Is on me, and the involuntary crime Is too severely punished: O Palmira, In vain was Seid virtuous: O if heaven Chastises thus our errors, what must crimes Like thine expect, detested Mahomet? What cause hast thou to tremble—O I die; Receive me, gracious heaven, and spare Palmira. [Dies.]

**Palmira**: 'Tis not, ye people, 'tis not angry heaven Pursues my Seid. No: he's poisoned—

**Mahomet**: [Interrupting her, and addressing himself to the people.] Learn From Seid's fate, ye unbelievers, how To reverence Mahomet whom heaven defends; Nature and death, ye see, have heard my voice, And this pale corpse hath witnessed their obedience; The sword of fate hangs o'er your heads, beware It fall not on you: thus will I reward All impious rebels, all vile infidels, And punish every word and thought against me. If I withhold my rage, and let you live, Remember, traitors, that you owe your beings To my indulgence; hasten to the temple. Prostrate yourselves before the throne of grace, And deprecate the wrath of Mahomet. [The people retire.]

**Palmira**: O stay, and hear me, people—the barbarian Poisoned my brother—monster, raised by crimes To empire thus, and deified by guilt, Thou murderer of Palmira's hapless race, Complete thy work, and take my wretched life: O my dear brother, let me follow thee! [She seizes her brother's sword and stabs herself.]

**Mahomet**: Seize, and prevent her—

**Palmira**: 'Tis too late; I die: And dying hope a God more just than thine Has yet in store a state of happiness For injured innocence: let Mahomet Reign here in peace: this world was made for tyrants. [Dies.]

**Mahomet**: She's gone; she's lost; the only dear reward I wished to keep of all my crimes: in vain I fought, and conquered; Mahomet is wretched Without Palmira: Conscience, now I feel thee, And feel that thou canst rive the guilty heart. O thou eternal God, whom I have made The instrument of ill, whom I have wronged, Braved, and blasphemed; O thou whom yet I fear, Behold me self-condemned, behold me wretched, Even whilst the world adores me: vain was all My boasted power: I have deceived mankind; But how shall I impose on my own heart? A murdered father, and two guiltless children Must be avenged: come, ye unhappy victims, And end me quickly!—Omar, we must strive To hide this shameful weakness, save my glory, And let me reign o'er a deluded world: For Mahomet depends on fraud alone, And to be worshipped never must be known.

**End**

# Amelia

## Contents

Dramatis Personæ. . . . . . . . . . . . . . . . . . . . . . . . . . . . . . . . . . . . . 456

Act I. . . . . . . . . . . . . . . . . . . . . . . . . . . . . . . . . . . . . . . . . . . . . . . . . 456

Act II. . . . . . . . . . . . . . . . . . . . . . . . . . . . . . . . . . . . . . . . . . . . . . . . 462

Act III. . . . . . . . . . . . . . . . . . . . . . . . . . . . . . . . . . . . . . . . . . . . . . . 466

Act IV. . . . . . . . . . . . . . . . . . . . . . . . . . . . . . . . . . . . . . . . . . . . . . . 473

Act V. . . . . . . . . . . . . . . . . . . . . . . . . . . . . . . . . . . . . . . . . . . . . . . . 477

## Dramatis Personæ

The Duke of Foix.
Amelia.
Vamir, Brother to the Duke of Foix.
Lisois.
Thais, Confidante of Amelia.
Emar, Friend of Vamir.

This tragedy is founded on historical truth. A duke of Brittany, in the year 1387, commanded the lord of Bavalan to assassinate the constable of Clisson: Bavalan, the day after, told the duke it was done: the duke becoming sensible of the horror of his crime, and apprehensive of the fatal consequences of it, abandoned himself to the most violent despair: Bavalan, after giving him time to repent, at length told him that he had loved him well enough to disobey his orders, etc.

The action is transported to another age and country for particular reasons.

## ACT I.

**SCENE I.**
Amelia, Lisois.

**Lisois:** Permit a soldier, in this seat of war, To steal a moment from the battle's rage, And greet the fair Amelia; to the king Thy noble heart is bound, I know, by ties Of dearest friendship; long and faithfully Hath Lisois served the valiant duke of Foix Who holds thee here a prisoner: well I know The violence of his passion for Amelia, Foresee the dreadful consequence, and come, With all the warmth of friendship, to advise And to consult, to lay my heart before thee Perhaps 'tis not unworthy of thy notice.

**Amelia:** The seal of truth is ever on thy lips, I know thy firm integrity; whate'er Thou sayest, I shall believe.

**Lisois:** Know then, though long I've served the duke with most unwearied zeal, Through years of peril, and unnumbered toils, Yet could I ne'er approve the fatal league That bound him to the Moor, and took from France The noblest of her princes; in these days Of public discord, I have ranged myself Beneath no banners but what honor raised, And followed but the dictates of my heart: Not that, the slave of prejudice, my soul Is blind to all the errors of a friend; With grief I see the duke's impatient warmth, The impetuous ardor of his boiling youth, I cannot shut my eyes against his follies: Ofttimes the torrent which I strive to stop Mocks my weak power, and throws down all before it; But he has virtues that will recompense His worst of faults: if we must follow none But perfect princes, whose unbiassed hearts Are free from every vice, and every weakness, Whom shall we serve? I love the duke; and yet 'Tis with regret I draw the hostile sword 'Gainst France: I wish he could be reconciled.

**Amelia:** If that could e'er be done, thy influence best Might reunite them: if he loves his glory, Sure this misguided prince will listen to thee. How fatal has his error been!

**Lisois:** In vain I've tried to bend his haughty spirit; oft Have I with harsh unwelcome truths attacked him, And sorely pierced his heart: but thou alone Canst bring him to his duty, and his king: That was my errand here: there was a time When on the fair Amelia I had placed My hopes of bliss; without abasement then I thought you might have listened to my vows; But heaven reserved thee for a nobler fate. Whilst I was absent, by the cruel Moors Thou wert enslaved; the happy conqueror came, The gallant Foix, and saved thee from their rage; His was the glory, his be the reward: His claims are strong, his youth, his rank, and power, His fame, and services, all plead for him; Amelia's justice and her gratitude Must bind her to him: I have no pretence, And therefore I am silent; but if merit Could make thee mine, I would dispute the prize Even with the sons of kings, nor yield Amelia To any but to him: he is my master, My leader, and my friend; he loves me well: I am not a half proud, half virtuous lover, But what I still would litigate with power, I give to friendship; nay, I can do more, I can subdue the weakness of my heart, And plead a rival's cause; point out the path Of glory to thee, show thee what is due To that illustrious hero who preserved thee, By whom thou livest: I can behold unmoved, And with unenvying eye, thy charms bestowed On him who best deserves them: take my heart Between you, and accept my honest service, This arm shall fight for both; I sacrifice My passions to your interest: friendship bids me, And I obey; my country too commands: Remember, if the prince is yours, he soon Will be the king's.

**Amelia**: Thy virtues, noble youth, Astonish me; thou givest the admiring world A rare example; canst thou be sincere? And sure thou art so, thus to conquer love, And give up all to friendship! all who know Must wonder at thee: thou hast served thy master. And canst not be an enemy to mine: A heart so generous sure must think with me: 'Tis not in souls like thine to hate their king. Shall I then ask one favor at thy hands?

**Lisois**: Amelia's orders shall be ever sacred: Command, and I obey.

**Amelia**: Thy generous counsel Hath urged me to accept a noble rank I looked not for, and offered by a prince: The choice, I own, does honor to Amelia, When I reflect, that, long before he told His love, he saved my liberty and life; Foe to his sovereign, though the rebel Moor Hath drawn him from his duty and allegiance, Yet he has poured so many favors on me, I cannot bear to hurt him, though, in spite Of all his goodness, and my gratitude, I must refuse him: his unhappy passion Afflicts me; 'tis distressful to my heart, For all his kindness thus to make him wretched. Fain would I spare myself the ungrateful task Of saying that I must not hear his vows: It is not for my feeble voice to tell A prince his duty; 'twere a dangerous power, And I am far from wishing to enjoy it; Who can direct him better than thyself? Alas! my lord, 'tis not a time for love; The royal army at our gates, and naught But war and slaughter all around us: blood On every side! himself against my master, Against his brother, now in arms; all these Are powerful reasons: O my lord, in you Is all my hope; forgive me; O complete The generous work, restore me to my king; Let him do that, 'tis all I ask; but add This effort more to what thou'st done already: Thou hast the strongest influence o'er his heart, A firm and manly soul, a friend like thee, Respected and beloved, will make the voice Of duty heard, his counsels will be laws.

**Lisois**: Alas! those counsels will have little weight Against the passions that possess his soul; His fiery temper gives me too much cause To fear him: he's inclined to jealousy, And if he hears I had a thought of thee, 'Twill drive his soul to madness, and perhaps Undo us all: he must be soothed by art; Leave him to me, and try to reconcile Your jarring interests; weigh his offers well. Henceforth I'll think no more of love and thee, But get me to the field, the soldier's duty Shall there engross me: if thou lovest thy country, If France be dear to thee, restore her hero, And she will bless thee for the deed: farewell.

## SCENE II.
Amelia, Thais.

**Amelia:** Restore him, said he? what! at the dear price Of all my happiness! it cannot be; 'Twere infamous and base, the worst of crimes.

**Thais:** But wherefore is the prince thus hateful to you? Why in these days of discord, war, and tumult, Whilst faction reigns, and of our royal race Brother 'gainst brother arms, and every hour Brings new afflictions, wherefore should Amelia, Whose gentler stars for other purposes Had formed her soul, to love and to be loved, Why should Amelia, with such sentiments Of scorn and hatred, meet a hero's vows Who had avenged her cause? The prince, thou knowest, Amongst his ancestors can boast the blood Of our first kings, and is himself a lord Of rich domains, and wide-extended power. He loves you, offers you his hand: can rank And title, objects that are envied still By all mankind, pursued with eagerness, And gained with rapture, can these only fill Thy heart with sorrow, and thy eyes with tears?

**Amelia:** Because he saved me once, has he a right Now to oppress me? Must Amelia fall A victim to his fatal aid? I know I'm much indebted to him, would I were not!

**Thais:** Nay, that's ungrateful.

**Amelia:** Thou shalt know my heart, My miseries, my duty, and my fate: I will no longer keep the secret from thee, 'Twere cruel to distrust thee; when thou knowest My story, thou mayst justify thy friend. I must not listen to the prince's vows, For know, my heart is given to his brother.

**Thais:** Ha! to the noble Vamir!

**Amelia:** Yes, my friend: With mutual oaths we sealed our mutual faith, And at Leucate I expected him, There to confirm it at the holy altar, When by the cruel Moors that rushed upon us I was surprised, and made a captive; then The prince, to these unconquered savages In firm alliance bound, appeared, and saved me; There's my distress: the life another saved Must be devoted to the faithful Vamir.

**Thais:** But why then thus conceal thy passion? why Nourish a hopeless flame thou shouldst extinguish? He would respect this sacred tie, and check His fruitless passion.

**Amelia:** O I must not tell him: The brothers, to complete my sorrows, armed Against each other, have taken different parties In this destructive war; the faithful Vamir Fights for his king. Thou knowest the violence Of his proud rival: all I can oppose To his fierce rage is melancholy silence; Even yet he knows not that in happier times The gallant Vamir had engaged my heart: To tell it him would fire his jealous soul, And only make Amelia more unhappy. 'Tis time to quit this fatal place, the king With pleasure will receive me: let us hence. The prisoners, Thais, from these walls even now Are breaking forth, and meditate their flight: They will conduct us: I defy all danger, Will hazard all for freedom and repose.

**Thais**: Behold the Duke.

**Amelia**: I cannot speak to him, The starting tear would soon betray me: what Would I not give forever to avoid him!

SCENE III.

Duke of Foix, Lisois, Thais.

**Duke**: [To Thais.] Avoid me! fly me! Thais, stay: thou knowest My sorrows, knowest I love her to distraction; My life depends on her: but let her not Abuse her power, and drive me to despair: I hate her cold respect, her poor return Of gratitude to all my warmth of passion: Delay is cruel, 'tis the worst refusal; 'Tis an affront my heart will ne'er forgive: In vain she boasts to me her loyal zeal, Her fond attachment to her royal master, 'Tis time that all should yield to love and me: Here let her find her country and her king; To me she owes her honor, and her life; And I owe all to her, I owe my love: United as we are by every claim, We must not part, the altar is prepared, She shall be mine; go, tell her all is ready.

SCENE IV.

The Duke, Lisois.

**Lisois**: My lord, remember that our kingdom's safety Depends on this decisive day.

**Duke**: I know it And am resolved to conquer or to die Amelia's husband.

**Lisois**: But the foe advances, And soon will be upon us.

**Duke**: Let him come, I mean to fight him; thinkest thou I'm a coward? Thinkest thou the tyrant love shall e'er extinguish My noble thirst of glory? though she hates, She shall admire me still: she boasts indeed Her sovereign empire o'er my captive heart, But shall not blast my virtue and my fame. No: thy reproaches are unjust; my friend Was too severe; condemn me not unjustly, Love ne'er unnerves the gallant sons of France: Even from the bosom of success and joy, Fearless they fly to arms, and rush on death: And I too will die worthy of Amelia.

**Lisois**: Say rather, worthy of thyself: I think To-day of nothing but the public welfare; I talk of battles, and thou speakest of love. My lord, I've seen the army of the foe: Vamir, so fame reports, is armed against us: From us, I know, he hath long since withdrawn His valiant troops. I know him not, but hear He's of a noble nature: if his soul, Inspired by duty, and by glory warmed, Still feels the tender tie that linked your hearts In earlier years, he may assist us now, And be the means of making wished-for peace. My cares—

**Duke**: Away: I would not be obliged Thus to a brother: shall I sue for peace, And ask forgiveness? yet it hurts my soul To think that Vamir is my foe: I still Remember our past friendship, and the love I bore him once; but since he will oppose me, Since he's no longer ours, why let him go, And serve his king.

**Lisois**: Thy fiery temper braves Too far the patience of an easy monarch.

**Duke**: A monarch! the mere phantom of a king, Unworthy of his race, a royal slave, In golden chains, and seated on a throne Subjected to a petty officer: I'm not afraid of Pepin, their arch-tyrant; I hate a subject that would frighten me, And I despise a king who can't command: If he permits a rebel to usurp The sovereign power, I'll still support my own: This heart's too proud to bend beneath the laws Of these new upstarts who oppress their king: Clovis, my royal ancestor, ne'er taught His sons to cringe beneath a haughty master. At least these faithful Arabs will avenge me; If I must feel a tyrant, let him be A stranger.

**Lisois**: You detest these governors, But they have saved our empire, which your friends, The Arabs, but for them had overthrown: I tremble at this new alliance: Spain Before you stands a terrible example: These savage plunderers, these new tyrants dig Our graves with our own hands. 'Twere better far To yield with prudence.

**Duke**: What, fall down and sue For mercy!

**Lisois**: Your true interest long forgotten—

**Duke**: Revenge is my first interest.

**Lisois**: Love and anger Too long have ruled the bosom of my friend.

**Duke**: I know they have, but cannot conquer nature.

**Lisois**: You may, you ought; nay, I'll not flatter you, But even though I condemn, I'll follow thee; 'Tis a friend's duty to point out the faults Of him he loves; to counsel, to exhort, To save him from the dangerous precipice: This I have done for thee, but thou wilt fall, And I must perish with thee.

**Duke**: O my friend, What hast thou said?

**Lisois**: But what I ought to say: And would to heaven that thou hadst listened to me! What dost thou purpose?

**Duke**: When my ardent hopes Shall be fulfilled, when the ungrateful maid Shall give sweet peace to my distracted mind, Then will I hear the counsels of my friend. What can I purpose now, or what design, Till I have seen the tyrant who must guide My future fate? let her determine for me, Let her save me, and I will save my country.

## ACT II.

**SCENE I.**
The Duke of Foix; [Alone.] She cannot sure again refuse to see me, And urge me to despair! she dare not do it: Fool that I am to give her thus the power; How weak is my proud heart to yield itself A voluntary slave! go, throw thyself, Mean as thou art, beneath the tyrant's feet; Go, make thy life dependent on a word, A look, a smile, from proud Amelia; pass From love to fury, and from tears to rage; 'Tis the last time I e'er will speak to her. I go—

**SCENE II.**
The Duke, Amelia and Thais Advancing from the Upper End of the Stage.
**Amelia**: There's hope, my Thais; yet I tremble. Would Vamir hazard this bold enterprise? 'Tis full of danger; ha! what do I see? [Advancing towards the Duke.]
**Duke**: Amelia, what hath this way led thy steps I know not, but thy eyes too plainly tell me That I was not the object of their search: What! still turn from me, still insult the heart That dotes upon thee! cruel tyrant, thus To blast the laurels planted on my brow: O if Amelia's hand had placed them there They might have flourished, but she has forgot Her plighted faith, and broke her flattering promise.
**Amelia**: Thou never hadst my faith, I never gave Thee promise, gratitude is all I owe thee.
**Duke**: Did I not offer thee my hand?
**Amelia**: Thou didst: It was an honor which I could not merit, And which I never sought, but I received it With due respect; you thought, no doubt, a rank So glorious must have dazzled poor Amelia. At length, my lord, 'tis time to undeceive you; I do it with regret, because I know It will offend you, but I must be plain: In short, my lord, I love my king too well To think of wedding with his foe: thy blood, I know, is noble; mine is spotless yet, Nor will be stained with foul disloyalty, And I inherit from my ancestors The fixed abhorrence of my country's foes: Nor will I e'er acknowledge for a master The friend of tyrants, be he e'er so great: Such is my firm resolve; perhaps, my lord, It may seem harsh, but you obliged me to it.
**Duke**: This is a language, madam, which I own I looked not for; I never could have thought That angry heaven, to make me doubly wretched, Would choose Amelia for its instrument Of vengeance: you have studied long in secret The arts of black ingratitude, of scorn And insult, and now open all your heart. I was a stranger to this patriot zeal, This most heroic ardor for thy country, This fetch of policy; but tell me, madam, Whom have you here but this insulted lover, The injured Foix, to succor and support you? Thou hast reproached me with my new

alliance, Those faithful friends on whom I here rely For all my safety, and for all my power: Without their aid thou hadst been still a captive; To them you owed your liberty and life, And am I thus rewarded?

**Amelia:** You prolonged My wretched days; but are they therefore yours, And may I not dispose them as I please? Did you preserve me but to make me wretched, To be a tyrant o'er the life you saved?

**Duke:** Ungrateful woman, thou deservest the name Of tyrant most, for now I read thy soul, See through the thin disguise, behold too plainly My own dishonor, and thy treacherous falsehood: I know thou lovest another, but whoe'er He be that thus hath robbed me of thy heart, Fear thou my love, and tremble at my rage; For, if he be on earth, I'll find the traitor, And tear him from thee: if amidst its horrors My soul could feel one momentary joy, 'Twould be to make thee wretched.

**Amelia:** No: my lord, Indeed it would not; reason will forbid it: Thy soul's too noble to oppress with woe A life which thou hadst saved; but if thy heart Should ever stoop so low, thy virtues still, Thy goodness in my memory shall live, And only thy unkindness be forgotten. I pity, and forgive thee; thou wilt blush Hereafter at the thought of injuring me; Spite of thy threats, my soul is yet unmoved, Nor dreads thy anger, nor defies thy power.

**Duke:** Forgive the transports of a mind disturbed, The rage of love embittered by despair; Lisois, I find, holds secret conference with you, Abets you falsehood, and defends your conduct; Leans to the royal party, and combines In vain with you to make a convert of me: It seems I'm to be governed by your will, And not my own: your converse is the same, The same your purpose; but why use these arms Against me? to persuade my easy heart, Why must Amelia seek a stranger's aid? A word will win me, if 'tis spoke by love.

**Amelia:** My heart, I own, hath opened to thy friend Its hopes and fears, but he hath done much more Than he had promised: pity then my tears, Pity my sorrows, be thyself again; Subdue a passion which Amelia must not, Cannot return: accept my gratitude, 'Tis all I have to give thee.

**Duke:** Lisois, then, And he alone, enjoys thy confidence, Thy friendship, more perhaps; I see it now.

**Amelia:** You may perhaps hereafter, but at present You have no right, sir, to control my thoughts, My actions, or my words; no right to blame me, Or to complain: I sought thy friend's assistance, And he has given it me; I wish, my lord, That you would learn to act and think like him.

### SCENE III.

**The Duke:** [Alone.] 'Tis well: this base, ungrateful, perjured woman, Without a blush, confesses all her falsehood; The mystery is unfolded now: one friend,

One only friend, I had, and he destroys me. Friendship! vain phantom, unsubstantial shade, So often sought for, and so seldom found, Thou ever hadst some wholesome draught to pour Into my cup of sorrow; but at last Thou, too, like love, hast cruelly deceived me! For the reward of all my errors past I have but this, that no allurements now, No flattering pleasures, henceforth shall betray me; For from this hour I will be fond—of nothing. But lo! the traitor comes with cruel hand To tear my wounds, and make them bleed afresh.

### SCENE IV.
The Duke, Lisois.

**Lisois**: My lord, I come obedient to thy orders: But why that frown, those eyes of discontent That scowl upon me? has thy soul, long time The sport of passion, weighed in reason's scale Thy interest, and thy happiness?

**Duke**: It has.

**Lisois**: And what was the result?

**Duke**: My eyes are opened To falsehood and deceit; I've learned to find A rival and a traitor in my friend.

**Lisois**: How's that!

**Duke**: It is enough.

**Lisois**: Too much, my lord: Who is the traitor?

**Duke**: Canst thou ask me who? Who but thyself was privy to the wrongs I have received, who else must answer for them? I know, Amelia hath conversed with thee Here, in the palace; when I mentioned thee She trembled: this affected silence speaks Your guilt more plainly, and I know not which Most to abhor, Amelia, or—my friend.

**Lisois**: Canst thou yet listen to that friend?

**Duke**: I can.

**Lisois**: Thinkest thou I still am anxious for my fame? Dost thou esteem, and canst thou yet believe me?

**Duke**: I will: for till this hour I thought thee virtuous, And held thee for my friend.

**Lisois**: Those noble titles Have hitherto conducted me through life; But wherefore justify myself to thee? Thou'st not deserved it: know, Amelia's charms Long since had touched my heart, before thy hand Had set her free, and saved her precious life, But by the ties of gratitude she's thine; Thou hast deserved her by thy services: For me, I'm more the soldier than the soft And tender lover; I despise the art Of base seduction, fit for courts alone, And flattery's smooth perfidiousness; my soul Is made of firmer stuff: I talked indeed Of marriage to her; and that sacred tie, Knit by esteem and fair equality Of fortune and condition, might have made her More happy far than rank and titles could, That

## Voltaire

stand upon a dangerous precipice: But yesternight, you know, I visited Your ramparts, when your jealous soul alarmed Discovered all its passion; I observed it: To-day I saw the object of your grief, Your loved Amelia, and beheld her charms With eyes of cold indifference: o'er myself I gained an easy conquest: I did more, Pleaded for thee, for an ungrateful friend, And urged a passion which I can't approve; Recalled the memory of thy bounties past, Thy glory and thy rank, acknowledged faults I knew you had, and numbered all your virtues; All this against myself I did for thee; For my friend's happiness gave up my own: And if the sacrifice is still imperfect, Show me the rival that still dares to oppose thee, And I will stake my life to do thee justice.

**Duke**: My friend, thou soarest above me; I am fallen, Abashed, confounded: who could see Amelia And not adore her? but to conquer thus Thy passion! O thou never couldst have loved her.

**Lisois**: I did: but love, like other passions, acts With different force on different minds.

**Duke**: I love Too well, my friend, and cannot imitate The virtue I admire: my foolish heart—

**Lisois**: I ask not for thy praises, but thy love; And if thou thinkest that I have merited Aught at thy hands, O do but serve thyself, Thy happiness is Lisois' best reward. Thou seest with what determined hate thy brother Pursues the Moor, I dread the consequence: The people groan beneath this foreign yoke, Soon, I foresee, the empire will unite Their scattered powers, new enemies still rise Against us, the pure blood of Clovis still Is worshipped by the crowd, and soon or late The branches of this sacred tree, that long Have bent beneath the storm, again shall rise, Spring with fresh verdure, and overshade the land. Placed by thy rank and fortunes near the throne, Long time thou wert thy king and country's friend; But in the days of public discord, fate Attached thee to another cause; perhaps New interests now may call for new connections, And what united may dissolve the tie; The power of these despotic governors May be restrained, and weakened by thy hand—

**Duke**: I wish it were so; thinkest thou then Amelia Would listen to me? if I should embrace The royal party, might she still be mine?

**Lisois**: I am a stranger to Amelia's heart; But what are her designs, her views to thee? Must love alone decide the nation's fate? In Touraine's field, when gallant Clovis fought, And, o'er the haughty conquerors of Rome Victorious, stopped the bloody Arian's hand, That dealt destruction round us, did he save His country, thinkest thou, but to please a mistress? This arm against a rival is prepared To serve my friend, but I would serve him more, Would cure him of this fond, destructive passion; This love deceives us, we're too fearful of him; We wound ourselves, and lay the blame on him; The coward's tyrant, and the hero's slave; He may be conquered; Lisois has subdued him, And shall he triumph o'er the blood of kings Who never yet submitted to a foe? Awake, my friend, and be our great example In every virtue.

**Duke**: Yes, I will do all, All for Amelia; she must yield at last. Her laws, her king, her master, shall be mine: I have no will but her, and in her eyes Will read my duty, and my fate: possessed Of the dear treasure, will be reconciled To every foe. O how my heart enjoys The pleasing hope! I had no cause to fear, I have no rival; if thou art not loved, I can have none: who in this court would dare To cast one look towards Amelia? now Her vain pretexts are vanished; reason, glory, My interest, and my birth, the sacred right Of my great ancestors, all, all unite To bind the nuptial chain, and make me happy. Henceforth I am the king's, and will support him So virtue bids, and beauty has commanded. On this blest day will I confirm the oaths I made to love: away, my friend, I leave My interest and my fortunes to thy care.

**Lisois**: Permit me, then, my lord, to seek the king: I could have wished that this important change Were to the hero, not the lover due; But be it as it may, the effect's too glorious To blame the cause: I triumph in thy weakness, And bless for once the lucky power of love.

### SCENE V.

The Duke, Lisois, an Officer.

**Officer**: My lord, the foe advances; we expect A fierce assault, and wait your orders; time Is precious.

**Duke**: Cruel fate! to counteract My noble purpose! then farewell to peace, And welcome, victory! I'll deserve Amelia: I heed not these rash fools: of all the foes I have to conquer, there's but one to fear, And that's—Amelia.

# ACT III.

### SCENE I.

Duke of Foix, Lisois.

**Duke**: The day is ours; thanks to thy friendly hand That guided my rash youth; thy noble soul, In peace or war, is my best counsellor.

**Lisois**: The glorious fire that animates thy heart Must always conquer, when 'tis checked by prudence, As here it was: preserve this happy virtue, 'Twill make thee happy, and 'twill make thee great; The coward is restless, but the hero calm.

**Duke**: How is the lover? can he ever taste Of sweet tranquillity? But say, my friend, This unknown chief, that mounted on our ramparts, And with his single arm so long suspended The doubtful victory: I grow jealous of him: Where is he? what became of him?

**Lisois:** Surrounded By slaughtered friends, alone long time he stood, And braved opposing legions; but what most Surprised us, when at length he had escaped From every danger, wondrous to relate! He yielded up himself a prisoner to us; Conceals his rank and name, accuses heaven, And begs for instant death. One friend alone Attends him, and partakes his sorrows.

**Duke:** Lisois, Who can this bold, this fearless soldier be? He wore his beaver down: some secret charm O'erpowered my trembling soul when I opposed him. Whether this fatal passion that enslaves me Hath spread its weakness o'er each faculty, And left the soft impression on my soul, Or that my bleeding country's voice alarmed This conscious heart, and silently reproached me.

**Lisois:** As for the weakness of thy soul, advice I know were vain, but sure thy country's voice May still be heard; now is the time to show The greatness of thy soul, and give us peace. Fortune, that smiled on us to-day, perhaps May frown to-morrow, and thy pride be forced To sue for pardon to a haughty foe. Since thou art happy, and Amelia's thine, Now rest thy glory on the common cause, This brave unknown may forward our designs; Let us improve the lucky moment.

**Duke:** Yes, My friend, I will do all to serve Amelia, Her cause is mine: I must prepare the minds Of my brave followers for the change; to thee, And to thy happy counsels, every bliss, Glory and peace, and hymeneal joys, To thee I owe, to friendship and to love.

## SCENE II.
Lisois, Vamir and Emarat the Farther End of the Stage.

**Lisois:** It is the noble prisoner, and his friend, If I mistake not: this way they advance; He seems o'erwhelmed with deep despair.

**Vamir:** O heaven! Where am I? whither dost thou lead me?

**Lisois:** Stranger, Whoe'er thou art, be comforted; thy fate Hath thrown thee into noble hands: thou'lt find A generous master, who can see desert Even in a foe: may I not ask thy name?

**Vamir:** I am a poor abandoned wretch, the sport Of fortune, one whose least affliction is To be a captive, and from every eye Would wish to hide the story of my fate: It is enough to be supremely wretched, Without this cruel witness of my woe: Too soon my name and sorrows will be known.

**Lisois:** Respect is due to misery like thine; I will not urge thee further, but retire: Perhaps even here thy soul may find relief In generous treatment, and a milder fate.

## SCENE III.
Vamir, Emar.

**Vamir:** A milder fate! I must not hope for it: O I have lived too long.

**Emar:** Thank heaven, my lord, That we are fallen amongst such noble foes, And shall not groan beneath a stranger's power.

**Vamir:** No yoke sometimes so galling as a brother's.

**Emar:** But you were bred together, and the ties Of tenderest friendship linked your hearts.

**Vamir:** They did: But O the friendship of our early years Soon takes its flight: he loved me once, and still This heart retains a brother's kindness for him: I cannot hate him, though he conquered me.

**Emar:** He knows not yet how great a captive comes To grace his triumph; knows not that a brother Is in his power, whom vengeance had inspired.

**Vamir:** No: Emar, never did a thought of vengeance Enter my heart; a different passion swayed The soul of Vamir: can it be, just heaven! Or is it but the lying voice of fame, That my Amelia's false, that she has broke Her solemn vows? for whom, too? added guilt To her, and double sorrow to thy friend! The sacred laws of nature, and the ties Of tender love, all broken, all betrayed! Unjust, inhuman brother!

**Emar:** Knows he then How dear a treasure he hath robbed thee of In thy Amelia? did not Vamir say That he was still a stranger to thy love?

**Vamir:** But she is not: she knows what solemn ties, What strict engagements, bound us to each other: That at the altar, ere we had confirmed Our mutual vows, the barbarous Moor rushed in, And tore her from me; the base ravishers Escaped my vengeance, and my happier brother Enjoys the precious treasure Vamir lost Ungrateful woman! came I here, my friend, But to reproach her? what will it avail? She will not listen to my fond complaint: But to my royal master I have lived A faithful servant, and to false Amelia, And faithful will I die: when she shall know How well I loved her, she may shed a tear, And in a brother's arms lament my fate.

**Emar:** Repress thy sorrows; see, the duke approaches.

**Vamir:** Be still, my heart.

SCENE IV.

Duke of Foix, Vamir, Emar.

**Duke:** This mystery alarms me: But I must see this noble captive: ha! He turns aside with horror.

**Vamir:** Hateful life! Must I support thee still? must I again Behold the faithless wretch?

**Duke:** What do I hear?

**Vamir:** Dost thou not know me?

**Duke:** Ha! my brother! Vamir!

Vamir: Alas! too sure I am that wretched brother, Thy vanquished foe, a poor abandoned captive.

Duke: Thou art my brother still, and I forgive thee; But 'tis most strange, and most unnatural: Could the king find no instrument but thee To execute his vengeance on my head? What had I done to Vamir?

Vamir: Made his life Unhappy: would that thou hadst taken it from me!

Duke: Dreadful effects of civil strife!

Vamir: More dreadful Are the deep wounds that pierce the heart of Vamir.

Duke: Against another foe I might have shown A soldier's courage, but I pity thee.

Vamir: Pity thyself, the wretch who has betrayed His country, and deceived the king that loved him; A traitor, and unworthy of thy race.

Duke: Brand me not, Vamir, with opprobrious name Of traitor, lest I should forget myself, And spurn thee for the insult: no, my brother, I'm not that base, ungrateful wretch thou thinkest me; Thou seest me ready to restore fair peace, And heal the wounds of my divided country.

Vamir: Thou heal our wounds! thou—

Duke: Yes: the day that seemed So fatal to thy peace shall quench the flames Of public discord, and unite us all.

Vamir: O 'tis a day of sorrow.

Duke: Of delight And joy, the day that crowns my wishes—

Vamir: How!

Duke: Yes, Vamir, all is changed, and I am happy.

Vamir: It may be so: I heard indeed thy heart These three months past has been the slave of love; And if report say true, most violent And fierce thy passion.

Duke: Thou hast heard aright; I love her even to madness: thou art come In happy hour to make our bliss complete. Yes: I will lay my friends, my foes, my every claim, Revenge and glory, all beneath her feet. Go, tell her two unhappy brothers, long [To his attendants.] By adverse fate to different interests bound, Wait but a look from her to be united. [To Vamir.] Blame not my passion, Vamir, when thou seest The lovely object, soon thou wilt approve it.

Vamir: [Aside.] And does she love thee? cruel thought!

Duke: At least She ought: one obstacle alone remained, And that shall be removed.

Vamir: [Aside.] Inhuman brother! Knowest thou what led me to this fatal place, And meanest thou to insult me?

Duke: Let us bury In deep oblivion every thought of discord; Behold, the fair Amelia comes.

**SCENE V.**
Duke of Foix, Vamir, Amelia.

**Amelia**: O heaven! What do I see? I die.

**Duke**: Amelia, listen, And mark how happiness ariseth oft From our misfortunes; this day I have conquered, And this day found a brother; thou, my Vamir, Shalt be a witness to the power of love. What nor Amelia's prayers, nor her reproaches, My generous friend, my country, and my king, Long time in vain solicited, her charms At length have won: to them I yield submissive. Amelia, whilst I was thy sovereign's foe, Thou wouldst not listen to my vows: henceforth I have no laws, no friends, no king, but thine: So love commands, and love shall be obeyed. Vamir, thou'rt free: be thou the messenger Of welcome tidings to the court: away, And tell the king I hasten to present His fair ally, the conqueror who subdued A rebel's heart, and of a dangerous foe Hath made a faithful subject; changed by her, And her alone.

**Vamir**: [Aside.] 'Tis as I wished: my fate Will soon be known: speak, and pronounce our doom.

**Duke**: Amelia, speak, art thou not satisfied With my submission? Is it not enough To see a conqueror thus humbly kneel Before thee? Can my life alone content Thy cruel heart? take it, ungrateful woman! I wished but to preserve it for thy sake; For thee alone I lived, for thee will die.

**Amelia**: I am astonished, and my faltering voice Will scarce give utterance to my words—my lord, If thy great soul laments thy country's fate, And feels for her distress, thy generous care Must spring from nobler motives than the wish To serve Amelia; thou hast heard the voice Of powerful nature: what hath love to do Where only honor hath a right to dictate?

**Duke**: 'Tis thy own work, Amelia, all thy own: O'er every interest, every passion, love Superior reigns; reproach me, cover me With shame, no matter: I must force thy heart; Come to the altar.

**Vamir**: Darest thou—

**Amelia**: No, my lord; I'd sooner die: my life's at thy command, But not my heart: there is a fatal bar Between us, and I never can be thine.

**Duke**: 'Tis well, ungrateful—dost thou hear her, Vamir? But I'll be calm: I'll not complain of thee, I see thee now: the soft persuasive arts That call our passions forth, the flattering hope That's given but to betray, the subtle poison Spread o'er our hearts, deceitful all and vain, No longer shall seduce my easy faith, The eye of reason hath detected them, And the same art that bound hath set me free: I will not blush before thee, Vamir: no, I will not be despised: but let me see This hidden rival, bring him here before me, And I will yield him up the worthless prize; For know, I have contempt enough for both To wish you were united; that alone Should be your punishment.

**Amelia:** Perhaps, my lord, 'Twere fittest for Amelia to retire In silence, but I hold my honor dear, And must defend it: I have been accused Before thy brother, and must answer thee. Know, then, I'm destined to another's arms; I own my love, my tender passion for him; Amelia were unworthy of his heart, Had she e'er given a distant hope to thee: But thou wouldst seize my faith and liberty, As if they were by right of conquest thine. I owed thee much, but injuries like these, My lord, discharge the debt of gratitude, And cancel all: I saw, and pitied long The violence of thy fruitless passion for me; Do not then make me hate thee: I rejected Thy proffered vows, but never scorned thy love: I wished for thy esteem, and gave thee mine.

**Duke:** Perfidious woman! naught hast thou deserved But my resentment, which thou soon shalt know Is equal to my love: thou waitedst then For Vamir to be witness of my shame! I should have thought he was himself the traitor, If—but he ne'er beheld thy fatal charms, My happier brother never knew Amelia. Who is this rival? let me know his name, But think not I will tamely yield to him. No: I deceived thee there, but cannot long Dissemble; I will drag thee to the altar, There, as he dies in torment, shall he see Our hands united; I will dip in blood The torch of Hymen: well I know that princes Have been despised for mean and vulgar slaves, But I shall find him.

**Vamir:** Why shouldst thou suppose This rival so contemptible?

**Duke:** And why Shouldst thou excuse him? Didst thou never know her? 'Tis dreadful to conceive it. If thou didst, Now, traitor, tremble.

**Vamir:** Vamir tremble? No: Too long already I have borne in silence Thy cruel insults; know me now, barbarian, Know a despair that's equal to thy own: Strike here; behold thy brother, and thy rival.

**Duke:** Thou, Vamir, thou?

**Vamir:** Yes: for these two years past We've been united in the strictest bonds Of tender love; the only good on earth I wished to keep, thy cruel hand hath strove To ravish from me, made my life unhappy: Judge of my miseries by thy own: we both Are jealous, both were born the slaves of passion: Hatred and love, resentment, and despair, Possess our souls, and all in the extreme: Thou wert my rival, therefore I opposed thee: Furious and blind, I ran, I flew to save The object of my love; not all thy power Restrained me, nor my weakness, time nor place, Not even thy noble courage; love prevailed O'er friendship, and the ties of blood: be thou Cruel like me, like me unnatural. Whilst I have life, thou never canst enjoy Thy conquest, never canst possess Amelia: Strike, then, and punish, shed thy brother's blood; But when thou draggest her with thee to the altar, Remember, she's thy sister, and my wife.

**Duke:** Guards, seize the traitor, take him from my sight.

**Amelia:** Stay, cruel prince; art thou inflexible, Deaf to the voice of nature? O, my lord!

**Vamir:** Sue not for me, Amelia, Vamir's fate Is to be envied: he most claims your pity Who hath betrayed his king, and injured thee: I am revenged, the victory is mine; For thou art hated here, and I'm beloved.

**Amelia:** [Kneeling to the Duke.] O dearest prince, my lord, see at your feet—

**Duke:** Away with him: rise, madam, for thy tears And fruitless prayers to save a traitor's life But pour fresh poison o'er my wounded heart That bleeds for thee; but I will die, Amelia, Not unrevenged: when thou shalt feel my rage Accuse thyself; the work is all thy own.

**Amelia:** I cannot leave thee: O my lord, yet hear—

**Duke:** If I must hear thee, speak, go on.

SCENE VI.

The Duke, Vamir, Amelia, Lisois.

**Lisois:** My lord, The people are in arms; at Vamir's name They rose tumultuous, and on every side Disorder reigns; the affrighted soldiers leave Their colors, and in wild confusion fly: Meantime the foe unites his scattered powers, And rushes on us.

**Duke:** Go, ungrateful woman! Thou hast not long to glory in thy crimes; Follow her— [To one of her attendants.] I must to the factious crowd And show myself: thou, Lisois, guard this traitor.

SCENE VII.

Vamir, Lisois.

**Lisois:** Art thou a traitor? couldst thou thus disgrace Thy noble blood, to violate the laws Of nature? could a prince so far forget His duty and himself?

**Vamir:** I never did: The people's just: my brother is a rebel, And has betrayed his master.

**Lisois:** Hear me, Vamir; My soul desires no greater happiness Than to unite you: long have I beheld With deep regret my bleeding country's woes, Our fields laid waste, and nature sacrificed To discord and revenge; the haughty Moor, Raised on our ruins, menacing the state, Which we have weakened by our own divisions. O if thou bearest a heart that's truly noble, And worthy of thy race, now save thy country; Exert thy power to reconcile the king, Soften thy brother, and put out the flames Of civil war.

**Vamir:** Impossible! thy cares Are fruitless all and vain: if naught but discord, Revenge and hatred, led me to the field, Had glory and ambition fired my breast, Thou mightest have hoped indeed to reunite us; But there's a bar more fatal still behind.

*Lisois*: What could it be! O tell me, Vamir.

*Vamir*: Love: Love that has filled this breast with savage fury, And made my brother cruel and inhuman.

*Lisois*: Good heaven! that vain caprice should thus destroy The noblest purposes! Almighty love, Canst thou reverse the laws of nature, fill With unrelenting hate the jealous hearts Of fondest brothers, and in every clime By private passions work the public ruin? Vamir, I feel for both, but long have served Thy brother; I must hence, and second him Against thy factious friends: the strife is dreadful, And much I fear will have a bloody end; But I must fly to succor him: farewell; Thou art my prisoner, but I leave thee here; Give me thy word, that shall suffice.

*Vamir*: I do.

*Lisois*: Would I could knit you in the bonds of peace! But much more to be feared than all thy foes And far more fatal, is the tyrant, love.

# ACT IV.

SCENE I.

Vamir, Amelia, Emar.

*Amelia*: O Vamir, how the hand of heaven hath marked My life with sad variety of woe! The chance of war, that tore me from thy arms. Once more hath joined us; but, alas! we meet On mournful terms, meet but to part; my Vamir, Didst thou not say it must be so?

*Vamir*: It must: Thou seest me chained by honor's laws beneath A rival's power: my sacred word is given: Vamir may die, but must not follow thee.

*Amelia*: Thou who hast dared to fight, art thou afraid To flee from him?

*Vamir*: I am: my honor binds me: Take thou advantage of the general tumult, Which favors thy retreat: a guard attends To aid thy flight; heaven will protect thy virtues; Hope for the best.

*Amelia*: What can Amelia hope, When thou art from her?

*Vamir*: 'Tis but for a day.

*Amelia*: O but that day will be an age to me. Grant, heaven! my tears and terrors may be vain. The Moor, I know, thirsts for my Vamir's blood; Thinkest thou thy brother will not give it him? He loves with fury, and he hates with rancor; His hatred, like his love, is in extreme: He is thy rival, and the Moor's ally. I tremble for thee.

*Vamir*: He would never dare—

*Amelia*: O his impetuous passion knows no bounds!

**Vamir**: He must be taught to know them soon; the king Comes to avenge us; half his force already Throngs to the royal standard; if thou lovest me, Fly, my Amelia, from the impending storm, From dreadful slaughter, and the din of arms, And all the terrors of a bloody field; But, above all, avoid my furious rival, Whose jealous love despised, will turn to rage; Avoid an insult Vamir must avenge, Or perish in the attempt: my dear Amelia, Hope of my life, the only good on earth I have to boast, do not expose thyself To needless dangers, but retire in safety.

**Amelia**: Why wilt thou hazard then thy precious life, And stay without Amelia?

**Vamir**: When thou art safe, I shall not fear my brother; soon perhaps Vamir may prove his best support: to-day I am his prisoner, but perchance to-morrow May be his patron, and persuade the king To spare a rebel: to protect my rival Were noble triumph. Haste, Amelia, leave This seat of danger.

**Amelia**: Wheresoever fate Shall cast my hapless lot, I'll carry with me My hatred and my love; 'midst every danger, In the wild desert, or the gloomy dungeon, In exile, or in chains, in death itself, Still shall I think of, still adore my Vamir: But O I cannot bear to live without thee!

**Vamir**: It is too much: thy griefs unman my soul. What noise was that? O thou hast staid too long!

### SCENE II.

Amelia, Vamir, Duke of Foix, Guards.

**Duke**: I hear his voice; 'tis he: stay, villain, thou Who hast betrayed me.

**Vamir**: I betrayed thee not. Now satiate thy revenge, and take my life; Lose not a moment, for the hand of heaven Is raised against thee: tremble, slave, thy king Approaches: thou hast conquered none but Vamir: Thy master comes, take heed.

**Duke**: He may avenge, But cannot save thee; for thy blood—

**Amelia**: O no, Amelia's guilty: let Amelia die, And not my Vamir: I deceived thy guards, And bartered with them to assist my flight From hated slavery, and a tyrant's power: Punish my crimes, but, O respect a brother, Respect thyself, thy own unblemished fame! He ne'er betrayed, but loves and would have served thee, Even when thy rage had doomed him to destruction. What crime has he committed? none, my lord, None but the crime of loving his Amelia.

**Duke**: The more thou pleadest for him, the more his guilt: Thou art his murderer: thou, whose fatal charms Have poisoned all our happiness, and armed Our hands against each other, may the blood Of both fall on thee! now thou weepest; thy tears No longer shall deceive me: I must die, But Vamir first shall perish. Yet I love thee, Even yet thou mayest escape the fatal blow: Accept my hand, attend me to the altar, And seal his pardon there.

**Amelia**: Who, I, my lord?

**Duke**: It is enough.

**Amelia**: Shall I be false to Vamir?

**Duke**: Stop—answer me.

**Amelia**: I cannot.

**Duke**: Let him die.

**Vamir**: Amelia, never let his threats o'ercome Thy noble faith, but love me well enough To see me perish: leave me to my fate; Now I shall fall triumphant: shouldst thou yield, Vamir must die by his Amelia's hand.

**Duke**: Guards, drag the traitor to the tower: away.

## SCENE III.
Duke, Amelia.

**Amelia**: And wilt thou make this horrid sacrifice? Pollute thee with the blood of innocence? Thou wilt not!

**Duke**: Yes: to hate thee, and to die, Is all I wish; to see thee more unhappy, More wretched than myself, to shed the blood That's dearest to thee, and to make thy days As full of woe as was that fatal hour Which hath destroyed us all. Away, and leave me; The sight of thee distracts me.

## SCENE IV.
Duke, Amelia, Lisois.

**Amelia**: From thy justice, And, that alone, I can expect relief. Help me to soften this obdurate heart: Assist me, Lisois.

**Duke**: If thou listenest to her, Thou art not my friend.

**Amelia**: I call just heaven to witness.

**Duke**: Hence from my sight: I loathe thee.

**Amelia**: Tyrant, go, For I abhor thee; spite of all thy rage, I thought a woman might at least command Some cold respect: but love, that softens all, Hath lost its tender influence o'er thy heart: I leave thee to thy rage; go, sacrifice Thy victims, amidst thy crimes be sure thou count Amelia's death, and with it count thy own, For vengeance comes, and in thy punishment Unites us all; inglorious shalt thou perish, And unlamented. Die, inhuman savage; And may that hatred, that contempt of thee, Which now I feel, pursue thy memory, And after ages execrate thy name!

## SCENE V.
Duke of Foix, Lisois.

**Duke:** Yes, cruel prophet, I expect the doom Pronounced by thee, that discord's fatal hand Shall seize on all, and join us in the tomb.

**Lisois:** Rage has o'erpowered him, and his senses fail.

**Duke:** What says my friend? am I to suffer shame And insult thus; and shall my haughty rival Bear off the false, perfidious, dear Amelia? Wilt thou bear this, or waitest thou till the traitor Shall raise a powerful faction to enslave me?

**Lisois:** Too well I see, my lord, the royal party Hath spread sedition through the multitude, And shook their faith.

**Duke:** Vamir lights up the flame: He has betrayed us all.

**Lisois:** I never meant To palliate Vamir's crimes, for much I dread The fatal consequence; already France Is armed against us. If the people seek Their safety in rebellion, all is lost, Danger's on every side.

**Duke:** What's to be done?

**Lisois:** Prevent it; rage and love must be subdued; Then may we conquer all. We must be firm And resolute; avoid, or brave the storm, Do as thou wilt, my hand is ready still To aid my friend. This morning thou hadst thoughts Of treating with the king: if thou commandest, I'll go, my lord, even now, and sue for peace; Or if we try the fortune of the day, The faithful Lisois shall attend thee still: There, if thou fallest, thy friend shall not survive thee.

**Duke:** Alone I will descend into the grave: Live thou, to serve my cause, and to avenge me. My hour is come, I must fulfil my fate: Who wishes but for death, is sure to find it; But mine should come with all his terrors round him; I must have vengeance; and whene'er I fall, Will drag my rival with me to the tomb.

**Lisois:** What horrid thoughts are these!

**Duke:** In yonder tower He is confined: 'tis under thy command, And thou didst promise, that whene'er—

**Lisois:** Of whom Speakest thou, my lord? a brother?

**Duke:** No: a traitor, My worst of foes, a rival who abhors me; One who has robbed me of my dearest treasure: The Moor demands his head, and I have promised To give it him.

**Lisois:** Ha! promised to shake off The bonds of nature and humanity!

**Duke:** Long since they had proscribed him.

**Lisois:** And to them, Thou yieldest his life?

**Duke:** Not to their vengeance only, But to my own, which shall be satisfied. What is the Moor to me, or what my country?

**Lisois:** To love then you would make the sacrifice, And I must be the executioner.

**Duke:** No: I expect not so much justice from thee; I am a wretch, abandoned and forlorn, Betrayed by love, deserted by my friend; But there are those who yet will keep their promise; Others, perhaps, may serve me, nor allege Such poor excuses for ingratitude.

**Lisois**: [After a long silence.] I am resolved; and be it guilt or justice, Ne'er shalt thou say that Lisois hath betrayed thee: Thou art unhappy: Vamir is a traitor. It is enough; I love thee, and consent: There is a time for desperate extremes, When duties the most sacred must give way To hard necessity: at such an hour I cannot suffer thee to try the faith Of any heart but mine: success alone Must prove my friendship: soon shalt thou determine Whether thy Lisois loved thee, and was faithful.

**Duke**: Once more in sorrow I behold a friend; Deserted by the world, in thee I find My only refuge: thou wilt not permit A haughty rival to insult my rage, To trample on my ashes, and enjoy My kingdom in the arms of my Amelia.

**Lisois**: I will not; but in recompense for this, I must demand another sacrifice.

**Duke**: What is it? speak.

**Lisois**: I cannot bear the Moor, Our insolent protector; cannot bear To see him lord it o'er thy noble subjects. I would not serve a tyrant, nor submit To shameful slavery for a poor support We do not want; 'tis in our power at least To die without him: leave to me, my lord, The conduct of this day, perhaps my service May claim it of thee: Lisois and the Moor Would ne'er agree: I must command alone, To the last hour.

**Duke**: Thou shalt: I'll give thee all Thou canst desire, let but Amelia feel Despair like mine, and weep in tears of blood Her treacherous lover: let me hear her groans In my last moments to delight my soul; And for the rest, 'tis equal all: to thee I trust my glory; go, dispose, command, Prepare thee for the field. I hope not now For victory, nor for honorable death; For what is honor to a heart like mine, Sunk in despair! O be the sad remembrance Of a false mistress, and a cruel rival, Buried with me in everlasting silence!

**Lisois**: Eternal night, if possible, should hide Such dreadful deeds: would death had closed our eyes Before this day of horrors; but I go To keep my word, and save my friend. Farewell.

# ACT V.

### SCENE I.
Duke of Foix, an Officer.

**Duke**: Perpetual misery! am I doomed to see Nothing but faction, treason, and revolt? Where are the rebels, do they mutiny?

**Officer**: At sight of you, my lord, the crowd dispersed.

**Duke**: On every side I am oppressed by Vamir; All hearts are his; my miseries are complete; But what hath Lisois done?

**Officer:** His watchful courage Defends our ramparts 'gainst the foe.

**Duke:** That soldier You brought to me in secret, has he done What I commanded?

**Officer:** Yes, my lord: ere now He's at the tower.

**Duke:** 'Tis well: a common arm Will do it best, and execute my vengeance Without remorse: Lisois' uncertain heart Was not to be depended on; methought He looked with too much coolness on my rage; We seldom try to mitigate a grief, Which we contemn: to other hands I'll trust My great revenge.—Go thou, and fetch my standard, Let it be brought upon the ramparts to me: New dangers press, and for the field again We must prepare: let the same zeal inspire thee, And the same courage, imitate thy master, And learn of him—to die, [Exit Officer.] Ere this 'tis done. A base, ungrateful woman dips my hands In brother's blood, and leads me to the tomb: A guilty murderer, ha! what means my heart? I've nourished vengeance long; and shall I not Enjoy it now? I tremble: and a voice, Solemn and sad, cries from my inmost soul, Stop, Foix, he is thy brother, hapless prince, Call back the murderer: Vamir was thy friend. O sweet remembrance of our infant years, When in the days of innocence our hearts Spoke nature's language, and imparted free Our mutual wishes! O how oft has Vamir Partook my griefs, and with a brother's hand, Wiped off the falling tears! and shall I now Destroy him? O thou fatal passion, where, Where hast thou led me? sure I was not born This savage, this barbarian: Vamir yet Was guilty; Vamir robbed me of my life, In my Amelia: still I am unjust; He loved; was that a crime to merit death? Alas! nor time, nor war, nor absence, cooled Their faithful passion; still their guiltless flame In purest lustre shone, before my heart Was poisoned by the cruel draught of love: But Vamir braves my wrath, and is my foe; Deceives me, hates me; yet he is my brother. He should have lived, he was beloved, and happy, And only I should perish: I will die But as I lived, with honor. Pity melts me, Nature determines, and I will forgive him. 'Tis time—

SCENE II.

Duke of Foix, an Officer.

**Duke:** Prevent a parricide: away, Haste to the tower, reverse my orders: go. And let my brother—

**Officer:** O my lord—

**Duke:** What sayest thou! Run, fly, obey me.

**Officer:** Near the gate this moment I saw a body covered o'er with blood, Carried in secret forth by Lisois' orders, And much I fear—

**Duke:** O heaven! my brother's dead And I yet live: earth hath not swallowed me, Nor lightning blasted: a base murderer, Foe to his country, an unnatural brother, How love has changed me! what a load of guilt Have I to answer for! the veil's removed; And now, alas! I know myself too well; I cannot be more guilty: O my brother! I feel I loved thee, yet I slew thee, Vamir.

**Officer**: Amelia comes, my lord, and begs to speak In private with you.

**Duke**: O I must not see her! Not for the world: I cannot bear it: no, She will avenge the murder in my blood: But let her come: I tremble to behold her.

## SCENE III.
Duke of Foix, Amelia, Thais.

**Amelia**: My lord, you have prevailed: and since that hatred (How can I call it by another name?) Which hath so long pursued me, now requires A brother's blood, or his Amelia's hand, Take it: the choice is made, and I am thine: Remember, I'm the purchase of thy guilt: Loosen his chains, and set my Vamir free, That I no more may tremble for his life, And I will give thee all, yield up my hopes Of happiness with him, and follow thee, Even to the altar; there the hand that gives My faith away shall punish all my weakness. Know, at the temple, where thy bridal vows— But thou desirest my hand, and that alone I have to give thee: ha! thou art silent: say, Is Vamir, is thy brother freed already?

**Duke**: My brother!

**Amelia**: Gracious heaven!—remove my fears, Thy eyes are bathed in tears.

**Duke**: Thou askest his life

**Amelia**: What do I hear? didst thou not promise me—

**Duke**: It is too late.

**Amelia**: Too late! O Vamir!

**Duke**: Yes, It is indeed; would it were not, Amelia; The cruel Lisois has obeyed my orders Too faithfully: O live, to punish me; Pierce this inhuman, this unnatural heart, That loved thee but too well: I killed my brother, But for thy sake: revenge on me the crimes Which but for thee I never had committed.

**Amelia**: [Falling into the arms of Thais.] Vamir is dead, barbarian!

**Duke**: And thy hand Shall shed the murderer's blood.

**Amelia**: [Fainting.] And is he gone? My Vamir—

**Duke**: Thy reproaches—

**Amelia**: Spare me, spare me, I'll not reproach thee; take thy sorrows hence, And thy repentance: let me but embrace him, And die.

**Duke**: Amelia, thou hast too much cause To grieve, but O for pity take this life That's hateful to me; but I've not deserved To perish by thy hand; but thou shalt guide—

## SCENE IV.
Duke, Amelia, Lisois.

**Lisois:** What would thy rashness do?

**Duke:** [They disarm him.] An act of justice: Punish myself.

**Amelia:** Wert thou his vile accomplice?

**Duke:** Thou minister of guilt, thou hast obeyed me.

**Lisois:** I promised you, my lord, and I have done But what I ought.

**Duke:** Thy stubborn virtue oft Hath checked my follies, and opposed my weakness; But when I bade thee be a murderer, And kill my brother, then thou wert obedient.

**Lisois:** When I refused but now to execute The bloody office, didst thou not employ Another hand?

**Duke:** Love, powerful love, that chained My reason down, and swayed my foolish heart, Love pleads for me; but thou whose wisdom calms Each rising passion, whose unaltered soul, Firm and unshaken, I so oft have feared, So oft respected, that thou, thus unmoved, Shouldst suffer such a deed of horror; O 'Tis terrible!

**Lisois:** Since sorrow and repentance, Virtue's best monitors, have pierced thy soul With just remorse: since, spite of all thy rashness, To save a brother's blood thou gladly now Wouldst give thy own; ye both shall find a friend. Keep thou thy penitence. [To the Duke.] Dry up thy tears. [To Amelia.] This is a day of triumph. Prince, come forth: Embrace thy brother. [The Scene opens, and discovers Vamir.]

**Amelia:** O my Vamir!

**Duke:** Ha! My brother!

**Amelia:** Gracious heaven!

**Duke:** Can it be? Vamir, advancing to the front. Again I see, again embrace my brother.

**Duke:** O thy forgiveness makes my crime still greater.

**Amelia:** O noble Lisois, thou hast given me life.

**Duke:** Life to us all.

**Lisois:** A base assassin raised His arm against Vamir, but I felled the traitor, And laid him breathless at my feet, then feigned That I had shed thy brother's blood: I knew Thou wouldst repent, and wish the deed undone.

**Duke:** This was a service I can ne'er reward But by endeavoring to be worthy of it: My crime sits heavy on me, and my eyes, Fixed on the earth, dare not look up to Vamir, And to the wronged Amelia.

**Vamir:** We would both Have served thee with our royal master; both Are still devoted to thee. What, my brother, Is thy design? O speak!

**Duke:** To do you justice: To expiate, by the greatest punishment, The greatest crime that love and fierce resentment Could e'er commit: long I adored Amelia; Even when I gave her Vamir up to death, I loved Amelia: I adore her still, Nay, more than ever, yet I yield her to thee, And sacrifice my heart to make you blest. Take her, be happy, and forgive thy brother.

**Vamir**: Behold me at thy feet, with gratitude Warm as thy bounty, as thy love sincere.

**Amelia**: Permit me to embrace thy knees with Vamir, Accept our tenderest friendship, for thy goodness Has amply paid for all my sufferings past.

**Duke**: No more of this, it doubles my misfortunes, And shows me but what happiness I've lost: But I will learn from you to follow virtue, My heart is yours: I'm now indeed thy brother, By thy example I will love my country. Let us away, and to the king relate My crimes, my sorrows, and thy happiness: Let Vamir's zeal and Vamir's truth be mine, Faithful to France, to friendship, and to thee; Foix shall deserve your pardon and your praise; Ye shall forget his follies and his crimes, And henceforth know him only by his virtues.

**End**

# Œdipus

## Contents

Dramatis Personæ. . . . . . . . . . . . . . . . . . . . . . . . . . . . . . . . . . . . 482
Act I. . . . . . . . . . . . . . . . . . . . . . . . . . . . . . . . . . . . . . . . . . . . . . 483
Act II. . . . . . . . . . . . . . . . . . . . . . . . . . . . . . . . . . . . . . . . . . . . . 487
Act III. . . . . . . . . . . . . . . . . . . . . . . . . . . . . . . . . . . . . . . . . . . . 493
Act IV. . . . . . . . . . . . . . . . . . . . . . . . . . . . . . . . . . . . . . . . . . . . 498
Act V. . . . . . . . . . . . . . . . . . . . . . . . . . . . . . . . . . . . . . . . . . . . . 503

## Dramatis Personæ

Œdipus, King of Thebes.
Jocaste, Queen of Thebes.
Philoctetes, Prince of Eubæa.
High Priest.
Araspes, Confidant of Œdipus.
Ægina, Confidante of Jocaste.
Dimas, Friend of Philoctetes.
Phorbas, an old Man of Thebes.
Icarus, an old Man of Corinth.
Chorus of Thebans.

**SCENE** Thebes.

Œdipus was written when M. de Voltaire was but nineteen years of age. It was played for the first time in 1718, and ran five-and-forty nights. Du Frêsne, a celebrated actor, and of the same age with the author, played the part of Œdipus; and Madame Desmarêts, a famous actress, did Jocaste, and soon after quitted the stage. In this edition, the part of Philoctetes is restored, and stands exactly as it was in the first representation.

# ACT I.

## SCENE I.
Philoctetes, Dimas.

**Dimas:** Is it my friend, my Philoctetes? Whence And wherefore comest thou to distempered Thebes In search of death, to brave the wrath of heaven? For, know, the gods on this devoted land Wreak their full vengeance: mortals dare not tread The guilty soil, to death and horror long Consigned, and from the living world cut off: Away, begone!

**Philoctetes:** It suits a wretch like me: Leave me, my friend, to my unhappy fate; And only tell me, if the wrath divine Hath, in its rapid progress, spared the queen.

**Dimas:** Jocaste lives; but round her throne still spreads The dire contagion; every fatal moment Deprives her of some faithful subject: death Steals closer by degrees, and seems to threat Her sacred life. But heaven, we trust, will soon Withdraw its vengeful arm: such scenes of blood Will sure appease its rage.

**Philoctetes:** What horrid crime Could bring down so severe a punishment?

**Dimas:** Since the king's death—

**Philoctetes:** The king! ha! Laius—

**Dimas:** Died Some four years since.

**Philoctetes:** Ha! Laius dead! indeed! What sweet seducing hope awakes my soul? Jocaste! will the gods at length be kind? May Philoctetes still be thine? But say, Dimas, how fell the king?

**Dimas:** 'Tis four years since For the last time towards Bœotia, led By fate, you came; scarce had you bent your way To Asia, e'er the unhappy Laius fell By some base hand.

**Philoctetes:** Assassinated, sayest thou?

**Dimas:** This was the cause, the source of all our ills, The ruin of this wretched country: shocked At the sad stroke, we wept the general loss, When lo! the minister of wrath divine, (Fatal to innocence, and favoring long Unpunished guilt) a dreadful monster came, (O Philoctetes, would thou hadst been here!) And ravaged all our borders, horrid form! Made for destruction by avenging heaven, With human voice, an eagle, woman, lion, Unnatural mixture! rage with cunning joined United to destroy us: naught remained To save but this alone; in phrase obscure The monster had proposed to affrighted Thebes A strange enigma, which who could unfold Should save his country; if he failed, must die. Reluctant we obeyed the hard decree. Instant the general voice aloud proclaimed The kingdom his reward, who, by the gods Inspired, should first unveil the mystery. The aged and the wise, by hope misled, With fruitless science braved the monster's rage; Vain knowledge all! all tried and trying fell, Till Œdipus, the heir to Corinth's throne, Endowed with wisdom far above his years, Fearless, and led by fortune, came, beheld, Unfolded all, and took the great reward; Lives still, and reigns o'er Thebes; but reigns, alas! O'er dying subjects, and a desert land. Vainly we hoped to see the wayward fates Chained to his throne, and yielding to the hand Of Œdipus, our great deliverer. A little time the gods propitious smiled, And blessed us with a gleam of transient peace; But barrenness and famine soon destroyed Our airy hopes: ills heaped on ills succeed, A dreadful plague unpeoples half the realms Of sickly Thebes, snatching the poor remains Just escaped from famine and the grave: high heaven Hath thus ordained, and such our hapless fate. But say, illustrious hero, whom the gods Have long approved, say, wherefore hast thou left The paths of glory, and the smiles of fortune, To seek the regions of affliction here?

**Philoctetes**: I come to join my sorrows and my tears, For know the world with me hath lost its best And noblest friend: ne'er shall these eyes behold The offspring of the gods, like them unconquered, Earth's best support, the guardian deity Of innocence oppressed: I mourn a friend, The world a father.

**Dimas**: Is Alcides dead?

**Philoctetes**: These hands performed the melancholy office, Laid on his funeral pile the first of men; The all-conquering arrows, those dear dreadful gifts The son of Jove bequeathed me, have I brought, With his cold ashes, here, where I will raise A tomb and altars to my valued friend. O! had he lived! had but indulgent heaven, In pity to mankind, prolonged his days, Far from Jocaste I had still remained; And, though I might have cherished still my vain And hopeless passion, had not wandered here, Or left Alcides for a woman's love.

**Dimas**: Oft have I pitied thy unhappy flame, Caught in thy earliest youth, increasing still And growing with thy growth: Jocaste, forced By a hard father to a hateful bed, Unwillingly partook the throne of Laius. Alas! what tears those fatal nuptials cost, What sorrows have they brought on wretched Thebes! How have I oft admired thy noble soul, Worthy of empire! conqueror o'er thyself: There first the hero shone, repressed his passion, And the first tyrant he subdued was love.

**Philoctetes**: There we must fly to conquer; I confess it: Long time I strove, I felt my weakness long; At length resolved to shun the fatal place, I took a last farewell of my Jocaste. The world then trembled at Alcides' name, And on his valor did suspend their fate; I joined the god-like man, partook his toils, Marched by his side, and twined his laurel wreath Round my own brows: then my enlightened soul Against the passions armed, and rose superior. A great man's friendship is the gift of heaven. In him I read my duty and my fate; I bound myself to virtue and to him: My valor strengthened, and my heart improved, Not hardened, I became like my Alcides. What had I been without him! a king's son, A common prince, the slave of every passion, Which Hercules hath taught me to subdue.

**Dimas:** Now then unmoved thou canst behold Jocaste, And her new husband.

**Philoctetes:** Ha! another husband! Saidst thou, another?

**Dimas:** Œdipus hath joined To hers his future fate

**Philoctetes:** He is too happy; But he is worthy: he who saved a kingdom Alone can merit her, and heaven is just.

**Dimas:** He comes, and with him his assembled people; Lo! the high-priest attends: this way they bend, To deprecate the wrath of angry heaven.

**Philoctetes:** It melts my soul; I weep for their misfortunes. O Hercules, from thy eternal seat Look down on thy afflicted country! hear Thy fellow citizens! O hear thy friend, Who joins his prayers, and be their guardian god!

## SCENE II.
High Priest, Chorus.

**First Person of the Chorus:** Ye blasting powers, who waste this wretched empire, And breathe contagion, death, and horrors round us, O quicken your slow wrath, be kind at last, And urge our lingering fate.

**Second Person of the Chorus:** Strike, strike, ye gods, Your victims are prepared; ye mountains, fall! Crush us, ye heavens! O death, deliver us, And we shall thank you for the boon.

**High Priest:** No more: Cease your loud plaints, the wretch's poor resource; Yield to the power supreme, who means to try His people by affliction; with a word He can destroy, and with a word can save: He knows that death is here; the cries of Thebes Have reached his throne. Behold! the king approaches, And heaven by me declares its will divine; The fates will soon to Œdipus unveil Their mysteries all, and happier days succeed.

## SCENE III.
Œdipus, Jocaste, High Priest, Ægina, Dimas, Araspes, Chorus.

**Œdipus:** O ye, who to this hallowed temple bring The mournful offering of your tears: O what, What shall I say to my afflicted people? Would I could turn the wrath of angry heaven Against myself, and quench the deadly flame? But O! in universal ills like these, Kings are but men, and only can partake The common danger. Say, thou minister Of the just gods, say, do they still refuse To hear the voice of misery; still relentless Will they behold us perish, are they deaf And silent still?

**High Priest:** King, people, listen all: This night did I behold the flame of heaven Descending on our altars; to my eyes The ghastly shade of Laius then appeared, Indignant frowned upon me, and thus spoke In fearful accents, terrible to hear: "The death of Laius is still unrevenged, The murderer lives in Thebes, and doth infect The wholesome air with his malignant breath; He must be known, he must be punished, And on his fate depends the people's safety."

**Œdipus:** Justly ye suffer, Thebans, for this crime; Laius was once your loved and honored king, And your neglect hath from his manes drawn This vengeance on you. Such is oft the fate Of the best sovereigns; whilst they live, respect Waits on their laws, their justice is admired, And they like gods are served, like gods adored; But after death they sink into oblivion. No longer then your flattering incense burns: The servile mind of wretched man still bends To interest; and when virtue is departed, 'Tis soon forgotten: therefore doth the blood Of murdered Laius now cry out against you, And sues for vengeance to offended heaven. To sprinkle on his tomb the murderer's blood Will better far than slaughtered hecatombs Appease his spirit: be it all our care To seek the guilty wretch. Can none remember Aught touching this sad deed? Amidst your signs And wonders, could no footsteps e'er be traced Of this unpunished crime? They always told me It was a Theban, who against his prince Uplifted his rebellious hand. For me [To Jocaste.] Who from thy hands received the crown, two years After the death of Laius did I mount The throne of Thebes, and never since that hour Would I recall the subject of thy tears, But in respectful silence waited still; Still have thy dangers busied all my soul, Nor left me time to think on aught but thee.

**Jocaste:** When fate, which had reserved me for thy arms, Deprived me of my late unhappy lord, Who, journeying o'er his kingdom's frontiers, fell By base assassins, Phorbas then alone Attended him, his loved and valued friend; To whom the king, relying on his wisdom, Entrusted half his power: he brought to Thebes The mangled corpse: himself half dead with wounds, And bathed in blood, fell at Jocaste's feet; "Villains unknown," he cried, "have slain the king; These eyes beheld it: I was dying too, But heaven hath restored me to prolong A wretched life." He said no more. My soul Distracted saw the melancholy truth Was still concealed; and therefore heaven perhaps Concealed the murderer too; perhaps accomplished Its own eternal will, and made us guilty, That it might punish. Soon the sphinx appeared, And laid our country waste: then hapless Thebes, Attentive to her safety, could not think On Laius' fate, whilst trembling for her own.

**Œdipus:** Where is that faithful Phorbas? lives he still?

**Jocaste:** Alas! his zeal and service ill repaid, Too powerful to be loved, the jealous state His secret foe, nobles and people joined To punish him for past felicity. The multitude accused him, even demanded Of me his death: sore pressed on every side, I knew not how to pardon or condemn, But to a neighboring castle I conveyed him, And hid the guiltless victim from their rage.

There four long winters hath the poor old man, To future favorites a sad example, Without a murmur or complaint remained, And hopes from innocence alone release.

**Œdipus**: It is enough, Jocaste. Fly, begone, [To his servants.] Open the prison, bring him hither straight, We will examine him before you all; Laius and Thebes shall be avenged together: Yes, we will hear and judge, will sound the depth Of this strange mystery. Ye gods of Thebes, Who hear our prayers, and know the murderer, now Reveal, and punish; and thou, Sun, withhold From his dark eyes thy blessed light! proscribed, Abandoned, let him wander o'er the earth A wretched miscreant, by his sons abhorred, And to his mother horrible! deprived Of burial, let his body be the prey Of hungry vultures!

**High Priest**: In these execrations We all unite.

**Œdipus**: Gods! let the guilty suffer, And they alone! or if the high decrees Of your eternal justice leave to me His punishment, at least indulgent grant, Where you command, the power to obey; If you pursue the guilty, O complete The glorious work, and make the victim known! [To the people.] Return, my people, to the temple; there Once more entreat the gods: perhaps your prayers May from their heavenly mansions draw them down To dwell among us: if they loved the king, They will avenge his death, and kind to him Who errs unknowing, will direct this arm For justice raised, and teach me where to strike.

# ACT II.

SCENE I.

Jocaste, Ægina, Araspes, Chorus.

**Araspe**: Believe me, 'tis too true, my royal mistress, Your dying people, with one common voice, Accuse the hapless Philoctetes: fate Hath sent him back to save this wretched kingdom.

**Jocaste**: What do I hear, ye powers?

**Ægina**: 'Tis wonderful.

**Jocaste**: Who? Philoctetes?

**Araspe**: Yes, it must be he: To whom can we impute it but to him? When last at Thebes, he seemed to meditate A deed like this; for much he hated Laius: From Œdipus his traitorous purpose scarce Could he conceal; for soon unwary youth Betrays itself: soon through the thin disguise Of ill dissembled loyalty, we saw The rancor of his heart. I know not what Provoked him, but too warm and open, ever The slave of passion, he would kindle oft At the king's name, and often pour forth threats Of vengeance: for some time he left the kingdom, But fate soon brought the restless wanderer back; And at that fatal time, which heaven distinguished By the detested shocking parricide, He was at Thebes: e'er since that dreadful hour, Suspicion justly falls on Philoctetes: But the high name which he had gained in war, His boasted title of earth's great avenger, And his heroic deeds, have stopped the tongue Of clamor, and suspended yet the stroke Of our resentment. Now the time is come When Thebes shall think no more of vain respect; His glory and his conquests plead no more; The hearts of an oppressed people groan; The gods require his blood, and must be heard.

**Chorus**: O queen! have pity on a wretched people, Who love and honor thee, revere the gods, And follow their example; yield up to us Their victim, and present our vows to heaven; For heaven will hear them, if they come from thee.

**Jocaste**: O! if my life can mitigate its wrath, I give it freely; take the sacrifice; Accept my blood; but O! demand no more. Thebans, be gone.

### SCENE II.

Jocaste, Ægina.

**Ægina**: How I lament thy fate!

**Jocaste**: Alas! I envy those whom death has freed From all their cares: but what remains for me, What pain and torment to a virtuous heart!

**Ægina**: 'Tis terrible indeed: the clamorous people, Warmed with false zeal, will cry aloud for vengeance, And soon demand their victim. I forbear To accuse him; but if he at last should prove The murderer of thy unhappy lord, How it must shock thy soul!

**Jocaste**: Impossible! Such guilt and baseness never dwelt in him. O my Ægina! since our bonds of love Were disunited, naught has pierced my heart Like this suspicion: this alone was wanting To make Jocaste most completely wretched: But I'll not bear to hear him thus accused; I loved him, and he must be innocent.

**Ægina**: That constant love—

**Jocaste**: Nay, think not that my heart Still nourishes a guilty passion for him; I conquered that long since; yet, dear Ægina, Howe'er the soul may act which virtue guides, Its secret motions, nature's children, still Must force their way: they will not be subdued, But in the folds and windings of the heart, Lurk still, and rush upon us; hid in fires We thought extinguished, from their ashes rise: In the hard conflict, rigid virtue may Resist the passions, but can ne'er destroy them.

**Ægina**: How just, and yet how noble is thy grief! Such sentiments!—

**Jocaste**: Jocaste is most wretched; Thou knowest my miseries, and thou knowest my heart, Ægina: twice hath Hymen lit his torch For me, and twice hath changed my slavery, For such it was; the only man I loved, Torn from my arms. Forgive me, ye just gods, The sad remembrance of a conquered passion.

Ægina, thou wert witness of our loves, Those ties, alas! dissolved as soon as made: Then Œdipus, my sovereign, sought and gained me, Spite of myself. I took the diadem, Begirt with sorrows. To forget the past Became my duty then; and I obeyed. Thou knowest I stifled every tender thought Of my first love, disguised an aching heart, Drank up my tears, and even from myself Strove to conceal my griefs.

**Ægina**: How could you venture The dangerous trial of a second marriage?

**Jocaste**: Alas!

**Ægina**: Will you forgive me? shall I speak?

**Jocaste**: Thou mayest.

**Ægina**: The king, the conqueror subdued thee: You gave your hand as a reward to him Who saved your country.

**Jocaste**: Gracious gods!

**Ægina**: Was he Happier than Laius? Was your Philoctetes Forgotten then, or did they share your heart?

**Jocaste**: Thebes, by a cruel monster then laid waste, Had promised its deliverer my hand; The conqueror of the sphinx was worthy of me.

**Ægina**: You loved him then?

**Jocaste**: I felt some tenderness For Œdipus; but O! 'twas far from love: 'Twas not, Ægina, that tumultuous passion, The impetuous offspring of my ravished senses, Not the fierce flame that burned for Philoctetes; Who, by his fatal charms, subdued my reason, And poured love's sweetest poison o'er my heart: Friendship sincere was all I could bestow On Œdipus, for much I prized his virtue; And pleased, beheld him mount the throne of Thebes Which he had saved; but, whilst I followed him, Even at the altar, my affrighted soul, Wherefore I knew not, was most strangely moved, And I retired with horror to his arms. To this a dreadful omen did succeed: Methought, Ægina, in the dead of night, I saw the gulf of hell yawn wide before me; When lo! the spirit of my murdered lord, Bloody and pale, with threatening aspect stood, And pointed to my son; that son, Ægina, Which I to Laius bore, and to the gods Offered, a cruel pious sacrifice. They beckoned me to follow them, and seemed To drag me with them to the horrid gloom Of Tartarus: my troubled soul long kept The sad idea, and must keep it ever. Now Philoctetes doubles every woe.

**Ægina**: I heard a noise that way, and, see he comes.

**Jocaste**: 'Tis he; I tremble: but I will avoid him.

## SCENE III.

Jocaste, Philoctetes.

**Philoctetes**: Do not avoid me, do not fly, Jocaste. From Philoctetes; turn, and look upon me: O speak to me, nor fear my jealous tears Should interrupt the new-born happiness Of thy late nuptials: think not that I came To cast reproaches on thee, or with sighs To win thy lost affection; vulgar arts, Unworthy of us both! the heart, Jocaste, That burned for thee, and if I may recall Thy plighted faith, was once not hateful to thee, Has learned, from thy example, not to feel Weakness like that.

**Jocaste**: I must approve thy conduct, And 'tis but fit I vindicate my own: I loved thee, Philoctetes; but my fate Tore me from thee, and gave me to another. Thou knowest what woes the horrid sphinx, by heaven Appointed to afflict us, brought on Thebes: Too well thou knowest that Œdipus—

**Philoctetes**: Is thine; I know it, and is worthy of the blessing: Young as he was, his wisdom saved thy country; His virtues, his fair deeds, and what still more Exalted him, Jocaste's love, have ranked Thy Œdipus among the first of men. Wherefore did cruel fortune, still resolved To punish Philoctetes, drive me hence, To seek vain trophies in a distant land? O! if the conqueror of the sphinx was doomed To conquer thee, why was not I at Thebes? I'd not have labored in the fruitless search Of idle mysteries, wrapped in words of darkness; This arm, to conquest long beneath thy smiles Accustomed, should have drawn the vengeful sword, And laid the howling monster at thy feet. But O! a happier arm has wrested from me That noblest triumph, and deserved Jocaste.

**Jocaste**: Alas! thou knowest not yet what ills await thee.

**Philoctetes**: Thee and Alcides I have lost already: Is there aught more to fear?

**Jocaste**: Thou dwellest at Thebes; The detestation of avenging gods; The baneful pestilence stalks forth amongst us; The blood of Laius cries aloud, and heaven Pursues us still: the murderer must bleed; He has been sought for; some have dared to say That he is found, and call him Philoctetes.

**Philoctetes**: Astonishment! the base suspicion shocks My soul, and bids my tongue be silent ever On the opprobrious theme: accused of murder! Murdering thy husband! thou canst never believe it.

**Jocaste**: O! never! 'twere injurious to thy honor To combat such imposture, or refute The vile aspersion; no, thou knowest my heart, Thou hadst my love, and couldst not do a deed Unworthy of it. Let them perish all, These worthless Thebans, who deserve their fate For thus suspecting thee: but, hence! begone! Our vows are fruitless: heaven reserves for thee Superior blessings. Thou wert born to serve The gods, whose wisdom would not bury here Virtues like thine, or suffer love to rule A heart designed for universal sway, And courage fit to save and bless mankind. Ill would it suit the follower of Alcides To lose his moments in the fond concerns, The little cares of love. Thy hours are due To the unhappy and the injured: they Will all thy time and all thy virtue claim. Already tyrants throng on every side; Alcides dead, new monsters rise; go, thou, And give the world another Hercules. Œdipus comes; permit me to retire; Not that I fear the weakness of my heart, But as Jocaste loved thee once, and he Is now my husband, I should blush before you.

SCENE IV.
Œdipus, Philoctetes, Araspes.

Œdipus: Sayst thou, Araspes, is he here, the prince, The noble Philoctetes?

Philoctetes: Yes; 'tis he; Led by blind fortune to this hapless clime, Where angry heaven hath made me suffer wrongs I am not used to bear. I know the crimes Laid to my charge; but think not that I mean To justify myself: too well I know thee To think that Œdipus would ever stoop To such low mean suspicions: no! thy fame Is mixed with mine; in the same steps of honor We trod together. Theseus, Hercules, And Philoctetes, pointed out to thee The paths of glory; do not then disgrace Their names, and taint thy own, by calumny, But keep their bright examples still before thee.

Œdipus: All that I wish is but to save my country, And if I can be useful to mankind, This is the ambition I would satisfy, And this the lesson which those heroes taught, Whom thou hast followed, and whom I admire. I meant not to accuse thee: had I chose The people's victim, it had been myself. I think it but the duty of a king To perish for his country: 'tis an honor Too great for common men. Then had I saved Once more my Thebans, yielded up my life, And sheltered thine: but 'twas not in my power. The blood of guilt must flow, thou standest accused. Defend thyself: if thou art innocent, None shall rejoice so much as Œdipus; Nor as a criminal shall then receive thee, But as my noble friend, as Philoctetes.

Philoctetes: I thought myself, indeed, above suspicion: From many a base assassin has this arm, While Jove's dread thunder slept, relieved mankind Whom we chastise, we seldom imitate.

Œdipus: I do not think thou wouldst disgrace thy name, And thy fair martial deeds, by such a crime. If Laius fell by thee, he fell with honor, I doubt it not, for I must do thee justice.

Philoctetes: If I had slain him, I had only gained One added triumph. Kings, indeed, are gods To their own subjects, but to Hercules, Or me, they were no more than common men. I have avenged the wrongs of mighty princes; And, therefore, little, thou mayest think, should fear To attack the bravest.

Œdipus: Heroes, like thyself, Are equal even to kings, I know they are: But still remember, prince, whoe'er slew Laius, His head must answer for the woes of Thebes; And thou—

Philoctetes: I slew him not; let that suffice. If I had done the deed, I would have owned, Nay boasted of it. Hear me, Œdipus, Though vulgar souls, by vulgar methods, deign To vindicate their injured honor; kings And heroes, when they speak, expect, no doubt, To be believed: perhaps thou dost suspect I murdered Laius. It becomes not thee, Of all men, to accuse me: to thy hand Devolved his sceptre and his queen. Who reaped The fruits of Laius's death, but Œdipus? Who took the spoils? Who filled his throne? Not I. That object never tempted Philoctetes: Alcides never would accept a crown: We knew no master, and desired no subjects: I have made kings, but never wished to be one. But 'tis beneath me to refute the falsehood, For innocence is lessened by defence.

**Œdipus**: Thy pride offends me, whilst thy virtue charms. If thou art guiltless, thou hast naught to fear From justice and the laws; thy innocence Will shine with double splendor: dwell with us, And wait the event.

**Philoctetes**: My honor is concerned, And therefore I shall stay; nor hence depart Till I have ample vengeance for the wrongs Thy base suspicions cast on Philoctetes.

SCENE V.
Œdipus, Araspes.

**Œdipus**: Araspes, I can never think him guilty: A heart like his, intrepid, brave, and fearless, Could never stoop to mean disguise; nor thoughts So noble e'er inspire the timid breast Of falsehood: no! such baseness is far from him: I even blushed to accuse him, and condemned My own injustice: hard and cruel fate Of royalty! alas! kings cannot read The hearts of men, and oft on innocence, Spite of ourselves unjust, inflict the pains Due to the guilty. How this Phorbas lingers! In him alone are all my hopes: the gods Refuse to hear or answer to our vows; Their silence shows how much they are offended.

**Araspe**: Rely then on thyself: the gods, whose aid This priest hath promised, do not always dwell Within their temples; tripods, caves, and cells, The brazen mouths that pour forth oracles, Which men had framed, by men may be inspired; We must not rest our faith on priests alone; Even in the sanctuary traitors oft May lurk unseen, exert their pious arts To enslave mankind, and bid the destinies Speak or be silent just as they command them. Search then, and find the truth, examine all; Phorbas, and Philoctetes, and Jocaste. Trust to yourself; let our own eyes determine; Be they our tripods, oracles, and gods.

**Œdipus**: Within the temple, thinkest thou, perfidy Like this can dwell: but if just heaven at last Should fix our fate, and Œdipus be called To execute its will, he will receive The precious trust, the safety of his country, Nor act unworthy of it. To the gods Once more I go, and with incessant prayer Will try to soothe their anger: thou, meantime, If thou wouldst wish to serve me, hasten onward The lingering Phorbas; in our hapless state, I must enquire the truth of gods and men.

# ACT III.

**SCENE I.**
Jocaste, Ægina.

**Jocaste:** Yes, my Ægina, I expect him here; 'Tis the last time these eyes shall e'er behold The wretched Philoctetes.

**Ægina:** Thou hast heard, My royal mistress, to what desperate height The clamorous people carry their resentment; Our dying Thebans from his punishment Expect their safety. Old men, women, children, United by misfortunes, breathe forth vengeance; Pronounce him guilty, and cry out that heaven Demands his blood: canst thou resist the torrent, Defend, or save him?

**Jocaste:** Yes: I will defend him; Even though Thebes should lift the murderous hand Against her queen, beneath her smoking walls To crush Jocaste, ne'er would I betray Such injured innocence; but still I fear The tongue of slander: well thou knowest my heart Once sighed for Philoctetes; now, Ægina, Will they not say I sacrifice to him My fame, my gods, my country, and my husband? Will they not say Jocaste loves him still?

**Ægina:** Calm thy vain fears; thy passion had no witness But me, and never—

**Jocaste:** Thinkest thou that a princess Can e'er conceal her hatred or her love? O no! on every side the eager eyes Of courtiers look upon us: through the veil Of feigned respect, with subtle treachery They search our hearts, and trace out every weakness. Naught can escape their sharp malignant sight; A little word, a sigh, or glance betrays us; Our very silence shall be made to speak Our thoughts; and when their busy artifice, Spite of ourselves, hath drawn the secret from us, Then their loud censures cast invidious light O'er all our actions, and the instructed world Is quickly taught to echo every weakness.

**Ægina:** But what hast thou to fear from calumny? What piercing eye can wound Jocaste's fame? Who knows thy love, will know thy conquest o'er it; Will know thy virtue still supported thee.

**Jocaste:** It is that virtue which distresses me; I look, perhaps, with too severe an eye On my own weakness, and accuse myself Unjustly; but the image still remains Of Philoctetes, engraved within my heart Too deep for time or virtue to efface it; And much I doubt, if when I strive to save him. I act not less from justice than from love: My pity hath too much of tenderness; I tremble oft, and oft reproach myself For my fond care; I could be more his friend, If he had been less dear to me.

**Ægina:** But say, Is it your will that he depart?

**Jocaste:** It is: And O! if he would listen to Jocaste, Never return, never behold me more; Fly from this fatal, this distressful scene, And save my life and fame. But what detains him? Why hastes he not? Ægina, fly—

## SCENE II.

Philoctetes, Ægina, Jocaste.

**Jocaste**: He's here. O prince, my soul is on the rack; I blush To see the man whom duty bids me shun, Which says I should forget and not betray thee. Doubtless thou knowest the dreadful fate that hangs O'er thy devoted head.

**Philoctetes**: The clamorous people Demand my life; but they have suffered much, And therefore, though unjust, I pity them.

**Jocaste**: Yield not thyself a victim to their rage: Away, begone; as yet thou art thyself The master of thy fate; but this perhaps Is the last minute that can give me power To save thee: far, O fly far from Jocaste; And, in return for added life, I beg thee But to forget 'twas I who thus preserved it.

**Philoctetes**: I could have wished, Jocaste, thou hadst shown More strength of mind, and less compassion for me; Preferred with me my honor to my life, And rather bade me die than meanly quit My station here: I yet am innocent, But in obeying thee I should be guilty. Of all the blessings heaven bestowed upon me, My honor and my fame alone remain Untouched. O! do not rob me of a treasure So precious to me; do not make me thus Unworthy of Jocaste. I have lived, Lived to fulfil the fate allotted to me; Have passed my sacred word to Œdipus, And whatsoever suspicions he may cherish, I am a stranger to the breach of honor.

**Jocaste**: O Philoctetes, let me here entreat thee, By the just gods, by that ill-fated passion, Which once inspired thy breast, if aught remains Of tender friendship, if thou still rememberest How much my happiness on thine depended, Deign to prolong a glorious life, and days That should have been united with Jocaste.

**Philoctetes**: To thee devoted I would have them still In equal tenor flow, and worthy of thee; I've lived far from thee, and shall die content, If thy regard attends me to the tomb Who knows but heaven may yet refuse to see This bloody sacrifice; perhaps, in mercy It guided me to Thebes to save Jocaste; Shortened my days, perhaps, to lengthen thine. Happy event! the blood of innocence May be accepted; mine is not unworthy.

## SCENE III.

Œdipus, Jocaste, Philoctetes, Ægina, Araspes, with Attendants.

**Œdipus**: Fear not the clamors of an idle crowd, That rage tumultuous, and demand thy death: Know, Philoctetes, I have calmed their rage And will myself, if needful, be thy guard. I judge not with the hasty multitude, But wish to see thy innocence appear: My doubtful mind, uncertain where to fix, Nor dares or to condemn, or to acquit thee: Heaven can alone determine all, which hears My ardent prayer; at length it seems appeased, And by its priest shall soon point out the victim. The gods shall soon decide 'twixt Thebes and thee.

**Philoctetes**: Great is thy love of truth, O king, but know Justice extreme is height of injury; We must not always hearken to the voice Of rigor: honor is the first of laws, Let us observe it. But thou seest me sunk Beneath myself, answering the slandrous tongues Of base defamers, whom I should despise. O let not Œdipus unite with such To ruin my fair fame! it is enough That I deny it; 'tis enough to call My life before thee. Let Alcides come, And bring with him the monsters I destroyed, The tyrants I subdued; let these stand forth My witnesses, and let my enemies confute them. But ask your priest whether his gods condemn me; I'll wait their sentence; not because I fear it, But to preserve thy persecuted people.

SCENE IV.

Œdipus, Jocaste, High Priest, Araspes, Philoctetes, Ægina, Attendants, Chorus.

**Œdipus**: Will heaven at last indulgent to our prayers Withdraw its vengeance? By what murderous hand Was it offended?

**Philoctetes**: Speak, whose blood must flow For expiation?

**High Priest**: Fatal gift of heaven! Unhappy knowledge! to what dangers oft Dost thou betray the heart of curious man! O would that fate, thus open to my view, Had o'er its secrets drawn the eternal veil To hide them from my sight!

**Philoctetes**: What evil bringest thou?

**Œdipus**: Comest thou the minister of wrath divine?

**Philoctetes**: Fear nothing.

**Œdipus**: Do the gods demand my life?

**High Priest**: If thou givest credit to me, ask me not.

**Œdipus**: Whatever be the fate which heaven decrees, The safety of my country is concerned, And I will know it.

**Philoctetes**: Speak.

**Œdipus**: Have pity on us, Pity the afflicted, pity—

**High Priest**: Œdipus Deserves more, much more, pity than his people.

**Leader of the Chorus.**: Œdipus loves them with paternal fondness; To his we join our prayers. O! hear us thou Interpreter of heaven; now hear, and save!

**Second Person of the Chorus**: We die, O save us! turn aside the wrath Of the angry gods; name the perfidious monster!

**Leader of the Chorus.**: Name him, and soon the parricide shall die

**High Priest**: Unhappy men! why will ye press me thus?

**Leader of the Chorus.**: Speak but the word, he dies, and we are saved.

**High Priest:** O! ye will tremble but to hear his name, When ye shall know what pangs he must endure. The God, who speaks by me, in pity dooms him To banishment alone; but dreadful ills Await the murderer: driven to fell despair His own rash hand shall to the wrath of heaven Add woes more deep and heavier punishment: Even you shall shudder at his fate, and own Your safety purchased at a rate too dear.

**Œdipus:** Obey then.

**Philoctetes:** Speak.

**Œdipus:** Still obstinate!

**High Priest:** Remember, If I must speak, that thou didst force me to it.

**Œdipus:** Insufferable delay! I'll bear no more.

**High Priest:** Since thou wilt hear it then, 'tis—

**Œdipus:** Ha! speak, who?

**High Priest:** 'Tis—Œdipus.

**Œdipus:** I?

**High Priest:** Thou, unhappy Prince, Thou art the man.

**Second Person of the Chorus:** Alas! what do I hear!

**Jocaste:** Say, can it be, interpreter of heaven? [To Œdipus.] Thou, Œdipus, the murderer of my husband! To whom Jocaste yielded with herself The throne of Thebes: the oracle is false; I know it is; thy virtues must confute it.

**Leader of the Chorus.:** O! heaven, whose power decrees the fate of mortals, O! name another, or to death devote us!

**Philoctetes:** [Turning to Œdipus.] Think not I mean to render ill for ill; Or from this strange reverse of fortune take A mean advantage, to return the wrongs I suffered from thy people and from thee: No, Œdipus, I'll do thee noble justice, That justice thou deniest to Philoctetes. Spite of the gods, I think thee innocent, And here I offer thee my willing hand Against thy foes: I cannot hesitate Which I should serve, a pontiff or a king. 'Tis a priest's business, whosoever he be, By whatsoever deity inspired, To pray for, not to curse, his royal master.

**Œdipus:** Transcendent virtue! execrable traitor! Here I behold a demi-god, and there A base impostor: see the glorious privilege Of altars; thanks to their protecting veil, With lips profane thou hast abused the power Given thee by heaven, to arraign thy king; And yet thou thinkest the sacred ministry Thou hast disgraced shall withhold my wrath: Traitor, thou shouldst have perished at the altar Before those gods whose voice thou hast usurped.

**High Priest:** My life is in thy hands, and thou art now The master of my fate: seize then the time Whilst yet thou art so, for to-day thy doom Will be pronounced. Tremble, unhappy Prince, Thy reign is past; a hand unseen suspends The fatal sword that glitters o'er thy head: Soon shall thy conscious soul with horror feel The weight of guilt; soon shalt thou quit the throne, Where now thou sittest secure, to wander forth A wretched exile in a distant land; Of wholesome water and of sacred fire Deprived, shalt take thy solitary way, And to the caves and hollow rocks complain. Where'er thou goest, a vengeful God shall still Pursue thy steps; still shalt thou call on death, But call in vain: heaven, that beholds thy fate, Shall hide itself in darkness from thy sight; To guilt and sorrow doomed, thou shall regret Thy life, and wish that thou hadst ne'er been born.

Œdipus: Thus far I have constrained my wrath, and heard thee. Priest, if thy blood were worthy of my sword, Thy life should answer for this insolence: But hence, begone, nor urge my temper further, Thou author of abominable falsehood.

High Priest: Thou callest me hypocrite, and base impostor; Thy father thought not so.

Œdipus: Who? Polybus? My father, saidst thou?

High Priest: Thou wilt know too soon Thy wretched fate: to-day shall give thee birth; To-day shall give thee death: unhappy man, Tell me who gave thee birth, or say with whom Thou livest, beset with sorrows and with crimes For thee alone reserved. O Corinth! Phocis! Detested nuptials! impious wretched race, Too like its parent stem! whose deadly rage Shall fill the world with horror and amaze. Farewell.

SCENE V.
Œdipus, Philoctetes, Jocaste.

Œdipus: His last words fix me to the earth Immovable; my passion is subsided; I know not where I am: methinks some god Descended from above to calm my rage; Who to his priest imparted power divine, And by his sacred voice pronounced my ruin.

Philoctetes: If thou hadst naught to oppose but king to king, I would have fought for Œdipus; but know That Priests are here more formidable foes, Because respected, feared and honored more. Supported by his oracles, the priest Shall often make his sovereign crouch beneath him; Whilst his weak people, dragged in holy chains, Embrace the idol, tread on sacred laws With pious zeal, and think they honor heaven When they betray their master and their king, But above all, when interest, fruitful parent Of riot and licentiousness, increase Their impious rage, and back their insolence.

Œdipus: Alas! thy virtue doubles all my woes, For great as my misfortunes is thy soul; Beneath the weight of care that hangs upon me; Who strives to comfort can but more oppress. What voice is this which from my inmost soul

Pours forth complaints? What crime have I committed? Say, vengeful gods, is Œdipus so guilty?

**Jocaste:** Talk not of guilt, my lord, your dying people Demand a victim; we must save our country; Delay it not: I was the wife of Laius, And I alone should perish: let me seek The wandering spirit of my murdered lord On the infernal shore, and calm his rage: Yes, I will go: may the kind gods accept My life and ask no other sacrifice! May thy Jocaste save her Œdipus!

**Œdipus:** And wouldest thou die! are there not woes enough Heaped on this head? O cease, my loved Jocaste, This mournful language, I am sunk already Too deep in grief without new miseries, Without thy death to fill my cup of sorrow. Let us go in: I must clear up a doubt Too justly formed, I fear: but follow me.

**Jocaste:** How couldst thou ever, my lord—

**Œdipus:** No more: come in, And there confirm my terrors, or remove them.

# ACT IV.

**SCENE I.**
Œdipus, Jocaste.

**Œdipus:** Jocaste, 'tis in vain: say what thou wilt, These terrible suspicions haunt me still; The priest affrights me; I acquit him now, And even, in secret, am my own accuser. O! I have asked myself some dreadful questions; A thousand strange events, which form my mind Were long effaced, now rush in crowds upon me, And harrow up my soul; the past obstructs, The present but confounds me, and the future Is big with horrid truths; on every side Guilt waits my footsteps.

**Jocaste:** Will not virtue guard thee? Art thou not sure that thou art innocent?

**Œdipus:** We're oft more guilty than we think we are.

**Jocaste:** Disdain the madness of a talking priest, Nor thus excuse him with unmanly fears.

**Œdipus:** Now in the name of the unhappy king, And angry heaven, let me entreat thee, say, When Laius undertook that fatal journey, Did guards attend him?

**Jocaste:** I've already told thee, One followed him alone.

**Œdipus:** And only one?

**Jocaste:** Superior even to the rank he bore. He was a king, who, like thyself, disdained All irksome pomp, and never would permit An idle train of slaves to march before him. Amidst his happy subjects fearless still, And still unguarded lived in peace and safety, And thought his people's love his best defence.

**Œdipus:** Thou best of kings, sent by indulgent heaven To mortals here; thou exemplary greatness! Could ever Œdipus his barbarous hand Lift against thee? but if thou canst, Jocaste, Describe him to me.

**Jocaste:** Since thou wilt recall The sad remembrance, hear what Laius was: Spite of the frost which hoary age had spread O'er his fair temples in declining age, Which yet was vigorous, his eyes sparkled still With all the fire of youth, his wrinkled forehead Beneath, his silver locks attracted awe And reverence from mankind: if I may dare To say it, Laius much resembled thee; With pleasure I behold in Œdipus His virtues and his features thus united. What have I said to alarm thee thus?—

**Œdipus:** I see Some strange misfortune will o'ertake me soon; The priest, I fear, was by the gods inspired, And but too truly hath foretold my fate: Could I do this, and was it possible?

**Jocaste:** Are then these holy instruments of heaven Infallible? Their ministry indeed Binds them to the altar, they approach the gods, But they are mortals still; and thinkest thou then Truth is dependent on the flight of birds? Thinkest thou, expiring by the sacred knife, The groaning heifer shall for them alone Remove the veil of dark futurity? Or the gay victims, crowned with flowery garlands, Within their entrails bear the fates of men? O no! to search for truth by ways like these Is to usurp the rights of power supreme; These priests are not what the vile rabble think them, Their knowledge springs from our credulity.

**Œdipus:** Would it were so! for then I might be happy.

**Jocaste:** It is: alas! my griefs bear witness to it. Once I was partial to them like thyself, But undeceived at length lament my folly; Heaven hath chastised me for my easy faith In dark mysterious lying oracles, That robbed me of my child; I hate the base Deluders all; had it not been for them, My son had still been living.

**Œdipus:** Ha! thy son! How didst thou lose him? By what oracles Did the gods speak concerning him?

**Jocaste:** I'll tell thee What from myself I would have gladly hidden. But 'twas a false one; therefore be not moved. Thou must have heard I had a son by Laius. A mother's fond disquietude provoked me To ask his fate of the great oracle. Alas! what madness 'tis to wrest from heaven Those secrets which it kindly would conceal: But I was a weak woman, and a mother. Before the priestess' feet I fell submissive, And thus her answer was; for O, too well I must remember what but to repeat Now makes me tremble; but thou wilt forgive me: "Thy son shall slay his father, sacrilegious, Incestuous parricide." Shall I go on?

**Œdipus:** Well, very well—

**Jocaste:** In short, it then foretold me, This son, this monster should pollute my bed; That I, his mother, should embrace my son, Just recent from the murder of his father. That thus united by these dreadful ties, I should bear children to this hapless child. You seem to be disordered at my story, And dread perhaps to hear the sad remainder.

Œdipus: Proceed: what did you with the wretched infant. Object of wrath divine?

Jocaste: Believed the gods; Piously cruel, sacrificed my child, And stifled all a mother's tenderness: In vain the clamors of parental love Condemned the rigid laws of partial heaven: Alas! I meant to save the tender victim From his hard fate that threatened future guilt, And doomed him to involuntary crimes: I thought to triumph o'er the oracle, And in compassion gave him up to death. Cruel compassion, and destructive too! Deceitful darkness of a false prediction! What did I reap from my inhuman care, Did it prolong my wretched husband's life? Alas! cut off in full prosperity, He fell by the unknown hands of base assassins, Not by his son. Thus were they both torn from me: I lost my child, and could not save his father. By my example taught, avoid my errors, Banish these idle fears, and calm thy soul.

Œdipus: After the dreadful secret thou hast told me, It were not fit I should conceal my own: Hear then my tale; perchance when thou shalt know The sad relation, which they bear each other, Thou too wilt tremble: Born the natural heir To Corinth's throne, from Corinth far removed, I look with horror on my native land: One day—that fatal day I well remember, For O! 'tis ever present to my thoughts, And dreadful to my soul—my youthful hands, For the first time their solemn gift prepared An offering to the gods, when lo! the gates Throughout the temple on a sudden stood Self-opened, and the pillars streamed with blood; The altars shook; a hand invisible Threw back my offerings, and in thunder thus A horrid voice addressed me: "Come not here, Stain not the holy threshold with thy feet, The gods have from the living cut thee off Indignant, nor will e'er accept thy gifts; Go, take thy offerings to the furies, seek The serpents that stand ready to devour thee; These are thy gods, begone, and worship them." While terror seized me at these dreadful words, Again the voice alarmed me, and foretold All those sad crimes which heaven to thee denounced Against thy son; said, I should slay my father, O gods! and be the husband of my mother.

Jocaste: Where am I? what malicious dæmon joined Our hands, to make us thus supremely wretched?

Œdipus: Reserve thy tears for something still more dreadful; Now list and tremble: fearful of myself, Lest I should e'er fulfil the dire prediction, Or oppose heaven, I left my native land, Broke from the arms of a distracted mother, Wandered from place to place, disguised my birth, My family, and name, by one kind friend Attended; yet, in my disastrous journey, The God who guided my sad footsteps oft Strengthened my arm, and crowned me with success: But happier had it been for Œdipus, If he had fallen with glory in the field, And by his death prevented all his woes: I was reserved to be a parricide: The hand of heaven, so long suspended o'er me, Hath from my eyes at length removed the veil Of Ignorance, and now I see it all: I do remember, in the fields of Phocis (Nor know I how I could so long forget The great event) that in a narrow way I met two warriors in a splendid car: The path was strait, and we disputed it: An idle contest for us both; but I Was young and haughty, from my earliest years Bred up to pride that flowed in with my blood; An unknown stranger in a foreign land, I thought myself upon my father's throne, And whomso'er I chanced to meet, esteemed As my own vassals, born but to obey me: I rushed upon them, and with furious arm Their rapid coursers stopped in full career; Hurled from their chariot the intrepid pair. Forward advanced in rage, and both attacked me: The combat was not long, for victory soon Declared for Œdipus. Immortal powers! Whether from hatred or from love I know not, But surely on that day ye fought for me. I saw them both expiring at my feet, And one of them, I do remember well, Who seemed in age well-stricken, as he lay Gasping on the earth, looked earnestly upon me, Held out his arms, and would have spoke: I saw The tears flow plenteous from his half-closed eyes: Methought when I did wound him my shocked soul, All conqueror as I was—you shake, Jocaste.

Jocaste: My lord, see Phorbas comes; this way they lead him.

Œdipus: 'Tis well: my doubts will then be satisfied.

## SCENE II.

Œdipus, Jocaste, Phorbas, Attendants.

Œdipus: Come hither, thou unfortunate old man; The sight of him alarms my conscious soul; Confused remembrance tortures me; I dread To look on, or to question him.

Phorbas: O queen, Is this the day appointed for my death; Hast thou decreed it? Never but to me Wert thou unjust.

Jocaste: Fear not, but hear the king, And answer him.

Phorbas: The king?

Jocaste: Thou standest before him.

Phorbas: Ye gods! is this the successor of Laius?

Œdipus: Waste not the time thus idly, but inform me, Thou wert the only witness of his death, And wounded, so 'tis said, in his defence.

Phorbas: He's dead, and let his ashes rest in peace; Embitter not my fate, nor thus insult A faithful subject wounded by thy hand.

Œdipus: I wound thee? I?

**Phorbas**: Now satiate thy revenge, And put an end to this unhappy life; The poor remains of blood which then escaped thee Now thou mayest shed; and since thou must remember The fatal place where Laius—

**Œdipus**: Spare the rest: It is enough: I see it now: 'twas I: Ye gods! my eyes are opened.

**Jocaste**: Can it be?

**Œdipus**: And art thou he whom my unhappy rage Attacked at Daulis in the narrow path? O yes it is, must be so: in vain myself Would I deceive, all speaks too plain against me, I know thee but too well.

**Phorbas**: I saw him fall, My royal master fall beneath thy hand: Thou didst the crime, and I have suffered for it: A prison was my fate, and thine a throne.

**Œdipus**: Away: I soon shall do thee ample justice, Thee and myself; leave then to me the care Of my own punishment: begone, and save me At least the painful sight of innocence, Which I have made unhappy.

## SCENE III.

Œdipus, Jocaste.

**Œdipus**: O Jocaste! For cruel fate forbids me ever more To call thee by the tender name of wife; Thou seest my crimes; no longer bound to love; Strike now, and free thyself from the dread thought Of being mine.

**Jocaste**: Alas!

**Œdipus**: Take, take this sword, The instrument of my unhappy rage; Receive, and use it for a noble purpose, And plunge it in my breast.

**Jocaste**: What wouldst thou do! O stop thy furious grief, be calm, and live.

**Œdipus**: Canst thou have pity on a wretch like me? No, I must die.

**Jocaste**: Thou must not: hear Jocaste, O hear her prayers!

**Œdipus**: I will not, must not hear thee. I slew thy husband.

**Jocaste**: And thou gavest me one.

**Œdipus**: I did, but 'twas by guilt.

**Jocaste**: Involuntary.

**Œdipus**: No matter, still 'twas guilt.

**Jocaste**: O height of woe!

**Œdipus**: O fatal nuptials! once such envied bliss!

**Jocaste**: Such be it still, for still thou art my husband.

**Œdipus**: O no! I am not; this destructive hand Hath broke the sacred tie, and deep involved Thy kingdom in my ruin. O! avoid me, Fear the vindictive God who still pursues The wretched Œdipus; I fear myself, My timid virtue serves but to confound me; Perhaps my fate may reach even thee, Jocaste; Pity thyself, pity the hapless victims That perish daily for my guilt; O strike, And save thy Œdipus from future crimes.

Jocaste: Do not accuse, do not condemn thyself; Thou art unhappy, but thou art not guilty: Thou didst not know whose blood thy hand had shed In Daulis' fatal conflict; when remembrance Calls forth the melancholy deed, I must Weep for myself, but should not punish thee. Live therefore—

Œdipus: No; it is impossible: Farewell, Jocaste! whither must I go, O whither must I drag this hateful being? What clime accursed, or what disastrous shore Shall hide my crimes, and bury my despair? Still must I wander on from clime to clime, Or rise by murder to another throne? Shall I to Corinth bend my way, where fate Hath heavier crimes in store for Œdipus? O Corinth! ne'er on thy detested borders—

SCENE IV.
Œdipus, Jocaste, Dimas.
Dimas: My lord, this moment is arrived a stranger, He says, from Corinth, and desires admittance.

Œdipus: I'll go and meet him—fare thee well, Jocaste: But stop thy tears; no more shalt thou behold The wretched Œdipus; it is determined: My reign is past; thou hast no husband now, I am no more a sovereign, nor Jocaste's. Oppressed with ills I go, in search of climes, Where far removed from thee and from my country, I still may act as shall become a king, Worthy of thee, and justify the tears Thou sheddest for Œdipus: farewell! forever.

# ACT V.

SCENE I.
Œdipus, Araspes, Dimas, Attendants.

Œdipus: Weep not for me, my friends, nor thus regret Your sovereign's fate: I wish for banishment; To me 'tis pleasure; for I know 'twill make My people happy: you must lose your king, But shall preserve his country. When I first Came to the throne of Thebes, I served it well; And, as I mounted, now I shall descend In glory: honor shall attend my fall: I leave my country, kingdom, children, all. Then hear me now, hear my last parting words; A king you must have; let him be my choice; Take Philoctetes: he is generous, noble, Virtuous, and brave; his father was a king, And he the friend of Hercules; let him Succeed me: I must hence.—Go, search out Phorbas; Bid him not fear, but come this moment hither, I must bequeath him something; he deserves it: I'll take my farewell as a monarch ought. Go, bring the stranger to me—stay ye here.

SCENE II.
Œdipus, Araspes, Icarus, Attendants.

Œdipus: Ha! is it thou, my much-loved Icarus! The faithful guardian of my infant years, Favorite and friend of Polybus, my father, What brought thee hither?

Icarus: Polybus is dead.

Œdipus: Alas? my father!

Icarus: 'Twas what we expected; For he had filled the measure of his days, And died in good old age; these eyes beheld it. Where are ye now, mistaken oracles! That shook my timid virtue, and foretold That I should prove a guilty parricide? My father's dead, ye meant but to deceive me; These hands are not polluted with his blood: The slave of error, I have wandered long In darkness, busied in a fruitless toil, And to remove imaginary ills, Have made my life a scene of real woes, The offspring of my fond credulity. How deep must be the color of my fate When miseries like this can bring relief! Bliss spring from sorrow, and a father's death Shall be accepted as the gift of heaven! But I must hence, and to his ashes pay The tribute due:—ha! silent, and in tears!

Icarus: Ought I to speak? O heaven!

Œdipus: Hast thou aught more Of ill to tell me?

Icarus: For a moment grant me Your private ear.

Œdipus: Retire.—[To the attendants.] What can this mean?

Icarus: Think not of Corinth: thither, if thou goest, Thy death is certain.

Œdipus: Who shall banish me From my own kingdom?

Icarus: To the throne of Corinth Another heir succeeds.

Œdipus: Ye gods! is this The last sad stroke which I am born to suffer, Or will ye still pursue me? Fate, go on And persecute, thou shalt not conquer me: Let us away to my rebellious subjects, I'll go to be their scourge, if not their king, And find at least an honorable death. But say, what stranger has usurped my throne?

Icarus: He is the son-in-law of Polybus, Who on his head did place the diadem In his last moments; the obedient people Hail their new sovereign.

Œdipus: Has my father too Betrayed me, sided with my faithless subjects, And drove me from my throne?

Icarus: He did but justice, For thou wert not his son.

Œdipus: Ha! Icarus!

Icarus: With terror and regret I must reveal The dreadful secret, Corinth—

Œdipus: Not his son!

Icarus: Thou art not. Polybus, oppressed by conscience, Dying declared it; to the royal blood Of Corinth's kings he yielded up his throne: I who alone enjoyed his confidence, And therefore dreaded the new sovereign's power, Fled to implore thy aid.

Œdipus: Who am I then, If not the son of Polybus?

**Icarus**: The gods, Who trusted to my hands thy infant years, In shades of darkest night conceal thy birth; I only know, that soon as born condemned To death, and on a desert hill exposed, Thou but for me hadst perished.

**Œdipus**: Thus with life Began my sorrows, a detested object Even from my cradle, and accursed by all. Where didst thou light on me?

**Icarus**: On mount Citheron,

**Œdipus**: Near Thebes?

**Icarus**: In that deserted place, a Theban, Who called himself thy father, left thee; there To perish: some kind God conducted me That way; I pitied, took thee in my arms, Revived, and cherished thee: to Corinth then Carried my little charge, and to the king Presented thee; who, mark thy wondrous fate! His child just dead, adopted thee his son, And by that stroke of policy confirmed His tottering power: As son of Polybus Thou wert brought up by him who had preserved thee: The throne of Corinth never was thy right, But conscience robbed thee of what chance bestowed.

**Œdipus**: Immortal powers, who rule the fate of kings! Am I thus doomed in one unhappy day To suffer such variety of woe! On a frail mortal shall your miracles Be thus exhausted! But inform me, friend, This old man, from whose hands you took me, say, Hast thou beheld him since that fatal hour?

**Icarus**: Never: perhaps he's dead, he who alone Could tell thee the strange secret of thy birth; But on my mind his image is engraved So deeply, I should know him well.

**Œdipus**: Alas! Wretch that I am! why should I wish to find him? Rather, submissive to the will of heaven Should I keep close the veil that o'er my eyes Spreads its benignant shade: too well already I see my fate; more knowledge would but show New horrors; and yet, spite of all my woes, Urged on by fatal curiosity, I thirst for more: I cannot bear to rest In sad suspense: to doubt is to be wretched: I dread the torch that lights me to my ruin: I fear to know myself, yet cannot long Remain unknown.

### SCENE III.
Œdipus, Icarus, Phorbas.

**Œdipus**: Ha! Phorbas! come this way.

**Icarus**: Surprising! sure the more I look, the more— 'Tis he, my lord, it must be he.

**Phorbas**: Forgive me [To Icarus] If still that face unknown—

**Icarus**: Dost thou remember? On mount Citheron—

**Phorbas**: How!

**Icarus**: The child you gave me, The child to death—

**Phorbas**: What dost thou say? remember, Remember what?

**Icarus**: Thou hast no cause to fear; Le not alarmed: thou mayest rejoice, that infant Was—Œdipus.

**Phorbas**: The lightning blast thee, wretch! What hast thou said?

**Icarus**: Doubt not, my lord, whatever [To Œdipus.] This Theban says, he gave thee to my arms; Thy fate is known; this old man is thy father.

**Œdipus**: What complicated misery! Alas! [To Phorbas.] If thou art indeed my father, will the gods Ever suffer me to shed thy blood?

**Phorbas**: O no! For thou art not my son.

**Œdipus**: And didst not thou Expose me in my infancy?

**Phorbas**: My lord, Permit me to retire, and hide from thee The dreadful truth.

**Œdipus**: No, Phorbas; by the gods I beg thee, tell me all.

**Phorbas**: Begone, avoid Thy children, and thy queen.

**Œdipus**: Now answer me, For to resist is vain: that infant, doomed To death by thee, say, didst thou give it him? [Pointing to **Icarus**: **Phorbas**: I did: and would that day had been my last!]

**Œdipus**: And of what country was that child?

**Phorbas**: Of Thebes.

**Œdipus**: And thou art not his father?

**Phorbas**: No: alas! Sprung from a nobler, but more wretched race—

**Œdipus**: Who was he then?

**Phorbas**: My lord, what would you do? [Throwing himself at the feet of Œdipus.]

**Œdipus**: Speak, speak, I say.

**Phorbas**: Jocaste was his mother.

**Icarus**: [Looking at Œdipus.] Behold the fruit of all my generous care!

**Phorbas**: What have we done?

**Œdipus**: I thought it must be so.

**Icarus**: My lord—

**Œdipus**: Away, begone, this moment leave me: The dreadful gifts ye have bestowed on me Must have their recompense; and ye have cause To fear my wrath, for ye preserved my life.

## SCENE IV.

**Œdipus**: At length the dire prediction is fulfilled, And Œdipus is now, though innocent, A base, incestuous parricide: O virtue! Thou fatal empty name; thou who didst guide My hapless days, thou hadst not power to stop The current of my fate: alas! I fell Into the snare by trying to avoid it: Heaven led me on to guilt, and sunk a pit Beneath my sliding feet: I was the slave Of some unknown, some unrelenting power, That used me for its instrument of vengeance: These are my crimes, remorseless cruel gods! Yours was the guilt, and ye have punished me. Where am I? what dark shade thus from my eyes Covers the light of heaven? the walls are stained With blood; the furies shake their torches at me; The lightnings flash; hell opens her wide gates: O Laius! O my father! art thou there? I see the deadly wound these hands had made; Revenge thee now on this abhorred monster, A monster who defiled the bed of her Who bore him: lead me to the dark abode, That I may strike fresh terror to the hearts Of guilty beings by my punishment: Lead on, I'll follow thee.

SCENE V.

Œdipus, Jocaste, Ægina, Chorus.

**Jocaste**: O Œdipus, Dispel my fears, thy dreadful cries alarm me.

**Œdipus**: Open, thou earth, and swallow me!

**Jocaste**: Alas! What sad misfortune moves thee thus?

**Œdipus**: My crimes.

**Jocaste**: My lord!—

lf0060-08_figure_005 **Œdipus**: Away, Jocaste.

**Jocaste**: Cruel husband!

**Œdipus**: O stop! what name is that? am I thy husband? Do not say husband: we shall hate each other.

**Jocaste**: What sayest thou?

**Œdipus**: 'Tis enough: I have fulfilled My horrid fate: know, Laius was my father; I am thy son.

**Leader of the Chorus.**: O guilt!

**Second Person of the Chorus**: O dreadful day!

**Jocaste**: Ægina, drag me from this horrid place!

**Ægina**: Alas!

**Jocaste**: If thou hast pity on Jocaste, If without horror thou canst now approach me, Assist me now, compassionate thy queen!

**Leader of the Chorus.**: Ye gods! and is it thus your vengeance ceases? Take back your cruel gifts, 'twere better far That we had suffered still.

SCENE VI.

Jocaste, Ægina, High Priest, Chorus.

**High Priest**: Attend, ye people, And know, a milder sun now beams upon you: At length the baleful pestilence is fled, The graves once more are closed, and death hath left us; The God of heaven and earth declares his goodness In peals of thunder: hark! [Thunder and lightning.]

**Jocaste**: What dreadful flashes! Where am I? heaven! what do I hear! Barbarians—

**High Priest**: 'Tis done: the gods are satisfied: no more Doth Laius from the tomb cry out for vengeance: Jocaste, thou mayest live and reign; the blood Of Œdipus sufficeth.

**Chorus**: Gracious heaven!

**Jocaste**: My son! and must I call him husband too! Dear dreadful names! is he then dead?

**High Priest**: He lives, But from the living and the dead cut off, Deprived of light: I saw him plunge this sword, Stained with his father's blood, into his eyes: This fatal moment has to Thebes restored Her safety: such are the decrees of heaven: Which, as it wills, decides the fate of mortals, All-powerful to save or to destroy. Its wrath is all exhausted on thy son, And thou art pardoned.

**Jocaste**: Punish then thyself. [Stabs herself.] Jocaste, thus reserved for horrid incest, Death is the only good remaining for me: Laius, receive my blood: I follow thee: I have lived virtuous, and shall die with pleasure.

**Chorus**: Unhappy queen, and sad calamity!

**Jocaste**: Weep only for my son, who still survives. Priests, and you Thebans, who were once my subjects, Honor my ashes, and remember ever, That midst the horrors which oppressed me, still I could reproach the gods; for heaven alone Was guilty of the crime, and not Jocaste.

End

# Mariamne

## Contents

Dramatis Personæ. . . . . . . . . . . . . . . . . . . . . . . . . . . . . . . . . . . . . 509

Act I. . . . . . . . . . . . . . . . . . . . . . . . . . . . . . . . . . . . . . . . . . . . . . 509

Act II. . . . . . . . . . . . . . . . . . . . . . . . . . . . . . . . . . . . . . . . . . . . . 514

Act III. . . . . . . . . . . . . . . . . . . . . . . . . . . . . . . . . . . . . . . . . . . . 519

Act IV. . . . . . . . . . . . . . . . . . . . . . . . . . . . . . . . . . . . . . . . . . . . 526

Act V. . . . . . . . . . . . . . . . . . . . . . . . . . . . . . . . . . . . . . . . . . . . . 530

## Dramatis Personæ

Varus, a Roman Prætor, Governor of Syria.
Herod, King of Palestine.
Mariamne, Wife of Herod.
Salome, Sister of Herod.
Albinus, Friend to Varus.
MAZAEL, Herod's Minister.
IDAMAS, Herod's Minister
Nabal, an old Officer under the Asmonæan Kings.
Eliza, Confidante of Mariamne.
Herod's Guard, Attendants on Varus, Herod, and Mariamne.
This piece was produced in 1724.

## ACT I.

SCENE, Jerusalem.

SCENE I.
Salome, Mazael.

**Mazael**: It is enough: the power of Salome, By all acknowledged, and by all obeyed, On its firm basis stands immovable: I fled to Azor, with the lightning's speed, Even from Samaria's plain to Jordan's spring, And quick returned: my presence there indeed Was needful, to cut off the aspiring hopes Of Israel's moody race: thy brother Herod, So long detained at Rome, was almost grown

A stranger in his kingdom; and the people, Ever capricious, turbulent, and bold, Still to their kings unjust, aloud proclaimed, That Herod was condemned to slavery By haughty Rome; and Mariamne, raised To the high rank of her proud ancestors, Would from the blood of our high-priests select A king, to rule o'er conquered Palestine. With grief I see, she is by all adored; Her name the dear delight of every tongue; Israel reveres the race from whence she sprang, Even to idolatry: her birth, her beauty, And, above all, her sorrows, melt the hearts Of the rude rabble, who, thou knowest, detest And rail at us. They call her their dear sovereign, And seem to threaten thee with swift destruction. I saw the fickle multitudes alarmed With idle tales like these, but soon I taught them Another lesson; soon I made them tremble: Told them great Herod, fraught with double power, And armed with vengeance, would ere long return: His name alone struck terror to their souls, They saw their folly then, and wept in silence.

**Salome**: Thou toldest them truth, for Herod comes, and soon Shall make rebellious Sion bend beneath him. Antony's favorite is Cæsar's friend; Fortune attends him, at his chariot wheels Submissive chained: his subtle policy Is equal to his courage, and he rises With added strength and glory from his fall: The senate crown him.

**Mazael**: But when Mariamne Shall see her husband, where will be thy power? That haughty rival o'er the king had ever A fatal influence that supplanted thee; And her proud spirit, still inflexible, And still revengeful, holds its enmity: Her safety must depend on thy destruction, And mutual injuries nourish mutual hate. Dost thou not dread her all-subduing charms, Those lordly tyrants o'er the vanquished Herod? For five years past, ever since their fatal marriage, Hath his strange passion for her still increased, By hatred fixed, and nourished by disdain. Oft have we seen the haughty monarch kneel Before her feet, her eyes indignant turned In fury from him, whilst in vain he sued For softer looks than she would deign to give. How have we seen him rage, and sigh, and weep, Abuse, and flatter, threaten and implore! Mean in his rage, and cruel in his love; Abroad a hero, and a slave at home: He punished an ungrateful barbarous race, And, reeking with the father's blood, adored The daughter; raised the dagger to her breast, Guided by thee, then dropped it at her feet. At Rome indeed, whilst from her sight removed, The chain was loosened; but 'twill re-unite When he returns, and shall again behold The fatal charms which he so long admired: Those powerful eyes are ever sure to please, And will resume their empire o'er his heart: Her foes will soon be humbled, and if she But gives the nod, must fall a sacrifice To her resentment. Let us guard against it, And court that power which we can never destroy: Respect well-feigned may win her to our purpose.

**Salome**: No: there are better methods to remove Our fears of Mariamne.

**Mazael**: Ha! what means?

**Salome:** Perhaps even now she dies.

**Mazael:** And wilt thou dare To do a deed so desperate? If the king—

**Salome:** The king assists me in the work of vengeance, And has consented: Zares is arrived At Solyma; my instrument of wrath Waits for his victim: know, the time, the place, The hand to execute, are ready all: To-day it must be done.

**Mazael:** Hast thou then gained At last the victory? Could the king believe thee? Spite of his passion, will he yield up all, And act as thou commandest?

**Salome:** Not so: my power Is more confined: scarce could I urge to vengeance, With all my arts, his long-reluctant soul, But I availed me of his absence from her: Whilst Herod lived, exposed to all her charms, Thou knowest I led a life of wretchedness, Of doubt and fear, uncertain of my fate; When, by a thousand crooked paths, at last I found a passage to his heart, and thought I had secured it, Mariamne came; And, when he saw her, all was lost again; My arts all baffled by a single glance: Yes, the proud queen was mistress of my life, And might have taken it: had she known the way To manage well her easy lover's fondness, Herod had signed the mandate for another, And not for Mariamne; then the blow I meant for her had fallen on Salome: But I have made her pride assist my vengeance, And I have only now to point the dart, Which her own hand hath fashioned, to destroy her. Thou mayest remember well the fatal time That blasted all our hopes; when, Antony Subdued, Augustus took the reins of empire, Each Eastern monarch trembled on his throne: Amongst the rest my hapless brother feared, With his protector, he had lost his crown. Resistance now was vain, and naught remained But to address the conqueror of the world In lowliest terms, and ask forgiveness of him. Call back that dreadful day, when Herod, driven Even to despair, beheld proud Mariamne Spurn at his offered love and kind farewell; Heard her with anguish heap reproaches on him; Call for a father's and a brother's blood, Shed by her tyrant husband: Herod flew To me, and told his griefs; I seized the moment Propitious to my vengeance, and regained A sister's power o'er his distressed heart; Inflamed his rage, and sharpened his despair; Dipped in fresh poison the envenomed dart That pierced his soul: then, desperate in his wrath, Thou heardest him swear to exterminate the race Of Hebrews, and destroy its poor remains; Condemn the mother, and cut off her sons From their inheritance: but soon to rage Succeeded love; one look from her disarmed His vengeance. I, with double eagerness, Pressed his departure, and at length prevailed: He left her; from that hour I was successful; My frequent letters kept up his resentment, And, absent from her, all his rage returned: He blushed in secret for his weakness past, And by degrees, as I removed the veil, His eyes were opened: Zares caught with me The favorable hour, and painted her In blackest colors; told him of her power, Her interest, friends, and the seditious faction, The partisans of the Asmonæan race. But I did more, I raised his jealousy; He trembled for his glory, and his life: Continual treasons had alarmed his soul, And left it ever open to suspicion: Whate'er he fears, still ready to believe, He is not able to distinguish guilt From innocence; in short, I fixed his soul, Guided his hand, and made him sign the mandate.

**Mazael**: 'Twas nobly done: but what will Varus say, The haughty prætor, will he see unmoved A deed so daring? he's thy master here, And, unconfirmed by Rome, thy power is nothing. From Varus' hand thy brother must receive His crown; nor can he act as sovereign here Till the proud prætor shall restore it to him. Will Varus, thinkest thou, e'er permit a queen, Left to his care, to fall a sacrifice? I know the Romans well, they ne'er forgive Such rude contempt of their authority. Thou wilt bring down the storm on Herod's head; Their thunder's always ready; those proud conquerors Are jealous of their rights, and take, thou knowest, Peculiar pleasure in the fall of kings.

**Salome**: Fear not for Herod, Cæsar is his friend, And Varus knows it, therefore will respect him: Perhaps this Roman means to manage all, But be it as it may, my aim is vengeance; I'm on the verge of glory or of shame; To-morrow, nay, to-day may change the scene: Who knows if e'er hereafter I shall find An hour propitious to me, who can tell If Herod will be steady to his purpose? I know his weakness, and I must prevent it, Nor give him time to say, it shall not be. When it is done, let Varus rage, and Rome Pour forth her threats, it shall not damp my joys: The Romans are not here my worst of foes; No, I have more to fear from Mariamne; I must subdue her rival powers, or perish: But Varus comes this way, we must avoid him: Zares ere now should have been here: I'll hence And meet him; fare thee well.—If there be need, My soldiers at the least alarm are ready, And will defend us.

### SCENE II.

Varus, Albinus, Mazael, Attendants Onvarus.

**Varus**: Salome and Mazael— They seem to shun us; in their eyes I read Their terrors; guilt hath reason to be fearful, And dread my presence.—Mazael, stay: go, tell Thy cruel master his designs are known; His wicked instrument is now in chains, And should have met the death he merited, But my regard for Herod bids me hope That he will soon behold the snare they laid. Punish the traitors, and revenge the cause Of injured virtue: if thou lovest thy king, If thou regardest his honor or his peace, Calm his wild rage, embitter not his soul With vile suspicions, and remember, slave, Rome is the scourge of villainy; remember That Varus knows thee; that he's master here, And that his eyes are open to detect thee Away: let Mariamne be obeyed, And treated like a queen; observe her well, And, if thy life be dear to thee, respect her.

**Mazael**: My lord—

**Varus**: Begone: you know my last commands; Reply not, but obey them.

SCENE III.
Varus, Albinus.
**Varus**: Without thee, And thy well-timed advice, thou seest, my friend, The beautous Mariamne had been lost.

**Albinus**: Zares' return raised my suspicions of him; His most officious care to avoid thy presence, And troubled features, I must own, alarmed me.

**Varus**: How much I owe thee for the important service! By thee she lives; by thee my heart once more Shall taste its noble happiness, the best And fairest treasure of the virtuous mind, The happiness to succor the oppressed.

**Albinus**: Such generous cares befit the soul of Varus; Thy arm was ever stretched to help the wretched; Still hast thou born Rome's thunder through the world, And only conquered but to bless mankind; Would I might say thy pity dictates here, And not thy love!

**Varus**: Must love then be the cause? Who would not cherish innocence like hers? What heart, howe'er indifferent, would not plead So fair a cause? who would not die to save her?

**Albinus**: Thus the deceitful passion hides itself In virtue's garb, and steals into the heart: Thy hapless flame—

**Varus**: Albinus, I confess it; The wretched Varus dotes on Mariamne: Thou seest my naked heart, which fears not thee, Because thou art my friend: judge then, Albinus, How must her dangers have alarmed my soul! Her safety and her welfare are my own; Death in its ugliest form were welcome to me, If it could make my Mariamne happy.

**Albinus**: How altered is the noble heart of Varus! Love has avenged himself of all thy flights; No longer do I see the virtuous Roman, Severe and unimpassioned, 'midst the crowd Of rival beauties, who solicited His wandering eyes, regardless of their charms.

**Varus**: To virtue then, thou knowest, and her alone, I paid my vows: in vain corrupted Rome Offered her venal beauties to my eyes; Their pride disgusted, and their arts displeased; False in their vows, and in their vengeance cruel: I saw their shameless fronts all covered o'er With foul dishonor: vanity, ambition, Caprice, and folly, bore the name of love; Such conquests were unworthy of thy friend. At length the power I had so long contemned Indignant saw me from his Eastern throne, And soon subdued; it was my fate to rule O'er Syria's melancholy plains: when heaven Had to Augustus given the vanquished world, And Herod, midst a crowd of kneeling kings, Fell at his feet, and sued for his protection, Hither I came, and fatal to my peace Was Palestine, for there I first beheld her. The melancholy theme of every tongue Was Mariamne's woes; all wept her fate, Doomed to the arms of an inhuman husband, Who slew the father of his lovely bride: Thou knowest what miseries she had suffered since, Her sorrows only equalled by her virtue: Truth, ever banished from the courts of kings, Dwells on her lips, and all the art she knows Is but the generous care to serve the wretched. Her duty is her law; her innocence, Calm and serene, contemns the tyrant's power, And pardons her oppressor; even solicits My aid to save the man who would destroy her. Her virtues, her misfortunes, and her charms United, are too powerful for my soul; I love her, my Albinus; but my love Is not a passion which one day creates, And in another is forgotten; no: The heart she has subdued is not the slave Of loose desire, but by her virtue fired, Means to revenge but never to betray her.

**Albinus**: But if the king, my lord, has gained from Rome Permission to return.

**Varus**: Ay, that I fear: Alas! myself did move the senate for him. Perhaps already he returns to empire, And this abhorred mandate is his own; The first sad proof of his authority: It may be fatal to him. Varus' power May soon be lost, but O! his love remains; Yes, I will die in Mariamne's cause; The world shall weep her fate, and I avenge it.

# ACT II.

### SCENE I.
Salome, Mazael.

**Salome**: Thou seest we are ruined; Mariamne triumphs, And Salome's undone: that lingering Zares, How tedious was his voyage, as if the sea Unwillingly transported him! whilst Herod Flies with the winds to empire and to love: But sea and land, the elements, the heavens, All, all conspire with Varus, to destroy me. Ambition, thou hast plunged me deep in woe; Why did I listen to thy fatal voice? I knew his foolish heart would soon relent; Even now I fear he has revoked the mandate, And all the harvest of my toil is grief And danger, that still wait on high condition Stripped of its power: already fawning crowds Adore my rival, and insult my fall: My feeble glories, all eclipsed by her, Shall shine no more, for this new deity Must now be worshipped: but this is not all, My death, I know, must crown the triumph; she Can never reign whilst Salome survives; She will not spare a life so fatal to her. And yet, O shame, O infamous submission! My pride must stoop to vile dissimulation, To soothe her vanity with feigned respect, And give her joy of—Salome's destruction.

**Mazael**: Despair not, Madam, arms may yet be found To conquer this proud queen: I ever feared Her powerful charms, and Herod's weakness for her; But if I may depend on Zares, still In the king's bosom dwells determined hate, And he has sworn that she shall die: the blow Is but suspended till he comes himself To execute his vengeance; but, meantime, Whether his heart be sharpened by resentment, Or moved by love, it is enough his hand Once signed the mandate: Mariamne soon Will swell the tempest, and eternal discord Shall rankle in their hearts: I know them well: Soon will she light again the torch of hatred, Revive his doubts, and work her own destruction: With new disdain will irritate his soul: Rely upon herself, and mark her ruin.

**Salome**: O! 'tis uncertain; I can never wait Such tardy vengeance; I have surer means; Danger has taught me wisdom: this loud rage, These violent transports of the impassioned Varus, If I observe aright, can never flow From generosity alone, and pity Is seldom known by marks like these: the queen Has charms, and Varus may have charms for her. I know the power of Mariamne's beauty, Nor envy her the crowd of gazing fools, Who throw their flattering incense at her feet; The dangerous happiness may cost her dear: Whether she listens to the Roman's vows, Or with the conquest only means to soothe Her fickle pride, it is enough for me, If it preserves that power I must not lose O'er Herod's heart. Take care my faithful spies Perform their office; let them be rewarded, And sell me precious secrets.—Ha! she comes, Must I then see her?

### SCENE II.
Mariamne, Eliza, Salome, Mazael, Nabal.

**Salome**: Joy to Mariamne: Herod returns, and Rome this day restores To me a brother, and to thee a husband. Thy cruel scorn had raised his just resentment, Which now subsides, and love has quenched the flame Which love alone inspired: his triumphs past, His future glories, all the senate's rights Reposed in him, the titles he has gained, All brought to lay at Mariamne's feet, Proclaim thy happiness: enjoy his heart; Enjoy his empire; I am pleased to see Thy virtues thus rewarded; Salome Shall lend her aid to join your hands together.

**Mariamne**: I neither looked for, nor desired your friendship: I know you, madam, and shall do you justice; I know by what mean arts, and treacherous falsehood, Your powerless malice has pursued my life. Perhaps thou thinkest my heart is like thy own, And therefore tremblest; but thou knowest me not: Fear nothing, for thy crimes and punishment Are both beneath my notice: I have seen Thy base designs, and have forgiven them: I leave thee to thy conscience, if a heart Guilty as thine is capable of feeling.

**Salome**: I've not deserved this bitterness and wrath From Mariamne: to my honest zeal, My conduct, and my brother, I appeal From thy suspicions.

**Mariamne**: I've already told thee, All is forgotten, I am satisfied, And I can pardon, though I can't believe thee.

**Mazael:** Now, by the power supreme, my royal mistress, Scarce could my pains—

**Mariamne:** Stop, Mazael, excuse Is added injury; obey the king, That is thy duty: sold to my oppressors, Thou art their instrument; perform thy office, I shall not stoop to make complaints of thee. Thou, Salome, mayest hence, and tell the king [To Salome.] The secrets of my soul; inflame his heart Once more with rage; I shall not strive to calm it: Instruct your creatures to deal forth their slander, I've left their vile attempts unpunished still; Content to use no arms against my foes, But blameless virtue, and a just disdain.

**Mazael:** What haughtiness!

**Salome:** 'Twill meet with its reward: It is the pride of art to punish folly.

### SCENE III.

Mariamne, Eliza, Nabal.

**Eliza:** Why, my loved mistress, would you thus provoke A foe who burns with ardor to destroy you? Perhaps the rage of Herod is suspended But for a time, and yet may burst upon you. Death was departing, and thou callest him back, When thou shouldst strive to turn his dart aside: Thou hast no friend to guard or to defend thee; Varus, thy kind protector, must obey The senate's orders, and to distant realms Convey its high commands: at his request, And by thy kind assistance, Herod gained His power, and now the tyrant will return With double terror: thou hast furnished him With arms against thyself, and must depend On this proud master, to be dreaded more Because he loves, because his passion soured By thy disdain—

**Mariamne:** My dear Eliza, fly, Bring Varus hither: thou art in the right; I see it all; but I have other cares; My soul is filled with more important business: Let Varus come: Nabal, stay thou with me.

### SCENE IV.

Mariamne, Nabal.

**Mariamne:** Thy virtues, thy experience, and thy zeal For Mariamne's welfare, have long since Deserved my confidence: thou knowest my heart, And all its purposes; the woes I feel, And those I fear: thou sawest my wretched mother, Driven to despair, with tears imploring me To share her flight: her mind, replete with terror, Sees every moment the impetuous Herod, Yet reeking with the blood of half her race, Assassinate her dearest Mariamne. Still she entreats me, with my helpless children, To fly his wrath, and leave this hated clime; The Roman vessels might transport us soon From Syria's borders to the Italian shore; From Varus I might hope some kind protection, And from Augustus; fortune points the way For my escape, the only path of safety: And yet, from virtue or from weakness, which I know not, but my foolish heart recoils At flying from a husband's arms, and keeps, Spite of myself, my lingering footsteps here.

**Nabal**: Thy fears are groundless; yet I must admire them, Because they flow from virtue: thy brave heart, That fears not death, yet trembles at the thought Even of imaginary guilt: but cease Your causeless doubts; consider where you are; Open your eyes, and mark this fatal palace, Wet with a father's and a brother's blood. In vain the king denies the horrid deed; Cæsar in vain absolves him from the crime, Whilst the whole East pronounce him guilty of it. Think of thy mother's fears, thy injured sons, Thy murdered father, the king's cruelty, Thy sister's hatred, and what scarce my tongue Can mention without horror, though thy virtue Regardless smiles, thy death this day determined. If, undismayed by such a scene of woe, Thou art resolved to meet and brave thy fate, O still remember, still defend thy children: The king hath taken away their hopes of empire, And well thou knowest what dreadful oracles Long since alarmed thy fears, when heaven foretold, That a strange hand should one day join thy sons To their unhappy father. A wild Arab, Implacable and pitiless, already Hath half fulfilled the terrible prediction: After a deed so horrid, may he not Accomplish all the rest? From Herod's rage Nothing is sacred; who can tell but now, Even now he comes to act his bloody purpose, And blot out all our Asmonæan race? 'Tis time to guard against him, to prevent His guilt, and stop his murderous hand; to save Those tender victims from a tyrant's sword, And hide them from the sight of such examples. Within thy palace from my earliest years Brought up, and by thy ancestors beloved, Thou seest me ready to partake thy fortunes Where'er thou goest: away then; break thy chains; Fly to the justice of a Roman senate; Implore them to adopt thy injured sons, And shelter their distress: such innocence And virtue will astonish great Augustus. If just and happy is his reign, as fame Reports, and conquered worlds in rapture bend The knee before him, if he merits all The honors he has gained, he must protect thee.

**Mariamne**: My doubts are vanished, and I yield to thee; To thy advice, and to a mother's tears; To my son's danger, to my own hard fate; Which dooms me yet perhaps to greater ills Than I have suffered. Go thou to my mother; When night shall throw her sable mantle o'er This seat of guilt, let some one give me notice That all is ready; since it must be done, I am prepared.

SCENE V.
Mariamne, Varus, Eliza.

**Varus:** I come, great queen, to know Your last commands; which, as the law of heaven. Shall be revered: say, must this arm avenge thee? Speak, and 'tis done: command, and I obey.

**Mariamne:** Varus, I'm much indebted to thy goodness, And, but my sorrows plead their own excuse, Should not be thus importunate; I know Thou lovest to help the wretched, therefore ask Thy generous aid: whilst Herod's doubtful fate Hung in the balance, and he knew not which Awaited him, a prison or a throne, I did solicit Varus in his favor; Spite of his cruelties, against my peace, Against my interest, I performed my duty. Now Mariamne for herself implores Thy kind protection; begs thee to preserve From most inhuman laws, her hapless sons, The poor remains of Syria's royal race. Long since I should have left these guilty walls, And asked the senate for some safe retreat; But whilst the sword of war filled half the world With blood and slaughter, 'twas in vain to seek For refuge in the scene of wild destruction: Augustus now hath given the nations peace, And spread his bounties o'er the face of nature: After the toils of hateful war, resolved To make the world, which he had conquered, happy: He sits supreme o'er tributary kings, And takes the poor and injured to his care: Who has so fair a title to his justice, As my unhappy, my defenceless children? Brought by their weeping mother from afar To ask his succor; he will shelter them, His generous hand will wipe off all our tears. I shall not ask him to revenge my cause, Or punish my proud foes; it is enough If my loved children, formed by his example, And by his justice taught, true Romans soon, Shall learn to rule of those who rule mankind. A mother's comfort, and her children's safety, Depend on thee: my woes will vanish all If thou wilt hear me; and thy noble heart Hath ever been the friend of injured virtue: To thee I owe my life: assist me now, Remove me, Varus, from this fatal palace; Grant my benighted steps a friendly guide To Sidon's ports, where now thy vessels lie. Not answer me! what means that look of sorrow? Why art thou silent? O! too well I see Thou wilt not hear the voice of wretchedness.

**Varus:** It is not so: I hear, and will obey thee: My guards shall follow thee to Rome: dispose Of them, of me; my heart, my life is thine. Flee from the tyrant, break the fatal tie; 'Tis punishment enough to be forsaken By Mariamne: never shall he behold thee; Thanks to his own injustice; and I feel Too well there cannot be a fate more cruel. Forgive me, but the thought of losing thee Hath drawn the fatal secret from my breast; I own my crime: but, spite of all my weakness, Know, my respect is equal to my love: Varus but wishes to protect thy virtue, But to avenge thy injuries, and die.

**Mariamne:** I hoped the great preserver of my life Would prove the guardian of my honor too; And to his pity only thought I owed His kind assistance; ne'er did I expect That he, of all men, should increase my sorrows; Or that, to crown the woes of Mariamne, I should be forced to tremble at thy goodness, And blush for every favor I received: Yet, think not, Varus, that thy passion, thus Declared, shall rob thee of my gratitude: My constant friendship shall be ever thine; I will forget thy love, but not thy virtues: Thou hadst my praise and my esteem till now, But longer converse may deprive thee of it; For thy sake therefore, Varus, I must leave thee.

### SCENE VI.
Varus, Albinus.

**Albinus**: I fear you're troubled, sir; your color changes.

**Varus**: Albinus, I must own, my spirits droop; Pity, my friend, the weakness of a heart That never loved before: alas! I knew not How strong my fetters were, but now I feel, Nor can I break them: with what sweet demeanor, And lovely softness, did she chide my passion; Calm and unruffled, how her tranquil prudence Taught me my duty, and enforced her own; How I adored her even when she repulsed me! I've lost all hope, yet love her more than ever: Gods! for what dreadful trial of my faith Am I reserved?

**Albinus**: Wilt thou then aid her flight?

**Varus**: 'Tis a sad office.

**Albinus**: Art thou pleased so well With her disdain, as thus to make thyself Unhappy, and promote thy own destruction? What dost thou purpose?

**Varus**: Can I e'er forsake her? Can I rebel against her laws? my heart Were then unworthy of her. Hence my doubts. 'Twas Mariamne spoke, and I obey: Quick, let her leave the tyrant; let her seek Augustus; she has cause to fly, and Varus Has none to murmur or complain; at least She leaves me the sweet pleasure to reflect, That I have lived and acted but for her; Have broke her chains, have saved her precious life: Nay more: for I will sacrifice my love, Fly from those dangerous charms that would betray me, And imitate the virtue I adore.

# ACT III.

### SCENE I.
Varus, Nabal, Albinus, attendants Onvarus.

**Nabal**: The king, my lord, the happy Herod, comes Triumphant, and the Hebrews flock in crowds To meet him: Salome, alarmed and fearful Of her declining interest, joins his train Of fawning courtiers, soothes his pride, and strives By every art to gain him to her purpose; The priests attend, and strew their palms before him. With Herod comes the faithful Idamas, Deputed by his sovereign to attend The noble Varus; he will soon be here. Still hath he proved himself the constant friend Of Mariamne, and by wholesome counsels Softened the rage of his impetuous master: The queen, still wavering and irresolute, Condemns herself; her rigid virtue fears To do what danger tells her must be done: She quits the palace, then returns; meanwhile Her anxious mother, falling at her feet, Bathes them in tears, points to her weeping children, And trembling begs her to depart: she stops, And doubts, and much I fear will stay too long: 'Tis thou must hasten her; on thee alone Depends the safety of the noblest being Heaven e'er gave birth to. O preserve her; save The race august sprung from a line of kings; Save Mariamne. Are your guards all ready? May I inform her of it?

**Varus**: All's prepared: I gave them orders: she may go this moment.

**Nabal**: And wilt thou too permit a faithful servant To follow his loved mistress?

**Varus**: Go with her, Wait on her steps, and guard her as thy life: This hateful place deserves her not: may heaven, In pity to her sorrows, smile upon her; Light up a fairer sun to gild her journey, And bid the waves in smoother currents flow, Obedient to the sacred charge they bear! Thou, good old man, mayest follow and attend her; Thou art too happy, but thou hast deserved it.

## SCENE II.

Varus, Albinus, Attendants Onvarus.

**Varus**: Already Herod comes; the trumpet's sound Speaks his return; unwelcome sound to me! I dread his presence: cruel as he is, Instant his wrath may fall on Mariamne: Would she had left forever these sad seats Of guilt and horror! would I might partake Her flight! but O! the more I love, the more I must avoid her: 'twere in me a crime To follow her; and all that Varus can— But Idamas approaches.

## SCENE III.

Varus, Idamas, Albinus, Attendants Onvarus.

**Idamas**: Ere the king, My royal master, comes, with gratitude To pay thy bounties, and receive from thee The holy sceptre, say, wilt thou permit me?—

**Varus**: No more: your king may spare this idle homage, These practised arts of visionary friendship Amongst the great, drawn forth with pompous splendor But to amuse the gaping multitude And foreign to the heart: but say, at length Rome has consented; Herod is your king; Doth he deserve to reign? Is the queen safe, And will he spare the blood of innocence.

**Idamas**: May the just gods, who hate the perjured man, Open his eyes, now blinded by imposture! But who shall dive into his secret thoughts, Or trace the emotions of his troubled soul? Naught can we draw from him but sullen silence;

Or if perchance the name of Mariamne Escape his lips, he sighs, and raves: this moment Gives secret orders, and the next revokes them: Herod detests the race from whence she sprang, And hates her more because he loved too well. Perfidious Zares, by thy order stopped, And by thy order freed, the artificer Of calumny and fraud, will serve the cause Of subtle Salome, whilst Mazael lends His secret aid: the jealous Herod listens To their suggestions; they besiege him closely; And their officious hatred still keeps truth At distance from him: this great conqueror, Who made so many potent monarchs tremble, This king, whose noble deeds even Rome admired, Whose name yet fills all Asia with alarms, In his own house beholds his glories fade: Torn by suspicions, and o'erwhelmed with grief; Led by his sister, hated by his wife: I pity him, and fear for Mariamne. Say, wilt thou not protect her?

**Varus**: 'Tis enough: Albinus, follow me, the queen's in danger: Away, for I must save the innocent.

**Idamas**: Will you not wait then for the king?

**Varus**: I know I should receive him here: it is my duty, For so the senate wills: but other cares Inspire me now, and other interests guide: 'Tis my first duty to protect the wretched. [Exit Varus.]

**Idamas**: What storms do I foresee? what new distresses Will soon o'ertake us? Now, O Israel's God, Change Herod's heart!

### SCENE IV.

Herod, Mazael, Idamas, attendants On **Herod**: **Herod**: Varus avoid me too! What horrors meet me here on every side! Good heaven! can Herod inspire naught but hatred And terror to mankind? Is every heart Thus shut against me? To myself disgustful, My people, and my queen; with grief oppressed I re-ascend my throne, and only come To see the sorrows my own hand hath made. O heaven!

**Mazael**: Be calm, my lord, let me entreat you.

**Herod**: Wretch that I am, what have I done!

**Mazael**: Ha! weeping! Shall Herod weep, the great, the illustrious king, The dread of Parthia, and the friend of Rome, For wisdom and for valor long renowned! O! think my lord, of those distinguished honors Which Antony and victory bestowed; Think of thy fame, when seen by great Augustus, He chose thee from a crowd of conquered kings, And marked thee for his friend: call back the time, When great Jerusalem, by thee subdued, Submitted to thy laws: by thee defended, Once more she shines with all her ancient lustre, And sees her sovereign crowned with fair success: Never was king in peace or war more happy.

**Herod**: There is no happiness on earth for me; Fate points its poisoned arrows at my breast; And, to complete my woes, I have deserved them.

**Idamas:** Permit me, sir, the freedom to observe, Your throne, by fears and jealousies surrounded, Would stand more firmly on love's nobler basis: The king who makes his people's happiness Secures his own; thy soul, thus racked with tortures, Might trace the poisoned waters to their spring. O, my lord, suffer not malicious tongues To wound the peace and honor of thy life; Nor servile flatterers to estrange the hearts Of those who long to serve their royal master: Israel shall then enamored with thy virtues—

**Herod:** And thinkest thou Herod might again be loved?

**Mazael:** Zares, my lord, still faithful to his charge, Burns with the same unwearied zeal to serve thee: He comes from Salome, and begs admittance.

**Herod:** What! both forever persecute me! No! Let not that monster e'er appear before me; I've heard too much already: hence, begone, And leave me to myself: what shall I do To calm my troubled soul? Stay, Idamas, And, Mazael, stay.

### SCENE V.

Herod, Mazael, Idamas.

**Herod:** Behold this dreadful monarch, This mighty king, who made the nations tremble; Who knew so well to conquer and to reign. To break his chains, and make the world admire His wisdom and his power: behold him now, Alas! how little like his former self!

**Mazael:** All own thy greatness, and adore thy virtues.

**Idamas:** One heart alone resists, and that perhaps May still be thine.

**Herod:** No: Herod's a barbarian, Unworthy of his throne.

**Idamas:** Thy grief is just, And if for Mariamne—

**Herod:** Fatal name! 'Tis that condemns me; that reproaches still My tortured soul with cruelty and weakness.

**Mazael:** My lord, your goodness but augments her hatred; She loathes your sight, and flies from your embraces.

**Herod:** I courted hers.

**Mazael:** Indeed, my lord?

**Herod:** I did: This sudden change, this grief that hangs upon me, These shameful tears, do they not all declare That Herod is returned from Mariamne? With love and hatred mingled in my soul, I left the crowd of flatterers in my court, And flew to her: but what was my reward? How did we meet! in anger, frowns, and strife: In her indignant eyes I read my fate, And my injustice: she scarce deigned to cast A look upon me; even my tears availed not; They only served to make her scorn me more.

**Mazael:** You see, my lord, her soul's implacable, And never will be softened by indulgence; It but inflames her pride.

**Herod**: I know she hates me; But I've deserved it, and I must forgive her: She has but too much cause from one so guilty.

**Mazael**: Guilty, my lord? hast thou forgot her flights, Contempt, and pride, and wrath, and fierce resentment; Her father's plot, her own designs against thee, And all her race thy mortal foes? Hircanus Had oft betrayed thee; the Asmonæan league Was firmly knit; and by such dangerous powers, That nothing but a master-stroke could save—

**Herod**: No matter: that Hircanus was her father, I should have spared him; but I only listened To proud ambition, and the love of empire: My cruel policy destroyed her race; I killed the father, and proscribed his daughter: I wanted but to hate and to oppress, And heaven, to punish me, hath made me love her.

**Idamas**: To feel a passion for a worthy object Is not a weakness in us, but a virtue, Worthy of every good which heaven hath given thee; Esteem thy love amongst its choicest blessings.

**Herod**: What hath my rashness done! ye sacred manes, Hircanus, Oh!

**Mazael**: Banish the sad remembrance, And grant, kind heaven, the queen too may forget it!

**Herod**: Unhappy father! more unhappy husband! The injuries I have done my Mariamne Make her more dear: O! if her heart—her faith— But I have stayed too long: now, Idamas, I'll make amends for all; go, haste, and tell her, My soul, obedient to her will, shall lay My throne, my life, my glory at her feet: Amongst her sons I'll choose a successor. She has accused my sister as the cause Of her misfortunes, henceforth I disclaim her; A nearer tie demands the sacrifice, And Salome must yield to Mariamne: My queen shall rule with power unlimited!

**Mazael**: My lord, you will not—

**Herod**: Yes: I am resolved: I know her now; she is the choicest gift Of bounteous heaven; as such I shall revere her: What cannot love, the mighty conqueror, do? To Mariamne I shall owe my virtue. In savage pomp, and barbarous majesty, Too long hath Asia seen her sovereign rule Respected by his people; feared, admired, Yet hated still; with crowds of worshippers, But not one friend. My sister, whom long time This foolish heart believed, hath ne'er consulted My happiness, my interest, or my fame: For Salome, more cruel than myself, And more revengeful, dipped her hands in blood, And ruled my subjects with a rod of iron: Whilst Mariamne felt for the unhappy, Forgot her own distress to pity theirs, And told me all their sorrows: but 'tis past: Henceforth I will be just, but not severe; I'll strive to please her by promoting still The public weal: Judah shall bless my reign, For I am changed. From this auspicious hour, Far from my throne, shall every jealous fear Be now removed: I will dry up the tears Of the oppressed, and reign o'er Palestine, Not as a tyrant, but a citizen; Gain every heart to merit Mariamne's. O seek her, tell her how my soul repents; That my remorse is equal to my rashness. Run, fly, begone, and instantly return. What do I see? my sister? hence: O heaven, Finish the woes of my unhappy life!

SCENE VI.
Herod, Salome.

**Salome**: Well, sir, you've seen your dear deceitful foe, And suffered more affronts; I know you have.

**Herod**: Madam, permit me to inform you, this Is not a time to add to my misfortunes; I would remove them: my imperious temper Made me more feared indeed, but more unhappy: Too long already o'er this house of sorrow Hath vengeance poured her black and deadly poison: The queen and you, thus at perpetual variance, Would be a spring of endless misery; therefore, My sister, for our mutual happiness, For thy repose and mine, 'tis best to part; Immediately, away: it must be so.

**Salome**: What do I hear! O fatal enemy!

**Herod**: A king commands, a brother begs it of thee: O may he ne'er again be forced to give One cruel order, ne'er take vengeance more, Nourish suspicions, or shed guiltless blood! Thou shalt no longer make my life a burden; Complain of me, lament thyself, but go.

**Salome**: Alas! my lord, I shall make no complaints; Since I am doomed to banishment by thee, It must be just, and fitting that I should be; For I have ever learned to make thy will My law: if thou commandest, I must obey; I never shall resent the injury, Or call on nature and the ties of blood, Or to attest, or vindicate my wrongs; The voice of nature's seldom heard by kings, The ties of blood are much too weak to bind them: I will not boast that tender friendship now Whose zeal offends thee; much less would I call To thy remembrance all my service past; One look I see from Mariamne soon Effaces all: but canst thou ever think She will forget the attempt upon her life Which Herod made? thee she must fear: thou therefore Shouldst dread her more: thou knowest her vows, her thoughts Are bent against thee, and whose counsels now Shall stay her vengeance? Where's the faithful heart Devoted to thee? where's the watchful eye, Ever awake, to guard the life of Herod? Who shall unravel all her subtle plots, Or who restrain her wrath? Dost thou believe, When thou hast put thy life within her power, That love will plead for thee? O no! such hate, Such scorn as hers, such desperate resentment—

**Herod**: Permit me, Salome, at least to doubt, At least delude me with the flattering hopes I may regain her heart: in this alone I wish to be deceived: show some regard, Some kind compassion for a brother's weakness: I must believe, thou knowest I've too much reason. Thy hatred was a barrier to our love: Thy malice hardened Mariamne's heart, And, but for thee, I had been less detested.

**Salome**: Couldst thou but know, O! couldst thou but conceive To what excess—

**Herod**: Sister, I'll hear no more: Let Mariamne threaten; let her take This loathesome life, for I am weary of it; So shall I perish by the hand I love.

**Salome**: It would be cruel to deceive you longer By guilty silence, or conceal her crimes: I know the dangerous hazard that I run By serving you; but I must speak, though death Were my reward: poor, blind, deluded husband, Enslaved by love for a vile worthless woman; Know Mariamne now, and know thy shame: 'Tis not her pride, her hatred, and disdain, Should make thee loathe her, but that—she is false; She loves another.

**Herod**: Mariamne love Another! barbarous sister! to suspect Her spotless virtue! Is it thus thou meanest To murder Herod? Are these poisoned darts The best farewell that thou canst leave thy brother? To light up discord, shame, and rage, and horror, In my distracted mind! Could Mariamne— But thou already hast too oft deceived me; Too long have I given credit to thy falsehood: Now heaven has punished my credulity, But it has ever been my fate to love Those who abhor me. You are all my foes; All sworn to persecute the wretched Herod.

**Salome**: Far from thy sight then—

**Herod**: Stir not hence, I charge thee; Another is beloved? Speak, tell me, who Must fall a sacrifice to Herod's vengeance? Pursue thy work, and make my woes complete.

**Salome**: Since I must speak—

**Herod**: Strike here: behold my heart: Who has dishonored me? Whoe'er he be, Thou, Salome, perhaps mayest answer for it, For thou art guilty: thou hast undeceived me: Now at thy peril speak.

**Salome**: No matter.

**Herod**: Well—

**Salome**: 'Tis—

### SCENE VII.

Herod, Salome, Mazael.

**Mazael**: Bear not this indignity, my lord, The queen is fled, accompanied by Varus.

**Herod**: Varus, and Mariamne! gods! where am I?

**Mazael**: Varus, my lord, and all his troops have left The palace, and a secret band is placed About the walls to favor her retreat; Your Mariamne will be lost forever.

**Herod**: The charm is broke, and day shines full upon me: Come, Salome, acknowledge now thy brother, And know him by his wrath; let us surprise The infidel: now judge if Herod still Acts like himself, and like himself revenges.

# ACT IV.

SCENE I.
Salome, Mazael.

**Mazael**: Never did fair appearance gild so well The specious covering of a happy falsehood: With what dexterity I played on him, And blended truth with artifice! But why Art thou dejected? art thou not restored To Herod's favor? Mariamne lost, Beyond recovery lost? Thou art avenged; The king's distracted. I am shocked myself When I behold the work of my own hands: Thou too hast seen the horrid spectacle, The trembling slaves all butchered by his hand. The queen half-dead, and fainting by their side, And Herod's arm uplifted as in act To murder her: the children bathed in tears Fall at his feet, and offer their own lives To save their mother's: canst thou wish for more, Or hast thou aught to fear?

**Salome**: I fear the king, I fear those fatal charms which he adores; That arm which oft uplifted falls as oft Inactive down; that anger which soon kindled Is soon extinct; which, doubtful still and blind, Exhausts its feeble powers in sudden transports: My triumphs, Mazael, are uncertain still; Twice has my fate been changed this day, and twice To hatred love succeeded: if he sees The queen again, we are undone.

SCENE II.
Herod, Salome, Mazael, Guards.

**Mazael**: He comes, And seems disturbed: what horror in his aspect!

**Salome**: Say, Herod, hast thou taken ample vengeance?

**Mazael**: I hope my royal master will forgive His faithful servant, who thus dares to speak Touching the queen: but Varus is her safeguard; Prevent his dark designs, and save thyself: The haughty prætor, resolute and bold, Will make a merit of destroying thee.

**Herod**: Alas! my sister, how have I been treated! Deceived, betrayed! help me to rail, to curse This dear ungrateful woman: now my heart Rests all its hopes on thy assisting friendship: Thou, Salome, wert made a sacrifice To my unhappy love for Mariamne; I numbered thee amongst my worst of foes; For her unkindness did I punish thee; But thou hast seen my tenderness betrayed, And, ere this day is past, we'll be revenged: Yes, she shall suffer for her fatal power O'er Herod's heart, that sighed for her alone. O how have I adored, and how detested, The faithless Mariamne! and thou, Varus, Shalt feel my wrath; thou art a Roman, therefore Thy life is safe; but I can punish thee In blood more precious, and a dearer self: Thou shalt behold the object of thy love, Who has preferred thee to her hated lord, Thou shalt behold her soon expire in torment Before thy eyes: dost thou not think Augustus Will praise my just severity?

*Salome*: No doubt He will, my lord, and would himself advise it. On the same altar where his friends adore him, He sheds the blood of foes: he teaches kings To rule and to be feared; let Herod mark And follow his example; thus alone Thy life can be secure: the queen must stand Condemned by all, and thou be justified.

*Mazael*: But make good use of this important moment, Whilst Varus is yet absent, and his forces Far from our walls; now seize her, and complete Thy easy vengeance.

*Salome*: Above all conceal From Israel's sons thy purpose and thy grief, And spare thyself the horror of a sight So dreadful; fly from this unhappy place, The witness of thy shame, that must recall A thousand mournful images; O hide From every eye thy sorrows and thy tears.

*Herod*: No: I must see her; face to face confound her; Force her to answer; hear her poor excuses: I'll make her tremble at the approach of death, And ask that pardon she shall never obtain.

*Salome*: My lord, you will not see her?

*Herod*: Fear me not; Her doom is fixed: vainly she hopes that love Will plead her cause; my heart is shut against her: Those eyes, which once were dangerous to my peace, Are harmless now; her presence will but raise My anger, not my love. Guards, bring her hither; I'll only see, and hear, and punish her. Sister, I would be private for a moment: [To the attendants.] Send Mariamne here: you may retire. [To the guards.]

## SCENE III.

*Herod*: [Alone.] Art thou resolved to see her then? O Herod, Canst thou depend on thy own treacherous heart? Is not her guilt too plain, and have I not Been basely injured? Why then seek for more? What profit can this interview afford me? I know her thoughts already, know she hates me; Why lives she yet? revenge, thou art too slow! Unworthy Herod, coward as thou art, Go, see her, pardon, sigh again, and court Your haughty tyrant. No: to-night she dies: I've sworn it; the Asmonæan blood shall flow; I hate the race, and am abhorred by them. But see, she comes; heaven! what a mournful sight!

## SCENE IV.

Mariamne, Herod, Eliza, Guards.

**Eliza**: Rouse up your spirits, madam, 'tis the king.

**Mariamne**: Where am I; whither do you lead me? O 'Tis death to look upon him.

**Herod**: How my soul Shudders at sight of her!

**Mariamne**: Eliza, help, Support me, I grow faint.

**Eliza**: This way.

**Mariamne**: What torment.

**Herod**: What shall I say to her? O heaven!

**Mariamne**: Well, sir, Your pleasure: wherefore am I ordered here? Is it to yield thee up the poor remains Of hated life, destructive to us both? Take it; strike here; I'll thank thee for the blow; The only gift I would accept from thee.

**Herod**: Then thou shalt have it: but first speak, defend, If possible, thy shameful flight, and tell me wherefore, When Herod's heart to thee alone indulgent, So oft offended, yet as oft forgave thee, The partner of my empire and my glory, What couldst thou purpose by so black a crime?

**Mariamne**: Is that a question fit for thee to ask? But 'tis not now a time for vain reproaches; Yet sure, my lord, if wretched Mariamne, Far from these walls had sought some kind retreat, If she for once had dared to violate A husband's rights, and swerve from her obedience, Think of my royal ancestors; remember My sufferings past, my present danger; think On these, my lord, and blame me if thou darest.

**Herod**: But when thy guilty passion for a traitor, For Varus—

**Mariamne**: Stop thy bold licentious tongue: My life is thine: but do not cover me With foul dishonor; let me pass at least Without a blush unspotted to the grave: Do not forget the sacred tie that bound us, That joined my honor and my fame with thine, As such I have preserved them: look on me; Strike here; thou art welcome: but remember still I am thy wife; pay some respect to me, And to thyself.

**Herod**: O! it becomes thee well To talk of sacred ties which thou hast broken: Perfidious woman! would not the proud scorn And hatred thou hast shown alone condemn thee?

**Mariamne**: Since thou already hast decreed my fate, What would avail my hatred or my love? What right hast thou to Mariamne's heart, Which thou hast filled with sorrow, and despair, And anguish: thou who, for these five years past, Hast marked my days with bitterness and woe; Thou fell destroyer of my guiltless parents. Where is my murdered father? cruel Herod! O! if thy rage had sought no blood but mine, Heaven be my witness, I had loved thee still, And blessed thee in my latest hour: but O! Do not pursue me, Herod, after death; Do not extend my woes beyond the grave, Preserve my children; do not punish them, Because they are mine, but act a father's part: Perhaps hereafter thou wilt know their mother; Perhaps shalt one day pity, when too late, The heart, which, never but by thee suspected, Could not disguise its griefs; the heart which still Preserved its virtue, and, but for thyself, Had loved thee, Herod.

**Herod**: Ha! what do I hear! What charm, what secret power controls my rage, And steals me from myself? O Mariamne!

**Mariamne**: O cruel Herod!

**Herod**: O my foolish heart!

**Mariamne**: For pity's sake behold my wretchedness, And take this hated life.

**Herod**: My own is thine, Forever thine; thou art my Mariamne: Banish thy fears; O thou wert sure to triumph When I beheld thee; make no more excuses, Thou art, thou must be innocent: I now Must tremble in my turn, and ask forgiveness: Wilt thou not pardon him who pardoned thee? Were our hearts made but to detest each other, To persecute ourselves? Let us at once End all our fears and all our pains together; Give me thy love, give me thy hand again.

**Mariamne**: Canst thou desire this hand? O heaven, thou knowest Herod's is stained with blood.

**Herod**: It is: I slew Thy father, and my king; but wherefore did it? To reign with thee: and what was my reward? Thy hatred; a reward I well deserved: I have no right to murmur or complain; Thy father's death, and the injustice done To thy unhappy children, are the least Of Herod's guilt; it reached even Mariamne, And for a moment I detested thee; Nay more, gave ear to foul suspicions of thee; 'Twill be the height of virtue to forgive me; The more my crimes, the more thy soul will show Its greatness: thou hast seen my weakness for thee, Take heed that thou abuse it not; for love And rage, thou knowest, by turns possess my soul; O give it ease; thou turnest aside thine eyes, Speak, Mariamne—

**Mariamne**: Such tumultuous transports Can never spring, I fear, from true repentance: Art thou sincere, and may I trust thee, Herod?

**Herod**: Thou mayest: what is there which thou canst not do If thou wilt cease to hate me? 'twas thy scorn That raised such furious tempests in my soul; It was the loss of Mariamne's heart That made me savage, barbarous, and inhuman: My tears shall wash away the mutual stain Of both our faults: and here I swear—

SCENE V.

Herod, Mariamne, Eliza, a Guard.

**Guard**: My lord, The people are in arms; they have destroyed The scaffold raised by Salome's command, And slain the officers of justice: Varus Assumes the sovereign power, he comes this way, And every moment we expect him here.

**Herod**: Ha! can it be! thus at the very instant When I was falling at thy feet, to raise Thy minion—

**Mariamne**: O my lord, can you believe—

**Herod**: Thou seekest my life, and thou shalt have it, traitress; But I will drag thee with me to the tomb, Spite of thyself, we there shall be united. A guard there, seize, and watch her.

### SCENE VI.
Herod, Mariamne, Salome, Mazael, Eliza, Guards.

**Salome**: O, my brother, Venture not forth; for the rebellious Hebrews Are raised against you, and demand your life, Repeating still the name of Mariamne: They come even now to seize and take her from thee.

**Herod**: Away. I'll meet them unappalled: but thou Shalt answer for this insult: to thy care I leave her, Salome, guard well thy charge.

**Mariamne**: I fear not death, but call high heaven to witness—

**Mazael**: My lord, the Romans are already here.

**Herod**: And must I leave the guilty wretch unpunished? No: she shall bleed: it must be so: alas! In my sad state I can determine nothing; Death would be welcome; I'll away and meet it.

# ACT V.

### SCENE I.
Mariamne, Eliza, Guards.

**Mariamne**: Soldiers, retire, and leave your queen at least The mournful privilege to weep alone. [The guards retire to a corner of the stage.] Just heaven! is this at last my wretched fate? My noble blood, my title to a throne, All that could promise years of happiness, And days of pleasure, turned to deadly poison, Have filled my cup with bitterness and woe. O birth! O youth! and thou destructive beauty, Whose dangerous lustre but enflamed my pride, Flattering delusion! unsubstantial shade Of fancied bliss, O how hast thou deceived me! Beneath my fatal throne forever lurked Anguish and care, digging the grave that now Gapes to receive the dying Mariamne. In Jordan's flood I saw my brother perish, My father massacred by bloody Herod, Who now has doomed to death a guiltless wife: My virtue still remained, and that the tongue Of slander strives to wound: thou power supreme! Whose chastisements severe are but the proofs Of innocence, I ask not for thy aid, Nor for thy vengeance; my great ancestors Taught me to look on death unmerited Without a fear: take then my guiltless blood, But O! defend my fame: command the tyrant To spare my memory; let not clamorous falsehood Insult my ashes: virtue is avenged When she's respected. But what new alarm, What dreadful shrieks are these? the palace rings With loud confusion, and the din of arms: I am perhaps the cause, they fight for me: They force the doors: ha! what do I see?

## SCENE II.

Mariamne, Varus, Eliza, Albinus, Soldiers.

**Varus**: Away: Hence ruffians; you who hold your queen in bondage, Vile Hebrews, hence:—you, Romans, do your office. [Herod's guards go off, chained by Varus's soldiers.] Now, Mariamne, thou art free; thou seest The tyrant could not bar my entrance here: Mazael lies bathed in his perfidious blood; At least my arm hath half avenged the cause Of injured majesty: haste, Mariamne, Seize the propitious moment, and secure A shelter from the storm: let us begone.

**Mariamne**: My lord, I cannot now accept thy bounty; After the vile reproach which Herod cast On my fair fame, I should indeed deserve it, Were I imprudent to receive the aid Thou profferest: I have much more cause to dread Thy kindness now than his barbarity; 'Twould be disgraceful thus to owe my life To Varus; honor says even this is guilt, And death alone can expiate my offence.

**Varus**: What wouldst thou do? alas! unhappy princess, A moment may destroy thee: the time presses; Still we're in arms, and Herod may succeed: Dost thou not fear his rage and his despair?

**Mariamne**: No: I fear naught but shame; and know my duty.

**Varus**: Am I then doomed forever to offend you? But I will do the work of vengeance for thee, Spite of thyself; once more I'll to the field; And, if the tyrant comes across me there, This arm—

**Mariamne**: Stop, Varus; I detest a triumph So dearly bought: know, sir, the life of Herod Demands my care: his rights—

**Varus**: Are forfeited By his ingratitude.

**Mariamne**: The sacred tie—

**Varus**: Is broken.

**Mariamne**: Duty hath united us.

**Varus**: But guilt divorces; therefore do not stay me, Revenge thyself, and save so many virtues.

**Mariamne**: Thou wouldst disgrace them.

**Varus**: He would take thy life.

**Mariamne**: Yet his is sacred still to Mariamne.

**Varus**: He killed thy father.

**Mariamne**: Varus, I know well What Herod did, and what I ought to do. Patient, I'll wait the fury of the storm, Nor by his crimes would justify my own.

**Varus**: O noble, brave, unconquerable heart! Ye gods, how many virtues have conspired To swell this tyrant's guilt! O Mariamne! The more thou shalt disclaim my proffered service, The more am I resolved to disobey thee. Thy honor disapproves what mine commands; But naught shall stop me, naught intimidate: I go to search the tyrant, and repair The hours I've lost in not avenging thee.

**Mariamne:** My lord—

SCENE III.
Mariamne, Eliza, Guards.
**Mariamne:** He's gone, and would not hear me: heaven! Let not more blood be shed; O spare my subjects; Pour all thy wrath on me, and spare even Herod!

SCENE IV.
Mariamne, Eliza, Nabal, Guards.
**Mariamne:** O Nabal, art thou here? what hast thou done With my dear children? where's my mother?
**Nabal:** Safe: The wrath of Herod reaches not to them: Thou art the only object of his fury, Which kindles at the hateful name of Varus: If he is conquered, Mariamne dies. The barbarous Zares is already sent With secret orders hither; thou mayest guess The purport, therefore now exert thy power: The people love thee; on their loyal zeal Thou mayest rely; the sight of thee will raise Their drooping hearts; let them behold thee: fly, My royal mistress, let us call the priests, All Judah's sons will rise to guard the race Of their loved kings: at length the hour is come, To conquer or to die: let me entreat thee—
**Mariamne:** True courage lies in knowing how to suffer, And not in stirring up rebellious crowds Against their sovereign: I should blush to think, That, anxious for itself, my fearful heart Had ever formed a wish for his destruction, Or raised my hopes of safety on his death: No: heaven this moment has inspired my breast With rage less guilty, and a nobler purpose: Herod suspects me, he shall know me now; I'll rush into the battle; strive to part The king and Varus; cast myself before My husband's feet, and yield him up my life. I fled this morning from that dreadful vengeance Which now I search for: banished by his crimes, His danger has recalled me: honor bids, And I obey: I go to save his life Who thirsts for mine.
**Nabal:** Alas! to what extremes—
**Mariamne:** I'm lost: 'tis Herod.

SCENE V.
Herod, Mariamne, Eliza, Nabal, Idamas, Guards.
**Herod:** Did they see each other? Now, faithless wretch, thou diest.
**Mariamne:** Do not, my lord, 'Tis the last boon that I shall crave; O do not—
**Herod:** Begone—guards, follow her. [Guards carry off Mariamne.]
**Nabal:** Eternal justice!

## SCENE VI.
Herod, Idamas, Guards.

**Herod**: Let me not hear her named: perfidious woman! Well, my brave soldiers, are there yet more foes?

**Idamas**: The Romans are subdued; the Hebrews bend Once more submissive to the yoke; and Varus, Covered with wounds, to thy victorious arm Gives up the field: O thou hast gained this day Eternal glory; but the prætor's blood, Shed by thy hand, will draw on thee the vengeance Of proud offended Rome: a crime like this—

**Herod**: And now for my revenge on Mariamne. Unworthy of my love I cast her from me, And from this moment shall begin to reign. O! I was blind, that fond destructive passion Was Herod's only weakness: let her die: Let me forget her charms, and her remembrance Be blotted now forever from my soul. Are all things ready for the execution?

**Idamas**: They are, my lord.

**Herod**: How quickly they obey me! Unhappy Herod! must she perish then? Didst thou say, Idamas, 'twas ready all?

**Idamas**: The guards have seized her person, and too soon Thy vengeance will be satisfied.

**Herod**: She courted Her own destruction, and obliged me to it: But she is gone: I'll think no more on it: Oh! I could have lived and died with Mariamne: To what hast thou compelled me?

## SCENE the last.
Herod, Idamas, Nabal.

**Herod**: Nabal, ha! Whither so fast? just heaven! and in tears! How my soul shakes with dreadful apprehension.

**Nabal**: My lord—

**Herod**: What wouldst thou say?

**Nabal**: My feeble voice Dies on my trembling lips.

**Herod**: O Mariamne!

**Nabal**: Superfluous sorrow!

**Herod**: Ha! 'tis past then, is it?

**Nabal**: She is no more.

**Herod**: Ha! dead! great God!

**Nabal**: My lord, Permit me, 'tis a debt I owe to thee, Due to her memory, to her virtues due, To show thee what a treasure thou hast lost, The worth of that dear blood which thou hast shed: Know, Herod, she was never faithless to thee; But, even whilst Varus fought for her, refused His offered hand, slighted his ardent vows, And hazarded her life to succor thee.

**Herod:** What do I hear? O wretched Herod! Nabal, What has thou told me?

**Nabal:** In that very moment, Even when her generous heart inspired her last And noblest act, thy cruel orders came, And she was led to death: thy barbarous sister Urged on her fate.

**Herod:** Inhuman Salome; Why did my justice spare that cruel monster? What punishments must be reserved for thee! But let thy blood and mine—Nabal, go on, And kill me with the melancholy tale.

**Nabal:** How shall I speak the rest! the guard, thou knowest, By thee directed, led her hence: she followed Without a murmur or reproach of thee; Without affected pride, or real fear; On her fair front sat graceful majesty, Tempered with softness; modest innocence And heart-felt virtue sparkled in her eyes; Her sorrows gave new lustre to her charms; Priests, Hebrews, all, with tears and shrieks besought her: The soldiers called for death, and wept the fate Of Mariamne—and of Herod too; For deep, they cried aloud, would be thy grief, And horror and remorse attend thee ever.

**Herod:** How every word strikes to my heart!

**Nabal:** She felt For their distress, and as she passed along, Spake comfort to them. To the fatal scaffold At length she came; there lifted up her hands, Loaded with shameful chains, and thus she spake: "Farewell, unhappy king; Herod, farewell! Thy dying Mariamne weeps for thee, And thee alone; may this be thy last act Of foul injustice! may thy reign henceforth Be happy! Take my people to thy care; Protect my children; love and cherish them; And I shall die content." She spake, and bent Her beauteous body to the axe; I saw, And wept her fall.

**Herod:** Then Mariamne's dead; And Herod lives: thou dear, and honored shade! Ye poor remains of all that once was fair And good, and virtuous, to the silent grave Soon will I follow thee—Ye shall not stop me, Perfidious subjects: from my murderous hand, Why will ye wrest my sword? O Mariamne! Come now, and be avenged: tear forth this heart That bleeds for thee. I faint, I die. [He faints.]

**Nabal:** His senses Are lost; his grief o'erpowers him.

**Herod:** What thick clouds O'erspread my troubled soul! deep melancholy Weighs down my senses; why am I abandoned, Left to my sorrows thus? No sister here; No Mariamne! How you stand and weep At distance from me! Dare you not approach me! All Judah flies before her wretched king. What have I done? why am I thus abhorred? Who will relieve me? who will soothe my grief? Fetch Mariamne to me.

**Nabal:** Mariamne, My lord!

**Herod:** Ay, bring her; for I know the sight Of her will calm at once my agony: When Mariamne's with me, my blessed hours Are all serene, and life glides sweetly on: Methinks her very name hath healed my woes, And lessened my affliction: let her come.

**Nabal**: My lord—

**Herod**: I'll see her.

**Nabal**: Sir, have you forgot That Mariamne's dead?

**Herod**: What sayest thou?

**Nabal**: Grief Transports him; his mind's hurt; he's not himself.

**Herod**: Ha! Mariamne dead! destructive reason, Why comest thou now to tell me this sad truth? Down with these hateful walls, this fatal palace, Stained with her blood, and let its ruins hide The accursed place where Mariamne perished! Is she then dead, and I her murderer! Punish this parricide, this horrid monster: Tear him in pieces, you who weep her loss, My subjects; and thou, heaven, who hast her now, Send down thy vengeful lightnings, and destroy me.

**End**

# Candide

## How Candide Was Brought up in a Magnificent Castle, and How He Was Expelled Thence.

In a castle of Westphalia, belonging to the Baron of Thunder-ten-Tronckh, lived a youth, whom nature had endowed with the most gentle manners. His countenance was a true picture of his soul. He combined a true judgment with simplicity of spirit, which was the reason, I apprehend, of his being called Candide. The old servants of the family suspected him to have been the son of the Baron's sister, by a good, honest gentleman of the neighborhood, whom that young lady would never marry because he had been able to prove only seventy-one quarterings, the rest of his genealogical tree having been lost through the injuries of time.

The Baron was one of the most powerful lords in Westphalia, for his castle had not only a gate, but windows. His great hall, even, was hung with tapestry. All the dogs of his farm-yards formed a pack of hounds at need; his grooms were his huntsmen; and the curate of the village was his grand almoner. They called him "My Lord," and laughed at all his stories.

The Baron's lady weighed about three hundred and fifty pounds, and was therefore a person of great consideration, and she did the honours of the house with a dignity that commanded still greater respect. Her daughter Cunegonde was seventeen years of age, fresh-coloured, comely, plump, and desirable. The Baron's son seemed to be in every respect worthy of his father. The Preceptor Pangloss[1] was the oracle of the family, and little Candide heard his lessons with all the good faith of his age and character.

Pangloss was professor of metaphysico-theologico-cosmolo-nigology. He proved admirably that there is no effect without a cause, and that, in this best of all possible worlds, the Baron's castle was the most magnificent of castles, and his lady the best of all possible Baronesses.

"It is demonstrable," said he, "that things cannot be otherwise than as they are; for all being created for an end, all is necessarily for the best end. Observe, that the nose has been formed to bear spectacles—thus we have spectacles. Legs are visibly designed for stockings—and we have stockings. Stones were made to be hewn, and to construct castles—therefore my lord has a magnificent castle; for the greatest baron in the province ought to be the best lodged. Pigs were made to be eaten—therefore we eat pork all the year round. Consequently they who assert that all is well have said a foolish thing, they should have said all is for the best."

Candide listened attentively and believed innocently; for he thought Miss Cunegonde extremely beautiful, though he never had the courage to tell her so. He concluded that after the happiness of being born of Baron of Thunder-ten-Tronckh, the second degree of happiness was to be Miss Cunegonde, the third that of seeing her every day, and the fourth that of hearing Master Pangloss, the greatest philosopher of the whole province, and consequently of the whole world.

One day Cunegonde, while walking near the castle, in a little wood which they called a park, saw between the bushes, Dr. Pangloss giving a lesson in experimental natural philosophy to her mother's chamber-maid, a little brown wench, very pretty and very docile. As Miss Cunegonde had a great disposition for the sciences, she breathlessly observed the repeated experiments of which she was a witness; she clearly perceived the force of the Doctor's reasons, the effects, and the causes; she turned back greatly flurried, quite pensive, and filled with the desire to be learned; dreaming that she might well be a sufficient reason for young Candide, and he for her.

She met Candide on reaching the castle and blushed; Candide blushed also; she wished him good morrow in a faltering tone, and Candide spoke to her without knowing what he said. The next day after dinner, as they went from table, Cunegonde and Candide found themselves behind a screen; Cunegonde let fall her handkerchief, Candide picked it up, she took him innocently by the hand, the youth as innocently kissed the young lady's hand with particular vivacity, sensibility, and grace; their lips met, their eyes sparkled, their knees trembled, their hands strayed. Baron Thunder-ten-Tronckh passed near the screen and beholding this cause and effect chased Candide from the castle with great kicks on the backside; Cunegonde fainted away; she was boxed on the ears by the Baroness, as soon as she came to herself; and all was consternation in this most magnificent and most agreeable of all possible castles.

# What Became of Candide among the Bulgarians.

Candide, driven from terrestrial paradise, walked a long while without knowing where, weeping, raising his eyes to heaven, turning them often towards the most magnificent of castles which imprisoned the purest of noble young ladies. He lay down to sleep without supper, in the middle of a field between two furrows. The snow fell in large flakes. Next day Candide, all benumbed, dragged himself towards the neighbouring town which was called Waldberghofftrarbk-dikdorff, having no money, dying of hunger and fatigue, he stopped sorrowfully at the door of an inn. Two men dressed in blue observed him.

"Comrade," said one, "here is a well-built young fellow, and of proper height."

They went up to Candide and very civilly invited him to dinner.

"Gentlemen," replied Candide, with a most engaging modesty, "you do me great honour, but I have not wherewithal to pay my share."

"Oh, sir," said one of the blues to him, "people of your appearance and of your merit never pay anything: are you not five feet five inches high?"

"Yes, sir, that is my height," answered he, making a low bow.

"Come, sir, seat yourself; not only will we pay your reckoning, but we will never suffer such a man as you to want money; men are only born to assist one another."

"You are right," said Candide; "this is what I was always taught by Mr. Pangloss, and I see plainly that all is for the best."

They begged of him to accept a few crowns. He took them, and wished to give them his note; they refused; they seated themselves at table.

"Love you not deeply?"

"Oh yes," answered he; "I deeply love Miss Cunegonde."

"No," said one of the gentlemen, "we ask you if you do not deeply love the King of the Bulgarians?"

"Not at all," said he; "for I have never seen him."

"What! he is the best of kings, and we must drink his health."

"Oh! very willingly, gentlemen," and he drank.

"That is enough," they tell him. "Now you are the help, the support, the defender, the hero of the Bulgarians. Your fortune is made, and your glory is assured."

Instantly they fettered him, and carried him away to the regiment. There he was made to wheel about to the right, and to the left, to draw his rammer, to return his rammer, to present, to fire, to march, and they gave him thirty blows with a cudgel. The next day he did his exercise a little less badly, and he received but twenty blows. The day following they gave him only ten, and he was regarded by his comrades as a prodigy.

Candide, all stupefied, could not yet very well realise how he was a hero. He resolved one fine day in spring to go for a walk, marching straight before him, believing that it was a privilege of the human as well as of the animal species to make use of their legs as they pleased. He had advanced two leagues when he was overtaken by four others, heroes of six feet, who bound him and carried him to a dungeon. He was asked which he would like the best, to be whipped six-and-thirty times through all the regiment, or to receive at once twelve balls of lead in his brain. He vainly said that human will is free, and that he chose neither the one nor the other. He was forced to make a choice; he determined, in virtue of that gift of God called liberty, to run the gauntlet six-and-thirty times. He bore this twice. The regiment was composed of two thousand men; that composed for him four thousand strokes, which laid bare all his muscles and nerves, from the nape of his neck quite down to his rump. As they were going to proceed to a third whipping, Candide, able to bear no more, begged as a favour that they would be so good as to shoot him. He obtained this favour; they bandaged his eyes, and bade him kneel down. The King of the Bulgarians passed at this moment and ascertained the nature of the crime. As he had great talent, he understood from all that he learnt of Candide that he was a young metaphysician, extremely ignorant of the things of this world, and he accorded him his pardon with a clemency which will bring him praise in all the journals, and throughout all ages.

An able surgeon cured Candide in three weeks by means of emollients taught by Dioscorides. He had already a little skin, and was able to march when the King of the Bulgarians gave battle to the King of the Abares.[2]

## How Candide Made His Escape from the Bulgarians, and What Afterwards Became of Him.

There was never anything so gallant, so spruce, so brilliant, and so well disposed as the two armies. Trumpets, fifes, hautboys, drums, and cannon made music such as Hell itself had never heard. The cannons first of all laid flat about six thousand men on each side; the muskets swept away from this best of worlds nine or ten thousand ruffians who infested its surface. The bayonet was also a sufficient reason for the death of several thousands. The whole might amount to thirty thousand souls. Candide, who trembled like a philosopher, hid himself as well as he could during this heroic butchery.

At length, while the two kings were causing Te Deum to be sung each in his own camp, Candide resolved to go and reason elsewhere on effects and causes. He passed over heaps of dead and dying, and first reached a neighbouring village; it was in cinders, it was an Abare village which the Bulgarians had burnt according to the laws of war. Here, old men covered with wounds, beheld their wives, hugging their children to their bloody breasts, massacred before their faces; there, their daughters, disembowelled and breathing their last after having satisfied the natural wants of Bulgarian heroes; while others, half burnt in the flames, begged to be despatched. The earth was strewed with brains, arms, and legs.

Candide fled quickly to another village; it belonged to the Bulgarians; and the Abarian heroes had treated it in the same way. Candide, walking always over palpitating limbs or across ruins, arrived at last beyond the seat of war, with a few provisions in his knapsack, and Miss Cunegonde always in his heart. His provisions failed him when he arrived in Holland; but having heard that everybody was rich in that country, and that they were Christians, he did not doubt but he should meet with the same treatment from them as he had met with in the Baron's castle, before Miss Cunegonde's bright eyes were the cause of his expulsion thence.

He asked alms of several grave-looking people, who all answered him, that if he continued to follow this trade they would confine him to the house of correction, where he should be taught to get a living.

The next he addressed was a man who had been haranguing a large assembly for a whole hour on the subject of charity. But the orator, looking askew, said:

"What are you doing here? Are you for the good cause?"

"There can be no effect without a cause," modestly answered Candide; "the whole is necessarily concatenated and arranged for the best. It was necessary for me to have been banished from the presence of Miss Cunegonde, to have afterwards run the gauntlet, and now it is necessary I should beg my bread until I learn to earn it; all this cannot be otherwise."

"My friend," said the orator to him, "do you believe the Pope to be Anti-Christ?"

"I have not heard it," answered Candide; "but whether he be, or whether he be not, I want bread."

"Thou dost not deserve to eat," said the other. "Begone, rogue; begone, wretch; do not come near me again."

The orator's wife, putting her head out of the window, and spying a man that doubted whether the Pope was Anti-Christ, poured over him a full.... Oh, heavens! to what excess does religious zeal carry the ladies.

A man who had never been christened, a good Anabaptist, named James, beheld the cruel and ignominious treatment shown to one of his brethren, an unfeathered biped with a rational soul, he took him home, cleaned him, gave him bread and beer, presented him with two florins, and even wished to teach him the manufacture of Persian stuffs which they make in Holland. Candide, almost prostrating himself before him, cried:

"Master Pangloss has well said that all is for the best in this world, for I am infinitely more touched by your extreme generosity than with the inhumanity of that gentleman in the black coat and his lady."

The next day, as he took a walk, he met a beggar all covered with scabs, his eyes diseased, the end of his nose eaten away, his mouth distorted, his teeth black, choking in his throat, tormented with a violent cough, and spitting out a tooth at each effort.

# How Candide Found His Old Master Pangloss, and What Happened to Them.

Candide, yet more moved with compassion than with horror, gave to this shocking beggar the two florins which he had received from the honest Anabaptist James. The spectre looked at him very earnestly, dropped a few tears, and fell upon his neck. Candide recoiled in disgust.

"Alas!" said one wretch to the other, "do you no longer know your dear Pangloss?"

"What do I hear? You, my dear master! you in this terrible plight! What misfortune has happened to you? Why are you no longer in the most magnificent of castles? What has become of Miss Cunegonde, the pearl of girls, and nature's masterpiece?"

"I am so weak that I cannot stand," said Pangloss.

Upon which Candide carried him to the Anabaptist's stable, and gave him a crust of bread. As soon as Pangloss had refreshed himself a little:

"Well," said Candide, "Cunegonde?"

"She is dead," replied the other.

Candide fainted at this word; his friend recalled his senses with a little bad vinegar which he found by chance in the stable. Candide reopened his eyes.

"Cunegonde is dead! Ah, best of worlds, where art thou? But of what illness did she die? Was it not for grief, upon seeing her father kick me out of his magnificent castle?"

"No," said Pangloss, "she was ripped open by the Bulgarian soldiers, after having been violated by many; they broke the Baron's head for attempting to defend her; my lady, her mother, was cut in pieces; my poor pupil was served just in the same manner as his sister; and as for the castle, they have not left one stone upon another, not a barn, nor a sheep, nor a duck, nor a tree; but we have had our revenge, for the Abares have done the very same thing to a neighbouring barony, which belonged to a Bulgarian lord."

At this discourse Candide fainted again; but coming to himself, and having said all that it became him to say, inquired into the cause and effect, as well as into the sufficient reason that had reduced Pangloss to so miserable a plight.

"Alas!" said the other, "it was love; love, the comfort of the human species, the preserver of the universe, the soul of all sensible beings, love, tender love."

"Alas!" said Candide, "I know this love, that sovereign of hearts, that soul of our souls; yet it never cost me more than a kiss and twenty kicks on the backside. How could this beautiful cause produce in you an effect so abominable?"

Pangloss made answer in these terms: "Oh, my dear Candide, you remember Paquette, that pretty wench who waited on our noble Baroness; in her arms I tasted the delights of paradise, which produced in me those hell torments with which you see me devoured; she was infected with them, she is perhaps dead of them. This present Paquette received of a learned Grey Friar, who had traced it to its source; he had had it of an old countess, who had received it from a cavalry captain, who owed it to a marchioness, who took it from a page, who had received it from a Jesuit, who when a novice had it in a direct line from one of the companions of Christopher Columbus.[3] For my part I shall give it to nobody, I am dying."

"Oh, Pangloss!" cried Candide, "what a strange genealogy! Is not the Devil the original stock of it?"

"Not at all," replied this great man, "it was a thing unavoidable, a necessary ingredient in the best of worlds; for if Columbus had not in an island of America caught this disease, which contaminates the source of life, frequently even hinders generation, and which is evidently opposed to the great end of nature, we should have neither chocolate nor cochineal. We are also to observe that upon our continent, this distemper is like religious controversy, confined to a particular spot. The Turks, the Indians, the Persians, the Chinese, the Siamese, the Japanese, know nothing of it; but there is a sufficient reason for believing that they will know it in their turn in a few centuries. In the meantime, it has made marvellous progress among us, especially in those great armies composed of honest well-disciplined hirelings, who decide the destiny of states; for we may safely affirm that when an army of thirty thousand men fights another of an equal number, there are about twenty thousand of them p-x-d on each side."

"Well, this is wonderful!" said Candide, "but you must get cured."

"Alas! how can I?" said Pangloss, "I have not a farthing, my friend, and all over the globe there is no letting of blood or taking a glister, without paying, or somebody paying for you."

These last words determined Candide; he went and flung himself at the feet of the charitable Anabaptist James, and gave him so touching a picture of the state to which his friend was reduced, that the good man did not scruple to take Dr. Pangloss into his house, and had him cured at his expense. In the cure Pangloss lost only an eye and an ear. He wrote well, and knew arithmetic perfectly. The Anabaptist James made him his bookkeeper. At the end of two months, being obliged to go to Lisbon about some mercantile affairs, he took the two philosophers with him in his ship. Pangloss explained to him how everything was so constituted that it could not be better. James was not of this opinion.

"It is more likely," said he, "mankind have a little corrupted nature, for they were not born wolves, and they have become wolves; God has given them neither cannon of four-and-twenty pounders, nor bayonets; and yet they have made cannon and bayonets to destroy one another. Into this account I might throw not only bankrupts, but Justice which seizes on the effects of bankrupts to cheat the creditors."

"All this was indispensable," replied the one-eyed doctor, "for private misfortunes make the general good, so that the more private misfortunes there are the greater is the general good."

While he reasoned, the sky darkened, the winds blew from the four quarters, and the ship was assailed by a most terrible tempest within sight of the port of Lisbon.

# Tempest, Shipwreck, Earthquake, and What Became of Doctor Pangloss, Candide, and James the Anabaptist.

Half dead of that inconceivable anguish which the rolling of a ship produces, one-half of the passengers were not even sensible of the danger. The other half shrieked and prayed. The sheets were rent, the masts broken, the vessel gaped. Work who would, no one heard, no one commanded. The Anabaptist being upon deck bore a hand; when a brutish sailor struck him roughly and laid him sprawling; but with the violence of the blow he himself tumbled head foremost overboard, and stuck upon a piece of the broken mast. Honest James ran to his assistance, hauled him up, and from the effort he made was precipitated into the sea in sight of the sailor, who left him to perish, without deigning to look at him. Candide drew near and saw his benefactor, who rose above the water one moment and was then swallowed up for ever. He was just going to jump after him, but was prevented by the philosopher Pangloss, who demonstrated to him that the Bay of Lisbon had been made on purpose for the Anabaptist to be drowned. While he was proving this à priori, the ship foundered; all perished except Pangloss, Candide, and that brutal sailor who had drowned the good Anabaptist. The villain swam safely to the shore, while Pangloss and Candide were borne thither upon a plank.

As soon as they recovered themselves a little they walked toward Lisbon. They had some money left, with which they hoped to save themselves from starving, after they had escaped drowning. Scarcely had they reached the city, lamenting the death of their benefactor, when they felt the earth tremble under their feet. The sea swelled and foamed in the harbour, and beat to pieces the vessels riding at anchor. Whirlwinds of fire and ashes covered the streets and public places; houses fell, roofs were flung upon the pavements, and the pavements were scattered. Thirty thousand inhabitants of all ages and sexes were crushed under the ruins.[4] The sailor, whistling and swearing, said there was booty to be gained here.

"What can be the sufficient reason of this phenomenon?" said Pangloss.

"This is the Last Day!" cried Candide.

The sailor ran among the ruins, facing death to find money; finding it, he took it, got drunk, and having slept himself sober, purchased the favours of the first good-natured wench whom he met on the ruins of the destroyed houses, and in the midst of the dying and the dead. Pangloss pulled him by the sleeve.

"My friend," said he, "this is not right. You sin against the universal reason; you choose your time badly."

"S'blood and fury!" answered the other; "I am a sailor and born at Batavia. Four times have I trampled upon the crucifix in four voyages to Japan[5]; a fig for thy universal reason."

Some falling stones had wounded Candide. He lay stretched in the street covered with rubbish.

"Alas!" said he to Pangloss, "get me a little wine and oil; I am dying."

"This concussion of the earth is no new thing," answered Pangloss. "The city of Lima, in America, experienced the same convulsions last year; the same cause, the same effects; there is certainly a train of sulphur under ground from Lima to Lisbon."

"Nothing more probable," said Candide; "but for the love of God a little oil and wine."

"How, probable?" replied the philosopher. "I maintain that the point is capable of being demonstrated."

Candide fainted away, and Pangloss fetched him some water from a neighbouring fountain. The following day they rummaged among the ruins and found provisions, with which they repaired their exhausted strength. After this they joined with others in relieving those inhabitants who had escaped death. Some, whom they had succoured, gave them as good a dinner as they could in such disastrous circumstances; true, the repast was mournful, and the company moistened their bread with tears; but Pangloss consoled them, assuring them that things could not be otherwise.

"For," said he, "all that is is for the best. If there is a volcano at Lisbon it cannot be elsewhere. It is impossible that things should be other than they are; for everything is right."

A little man dressed in black, Familiar of the Inquisition, who sat by him, politely took up his word and said:

"Apparently, then, sir, you do not believe in original sin; for if all is for the best there has then been neither Fall nor punishment."

"I humbly ask your Excellency's pardon," answered Pangloss, still more politely; "for the Fall and curse of man necessarily entered into the system of the best of worlds."

"Sir," said the Familiar, "you do not then believe in liberty?"

"Your Excellency will excuse me," said Pangloss; "liberty is consistent with absolute necessity, for it was necessary we should be free; for, in short, the determinate will—"

Pangloss was in the middle of his sentence, when the Familiar beckoned to his footman, who gave him a glass of wine from Porto or Opporto.

## How the Portuguese Made a Beautiful Auto-da-fé, to Prevent Any Further Earthquakes; and How Candide Was Publicly Whipped.

After the earthquake had destroyed three-fourths of Lisbon, the sages of that country could think of no means more effectual to prevent utter ruin than to give the people a beautiful auto-da-fé[6]; for it had been decided by the University of Coimbra, that the burning of a few people alive by a slow fire, and with great ceremony, is an infallible secret to hinder the earth from quaking.

In consequence hereof, they had seized on a Biscayner, convicted of having married his godmother, and on two Portuguese, for rejecting the bacon which larded a chicken they were eating[7]; after dinner, they came and secured Dr. Pangloss, and his disciple Candide, the one for speaking his mind, the other for having listened with an air of approbation. They were conducted to separate apartments, extremely cold, as they were never incommoded by the sun. Eight days after they were dressed in san-benitos[8] and their heads ornamented with paper mitres. The mitre and san-benito belonging to Candide were painted with reversed flames and with devils that had neither tails nor claws; but Pangloss's devils had claws and tails and the flames were upright. They marched in procession thus habited and heard a very pathetic sermon, followed by fine church music. Candide was whipped in cadence while they were singing; the Biscayner, and the two men who had refused to eat bacon, were burnt; and Pangloss was hanged, though that was not the custom. The same day the earth sustained a most violent concussion.

Candide, terrified, amazed, desperate, all bloody, all palpitating, said to himself:

"If this is the best of possible worlds, what then are the others? Well, if I had been only whipped I could put up with it, for I experienced that among the Bulgarians; but oh, my dear Pangloss! thou greatest of philosophers, that I should have seen you hanged, without knowing for what! Oh, my dear Anabaptist, thou best of men, that thou should'st have been drowned in the very harbour! Oh, Miss Cunegonde, thou pearl of girls! that thou should'st have had thy belly ripped open!"

Thus he was musing, scarce able to stand, preached at, whipped, absolved, and blessed, when an old woman accosted him saying:

"My son, take courage and follow me."

# How the Old Woman Took Care of Candide, and How He Found the Object He Loved.

Candide did not take courage, but followed the old woman to a decayed house, where she gave him a pot of pomatum to anoint his sores, showed him a very neat little bed, with a suit of clothes hanging up, and left him something to eat and drink.

"Eat, drink, sleep," said she, "and may our lady of Atocha,[9] the great St. Anthony of Padua, and the great St. James of Compostella, receive you under their protection. I shall be back to-morrow."

Candide, amazed at all he had suffered and still more with the charity of the old woman, wished to kiss her hand.

"It is not my hand you must kiss," said the old woman; "I shall be back to-morrow. Anoint yourself with the pomatum, eat and sleep."

Candide, notwithstanding so many disasters, ate and slept. The next morning the old woman brought him his breakfast, looked at his back, and rubbed it herself with another ointment: in like manner she brought him his dinner; and at night she returned with his supper. The day following she went through the very same ceremonies.

"Who are you?" said Candide; "who has inspired you with so much goodness? What return can I make you?"

The good woman made no answer; she returned in the evening, but brought no supper.

"Come with me," she said, "and say nothing."

She took him by the arm, and walked with him about a quarter of a mile into the country; they arrived at a lonely house, surrounded with gardens and canals. The old woman knocked at a little door, it opened, she led Candide up a private staircase into a small apartment richly furnished. She left him on a brocaded sofa, shut the door and went away. Candide thought himself in a dream; indeed, that he had been dreaming unluckily all his life, and that the present moment was the only agreeable part of it all.

The old woman returned very soon, supporting with difficulty a trembling woman of a majestic figure, brilliant with jewels, and covered with a veil.

"Take off that veil," said the old woman to Candide.

The young man approaches, he raises the veil with a timid hand. Oh! what a moment! what surprise! he believes he beholds Miss Cunegonde? he really sees her! it is herself! His strength fails him, he cannot utter a word, but drops at her feet. Cunegonde falls upon the sofa. The old woman supplies a smelling bottle; they come to themselves and recover their speech. As they began with broken accents, with questions and answers interchangeably interrupted with sighs, with tears, and cries. The old woman desired they would make less noise and then she left them to themselves.

"What, is it you?" said Candide, "you live? I find you again in Portugal? then you have not been ravished? then they did not rip open your belly as Doctor Pangloss informed me?"

"Yes, they did," said the beautiful Cunegonde; "but those two accidents are not always mortal."

"But were your father and mother killed?"

"It is but too true," answered Cunegonde, in tears.

"And your brother?"

"My brother also was killed."

"And why are you in Portugal? and how did you know of my being here? and by what strange adventure did you contrive to bring me to this house?"

"I will tell you all that," replied the lady, "but first of all let me know your history, since the innocent kiss you gave me and the kicks which you received."

Candide respectfully obeyed her, and though he was still in a surprise, though his voice was feeble and trembling, though his back still pained him, yet he gave her a most ingenuous account of everything that had befallen him since the moment of their separation. Cunegonde lifted up her eyes to heaven; shed tears upon hearing of the death of the good Anabaptist and of Pangloss; after which she spoke as follows to Candide, who did not lose a word and devoured her with his eyes.

# The History of Cunegonde.

"I was in bed and fast asleep when it pleased God to send the Bulgarians to our delightful castle of Thunder-ten-Tronckh; they slew my father and brother, and cut my mother in pieces. A tall Bulgarian, six feet high, perceiving that I had fainted away at this sight, began to ravish me; this made me recover; I regained my senses, I cried, I struggled, I bit, I scratched, I wanted to tear out the tall Bulgarian's eyes—not knowing that what happened at my father's house was the usual practice of war. The brute gave me a cut in the left side with his hanger, and the mark is still upon me."

"Ah! I hope I shall see it," said honest Candide.

"You shall," said Cunegonde, "but let us continue."

"Do so," replied Candide.

Thus she resumed the thread of her story:

"A Bulgarian captain came in, saw me all bleeding, and the soldier not in the least disconcerted. The captain flew into a passion at the disrespectful behaviour of the brute, and slew him on my body. He ordered my wounds to be dressed, and took me to his quarters as a prisoner of war. I washed the few shirts that he had, I did his cooking; he thought me very pretty—he avowed it; on the other hand, I must own he had a good shape, and a soft and white skin; but he had little or no mind or philosophy, and you might see plainly that he had never been instructed by Doctor Pangloss. In three months time, having lost all his money, and being grown tired of my company, he sold me to a Jew, named Don Issachar, who traded to Holland and Portugal, and had a strong passion for women. This Jew was much attached to my person, but could not triumph over it; I resisted him better than the Bulgarian soldier. A modest woman may be ravished once, but her virtue is strengthened by it. In order to render me more tractable, he brought me to this country house. Hitherto I had imagined that nothing could equal the beauty of Thunder-ten-Tronckh Castle; but I found I was mistaken.

"The Grand Inquisitor, seeing me one day at Mass, stared long at me, and sent to tell me that he wished to speak on private matters. I was conducted to his palace, where I acquainted him with the history of my family, and he represented to me how much it was beneath my rank to belong to an Israelite. A proposal was then made to Don Issachar that he should resign me to my lord. Don Issachar, being the court banker, and a man of credit, would hear nothing of it. The Inquisitor threatened him with an auto-da-fé. At last my Jew, intimidated, concluded a bargain, by which the house and myself should belong to both in common; the Jew should have for himself Monday, Wednesday, and Saturday, and the Inquisitor should have the rest of the week. It is now six months since this agreement was made. Quarrels have not been wanting, for they could not decide whether the night from Saturday to Sunday belonged to the old law or to the new. For my part, I have so far held out against both, and I verily believe that this is the reason why I am still beloved.

"At length, to avert the scourge of earthquakes, and to intimidate Don Issachar, my Lord Inquisitor was pleased to celebrate an auto-da-fé. He did me the honour to invite me to the ceremony. I had a very good seat, and the ladies were served with refreshments between Mass and the execution. I was in truth seized with horror at the burning of those two Jews, and of the honest Biscayner who had married his godmother; but what was my surprise, my fright, my trouble, when I saw in a san-benito and mitre a figure which resembled that of Pangloss! I rubbed my eyes, I looked at him attentively, I saw him hung; I fainted. Scarcely had I recovered my senses than I saw you stripped, stark naked, and this was the height of my horror, consternation, grief, and despair. I tell you, truthfully, that your skin is yet whiter and of a more perfect colour than that of my Bulgarian captain. This spectacle redoubled all the feelings which overwhelmed and devoured me. I screamed out, and would have said, 'Stop, barbarians!' but my voice failed me, and my cries would have been useless after you had been severely whipped. How is it possible, said I, that the beloved Candide and the wise Pangloss should both be at Lisbon, the one to receive a hundred lashes, and the other to be hanged by the Grand Inquisitor, of whom I am the well-beloved? Pangloss most cruelly deceived me when he said that everything in the world is for the best.

"Agitated, lost, sometimes beside myself, and sometimes ready to die of weakness, my mind was filled with the massacre of my father, mother, and brother, with the insolence of the ugly Bulgarian soldier, with the stab that he gave me, with my servitude under the Bulgarian captain, with my hideous Don Issachar, with my abominable Inquisitor, with the execution of Doctor Pangloss, with the grand Miserere to which they whipped you, and especially with the kiss I gave you behind the screen the day that I had last seen you. I praised God for bringing you back to me after so many trials, and I charged my old woman to take care of you, and to conduct you hither as soon as possible. She has executed her commission perfectly well; I have tasted the inexpressible pleasure of seeing you again, of hearing you, of speaking with you. But you must be hungry, for myself, I am famished; let us have supper."

They both sat down to table, and, when supper was over, they placed themselves once more on the sofa; where they were when Signor Don Issachar arrived. It was the Jewish Sabbath, and Issachar had come to enjoy his rights, and to explain his tender love.

# What Became of Cunegonde, Candide, the Grand Inquisitor, and the Jew.

This Issachar was the most choleric Hebrew that had ever been seen in Israel since the Captivity in Babylon.

"What!" said he, "thou bitch of a Galilean, was not the Inquisitor enough for thee? Must this rascal also share with me?"

In saying this he drew a long poniard which he always carried about him; and not imagining that his adversary had any arms he threw himself upon Candide: but our honest Westphalian had received a handsome sword from the old woman along with the suit of clothes. He drew his rapier, despite his gentleness, and laid the Israelite stone dead upon the cushions at Cunegonde's feet.

"Holy Virgin!" cried she, "what will become of us? A man killed in my apartment! If the officers of justice come, we are lost!"

"Had not Pangloss been hanged," said Candide, "he would give us good counsel in this emergency, for he was a profound philosopher. Failing him let us consult the old woman."

She was very prudent and commenced to give her opinion when suddenly another little door opened. It was an hour after midnight, it was the beginning of Sunday. This day belonged to my lord the Inquisitor. He entered, and saw the whipped Candide, sword in hand, a dead man upon the floor, Cunegonde aghast, and the old woman giving counsel.

At this moment, the following is what passed in the soul of Candide, and how he reasoned:

If this holy man call in assistance, he will surely have me burnt; and Cunegonde will perhaps be served in the same manner; he was the cause of my being cruelly whipped; he is my rival; and, as I have now begun to kill, I will kill away, for there is no time to hesitate. This reasoning was clear and instantaneous; so that without giving time to the Inquisitor to recover from his surprise, he pierced him through and through, and cast him beside the Jew.

"Yet again!" said Cunegonde, "now there is no mercy for us, we are excommunicated, our last hour has come. How could you do it? you, naturally so gentle, to slay a Jew and a prelate in two minutes!"

"My beautiful young lady," responded Candide, "when one is a lover, jealous and whipped by the Inquisition, one stops at nothing."

The old woman then put in her word, saying:

"There are three Andalusian horses in the stable with bridles and saddles, let the brave Candide get them ready; madame has money, jewels; let us therefore mount quickly on horseback, though I can sit only on one buttock; let us set out for Cadiz, it is the finest weather in the world, and there is great pleasure in travelling in the cool of the night."

Immediately Candide saddled the three horses, and Cunegonde, the old woman and he, travelled thirty miles at a stretch. While they were journeying, the Holy Brotherhood entered the house; my lord the Inquisitor was interred in a handsome church, and Issachar's body was thrown upon a dunghill.

Candide, Cunegonde, and the old woman, had now reached the little town of Avacena in the midst of the mountains of the Sierra Morena, and were speaking as follows in a public inn.

# In What Distress Candide, Cunegonde, and the Old Woman Arrived at Cadiz; and of Their Embarkation.

"Who was it that robbed me of my money and jewels?" said Cunegonde, all bathed in tears. "How shall we live? What shall we do? Where find Inquisitors or Jews who will give me more?"

"Alas!" said the old woman, "I have a shrewd suspicion of a reverend Grey Friar, who stayed last night in the same inn with us at Badajos. God preserve me from judging rashly, but he came into our room twice, and he set out upon his journey long before us."

"Alas!" said Candide, "dear Pangloss has often demonstrated to me that the goods of this world are common to all men, and that each has an equal right to them. But according to these principles the Grey Friar ought to have left us enough to carry us through our journey. Have you nothing at all left, my dear Cunegonde?"

"Not a farthing," said she.

"What then must we do?" said Candide.

"Sell one of the horses," replied the old woman. "I will ride behind Miss Cunegonde, though I can hold myself only on one buttock, and we shall reach Cadiz."

In the same inn there was a Benedictine prior who bought the horse for a cheap price. Candide, Cunegonde, and the old woman, having passed through Lucena, Chillas, and Lebrixa, arrived at length at Cadiz. A fleet was there getting ready, and troops assembling to bring to reason the reverend Jesuit Fathers of Paraguay, accused of having made one of the native tribes in the neighborhood of San Sacrament revolt against the Kings of Spain and Portugal. Candide having been in the Bulgarian service, performed the military exercise before the general of this little army with so graceful an address, with so intrepid an air, and with such agility and expedition, that he was given the command of a company of foot. Now, he was a captain! He set sail with Miss Cunegonde, the old woman, two valets, and the two Andalusian horses, which had belonged to the grand Inquisitor of Portugal.

During their voyage they reasoned a good deal on the philosophy of poor Pangloss.

"We are going into another world," said Candide; "and surely it must be there that all is for the best. For I must confess there is reason to complain a little of what passeth in our world in regard to both natural and moral philosophy."

"I love you with all my heart," said Cunegonde; "but my soul is still full of fright at that which I have seen and experienced."

"All will be well," replied Candide; "the sea of this new world is already better than our European sea; it is calmer, the winds more regular. It is certainly the New World which is the best of all possible worlds."

"God grant it," said Cunegonde; "but I have been so horribly unhappy there that my heart is almost closed to hope."

"You complain," said the old woman; "alas! you have not known such misfortunes as mine."

Cunegonde almost broke out laughing, finding the good woman very amusing, for pretending to have been as unfortunate as she.

"Alas!" said Cunegonde, "my good mother, unless you have been ravished by two Bulgarians, have received two deep wounds in your belly, have had two castles demolished, have had two mothers cut to pieces before your eyes, and two of your lovers whipped at an auto-da-fé, I do not conceive how you could be more unfortunate than I. Add that I was born a baroness of seventy-two quarterings—and have been a cook!"

"Miss," replied the old woman, "you do not know my birth; and were I to show you my backside, you would not talk in that manner, but would suspend your judgment."

This speech having raised extreme curiosity in the minds of Cunegonde and Candide, the old woman spoke to them as follows.

# History of the Old Woman.

"I had not always bleared eyes and red eyelids; neither did my nose always touch my chin; nor was I always a servant. I am the daughter of Pope Urban X,[10] and of the Princess of Palestrina. Until the age of fourteen I was brought up in a palace, to which all the castles of your German barons would scarcely have served for stables; and one of my robes was worth more than all the magnificence of Westphalia. As I grew up I improved in beauty, wit, and every graceful accomplishment, in the midst of pleasures, hopes, and respectful homage. Already I inspired love. My throat was formed, and such a throat! white, firm, and shaped like that of the Venus of Medici; and what eyes! what eyelids! what black eyebrows! such flames darted from my dark pupils that they eclipsed the scintillation of the stars—as I was told by the poets in our part of the world. My waiting women, when dressing and undressing me, used to fall into an ecstasy, whether they viewed me before or behind; how glad would the gentlemen have been to perform that office for them!

"I was affianced to the most excellent Prince of Massa Carara. Such a prince! as handsome as myself, sweet-tempered, agreeable, brilliantly witty, and sparkling with love. I loved him as one loves for the first time—with idolatry, with transport. The nuptials were prepared. There was surprising pomp and magnificence; there were fêtes, carousals, continual opera bouffe; and all Italy composed sonnets in my praise, though not one of them was passable. I was just upon the point of reaching the summit of bliss, when an old marchioness who had been mistress to the Prince, my husband, invited him to drink chocolate with her. He died in less than two hours of most terrible convulsions. But this is only a bagatelle. My mother, in despair, and scarcely less afflicted than myself, determined to absent herself for some time from so fatal a place. She had a very fine estate in the neighbourhood of Gaeta. We embarked on board a galley of the country which was gilded like the great altar of St. Peter's at Rome. A Sallee corsair swooped down and boarded us. Our men defended themselves like the Pope's soldiers; they flung themselves upon their knees, and threw down their arms, begging of the corsair an absolution in articulo mortis.

"Instantly they were stripped as bare as monkeys; my mother, our maids of honour, and myself were all served in the same manner. It is amazing with what expedition those gentry undress people. But what surprised me most was, that they thrust their fingers into the part of our bodies which the generality of women suffer no other instrument but—pipes to enter. It appeared to me a very strange kind of ceremony; but thus one judges of things when one has not seen the world. I afterwards learnt that it was to try whether we had concealed any diamonds. This is the practice established from time immemorial, among civilised nations that scour the seas. I was informed that the very religious Knights of Malta never fail to make this search when they take any Turkish prisoners of either sex. It is a law of nations from which they never deviate.

"I need not tell you how great a hardship it was for a young princess and her mother to be made slaves and carried to Morocco. You may easily imagine all we had to suffer on board the pirate vessel. My mother was still very handsome; our maids of honour, and even our waiting women, had more charms than are to be found in all Africa. As for myself, I was ravishing, was exquisite, grace itself, and I was a virgin! I did not remain so long; this flower, which had been reserved for the handsome Prince of Massa Carara, was plucked by the corsair captain. He was an abominable negro, and yet believed that he did me a great deal of honour. Certainly the Princess of Palestrina and myself must have been very strong to go through all that we experienced until our arrival at Morocco. But let us pass on; these are such common things as not to be worth mentioning.

"Morocco swam in blood when we arrived. Fifty sons of the Emperor Muley-Ismael[11] had each their adherents; this produced fifty civil wars, of blacks against blacks, and blacks against tawnies, and tawnies against tawnies, and mulattoes against mulattoes. In short it was a continual carnage throughout the empire.

"No sooner were we landed, than the blacks of a contrary faction to that of my captain attempted to rob him of his booty. Next to jewels and gold we were the most valuable things he had. I was witness to such a battle as you have never seen in your European climates. The northern nations have not that heat in their blood, nor that raging lust for women, so common in Africa. It seems that you Europeans have only milk in your veins; but it is vitriol, it is fire which runs in those of the inhabitants of Mount Atlas and the neighbouring countries. They fought with the fury of the lions, tigers, and serpents of the country, to see who should have us. A Moor seized my mother by the right arm, while my captain's lieutenant held her by the left; a Moorish soldier had hold of her by one leg, and one of our corsairs held her by the other. Thus almost all our women were drawn in quarters by four men. My captain concealed me behind him; and with his drawn scimitar cut and slashed every one that opposed his fury. At length I saw all our Italian women, and my mother herself, torn, mangled, massacred, by the monsters who disputed over them. The slaves, my companions, those who had taken them, soldiers, sailors, blacks, whites, mulattoes, and at last my captain, all were killed, and I remained dying on a heap of dead. Such scenes as this were transacted through an extent of three hundred leagues—and yet they never missed the five prayers a day ordained by Mahomet.

"With difficulty I disengaged myself from such a heap of slaughtered bodies, and crawled to a large orange tree on the bank of a neighbouring rivulet, where I fell, oppressed with fright, fatigue, horror, despair, and hunger. Immediately after, my senses, overpowered, gave themselves up to sleep, which was yet more swooning than repose. I was in this state of weakness and insensibility, between life and death, when I felt myself pressed by something that moved upon my body. I opened my eyes, and saw a white man, of good countenance, who sighed, and who said between his teeth: 'O che sciagura d'essere senza coglioni!'"[12]

# The Adventures of the Old Woman Continued.

"Astonished and delighted to hear my native language, and no less surprised at what this man said, I made answer that there were much greater misfortunes than that of which he complained. I told him in a few words of the horrors which I had endured, and fainted a second time. He carried me to a neighbouring house, put me to bed, gave me food, waited upon me, consoled me, flattered me; he told me that he had never seen any one so beautiful as I, and that he never so much regretted the loss of what it was impossible to recover.

"'I was born at Naples,' said he, 'there they geld two or three thousand children every year; some die of the operation, others acquire a voice more beautiful than that of women, and others are raised to offices of state.[13] This operation was performed on me with great success and I was chapel musician to madam, the Princess of Palestrina.'

"'To my mother!' cried I.

"'Your mother!' cried he, weeping. 'What! can you be that young princess whom I brought up until the age of six years, and who promised so early to be as beautiful as you?'

"'It is I, indeed; but my mother lies four hundred yards hence, torn in quarters, under a heap of dead bodies.'

"I told him all my adventures, and he made me acquainted with his; telling me that he had been sent to the Emperor of Morocco by a Christian power, to conclude a treaty with that prince, in consequence of which he was to be furnished with military stores and ships to help to demolish the commerce of other Christian Governments.

"'My mission is done,' said this honest eunuch; 'I go to embark for Ceuta, and will take you to Italy. Ma che sciagura d'essere senza coglioni!'

"I thanked him with tears of commiseration; and instead of taking me to Italy he conducted me to Algiers, where he sold me to the Dey. Scarcely was I sold, than the plague which had made the tour of Africa, Asia, and Europe, broke out with great malignancy in Algiers. You have seen earthquakes; but pray, miss, have you ever had the plague?"

"Never," answered Cunegonde.

"If you had," said the old woman, "you would acknowledge that it is far more terrible than an earthquake. It is common in Africa, and I caught it. Imagine to yourself the distressed situation of the daughter of a Pope, only fifteen years old, who, in less than three months, had felt the miseries of poverty and slavery, had been ravished almost every day, had beheld her mother drawn in quarters, had experienced famine and war, and was dying of the plague in Algiers. I did not die, however, but my eunuch, and the Dey, and almost the whole seraglio of Algiers perished.

"As soon as the first fury of this terrible pestilence was over, a sale was made of the Dey's slaves; I was purchased by a merchant, and carried to Tunis; this man sold me to another merchant, who sold me again to another at Tripoli; from Tripoli I was sold to Alexandria, from Alexandria to Smyrna, and from Smyrna to Constantinople. At length I became the property of an Aga of the Janissaries, who was soon ordered away to the defence of Azof, then besieged by the Russians.

"The Aga, who was a very gallant man, took his whole seraglio with him, and lodged us in a small fort on the Palus Méotides, guarded by two black eunuchs and twenty soldiers. The Turks killed prodigious numbers of the Russians, but the latter had their revenge. Azof was destroyed by fire, the inhabitants put to the sword, neither sex nor age was spared; until there remained only our little fort, and the enemy wanted to starve us out. The twenty Janissaries had sworn they would never surrender. The extremities of famine to which they were reduced, obliged them to eat our two eunuchs, for fear of violating their oath. And at the end of a few days they resolved also to devour the women.

"We had a very pious and humane Iman, who preached an excellent sermon, exhorting them not to kill us all at once.

"'Only cut off a buttock of each of those ladies,' said he, 'and you'll fare extremely well; if you must go to it again, there will be the same entertainment a few days hence; heaven will accept of so charitable an action, and send you relief.'

"He had great eloquence; he persuaded them; we underwent this terrible operation. The Iman applied the same balsam to us, as he does to children after circumcision; and we all nearly died.

"Scarcely had the Janissaries finished the repast with which we had furnished them, than the Russians came in flat-bottomed boats; not a Janissary escaped. The Russians paid no attention to the condition we were in. There are French surgeons in all parts of the world; one of them who was very clever took us under his care—he cured us; and as long as I live I shall remember that as soon as my wounds were healed he made proposals to me. He bid us all be of good cheer, telling us that the like had happened in many sieges, and that it was according to the laws of war.

"As soon as my companions could walk, they were obliged to set out for Moscow. I fell to the share of a Boyard who made me his gardener, and gave me twenty lashes a day. But this nobleman having in two years' time been broke upon the wheel along with thirty more Boyards for some broils at court, I profited by that event; I fled. I traversed all Russia; I was a long time an inn-holder's servant at Riga, the same at Rostock, at Vismar, at Leipzig, at Cassel, at Utrecht, at Leyden, at the Hague, at Rotterdam. I waxed old in misery and disgrace, having only one-half of my posteriors, and always remembering I was a Pope's daughter. A hundred times I was upon the point of killing myself; but still I loved life. This ridiculous foible is perhaps one of our most fatal characteristics; for is there anything more absurd than to wish to carry continually a burden which one can always throw down? to detest existence and yet to cling to one's existence? in brief, to caress the serpent which devours us, till he has eaten our very heart?

"In the different countries which it has been my lot to traverse, and the numerous inns where I have been servant, I have taken notice of a vast number of people who held their own existence in abhorrence, and yet I never knew of more than eight who voluntarily put an end to their misery; three negroes, four Englishmen, and a German professor named Robek.[14] I ended by being servant to the Jew, Don Issachar, who placed me near your presence, my fair lady. I am determined to share your fate, and have been much more affected with your misfortunes than with my own. I would never even have spoken to you of my misfortunes, had you not piqued me a little, and if it were not customary to tell stories on board a ship in order to pass away the time. In short, Miss Cunegonde, I have had experience, I know the world; therefore I advise you to divert yourself, and prevail upon each passenger to tell his story; and if there be one of them all, that has not cursed his life many a time, that has not frequently looked upon himself as the unhappiest of mortals, I give you leave to throw me headforemost into the sea."

# How Candide Was Forced Away from His Fair Cunegonde and the Old Woman.

The beautiful Cunegonde having heard the old woman's history, paid her all the civilities due to a person of her rank and merit. She likewise accepted her proposal, and engaged all the passengers, one after the other, to relate their adventures; and then both she and Candide allowed that the old woman was in the right.

"It is a great pity," said Candide, "that the sage Pangloss was hanged contrary to custom at an auto-da-fé; he would tell us most amazing things in regard to the physical and moral evils that overspread earth and sea, and I should be able, with due respect, to make a few objections."

While each passenger was recounting his story, the ship made her way. They landed at Buenos Ayres. Cunegonde, Captain Candide, and the old woman, waited on the Governor, Don Fernando d'Ibaraa, y Figueora, y Mascarenes, y Lampourdos, y Souza. This nobleman had a stateliness becoming a person who bore so many names. He spoke to men with so noble a disdain, carried his nose so loftily, raised his voice so unmercifully, assumed so imperious an air, and stalked with such intolerable pride, that those who saluted him were strongly inclined to give him a good drubbing. Cunegonde appeared to him the most beautiful he had ever met. The first thing he did was to ask whether she was not the captain's wife. The manner in which he asked the question alarmed Candide; he durst not say she was his wife, because indeed she was not; neither durst he say she was his sister, because it was not so; and although this obliging lie had been formerly much in favour among the ancients, and although it could be useful to the moderns, his soul was too pure to betray the truth.

"Miss Cunegonde," said he, "is to do me the honour to marry me, and we beseech your excellency to deign to sanction our marriage."

Don Fernando d'Ibaraa, y Figueora, y Mascarenes, y Lampourdos, y Souza, turning up his moustachios, smiled mockingly, and ordered Captain Candide to go and review his company. Candide obeyed, and the Governor remained alone with Miss Cunegonde. He declared his passion, protesting he would marry her the next day in the face of the church, or otherwise, just as should be agreeable to herself. Cunegonde asked a quarter of an hour to consider of it, to consult the old woman, and to take her resolution.

The old woman spoke thus to Cunegonde:

"Miss, you have seventy-two quarterings, and not a farthing; it is now in your power to be wife to the greatest lord in South America, who has very beautiful moustachios. Is it for you to pique yourself upon inviolable fidelity? You have been ravished by Bulgarians; a Jew and an Inquisitor have enjoyed your favours. Misfortune gives sufficient excuse. I own, that if I were in your place, I should have no scruple in marrying the Governor and in making the fortune of Captain Candide."

While the old woman spoke with all the prudence which age and experience gave, a small ship entered the port on board of which were an Alcalde and his alguazils, and this was what had happened.

As the old woman had shrewdly guessed, it was a Grey Friar who stole Cunegonde's money and jewels in the town of Badajos, when she and Candide were escaping. The Friar wanted to sell some of the diamonds to a jeweller; the jeweller knew them to be the Grand Inquisitor's. The Friar before he was hanged confessed he had stolen them. He described the persons, and the route they had taken. The flight of Cunegonde and Candide was already known. They were traced to Cadiz. A vessel was immediately sent in pursuit of them. The vessel was already in the port of Buenos Ayres. The report spread that the Alcalde was going to land, and that he was in pursuit of the murderers of my lord the Grand Inquisitor. The prudent old woman saw at once what was to be done.

"You cannot run away," said she to Cunegonde, "and you have nothing to fear, for it was not you that killed my lord; besides the Governor who loves you will not suffer you to be ill-treated; therefore stay."

She then ran immediately to Candide.

"Fly," said she, "or in an hour you will be burnt."

There was not a moment to lose; but how could he part from Cunegonde, and where could he flee for shelter?

## How Candide and Cacambo Were Received by the Jesuits of Paraguay.

Candide had brought such a valet with him from Cadiz, as one often meets with on the coasts of Spain and in the American colonies. He was a quarter Spaniard, born of a mongrel in Tucuman; he had been singing-boy, sacristan, sailor, monk, pedlar, soldier, and lackey. His name was Cacambo, and he loved his master, because his master was a very good man. He quickly saddled the two Andalusian horses.

"Come, master, let us follow the old woman's advice; let us start, and run without looking behind us."

Candide shed tears.

"Oh! my dear Cunegonde! must I leave you just at a time when the Governor was going to sanction our nuptials? Cunegonde, brought to such a distance what will become of you?"

"She will do as well as she can," said Cacambo; "the women are never at a loss, God provides for them, let us run."

"Whither art thou carrying me? Where shall we go? What shall we do without Cunegonde?" said Candide.

"By St. James of Compostella," said Cacambo, "you were going to fight against the Jesuits; let us go to fight for them; I know the road well, I'll conduct you to their kingdom, where they will be charmed to have a captain that understands the Bulgarian exercise. You'll make a prodigious fortune; if we cannot find our account in one world we shall in another. It is a great pleasure to see and do new things."

"You have before been in Paraguay, then?" said Candide.

"Ay, sure," answered Cacambo, "I was servant in the College of the Assumption, and am acquainted with the government of the good Fathers as well as I am with the streets of Cadiz. It is an admirable government. The kingdom is upwards of three hundred leagues in diameter, and divided into thirty provinces; there the Fathers possess all, and the people nothing; it is a masterpiece of reason and justice. For my part I see nothing so divine as the Fathers who here make war upon the kings of Spain and Portugal, and in Europe confess those kings; who here kill Spaniards, and in Madrid send them to heaven; this delights me, let us push forward. You are going to be the happiest of mortals. What pleasure will it be to those Fathers to hear that a captain who knows the Bulgarian exercise has come to them!"

As soon as they reached the first barrier, Cacambo told the advanced guard that a captain wanted to speak with my lord the Commandant. Notice was given to the main guard, and immediately a Paraguayan officer ran and laid himself at the feet of the Commandant, to impart this news to him. Candide and Cacambo were disarmed, and their two Andalusian horses seized. The strangers were introduced between two files of musketeers; the Commandant was at the further end, with the three-cornered cap on his head, his gown tucked up, a sword by his side, and a spontoon[15] in his hand. He beckoned, and straightway the new-comers were encompassed by four-and-twenty soldiers. A sergeant told them they must wait, that the Commandant could not speak to them, and that the reverend Father Provincial does not suffer any Spaniard to open his mouth but in his presence, or to stay above three hours in the province.

"And where is the reverend Father Provincial?" said Cacambo.

"He is upon the parade just after celebrating mass," answered the sergeant, "and you cannot kiss his spurs till three hours hence."

"However," said Cacambo, "the captain is not a Spaniard, but a German, he is ready to perish with hunger as well as myself; cannot we have something for breakfast, while we wait for his reverence?"

The sergeant went immediately to acquaint the Commandant with what he had heard.

"God be praised!" said the reverend Commandant, "since he is a German, I may speak to him; take him to my arbour."

Candide was at once conducted to a beautiful summer-house, ornamented with a very pretty colonnade of green and gold marble, and with trellises, enclosing parraquets, humming-birds, fly-birds, guinea-hens, and all other rare birds. An excellent breakfast was provided in vessels of gold; and while the Paraguayans were eating maize out of wooden dishes, in the open fields and exposed to the heat of the sun, the reverend Father Commandant retired to his arbour.

He was a very handsome young man, with a full face, white skin but high in colour; he had an arched eyebrow, a lively eye, red ears, vermilion lips, a bold air, but such a boldness as neither belonged to a Spaniard nor a Jesuit. They returned their arms to Candide and Cacambo, and also the two Andalusian horses; to whom Cacambo gave some oats to eat just by the arbour, having an eye upon them all the while for fear of a surprise.

Candide first kissed the hem of the Commandant's robe, then they sat down to table.

"You are, then, a German?" said the Jesuit to him in that language.

"Yes, reverend Father," answered Candide.

As they pronounced these words they looked at each other with great amazement, and with such an emotion as they could not conceal.

"And from what part of Germany do you come?" said the Jesuit.

"I am from the dirty province of Westphalia," answered Candide; "I was born in the Castle of Thunder-ten-Tronckh."

"Oh! Heavens! is it possible?" cried the Commandant.

"What a miracle!" cried Candide.

"Is it really you?" said the Commandant.

"It is not possible!" said Candide.

They drew back; they embraced; they shed rivulets of tears.

"What, is it you, reverend Father? You, the brother of the fair Cunegonde! You, that was slain by the Bulgarians! You, the Baron's son! You, a Jesuit in Paraguay! I must confess this is a strange world that we live in. Oh, Pangloss! Pangloss! how glad you would be if you had not been hanged!"

The Commandant sent away the negro slaves and the Paraguayans, who served them with liquors in goblets of rock-crystal. He thanked God and St. Ignatius a thousand times; he clasped Candide in his arms; and their faces were all bathed with tears.

"You will be more surprised, more affected, and transported," said Candide, "when I tell you that Cunegonde, your sister, whom you believe to have been ripped open, is in perfect health."

"Where?"

"In your neighbourhood, with the Governor of Buenos Ayres; and I was going to fight against you."

Every word which they uttered in this long conversation but added wonder to wonder. Their souls fluttered on their tongues, listened in their ears, and sparkled in their eyes. As they were Germans, they sat a good while at table, waiting for the reverend Father Provincial, and the Commandant spoke to his dear Candide as follows.

# How Candide Killed the Brother of His Dear Cunegonde.

"I shall have ever present to my memory the dreadful day, on which I saw my father and mother killed, and my sister ravished. When the Bulgarians retired, my dear sister could not be found; but my mother, my father, and myself, with two maid-servants and three little boys all of whom had been slain, were put in a hearse, to be conveyed for interment to a chapel belonging to the Jesuits, within two leagues of our family seat. A Jesuit sprinkled us with some holy water; it was horribly salt; a few drops of it fell into my eyes; the father perceived that my eyelids stirred a little; he put his hand upon my heart and felt it beat. I received assistance, and at the end of three weeks I recovered. You know, my dear Candide, I was very pretty; but I grew much prettier, and the reverend Father Didrie,[16] Superior of that House, conceived the tenderest friendship for me; he gave me the habit of the order, some years after I was sent to Rome. The Father-General needed new levies of young German-Jesuits. The sovereigns of Paraguay admit as few Spanish Jesuits as possible; they prefer those of other nations as being more subordinate to their commands. I was judged fit by the reverend Father-General to go and work in this vineyard. We set out—a Pole, a Tyrolese, and myself. Upon my arrival I was honoured with a sub-deaconship and a lieutenancy. I am to-day colonel and priest. We shall give a warm reception to the King of Spain's troops; I will answer for it that they shall be excommunicated and well beaten. Providence sends you here to assist us. But is it, indeed, true that my dear sister Cunegonde is in the neighbourhood, with the Governor of Buenos Ayres?"

Candide assured him on oath that nothing was more true, and their tears began afresh.

The Baron could not refrain from embracing Candide; he called him his brother, his saviour.

"Ah! perhaps," said he, "we shall together, my dear Candide, enter the town as conquerors, and recover my sister Cunegonde."

"That is all I want," said Candide, "for I intended to marry her, and I still hope to do so."

"You insolent!" replied the Baron, "would you have the impudence to marry my sister who has seventy-two quarterings! I find thou hast the most consummate effrontery to dare to mention so presumptuous a design!"

Candide, petrified at this speech, made answer:

"Reverend Father, all the quarterings in the world signify nothing; I rescued your sister from the arms of a Jew and of an Inquisitor; she has great obligations to me, she wishes to marry me; Master Pangloss always told me that all men are equal, and certainly I will marry her."

"We shall see that, thou scoundrel!" said the Jesuit Baron de Thunder-ten-Tronckh, and that instant struck him across the face with the flat of his sword. Candide in an instant drew his rapier, and plunged it up to the hilt in the Jesuit's belly; but in pulling it out reeking hot, he burst into tears.

"Good God!" said he, "I have killed my old master, my friend, my brother-in-law! I am the best-natured creature in the world, and yet I have already killed three men, and of these three two were priests."

Cacambo, who stood sentry by the door of the arbour, ran to him.

"We have nothing more for it than to sell our lives as dearly as we can," said his master to him, "without doubt some one will soon enter the arbour, and we must die sword in hand."

Cacambo, who had been in a great many scrapes in his lifetime, did not lose his head; he took the Baron's Jesuit habit, put it on Candide, gave him the square cap, and made him mount on horseback. All this was done in the twinkling of an eye.

"Let us gallop fast, master, everybody will take you for a Jesuit, going to give directions to your men, and we shall have passed the frontiers before they will be able to overtake us."

He flew as he spoke these words, crying out aloud in Spanish:

"Make way, make way, for the reverend Father Colonel."

# Adventures of the Two Travellers, with Two Girls, Two Monkeys, and the Savages Called Oreillons.

Candide and his valet had got beyond the barrier, before it was known in the camp that the German Jesuit was dead. The wary Cacambo had taken care to fill his wallet with bread, chocolate, bacon, fruit, and a few bottles of wine. With their Andalusian horses they penetrated into an unknown country, where they perceived no beaten track. At length they came to a beautiful meadow intersected with purling rills. Here our two adventurers fed their horses. Cacambo proposed to his master to take some food, and he set him an example.

"How can you ask me to eat ham," said Candide, "after killing the Baron's son, and being doomed never more to see the beautiful Cunegonde? What will it avail me to spin out my wretched days and drag them far from her in remorse and despair? And what will the Journal of Trevoux[17] say?"

While he was thus lamenting his fate, he went on eating. The sun went down. The two wanderers heard some little cries which seemed to be uttered by women. They did not know whether they were cries of pain or joy; but they started up precipitately with that inquietude and alarm which every little thing inspires in an unknown country. The noise was made by two naked girls, who tripped along the mead, while two monkeys were pursuing them and biting their buttocks. Candide was moved with pity; he had learned to fire a gun in the Bulgarian service, and he was so clever at it, that he could hit a filbert in a hedge without touching a leaf of the tree. He took up his double-barrelled Spanish fusil, let it off, and killed the two monkeys.

"God be praised! My dear Cacambo, I have rescued those two poor creatures from a most perilous situation. If I have committed a sin in killing an Inquisitor and a Jesuit, I have made ample amends by saving the lives of these girls. Perhaps they are young ladies of family; and this adventure may procure us great advantages in this country."

He was continuing, but stopped short when he saw the two girls tenderly embracing the monkeys, bathing their bodies in tears, and rending the air with the most dismal lamentations.

"Little did I expect to see such good-nature," said he at length to Cacambo; who made answer:

"Master, you have done a fine thing now; you have slain the sweethearts of those two young ladies."

"The sweethearts! Is it possible? You are jesting, Cacambo, I can never believe it!"

"Dear master," replied Cacambo; "you are surprised at everything. Why should you think it so strange that in some countries there are monkeys which insinuate themselves into the good graces of the ladies; they are a fourth part human, as I am a fourth part Spaniard."

"Alas!" replied Candide, "I remember to have heard Master Pangloss say, that formerly such accidents used to happen; that these mixtures were productive of Centaurs, Fauns, and Satyrs; and that many of the ancients had seen such monsters, but I looked upon the whole as fabulous."

"You ought now to be convinced," said Cacambo, "that it is the truth, and you see what use is made of those creatures, by persons that have not had a proper education; all I fear is that those ladies will play us some ugly trick."

These sound reflections induced Candide to leave the meadow and to plunge into a wood. He supped there with Cacambo; and after cursing the Portuguese inquisitor, the Governor of Buenos Ayres, and the Baron, they fell asleep on moss. On awaking they felt that they could not move; for during the night the Oreillons, who inhabited that country, and to whom the ladies had denounced them, had bound them with cords made of the bark of trees. They were encompassed by fifty naked Oreillons, armed with bows and arrows, with clubs and flint hatchets. Some were making a large cauldron boil, others were preparing spits, and all cried:

"A Jesuit! a Jesuit! we shall be revenged, we shall have excellent cheer, let us eat the Jesuit, let us eat him up!"

"I told you, my dear master," cried Cacambo sadly, "that those two girls would play us some ugly trick."

Candide seeing the cauldron and the spits, cried:

"We are certainly going to be either roasted or boiled. Ah! what would Master Pangloss say, were he to see how pure nature is formed? Everything is right, may be, but I declare it is very hard to have lost Miss Cunegonde and to be put upon a spit by Oreillons."

Cacambo never lost his head.

"Do not despair," said he to the disconsolate Candide, "I understand a little of the jargon of these people, I will speak to them."

"Be sure," said Candide, "to represent to them how frightfully inhuman it is to cook men, and how very un-Christian."

"Gentlemen," said Cacambo, "you reckon you are to-day going to feast upon a Jesuit. It is all very well, nothing is more unjust than thus to treat your enemies. Indeed, the law of nature teaches us to kill our neighbour, and such is the practice all over the world. If we do not accustom ourselves to eating them, it is because we have better fare. But you have not the same resources as we; certainly it is much better to devour your enemies than to resign to the crows and rooks the fruits of your victory. But, gentlemen, surely you would not choose to eat your friends. You believe that you are going to spit a Jesuit, and he is your defender. It is the enemy of your enemies that you are going to roast. As for myself, I was born in your country; this gentleman is my master, and, far from being a Jesuit, he has just killed one, whose spoils he wears; and thence comes your mistake. To convince you of the truth of what I say, take his habit and carry it to the first barrier of the Jesuit kingdom, and inform yourselves whether my master did not kill a Jesuit officer. It will not take you long, and you can always eat us if you find that I have lied to you. But I have told you the truth. You are too well acquainted with the principles of public law, humanity, and justice not to pardon us."

The Oreillons found this speech very reasonable. They deputed two of their principal people with all expedition to inquire into the truth of the matter; these executed their commission like men of sense, and soon returned with good news. The Oreillons untied their prisoners, showed them all sorts of civilities, offered them girls, gave them refreshment, and reconducted them to the confines of their territories, proclaiming with great joy:

"He is no Jesuit! He is no Jesuit!"

Candide could not help being surprised at the cause of his deliverance.

"What people!" said he; "what men! what manners! If I had not been so lucky as to run Miss Cunegonde's brother through the body, I should have been devoured without redemption. But, after all, pure nature is good, since these people, instead of feasting upon my flesh, have shown me a thousand civilities, when then I was not a Jesuit."

# Arrival of Candide and His Valet at El Dorado, and What They Saw There.

"You see," said Cacambo to Candide, as soon as they had reached the frontiers of the Oreillons, "that this hemisphere is not better than the others, take my word for it; let us go back to Europe by the shortest way."

"How go back?" said Candide, "and where shall we go? to my own country? The Bulgarians and the Abares are slaying all; to Portugal? there I shall be burnt; and if we abide here we are every moment in danger of being spitted. But how can I resolve to quit a part of the world where my dear Cunegonde resides?"

"Let us turn towards Cayenne," said Cacambo, "there we shall find Frenchmen, who wander all over the world; they may assist us; God will perhaps have pity on us."

It was not easy to get to Cayenne; they knew vaguely in which direction to go, but rivers, precipices, robbers, savages, obstructed them all the way. Their horses died of fatigue. Their provisions were consumed; they fed a whole month upon wild fruits, and found themselves at last near a little river bordered with cocoa trees, which sustained their lives and their hopes.

Cacambo, who was as good a counsellor as the old woman, said to Candide:

"We are able to hold out no longer; we have walked enough. I see an empty canoe near the river-side; let us fill it with cocoanuts, throw ourselves into it, and go with the current; a river always leads to some inhabited spot. If we do not find pleasant things we shall at least find new things."

"With all my heart," said Candide, "let us recommend ourselves to Providence."

They rowed a few leagues, between banks, in some places flowery, in others barren; in some parts smooth, in others rugged. The stream ever widened, and at length lost itself under an arch of frightful rocks which reached to the sky. The two travellers had the courage to commit themselves to the current. The river, suddenly contracting at this place, whirled them along with a dreadful noise and rapidity. At the end of four-and-twenty hours they saw daylight again, but their canoe was dashed to pieces against the rocks. For a league they had to creep from rock to rock, until at length they discovered an extensive plain, bounded by inaccessible mountains. The country was cultivated as much for pleasure as for necessity. On all sides the useful was also the beautiful. The roads were covered, or rather adorned, with carriages of a glittering form and substance, in which were men and women of surprising beauty, drawn by large red sheep which surpassed in fleetness the finest coursers of Andalusia, Tetuan, and Mequinez.[18]

"Here, however, is a country," said Candide, "which is better than Westphalia."

He stepped out with Cacambo towards the first village which he saw. Some children dressed in tattered brocades played at quoits on the outskirts. Our travellers from the other world amused themselves by looking on. The quoits were large round pieces, yellow, red, and green, which cast a singular lustre! The travellers picked a few of them off the ground; this was of gold, that of emeralds, the other of rubies—the least of them would have been the greatest ornament on the Mogul's throne.

"Without doubt," said Cacambo, "these children must be the king's sons that are playing at quoits!"

The village schoolmaster appeared at this moment and called them to school.

"There," said Candide, "is the preceptor of the royal family."

The little truants immediately quitted their game, leaving the quoits on the ground with all their other playthings. Candide gathered them up, ran to the master, and presented them to him in a most humble manner, giving him to understand by signs that their royal highnesses had forgotten their gold and jewels. The schoolmaster, smiling, flung them upon the ground; then, looking at Candide with a good deal of surprise, went about his business.

The travellers, however, took care to gather up the gold, the rubies, and the emeralds.

"Where are we?" cried Candide. "The king's children in this country must be well brought up, since they are taught to despise gold and precious stones."

Cacambo was as much surprised as Candide. At length they drew near the first house in the village. It was built like an European palace. A crowd of people pressed about the door, and there were still more in the house. They heard most agreeable music, and were aware of a delicious odour of cooking. Cacambo went up to the door and heard they were talking Peruvian; it was his mother tongue, for it is well known that Cacambo was born in Tucuman, in a village where no other language was spoken.

"I will be your interpreter here," said he to Candide; "let us go in, it is a public-house."

Immediately two waiters and two girls, dressed in cloth of gold, and their hair tied up with ribbons, invited them to sit down to table with the landlord. They served four dishes of soup, each garnished with two young parrots; a boiled condor[19] which weighed two hundred pounds; two roasted monkeys, of excellent flavour; three hundred humming-birds in one dish, and six hundred fly-birds in another; exquisite ragouts; delicious pastries; the whole served up in dishes of a kind of rock-crystal. The waiters and girls poured out several liqueurs drawn from the sugar-cane.

Most of the company were chapmen and waggoners, all extremely polite; they asked Cacambo a few questions with the greatest circumspection, and answered his in the most obliging manner.

As soon as dinner was over, Cacambo believed as well as Candide that they might well pay their reckoning by laying down two of those large gold pieces which they had picked up. The landlord and landlady shouted with laughter and held their sides. When the fit was over:

"Gentlemen," said the landlord, "it is plain you are strangers, and such guests we are not accustomed to see; pardon us therefore for laughing when you offered us the pebbles from our highroads in payment of your reckoning. You doubtless have not the money of the country; but it is not necessary to have any money at all to dine in this house. All hostelries established for the convenience of commerce are paid by the government. You have fared but very indifferently because this is a poor village; but everywhere else, you will be received as you deserve."

Cacambo explained this whole discourse with great astonishment to Candide, who was as greatly astonished to hear it.

"What sort of a country then is this," said they to one another; "a country unknown to all the rest of the world, and where nature is of a kind so different from ours? It is probably the country where all is well; for there absolutely must be one such place. And, whatever Master Pangloss might say, I often found that things went very ill in Westphalia."

# What They Saw in the Country of El Dorado.

Cacambo expressed his curiosity to the landlord, who made answer:

"I am very ignorant, but not the worse on that account. However, we have in this neighbourhood an old man retired from Court who is the most learned and most communicative person in the kingdom."

At once he took Cacambo to the old man. Candide acted now only a second character, and accompanied his valet. They entered a very plain house, for the door was only of silver, and the ceilings were only of gold, but wrought in so elegant a taste as to vie with the richest. The antechamber, indeed, was only encrusted with rubies and emeralds, but the order in which everything was arranged made amends for this great simplicity.

The old man received the strangers on his sofa, which was stuffed with humming-birds' feathers, and ordered his servants to present them with liqueurs in diamond goblets; after which he satisfied their curiosity in the following terms:

"I am now one hundred and seventy-two years old, and I learnt of my late father, Master of the Horse to the King, the amazing revolutions of Peru, of which he had been an eyewitness. The kingdom we now inhabit is the ancient country of the Incas, who quitted it very imprudently to conquer another part of the world, and were at length destroyed by the Spaniards.

"More wise by far were the princes of their family, who remained in their native country; and they ordained, with the consent of the whole nation, that none of the inhabitants should ever be permitted to quit this little kingdom; and this has preserved our innocence and happiness. The Spaniards have had a confused notion of this country, and have called it El Dorado; and an Englishman, whose name was Sir Walter Raleigh, came very near it about a hundred years ago; but being surrounded by inaccessible rocks and precipices, we have hitherto been sheltered from the rapaciousness of European nations, who have an inconceivable passion for the pebbles and dirt of our land, for the sake of which they would murder us to the last man."

The conversation was long: it turned chiefly on their form of government, their manners, their women, their public entertainments, and the arts. At length Candide, having always had a taste for metaphysics, made Cacambo ask whether there was any religion in that country.

The old man reddened a little.

"How then," said he, "can you doubt it? Do you take us for ungrateful wretches?"

Cacambo humbly asked, "What was the religion in El Dorado?"

The old man reddened again.

"Can there be two religions?" said he. "We have, I believe, the religion of all the world: we worship God night and morning."

"Do you worship but one God?" said Cacambo, who still acted as interpreter in representing Candide's doubts.

"Surely," said the old man, "there are not two, nor three, nor four. I must confess the people from your side of the world ask very extraordinary questions."

Candide was not yet tired of interrogating the good old man; he wanted to know in what manner they prayed to God in El Dorado.

"We do not pray to Him," said the worthy sage; "we have nothing to ask of Him; He has given us all we need, and we return Him thanks without ceasing."

Candide having a curiosity to see the priests asked where they were. The good old man smiled.

"My friend," said he, "we are all priests. The King and all the heads of families sing solemn canticles of thanksgiving every morning, accompanied by five or six thousand musicians."

"What! have you no monks who teach, who dispute, who govern, who cabal, and who burn people that are not of their opinion?"

"We must be mad, indeed, if that were the case," said the old man; "here we are all of one opinion, and we know not what you mean by monks."

During this whole discourse Candide was in raptures, and he said to himself:

"This is vastly different from Westphalia and the Baron's castle. Had our friend Pangloss seen El Dorado he would no longer have said that the castle of Thunder-ten-Tronckh was the finest upon earth. It is evident that one must travel."

After this long conversation the old man ordered a coach and six sheep to be got ready, and twelve of his domestics to conduct the travellers to Court.

"Excuse me," said he, "if my age deprives me of the honour of accompanying you. The King will receive you in a manner that cannot displease you; and no doubt you will make an allowance for the customs of the country, if some things should not be to your liking."

Candide and Cacambo got into the coach, the six sheep flew, and in less than four hours they reached the King's palace situated at the extremity of the capital. The portal was two hundred and twenty feet high, and one hundred wide; but words are wanting to express the materials of which it was built. It is plain such materials must have prodigious superiority over those pebbles and sand which we call gold and precious stones.

Twenty beautiful damsels of the King's guard received Candide and Cacambo as they alighted from the coach, conducted them to the bath, and dressed them in robes woven of the down of humming-birds; after which the great crown officers, of both sexes, led them to the King's apartment, between two files of musicians, a thousand on each side. When they drew near to the audience chamber Cacambo asked one of the great officers in what way he should pay his obeisance to his Majesty; whether they should throw themselves upon their knees or on their stomachs; whether they should put their hands upon their heads or behind their backs; whether they should lick the dust off the floor; in a word, what was the ceremony?

"The custom," said the great officer, "is to embrace the King, and to kiss him on each cheek."

Candide and Cacambo threw themselves round his Majesty's neck. He received them with all the goodness imaginable, and politely invited them to supper.

While waiting they were shown the city, and saw the public edifices raised as high as the clouds, the market places ornamented with a thousand columns, the fountains of spring water, those of rose water, those of liqueurs drawn from sugar-cane, incessantly flowing into the great squares, which were paved with a kind of precious stone, which gave off a delicious fragrancy like that of cloves and cinnamon. Candide asked to see the court of justice, the parliament. They told him they had none, and that they were strangers to lawsuits. He asked if they had any prisons, and they answered no. But what surprised him most and gave him the greatest pleasure was the palace of sciences, where he saw a gallery two thousand feet long, and filled with instruments employed in mathematics and physics.

After rambling about the city the whole afternoon, and seeing but a thousandth part of it, they were reconducted to the royal palace, where Candide sat down to table with his Majesty, his valet Cacambo, and several ladies. Never was there a better entertainment, and never was more wit shown at a table than that which fell from his Majesty. Cacambo explained the King's bon-mots to Candide, and notwithstanding they were translated they still appeared to be bon-mots. Of all the things that surprised Candide this was not the least.

They spent a month in this hospitable place. Candide frequently said to Cacambo:

"I own, my friend, once more that the castle where I was born is nothing in comparison with this; but, after all, Miss Cunegonde is not here, and you have, without doubt, some mistress in Europe. If we abide here we shall only be upon a footing with the rest, whereas, if we return to our old world, only with twelve sheep laden with the pebbles of El Dorado, we shall be richer than all the kings in Europe. We shall have no more Inquisitors to fear, and we may easily recover Miss Cunegonde."

This speech was agreeable to Cacambo; mankind are so fond of roving, of making a figure in their own country, and of boasting of what they have seen in their travels, that the two happy ones resolved to be no longer so, but to ask his Majesty's leave to quit the country.

"You are foolish," said the King. "I am sensible that my kingdom is but a small place, but when a person is comfortably settled in any part he should abide there. I have not the right to detain strangers. It is a tyranny which neither our manners nor our laws permit. All men are free. Go when you wish, but the going will be very difficult. It is impossible to ascend that rapid river on which you came as by a miracle, and which runs under vaulted rocks. The mountains which surround my kingdom are ten thousand feet high, and as steep as walls; they are each over ten leagues in breadth, and there is no other way to descend them than by precipices. However, since you absolutely wish to depart, I shall give orders to my engineers to construct a machine that will convey you very safely. When we have conducted you over the mountains no one can accompany you further, for my subjects have made a vow never to quit the kingdom, and they are too wise to break it. Ask me besides anything that you please."

"We desire nothing of your Majesty," says Candide, "but a few sheep laden with provisions, pebbles, and the earth of this country."

The King laughed.

"I cannot conceive," said he, "what pleasure you Europeans find in our yellow clay, but take as much as you like, and great good may it do you."

At once he gave directions that his engineers should construct a machine to hoist up these two extraordinary men out of the kingdom. Three thousand good mathematicians went to work; it was ready in fifteen days, and did not cost more than twenty million sterling in the specie of that country. They placed Candide and Cacambo on the machine. There were two great red sheep saddled and bridled to ride upon as soon as they were beyond the mountains, twenty pack-sheep laden with provisions, thirty with presents of the curiosities of the country, and fifty with gold, diamonds, and precious stones. The King embraced the two wanderers very tenderly.

Their departure, with the ingenious manner in which they and their sheep were hoisted over the mountains, was a splendid spectacle. The mathematicians took their leave after conveying them to a place of safety, and Candide had no other desire, no other aim, than to present his sheep to Miss Cunegonde.

"Now," said he, "we are able to pay the Governor of Buenos Ayres if Miss Cunegonde can be ransomed. Let us journey towards Cayenne. Let us embark, and we will afterwards see what kingdom we shall be able to purchase."

# What Happened to Them at Surinam and How Candide Got Acquainted with Martin.

Our travellers spent the first day very agreeably. They were delighted with possessing more treasure than all Asia, Europe, and Africa could scrape together. Candide, in his raptures, cut Cunegonde's name on the trees. The second day two of their sheep plunged into a morass, where they and their burdens were lost; two more died of fatigue a few days after; seven or eight perished with hunger in a desert; and others subsequently fell down precipices. At length, after travelling a hundred days, only two sheep remained. Said Candide to Cacambo:

"My friend, you see how perishable are the riches of this world; there is nothing solid but virtue, and the happiness of seeing Cunegonde once more."

"I grant all you say," said Cacambo, "but we have still two sheep remaining, with more treasure than the King of Spain will ever have; and I see a town which I take to be Surinam, belonging to the Dutch. We are at the end of all our troubles, and at the beginning of happiness."

As they drew near the town, they saw a negro stretched upon the ground, with only one moiety of his clothes, that is, of his blue linen drawers; the poor man had lost his left leg and his right hand.

"Good God!" said Candide in Dutch, "what art thou doing there, friend, in that shocking condition?"

"I am waiting for my master, Mynheer Vanderdendur, the famous merchant," answered the negro.

"Was it Mynheer Vanderdendur," said Candide, "that treated thee thus?"

"Yes, sir," said the negro, "it is the custom. They give us a pair of linen drawers for our whole garment twice a year. When we work at the sugar-canes, and the mill snatches hold of a finger, they cut off the hand; and when we attempt to run away, they cut off the leg; both cases have happened to me. This is the price at which you eat sugar in Europe. Yet when my mother sold me for ten patagons[20] on the coast of Guinea, she said to me: 'My dear child, bless our fetiches, adore them for ever; they will make thee live happily; thou hast the honour of being the slave of our lords, the whites, which is making the fortune of thy father and mother.' Alas! I know not whether I have made their fortunes; this I know, that they have not made mine. Dogs, monkeys, and parrots are a thousand times less wretched than I. The Dutch fetiches, who have converted me, declare every Sunday that we are all of us children of Adam—blacks as well as whites. I am not a genealogist, but if these preachers tell truth, we are all second cousins. Now, you must agree, that it is impossible to treat one's relations in a more barbarous manner."

"Oh, Pangloss!" cried Candide, "thou hadst not guessed at this abomination; it is the end. I must at last renounce thy optimism."

"What is this optimism?" said Cacambo.

"Alas!" said Candide, "it is the madness of maintaining that everything is right when it is wrong."

Looking at the negro, he shed tears, and weeping, he entered Surinam.

The first thing they inquired after was whether there was a vessel in the harbour which could be sent to Buenos Ayres. The person to whom they applied was a Spanish sea-captain, who offered to agree with them upon reasonable terms. He appointed to meet them at a public-house, whither Candide and the faithful Cacambo went with their two sheep, and awaited his coming.

Candide, who had his heart upon his lips, told the Spaniard all his adventures, and avowed that he intended to elope with Miss Cunegonde.

"Then I will take good care not to carry you to Buenos Ayres," said the seaman. "I should be hanged, and so would you. The fair Cunegonde is my lord's favourite mistress."

This was a thunderclap for Candide: he wept for a long while. At last he drew Cacambo aside.

"Here, my dear friend," said he to him, "this thou must do. We have, each of us in his pocket, five or six millions in diamonds; you are more clever than I; you must go and bring Miss Cunegonde from Buenos Ayres. If the Governor makes any difficulty, give him a million; if he will not relinquish her, give him two; as you have not killed an Inquisitor, they will have no suspicion of you; I'll get another ship, and go and wait for you at Venice; that's a free country, where there is no danger either from Bulgarians, Abares, Jews, or Inquisitors."

Cacambo applauded this wise resolution. He despaired at parting from so good a master, who had become his intimate friend; but the pleasure of serving him prevailed over the pain of leaving him. They embraced with tears; Candide charged him not to forget the good old woman. Cacambo set out that very same day. This Cacambo was a very honest fellow.

Candide stayed some time longer in Surinam, waiting for another captain to carry him and the two remaining sheep to Italy. After he had hired domestics, and purchased everything necessary for a long voyage, Mynheer Vanderdendur, captain of a large vessel, came and offered his services.

"How much will you charge," said he to this man, "to carry me straight to Venice—me, my servants, my baggage, and these two sheep?"

The skipper asked ten thousand piastres. Candide did not hesitate.

"Oh! oh!" said the prudent Vanderdendur to himself, "this stranger gives ten thousand piastres unhesitatingly! He must be very rich."

Returning a little while after, he let him know that upon second consideration, he could not undertake the voyage for less than twenty thousand piastres.

"Well, you shall have them," said Candide.

"Ay!" said the skipper to himself, "this man agrees to pay twenty thousand piastres with as much ease as ten."

He went back to him again, and declared that he could not carry him to Venice for less than thirty thousand piastres.

"Then you shall have thirty thousand," replied Candide.

"Oh! oh!" said the Dutch skipper once more to himself, "thirty thousand piastres are a trifle to this man; surely these sheep must be laden with an immense treasure; let us say no more about it. First of all, let him pay down the thirty thousand piastres; then we shall see."

Candide sold two small diamonds, the least of which was worth more than what the skipper asked for his freight. He paid him in advance. The two sheep were put on board. Candide followed in a little boat to join the vessel in the roads. The skipper seized his opportunity, set sail, and put out to sea, the wind favouring him. Candide, dismayed and stupefied, soon lost sight of the vessel.

"Alas!" said he, "this is a trick worthy of the old world!"

He put back, overwhelmed with sorrow, for indeed he had lost sufficient to make the fortune of twenty monarchs. He waited upon the Dutch magistrate, and in his distress he knocked over loudly at the door. He entered and told his adventure, raising his voice with unnecessary vehemence. The magistrate began by fining him ten thousand piastres for making a noise; then he listened patiently, promised to examine into his affair at the skipper's return, and ordered him to pay ten thousand piastres for the expense of the hearing.

This drove Candide to despair; he had, indeed, endured misfortunes a thousand times worse; the coolness of the magistrate and of the skipper who had robbed him, roused his choler and flung him into a deep melancholy. The villainy of mankind presented itself before his imagination in all its deformity, and his mind was filled with gloomy ideas. At length hearing that a French vessel was ready to set sail for Bordeaux, as he had no sheep laden with diamonds to take along with him he hired a cabin at the usual price. He made it known in the town that he would pay the passage and board and give two thousand piastres to any honest man who would make the voyage with him, upon condition that this man was the most dissatisfied with his state, and the most unfortunate in the whole province.

Such a crowd of candidates presented themselves that a fleet of ships could hardly have held them. Candide being desirous of selecting from among the best, marked out about one-twentieth of them who seemed to be sociable men, and who all pretended to merit his preference. He assembled them at his inn, and gave them a supper on condition that each took an oath to relate his history faithfully, promising to choose him who appeared to be most justly discontented with his state, and to bestow some presents upon the rest.

They sat until four o'clock in the morning. Candide, in listening to all their adventures, was reminded of what the old woman had said to him in their voyage to Buenos Ayres, and of her wager that there was not a person on board the ship but had met with very great misfortunes. He dreamed of Pangloss at every adventure told to him.

"This Pangloss," said he, "would be puzzled to demonstrate his system. I wish that he were here. Certainly, if all things are good, it is in El Dorado and not in the rest of the world."

At length he made choice of a poor man of letters, who had worked ten years for the booksellers of Amsterdam. He judged that there was not in the whole world a trade which could disgust one more.

This philosopher was an honest man; but he had been robbed by his wife, beaten by his son, and abandoned by his daughter who got a Portuguese to run away with her. He had just been deprived of a small employment, on which he subsisted; and he was persecuted by the preachers of Surinam, who took him for a Socinian. We must allow that the others were at least as wretched as he; but Candide hoped that the philosopher would entertain him during the voyage. All the other candidates complained that Candide had done them great injustice; but he appeased them by giving one hundred piastres to each.

# What Happened at Sea to Candide and Martin.

The old philosopher, whose name was Martin, embarked then with Candide for Bordeaux. They had both seen and suffered a great deal; and if the vessel had sailed from Surinam to Japan, by the Cape of Good Hope, the subject of moral and natural evil would have enabled them to entertain one another during the whole voyage.

Candide, however, had one great advantage over Martin, in that he always hoped to see Miss Cunegonde; whereas Martin had nothing at all to hope. Besides, Candide was possessed of money and jewels, and though he had lost one hundred large red sheep, laden with the greatest treasure upon earth; though the knavery of the Dutch skipper still sat heavy upon his mind; yet when he reflected upon what he had still left, and when he mentioned the name of Cunegonde, especially towards the latter end of a repast, he inclined to Pangloss's doctrine.

"But you, Mr. Martin," said he to the philosopher, "what do you think of all this? what are your ideas on moral and natural evil?"

"Sir," answered Martin, "our priests accused me of being a Socinian, but the real fact is I am a Manichean."[21]

"You jest," said Candide; "there are no longer Manicheans in the world."

"I am one," said Martin. "I cannot help it; I know not how to think otherwise."

"Surely you must be possessed by the devil," said Candide.

"He is so deeply concerned in the affairs of this world," answered Martin, "that he may very well be in me, as well as in everybody else; but I own to you that when I cast an eye on this globe, or rather on this little ball, I cannot help thinking that God has abandoned it to some malignant being. I except, always, El Dorado. I scarcely ever knew a city that did not desire the destruction of a neighbouring city, nor a family that did not wish to exterminate some other family. Everywhere the weak execrate the powerful, before whom they cringe; and the powerful beat them like sheep whose wool and flesh they sell. A million regimented assassins, from one extremity of Europe to the other, get their bread by disciplined depredation and murder, for want of more honest employment. Even in those cities which seem to enjoy peace, and where the arts flourish, the inhabitants are devoured by more envy, care, and uneasiness than are experienced by a besieged town. Secret griefs are more cruel than public calamities. In a word I have seen so much, and experienced so much that I am a Manichean."

"There are, however, some things good," said Candide.

"That may be," said Martin; "but I know them not."

In the middle of this dispute they heard the report of cannon; it redoubled every instant. Each took out his glass. They saw two ships in close fight about three miles off. The wind brought both so near to the French vessel that our travellers had the pleasure of seeing the fight at their ease. At length one let off a broadside, so low and so truly aimed, that the other sank to the bottom. Candide and Martin could plainly perceive a hundred men on the deck of the sinking vessel; they raised their hands to heaven and uttered terrible outcries, and the next moment were swallowed up by the sea.

"Well," said Martin, "this is how men treat one another."

"It is true," said Candide; "there is something diabolical in this affair."

While speaking, he saw he knew not what, of a shining red, swimming close to the vessel. They put out the long-boat to see what it could be: it was one of his sheep! Candide was more rejoiced at the recovery of this one sheep than he had been grieved at the loss of the hundred laden with the large diamonds of El Dorado.

The French captain soon saw that the captain of the victorious vessel was a Spaniard, and that the other was a Dutch pirate, and the very same one who had robbed Candide. The immense plunder which this villain had amassed, was buried with him in the sea, and out of the whole only one sheep was saved.

"You see," said Candide to Martin, "that crime is sometimes punished. This rogue of a Dutch skipper has met with the fate he deserved."

"Yes," said Martin; "but why should the passengers be doomed also to destruction? God has punished the knave, and the devil has drowned the rest."

The French and Spanish ships continued their course, and Candide continued his conversation with Martin. They disputed fifteen successive days, and on the last of those fifteen days, they were as far advanced as on the first. But, however, they chatted, they communicated ideas, they consoled each other. Candide caressed his sheep.

"Since I have found thee again," said he, "I may likewise chance to find my Cunegonde."

## Candide and Martin, Reasoning, Draw near the Coast of France.

At length they descried the coast of France.

"Were you ever in France, Mr. Martin?" said Candide.

"Yes," said Martin, "I have been in several provinces. In some one-half of the people are fools, in others they are too cunning; in some they are weak and simple, in others they affect to be witty; in all, the principal occupation is love, the next is slander, and the third is talking nonsense."

"But, Mr. Martin, have you seen Paris?"

"Yes, I have. All these kinds are found there. It is a chaos—a confused multitude, where everybody seeks pleasure and scarcely any one finds it, at least as it appeared to me. I made a short stay there. On my arrival I was robbed of all I had by pickpockets at the fair of St. Germain. I myself was taken for a robber and was imprisoned for eight days, after which I served as corrector of the press to gain the money necessary for my return to Holland on foot. I knew the whole scribbling rabble, the party rabble, the fanatic rabble. It is said that there are very polite people in that city, and I wish to believe it."

"For my part, I have no curiosity to see France," said Candide. "You may easily imagine that after spending a month at El Dorado I can desire to behold nothing upon earth but Miss Cunegonde. I go to await her at Venice. We shall pass through France on our way to Italy. Will you bear me company?"

"With all my heart," said Martin. "It is said that Venice is fit only for its own nobility, but that strangers meet with a very good reception if they have a good deal of money. I have none of it; you have, therefore I will follow you all over the world."

"But do you believe," said Candide, "that the earth was originally a sea, as we find it asserted in that large book belonging to the captain?"

"I do not believe a word of it," said Martin, "any more than I do of the many ravings which have been published lately."

"But for what end, then, has this world been formed?" said Candide.

"To plague us to death," answered Martin.

"Are you not greatly surprised," continued Candide, "at the love which these two girls of the Oreillons had for those monkeys, of which I have already told you?"

"Not at all," said Martin. "I do not see that that passion was strange. I have seen so many extraordinary things that I have ceased to be surprised."

"Do you believe," said Candide, "that men have always massacred each other as they do to-day, that they have always been liars, cheats, traitors, ingrates, brigands, idiots, thieves, scoundrels, gluttons, drunkards, misers, envious, ambitious, bloody-minded, calumniators, debauchees, fanatics, hypocrites, and fools?"

"Do you believe," said Martin, "that hawks have always eaten pigeons when they have found them?"

"Yes, without doubt," said Candide.

"Well, then," said Martin, "if hawks have always had the same character why should you imagine that men may have changed theirs?"

"Oh!" said Candide, "there is a vast deal of difference, for free will—"

And reasoning thus they arrived at Bordeaux.

# What Happened in France to Candide and Martin.

Candide stayed in Bordeaux no longer than was necessary for the selling of a few of the pebbles of El Dorado, and for hiring a good chaise to hold two passengers; for he could not travel without his Philosopher Martin. He was only vexed at parting with his sheep, which he left to the Bordeaux Academy of Sciences, who set as a subject for that year's prize, "to find why this sheep's wool was red;" and the prize was awarded to a learned man of the North, who demonstrated by A plus B minus C divided by Z, that the sheep must be red, and die of the rot.

Meanwhile, all the travellers whom Candide met in the inns along his route, said to him, "We go to Paris." This general eagerness at length gave him, too, a desire to see this capital; and it was not so very great a détour from the road to Venice.

He entered Paris by the suburb of St. Marceau, and fancied that he was in the dirtiest village of Westphalia.

Scarcely was Candide arrived at his inn, than he found himself attacked by a slight illness, caused by fatigue. As he had a very large diamond on his finger, and the people of the inn had taken notice of a prodigiously heavy box among his baggage, there were two physicians to attend him, though he had never sent for them, and two devotees who warmed his broths.

"I remember," Martin said, "also to have been sick at Paris in my first voyage; I was very poor, thus I had neither friends, devotees, nor doctors, and I recovered."

However, what with physic and bleeding, Candide's illness became serious. A parson of the neighborhood came with great meekness to ask for a bill for the other world payable to the bearer. Candide would do nothing for him; but the devotees assured him it was the new fashion. He answered that he was not a man of fashion. Martin wished to throw the priest out of the window. The priest swore that they would not bury Candide. Martin swore that he would bury the priest if he continued to be troublesome. The quarrel grew heated. Martin took him by the shoulders and roughly turned him out of doors; which occasioned great scandal and a law-suit.

Candide got well again, and during his convalescence he had very good company to sup with him. They played high. Candide wondered why it was that the ace never came to him; but Martin was not at all astonished.

Among those who did him the honours of the town was a little Abbé of Perigord, one of those busybodies who are ever alert, officious, forward, fawning, and complaisant; who watch for strangers in their passage through the capital, tell them the scandalous history of the town, and offer them pleasure at all prices. He first took Candide and Martin to La Comédie, where they played a new tragedy. Candide happened to be seated near some of the fashionable wits. This did not prevent his shedding tears at the well-acted scenes. One of these critics at his side said to him between the acts:

"Your tears are misplaced; that is a shocking actress; the actor who plays with her is yet worse; and the play is still worse than the actors. The author does not know a word of Arabic, yet the scene is in Arabia; moreover he is a man that does not believe in innate ideas; and I will bring you, to-morrow, twenty pamphlets written against him."[22]

"How many dramas have you in France, sir?" said Candide to the Abbé.

"Five or six thousand."

"What a number!" said Candide. "How many good?"

"Fifteen or sixteen," replied the other.

"What a number!" said Martin.

Candide was very pleased with an actress who played Queen Elizabeth in a somewhat insipid tragedy[23] sometimes acted.

"That actress," said he to Martin, "pleases me much; she has a likeness to Miss Cunegonde; I should be very glad to wait upon her."

The Perigordian Abbé offered to introduce him. Candide, brought up in Germany, asked what was the etiquette, and how they treated queens of England in France.

"It is necessary to make distinctions," said the Abbé. "In the provinces one takes them to the inn; in Paris, one respects them when they are beautiful, and throws them on the highway when they are dead."[24]

"Queens on the highway!" said Candide.

"Yes, truly," said Martin, "the Abbé is right. I was in Paris when Miss Monime passed, as the saying is, from this life to the other. She was refused what people call the honours of sepulture—that is to say, of rotting with all the beggars of the neighbourhood in an ugly cemetery; she was interred all alone by her company at the corner of the Rue de Bourgogne, which ought to trouble her much, for she thought nobly."

"That was very uncivil," said Candide.

"What would you have?" said Martin; "these people are made thus. Imagine all contradictions, all possible incompatibilities—you will find them in the government, in the law-courts, in the churches, in the public shows of this droll nation."

"Is it true that they always laugh in Paris?" said Candide.

"Yes," said the Abbé, "but it means nothing, for they complain of everything with great fits of laughter; they even do the most detestable things while laughing."

"Who," said Candide, "is that great pig who spoke so ill of the piece at which I wept, and of the actors who gave me so much pleasure?"

"He is a bad character," answered the Abbé, "who gains his livelihood by saying evil of all plays and of all books. He hates whatever succeeds, as the eunuchs hate those who enjoy; he is one of the serpents of literature who nourish themselves on dirt and spite; he is a folliculaire."

"What is a folliculaire?" said Candide.

"It is," said the Abbé, "a pamphleteer—a Fréron."[25]

Thus Candide, Martin, and the Perigordian conversed on the staircase, while watching every one go out after the performance.

"Although I am eager to see Cunegonde again," said Candide, "I should like to sup with Miss Clairon, for she appears to me admirable."

The Abbé was not the man to approach Miss Clairon, who saw only good company.

"She is engaged for this evening," he said, "but I shall have the honour to take you to the house of a lady of quality, and there you will know Paris as if you had lived in it for years."

Candide, who was naturally curious, let himself be taken to this lady's house, at the end of the Faubourg St. Honoré. The company was occupied in playing faro; a dozen melancholy punters held each in his hand a little pack of cards; a bad record of his misfortunes. Profound silence reigned; pallor was on the faces of the punters, anxiety on that of the banker, and the hostess, sitting near the unpitying banker, noticed with lynx-eyes all the doubled and other increased stakes, as each player dog's-eared his cards; she made them turn down the edges again with severe, but polite attention; she showed no vexation for fear of losing her customers. The lady insisted upon being called the Marchioness of Parolignac. Her daughter, aged fifteen, was among the punters, and notified with a covert glance the cheatings of the poor people who tried to repair the cruelties of fate. The Perigordian Abbé, Candide and Martin entered; no one rose, no one saluted them, no one looked at them; all were profoundly occupied with their cards.

"The Baroness of Thunder-ten-Tronckh was more polite," said Candide.

However, the Abbé whispered to the Marchioness, who half rose, honoured Candide with a gracious smile, and Martin with a condescending nod; she gave a seat and a pack of cards to Candide, who lost fifty thousand francs in two deals, after which they supped very gaily, and every one was astonished that Candide was not moved by his loss; the servants said among themselves, in the language of servants:—

"Some English lord is here this evening."

The supper passed at first like most Parisian suppers, in silence, followed by a noise of words which could not be distinguished, then with pleasantries of which most were insipid, with false news, with bad reasoning, a little politics, and much evil speaking; they also discussed new books.

"Have you seen," said the Perigordian Abbé, "the romance of Sieur Gauchat, doctor of divinity?"[26]

"Yes," answered one of the guests, "but I have not been able to finish it. We have a crowd of silly writings, but all together do not approach the impertinence of 'Gauchat, Doctor of Divinity.' I am so satiated with the great number of detestable books with which we are inundated that I am reduced to punting at faro."

"And the Mélanges of Archdeacon Trublet,[27] what do you say of that?" said the Abbé.

"Ah!" said the Marchioness of Parolignac, "the wearisome mortal! How curiously he repeats to you all that the world knows! How heavily he discusses that which is not worth the trouble of lightly remarking upon! How, without wit, he appropriates the wit of others! How he spoils what he steals! How he disgusts me! But he will disgust me no longer—it is enough to have read a few of the Archdeacon's pages."

There was at table a wise man of taste, who supported the Marchioness. They spoke afterwards of tragedies; the lady asked why there were tragedies which were sometimes played and which could not be read. The man of taste explained very well how a piece could have some interest, and have almost no merit; he proved in few words that it was not enough to introduce one or two of those situations which one finds in all romances, and which always seduce the spectator, but that it was necessary to be new without being odd, often sublime and always natural, to know the human heart and to make it speak; to be a great poet without allowing any person in the piece to appear to be a poet; to know language perfectly—to speak it with purity, with continuous harmony and without rhythm ever taking anything from sense.

"Whoever," added he, "does not observe all these rules can produce one or two tragedies, applauded at a theatre, but he will never be counted in the ranks of good writers. There are very few good tragedies; some are idylls in dialogue, well written and well rhymed, others political reasonings which lull to sleep, or amplifications which repel; others demoniac dreams in barbarous style, interrupted in sequence, with long apostrophes to the gods, because they do not know how to speak to men, with false maxims, with bombastic commonplaces!"

Candide listened with attention to this discourse, and conceived a great idea of the speaker, and as the Marchioness had taken care to place him beside her, he leaned towards her and took the liberty of asking who was the man who had spoken so well.

"He is a scholar," said the lady, "who does not play, whom the Abbé sometimes brings to supper; he is perfectly at home among tragedies and books, and he has written a tragedy which was hissed, and a book of which nothing has ever been seen outside his bookseller's shop excepting the copy which he dedicated to me."

"The great man!" said Candide. "He is another Pangloss!"

Then, turning towards him, he said:

"Sir, you think doubtless that all is for the best in the moral and physical world, and that nothing could be otherwise than it is?"

"I, sir!" answered the scholar, "I know nothing of all that; I find that all goes awry with me; that no one knows either what is his rank, nor what is his condition, what he does nor what he ought to do; and that except supper, which is always gay, and where there appears to be enough concord, all the rest of the time is passed in impertinent quarrels; Jansenist against Molinist, Parliament against the Church, men of letters against men of letters, courtesans against courtesans, financiers against the people, wives against husbands, relatives against relatives—it is eternal war."

"I have seen the worst," Candide replied. "But a wise man, who since has had the misfortune to be hanged, taught me that all is marvellously well; these are but the shadows on a beautiful picture."

"Your hanged man mocked the world," said Martin. "The shadows are horrible blots."

"They are men who make the blots," said Candide, "and they cannot be dispensed with."

"It is not their fault then," said Martin.

Most of the punters, who understood nothing of this language, drank, and Martin reasoned with the scholar, and Candide related some of his adventures to his hostess.

After supper the Marchioness took Candide into her boudoir, and made him sit upon a sofa.

"Ah, well!" said she to him, "you love desperately Miss Cunegonde of Thunder-ten-Tronckh?"

"Yes, madame," answered Candide.

The Marchioness replied to him with a tender smile:

"You answer me like a young man from Westphalia. A Frenchman would have said, 'It is true that I have loved Miss Cunegonde, but seeing you, madame, I think I no longer love her.'"

"Alas! madame," said Candide, "I will answer you as you wish."

"Your passion for her," said the Marchioness, "commenced by picking up her handkerchief. I wish that you would pick up my garter."

"With all my heart," said Candide. And he picked it up.

"But I wish that you would put it on," said the lady.

And Candide put it on.

"You see," said she, "you are a foreigner. I sometimes make my Parisian lovers languish for fifteen days, but I give myself to you the first night because one must do the honours of one's country to a young man from Westphalia."

The lady having perceived two enormous diamonds upon the hands of the young foreigner praised them with such good faith that from Candide's fingers they passed to her own.

Candide, returning with the Perigordian Abbé, felt some remorse in having been unfaithful to Miss Cunegonde. The Abbé sympathised in his trouble; he had had but a light part of the fifty thousand francs lost at play and of the value of the two brilliants, half given, half extorted. His design was to profit as much as he could by the advantages which the acquaintance of Candide could procure for him. He spoke much of Cunegonde, and Candide told him that he should ask forgiveness of that beautiful one for his infidelity when he should see her in Venice.

The Abbé redoubled his politeness and attentions, and took a tender interest in all that Candide said, in all that he did, in all that he wished to do.

"And so, sir, you have a rendezvous at Venice?"

"Yes, monsieur Abbé," answered Candide. "It is absolutely necessary that I go to meet Miss Cunegonde."

And then the pleasure of talking of that which he loved induced him to relate, according to his custom, part of his adventures with the fair Westphalian.

"I believe," said the Abbé, "that Miss Cunegonde has a great deal of wit, and that she writes charming letters?"

"I have never received any from her," said Candide, "for being expelled from the castle on her account I had not an opportunity for writing to her. Soon after that I heard she was dead; then I found her alive; then I lost her again; and last of all, I sent an express to her two thousand five hundred leagues from here, and I wait for an answer."

The Abbé listened attentively, and seemed to be in a brown study. He soon took his leave of the two foreigners after a most tender embrace. The following day Candide received, on awaking, a letter couched in these terms:

"My very dear love, for eight days I have been ill in this town. I learn that you are here. I would fly to your arms if I could but move. I was informed of your passage at Bordeaux, where I left faithful Cacambo and the old woman, who are to follow me very soon. The Governor of Buenos Ayres has taken all, but there remains to me your heart. Come! your presence will either give me life or kill me with pleasure."

This charming, this unhoped-for letter transported Candide with an inexpressible joy, and the illness of his dear Cunegonde overwhelmed him with grief. Divided between those two passions, he took his gold and his diamonds and hurried away, with Martin, to the hotel where Miss Cunegonde was lodged. He entered her room trembling, his heart palpitating, his voice sobbing; he wished to open the curtains of the bed, and asked for a light.

"Take care what you do," said the servant-maid; "the light hurts her," and immediately she drew the curtain again.

"My dear Cunegonde," said Candide, weeping, "how are you? If you cannot see me, at least speak to me."

"She cannot speak," said the maid.

The lady then put a plump hand out from the bed, and Candide bathed it with his tears and afterwards filled it with diamonds, leaving a bag of gold upon the easy chair.

In the midst of these transports in came an officer, followed by the Abbé and a file of soldiers.

"There," said he, "are the two suspected foreigners," and at the same time he ordered them to be seized and carried to prison.

"Travellers are not treated thus in El Dorado," said Candide.

"I am more a Manichean now than ever," said Martin.

"But pray, sir, where are you going to carry us?" said Candide.

"To a dungeon," answered the officer.

Martin, having recovered himself a little, judged that the lady who acted the part of Cunegonde was a cheat, that the Perigordian Abbé was a knave who had imposed upon the honest simplicity of Candide, and that the officer was another knave whom they might easily silence.

Candide, advised by Martin and impatient to see the real Cunegonde, rather than expose himself before a court of justice, proposed to the officer to give him three small diamonds, each worth about three thousand pistoles.

"Ah, sir," said the man with the ivory baton, "had you committed all the imaginable crimes you would be to me the most honest man in the world. Three diamonds! Each worth three thousand pistoles! Sir, instead of carrying you to jail I would lose my life to serve you. There are orders for arresting all foreigners, but leave it to me. I have a brother at Dieppe in Normandy! I'll conduct you thither, and if you have a diamond to give him he'll take as much care of you as I would."

"And why," said Candide, "should all foreigners be arrested?"

"It is," the Perigordian Abbé then made answer, "because a poor beggar of the country of Atrébatie[28] heard some foolish things said. This induced him to commit a parricide, not such as that of 1610 in the month of May,[29] but such as that of 1594 in the month of December,[30] and such as others which have been committed in other years and other months by other poor devils who had heard nonsense spoken."

The officer then explained what the Abbé meant.

"Ah, the monsters!" cried Candide. "What horrors among a people who dance and sing! Is there no way of getting quickly out of this country where monkeys provoke tigers? I have seen no bears in my country, but men I have beheld nowhere except in El Dorado. In the name of God, sir, conduct me to Venice, where I am to await Miss Cunegonde."

"I can conduct you no further than lower Normandy," said the officer.

Immediately he ordered his irons to be struck off, acknowledged himself mistaken, sent away his men, set out with Candide and Martin for Dieppe, and left them in the care of his brother.

There was then a small Dutch ship in the harbour. The Norman, who by the virtue of three more diamonds had become the most subservient of men, put Candide and his attendants on board a vessel that was just ready to set sail for Portsmouth in England.

This was not the way to Venice, but Candide thought he had made his way out of hell, and reckoned that he would soon have an opportunity for resuming his journey.

## Candide and Martin Touched upon the Coast of England, and What They Saw There.

"Ah, Pangloss! Pangloss! Ah, Martin! Martin! Ah, my dear Cunegonde, what sort of a world is this?" said Candide on board the Dutch ship.

"Something very foolish and abominable," said Martin.

"You know England? Are they as foolish there as in France?"

"It is another kind of folly," said Martin. "You know that these two nations are at war for a few acres of snow in Canada,[31] and that they spend over this beautiful war much more than Canada is worth. To tell you exactly, whether there are more people fit to send to a madhouse in one country than the other, is what my imperfect intelligence will not permit. I only know in general that the people we are going to see are very atrabilious."

Talking thus they arrived at Portsmouth. The coast was lined with crowds of people, whose eyes were fixed on a fine man kneeling, with his eyes bandaged, on board one of the men of war in the harbour. Four soldiers stood opposite to this man; each of them fired three balls at his head, with all the calmness in the world; and the whole assembly went away very well satisfied.

"What is all this?" said Candide; "and what demon is it that exercises his empire in this country?"

He then asked who was that fine man who had been killed with so much ceremony. They answered, he was an Admiral.[32]

"And why kill this Admiral?"

"It is because he did not kill a sufficient number of men himself. He gave battle to a French Admiral; and it has been proved that he was not near enough to him."

"But," replied Candide, "the French Admiral was as far from the English Admiral."

"There is no doubt of it; but in this country it is found good, from time to time, to kill one Admiral to encourage the others."

Candide was so shocked and bewildered by what he saw and heard, that he would not set foot on shore, and he made a bargain with the Dutch skipper (were he even to rob him like the Surinam captain) to conduct him without delay to Venice.

The skipper was ready in two days. They coasted France; they passed in sight of Lisbon, and Candide trembled. They passed through the Straits, and entered the Mediterranean. At last they landed at Venice.

"God be praised!" said Candide, embracing Martin. "It is here that I shall see again my beautiful Cunegonde. I trust Cacambo as myself. All is well, all will be well, all goes as well as possible."

## Of Paquette and Friar Giroflée.

Upon their arrival at Venice, Candide went to search for Cacambo at every inn and coffee-house, and among all the ladies of pleasure, but to no purpose. He sent every day to inquire on all the ships that came in. But there was no news of Cacambo.

"What!" said he to Martin, "I have had time to voyage from Surinam to Bordeaux, to go from Bordeaux to Paris, from Paris to Dieppe, from Dieppe to Portsmouth, to coast along Portugal and Spain, to cross the whole Mediterranean, to spend some months, and yet the beautiful Cunegonde has not arrived! Instead of her I have only met a Parisian wench and a Perigordian Abbé. Cunegonde is dead without doubt, and there is nothing for me but to die. Alas! how much better it would have been for me to have remained in the paradise of El Dorado than to come back to this cursed Europe! You are in the right, my dear Martin: all is misery and illusion."

He fell into a deep melancholy, and neither went to see the opera, nor any of the other diversions of the Carnival; nay, he was proof against the temptations of all the ladies.

"You are in truth very simple," said Martin to him, "if you imagine that a mongrel valet, who has five or six millions in his pocket, will go to the other end of the world to seek your mistress and bring her to you to Venice. If he find her, he will keep her to himself; if he do not find her he will get another. I advise you to forget your valet Cacambo and your mistress Cunegonde."

Martin was not consoling. Candide's melancholy increased; and Martin continued to prove to him that there was very little virtue or happiness upon earth, except perhaps in El Dorado, where nobody could gain admittance.

While they were disputing on this important subject and waiting for Cunegonde, Candide saw a young Theatin friar in St. Mark's Piazza, holding a girl on his arm. The Theatin looked fresh coloured, plump, and vigorous; his eyes were sparkling, his air assured, his look lofty, and his step bold. The girl was very pretty, and sang; she looked amorously at her Theatin, and from time to time pinched his fat cheeks.

"At least you will allow me," said Candide to Martin, "that these two are happy. Hitherto I have met with none but unfortunate people in the whole habitable globe, except in El Dorado; but as to this pair, I would venture to lay a wager that they are very happy."

"I lay you they are not," said Martin.

"We need only ask them to dine with us," said Candide, "and you will see whether I am mistaken."

Immediately he accosted them, presented his compliments, and invited them to his inn to eat some macaroni, with Lombard partridges, and caviare, and to drink some Montepulciano, Lachrymæ Christi, Cyprus and Samos wine. The girl blushed, the Theatin accepted the invitation and she followed him, casting her eyes on Candide with confusion and surprise, and dropping a few tears. No sooner had she set foot in Candide's apartment than she cried out:

"Ah! Mr. Candide does not know Paquette again."

Candide had not viewed her as yet with attention, his thoughts being entirely taken up with Cunegonde; but recollecting her as she spoke.

"Alas!" said he, "my poor child, it is you who reduced Doctor Pangloss to the beautiful condition in which I saw him?"

"Alas! it was I, sir, indeed," answered Paquette. "I see that you have heard all. I have been informed of the frightful disasters that befell the family of my lady Baroness, and the fair Cunegonde. I swear to you that my fate has been scarcely less sad. I was very innocent when you knew me. A Grey Friar, who was my confessor, easily seduced me. The consequences were terrible. I was obliged to quit the castle some time after the Baron had sent you away with kicks on the backside. If a famous surgeon had not taken compassion on me, I should have died. For some time I was this surgeon's mistress, merely out of gratitude. His wife, who was mad with jealousy, beat me every day unmercifully; she was a fury. The surgeon was one of the ugliest of men, and I the most wretched of women, to be continually beaten for a man I did not love. You know, sir, what a dangerous thing it is for an ill-natured woman to be married to a doctor. Incensed at the behaviour of his wife, he one day gave her so effectual a remedy to cure her of a slight cold, that she died two hours after, in most horrid convulsions. The wife's relations prosecuted the husband; he took flight, and I was thrown into jail. My innocence would not have saved me if I had not been good-looking. The judge set me free, on condition that he succeeded the surgeon. I was soon supplanted by a rival, turned out of doors quite destitute, and obliged to continue this abominable trade, which appears so pleasant to you men, while to us women it is the utmost abyss of misery. I have come to exercise the profession at Venice. Ah! sir, if you could only imagine what it is to be obliged to caress indifferently an old merchant, a lawyer, a monk, a gondolier, an abbé, to be exposed to abuse and insults; to be often reduced to borrowing a petticoat, only to go and have it raised by a disagreeable man; to be robbed by one of what one has earned from another; to be subject to the extortions of the officers of justice; and to have in prospect only a frightful old age, a hospital, and a dung-hill; you would conclude that I am one of the most unhappy creatures in the world."[33]

Paquette thus opened her heart to honest Candide, in the presence of Martin, who said to his friend:

"You see that already I have won half the wager."

Friar Giroflée stayed in the dining-room, and drank a glass or two of wine while he was waiting for dinner.

"But," said Candide to Paquette, "you looked so gay and content when I met you; you sang and you behaved so lovingly to the Theatin, that you seemed to me as happy as you pretend to be now the reverse."

"Ah! sir," answered Paquette, "this is one of the miseries of the trade. Yesterday I was robbed and beaten by an officer; yet to-day I must put on good humour to please a friar."

Candide wanted no more convincing; he owned that Martin was in the right. They sat down to table with Paquette and the Theatin; the repast was entertaining; and towards the end they conversed with all confidence.

"Father," said Candide to the Friar, "you appear to me to enjoy a state that all the world might envy; the flower of health shines in your face, your expression makes plain your happiness; you have a very pretty girl for your recreation, and you seem well satisfied with your state as a Theatin."

"My faith, sir," said Friar Giroflée, "I wish that all the Theatins were at the bottom of the sea. I have been tempted a hundred times to set fire to the convent, and go and become a Turk. My parents forced me at the age of fifteen to put on this detestable habit, to increase the fortune of a cursed elder brother, whom God confound. Jealousy, discord, and fury, dwell in the convent. It is true I have preached a few bad sermons that have brought me in a little money, of which the prior stole half, while the rest serves to maintain my girls; but when I return at night to the monastery, I am ready to dash my head against the walls of the dormitory; and all my fellows are in the same case."

Martin turned towards Candide with his usual coolness.

"Well," said he, "have I not won the whole wager?"

Candide gave two thousand piastres to Paquette, and one thousand to Friar Giroflée.

"I'll answer for it," said he, "that with this they will be happy."

"I do not believe it at all," said Martin; "you will, perhaps, with these piastres only render them the more unhappy."

"Let that be as it may," said Candide, "but one thing consoles me. I see that we often meet with those whom we expected never to see more; so that, perhaps, as I have found my red sheep and Paquette, it may well be that I shall also find Cunegonde."

"I wish," said Martin, "she may one day make you very happy; but I doubt it very much."

"You are very hard of belief," said Candide.

"I have lived," said Martin.

"You see those gondoliers," said Candide, "are they not perpetually singing?"

"You do not see them," said Martin, "at home with their wives and brats. The Doge has his troubles, the gondoliers have theirs. It is true that, all things considered, the life of a gondolier is preferable to that of a Doge; but I believe the difference to be so trifling that it is not worth the trouble of examining."

"People talk," said Candide, "of the Senator Pococurante, who lives in that fine palace on the Brenta, where he entertains foreigners in the politest manner. They pretend that this man has never felt any uneasiness."

"I should be glad to see such a rarity," said Martin.

Candide immediately sent to ask the Lord Pococurante permission to wait upon him the next day.

# The Visit to Lord Pococurante, a Noble Venetian.

Candide and Martin went in a gondola on the Brenta, and arrived at the palace of the noble Signor Pococurante. The gardens, laid out with taste, were adorned with fine marble statues. The palace was beautifully built. The master of the house was a man of sixty, and very rich. He received the two travellers with polite indifference, which put Candide a little out of countenance, but was not at all disagreeable to Martin.

First, two pretty girls, very neatly dressed, served them with chocolate, which was frothed exceedingly well. Candide could not refrain from commending their beauty, grace, and address.

"They are good enough creatures," said the Senator. "I make them lie with me sometimes, for I am very tired of the ladies of the town, of their coquetries, of their jealousies, of their quarrels, of their humours, of their pettinesses, of their prides, of their follies, and of the sonnets which one must make, or have made, for them. But after all, these two girls begin to weary me."

After breakfast, Candide walking into a long gallery was surprised by the beautiful pictures. He asked, by what master were the two first.

"They are by Raphael," said the Senator. "I bought them at a great price, out of vanity, some years ago. They are said to be the finest things in Italy, but they do not please me at all. The colours are too dark, the figures are not sufficiently rounded, nor in good relief; the draperies in no way resemble stuffs. In a word, whatever may be said, I do not find there a true imitation of nature. I only care for a picture when I think I see nature itself; and there are none of this sort. I have a great many pictures, but I prize them very little."

While they were waiting for dinner Pococurante ordered a concert. Candide found the music delicious.

"This noise," said the Senator, "may amuse one for half an hour; but if it were to last longer it would grow tiresome to everybody, though they durst not own it. Music, to-day, is only the art of executing difficult things, and that which is only difficult cannot please long. Perhaps I should be fonder of the opera if they had not found the secret of making of it a monster which shocks me. Let who will go to see bad tragedies set to music, where the scenes are contrived for no other end than to introduce two or three songs ridiculously out of place, to show off an actress's voice. Let who will, or who can, die away with pleasure at the sight of an eunuch quavering the rôle of Cæsar, or of Cato, and strutting awkwardly upon the stage. For my part I have long since renounced those paltry entertainments which constitute the glory of modern Italy, and are purchased so dearly by sovereigns."

Candide disputed the point a little, but with discretion. Martin was entirely of the Senator's opinion.

They sat down to table, and after an excellent dinner they went into the library. Candide, seeing a Homer magnificently bound, commended the virtuoso on his good taste.

"There," said he, "is a book that was once the delight of the great Pangloss, the best philosopher in Germany."

"It is not mine," answered Pococurante coolly. "They used at one time to make me believe that I took a pleasure in reading him. But that continual repetition of battles, so extremely like one another; those gods that are always active without doing anything decisive; that Helen who is the cause of the war, and who yet scarcely appears in the piece; that Troy, so long besieged without being taken; all these together caused me great weariness. I have sometimes asked learned men whether they were not as weary as I of that work. Those who were sincere have owned to me that the poem made them fall asleep; yet it was necessary to have it in their library as a monument of antiquity, or like those rusty medals which are no longer of use in commerce."

"But your Excellency does not think thus of Virgil?" said Candide.

"I grant," said the Senator, "that the second, fourth, and sixth books of his Æneid are excellent, but as for his pious Æneas, his strong Cloanthus, his friend Achates, his little Ascanius, his silly King Latinus, his bourgeois Amata, his insipid Lavinia, I think there can be nothing more flat and disagreeable. I prefer Tasso a good deal, or even the soporific tales of Ariosto."

"May I presume to ask you, sir," said Candide, "whether you do not receive a great deal of pleasure from reading Horace?"

"There are maxims in this writer," answered Pococurante, "from which a man of the world may reap great benefit, and being written in energetic verse they are more easily impressed upon the memory. But I care little for his journey to Brundusium, and his account of a bad dinner, or of his low quarrel between one Rupilius whose words he says were full of poisonous filth, and another whose language was imbued with vinegar. I have read with much distaste his indelicate verses against old women and witches; nor do I see any merit in telling his friend Mæcenas that if he will but rank him in the choir of lyric poets, his lofty head shall touch the stars. Fools admire everything in an author of reputation. For my part, I read only to please myself. I like only that which serves my purpose."

Candide, having been educated never to judge for himself, was much surprised at what he heard. Martin found there was a good deal of reason in Pococurante's remarks.

"Oh! here is Cicero," said Candide. "Here is the great man whom I fancy you are never tired of reading."

"I never read him," replied the Venetian. "What is it to me whether he pleads for Rabirius or Cluentius? I try causes enough myself; his philosophical works seem to me better, but when I found that he doubted of everything, I concluded that I knew as much as he, and that I had no need of a guide to learn ignorance."

"Ha! here are four-score volumes of the Academy of Sciences," cried Martin. "Perhaps there is something valuable in this collection."

"There might be," said Pococurante, "if only one of those rakers of rubbish had shown how to make pins; but in all these volumes there is nothing but chimerical systems, and not a single useful thing."

"And what dramatic works I see here," said Candide, "in Italian, Spanish, and French."

"Yes," replied the Senator, "there are three thousand, and not three dozen of them good for anything. As to those collections of sermons, which altogether are not worth a single page of Seneca, and those huge volumes of theology, you may well imagine that neither I nor any one else ever opens them."

Martin saw some shelves filled with English books.

"I have a notion," said he, "that a Republican must be greatly pleased with most of these books, which are written with a spirit of freedom."

"Yes," answered Pococurante, "it is noble to write as one thinks; this is the privilege of humanity. In all our Italy we write only what we do not think; those who inhabit the country of the Cæsars and the Antoninuses dare not acquire a single idea without the permission of a Dominican friar. I should be pleased with the liberty which inspires the English genius if passion and party spirit did not corrupt all that is estimable in this precious liberty."

Candide, observing a Milton, asked whether he did not look upon this author as a great man.

"Who?" said Pococurante, "that barbarian, who writes a long commentary in ten books of harsh verse on the first chapter of Genesis; that coarse imitator of the Greeks, who disfigures the Creation, and who, while Moses represents the Eternal producing the world by a word, makes the Messiah take a great pair of compasses from the armoury of heaven to circumscribe His work? How can I have any esteem for a writer who has spoiled Tasso's hell and the devil, who transforms Lucifer sometimes into a toad and other times into a pigmy, who makes him repeat the same things a hundred times, who makes him dispute on theology, who, by a serious imitation of Ariosto's comic invention of firearms, represents the devils cannonading in heaven? Neither I nor any man in Italy could take pleasure in those melancholy extravagances; and the marriage of Sin and Death, and the snakes brought forth by Sin, are enough to turn the stomach of any one with the least taste, [and his long description of a pest-house is good only for a grave-digger]. This obscure, whimsical, and disagreeable poem was despised upon its first publication, and I only treat it now as it was treated in its own country by contemporaries. For the matter of that I say what I think, and I care very little whether others think as I do."

Candide was grieved at this speech, for he had a respect for Homer and was fond of Milton.

"Alas!" said he softly to Martin, "I am afraid that this man holds our German poets in very great contempt."

"There would not be much harm in that," said Martin.

"Oh! what a superior man," said Candide below his breath. "What a great genius is this Pococurante! Nothing can please him."

After their survey of the library they went down into the garden, where Candide praised its several beauties.

"I know of nothing in so bad a taste," said the master. "All you see here is merely trifling. After to-morrow I will have it planted with a nobler design."

"Well," said Candide to Martin when they had taken their leave, "you will agree that this is the happiest of mortals, for he is above everything he possesses."

"But do you not see," answered Martin, "that he is disgusted with all he possesses? Plato observed a long while ago that those stomachs are not the best that reject all sorts of food."

"But is there not a pleasure," said Candide, "in criticising everything, in pointing out faults where others see nothing but beauties?"

"That is to say," replied Martin, "that there is some pleasure in having no pleasure."

"Well, well," said Candide, "I find that I shall be the only happy man when I am blessed with the sight of my dear Cunegonde."

"It is always well to hope," said Martin.

However, the days and the weeks passed. Cacambo did not come, and Candide was so overwhelmed with grief that he did not even reflect that Paquette and Friar Giroflée did not return to thank him.

# Of a Supper Which Candide and Martin Took with Six Strangers, and Who They Were.[34]

One evening that Candide and Martin were going to sit down to supper with some foreigners who lodged in the same inn, a man whose complexion was as black as soot, came behind Candide, and taking him by the arm, said:

"Get yourself ready to go along with us; do not fail."

Upon this he turned round and saw—Cacambo! Nothing but the sight of Cunegonde could have astonished and delighted him more. He was on the point of going mad with joy. He embraced his dear friend.

"Cunegonde is here, without doubt; where is she? Take me to her that I may die of joy in her company."

"Cunegonde is not here," said Cacambo, "she is at Constantinople."

"Oh, heavens! at Constantinople! But were she in China I would fly thither; let us be off."

"We shall set out after supper," replied Cacambo. "I can tell you nothing more; I am a slave, my master awaits me, I must serve him at table; speak not a word, eat, and then get ready."

Candide, distracted between joy and grief, delighted at seeing his faithful agent again, astonished at finding him a slave, filled with the fresh hope of recovering his mistress, his heart palpitating, his understanding confused, sat down to table with Martin, who saw all these scenes quite unconcerned, and with six strangers who had come to spend the Carnival at Venice.

Cacambo waited at table upon one of the strangers; towards the end of the entertainment he drew near his master, and whispered in his ear:

"Sire, your Majesty may start when you please, the vessel is ready."

On saying these words he went out. The company in great surprise looked at one another without speaking a word, when another domestic approached his master and said to him:

"Sire, your Majesty's chaise is at Padua, and the boat is ready."

The master gave a nod and the servant went away. The company all stared at one another again, and their surprise redoubled. A third valet came up to a third stranger, saying:

"Sire, believe me, your Majesty ought not to stay here any longer. I am going to get everything ready."

And immediately he disappeared. Candide and Martin did not doubt that this was a masquerade of the Carnival. Then a fourth domestic said to a fourth master:

"Your Majesty may depart when you please."

Saying this he went away like the rest. The fifth valet said the same thing to the fifth master. But the sixth valet spoke differently to the sixth stranger, who sat near Candide. He said to him:

"Faith, Sire, they will no longer give credit to your Majesty nor to me, and we may perhaps both of us be put in jail this very night. Therefore I will take care of myself. Adieu."

The servants being all gone, the six strangers, with Candide and Martin, remained in a profound silence. At length Candide broke it.

"Gentlemen," said he, "this is a very good joke indeed, but why should you all be kings? For me I own that neither Martin nor I is a king."

Cacambo's master then gravely answered in Italian:

"I am not at all joking. My name is Achmet III. I was Grand Sultan many years. I dethroned my brother; my nephew dethroned me, my viziers were beheaded, and I am condemned to end my days in the old Seraglio. My nephew, the great Sultan Mahmoud, permits me to travel sometimes for my health, and I am come to spend the Carnival at Venice."

A young man who sat next to Achmet, spoke then as follows:

"My name is Ivan. I was once Emperor of all the Russias, but was dethroned in my cradle. My parents were confined in prison and I was educated there; yet I am sometimes allowed to travel in company with persons who act as guards; and I am come to spend the Carnival at Venice."

The third said:

"I am Charles Edward, King of England; my father has resigned all his legal rights to me. I have fought in defence of them; and above eight hundred of my adherents have been hanged, drawn, and quartered. I have been confined in prison; I am going to Rome, to pay a visit to the King, my father, who was dethroned as well as myself and my grandfather, and I am come to spend the Carnival at Venice."

The fourth spoke thus in his turn:

"I am the King of Poland; the fortune of war has stripped me of my hereditary dominions; my father underwent the same vicissitudes; I resign myself to Providence in the same manner as Sultan Achmet, the Emperor Ivan, and King Charles Edward, whom God long preserve; and I am come to the Carnival at Venice."

The fifth said:

"I am King of Poland also; I have been twice dethroned; but Providence has given me another country, where I have done more good than all the Sarmatian kings were ever capable of doing on the banks of the Vistula; I resign myself likewise to Providence, and am come to pass the Carnival at Venice."

It was now the sixth monarch's turn to speak:

"Gentlemen," said he, "I am not so great a prince as any of you; however, I am a king. I am Theodore, elected King of Corsica; I had the title of Majesty, and now I am scarcely treated as a gentleman. I have coined money, and now am not worth a farthing; I have had two secretaries of state, and now I have scarce a valet; I have seen myself on a throne, and I have seen myself upon straw in a common jail in London. I am afraid that I shall meet with the same treatment here though, like your majesties, I am come to see the Carnival at Venice."

The other five kings listened to this speech with generous compassion. Each of them gave twenty sequins to King Theodore to buy him clothes and linen; and Candide made him a present of a diamond worth two thousand sequins.

"Who can this private person be," said the five kings to one another, "who is able to give, and really has given, a hundred times as much as any of us?"

Just as they rose from table, in came four Serene Highnesses, who had also been stripped of their territories by the fortune of war, and were come to spend the Carnival at Venice. But Candide paid no regard to these newcomers, his thoughts were entirely employed on his voyage to Constantinople, in search of his beloved Cunegonde.

# Candide's Voyage to Constantinople.

The faithful Cacambo had already prevailed upon the Turkish skipper, who was to conduct the Sultan Achmet to Constantinople, to receive Candide and Martin on his ship. They both embarked after having made their obeisance to his miserable Highness.

"You see," said Candide to Martin on the way, "we supped with six dethroned kings, and of those six there was one to whom I gave charity. Perhaps there are many other princes yet more unfortunate. For my part, I have only lost a hundred sheep; and now I am flying into Cunegonde's arms. My dear Martin, yet once more Pangloss was right: all is for the best."

"I wish it," answered Martin.

"But," said Candide, "it was a very strange adventure we met with at Venice. It has never before been seen or heard that six dethroned kings have supped together at a public inn."

"It is not more extraordinary," said Martin, "than most of the things that have happened to us. It is a very common thing for kings to be dethroned; and as for the honour we have had of supping in their company, it is a trifle not worth our attention."

No sooner had Candide got on board the vessel than he flew to his old valet and friend Cacambo, and tenderly embraced him.

"Well," said he, "what news of Cunegonde? Is she still a prodigy of beauty? Does she love me still? How is she? Thou hast doubtless bought her a palace at Constantinople?"

"My dear master," answered Cacambo, "Cunegonde washes dishes on the banks of the Propontis, in the service of a prince, who has very few dishes to wash; she is a slave in the family of an ancient sovereign named Ragotsky,[35] to whom the Grand Turk allows three crowns a day in his exile. But what is worse still is, that she has lost her beauty and has become horribly ugly."

"Well, handsome or ugly," replied Candide, "I am a man of honour, and it is my duty to love her still. But how came she to be reduced to so abject a state with the five or six millions that you took to her?"

"Ah!" said Cacambo, "was I not to give two millions to Senor Don Fernando d'Ibaraa, y Figueora, y Mascarenes, y Lampourdos, y Souza, Governor of Buenos Ayres, for permitting Miss Cunegonde to come away? And did not a corsair bravely rob us of all the rest? Did not this corsair carry us to Cape Matapan, to Milo, to Nicaria, to Samos, to Petra, to the Dardanelles, to Marmora, to Scutari?

Cunegonde and the old woman serve the prince I now mentioned to you, and I am slave to the dethroned Sultan."

"What a series of shocking calamities!" cried Candide. "But after all, I have some diamonds left; and I may easily pay Cunegonde's ransom. Yet it is a pity that she is grown so ugly."

Then, turning towards Martin: "Who do you think," said he, "is most to be pitied—the Sultan Achmet, the Emperor Ivan, King Charles Edward, or I?"

"How should I know!" answered Martin. "I must see into your hearts to be able to tell."

"Ah!" said Candide, "if Pangloss were here, he could tell."

"I know not," said Martin, "in what sort of scales your Pangloss would weigh the misfortunes of mankind and set a just estimate on their sorrows. All that I can presume to say is, that there are millions of people upon earth who have a hundred times more to complain of than King Charles Edward, the Emperor Ivan, or the Sultan Achmet."

"That may well be," said Candide.

In a few days they reached the Bosphorus, and Candide began by paying a very high ransom for Cacambo. Then without losing time, he and his companions went on board a galley, in order to search on the banks of the Propontis for his Cunegonde, however ugly she might have become.

Among the crew there were two slaves who rowed very badly, and to whose bare shoulders the Levantine captain would now and then apply blows from a bull's pizzle. Candide, from a natural impulse, looked at these two slaves more attentively than at the other oarsmen, and approached them with pity. Their features though greatly disfigured, had a slight resemblance to those of Pangloss and the unhappy Jesuit and Westphalian Baron, brother to Miss Cunegonde. This moved and saddened him. He looked at them still more attentively.

"Indeed," said he to Cacambo, "if I had not seen Master Pangloss hanged, and if I had not had the misfortune to kill the Baron, I should think it was they that were rowing."

At the names of the Baron and of Pangloss, the two galley-slaves uttered a loud cry, held fast by the seat, and let drop their oars. The captain ran up to them and redoubled his blows with the bull's pizzle.

"Stop! stop! sir," cried Candide. "I will give you what money you please."

"What! it is Candide!" said one of the slaves.

"What! it is Candide!" said the other.

"Do I dream?" cried Candide; "am I awake? or am I on board a galley? Is this the Baron whom I killed? Is this Master Pangloss whom I saw hanged?"

"It is we! it is we!" answered they.

"Well! is this the great philosopher?" said Martin.

"Ah! captain," said Candide, "what ransom will you take for Monsieur de Thunder-ten-Tronckh, one of the first barons of the empire, and for Monsieur Pangloss, the profoundest metaphysician in Germany?"

"Dog of a Christian," answered the Levantine captain, "since these two dogs of Christian slaves are barons and metaphysicians, which I doubt not are high dignities in their country, you shall give me fifty thousand sequins."

"You shall have them, sir. Carry me back at once to Constantinople, and you shall receive the money directly. But no; carry me first to Miss Cunegonde."

Upon the first proposal made by Candide, however, the Levantine captain had already tacked about, and made the crew ply their oars quicker than a bird cleaves the air.

Candide embraced the Baron and Pangloss a hundred times.

"And how happened it, my dear Baron, that I did not kill you? And, my dear Pangloss, how came you to life again after being hanged? And why are you both in a Turkish galley?"

"And it is true that my dear sister is in this country?" said the Baron.

"Yes," answered Cacambo.

"Then I behold, once more, my dear Candide," cried Pangloss.

Candide presented Martin and Cacambo to them; they embraced each other, and all spoke at once. The galley flew; they were already in the port. Instantly Candide sent for a Jew, to whom he sold for fifty thousand sequins a diamond worth a hundred thousand, though the fellow swore to him by Abraham that he could give him no more. He immediately paid the ransom for the Baron and Pangloss. The latter threw himself at the feet of his deliverer, and bathed them with his tears; the former thanked him with a nod, and promised to return him the money on the first opportunity.

"But is it indeed possible that my sister can be in Turkey?" said he.

"Nothing is more possible," said Cacambo, "since she scours the dishes in the service of a Transylvanian prince."

Candide sent directly for two Jews and sold them some more diamonds, and then they all set out together in another galley to deliver Cunegonde from slavery.

# What Happened to Candide, Cunegonde, Pangloss, Martin, Etc.

"I ask your pardon once more," said Candide to the Baron, "your pardon, reverend father, for having run you through the body."

"Say no more about it," answered the Baron. "I was a little too hasty, I own, but since you wish to know by what fatality I came to be a galley-slave I will inform you. After I had been cured by the surgeon of the college of the wound you gave me, I was attacked and carried off by a party of Spanish troops, who confined me in prison at Buenos Ayres at the very time my sister was setting out thence. I asked leave to return to Rome to the General of my Order. I was appointed chaplain to the French Ambassador at Constantinople. I had not been eight days in this employment when one evening I met with a young Ichoglan, who was a very handsome fellow. The weather was warm. The young man wanted to bathe, and I took this opportunity of bathing also. I did not know that it was a capital crime for a Christian to be found naked with a young Mussulman. A cadi ordered me a hundred blows on the soles of the feet, and condemned me to the galleys. I do not think there ever was a greater act of injustice. But I should be glad to know how my sister came to be scullion to a Transylvanian prince who has taken shelter among the Turks."

"But you, my dear Pangloss," said Candide, "how can it be that I behold you again?"

"It is true," said Pangloss, "that you saw me hanged. I should have been burnt, but you may remember it rained exceedingly hard when they were going to roast me; the storm was so violent that they despaired of lighting the fire, so I was hanged because they could do no better. A surgeon purchased my body, carried me home, and dissected me. He began with making a crucial incision on me from the navel to the clavicula. One could not have been worse hanged than I was. The executioner of the Holy Inquisition was a sub-deacon, and knew how to burn people marvellously well, but he was not accustomed to hanging. The cord was wet and did not slip properly, and besides it was badly tied; in short, I still drew my breath, when the crucial incision made me give such a frightful scream that my surgeon fell flat upon his back, and imagining that he had been dissecting the devil he ran away, dying with fear, and fell down the staircase in his flight. His wife, hearing the noise, flew from the next room. She saw me stretched out upon the table with my crucial incision. She was seized with yet greater fear than her husband, fled, and tumbled over him. When they came to themselves a little, I heard the wife say to her husband: 'My dear, how could you take it into your head to dissect a heretic? Do you not know that these people always have the devil in their bodies? I will go and fetch a priest this minute to exorcise him.' At this proposal I shuddered, and mustering up what little courage I had still remaining I cried out aloud, 'Have mercy on me!' At length the Portuguese barber plucked up his spirits. He sewed up my wounds; his wife even nursed me. I was upon my legs at the end of fifteen days. The barber found me a place as lackey to a knight of Malta who was going to Venice, but finding that my master had no money to pay me my wages I entered the service of a Venetian merchant, and went with him to Constantinople. One day I took it into my head to step into a mosque, where I saw an old Iman and a very pretty young devotee who was saying her paternosters. Her bosom was uncovered, and between her breasts she had a beautiful bouquet of tulips, roses, anemones, ranunculus, hyacinths, and auriculas. She dropped her bouquet; I picked it up, and presented it to her with a profound reverence. I was so long in delivering it that the Iman began to get angry, and seeing that I was a Christian he called out for help. They carried me before the cadi, who ordered me a hundred lashes on the soles of the feet and sent me to the galleys. I was chained to the very same galley and the same bench as the young Baron. On board this galley there were four young men from Marseilles, five Neapolitan priests, and two monks from Corfu, who told us similar adventures happened daily. The Baron maintained that he had suffered greater injustice than I, and I insisted that it was far more innocent to take up a bouquet and place it again on a woman's bosom than to be found stark naked with an Ichoglan. We were continually disputing, and received twenty lashes with a bull's pizzle when the concatenation of universal events brought you to our galley, and you were good enough to ransom us."

"Well, my dear Pangloss," said Candide to him, "when you had been hanged, dissected, whipped, and were tugging at the oar, did you always think that everything happens for the best?"

"I am still of my first opinion," answered Pangloss, "for I am a philosopher and I cannot retract, especially as Leibnitz could never be wrong; and besides, the pre-established harmony is the finest thing in the world, and so is his plenum and materia subtilis."

# How Candide Found Cunegonde and the Old Woman Again.

While Candide, the Baron, Pangloss, Martin, and Cacambo were relating their several adventures, were reasoning on the contingent or non-contingent events of the universe, disputing on effects and causes, on moral and physical evil, on liberty and necessity, and on the consolations a slave may feel even on a Turkish galley, they arrived at the house of the Transylvanian prince on the banks of the Propontis. The first objects which met their sight were Cunegonde and the old woman hanging towels out to dry.

The Baron paled at this sight. The tender, loving Candide, seeing his beautiful Cunegonde embrowned, with blood-shot eyes, withered neck, wrinkled cheeks, and rough, red arms, recoiled three paces, seized with horror, and then advanced out of good manners. She embraced Candide and her brother; they embraced the old woman, and Candide ransomed them both.

There was a small farm in the neighbourhood which the old woman proposed to Candide to make a shift with till the company could be provided for in a better manner. Cunegonde did not know she had grown ugly, for nobody had told her of it; and she reminded Candide of his promise in so positive a tone that the good man durst not refuse her. He therefore intimated to the Baron that he intended marrying his sister.

"I will not suffer," said the Baron, "such meanness on her part, and such insolence on yours; I will never be reproached with this scandalous thing; my sister's children would never be able to enter the church in Germany. No; my sister shall only marry a baron of the empire."

Cunegonde flung herself at his feet, and bathed them with her tears; still he was inflexible.

"Thou foolish fellow," said Candide; "I have delivered thee out of the galleys, I have paid thy ransom, and thy sister's also; she was a scullion, and is very ugly, yet I am so condescending as to marry her; and dost thou pretend to oppose the match? I should kill thee again, were I only to consult my anger."

"Thou mayest kill me again," said the Baron, "but thou shalt not marry my sister, at least whilst I am living."

# The Conclusion.

At the bottom of his heart Candide had no wish to marry Cunegonde. But the extreme impertinence of the Baron determined him to conclude the match, and Cunegonde pressed him so strongly that he could not go from his word. He consulted Pangloss, Martin, and the faithful Cacambo. Pangloss drew up an excellent memorial, wherein he proved that the Baron had no right over his sister, and that according to all the laws of the empire, she might marry Candide with her left hand. Martin was for throwing the Baron into the sea; Cacambo decided that it would be better to deliver him up again to the captain of the galley, after which they thought to send him back to the General Father of the Order at Rome by the first ship. This advice was well received, the old woman approved it; they said not a word to his sister; the thing was executed for a little money, and they had the double pleasure of entrapping a Jesuit, and punishing the pride of a German baron.

It is natural to imagine that after so many disasters Candide married, and living with the philosopher Pangloss, the philosopher Martin, the prudent Cacambo, and the old woman, having besides brought so many diamonds from the country of the ancient Incas, must have led a very happy life. But he was so much imposed upon by the Jews that he had nothing left except his small farm; his wife became uglier every day, more peevish and unsupportable; the old woman was infirm and even more fretful than Cunegonde. Cacambo, who worked in the garden, and took vegetables for sale to Constantinople, was fatigued with hard work, and cursed his destiny. Pangloss was in despair at not shining in some German university. For Martin, he was firmly persuaded that he would be as badly off elsewhere, and therefore bore things patiently. Candide, Martin, and Pangloss sometimes disputed about morals and metaphysics. They often saw passing under the windows of their farm boats full of Effendis, Pashas, and Cadis, who were going into banishment to Lemnos, Mitylene, or Erzeroum. And they saw other Cadis, Pashas, and Effendis coming to supply the place of the exiles, and afterwards exiled in their turn. They saw heads decently impaled for presentation to the Sublime Porte. Such spectacles as these increased the number of their dissertations; and when they did not dispute time hung so heavily upon their hands, that one day the old woman ventured to say to them:

"I want to know which is worse, to be ravished a hundred times by negro pirates, to have a buttock cut off, to run the gauntlet among the Bulgarians, to be whipped and hanged at an auto-da-fé, to be dissected, to row in the galleys—in short, to go through all the miseries we have undergone, or to stay here and have nothing to do?"

"It is a great question," said Candide.

This discourse gave rise to new reflections, and Martin especially concluded that man was born to live either in a state of distracting inquietude or of lethargic disgust. Candide did not quite agree to that, but he affirmed nothing. Pangloss owned that he had always suffered horribly, but as he had once asserted that everything went wonderfully well, he asserted it still, though he no longer believed it.

What helped to confirm Martin in his detestable principles, to stagger Candide more than ever, and to puzzle Pangloss, was that one day they saw Paquette and Friar Giroflée land at the farm in extreme misery. They had soon squandered their three thousand piastres, parted, were reconciled, quarrelled again, were thrown into gaol, had escaped, and Friar Giroflée had at length become Turk. Paquette continued her trade wherever she went, but made nothing of it.

"I foresaw," said Martin to Candide, "that your presents would soon be dissipated, and only make them the more miserable. You have rolled in millions of money, you and Cacambo; and yet you are not happier than Friar Giroflée and Paquette."

"Ha!" said Pangloss to Paquette, "Providence has then brought you amongst us again, my poor child! Do you know that you cost me the tip of my nose, an eye, and an ear, as you may see? What a world is this!"

And now this new adventure set them philosophising more than ever.

In the neighbourhood there lived a very famous Dervish who was esteemed the best philosopher in all Turkey, and they went to consult him. Pangloss was the speaker.

"Master," said he, "we come to beg you to tell why so strange an animal as man was made."

"With what meddlest thou?" said the Dervish; "is it thy business?"

"But, reverend father," said Candide, "there is horrible evil in this world."

"What signifies it," said the Dervish, "whether there be evil or good? When his highness sends a ship to Egypt, does he trouble his head whether the mice on board are at their ease or not?"

"What, then, must we do?" said Pangloss.

"Hold your tongue," answered the Dervish.

"I was in hopes," said Pangloss, "that I should reason with you a little about causes and effects, about the best of possible worlds, the origin of evil, the nature of the soul, and the pre-established harmony."

At these words, the Dervish shut the door in their faces.

During this conversation, the news was spread that two Viziers and the Mufti had been strangled at Constantinople, and that several of their friends had been impaled. This catastrophe made a great noise for some hours. Pangloss, Candide, and Martin, returning to the little farm, saw a good old man taking the fresh air at his door under an orange bower. Pangloss, who was as inquisitive as he was argumentative, asked the old man what was the name of the strangled Mufti.

"I do not know," answered the worthy man, "and I have not known the name of any Mufti, nor of any Vizier. I am entirely ignorant of the event you mention; I presume in general that they who meddle with the administration of public affairs die sometimes miserably, and that they deserve it; but I never trouble my head about what is transacting at Constantinople; I content myself with sending there for sale the fruits of the garden which I cultivate."

Having said these words, he invited the strangers into his house; his two sons and two daughters presented them with several sorts of sherbet, which they made themselves, with Kaimak enriched with the candied-peel of citrons, with oranges, lemons, pine-apples, pistachio-nuts, and Mocha coffee unadulterated with the bad coffee of Batavia or the American islands. After which the two daughters of the honest Mussulman perfumed the strangers' beards.

"You must have a vast and magnificent estate," said Candide to the Turk.

"I have only twenty acres," replied the old man; "I and my children cultivate them; our labour preserves us from three great evils—weariness, vice, and want."

Candide, on his way home, made profound reflections on the old man's conversation.

"This honest Turk," said he to Pangloss and Martin, "seems to be in a situation far preferable to that of the six kings with whom we had the honour of supping."

"Grandeur," said Pangloss, "is extremely dangerous according to the testimony of philosophers. For, in short, Eglon, King of Moab, was assassinated by Ehud; Absalom was hung by his hair, and pierced with three darts; King Nadab, the son of Jeroboam, was killed by Baasa; King Ela by Zimri; Ahaziah by Jehu; Athaliah by Jehoiada; the Kings Jehoiakim, Jeconiah, and Zedekiah, were led into captivity. You know how perished Crœsus, Astyages, Darius, Dionysius of Syracuse, Pyrrhus, Perseus, Hannibal, Jugurtha, Ariovistus, Cæsar, Pompey, Nero, Otho, Vitellius, Domitian, Richard II. of England, Edward II., Henry VI., Richard III., Mary Stuart, Charles I., the three Henrys of France, the Emperor Henry IV.! You know—"

"I know also," said Candide, "that we must cultivate our garden."

"You are right," said Pangloss, "for when man was first placed in the Garden of Eden, he was put there ut operaretur eum, that he might cultivate it; which shows that man was not born to be idle."

"Let us work," said Martin, "without disputing; it is the only way to render life tolerable."

The whole little society entered into this laudable design, according to their different abilities. Their little plot of land produced plentiful crops. Cunegonde was, indeed, very ugly, but she became an excellent pastry cook; Paquette worked at embroidery; the old woman looked after the linen. They were all, not excepting Friar Giroflée, of some service or other; for he made a good joiner, and became a very honest man.

Pangloss sometimes said to Candide:

"There is a concatenation of events in this best of all possible worlds: for if you had not been kicked out of a magnificent castle for love of Miss Cunegonde: if you had not been put into the Inquisition: if you had not walked over America: if you had not stabbed the Baron: if you had not lost all your sheep from the fine country of El Dorado: you would not be here eating preserved citrons and pistachio-nuts."

"All that is very well," answered Candide, "but let us cultivate our garden."

**FOOTNOTES:**

[1] The name Pangloss is derived from two Greek words signifying "all" and "language."

[2] The Abares were a tribe of Tartars settled on the shores of the Danube, who later dwelt in part of Circassia.

[3] Venereal disease was said to have been first brought from Hispaniola, in the West Indies, by some followers of Columbus who were later employed in the siege of Naples. From this latter circumstance it was at one time known as the Neapolitan disease.

[4] The great earthquake of Lisbon happened on the first of November, 1755.

[5] Such was the aversion of the Japanese to the Christian faith that they compelled Europeans trading with their islands to trample on the cross, renounce all marks of Christianity, and swear that it was not their religion. See chap. xi. of the voyage to Laputa in Swift's Gulliver's Travels.

[6] This auto-da-fé actually took place, some months after the earthquake, on June 20, 1756.

[7] The rejection of bacon convicting them, of course, of being Jews, and therefore fitting victims for an auto-da-fé.

[8]The San-benito was a kind of loose over-garment painted with flames, figures of devils, the victim's own portrait, etc., worn by persons condemned to death by the Inquisition when going to the stake on the occasion of an auto-da-fé. Those who expressed repentance for their errors wore a garment of the same kind covered with flames directed downwards, while that worn by Jews, sorcerers, and renegades bore a St. Andrew's cross before and behind.

[9]"This Notre-Dame is of wood; every year she weeps on the day of her fête, and the people weep also. One day the preacher, seeing a carpenter with dry eyes, asked him how it was that he did not dissolve in tears when the Holy Virgin wept. 'Ah, my reverend father,' replied he, 'it is I who refastened her in her niche yesterday. I drove three great nails through her behind; it is then she would have wept if she had been able.'"—Voltaire, Mélanges.

[10]The following posthumous note of Voltaire's was first added to M. Beuchot's edition of his works issued in 1829; "See the extreme discretion of the author; there has not been up to the present any Pope named Urban X.; he feared to give a bastard to a known Pope. What circumspection! What delicacy of conscience!" The last Pope Urban was the eighth, and he died in 1644.

[11]Muley-Ismael was Emperor of Morocco from 1672 to 1727, and was a notoriously cruel tyrant.

[12]"Oh, what a misfortune to be an eunuch!"

[13]Carlo Broschi, called Farinelli, an Italian singer, born at Naples in 1705, without being exactly Minister, governed Spain under Ferdinand VI.; he died in 1782. He has been made one of the chief persons in one of the comic operas of MM. Auber and Scribe.

[14]Jean Robeck, a Swede, who was born in 1672, will be found mentioned in Rousseau's Nouvelle Héloïse. He drowned himself in the Weser at Bremen in 1729, and was the author of a Latin treatise on voluntary death, first printed in 1735.

[15]A spontoon was a kind of half-pike, a military weapon carried by officers of infantry and used as a medium for signalling orders to the regiment.

[16]Later Voltaire substituted the name of the Father Croust for that of Didrie. Of Croust he said in the Dictionnaire Philosophique that he was "the most brutal of the Society."

[17]By the Journal of Trevoux Voltaire meant a critical periodical printed by the Jesuits at Trevoux under the title of Mémoires pour servir à l'Historie des Sciences et des Beaux-Arts. It existed from 1701 until 1767, during which period its title underwent many changes.

[18]It has been suggested that Voltaire, in speaking of red sheep, referred to the llama, a South American ruminant allied to the camel. These animals are

sometimes of a reddish colour, and were notable as pack-carriers and for their fleetness.

[19] The first English translator curiously gives "a tourene of bouilli that weighed two hundred pounds," as the equivalent of "un contour bouilli qui pesait deux cent livres." The French editor of the 1869 reprint points out that the South American vulture, or condor, is meant; the name of this bird, it may be added, is taken from "cuntur," that given it by the aborigines.

[20] Spanish half-crowns.

[21] Socinians; followers of the teaching of Lalius and Faustus Socinus (16th century), which denied the doctrine of the Trinity, the deity of Christ, the personality of the devil, the native and total depravity of man, the vicarious atonement and eternal punishment. The Socinians are now represented by the Unitarians. Manicheans; followers of Manes or Manichæus (3rd century), a Persian who maintained that there are two principles, the one good and the other evil, each equally powerful in the government of the world.

[22] In the 1759 editions, in place of the long passage in brackets, there was only the following: "'Sir,' said the Perigordian Abbé to him, 'have you noticed that young person who has so roguish a face and so fine a figure? You may have her for ten thousand francs a month, and fifty thousand crowns in diamonds.' 'I have only a day or two to give her,' answered Candide, 'because I have a rendezvous at Venice.' In the evening after supper the insinuating Perigordian redoubled his politeness and attentions."

[23] The play referred to is supposed to be "Le Comte d'Essex," by Thomas Corneille.

[24] In France actors were at one time looked upon as excommunicated persons, not worthy of burial in holy ground or with Christian rites. In 1730 the "honours of sepulture" were refused to Mademoiselle Lecouvreur (doubtless the Miss Monime of this passage). Voltaire's miscellaneous works contain a paper on the matter.

[25] Élie-Catherine Fréron was a French critic (1719-1776) who incurred the enmity of Voltaire. In 1752 Fréron, in Lettres sur quelques écrits du temps, wrote pointedly of Voltaire as one who chose to be all things to all men, and Voltaire retaliated by references such as these in Candide.

[26] Gabriel Gauchat (1709-1779), French ecclesiastical writer, was author of a number of works on religious subjects.

[27] Nicholas Charles Joseph Trublet (1697-1770) was a French writer whose criticism of Voltaire was revenged in passages such as this one in Candide, and one in the Pauvre Diable beginning:

L'abbé Trublet avait alors le rage
D'être à Paris un petit personage.

[28] Damiens, who attempted the life of Louis XV. in 1757, was born at Arras, capital of Artois (Atrébatie).

[29] On May 14, 1610, Ravaillac assassinated Henry VI.

[30] On December 27, 1594, Jean Châtel attempted to assassinate Henry IV.

[31] This same curiously inept criticism of the war which cost France her American provinces occurs in Voltaire's Memoirs, wherein he says, "In 1756 England made a piratical war upon France for some acres of snow." See also his Précis du Siècle de Louis XV.

[32] Admiral Byng was shot on March 14, 1757.

[33] Commenting upon this passage, M. Sarcey says admirably: "All is there! In those ten lines Voltaire has gathered all the griefs and all the terrors of these creatures; the picture is admirable for its truth and power! But do you not feel the pity and sympathy of the painter? Here irony becomes sad, and in a way an avenger. Voltaire cries out with horror against the society which throws some of its members into such an abyss. He has his 'Bartholomew' fever; we tremble with him through contagion."

[34] The following particulars of the six monarchs may prove not uninteresting. Achmet III. (b. 1673, d. 1739) was dethroned in 1730. Ivan VI. (b. 1740, d. 1762) was dethroned in 1741. Charles Edward Stuart, the Pretender (b. 1720, d. 1788). Auguste III. (b. 1696, d. 1763). Stanislaus (b. 1682, d. 1766). Theodore (b. 1690, d. 1755). It will be observed that, although quite impossible for the six kings ever to have met, five of them might have been made to do so without any anachronism.

[35] François Leopold Ragotsky (1676-1735).

# Zadig

## THE BLIND OF ONE EYE

There lived at Babylon, in the reign of King Moabdar, a young man named Zadig, of a good natural disposition, strengthened and improved by education. Though rich and young, he had learned to moderate his passions; he had nothing stiff or affected in his behavior, he did not pretend to examine every action by the strict rules of reason, but was always ready to make proper allowances for the weakness of mankind.

It was matter of surprise that, notwithstanding his sprightly wit, he never exposed by his raillery those vague, incoherent, and noisy discourses, those rash censures, ignorant decisions, coarse jests, and all that empty jingle of words which at Babylon went by the name of conversation. He had learned, in the first book of Zoroaster, that self love is a football swelled with wind, from which, when pierced, the most terrible tempests issue forth.

Above all, Zadig never boasted of his conquests among the women, nor affected to entertain a contemptible opinion of the fair sex. He was generous, and was never afraid of obliging the ungrateful; remembering the grand precept of Zoroaster, "When thou eatest, give to the dogs, should they even bite thee." He was as wise as it is possible for man to be, for he sought to live with the wise.

Instructed in the sciences of the ancient Chaldeans, he understood the principles of natural philosophy, such as they were then supposed to be; and knew as much of metaphysics as hath ever been known in any age, that is, little or nothing at all. He was firmly persuaded, notwithstanding the new philosophy of the times, that the year consisted of three hundred and sixty-five days and six hours, and that the sun was in the center of the world. But when the principal magi told him, with a haughty and contemptuous air, that his sentiments were of a dangerous tendency, and that it was to be an enemy to the state to believe that the sun revolved round its own axis, and that the year had twelve months, he held his tongue with great modesty and meekness.

Possessed as he was of great riches, and consequently of many friends, blessed with a good constitution, a handsome figure, a mind just and moderate, and a heart noble and sincere, he fondly imagined that he might easily be happy. He was going to be married to Semira, who, in point of beauty, birth, and fortune, was the first match in Babylon. He had a real and virtuous affection for this lady, and she loved him with the most passionate fondness.

The happy moment was almost arrived that was to unite them forever in the bands of wedlock, when happening to take a walk together toward one of the gates of Babylon, under the palm trees that adorn the banks of the Euphrates, they saw some men approaching, armed with sabers and arrows. These were the attendants of young Orcan, the minister's nephew, whom his uncle's creatures had flattered into an opinion that he might do everything with impunity. He had none of the graces nor virtues of Zadig; but thinking himself a much more accomplished man, he was enraged to find that the other was preferred before him. This jealousy, which was merely the effect of his vanity, made him imagine that he was desperately in love with Semira; and accordingly he resolved to carry her off. The ravishers seized her; in the violence of the outrage they wounded her, and made the blood flow from her person, the sight of which would have softened the tigers of Mount Imaus. She pierced the heavens with her complaints. She cried out, "My dear husband! they tear me from the man I adore." Regardless of her own danger, she was only concerned for the fate of her dear Zadig, who, in the meantime, defended himself with all the strength that courage and love could inspire. Assisted only by two slaves, he put the ravishers to flight and carried home Semira, insensible and bloody as she was.

On opening her eyes and beholding her deliverer. "O Zadig!" said she, "I loved thee formerly as my intended husband; I now love thee as the preserver of my honor and my life." Never was heart more deeply affected than that of Semira. Never did a more charming mouth express more moving sentiments, in those glowing words inspired by a sense of the greatest of all favors, and by the most tender transports of a lawful passion.

Her wound was slight and was soon cured. Zadig was more dangerously wounded; an arrow had pierced him near his eye, and penetrated to a considerable depth. Semira wearied Heaven with her prayers for the recovery of her lover. Her eyes were constantly bathed in tears; she anxiously awaited the happy moment when those of Zadig should be able to meet hers; but an abscess growing on the wounded eye gave everything to fear. A messenger was immediately dispatched to Memphis for the great physician Hermes, who came with a numerous retinue. He visited the patient and declared that he would lose his eye. He even foretold the day and hour when this fatal event would happen. "Had it been the right eye," said he, "I could easily have cured it; but the wounds of the left eye are incurable." All Babylon lamented the fate of Zadig, and admired the profound knowledge of Hermes.

In two days the abscess broke of its own accord and Zadig was perfectly cured. Hermes wrote a book to prove that it ought not to have been cured. Zadig did not read it; but, as soon as he was able to go abroad, he went to pay a visit to her in whom all his hopes of happiness were centered, and for whose sake alone he wished to have eyes. Semira had been in the country for three days past. He learned on the road that that fine lady, having openly declared that she had an unconquerable aversion to one-eyed men, had the night before given her hand to Orcan. At this news he fell speechless to the ground. His sorrow brought him almost to the brink of the grave. He was long indisposed; but reason at last got the better of his affliction, and the severity of his fate served to console him.

"Since," said he, "I have suffered so much from the cruel caprice of a woman educated at court, I must now think of marrying the daughter of a citizen." He pitched upon Azora, a lady of the greatest prudence, and of the best family in town. He married her and lived with her for three months in all the delights of the most tender union. He only observed that she had a little levity; and was too apt to find that those young men who had the most handsome persons were likewise possessed of most wit and virtue.

## THE NOSE

One morning Azora returned from a walk in a terrible passion, and uttering the most violent exclamations. "What aileth thee," said he, "my dear spouse? What is it that can thus have discomposed thee?"

"Alas," said she, "thou wouldst be as much enraged as I am hadst thou seen what I have just beheld. I have been to comfort the young widow Cosrou, who, within these two days, hath raised a tomb to her young husband, near the rivulet that washes the skirts of this meadow. She vowed to heaven, in the bitterness of her grief, to remain at this tomb while the water of the rivulet should continue to run near it."~"Well," said Zadig, "she is an excellent woman, and loved her husband with the most sincere affection."

"Ah," replied Azora, "didst thou but know in what she was employed when I went to wait upon her!"

"In what, pray, beautiful Azora? Was she turning the course of the rivulet?"

Azora broke out into such long invectives and loaded the young widow with such bitter reproaches, that Zadig was far from being pleased with this ostentation of virtue.

Zadig had a friend named Cador, one of those young men in whom his wife discovered more probity and merit than in others. He made him his confidant, and secured his fidelity as much as possible by a considerable present. Azora, having passed two days with a friend in the country, returned home on the third. The servants told her, with tears in their eyes, that her husband died suddenly the night before; that they were afraid to send her an account of this mournful event; and that they had just been depositing his corpse in the tomb of his ancestors, at the end of the garden.

She wept, she tore her hair, and swore she would follow him to the grave.

In the evening Cador begged leave to wait upon her, and joined his tears with hers. Next day they wept less, and dined together. Cador told her that his friend had left him the greatest part of his estate; and that he should think himself extremely happy in sharing his fortune with her. The lady wept, fell into a passion, and at last became more mild and gentle. They sat longer at supper than at dinner. They now talked with greater confidence. Azora praised the deceased; but owned that he had many failings from which Cador was free.

During supper Cador complained of a violent pain in his side. The lady, greatly concerned, and eager to serve him, caused all kinds of essences to be brought, with which she anointed him, to try if some of them might not possibly ease him of his pain. She lamented that the great Hermes was not still in Babylon. She even condescended to touch the side in which Cador felt such exquisite pain.

"Art thou subject to this cruel disorder?" said she to him with a compassionate air.

"It sometimes brings me," replied Cador, "to the brink of the grave; and there is but one remedy that can give me relief, and that is to apply to my side the nose of a man who is lately dead."

"A strange remedy, indeed!" said Azora.

"Not more strange," replied he, "than the sachels of Arnon against the apoplexy." This reason, added to the great merit of the young man, at last determined the lady.

"After all," says she, "when my husband shall cross the bridge Tchinavar, in his journey to the other world, the angel Asrael will not refuse him a passage because his nose is a little shorter in the second life than it was in the first." She then took a razor, went to her husband's tomb, bedewed it with her tears, and drew near to cut off the nose of Zadig, whom she found extended at full length in the tomb. Zadig arose, holding his nose with one hand, and, putting back the razor with the other, "Madam," said he, "don't exclaim so violently against young Cosrou; the project of cutting off my nose is equal to that of turning the course of a rivulet." Zadig found by experience that the first month of marriage, as it is written in the book of Zend, is the moon of honey, and that the second is the moon of wormwood. He was some time after obliged to repudiate Azora, who became too difficult to be pleased; and he then sought for happiness in the study of nature. "No man," said he, "can be happier than a philosopher who reads in this great book which God hath placed before our eyes. The truths he discovers are his own; he nourishes and exalts his soul; he lives in peace; he fears nothing from men; and his tender spouse will not come to cut off his nose."

Possessed of these ideas he retired to a country house on the banks of the Euphrates. There he did not employ himself in calculating how many inches of water flow in a second of time under the arches of a bridge, or whether there fell a cube line of rain in the month of the Mouse more than in the month of the Sheep. He never dreamed of making silk of cobwebs, or porcelain of broken bottles; but he chiefly studied the properties of plants and animals; and soon acquired a sagacity that made him discover a thousand differences where other men see nothing but uniformity.

One day, as he was walking near a little wood, he saw one of the queen's eunuchs running toward him, followed by several officers, who appeared to be in great perplexity, and who ran to and fro like men distracted, eagerly searching for something they had lost of great value. "Young man," said the first eunuch, "hast thou seen the queen's dog?" "It is a female," replied Zadig. "Thou art in the right," returned the first eunuch. "It is a very small she spaniel," added Zadig; "she has lately whelped; she limps on the left forefoot, and has very long ears." "Thou hast seen her," said the first eunuch, quite out of breath. "No," replied Zadig, "I have not seen her, nor did I so much as know that the queen had a dog."

Exactly at the same time, by one of the common freaks of fortune, the finest horse in the king's stable had escaped from the jockey in the plains of Babylon. The principal huntsman and all the other officers ran after him with as much eagerness and anxiety as the first eunuch had done after the spaniel. The principal huntsman addressed himself to Zadig, and asked him if he had not seen the king's horse passing by. "He is the fleetest horse in the king's stable," replied Zadig; "he is five feet high, with very small hoofs, and a tail three feet and a half in length; the studs on his bit are gold of twenty-three carats, and his shoes are silver of eleven pennyweights." "What way did he take? where is he?" demanded the chief huntsman. "I have not seen him," replied Zadig, "and never heard talk of him before."

The principal huntsman and the first eunuch never doubted but that Zadig had stolen the king's horse and the queen's spaniel. They therefore had him conducted before the assembly of the grand desterham, who condemned him to the knout, and to spend the rest of his days in Siberia. Hardly was the sentence passed when the horse and the spaniel were both found. The judges were reduced to the disagreeable necessity of reversing their sentence; but they condemned Zadig to pay four hundred ounces of gold for having said that he had not seen what he had seen. This fine he was obliged to pay; after which he was permitted to plead his cause before the counsel of the grand desterham, when he spoke to the following effect:

"Ye stars of justice, abyss of sciences, mirrors of truth, who have the weight of lead, the hardness of iron, the splendor of the diamond, and many properties of gold: Since I am permitted to speak before this august assembly, I swear to you by Oramades that I have never seen the queen's respectable spaniel, nor the sacred horse of the king of kings. The truth of the matter was as follows: I was walking toward the little wood, where I afterwards met the venerable eunuch, and the most illustrious chief huntsman. I observed on the sand the traces of an animal, and could easily perceive them to be those of a little dog. The light and long furrows impressed on little eminences of sand between the marks of the paws plainly discovered that it was a female, whose dugs were hanging down, and that therefore she must have whelped a few days before. Other traces of a different kind, that always appeared to have gently brushed the surface of the sand near the marks of the forefeet, showed me that she had very long ears; and as I remarked that there was always a slighter impression made on the sand by one foot than the other three, I found that the spaniel of our august queen was a little lame, if I may be allowed the expression.

"With regard to the horse of the king of kings, you will be pleased to know that, walking in the lanes of this wood, I observed the marks of a horse's shoes, all at equal distances. This must be a horse, said I to myself, that gallops excellently. The dust on the trees in the road that was but seven feet wide was a little brushed off, at the distance of three feet and a half from the middle of the road. This horse, said I, has a tail three feet and a half long, which being whisked to the right and left, has swept away the dust. I observed under the trees that formed an arbor five feet in height, that the leaves of the branches were newly fallen; from whence I inferred that the horse had touched them, and that he must therefore be five feet high. As to his bit, it must be gold of twenty-three carats, for he had rubbed its bosses against a stone which I knew to be a touchstone, and which I have tried. In a word, from the marks made by his shoes on flints of another kind, I concluded that he was shod with silver eleven deniers fine."

All the judges admired Zadig for his acute and profound discernment. The news of this speech was carried even to the king and queen. Nothing was talked of but Zadig in the antechambers, the chambers, and the cabinet; and though many of the magi were of opinion that he ought to be burned as a sorcerer, the king ordered his officers to restore him the four hundred ounces of gold which he had been obliged to pay. The register, the attorneys, and bailiffs went to his house with great formality, to carry him back his four hundred ounces. They only retained three hundred and ninety-eight of them to defray the expenses of justice; and their servants demanded their fees.

Zadig saw how extremely dangerous it sometimes is to appear too knowing, and therefore resolved that on the next occasion of the like nature he would not tell what he had seen.

Such an opportunity soon offered. A prisoner of state made his escape, and passed under the window of Zadig's house. Zadig was examined and made no answer. But it was proved that he had looked at the prisoner from this window. For this crime he was condemned to pay five hundred ounces of gold; and, according to the polite custom of Babylon, he thanked his judges for their indulgence.

"Great God!" said he to himself, "what a misfortune it is to walk in a wood through which the queen's spaniel or the king's horse has passed! how dangerous to look out at a window! and how difficult to be happy in this life!"

## THE ENVIOUS MAN

Zadig resolved to comfort himself by philosophy and friendship for the evils he had suffered from fortune. He had in the suburbs of Babylon a house elegantly furnished, in which he assembled all the arts and all the pleasures worthy the pursuit of a gentleman. In the morning his library was open to the learned. In the evening his table was surrounded by good company. But he soon found what very dangerous guests these men of letters are. A warm dispute arose on one of Zoroaster's laws, which forbids the eating of a griffin. "Why," said some of them, "prohibit the eating of a griffin, if there is no such an animal in nature?" "There must necessarily be such an animal," said the others, "since Zoroaster forbids us to eat it." Zadig would fain have reconciled them by saying, "If there are no griffins, we cannot possibly eat them; and thus either way we shall obey Zoroaster."

A learned man who had composed thirteen volumes on the properties of the griffin, and was besides the chief theurgite, hastened away to accuse Zadig before one of the principal magi, named Yebor, the greatest blockhead and therefore the greatest fanatic among the Chaldeans. This man would have impaled Zadig to do honors to the sun, and would then have recited the breviary of Zoroaster with greater satisfaction. The friend Cador (a friend is better than a hundred priests) went to Yebor, and said to him, "Long live the sun and the griffins; beware of punishing Zadig; he is a saint; he has griffins in his inner court and does not eat them; and his accuser is an heretic, who dares to maintain that rabbits have cloven feet and are not unclean."

"Well," said Yebor, shaking his bald pate, "we must impale Zadig for having thought contemptuously of griffins, and the other for having spoken disrespectfully of rabbits." Cador hushed up the affair by means of a maid of honor with whom he had a love affair, and who had great interest in the College of the Magi. Nobody was impaled.

This levity occasioned a great murmuring among some of the doctors, who from thence predicted the fall of Babylon. "Upon what does happiness depend?" said Zadig. "I am persecuted by everything in the world, even on account of beings that have no existence." He cursed those men of learning, and resolved for the future to live with none but good company.

He assembled at his house the most worthy men and the most beautiful ladies of Babylon. He gave them delicious suppers, often preceded by concerts of music, and always animated by polite conversation, from which he knew how to banish that affectation of wit which is the surest method of preventing it entirely, and of spoiling the pleasure of the most agreeable society. Neither the choice of his friends nor that of the dishes was made by vanity; for in everything he preferred the substance to the shadow; and by these means he procured that real respect to which he did not aspire.

Opposite to his house lived one Arimazes, a man whose deformed countenance was but a faint picture of his still more deformed mind. His heart was a mixture of malice, pride, and envy. Having never been able to succeed in any of his undertakings, he revenged himself on all around him by loading them with the blackest calumnies. Rich as he was, he found it difficult to procure a set of flatterers. The rattling of the chariots that entered Zadig's court in the evening filled him with uneasiness; the sound of his praises enraged him still more. He sometimes went to Zadig's house, and sat down at table without being desired; where he spoiled all the pleasure of the company, as the harpies are said to infect the viands they touch. It happened that one day he took it in his head to give an entertainment to a lady, who, instead of accepting it, went to sup with Zadig. At another time, as he was talking with Zadig at court, a minister of state came up to them, and invited Zadig to supper without inviting Arimazes. The most implacable hatred has seldom a more solid foundation. This man, who in Babylon was called the Envious, resolved to ruin Zadig because he was called the Happy. "The opportunity of doing mischief occurs a hundred times in a day, and that of doing good but once a year," as sayeth the wise Zoroaster.

The envious man went to see Zadig, who was walking in his garden with two friends and a lady, to whom he said many gallant things, without any other intention than that of saying them. The conversation turned upon a war which the king had just brought to a happy conclusion against the prince of Hircania, his vassal. Zadig, who had signalized his courage in this short war, bestowed great praises on the king, but greater still on the lady. He took out his pocket-book, and wrote four lines extempore, which he gave to this amiable person to read. His friends begged they might see them; but modesty, or rather a well-regulated self love, would not allow him to grant their request. He knew that extemporary verses are never approved of by any but by the person in whose honor they are written. He therefore tore in two the leaf on which he had wrote them, and threw both the pieces into a thicket of rose-bushes, where the rest of the company sought for them in vain. A slight shower falling soon after obliged them to return to the house. The envious man, who stayed in the garden, continued the search till at last he found a piece of the leaf. It had been torn in such a manner that each half of a line formed a complete sense, and even a verse of a shorter measure; but what was still more surprising, these short verses were found to contain the most injurious reflections on the king. They ran thus:

To flagrant crimes His crown he owes,
To peaceful times The worst of foes.

The envious man was now happy for the first time of his life. He had it in his power to ruin a person of virtue and merit. Filled with this fiendlike joy, he found means to convey to the king the satire written by the hand of Zadig, who, together with the lady and his two friends, was thrown into prison.

His trial was soon finished, without his being permitted to speak for himself. As he was going to receive his sentence, the envious man threw himself in his way and told him with a loud voice that his verses were good for nothing. Zadig did not value himself on being a good poet; but it filled him with inexpressible concern to find that he was condemned for high treason; and that the fair lady and his two friends were confined in prison for a crime of which they were not guilty. He was not allowed to speak because his writing spoke for him. Such was the law of Babylon. Accordingly he was conducted to the place of execution, through an immense crowd of spectators, who durst not venture to express their pity for him, but who carefully examined his countenance to see if he died with a good grace. His relations alone were inconsolable, for they could not succeed to his estate. Three-fourths of his wealth were confiscated into the king's treasury, and the other fourth was given to the envious man.

Just as he was preparing for death the king's parrot flew from its cage and alighted on a rosebush in Zadig's garden. A peach had been driven thither by the wind from a neighboring tree, and had fallen on a piece of the written leaf of the pocketbook to which it stuck. The bird carried off the peach and the paper and laid them on the king's knee. The king took up the paper with great eagerness and read the words, which formed no sense, and seemed to be the endings of verses. He loved poetry; and there is always some mercy to be expected from a prince of that disposition. The adventure of the parrot set him a-thinking.

The queen, who remembered what had been written on the piece of Zadig's pocketbook, caused it to be brought. They compared the two pieces together and found them to tally exactly; they then read the verses as Zadig had wrote them.

Tyrants Are Prone to Flagrant Crimes.
To Clemency His Crown He Owes.
To Concord and to Peaceful Times.
Love Only Is the Worst of Foes.

The king gave immediate orders that Zadig should be brought before him, and that his two friends and the lady should be set at liberty. Zadig fell prostrate on the ground before the king and queen; humbly begged their pardon for having made such bad verses and spoke with so much propriety, wit, and good sense, that their majesties desired they might see him again. He did himself that honor, and insinuated himself still farther into their good graces. They gave him all the wealth of the envious man; but Zadig restored him back the whole of it. And this instance of generosity gave no other pleasure to the envious man than that of having preserved his estate.

The king's esteem for Zadig increased every day. He admitted him into all his parties of pleasure, and consulted him in all affairs of state. From that time the queen began to regard him with an eye of tenderness that might one day prove dangerous to herself, to the king, her august comfort, to Zadig, and to the kingdom in general. Zadig now began to think that happiness was not so unattainable as he had formerly imagined.

## THE GENEROUS

The time now arrived for celebrating a grand festival, which returned every five years. It was a custom in Babylon solemnly to declare at the end of every five years which of the citizens had performed the most generous action. The grandees and the magi were the judges. The first satrap, who was charged with the government of the city, published the most noble actions that had passed under his administration. The competition was decided by votes; and the king pronounced the sentence. People came to this solemnity from the extremities of the earth. The conqueror received from the monarch's hand a golden cup adorned with precious stones, his majesty at the same time making him this compliment:

"Receive this reward of thy generosity, and may the gods grant me many subjects like to thee."

This memorable day being come, the king appeared on his throne, surrounded by the grandees, the magi, and the deputies of all nations that came to these games, where glory was acquired not by the swiftness of horses, nor by strength of body, but by virtue. The first satrap recited, with an audible voice, such actions as might entitle the authors of them to this invaluable prize. He did not mention the greatness of soul with which Zadig had restored the envious man his fortune, because it was not judged to be an action worthy of disputing the prize.

He first presented a judge who, having made a citizen lose a considerable cause by a mistake, for which, after all, he was not accountable, had given him the whole of his own estate, which was just equal to what the other had lost.

He next produced a young man who, being desperately in love with a lady whom he was going to marry, had yielded her up to his friend, whose passion for her had almost brought him to the brink of the grave, and at the same time had given him the lady's fortune.

He afterwards produced a soldier who, in the wars of Hircania, had given a still more noble instance of generosity. A party of the enemy having seized his mistress, he fought in her defense with great intrepidity. At that very instant he was informed that another party, at the distance of a few paces, were carrying off his mother; he therefore left his mistress with tears in his eyes and flew to the assistance of his mother. At last he returned to the dear object of his love and found her expiring. He was just going to plunge his sword in his own bosom; but his mother remonstrating against such a desperate deed, and telling him that he was the only support of her life, he had the courage to endure to live.

The judges were inclined to give the prize to the soldier. But the king took up the discourse and said: "The action of the soldier, and those of the other two, are doubtless very great, but they have nothing in them surprising. Yesterday Zadig performed an action that filled me with wonder. I had a few days before disgraced Coreb, my minister and favorite. I complained of him in the most violent and bitter terms; all my courtiers assured me that I was too gentle and seemed to vie with each other in speaking ill of Coreb. I asked Zadig what he thought of him, and he had the courage to commend him. I have read in our histories of many people who have atoned for an error by the surrender of their fortune; who have resigned a mistress; or preferred a mother to the object of their affection; but never before did I hear of a courtier who spoke favorably of a disgraced minister that labored under the displeasure of his sovereign. I give to each of those whose generous actions have been now recited twenty thousand pieces of gold; but the cup I give to Zadig."

"May it please your majesty," said Zadig, "thyself alone deservest the cup; thou hast performed an action of all others the most uncommon and meritorious, since, notwithstanding thy being a powerful king, thou wast not offended at thy slave when he presumed to oppose thy passion." The king and Zadig were equally the object of admiration. The judge, who had given his estate to his client; the lover, who had resigned his mistress to a friend; and the soldier, who had preferred the safety of his mother to that of his mistress, received the king's presents and saw their names enrolled in the catalogue of generous men. Zadig had the cup, and the king acquired the reputation of a good prince, which he did not long enjoy. The day was celebrated by feasts that lasted longer than the law enjoined; and the memory of it is still preserved in Asia. Zadig said, "Now I am happy at last;" but he found himself fatally deceived.

## THE MINISTER

The king had lost his first minister and chose Zadig to supply his place. All the ladies in Babylon applauded the choice; for since the foundation of the empire there had never been such a young minister. But all the courtiers were filled with jealousy and vexation. The envious man in particular was troubled with a spitting of blood and a prodigious inflammation in his nose. Zadig, having thanked the king and queen for their goodness, went likewise to thank the parrot. "Beautiful bird," said he, "'tis thou that hast saved my life and made me first minister. The queen's spaniel and the king's horse did me a great deal of mischief; but thou hast done me much good. Upon such slender threads as these do the fates of mortals hang! But," added he, "this happiness perhaps will vanish very soon."

"Soon," replied the parrot.

Zadig was somewhat startled at this word. But as he was a good natural philosopher and did not believe parrots to be prophets, he quickly recovered his spirits and resolved to execute his duty to the best of his power.

He made everyone feel the sacred authority of the laws, but no one felt the weight of his dignity. He never checked the deliberation of the diran; and every vizier might give his opinion without the fear of incurring the minister's displeasure. When he gave judgment, it was not he that gave it, it was the law; the rigor of which, however, whenever it was too severe, he always took care to soften; and when laws were wanting, the equity of his decisions was such as might easily have made them pass for those of Zoroaster. It is to him that the nations are indebted for this grand principle, to wit, that it is better to run the risk of sparing the guilty than to condemn the innocent. He imagined that laws were made as well to secure the people from the suffering of injuries as to restrain them from the commission of crimes. His chief talent consisted in discovering the truth, which all men seek to obscure.

This great talent he put in practice from the very beginning of his administration. A famous merchant of Babylon, who died in the Indies, divided his estate equally between his two sons, after having disposed of their sister in marriage, and left a present of thirty thousand pieces of gold to that son who should be found to have loved him best. The eldest raised a tomb to his memory; the youngest increased his sister's portion, by giving her part of his inheritance. Everyone said that the eldest son loved his father best, and the youngest his sister; and that the thirty thousand pieces belonged to the eldest.

Zadig sent for both of them, the one after the other. To the eldest he said: "Thy father is not dead; he is recovered of his last illness, and is returning to Babylon," "God be praised," replied the young man; "but his tomb cost me a considerable sum." Zadig afterwards said the same to the youngest. "God be praised," said he, "I will go and restore to my father all that I have; but I could wish that he would leave my sister what I have given her." "Thou shalt restore nothing," replied Zadig, "and thou shalt have the thirty thousand pieces, for thou art the son who loves his father best."

## THE DISPUTES AND THE AUDIENCES

In this manner he daily discovered the subtilty of his genius and the goodness of his heart. The people at once admired and loved him. He passed for the happiest man in the world. The whole empire resounded with his name. All the ladies ogled him. All the men praised him for his justice. The learned regarded him as an oracle; and even the priests confessed that he knew more than the old archmage Yebor. They were now so far from prosecuting him on account of the griffin, that they believed nothing but what he thought credible.

There had reigned in Babylon, for the space of fifteen hundred years, a violent contest that had divided the empire into two sects. The one pretended that they ought to enter the temple of Mitra with the left foot foremost; the other held this custom in detestation and always entered with the right foot first. The people waited with great impatience for the day on which the solemn feast of the sacred fire was to be celebrated, to see which sect Zadig would favor. All the world had their eyes fixed on his two feet, and the whole city was in the utmost suspense and perturbation. Zadig jumped into the temple with his feet joined together, and afterwards proved, in an eloquent discourse, that the Sovereign of heaven and earth, who accepted not the persons of men, makes no distinction between the right and left foot. The envious man and his wife alleged that his discourse was not figurative enough, and that he did not make the rocks and mountains to dance with sufficient agility.

"He is dry." said they, "and void of genius: he does not make the flea to fly, and stars to fall, nor the sun to melt wax; he has not the true Oriental style." Zadig contented himself with having the style of reason. All the world favored him, not because he was in the right road or followed the dictates of reason, or was a man of real merit, but because he was prime vizier.

He terminated with the same happy address the grand difference between the white and the black magi. The former maintained that it was the height of impiety to pray to God with the face turned toward the east in winter; the latter asserted that God abhorred the prayers of those who turned toward the west in summer. Zadig decreed that every man should be allowed to turn as he pleased.

Thus he found out the happy secret of finishing all affairs, whether of a private or a public nature, in the morning. The rest of the day he employed in superintending and promoting the embellishments of Babylon. He exhibited tragedies that drew tears from the eyes of the spectators, and comedies that shook their sides with laughter; a custom which had long been disused, and which his good taste now induced him to revive. He never affected to be more knowing in the polite arts than the artists themselves; he encouraged them by rewards and honors, and was never jealous of their talents. In the evening the king was highly entertained with his conversation, and the queen still more. "Great minister!" said the king. "Amiable minister!" said the queen; and both of them added, "It would have been a great loss to the state had such a man been hanged."

Never was a man in power obliged to give so many audiences to the ladies. Most of them came to consult him about no business at all, that so they might have some business with him. But none of them won his attention.

Meanwhile Zadig perceived that his thoughts were always distracted, as well when he gave audience as when he sat in judgment. He did not know to what to attribute this absence of mind; and that was his only sorrow.

He had a dream in which he imagined that he laid himself down upon a heap of dry herbs, among which there were many prickly ones that gave him great uneasiness, and that he afterwards reposed himself on a soft bed of roses from which there sprung a serpent that wounded him to the heart with its sharp and venomed tongue. "Alas," said he, "I have long lain on these dry and prickly herbs, I am now on the bed of roses; but what shall be the serpent?"

## JEALOUSY

Zadig's calamities sprung even from his happiness and especially from his merit. He every day conversed with the king and Astarte, his august comfort. The charms of his conversation were greatly heightened by that desire of pleasing, which is to the mind what dress is to beauty. His youth and graceful appearance insensibly made an impression on Astarte, which she did not at first perceive. Her passion grew and flourished in the bosom of innocence. Without fear or scruple, she indulged the pleasing satisfaction of seeing and hearing a man who was so dear to her husband and to the empire in general. She was continually praising him to the king. She talked of him to her women, who were always sure to improve on her praises. And thus everything contributed to pierce her heart with a dart, of which she did not seem to be sensible. She made several presents to Zadig, which discovered a greater spirit of gallantry than she imagined. She intended to speak to him only as a queen satisfied with his services and her expressions were sometimes those of a woman in love.

Astarte was much more beautiful than that Semira who had such a strong aversion to one-eyed men, or that other woman who had resolved to cut off her husband's nose. Her unreserved familiarity, her tender expressions, at which she began to blush; and her eyes, which, though she endeavored to divert them to other objects, were always fixed upon his, inspired Zadig with a passion that filled him with astonishment. He struggled hard to get the better of it. He called to his aid the precepts of philosophy, which had always stood him in stead; but from thence, though he could derive the light of knowledge, he could procure no remedy to cure the disorders of his lovesick heart. Duty, gratitude, and violated majesty presented themselves to his mind as so many avenging gods. He struggled; he conquered; but this victory, which he was obliged to purchase afresh every moment, cost him many sighs and tears. He no longer dared to speak to the queen with that sweet and charming familiarity which had been so agreeable to them both. His countenance was covered with a cloud. His conversation was constrained and incoherent. His eyes were fixed on the ground; and when, in spite of all his endeavors to the contrary, they encountered those of the queen, they found them bathed in tears and darting arrows of flame. They seemed to say, We adore each other and yet are afraid to love; we both burn with a fire which we both condemn.

Zadig left the royal presence full of perplexity and despair, and having his heart oppressed with a burden which he was no longer able to bear. In the violence of his perturbation he involuntarily betrayed the secret to his friend Cador, in the same manner as a man who, having long supported the fits of a cruel disease, discovers his pain by a cry extorted from him by a more severe fit and by the cold sweat that covers his brow.

"I have already discovered," said Cador, "the sentiments which thou wouldst fain conceal from thyself. The symptoms by which the passions show themselves are certain and infallible. Judge, my dear Zadig, since I have read thy heart, whether the king will not discover something in it that may give him offense. He has no other fault but that of being the most jealous man in the world. Thou canst resist the violence of thy passion with greater fortitude than the queen because thou art a philosopher, and because thou art Zadig. Astarte is a woman: she suffers her eyes to speak with so much the more imprudence, as she does not as yet think herself guilty. Conscious of her innocence, she unhappily neglects those external appearances which are so necessary. I shall tremble for her so long as she has nothing wherewithal to reproach herself. Were ye both of one mind, ye might easily deceive the whole world. A growing passion, which we endeavor to suppress, discovers itself in spite of all our efforts to the contrary; but love, when gratified, is easily concealed."

Zadig trembled at the proposal of betraying the king, his benefactor; and never was he more faithful to his prince than when guilty of an involuntary crime against him.

Meanwhile the queen mentioned the name of Zadig so frequently and with such a blushing and downcast look; she was sometimes so lively and sometimes so perplexed when she spoke to him in the king's presence, and was seized with such deep thoughtfulness at his going away, that the king began to be troubled. He believed all that he saw and imagined all that he did not see. He particularly remarked that his wife's shoes were blue and that Zadig's shoes were blue; that his wife's ribbons were yellow and that Zadig's bonnet was yellow; and these were terrible symptoms to a prince of so much delicacy. In his jealous mind suspicions were turned into certainty.

All the slaves of kings and queens are so many spies over their hearts. They soon observed that Astarte was tender and that Moabdar was jealous. The envious man brought false reports to the king. The monarch now thought of nothing but in what manner he might best execute his vengeance. He one night resolved to poison the queen and in the morning to put Zadig to death by the bowstring. The orders were given to a merciless eunuch, who commonly executed his acts of vengeance. There happened at that time to be in the king's chamber a little dwarf, who, though dumb, was not deaf. He was allowed, on account of his insignificance, to go wherever he pleased, and, as a domestic animal, was a witness of what passed in the most profound secrecy. This little mute was strongly attached to the queen and Zadig. With equal horror and surprise he heard the cruel orders given. But how to prevent the fatal sentence that in a few hours was to be carried into execution! He could not write, but he could paint; and excelled particularly in drawing a striking resemblance. He employed a part of the night in sketching out with his pencil what he meant to impart to the queen. The piece represented the king in one corner, boiling with rage, and giving orders to the eunuch; a bowstring, and a bowl on a table; the queen in the middle of the picture, expiring in the arms of her woman, and Zadig strangled at her feet The horizon, represented a rising sun, to express that this shocking execution was to be performed in the morning. As soon as he had finished the picture he ran to one of Astarte's women, awakened her, and made her understand that she must immediately carry it to the queen.

At midnight a messenger knocks at Zadig's door, awakes him, and gives him a note from the queen. He doubts whether it is a dream; and opens the letter with a trembling hand. But how great was his surprise! and who can express the consternation and despair into which he was thrown upon reading these words: "Fly this instant, or thou art a dead man. Fly, Zadig, I conjure thee by our mutual love and my yellow ribbons. I have not been guilty, but I find I must die like a criminal."

Zadig was hardly able to speak. He sent for Cador, and, without uttering a word, gave him the note. Cador forced him to obey, and forthwith to take the road to Memphis. "Shouldst thou dare," said he, "to go in search of the queen, thou wilt hasten her death. Shouldst thou speak to the king, thou wilt infallibly ruin her. I will take upon me the charge of her destiny; follow thy own. I will spread a report that thou hast taken the road to India. I will soon follow thee, and inform thee of all that shall have passed in Babylon." At that instant, Cador caused two of the swiftest dromedaries to be brought to a private gate of the palace. Upon one of these he mounted Zadig, whom he was obliged to carry to the door, and who was ready to expire with grief. He was accompanied by a single domestic; and Cador, plunged in sorrow and astonishment, soon lost sight of his friend.

This illustrious fugitive arriving on the side of a hill, from whence he could take a view of Babylon, turned his eyes toward the queen's palace, and fainted away at the sight; nor did he recover his senses but to shed a torrent of tears and to wish for death. At length, after his thoughts had been long engrossed in lamenting the unhappy fate of the loveliest woman and the greatest queen in the world, he for a moment turned his views on himself and cried: "What then is human life? O virtue, how hast thou served me! Two women have basely deceived me, and now a third, who is innocent, and more beautiful than both the others, is going to be put to death! Whatever good I have done hath been to me a continual source of calamity and affliction; and I have only been raised to the height of grandeur, to be tumbled down the most horrid precipice of misfortune." Filled with these gloomy reflections, his eyes overspread with the veil of grief, his countenance covered with the paleness of death, and his soul plunged in an abyss of the blackest despair, he continued his journey toward Egypt.

## THE WOMAN BEATEN

Zadig directed his course by the stars. The constellation of Orion and the splendid Dog Star guided his steps toward the pole of Cassiopeia. He admired those vast globes of light, which appear to our eyes but as so many little sparks, while the earth, which in reality is only an imperceptible point in nature, appears to our fond imaginations as something so grand and noble.

He then represented to himself the human species as it really is, as a parcel of insects devouring one another on a little atom of clay. This true image seemed to annihilate his misfortunes, by making him sensible of the nothingness of his own being, and of that of Babylon. His soul launched out into infinity, and, detached from the senses, contemplated the immutable order of the universe. But when afterwards, returning to himself, and entering into his own heart, he considered that Astarte had perhaps died for him, the universe vanished from his sight, and he beheld nothing in the whole compass of nature but Astarte; expiring and Zadig unhappy. While he thus alternately gave up his mind to this flux and reflux of sublime philosophy and intolerable grief, he advanced toward the frontiers of Egypt; and his faithful domestic was already in the first village, in search of a lodging.

Upon reaching the village Zadig generously took the part of a woman attacked by her jealous lover. The combat grew so fierce that Zadig slew the lover. The Egyptians were then just and humane. The people conducted Zadig to the town house. They first of all ordered his wounds to be dressed and then examined him and his servant apart, in order to discover the truth. They found that Zadig was not an assassin; but as he was guilty of having killed a man, the law condemned him to be a slave. His two camels were sold for the benefit of the town; all the gold he had brought with him was distributed among the inhabitants; and his person, as well as that of the companion of his journey, was exposed to sale in the marketplace.

An Arabian merchant, named Setoc, made the purchase; but as the servant was fitter for labor than the master, he was sold at a higher price. There was no comparison between the two men. Thus Zadig became a slave subordinate to his own servant. They were linked together by a chain fastened to their feet, and in this condition they followed the Arabian merchant to his house.

BY the way Zadig comforted his servant, and exhorted him to patience; but he could not help making, according to his usual custom, some reflections on human life. "I see," said he, "that the unhappiness of my fate hath an influence on thine. Hitherto everything has turned out to me in a most unaccountable manner. I have been condemned to pay a fine for having seen the marks of a spaniel's feet. I thought that I should once have been impaled on account of a griffin. I have been sent to execution for having made some verses in praise of the king. I have been upon the point of being strangled because the queen had yellow ribbons; and now I am a slave with thee, because a brutal wretch beat his mistress. Come, let us keep a good heart; all this perhaps will have an end. The Arabian merchants must necessarily have slaves; and why not me as well as another, since, as well as another, I am a man? This merchant will not be cruel; he must treat his slaves well, if he expects any advantage from them." But while he spoke thus, his heart was entirely engrossed by the fate of the Queen of Babylon.

Two days after, the merchant Setoc set out for Arabia Deserta, with his slaves and his camels. His tribe dwelt near the Desert of Oreb. The journey was long and painful. Setoc set a much greater value on the servant than the master, because the former was more expert in loading the camels; and all the little marks of distinction were shown to him. A camel having died within two days' journey of Oreb, his burden was divided and laid on the backs of the servants; and Zadig had his share among the rest.

Setoc laughed to see all his slaves walking with their bodies inclined. Zadig took the liberty to explain to him the cause, and inform him of the laws of the balance. The merchant was astonished, and began to regard him with other eyes. Zadig, finding he had raised his curiosity, increased it still further by acquainting him with many things that related to commerce, the specific gravity of metals, and commodities under an equal bulk; the properties of several useful animals; and the means of rendering those useful that are not naturally so. At last Setoc began to consider Zadig as a sage, and preferred him to his companion, whom he had formerly so much esteemed. He treated him well and had no cause to repent of his kindness.

## THE STONE

As soon as Setoc arrived among his own tribe he demanded the payment of five hundred ounces of silver, which he had lent to a Jew in presence of two witnesses; but as the witnesses were dead, and the debt could not be proved, the Hebrew appropriated the merchant's money to himself, and piously thanked God for putting it in his power to cheat an Arabian. Setoc imparted this troublesome affair to Zadig, who was now become his counsel.

"In what place," said Zadig, "didst thou lend the five hundred ounces to this infidel?"

"Upon a large stone," replied the merchant, "that lies near Mount Oreb."

"What is the character of thy debtor?" said Zadig. "That of a knave," returned Setoc.

"But I ask thee whether he is lively or phlegmatic, cautious or imprudent?"

"He is, of all bad payers," said Setoc, "the most lively fellow I ever knew."

"Well," resumed Zadig, "allow me to plead thy cause." In effect Zadig, having summoned the Jew to the tribunal, addressed the judge in the following terms: "Pillar of the throne of equity, I come to demand of this man, in the name of my master, five hundred ounces of silver, which he refuses to pay."

"Hast thou any witnesses?" said the judge.

"No, they are dead; but there remains a large stone upon which the money was counted; and if it please thy grandeur to order the stone to be sought for, I hope that it will bear witness. The Hebrew and I will tarry here till the stone arrives; I will send for it at my master's expense."

"With all my heart," replied the judge, and immediately applied himself to the discussion of other affairs.

When the court was going to break up, the judge said to Zadig. "Well, friend, is not thy stone come yet?"

The Hebrew replied with a smile, "Thy grandeur may stay here till the morrow, and after all not see the stone. It is more than six miles from hence; and it would require fifteen men to move it."

"Well," cried Zadig, "did not I say that the stone would bear witness? Since this man knows where it is, he thereby confesses that it was upon it that the money was counted." The Hebrew was disconcerted, and was soon after obliged to confess the truth. The judge ordered him to be fastened to the stone, without meat or drink, till he should restore the five hundred ounces, which were soon after paid.

The slave Zadig and the stone were held in great repute in Arabia.

THE FUNERAL PILE

Setoc, charmed with the happy issue of this affair, made his slave his intimate friend. He had now conceived as great esteem for him as ever the King of Babylon had done; and Zadig was glad that Setoc had no wife. He discovered in his master a good natural disposition, much probity of heart, and a great share of good sense; but he was sorry to see that, according to the ancient custom of Arabia, he adored the host of heaven; that is, the sun, moon, and stars. He sometimes spoke to him on this subject with great prudence and discretion. At last he told him that these bodies were like all other bodies in the universe, and no more deserving of our homage than a tree or a rock.

"But," said Setoc, "they are eternal beings; and it is from them we derive all we enjoy. They animate nature; they regulate the seasons; and, besides, are removed at such an immense distance from us that we cannot help revering them."

"Thou receivest more advantage," replied Zadig, "from the waters of the Red Sea, which carry thy merchandise to the Indies. Why may not it be as ancient as the stars? And if thou adorest what is placed at a distance from thee, thou oughtest to adore the land of the Gangarides, which lies at the extremity of the earth."

"No," said Setoc, "the brightness of the stars commands my adoration."

At night Zadig lighted up a great number of candles in the tent where he was to sup with Setoc; and the moment his patron appeared, he fell on his knees before these lighted tapers, and said, "Eternal and shining luminaries! be ye always propitious to me." Having thus said, he sat down at table, without taking the least notice of Setoc.

"What art thou doing?" said Setoc to him in amaze.

"I act like thee," replied Zadig, "I adore these candles, and neglect their master and mine." Setoc comprehended the profound sense of this apologue. The wisdom of his slave sunk deep into his soul; he no longer offered incense to the creatures, but adored the eternal Being who made them.

There prevailed at that time in Arabia a shocking custom, sprung originally from Leythia, and which, being established in the Indies by the credit of the Brahmans, threatened to overrun all the East. When a married man died, and his beloved wife aspired to the character of a saint, she burned herself publicly on the body of her husband. This was a solemn feast and was called the Funeral Pile of Widowhood, and that tribe in which most women had been burned was the most respected.

An Arabian of Setoc's tribe being dead, his widow, whose name was Almona, and who was very devout, published the day and hour when she intended to throw herself into the fire, amidst the sound of drums and trumpets. Zadig remonstrated against this horrible custom; he showed Setoc how inconsistent it was with the happiness of mankind to suffer young widows to burn themselves every other day, widows who were capable of giving children to the state, or at least of educating those they already had; and he convinced him that it was his duty to do all that lay in his power to abolish such a barbarous practice.

"The women," said Setoc, "have possessed the right of burning themselves for more than a thousand years; and who shall dare to abrogate a law which time hath rendered sacred? Is there anything more respectable than ancient abuses?"

"Reason is more ancient," replied Zadig; "meanwhile, speak thou to the chiefs of the tribes and I will go to wait on the young widow."

Accordingly he was introduced to her; and, after having insinuated himself into her good graces by some compliments on her beauty and told her what a pity it was to commit so many charms to the flames, he at last praised her for her constancy and courage. "Thou must surely have loved thy husband," said he to her, "with the most passionate fondness."

"Who, I?" replied the lady. "I loved him not at all. He was a brutal, jealous, insupportable wretch; but I am firmly resolved to throw myself on his funeral pile."

"It would appear then," said Zadig, "that there must be a very delicious pleasure in being burned alive."

"Oh! it makes nature shudder," replied the lady, "but that must be overlooked. I am a devotee, and I should lose my reputation and all the world would despise me if I did not burn myself."

Zadig having made her acknowledge that she burned herself to gain the good opinion of others and to gratify her own vanity, entertained her with a long discourse, calculated to make her a little in love with life, and even went so far as to inspire her with some degree of good will for the person who spoke to her.

"Alas!" said the lady, "I believe I should desire thee to marry me."

Zadig's mind was too much engrossed with the idea of Astarte not to elude this declaration; but he instantly went to the chiefs of the tribes, told them what had passed, and advised them to make a law, by which a widow should not be permitted to burn herself till she had conversed privately with a young man for the space of an hour. Since that time not a single woman hath burned herself in Arabia. They were indebted to Zadig alone for destroying in one day a cruel custom that had lasted for so many ages and thus he became the benefactor of Arabia.

## THE SUPPER

Setoc, who could not separate himself from this man, in whom dwelt wisdom, carried him to the great fair of Balzora, whither the richest merchants in the earth resorted. Zadig was highly pleased to see so many men of different countries united in the same place. He considered the whole universe as one large family assembled at Balzora.

Setoc, after having sold his commodities at a very high price, returned to his own tribe with his friend Zadig; who learned upon his arrival that he had been tried in his absence and was now going to be burned by a slow fire. Only the friendship of Almona saved his life. Like so many pretty women she possessed great influence with the priesthood. Zadig thought it best to leave Arabia.

Setoc was so charmed with the ingenuity and address of Almona that he made her his wife. Zadig departed, after having thrown himself at the feet of his fair deliverer. Setoc and he took leave of each other with tears in their eyes, swearing an eternal friendship, and promising that the first of them that should acquire a large fortune should share it with the other.

Zadig directed his course along the frontiers of Assyria, still musing on the unhappy Astarte, and reflecting on the severity of fortune which seemed determined to make him the sport of her cruelty and the object of her persecution.

"What," said he to himself, "four hundred ounces of gold for having seen a spaniel! condemned to lose my head for four bad verses in praise of the king! ready to be strangled because the queen had shoes of the color of my bonnet! reduced to slavery for having succored a woman who was beat! and on the point of being burned for having saved the lives of all the young widows of Arabia!"

## THE ROBBER

Arriving on the frontiers which divide Arabia Petraea from Syria, he passed by a pretty strong castle, from which a party of armed Arabians sallied forth. They instantly surrounded him and cried, "All thou hast belongs to us, and thy person is the property of our master." Zadig replied by drawing his sword; his servant, who was a man of courage, did the same. They killed the first Arabians that presumed to lay hands on them; and, though the number was redoubled, they were not dismayed, but resolved to perish in the conflict. Two men defended themselves against a multitude; and such a combat could not last long.

The master of the castle, whose name was Arbogad, having observed from a window the prodigies of valor performed by Zadig, conceived a high esteem for this heroic stranger. He descended in haste and went in person to call off his men and deliver the two travelers.

"All that passes over my lands," said he, "belongs to me, as well as what I find upon the lands of others; but thou seemest to be a man of such undaunted courage that I will exempt thee from the common law." He then conducted him to his castle, ordering his men to treat him well; and in the evening Arbogad supped with Zadig.

The lord of the castle was one of those Arabians who are commonly called robbers; but he now and then performed some good actions amid a multitude of bad ones. He robbed with a furious rapacity, and granted favors with great generosity; he was intrepid in action; affable in company; a debauchee at table, but gay in debauchery; and particularly remarkable for his frank and open behavior. He was highly pleased with Zadig, whose lively conversation lengthened the repast.

At last Arbogad said to him; "I advise thee to enroll thy name in my catalogue; thou canst not do better; this is not a bad trade; and thou mayest one day become what I am at present."

"May I take the liberty of asking thee," said Zadig, "how long thou hast followed this noble profession?"

"From my most tender youth," replied the lord. "I was a servant to a pretty good-natured Arabian, but could not endure the hardships of my situation. I was vexed to find that fate had given me no share of the earth, which equally belongs to all men. I imparted the cause of my uneasiness to an old Arabian, who said to me: 'My son, do not despair; there was once a grain of sand that lamented that it was no more than a neglected atom in the desert; at the end of a few years it became a diamond; and is now the brightest ornament in the crown of the king of the Indies.' This discourse made a deep impression on my mind. I was the grain of sand, and I resolved to become the diamond. I began by stealing two horses; I soon got a party of companions; I put myself in a condition to rob small caravans; and thus, by degrees, I destroyed the difference which had formerly subsisted between me and other men. I had my share of the good things of this world; and was even recompensed with usury for the hardships I had suffered. I was greatly respected, and became the captain of a band of robbers. I seized this castle by force. The Satrap of Syria had a mind to dispossess me of it; but I was too rich to have any thing to fear. I gave the satrap a handsome present, by which means I preserved my castle and increased my possessions. He even appointed me treasurer of the tributes which Arabia Petraea pays to the king of kings. I perform my office of receiver with great punctuality; but take the freedom to dispense with that of paymaster.

"The grand Desterham of Babylon sent hither a pretty satrap in the name of King Moabdar, to have me strangled. This man arrived with his orders: I was apprised of all; I caused to be strangled in his presence the four persons he had brought with him to draw the noose; after which I asked him how much his commission of strangling me might be worth. He replied, that his fees would amount to about three hundred pieces of gold. I then convinced him that he might gain more by staying with me. I made him an inferior robber; and he is now one of my best and richest officers. If thou wilt take my advice thy success may be equal to his; never was there a better season for plunder, since King Moabdar is killed, and all Babylon thrown into confusion."

"Moabdar killed!" said Zadig, "and what is become of Queen Astarte?"

"I know not," replied Arbogad. "All I know is, that Moabdar lost his senses and was killed; that Babylon is a scene of disorder and bloodshed; that all the empire is desolated; that there are some fine strokes to be struck yet; and that, for my own part, I have struck some that are admirable."

"But the queen," said Zadig; "for heaven's sake, knowest thou nothing of the queen's fate?"

"Yes," replied he, "I have heard something of a prince of Hircania; if she was not killed in the tumult, she is probably one of his concubines; but I am much fonder of booty than news. I have taken several women in my excursions; but I keep none of them. I sell them at a high price, when they are beautiful, without inquiring who they are. In commodities of this kind rank makes no difference, and a queen that is ugly will never find a merchant. Perhaps I may have sold Queen Astarte; perhaps she is dead; but, be it as it will, it is of little consequence to me, and I should imagine of as little to thee." So saying he drank a large draught which threw all his ideas into such confusion that Zadig could obtain no further information.

Zadig remained for some time without speech, sense, or motion. Arbogad continued drinking; told stories; constantly repeated that he was the happiest man in the world; and exhorted Zadig to put himself in the same condition. At last the soporiferous fumes of the wine lulled him into a gentle repose.

Zadig passed the night in the most violent perturbation. "What," said he, "did the king lose his senses? and is he killed? I cannot help lamenting his fate. The empire is rent in pieces; and this robber is happy. O fortune! O destiny! A robber is happy, and the most beautiful of nature's works hath perhaps perished in a barbarous manner or lives in a state worse than death. O Astarte! what is become of thee?"

At daybreak he questioned all those he met in the castle; but they were all busy, and he received no answer. During the night they had made a new capture, and they were now employed in dividing the spoils. All he could obtain in this hurry and confusion was an opportunity of departing, which he immediately embraced, plunged deeper than ever in the most gloomy and mournful reflections.

Zadig proceeded on his journey with a mind full of disquiet and perplexity, and wholly employed on the unhappy Astarte, on the King of Babylon, on his faithful friend Cador, on the happy robber Arbogad; in a word, on all the misfortunes and disappointments he had hitherto suffered.

## THE FISHERMAN

At a few leagues' distance from Arbogad's castle he came to the banks of a small river, still deploring his fate, and considering himself as the most wretched of mankind. He saw a fisherman lying on the brink of the river, scarcely holding, in his weak and feeble hand, a net which he seemed ready to drop, and lifting up his eyes to Heaven.

"I am certainly," said the fisherman, "the most unhappy man in the world. I was universally allowed to be the most famous dealer in cream cheese in Babylon, and yet I am ruined. I had the most handsome wife that any man in my station could have; and by her I have been betrayed. I had still left a paltry house, and that I have seen pillaged and destroyed. At last I took refuge in this cottage, where I have no other resource than fishing, and yet I cannot catch a single fish. Oh, my net! no more will I throw thee into the water; I will throw myself in thy place." So saying, he arose and advanced forward, in the attitude of a man ready to throw himself into the river, and thus to finish his life.

"What!" said Zadig to himself, "are there men as wretched as I?" His eagerness to save the fisherman's life was as this reflection. He ran to him, stopped him, and spoke to him with a tender and compassionate air. It is commonly supposed that we are less miserable when we have companions in our misery. This, according to Zoroaster, does not proceed from _malice_, but necessity. We feel ourselves insensibly drawn to an unhappy person as to one like ourselves. The joy of the happy would be an insult; but two men in distress are like two slender trees, which, mutually supporting each other, fortify themselves against the storm.

"Why," said Zadig to the fisherman, "dost thou sink under thy misfortunes?"

"Because," replied he, "I see no means of relief. I was the most considerable man in the village of Derlback, near Babylon, and with the assistance of my wife I made the best cream cheese in the empire. Queen Astarte and the famous minister Zadig were extremely fond of them."

Zadig, transported, said, "What, knowest thou nothing of the queen's fate?"

"No, my lord," replied the fisherman; "but I know that neither the queen nor Zadig has paid me for my cream cheeses; that I have lost my wife, and am now reduced to despair."

"I flatter myself," said Zadig, "that thou wilt not lose all thy money. I have heard of this Zadig; he is an honest man; and if he returns to Babylon, as he expects, he will give thee more than he owes thee. Believe me, go to Babylon. I shall be there before thee, because I am on horseback, and thou art on foot. Apply to the illustrious Cador; tell him thou hast met his friend; wait for me at his house; go, perhaps thou wilt not always be unhappy."

"Oh, powerful Oromazes!" continued he, "thou employest me to comfort this man; whom wilt thou employ to give me consolation?" So saying, he gave the fisherman half the money he had brought from Arabia. The fisherman, struck with surprise and ravished with joy, kissed the feet of the friend of Cador, and said, "Thou art surely an angel sent from Heaven to save me!"

Meanwhile, Zadig continued to make fresh inquiries, and to shed tears. "What, my lord!" cried the fisherman, "art thou then so unhappy, thou who bestowest favors?"

"An hundred times more unhappy than thou art," replied Zadig.

"But how is it possible," said the good man, "that the giver can be more wretched than the receiver?"

"Because," replied Zadig, "thy greatest misery arose from poverty, and mine is seated in the heart."

"Did Orcan take thy wife from thee?" said the fisherman.

This word recalled to Zadig's mind the whole of his adventures.

He repeated the catalogue of his misfortunes, beginning with the queen's spaniel, and ending with his arrival at the castle of the robber Arbogad. "Ah!" said he to the fisherman, "Orcan deserves to be punished; but it is commonly such men as those that are the favorites of fortune. However, go thou to the house of Lord Cador, and there wait my arrival." They then parted, the fisherman walked, thanking Heaven for the happiness of his condition; and Zadig rode, accusing fortune for the hardness of his lot.

## THE BASILISK

Arriving in a beautiful meadow, he there saw several women, who were searching for something with great application. He took the liberty to approach one of them, and to ask if he might have the honor to assist them in their search. "Take care that thou dost not," replied the Syrian; "what we are searching for can be touched only by women."

"Strange," said Zadig, "may I presume to ask thee what it is that women only are permitted to touch?"

"It is a basilisk," said she.

"A basilisk, madam! and for what purpose, pray, dost thou seek for a basilisk?"

"It is for our lord and master Ogul, whose cattle thou seest on the bank of that river at the end of the meadow. We are his most humble slaves. The lord Ogul is sick. His physician hath ordered him to eat a basilisk, stewed in rose water; and as it is a very rare animal, and can only be taken by women, the lord Ogul hath promised to choose for his well-beloved wife the woman that shall bring him a basilisk; let me go on in my search; for thou seest what I shall lose if I am prevented by my companions."

Zadig left her and the other Assyrians to search for their basilisk, and continued to walk in the meadow; when coming to the brink of a small rivulet, he found another lady lying on the grass, and who was not searching for anything. Her person worried to be majestic; but her face was covered with a veil. She was inclined toward the rivulet, and profound sighs proceeded from her mouth. In her hand she held a small rod with which she was tracing characters on the fine sand that lay between the turf and the brook. Zadig had the curiosity to examine what this woman was writing. He drew near; he saw the letter Z, then an A; he was astonished; then appeared a D; he started. But never was surprise equal to his when he saw the last letters of his name.

He stood for some time immovable. At last, breaking silence with a faltering voice: "O generous lady! pardon a stranger, an unfortunate man, for presuming to ask thee by what surprising adventure I here find the name of Zadig traced out by thy divine hand!"

At this voice and these words, the lady lifted up the veil with a trembling hand, looked at Zadig, sent forth a cry of tenderness, surprise and joy, and sinking under the various emotions which at once assaulted her soul, fell speechless into his arms. It was Astarte herself; it was the Queen of Babylon; it was she whom Zadig adored, and whom he had reproached himself for adoring; it was she whose misfortunes he had so deeply lamented, and for whose fate he had been so anxiously concerned.

He was for a moment deprived of the use of his senses, when he had fixed his eyes on those of Astarte, which now began to open again with a languor mixed with confusion and tenderness: "O ye immortal powers!" cried he, "who preside over the fates of weak mortals, do ye indeed restore Astarte to me! at what a time, in what a place, and in what a condition do I again behold her!" He fell on his knees before Astarte and laid his face in the dust at her feet. The Queen of Babylon raised him up, and made him sit by her side on the brink of the rivulet. She frequently wiped her eyes, from which the tears continued to flow afresh. She twenty times resumed her discourse, which her sighs as often interrupted; she asked by what strange accident they were brought together, and suddenly prevented his answers by other questions; she waived the account of her own misfortunes, and desired to be informed of those of Zadig.

At last, both of them having a little composed the tumult of their souls, Zadig acquainted her in a few words by what adventure he was brought into that meadow. "But, O unhappy and respectable queen! by what means do I find thee in this lonely place, clothed in the habit of a slave, and accompanied by other female slaves, who are searching for a basilisk, which, by order of the physician, is to be stewed in rose water?"

"While they are searching for their basilisk," said the fair Astarte, "I will inform thee of all I have suffered, for which Heaven has sufficiently recompensed me by restoring thee to my sight. Thou knowest that the king, my husband, was vexed to see thee the most amiable of mankind; and that for this reason he one night resolved to strangle thee and poison me. Thou knowest how Heaven permitted my little mute to inform me of the orders of his sublime majesty. Hardly had the faithful Cador advised thee to depart, in obedience to my command, when he ventured to enter my apartment at midnight by a secret passage. He carried me off and conducted me to the temple of Oromazes, where the mage his brother shut me up in that huge statue whose base reaches to the foundation of the temple and whose top rises to the summit of the dome. I was there buried in a manner; but was saved by the mage; and supplied with all the necessaries of life. At break of day his majesty's apothecary entered my chamber with a potion composed of a mixture of henbane, opium, hemlock, black hellebore, and aconite; and another officer went to thine with a bowstring of blue silk. Neither of us was to be found. Cador, the better to deceive the king, pretended to come and accuse us both. He said that thou hadst taken the road to the Indies, and I that to Memphis, on which the king's guards were immediately dispatched in pursuit of us both.

"The couriers who pursued me did not know me. I had hardly ever shown my face to any but thee, and to thee only in the presence and by the order of my husband. They conducted themselves in the pursuit by the description that had been given them of my person. On the frontiers of Egypt they met with a woman of the same stature with me, and possessed perhaps of greater charms. She was weeping and wandering. They made no doubt but that this woman was the Queen of Babylon and accordingly brought her to Moabdar. Their mistake at first threw the king into a violent passion; but having viewed this woman more attentively, he found her extremely handsome and was comforted. She was called Missouf. I have since been informed that this name in the Egyptian language signifies the capricious fair one. She was so in reality; but she had as much cunning as caprice. She pleased Moabdar and gained such an ascendancy over him as to make him choose her for his wife. Her character then began to appear in its true colors. She gave herself up, without scruple, to all the freaks of a wanton imagination. She would have obliged the chief of the magi, who was old and gouty, to dance before her; and on his refusal, she persecuted him with the most unrelenting cruelty. She ordered her master of the horse to make her a pie of sweetmeats. In vain did he represent that he was not a pastry-cook; he was obliged to make it, and lost his place, because it was baked a little too hard. The post of master of the horse she gave to her dwarf, and that of chancellor to her page. In this manner did she govern Babylon. Everybody regretted the loss of me. The king, who till the moment of his resolving to poison me and strangle thee had been a tolerably good kind of man, seemed now to have drowned all his virtues in his immoderate fondness for this capricious fair one. He came to the temple on the great day of the feast held in honor of the sacred fire. I saw him implore the gods in behalf of Missouf, at the feet of the statue in which I was inclosed. I raised my voice, I cried out, 'The gods reject the prayers of a king who is now become a tyrant, and who attempted to murder a reasonable wife, in order to marry a woman remarkable for nothing but her folly and extravagance.' At these words Moabdar was confounded and his head became disordered. The oracle I had pronounced, and the tyranny of Missouf, conspired to deprive him of his judgment, and in a few days his reason entirely forsook him.

"Moabdar's madness, which seemed to be the judgment of Heaven, was the signal to a revolt. The people rose and ran to arms; and Babylon, which had been so long immersed in idleness and effeminacy, became the theater of a bloody civil war. I was taken from the heart of my statue and placed at the head of a party. Cador flew to Memphis to bring thee back to Babylon. The Prince of Hircania, informed of these fatal events, returned with his army and made a third party in Chaldea. He attacked the king, who fled before him with his capricious Egyptian. Moabdar died pierced with wounds. I myself had the misfortune to be taken by a party of Hircanians, who conducted me to their prince's tent, at the very moment that Missouf was brought before him. Thou wilt doubtless be pleased to hear that the prince thought me beautiful; but thou wilt be sorry to be informed that he designed me for his seraglio. He told me, with a blunt and resolute air, that as soon as he had finished a military expedition, which he was just going to undertake, he would come to me. Judge how great must have been my grief. My ties with Moabdar were already dissolved; I might have been the wife of Zadig; and I was fallen into the hands of a barbarian. I answered him with all the pride which my high rank and noble sentiment could inspire. I had always heard it affirmed that Heaven stamped on persons of my condition a mark of grandeur, which, with a single word or glance, could reduce to the lowliness of the most profound respect those rash and forward persons who presume to deviate from the rules of politeness. I spoke like a queen, but was treated like a maidservant. The Hircanian, without even deigning to speak to me, told his black eunuch that I was impertinent, but that he thought me handsome. He ordered him to take care of me, and to put me under the regimen of favorites, that so my complexion being improved, I might be the more worthy of his favors when he should be at leisure to honor me with them, I told him that rather than submit to his desires I would put an end to my life. He replied, with a smile, that women, he believed, were not, so bloodthirsty, and that he was accustomed to such violent expressions; and then left me with the air of a man who had just put another parrot into his aviary. What a state for the first queen of the universe, and, what is more, for a heart devoted to Zadig!"

At these words Zadig threw himself at her feet and bathed them with his tears. Astarte raised him with great tenderness and thus continued her story: "I now saw myself in the power of a barbarian and rival to the foolish woman with whom I was confined. She gave me an account of her adventures in Egypt. From the description she gave me of your person, from the time, from the dromedary on which you were mounted, and from every other circumstance, I inferred that Zadig was the man who had fought for her. I doubted not but that you were at Memphis, and, therefore, resolved to repair thither. Beautiful Missouf, said I, thou art more handsome than I, and will please the Prince of Hircania much better. Assist me in contriving the means of my escape; thou wilt then reign alone; thou wilt at once make me happy and rid thyself of a rival. Missouf concerted with me the means of my flight; and I departed secretly with a female Egyptian slave.

"As I approached the frontiers of Arabia, a famous robber, named Arbogad, seized me and sold me to some merchants, who brought me to this castle, where Lord Ogul resides. He bought me without knowing who I was. He is a voluptuary, ambitious of nothing but good living, and thinks that God sent him into the world for no other purpose than to sit at table. He is so extremely corpulent that he is always in danger of suffocation. His physician, who has but little credit with him when he has a good digestion, governs him with a despotic sway when he has eaten too much. He has persuaded him that a basilisk stewed in rose water will effect a complete cure. The Lord Ogul hath promised his hand to the female slave that brings him a basilisk. Thou seest that I leave them to vie with each other in meriting this honor; and never was I less desirous of finding the basilisk than since Heaven hath restored thee to my sight."

This account was succeeded by a long conversation between Astarte and Zadig, consisting of everything that their long-suppressed sentiments, their great sufferings, and their mutual love could inspire in hearts the most noble and tender; and the genii who preside over love carried their words to the sphere of Venus.

The woman returned to Ogul without having found the basilisk. Zadig was introduced to this mighty lord and spoke to him in the following terms: "May immortal health descend from heaven to bless all thy days! I am a physician; at the first report of thy indisposition I flew to thy castle and have now brought thee a basilisk stewed in rose water. Not that I pretend to marry thee. All I ask is the liberty of a Babylonian slave, who hath been in thy possession for a few days; and, if I should not be so happy as to cure thee, magnificent Lord Ogul, I consent to remain a slave in her place."

The proposal was accepted. Astarte set out for Babylon with Zadig's servant, promising, immediately upon her arrival, to send a courier to inform him of all that had happened. Their parting was as tender as their meeting. The moment of meeting and that of parting are the two greatest epochs of life, as sayeth the great book of Zend. Zadig loved the queen with as much ardor as he professed; and the queen loved him more than she thought proper to acknowledge.

Meanwhile Zadig spoke thus to Ogul: "My lord, my basilisk is not to be eaten; all its virtues must enter through thy pores. I have inclosed it in a little ball, blown up and covered with a fine skin. Thou must strike this ball with all thy might and I must strike it back for a considerable time; and by observing this regimen for a few days thou wilt see the effects of my art." The first day Ogul was out of breath and thought he should have died with fatigue. The second he was less fatigued, slept better. In eight days he recovered all the strength, all the health, all the agility and cheerfulness of his most agreeable years.

"Thou hast played at ball, and thou hast been temperate," said Zadig; "know that there is no such thing in nature as a basilisk; that temperance and exercise are the two great preservatives of health; and that the art of reconciling intemperance and health is as chimerical as the philosopher's stone, judicial astrology, or the theology of the magi."

Ogul's first physician, observing how dangerous this man might prove to the medical art, formed a design, in conjunction with the apothecary, to send Zadig to search for a basilisk in the other world. Thus, having suffered such a long train of calamities on account of his good actions, he was now upon the point of losing his life for curing a gluttonous lord. He was invited to an excellent dinner and was to have been poisoned in the second course, but, during the first, he happily received a courier from the fair Astarte. "When one is beloved by a beautiful woman," says the great Zoroaster, "he hath always the good fortune to extricate himself out of every kind of difficulty and danger."

## THE COMBATS

The queen was received at Babylon with all those transports of joy which are ever felt on the return of a beautiful princess who hath been involved in calamities. Babylon was now in greater tranquillity. The Prince of Hircania had been killed in battle. The victorious Babylonians declared that the queen should marry the man whom they should choose for their sovereign. They were resolved that the first place in the world, that of being husband to Astarte and King of Babylon, should not depend on cabals and intrigues. They swore to acknowledge for king the man who, upon trial, should be found to be possessed of the greatest valor and the greatest wisdom. Accordingly, at the distance of a few leagues from the city, a spacious place was marked out for the list, surrounded with magnificent amphitheaters. Thither the combatants were to repair in complete armor. Each of them had a separate apartment behind the amphitheaters, where they were neither to be seen nor known by anyone. Each was to encounter four knights, and those that were so happy as to conquer four were then to engage with one another; so that he who remained the last master of the field would be proclaimed conqueror at the games.

Four days after he was to return with the same arms and to explain the enigmas proposed by the magi. If he did not explain the enigmas he was not king; and the running at the lances was to be begun afresh till a man would be found who was conqueror in both these combats; for they were absolutely determined to have a king possessed of the greatest wisdom and the most invincible courage. The queen was all the while to be strictly guarded: she was only allowed to be present at the games, and even there she was to be covered with a veil; but was not permitted to speak to any of the competitors, that so they might neither receive favor, nor suffer injustice.

These particulars Astarte communicated to her lover, hoping that in order to obtain her he would show himself possessed of greater courage and wisdom than any other person. Zadig set out on his journey, beseeching Venus to fortify his courage and enlighten his understanding. He arrived on the banks of the Euphrates on the eve of this great day. He caused his device to be inscribed among those of the combatants, concealing his face and his name, as the law ordained; and then went to repose himself in the apartment that fell to him by lot. His friend Cador, who, after the fruitless search he had made for him in Egypt, was now returned to Babylon, sent to his tent a complete suit of armor, which was a present from the queen; as also, from himself, one of the finest horses in Persia. Zadig presently perceived that these presents were sent by Astarte; and from thence his courage derived fresh strength, and his love the most animating hopes.

Next day, the queen being seated under a canopy of jewels, and the amphitheaters filled with all the gentlemen and ladies of rank in Babylon, the combatants appeared in the circus. Each of them came and laid his device at the feet of the grand magi. They drew their devices by lot; and that of Zadig was the last. The first who advanced was a certain lord, named Itobad, very rich and very vain, but possessed of little courage, of less address, and hardly of any judgment at all. His servants had persuaded him that such a man as he ought to be king; he had said in reply, "Such a man as I ought to reign"; and thus they had armed him cap-a-pie. He wore an armor of gold enameled with green, a plume of green feathers, and a lance adorned with green ribbons. It was instantly perceived by the manner in which Itobad managed his horse, that it was not for such a man as he that Heaven reserved the scepter of Babylon. The first knight that ran against him threw him out of his saddle; the second laid him flat on his horse's buttocks, with his legs in the air, and his arms extended. Itobad recovered himself, but with so bad a grace that the whole amphitheater burst out a-laughing. The third knight disdained to make use of his lance; but, making a pass at him, took him by the right leg and, wheeling him half round, laid him prostrate on the sand. The squires of the game ran to him laughing, and replaced him in his saddle. The fourth combatant took him by the left leg, and tumbled him down on the other side. He was conducted back with scornful shouts to his tent, where, according to the law, he was to pass the night; and as he climbed along with great difficulty he said, "What an adventure for such a man as I!"

The other knights acquitted themselves with greater ability and success. Some of them conquered two combatants; a few of them vanquished three; but none but Prince Otamus conquered four. At last Zadig fought him in his turn. He successively threw four knights off their saddles with all the grace imaginable. It then remained to be seen who should be conqueror, Otamus or Zadig. The arms of the first were gold and blue, with a plume of the same color; those of the last were white. The wishes of all the spectators were divided between the knight in blue and the knight in white. The queen, whose heart was in a violent palpitation, offered prayers to Heaven for the success of the white color.

The two champions made their passes and vaults with so much agility, they mutually gave and received such dexterous blows with their lances, and sat so firmly in their saddles, that everybody but the queen wished there might be two kings in Babylon. At length, their horses being tired and their lances broken, Zadig had recourse to this stratagem: He passes behind the blue prince; springs upon the buttocks of his horse; seizes him by the middle; throws him on the earth; places himself in the saddle; and wheels around Otamus as he lay extended on the ground. All the amphitheater cried out, "Victory to the white knight!"

Otamus rises in a violent passion, and draws his sword; Zadig leaps from his horse with his saber in his hand. Both of them are now on the ground, engaged in a new combat, where strength and agility triumph by turns. The plumes of their helmets, the studs of their bracelets, the rings of their armor, are driven to a great distance by the violence of a thousand furious blows. They strike with the point and the edge; to the right, to the left, on the head, on the breast; they retreat; they advance; they measure swords; they close; they seize each other; they bend like serpents; they attack like lions; and the fire every moment flashes from their blows.

At last Zadig, having recovered his spirits, stops; makes a feint; leaps upon Otamus; throws him on the ground and disarms him; and Otamus cries out, "It is thou alone, O white knight, that oughtest to reign over Babylon!" The queen was now at the height of her joy. The knight in blue armor and the knight in white were conducted each to his own apartment, as well as all the others, according to the intention of the law. Mutes came to wait upon them and to serve them at table. It may be easily supposed that the queen's little mute waited upon Zadig. They were then left to themselves to enjoy the sweets of repose till next morning, at which time the conqueror was to bring his device to the grand magi, to compare it with that which he had left, and make himself known.

Zadig though deeply in love, was so much fatigued that he could not help sleeping. Itobad, who lay near him, never closed his eyes. He arose in the night, entered his apartment, took the white arms and the device of Zadig, and put his green armor in their place. At break of day he went boldly to the grand magi to declare that so great a man as he was conqueror. This was little expected; however, he was proclaimed while Zadig was still asleep. Astarte, surprised and filled with despair, returned to Babylon. The amphitheater was almost empty when Zadig awoke; he sought for his arms, but could find none but the green armor. With this he was obliged to cover himself, having nothing else near him. Astonished and enraged, he put it on in a furious passion, and advanced in this equipage.

The people that still remained in the amphitheater and the circus received him with hoots and hisses. They surrounded him and insulted him to his face. Never did man suffer such cruel mortifications. He lost his patience; with his saber he dispersed such of the populace as dared to affront him; but he knew not what course to take. He could not see the queen; he could not claim the white armor she had sent him without exposing her; and thus, while she was plunged in grief, he was filled with fury and distraction. He walked on the banks of the Euphrates, fully persuaded that his star had destined him to inevitable misery, and resolving in his own mind all his misfortunes, from the adventure of the woman who hated one-eyed men to that of his armor. "This," said he, "is the consequence of my having slept too long. Had I slept less, I should now have been King of Babylon and in possession of Astarte. Knowledge, virtue, and courage have hitherto served only to make me miserable." He then let fall some secret murmurings against Providence, and was tempted to believe that the world was governed by a cruel destiny, which oppressed the good and prospered knights in green armor. One of his greatest mortifications was his being obliged to wear that green armor which had exposed him to such contumelious treatment. A merchant happening to pass by, he sold it to him for a trifle and bought a gown and a long bonnet. In this garb he proceeded along the banks of the Euphrates, filled with despair, and secretly accusing Providence, which thus continued to persecute him with unremitting severity.

## THE HERMIT

While he was thus sauntering he met a hermit, whose white and venerable beard hung down to his girdle. He held a book in his hand, which he read with great attention. Zadig stopped, and made him a profound obeisance. The hermit returned the compliment with such a noble and engaging air, that Zadig had the curiosity to enter into conversation with him. He asked him what book it was that he had been reading? "It is the Book of Destinies," said the hermit; "wouldst thou choose to look into it?" He put the book into the hands of Zadig, who, thoroughly versed as he was in several languages, could not decipher a single character of it. This only redoubled his curiosity.

"Thou seemest," said this good father, "to be in great distress."

"Alas," replied Zadig, "I have but too much reason."

"If thou wilt permit me to accompany thee," resumed the old man, "perhaps I may be of some service to thee. I have often poured the balm of consolation into the bleeding heart of the unhappy."

Zadig felt himself inspired with respect for the air, the beard, and the book of the hermit. He found, in the course of the conversation, that he was possessed of superior degrees of knowledge. The hermit talked of fate, of justice, of morals, of the chief good, of human weakness, and of virtue and vice, with such a spirited and moving eloquence, that Zadig felt himself drawn toward him by an irresistible charm. He earnestly entreated the favor of his company till their return to Babylon.

"I ask the same favor of thee," said the old man; "swear to me by Oromazes, that whatever I do, thou wilt not leave me for some days." Zadig swore, and they set out together.

In the evening the two travelers arrived in a superb castle. The hermit entreated a hospitable reception for himself and the young man who accompanied him. The porter, whom one might have easily mistaken for a great lord, introduced them with a kind of disdainful civility. He presented them to a principal domestic, who showed them his master's magnificent apartments. They were admitted to the lower end of the table, without being honored with the least mark of regard by the lord of the castle; but they were served, like the rest, with delicacy and profusion. They were then presented with water to wash their hands, in a golden basin adorned with emeralds and rubies. At last they were conducted to bed in a beautiful apartment; and in the morning a domestic brought each of them a piece of gold, after which they took their leave and departed.

"The master of the house," said Zadig, as they were proceeding on the journey, "appears to be a generous man, though somewhat too proud; he nobly performs the duties of hospitality." At that instant he observed that a kind of large pocket, which the hermit had, was filled and distended; and upon looking more narrowly he found that it contained the golden basin adorned with precious stones, which the hermit had stolen. He durst not take any notice of it, but he was filled with a strange surprise.

About noon, the hermit came to the door of a paltry house inhabited by a rich miser, and begged the favor of an hospitable reception for a few hours. An old servant, in a tattered garb, received them with a blunt and rude air, and led them into the stable, where he gave them some rotten olives, moldy bread, and sour beer. The hermit ate and drank with as much seeming satisfaction as he had done the evening before; and then addressing himself to the old servant, who watched them both, to prevent their stealing anything, and rudely pressed them to depart, he gave him the two pieces of gold he had received in the morning, and thanked him for his great civility.

"Pray," added he, "allow me to speak to thy master." The servant, filled with astonishment, introduced the two travelers. "Magnificent lord," said the hermit, "I cannot but return thee my most humble thanks for the noble manner in which thou hast entertained us. Be pleased to accept this golden basin as a small mark of my gratitude." The miser started, and was ready to fall backward; but the hermit, without giving him time to recover from his surprise, instantly departed with his young fellow traveler.

"Father," said Zadig, "what is the meaning of all this? Thou seemest to me to be entirely different from other men; thou stealest a golden basin adorned with precious stones from a lord who received thee magnificently, and givest it to a miser who treats thee with indignity."

"Son," replied the old man, "this magnificent lord, who receives strangers only from vanity and ostentation, will hereby be rendered more wise; and the miser will learn to practice the duties of hospitality. Be surprised at nothing, but follow me."

Zadig knew not as yet whether he was in company with the most foolish or the most prudent of mankind; but the hermit spoke with such an ascendancy, that Zadig, who was moreover bound by his oath, could not refuse to follow him.

In the evening they arrived at a house built with equal elegance and simplicity, where nothing savored either of prodigality or avarice. The master of it was a philosopher, who had retired from the world, and who cultivated in peace the study of virtue and wisdom, without any of that rigid and morose severity so commonly to be found in men of his character. He had chosen to build this country house, in which he received strangers with a generosity free from ostentation. He went himself to meet the two travelers, whom he led into a commodious apartment, where he desired them to repose themselves a little. Soon after he came and invited them to a decent and well-ordered repast during which he spoke with great judgment of the last revolutions in Babylon. He seemed to be strongly attached to the queen, and wished that Zadig had appeared in the lists to dispute the crown. "But the people," added he, "do not deserve to have such a king as Zadig."

Zadig blushed, and felt his griefs redoubled. They agreed, in the course of the conversation, that the things of this world did not always answer the wishes of the wise. The hermit still maintained that the ways of Providence were inscrutable; and that men were in the wrong to judge of a whole, of which they understood but the smallest part.

They talked of passions. "Ah," said Zadig, "how fatal are their effects!"

"They are in the winds," replied the hermit, "that swell the sails of the ship; it is true, they sometimes sink her, but without them she could not sail at all. The bile makes us sick and choleric; but without bile we could not live. Everything in this world is dangerous, and yet everything is necessary."

The conversation turned on pleasure; and the hermit proved that it was a present bestowed by the Deity. "For," said he, "man cannot give himself either sensations or ideas; he receives all; and pain and pleasure proceed from a foreign cause as well as his being."

Zadig was surprised to see a man, who had been guilty of such extravagant actions, capable of reasoning with so much judgment and propriety. At last, after a conversation equally entertaining and instructive, the host led back his two guests to their apartment, blessing Heaven for having sent him two men possessed of so much wisdom and virtue. He offered them money with such an easy and noble air as could not possibly give any offense. The hermit refused it, and said that he must now take his leave of him, as he set out for Babylon before it was light. Their parting Was tender; Zadig especially felt himself filled with esteem and affection for a man of such an amiable character.

When he and the hermit were alone in their apartment, they spent a long time praising their host. At break of day the old man awakened his companion. "We must now depart," said he, "but while all the family are still asleep, I will leave this man a mark of my esteem and affection." So saying, he took a candle and set fire to the house.

Zadig, struck with horror, cried aloud, and endeavored to hinder him from committing such a barbarous action; but the hermit drew him away by a superior force, and the house was soon in flames. The hermit, who, with his companion, was already at a considerable distance, looked back to the conflagration with great tranquillity.

"Thanks be to God," said he, "the house of my dear host is entirely destroyed! Happy man!"

At these words Zadig was at once tempted to burst out a-laughing, to reproach the reverend father, to beat him, and to run away. But he did none of all of these, for still subdued by the powerful ascendancy of the hermit, he followed him, in spite of himself, to the next stage.

This was at the house of a charitable and virtuous widow, who had a nephew fourteen years of age, a handsome and promising youth, and her only hope. She performed the honors of her house as well as she could. Next day, she ordered her nephew to accompany the strangers to a bridge, which being lately broken down, was become extremely dangerous in passing. The young man walked before them with great alacrity. As they were crossing the bridge, "Come" said the hermit to the youth, "I must show my gratitude to thy aunt." He then took him by the hair and plunged him into the river. The boy sunk, appeared again on the surface of the water, and was swallowed up by the current.

"O monster! O thou most wicked of mankind!" cried Zadig.

"Thou promisedst to behave with greater patience," said the hermit, interrupting him. "Know that under the ruins of that house which Providence hath set on fire the master hath found an immense treasure. Know that this young, man, whose life Providence hath shortened, would have assassinated his aunt in the space of a year, and thee in that of two."

"Who told thee so, barbarian?" cried Zadig; "and though thou hadst read this event in thy Book of Destinies, art thou permitted to drown a youth who never did thee any harm?"

While the Babylonian was thus exclaiming, he observed that the old man had no longer a beard, and that his countenance assumed the features and complexion of youth. The hermit's habit disappeared, and four beautiful wings covered a majestic body resplendent with light.

"O sent of heaven! O divine angel!" cried Zadig, humbly prostrating himself on the ground, "hast thou then descended from the Empyrean to teach a weak mortal to submit to the eternal decrees of Providence?"

"Men," said the angel Jesrad, "judge of all without knowing anything; and, of all men, thou best deservest to be enlightened."

Zadig begged to be permitted to speak. "I distrust myself," said he, "but may I presume to ask the favor of thee to clear up one doubt that still remains in my mind? Would it not have been better to have corrected this youth, and made him virtuous, than to have drowned him?"

"Had he been virtuous," replied Jesrad, "and enjoyed a longer life, it would have been his fate to be assassinated himself, together with the wife he would have married, and the child he would have had by her."

"But why," said Zadig, "is it necessary that there should be crimes and misfortunes, and that these misfortunes should fall on the good?"

"The wicked," replied Jesrad, "are always unhappy; they serve to prove and try the small number of the just that are scattered through the earth; and there is no evil that is not productive of some good."

"But," said Zadig, "suppose there were nothing but good and no evil at all."

"Then," replied Jesrad, "this earth would be another earth. The chain of events would be ranged in another order and directed by wisdom; but this other order, which would be perfect, can exist only in the eternal abode of the Supreme Being, to which no evil can approach. The Deity hath created millions of worlds among which there is not one that resembles another. This immense variety is the effect of His immense power. There are not two leaves among the trees of the earth, nor two globes in the unlimited expanse of heaven that are exactly similar; and all that thou seest on the little atom in which thou art born, ought to be in its proper time and place, according to the immutable decree of Him who comprehends all. Men think that this child who hath just perished is fallen into the water by chance; and that it is by the same chance that this house is burned; but there is no such thing as chance; all is either a trial, or a punishment, or a reward, or a foresight. Remember the fisherman who thought himself the most wretched of mankind. Oromazes sent thee to change his fate. Cease, then, frail mortal, to dispute against what thou oughtest to adore."

"But," said Zadig~as he pronounced the word "But," the angel took his flight toward the tenth sphere. Zadig on his knees adored Providence, and submitted. The angel cried to him from on high, "Direct thy course toward Babylon."

## THE ENIGMAS

Zadig, entranced, as it were, and like a man about whose head the thunder had burst, walked at random. He entered Babylon on the very day when those who had fought at the tournaments were assembled in the grand vestibule of the palace to explain the enigmas and to answer the questions of the grand magi. All the knights were already arrived, except the knight in green armor. As soon as Zadig appeared in the city the people crowded round him; every eye was fixed on him; every mouth blessed him, and every heart wished him the empire. The envious man saw him pass; he frowned and turned aside. The people conducted him to the place where the assembly was held. The queen, who was informed of his arrival, became a prey to the most violent agitations of hope and fear. She was filled with anxiety and apprehension. She could not comprehend why Zadig was without arms, nor why Itobad wore the white armor. A confused murmur arose at the sight of Zadig. They were equally surprised and charmed to see him; but none but the knights who had fought were permitted to appear in the assembly.

"I have fought as well as the other knights," said Zadig, "but another here wears my arms; and while I wait for the honor of proving the truth of my assertion, I demand the liberty of presenting myself to explain the enigmas." The question was put to the vote, and his reputation for probity was still so deeply impressed in their minds, that they admitted him without scruple.

The first question proposed by the grand magi was: "What, of all things in the world, is the longest and the shortest, the swiftest and the slowest, the most divisible and the most extended the most neglected and the most regretted, without which nothing can be done, which devours all that is little, and enlivens all that is great?"

Itobad was to speak. He replied that so great a man as he did not understand enigmas, and that it was sufficient for him to have conquered by his strength and valor. Some said that the meaning of the enigma was Fortune; some, the Earth; and others the Light. Zadig said that it was Time. "Nothing," added he, "is longer, since it is the measure of eternity; nothing is shorter, since it is insufficient for the accomplishment of our projects; nothing more slow to him that expects, nothing more rapid to him that enjoys; in greatness, it extends to infinity; in smallness, it is infinitely divisible; all men neglect it; all regret the loss of it; nothing can be done without it; it consigns to oblivion whatever is unworthy of being transmitted to posterity, and it immortalizes such actions as are truly great." The assembly acknowledged that Zadig was in the right.

The next question was: "What is the thing which we receive without thanks, which we enjoy without knowing how, which we give to others when we know not where we are, and which we lose without perceiving it?"

Everyone gave his own explanation. Zadig alone guessed that it was Life, and explained all the other enigmas with the same facility. Itobad always said that nothing was more easy, and that he could have answered them with the same readiness had he chosen to have given himself the trouble. Questions were then proposed on justice, on the sovereign good, and on the art of government. Zadig's answers were judged to be the most solid. "What a pity is it," said they, "that such a great genius should be so bad a knight!"

"Illustrious lords," said Zadig, "I have had the honor of conquering in the tournaments. It is to me that the white armor belongs. Lord Itobad took possession of it during my sleep. He probably thought that it would fit him better than the green. I am now ready to prove in your presence, with my gown and sword, against all that beautiful white armor which he took from me, that it is I who have had the honor of conquering the brave Otamus."

Itobad accepted the challenge with the greatest confidence. He never doubted but that, armed as he was, with a helmet, a cuirass, and brassarts, he would obtain an easy victory over a champion in a cap and nightgown. Zadig drew his sword, saluting the queen, who looked at him with a mixture of fear and joy. Itobad drew his without saluting anyone. He rushed upon Zadig, like a man who had nothing to fear; he was ready to cleave him in two. Zadig knew how to ward off his blows, by opposing the strongest part of his sword to the weakest of that of his adversary, in such a manner that Itobad's sword was broken. Upon which Zadig, seizing his enemy by the waist, threw him on the ground; and firing the point of his sword at the breastplate, "Suffer thyself to be disarmed," said he, "or thou art a dead man."

Itobad, always surprised at the disgraces that happened to such a man as he, was obliged to yield to Zadig, who took from him with great composure his magnificent helmet, his superb cuirass, his fine brassarts, his shining cuishes; clothed himself with them, and in this dress ran to throw himself at the feet of Astarte. Cador easily proved that the armor belonged to Zadig. He was acknowledged king by the unanimous consent of the whole nation, and especially by that of Astarte, who, after so many calamities, now tasted the exquisite pleasure of seeing her lover worthy, in the eyes of all the world, to be her husband. Itobad went home to be called lord in his own house. Zadig was king, and was happy. The queen and Zadig adored Providence. He sent in search of the robber Arbogad, to whom he gave an honorable post in his army, promising to advance him to the first dignities if he behaved like a true warrior, and threatening to hang him if he followed the profession of a robber.

Setoc, with the fair Almona, was called from the heart of Arabia and placed at the head of the commerce of Babylon. Cador was preferred and distinguished according to his great services. He was the friend of the king; and the king was then the only monarch on earth that had a friend. The little mute was not forgotten.

But neither could the beautiful Semira be comforted for having believed that Zadig would be blind of an eye; nor did Azora cease to lament her having attempted to cut off his nose. Their griefs, however, he softened by his presents. The envious man died of rage and shame. The empire enjoyed peace, glory, and plenty. This was the happiest age of the earth; it was governed by love and justice. The people blessed Zadig, and Zadig blessed Heaven.

www.ingramcontent.com/pod-product-compliance
Lightning Source LLC
Chambersburg PA
CBHW020344170426
43200CB00005B/40